PREACHER

Book One

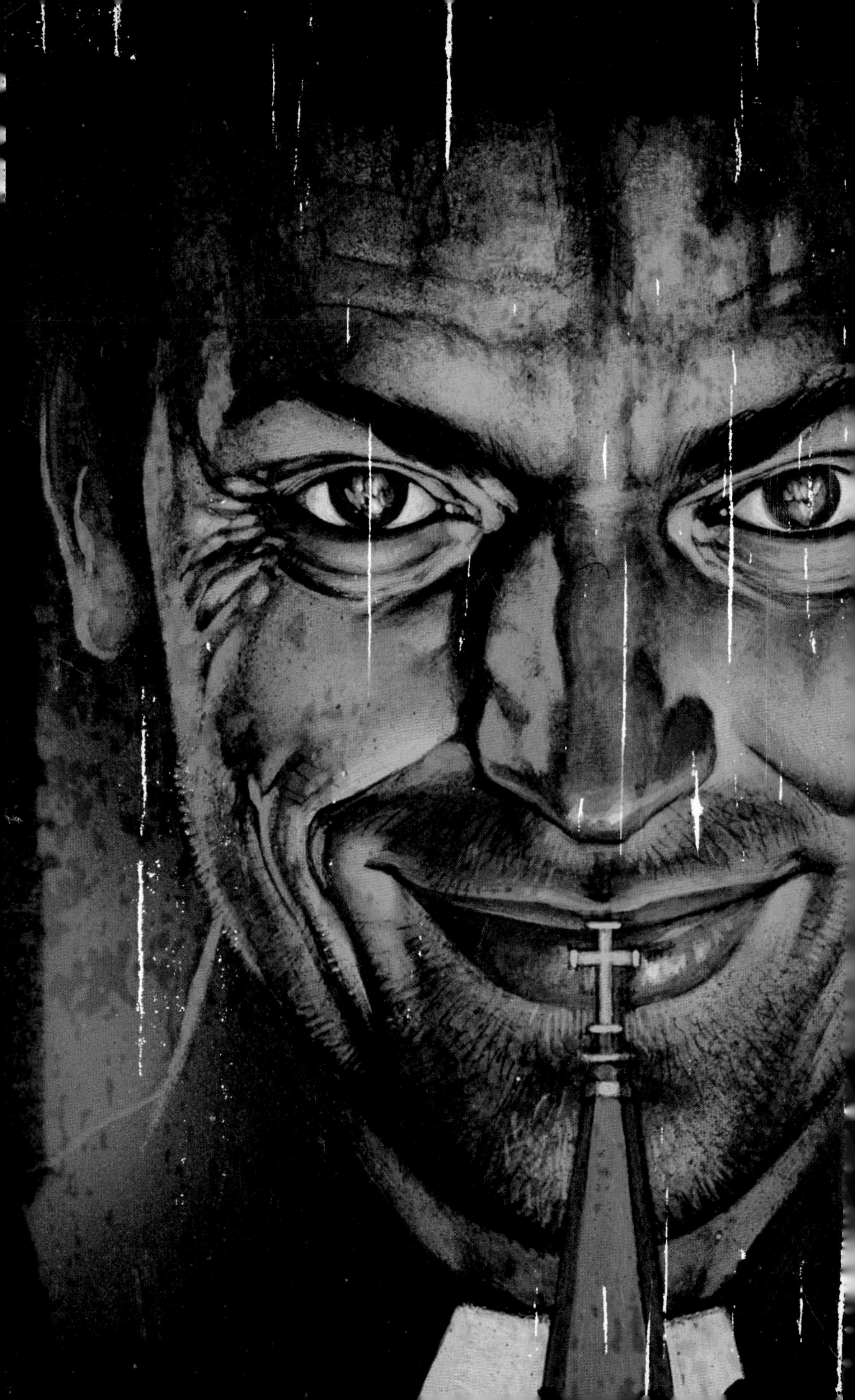

PREACHER

Book One

Garth Ennis Writer **Steve Dillon** Artist

Matt Hollingsworth Pamela Rambo Colorists

Clem Robins Letterer   Original Series Cover Art by **Glenn Fabry**

Preacher created by **Garth Ennis** and **Steve Dillon.**

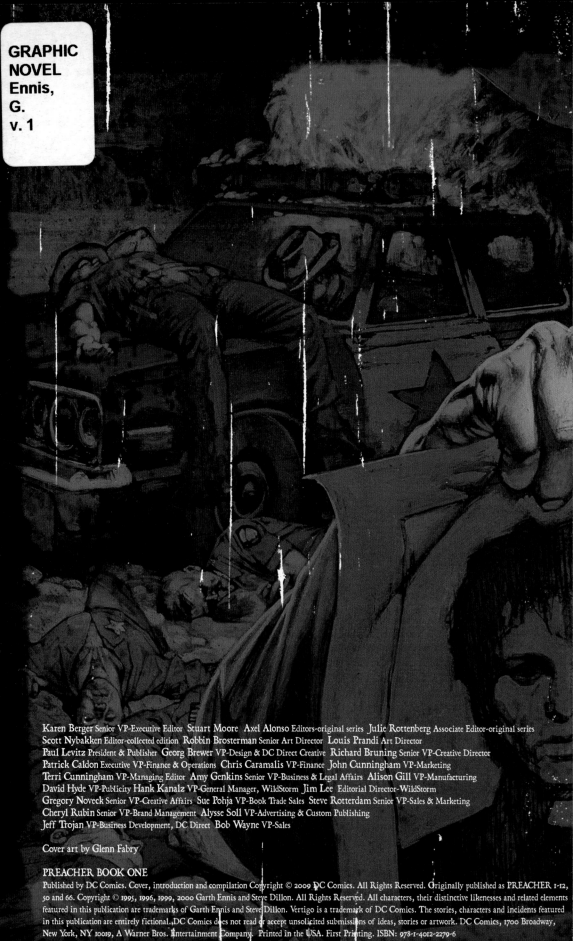

Karen Berger Senior VP-Executive Editor Stuart Moore Axel Alonso Editors-original series Julie Rottenberg Associate Editor-original series
Scott Nybakken Editor-collected edition Robbin Brosterman Senior Art Director Louis Prandi Art Director
Paul Levitz President & Publisher Georg Brewer VP-Design & DC Direct Creative Richard Bruning Senior VP-Creative Director
Patrick Caldon Executive VP-Finance & Operations Chris Caramalis VP-Finance John Cunningham VP-Marketing
Terri Cunningham VP-Managing Editor Amy Genkins Senior VP-Business & Legal Affairs Alison Gill VP-Manufacturing
David Hyde VP-Publicity Hank Kanalz VP-General Manager, WildStorm Jim Lee Editorial Director-WildStorm
Gregory Noveck Senior VP-Creative Affairs Sue Pohja VP-Book Trade Sales Steve Rotterdam Senior VP-Sales & Marketing
Cheryl Rubin Senior VP-Brand Management Alysse Soll VP-Advertising & Custom Publishing
Jeff Trojan VP-Business Development, DC Direct Bob Wayne VP-Sales

Cover art by Glenn Fabry

PREACHER BOOK ONE

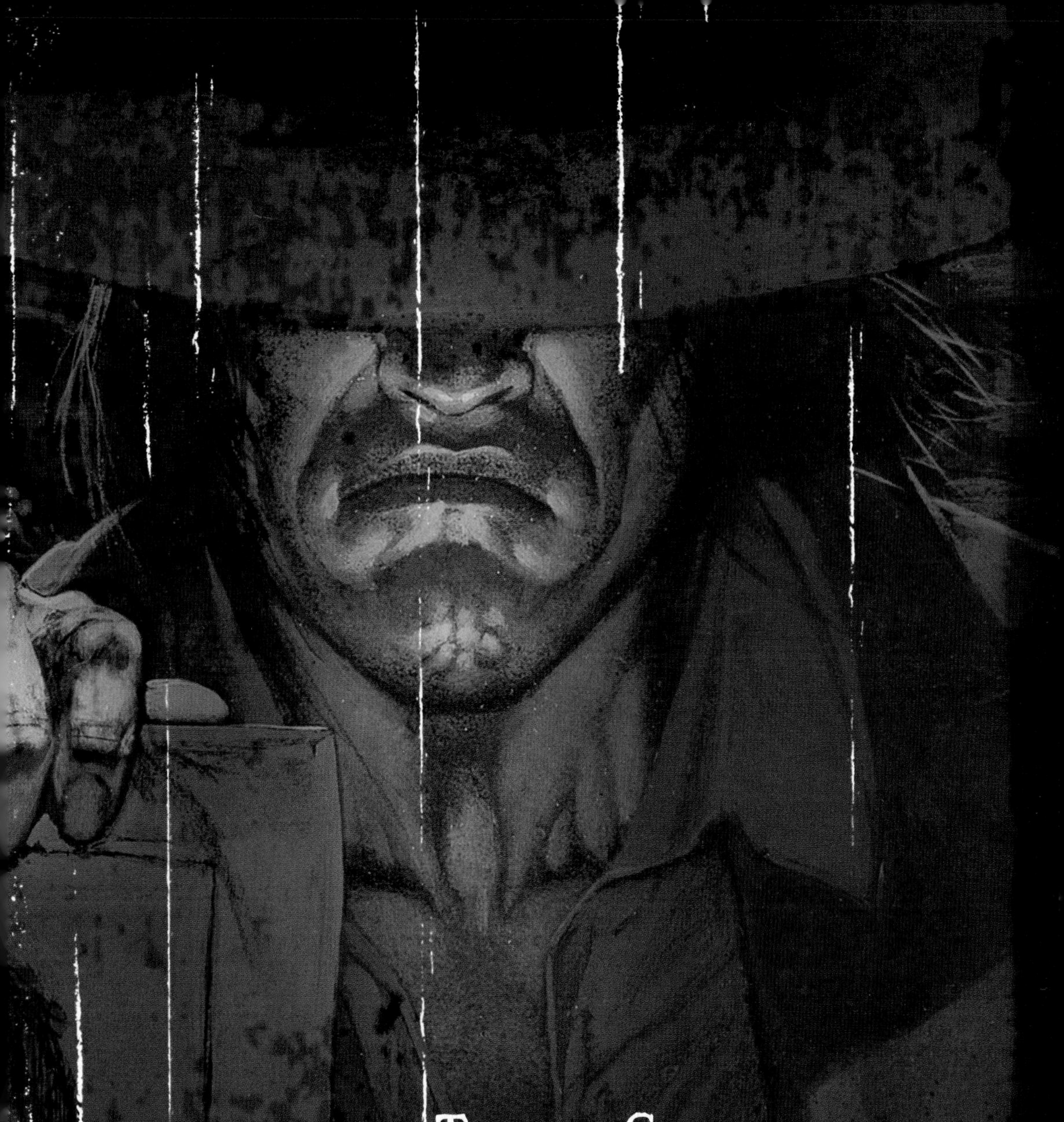

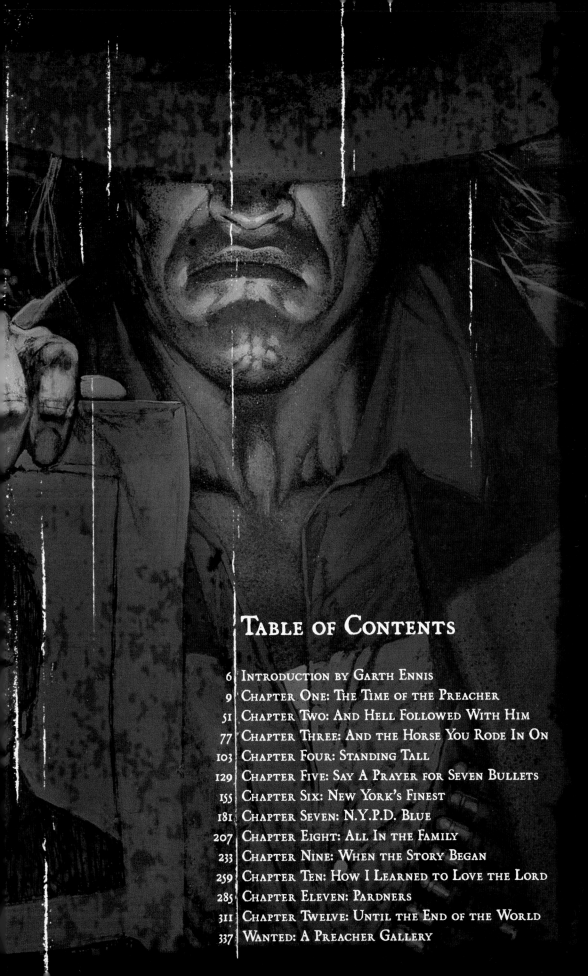

Table of Contents

The Greatest Thing Since Sliced Bread

Memorably described by British comics old contemptible Dave Gibbons as "uncalled for," and by Marvel Comics editor-in-chief Joe Quesada as "a good, one-dump read," PREACHER was many things to many people. Some liked it, some loathed it. A few constantly railed against it, realizing too late that their howls of protest translated directly into increased sales for the object of their frustration. Most understood that we were going all the way to issue 66 come hell or high water, and that the smart thing to do was either bale out or come along for the ride.

What does PREACHER mean to me? Enormous enjoyment is the expression that first comes to mind; there are far, far worse ways to spend five years than writing a story you love about characters you've created yourself. "Whopping great wodges of cash" is another relevant phrase; there seems little point in trying to deny it. Finally, the book established my name in a way that led to many more enjoyable projects, and continues to do to this day. So big thumbs-up all round, that would be my verdict.

Now, as I stroll the battlements of La Casa delle Pistole di Navarone, enjoying the Tuscan evening with my mongoose Charlie at my heels, my thoughts drift back to those heady times and to the people that I shared them with. I watch the sun sink behind a line of trees on the horizon, those ones that always seem so perfectly aligned for a nice stock establishing shot of the Italian countryside, and I recall the comrades with whom I embarked on that extraordinary journey. Where are they now, my dearest PREACHER chums? Gone, all gone. All swept away and scattered to the winds, each one individually violated by the fickle finger of fate. I take another sip of whatever wizard Eyetie plonk it is I'm quaffing... and I remember.

Original editor *Stuart Moore's* career in stand-up comedy went nowhere, largely due to his crippling inability to tell a joke. The Mother-In-Law stuff was one thing, but the infamous "Flintstone Incident" was the final nail in his coffin. Soon afterwards, he joined the Legion to forget.

His replacement *Axel Alonso* runs D-Block in Riker's now. "Don't be messin' wit' the Double-A," newcomers are told, "or he be all up in yo' shit wit' a quickness." For the price of twenty menthol Kools a day, a sensible inmate can usually avoid Alonso's ire; but woe betide the "hapless muthafucka" whom he decides to make his "bitch."

Dreadful oik and, yes, I suppose, talented colorist *Matt Hollingsworth* has left his native land for pastures new, where he lies in wait for the credulous. Obviously there's always been trouble in the Balkans, but the granting of his permanent visa seems like an act of pure recklessness. Any Archdukes in the vicinity are advised to keep a wary eye out.

We were all delighted when good egg and ace talent *Pam Rambo* took over from the beastly Hollingsworth. Personally, I can't decide if the best bit was when the giant bomb went off, or if it was when the truck driver slid out of the cab in several wet, meaty slices. But a splendid return to form, I think we can all agree on that.

Clem Robbins succumbed to a drubbing.

Glenn Fabry's ghastly wraith haunts the barren moorlands of Brighton to this day. Charming and debonair even in undeath, somehow his tormented howls retain the good humor, split-second comic timing and sheer wit that always made the man such splendid company. His specter is available for private commissions. Still a hell of a talent.

And *Steve Dillon*? Co-creator, artistic genius, storyteller without compare, Steve's contribution to the success of PREACHER cannot be overestimated. It was all very well for me to script the madness one week out of every month and then move on to another project, but Steve had to live with it — *and make it work* — day in, day out, for five and a half years. I have, indeed, always gone to some lengths to make this very point, so it is with some sadness that I must acknowledge the low esteem with which my former oppo now regards me. Hanging in the cum-dungeons of Lord Flarg The Octo-Cocked, his lot is obviously not a happy one, but in my defense I would just like to establish that a) the contract clearly said "eternal *soul*" (singular), and b) of course that wasn't a doubled-headed coin. Whoever heard of such a thing, outside the pages of some penny dreadful or similar flight of fiction?

But enough of this cloying sentimentality, this sugar-coated scamper down the paths of yesteryear. Why let misplaced guilt interfere with such a perfect evening? Twilight settles on the land like a pissed-up fat lad sprawling on his couch, and soon the chorus of the night begins. The rabbit drops a euro in the jukebox. The badger kicks the living shit out of the weasel. The nightjar fills itself with jam. All is well.

The sensible thing to do would be to open another bottle, but that would make eight for the day. Hmm... heads I do, tails I don't... well, well.

Heads again.

— **Garth Ennis**
Wombling free, February 2009

PREACHER

Book One

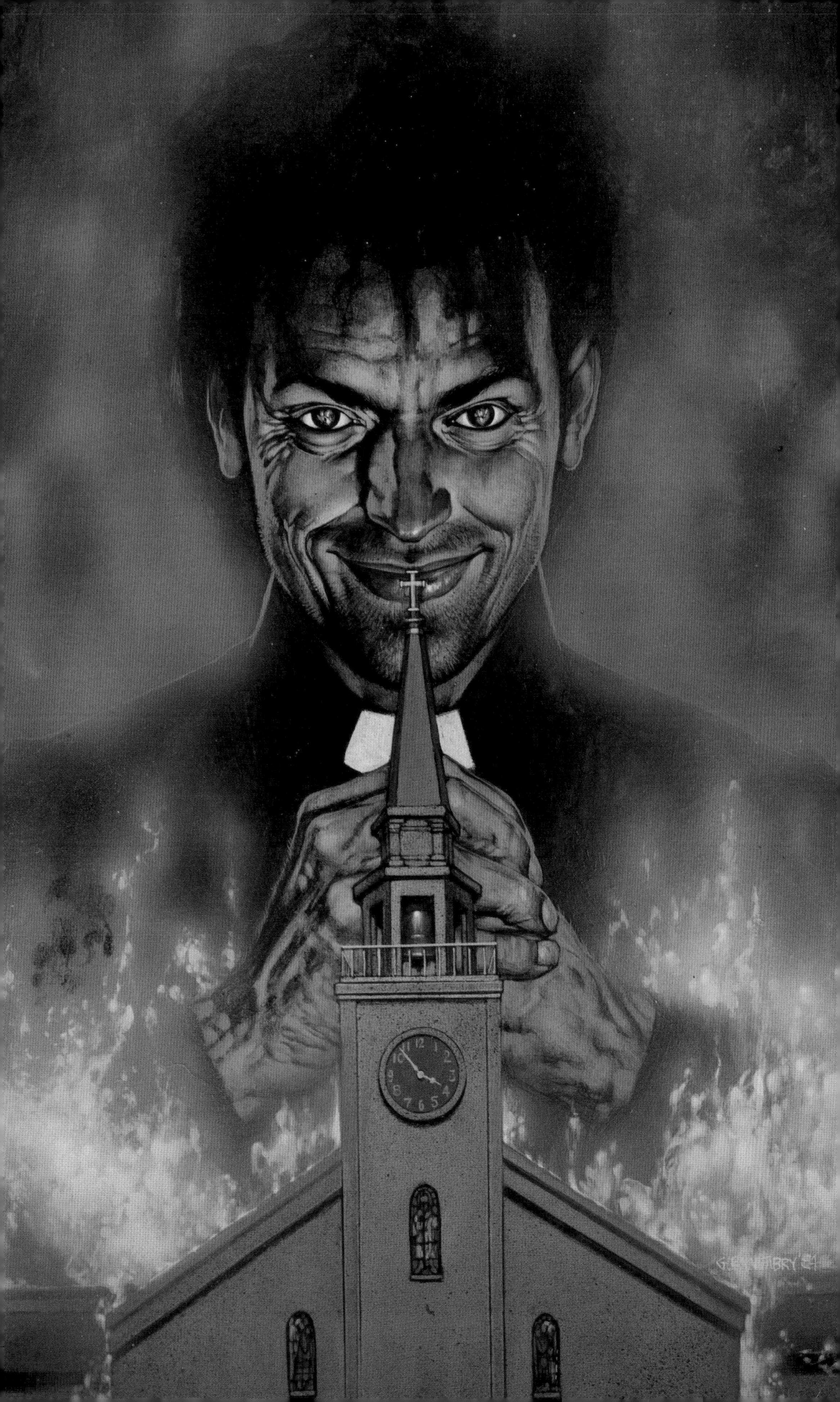

"Whatever it tells me, whatever it says —
it sounds like the word of God."

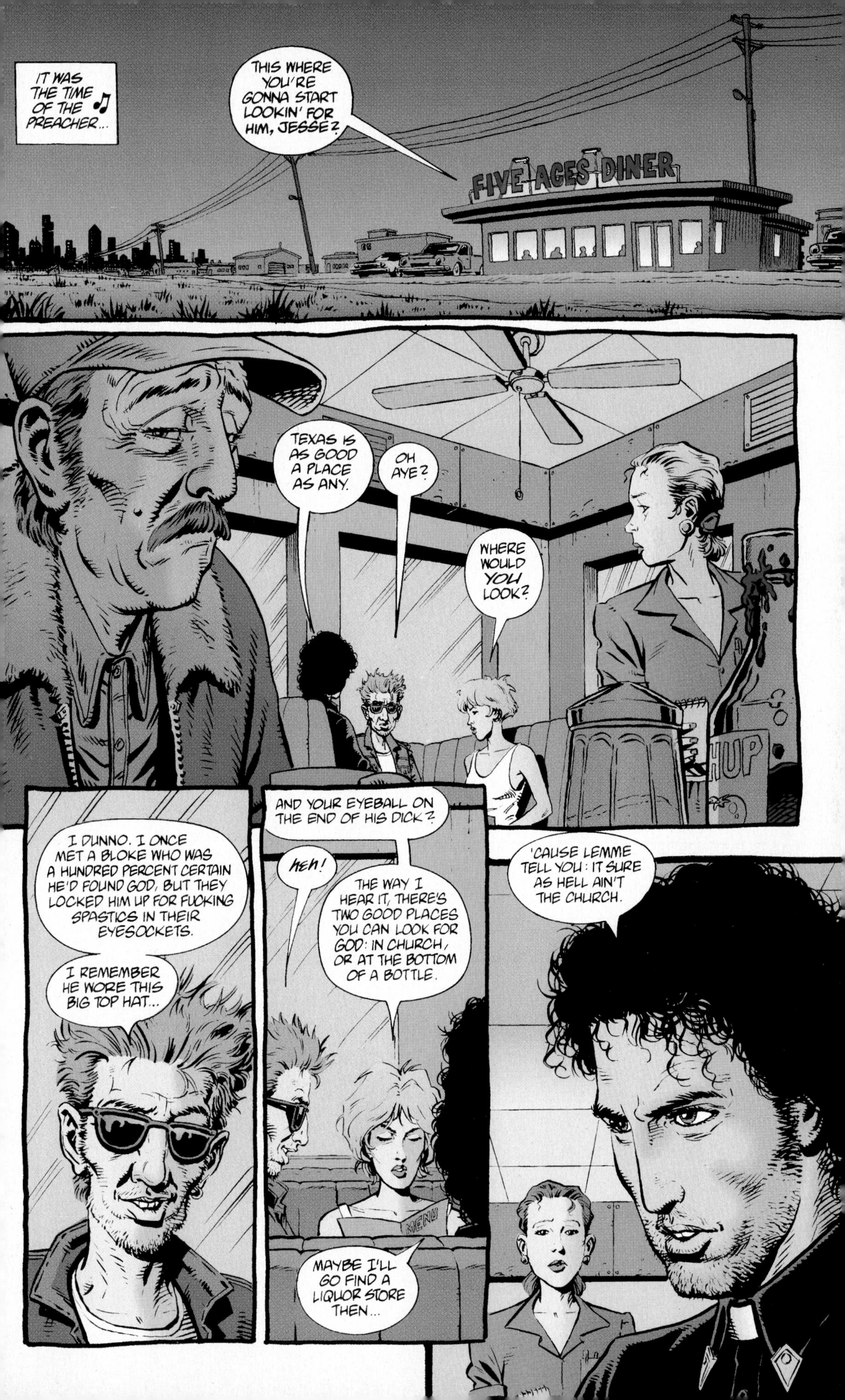
IT WAS THE TIME OF THE ♫ PREACHER...
THIS WHERE YOU'RE GONNA START LOOKIN' FOR HIM, JESSE?
FIVE AGES DINER
TEXAS IS AS GOOD A PLACE AS ANY.
OH AYE?
WHERE WOULD YOU LOOK?
HUP
I DUNNO. I ONCE MET A BLOKE WHO WAS A HUNDRED PERCENT CERTAIN HE'D FOUND GOD, BUT THEY LOCKED HIM UP FOR FUCKING SPASTICS IN THEIR EYESOCKETS.
I REMEMBER HE WORE THIS BIG TOP HAT...
AND YOUR EYEBALL ON THE END OF HIS DICK?
HEH!
THE WAY I HEAR IT, THERE'S TWO GOOD PLACES YOU CAN LOOK FOR GOD: IN CHURCH, OR AT THE BOTTOM OF A BOTTLE.
MENU
MAYBE I'LL GO FIND A LIQUOR STORE THEN...
'CAUSE LEMME TELL YOU: IT SURE AS HELL AIN'T THE CHURCH.

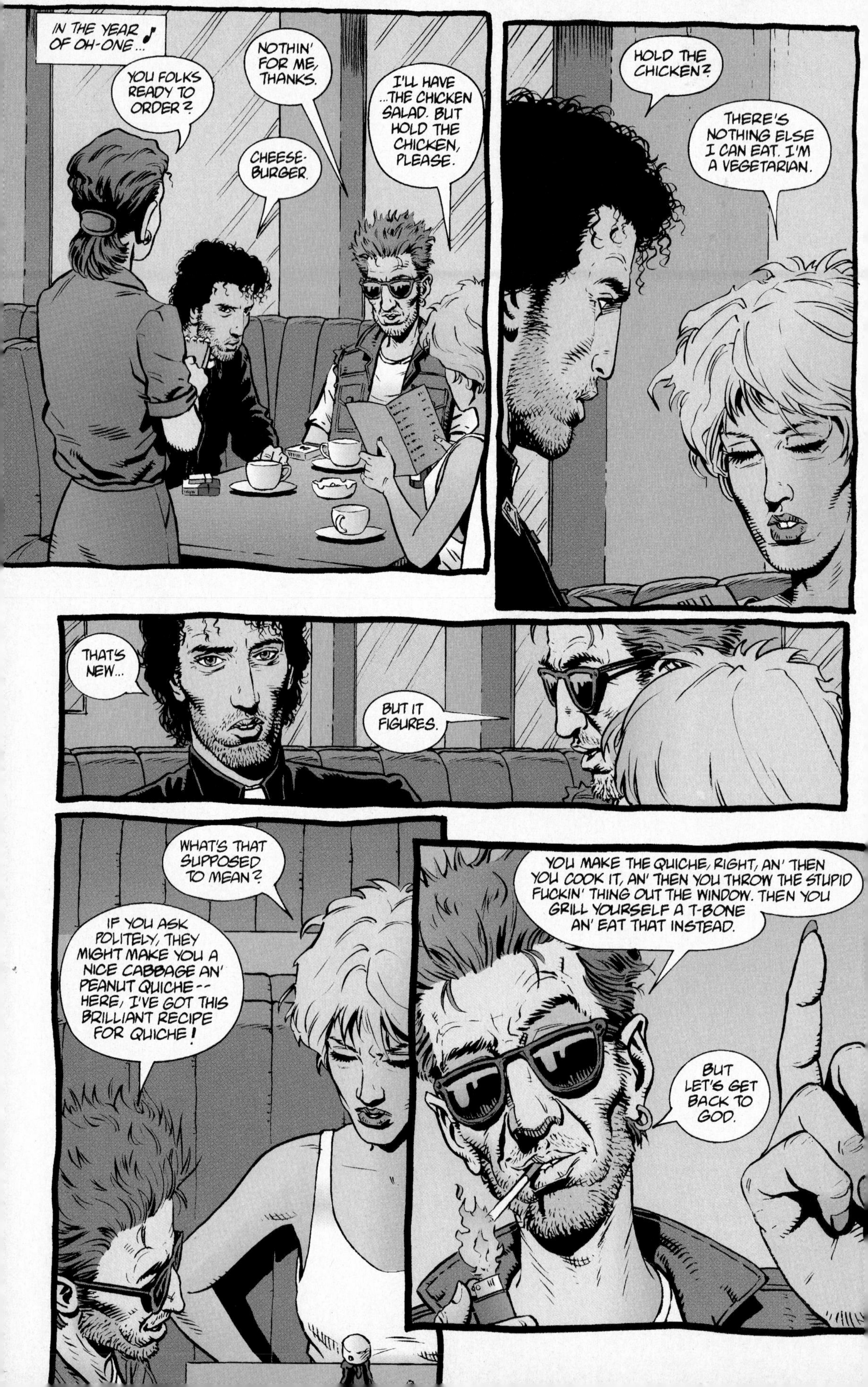
IN THE YEAR OF OH-ONE...
YOU FOLKS READY TO ORDER?
NOTHIN' FOR ME, THANKS.
CHEESE-BURGER.
I'LL HAVE ...THE CHICKEN SALAD. BUT HOLD THE CHICKEN, PLEASE.
HOLD THE CHICKEN?
THERE'S NOTHING ELSE I CAN EAT. I'M A VEGETARIAN.
THAT'S NEW...
BUT IT FIGURES.
WHAT'S THAT SUPPOSED TO MEAN?
IF YOU ASK POLITELY, THEY MIGHT MAKE YOU A NICE CABBAGE AN' PEANUT QUICHE-- HERE, I'VE GOT THIS BRILLIANT RECIPE FOR QUICHE!
YOU MAKE THE QUICHE, RIGHT, AN' THEN YOU COOK IT, AN' THEN YOU THROW THE STUPID FUCKIN' THING OUT THE WINDOW. THEN YOU GRILL YOURSELF A T-BONE AN' EAT THAT INSTEAD.
BUT LET'S GET BACK TO GOD.

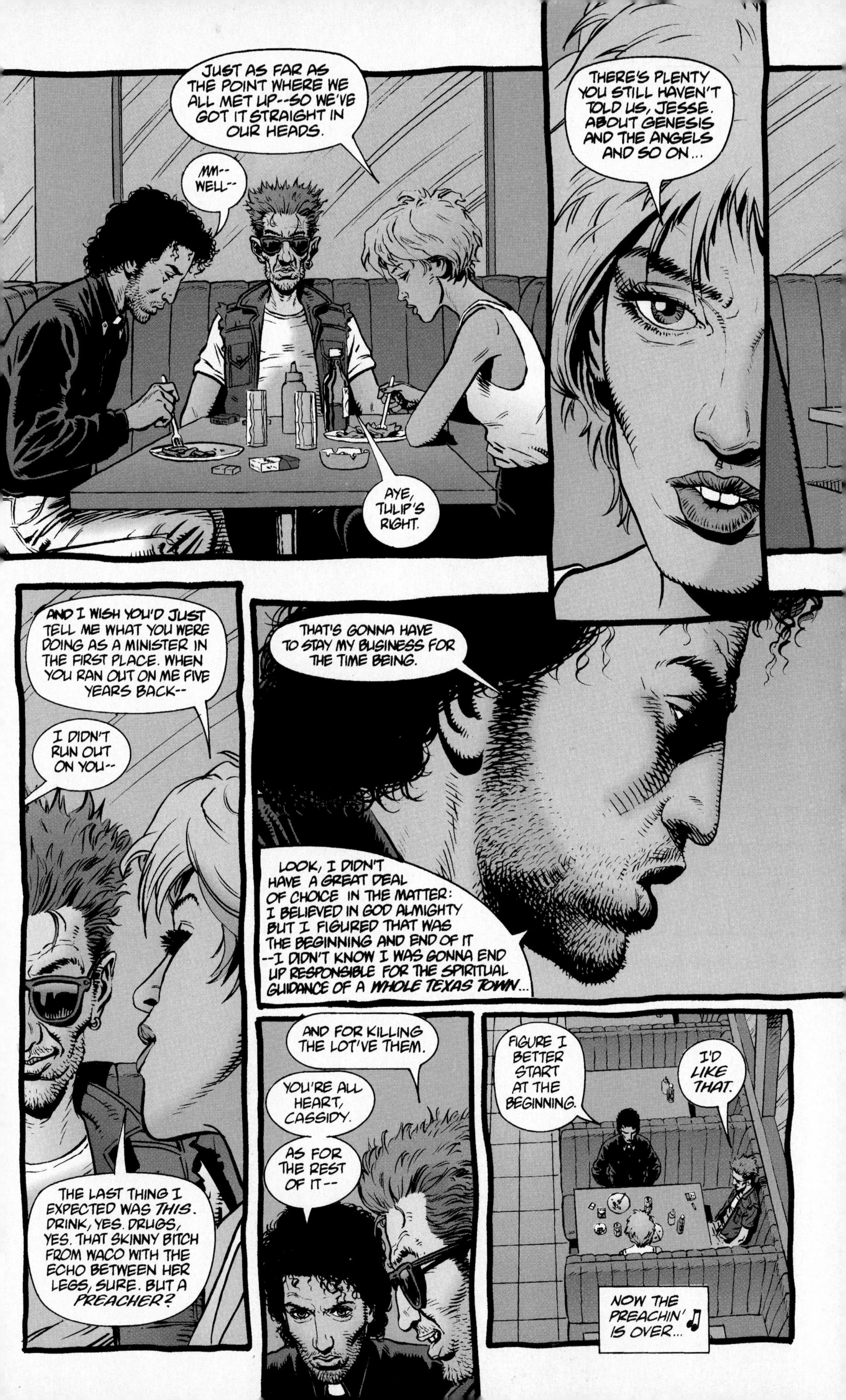
JUST AS FAR AS THE POINT WHERE WE ALL MET UP--SO WE'VE GOT IT STRAIGHT IN OUR HEADS.
MM-- WELL--
AYE, TULIP'S RIGHT.
THERE'S PLENTY YOU STILL HAVEN'T TOLD US, JESSE. ABOUT GENESIS AND THE ANGELS AND SO ON...
AND I WISH YOU'D JUST TELL ME WHAT YOU WERE DOING AS A MINISTER IN THE FIRST PLACE. WHEN YOU RAN OUT ON ME FIVE YEARS BACK--
I DIDN'T RUN OUT ON YOU--
THE LAST THING I EXPECTED WAS THIS. DRINK, YES. DRUGS, YES. THAT SKINNY BITCH FROM WACO WITH THE ECHO BETWEEN HER LEGS, SURE. BUT A PREACHER?
THAT'S GONNA HAVE TO STAY MY BUSINESS FOR THE TIME BEING.
LOOK, I DIDN'T HAVE A GREAT DEAL OF CHOICE IN THE MATTER: I BELIEVED IN GOD ALMIGHTY BUT I FIGURED THAT WAS THE BEGINNING AND END OF IT --I DIDN'T KNOW I WAS GONNA END UP RESPONSIBLE FOR THE SPIRITUAL GUIDANCE OF A WHOLE TEXAS TOWN...
AND FOR KILLING THE LOT'VE THEM.
YOU'RE ALL HEART, CASSIDY.
AS FOR THE REST OF IT --
FIGURE I BETTER START AT THE BEGINNING.
I'D LIKE THAT.
NOW THE PREACHIN' IS OVER...

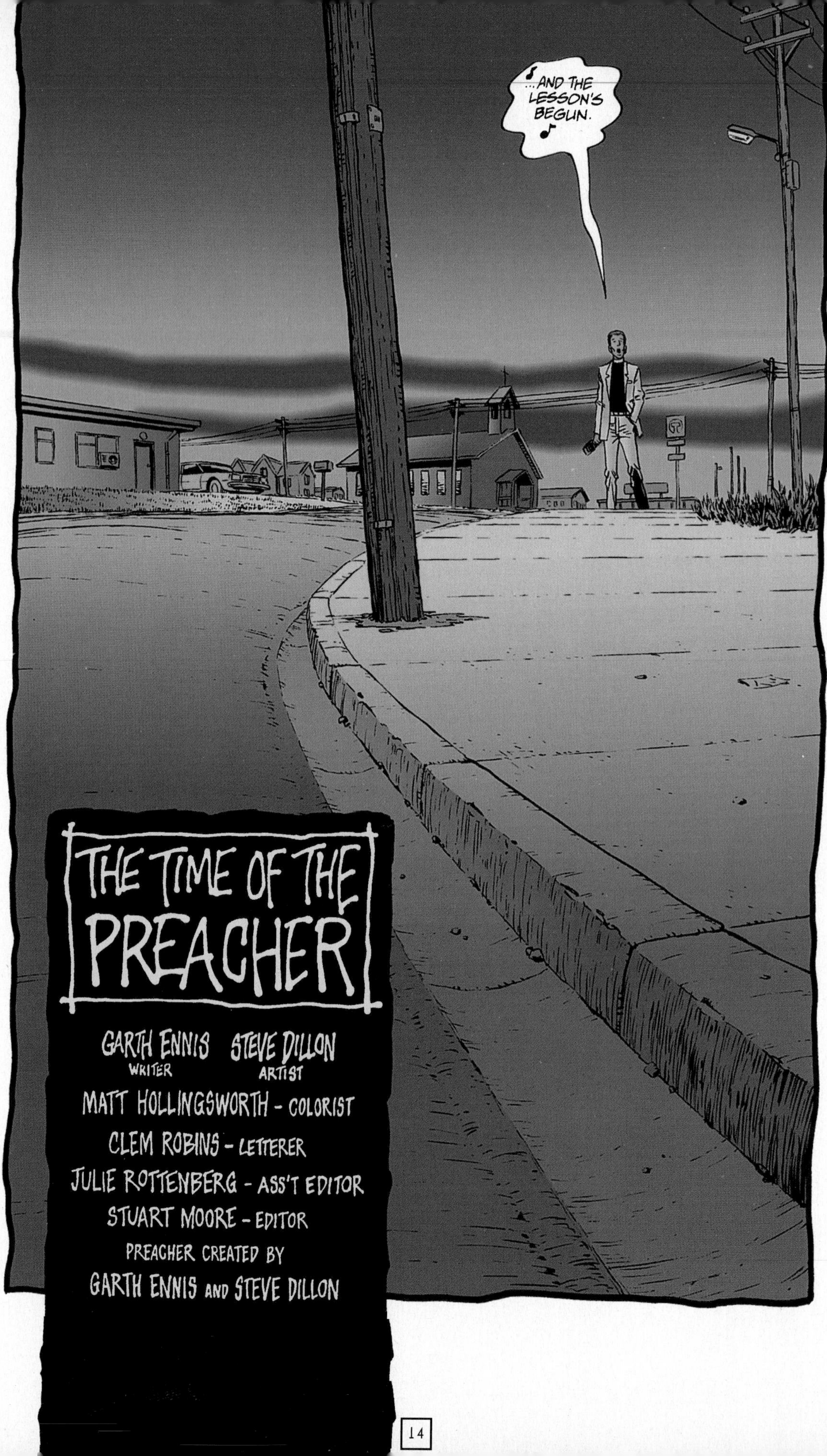
...AND THE LESSON'S BEGUN.
THE TIME OF THE PREACHER
GARTH ENNIS WRITER
STEVE DILLON ARTIST
MATT HOLLINGSWORTH - COLORIST
CLEM ROBINS - LETTERER
JULIE ROTTENBERG - ASS'T EDITOR
STUART MOORE - EDITOR
PREACHER CREATED BY GARTH ENNIS AND STEVE DILLON

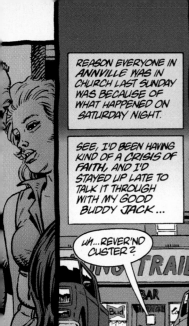

REASON EVERYONE IN ANNVILLE WAS IN CHURCH LAST SUNDAY WAS BECAUSE OF WHAT HAPPENED ON SATURDAY NIGHT.

SEE, I'D BEEN HAVING KIND OF A *CRISIS OF FAITH,* AND I'D STAYED UP LATE TO TALK IT THROUGH WITH MY GOOD BUDDY *JACK...*

UH...REVER'ND CUSTER?

JESSE'LL DO JUST FINE, LEONARD.

JESSE... SURE. JUST WE DON'T SEE TOO MUCH OF YOU IN HERE, IS ALL.

BEEN MEANING TO *FIX* THAT. HOW 'BOUT A BEER?

...COMIN' UP.

ALL RIGHT IF I SIT HERE?

SURE.

AAHHHH.

THAT'S *GOOD* BEER, LEONARD.

HELL, YOU CAN ALMOST TASTE IT THROUGH THE *GODDAMN* WATER.

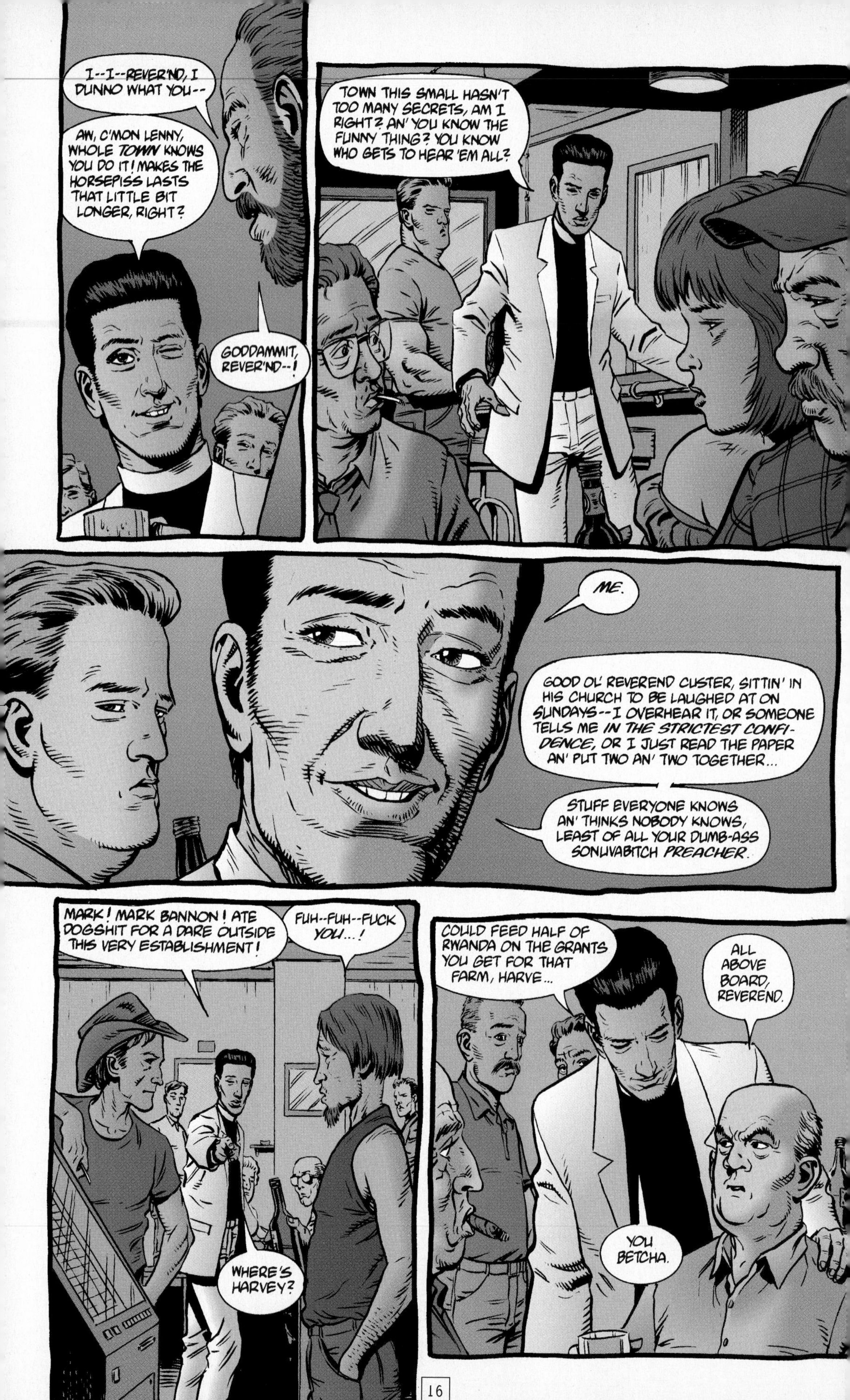

I--I--REVER'ND, I DUNNO WHAT YOU--
AW, C'MON LENNY, WHOLE *TOWN* KNOWS YOU DO IT! MAKES THE HORSEPISS LASTS THAT LITTLE BIT LONGER, RIGHT?
GODDAMMIT, REVER'ND--!
TOWN THIS SMALL HASN'T TOO MANY SECRETS, AM I RIGHT? AN' YOU KNOW THE FUNNY THING? YOU KNOW WHO GETS TO HEAR 'EM ALL?
ME.
GOOD OL' REVEREND CUSTER, SITTIN' IN HIS CHURCH TO BE LAUGHED AT ON SUNDAYS--I OVERHEAR IT, OR SOMEONE TELLS ME *IN THE STRICTEST CONFI-DENCE,* OR I JUST READ THE PAPER AN' PUT TWO AN' TWO TOGETHER...
STUFF EVERYONE KNOWS AN' THINKS NOBODY KNOWS, LEAST OF ALL YOUR DUMB-ASS SONUVABITCH *PREACHER.*
MARK! MARK BANNON! ATE DOGSHIT FOR A DARE OUTSIDE THIS VERY ESTABLISHMENT!
FUH--FUH--FUCK *YOU*...!
WHERE'S HARVEY?
COULD FEED HALF OF RWANDA ON THE GRANTS YOU GET FOR THAT FARM, HARVE...
ALL ABOVE BOARD, REVEREND.
YOU BETCHA.

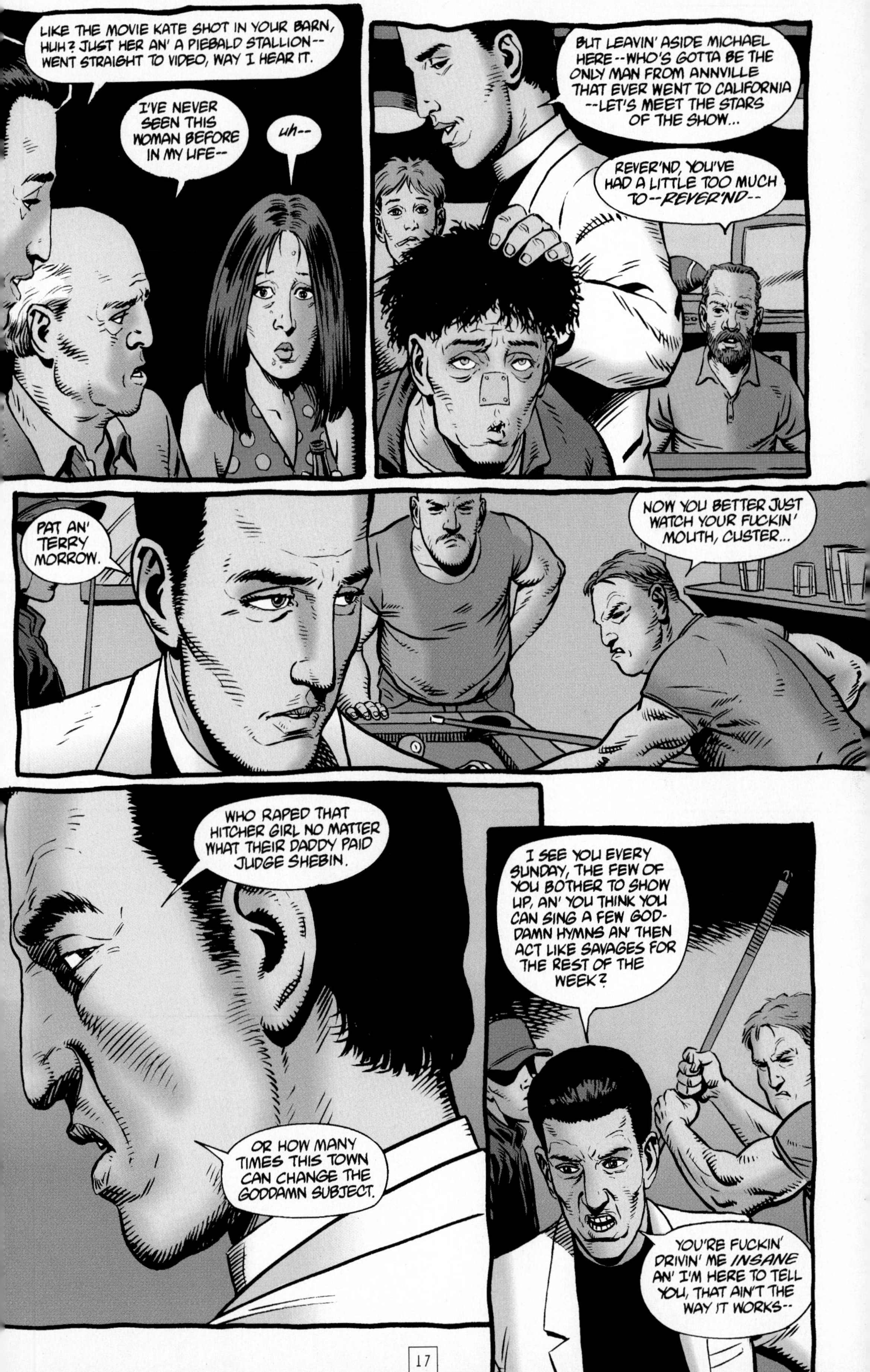
LIKE THE MOVIE KATE SHOT IN YOUR BARN, HUH? JUST HER AN' A PIEBALD STALLION--WENT STRAIGHT TO VIDEO, WAY I HEAR IT.
I'VE NEVER SEEN THIS WOMAN BEFORE IN MY LIFE--
uh--
BUT LEAVIN' ASIDE MICHAEL HERE--WHO'S GOTTA BE THE ONLY MAN FROM ANNVILLE THAT EVER WENT TO CALIFORNIA--LET'S MEET THE STARS OF THE SHOW...
REVER'ND, YOU'VE HAD A LITTLE TOO MUCH TO--*REVER'ND*--
PAT AN' TERRY MORROW.
NOW YOU BETTER JUST WATCH YOUR FUCKIN' MOUTH, CUSTER...
WHO RAPED THAT HITCHER GIRL NO MATTER WHAT THEIR DADDY PAID JUDGE SHEBIN.
OR HOW MANY TIMES THIS TOWN CAN CHANGE THE GODDAMN SUBJECT.
I SEE YOU EVERY SUNDAY, THE FEW OF YOU BOTHER TO SHOW UP, AN' YOU THINK YOU CAN SING A FEW GOD-DAMN HYMNS AN' THEN ACT LIKE SAVAGES FOR THE REST OF THE WEEK?
YOU'RE FUCKIN' DRIVIN' ME *INSANE* AN' I'M HERE TO TELL YOU, THAT AIN'T THE WAY IT WORKS--

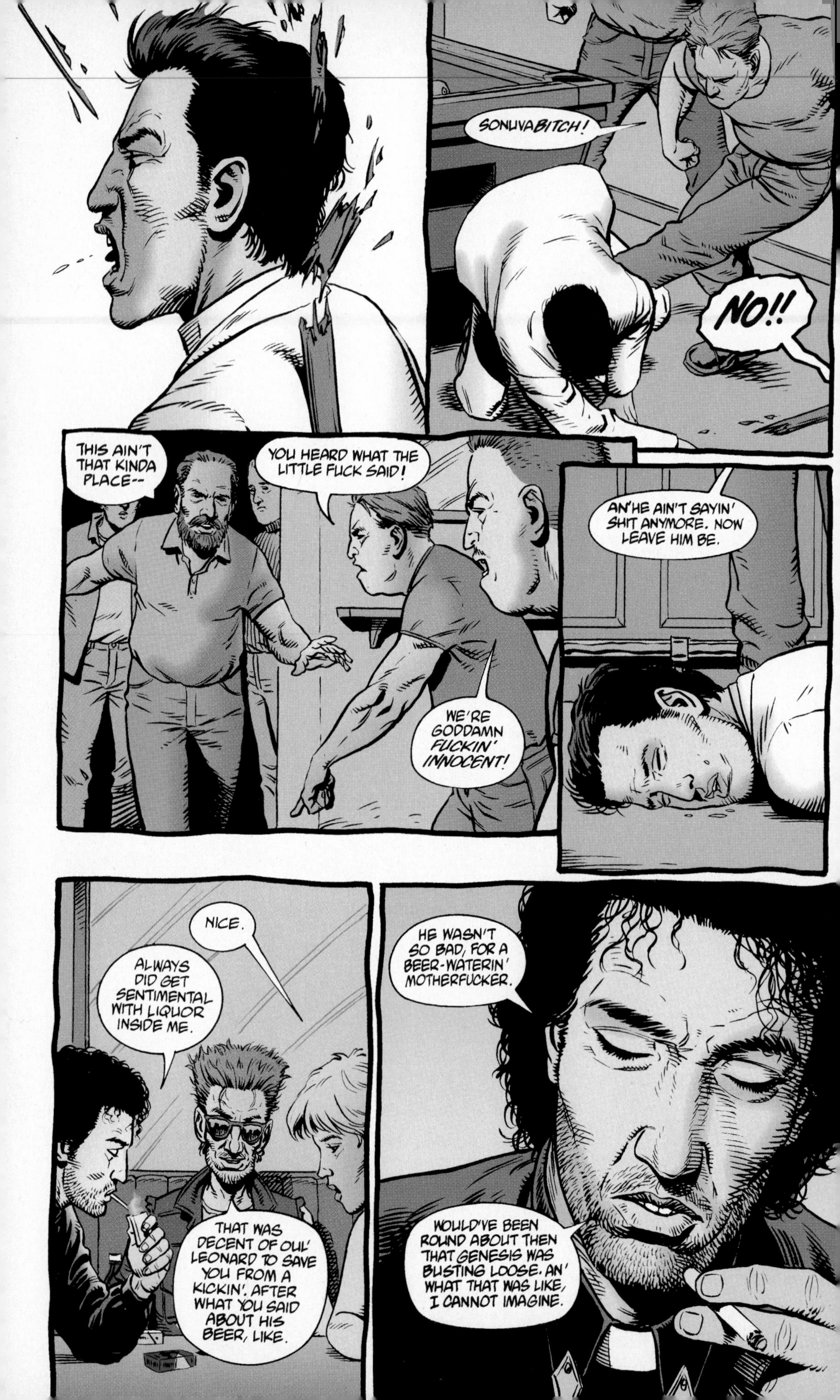
SONUVA BITCH!
NO!!
THIS AIN'T THAT KINDA PLACE--
YOU HEARD WHAT THE LITTLE FUCK SAID!
WE'RE GODDAMN FUCKIN' INNOCENT!
AN'HE AIN'T SAYIN' SHIT ANYMORE. NOW LEAVE HIM BE.
NICE.
ALWAYS DID GET SENTIMENTAL WITH LIQUOR INSIDE ME.
THAT WAS DECENT OF OUL' LEONARD TO SAVE YOU FROM A KICKIN', AFTER WHAT YOU SAID ABOUT HIS BEER, LIKE.
HE WASN'T SO BAD, FOR A BEER-WATERIN' MOTHERFUCKER.
WOULD'VE BEEN ROUND ABOUT THEN THAT GENESIS WAS BUSTING LOOSE. AN' WHAT THAT WAS LIKE, I CANNOT IMAGINE.

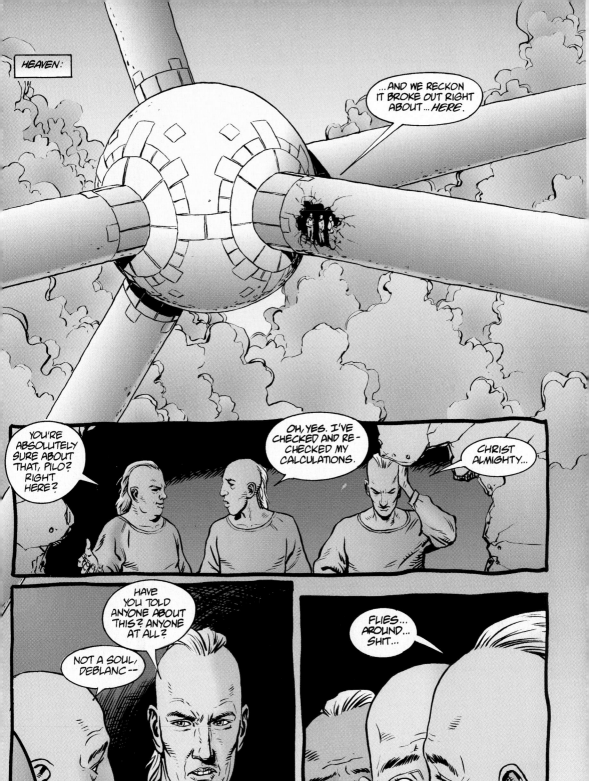

HEAVEN:

...AND WE RECKON IT BROKE OUT RIGHT ABOUT... *HERE.*

YOU'RE ABSOLUTELY SURE ABOUT THAT, PILO? RIGHT HERE?

OH, YES. I'VE CHECKED AND RE-CHECKED MY CALCULATIONS.

CHRIST ALMIGHTY...

HAVE YOU TOLD ANYONE ABOUT THIS? ANYONE AT ALL?

NOT A SOUL, DEBLANC --

BECAUSE THE LAST THING WE NEED NOW IS FOR THE SERAPHI TO FIND OUT. ONE SNIFF OF IT AND THE BASTARDS'LL BE DOWN ON US LIKE...

FLIES... AROUND... SHIT...

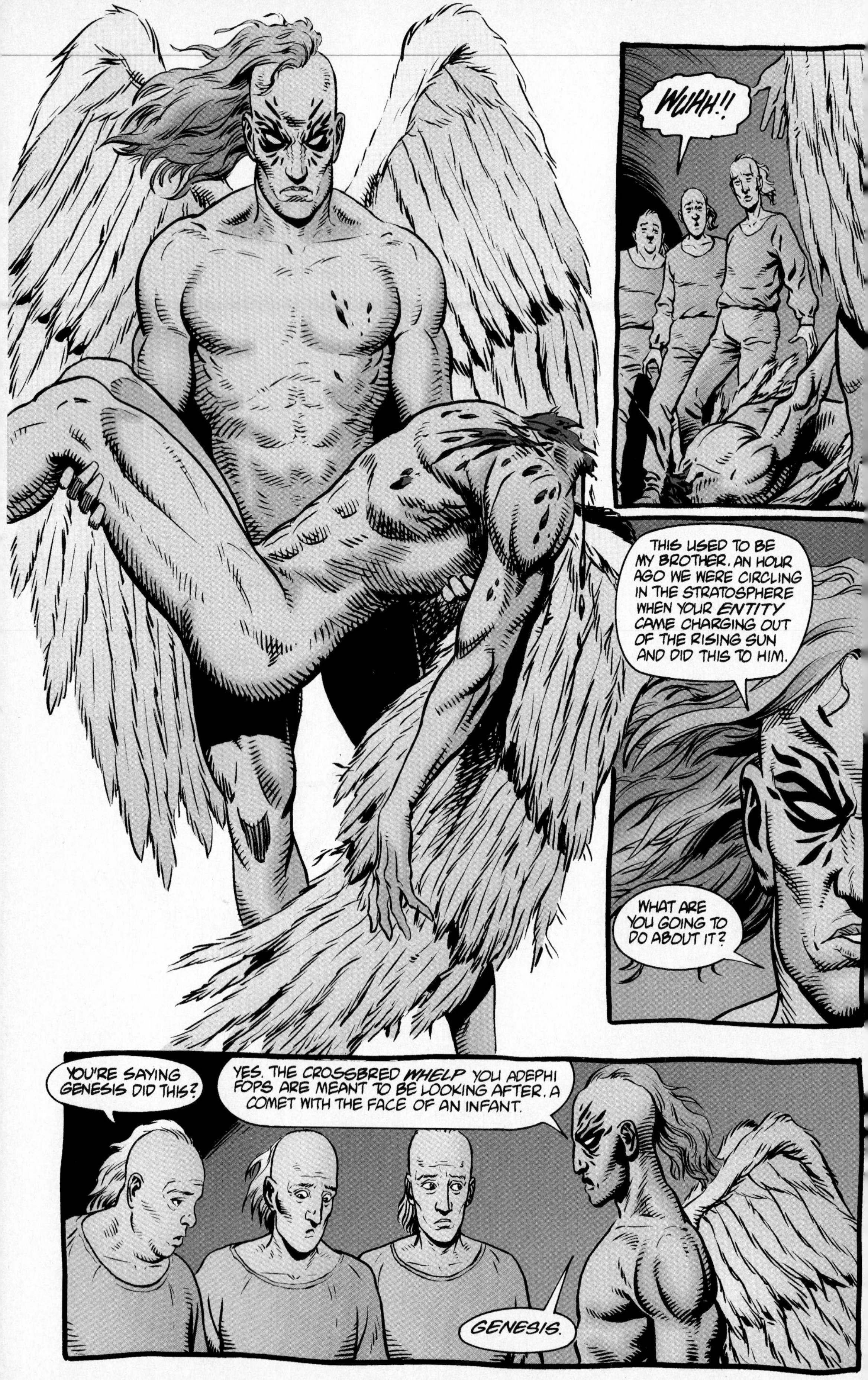
WUHH!!
THIS USED TO BE MY BROTHER. AN HOUR AGO WE WERE CIRCLING IN THE STRATOSPHERE WHEN YOUR ENTITY CAME CHARGING OUT OF THE RISING SUN AND DID THIS TO HIM.
WHAT ARE YOU GOING TO DO ABOUT IT?
YOU'RE SAYING GENESIS DID THIS?
YES. THE CROSSBRED WHELP YOU ADEPHI FOPS ARE MEANT TO BE LOOKING AFTER. A COMET WITH THE FACE OF AN INFANT.
GENESIS.

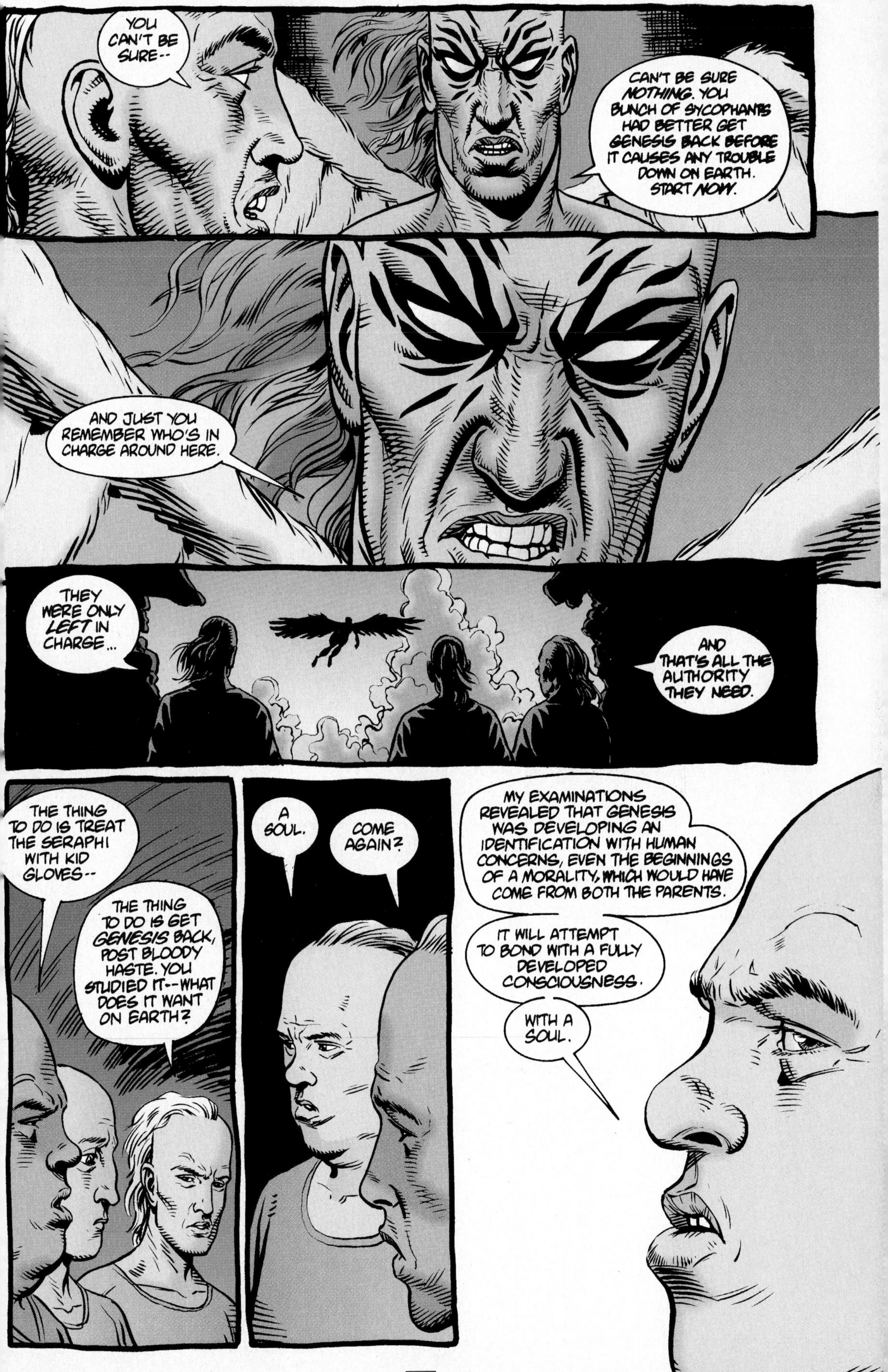
YOU CAN'T BE SURE--
CAN'T BE SURE NOTHING. YOU BUNCH OF SYCOPHANTS HAD BETTER GET GENESIS BACK BEFORE IT CAUSES ANY TROUBLE DOWN ON EARTH. START NOW.
AND JUST YOU REMEMBER WHO'S IN CHARGE AROUND HERE.
THEY WERE ONLY LEFT IN CHARGE...
AND THAT'S ALL THE AUTHORITY THEY NEED.
THE THING TO DO IS TREAT THE SERAPHI WITH KID GLOVES--
THE THING TO DO IS GET GENESIS BACK, POST BLOODY HASTE. YOU STUDIED IT--WHAT DOES IT WANT ON EARTH?
A SOUL.
COME AGAIN?
MY EXAMINATIONS REVEALED THAT GENESIS WAS DEVELOPING AN IDENTIFICATION WITH HUMAN CONCERNS, EVEN THE BEGINNINGS OF A MORALITY, WHICH WOULD HAVE COME FROM BOTH THE PARENTS.
IT WILL ATTEMPT TO BOND WITH A FULLY DEVELOPED CONSCIOUSNESS.
WITH A SOUL.

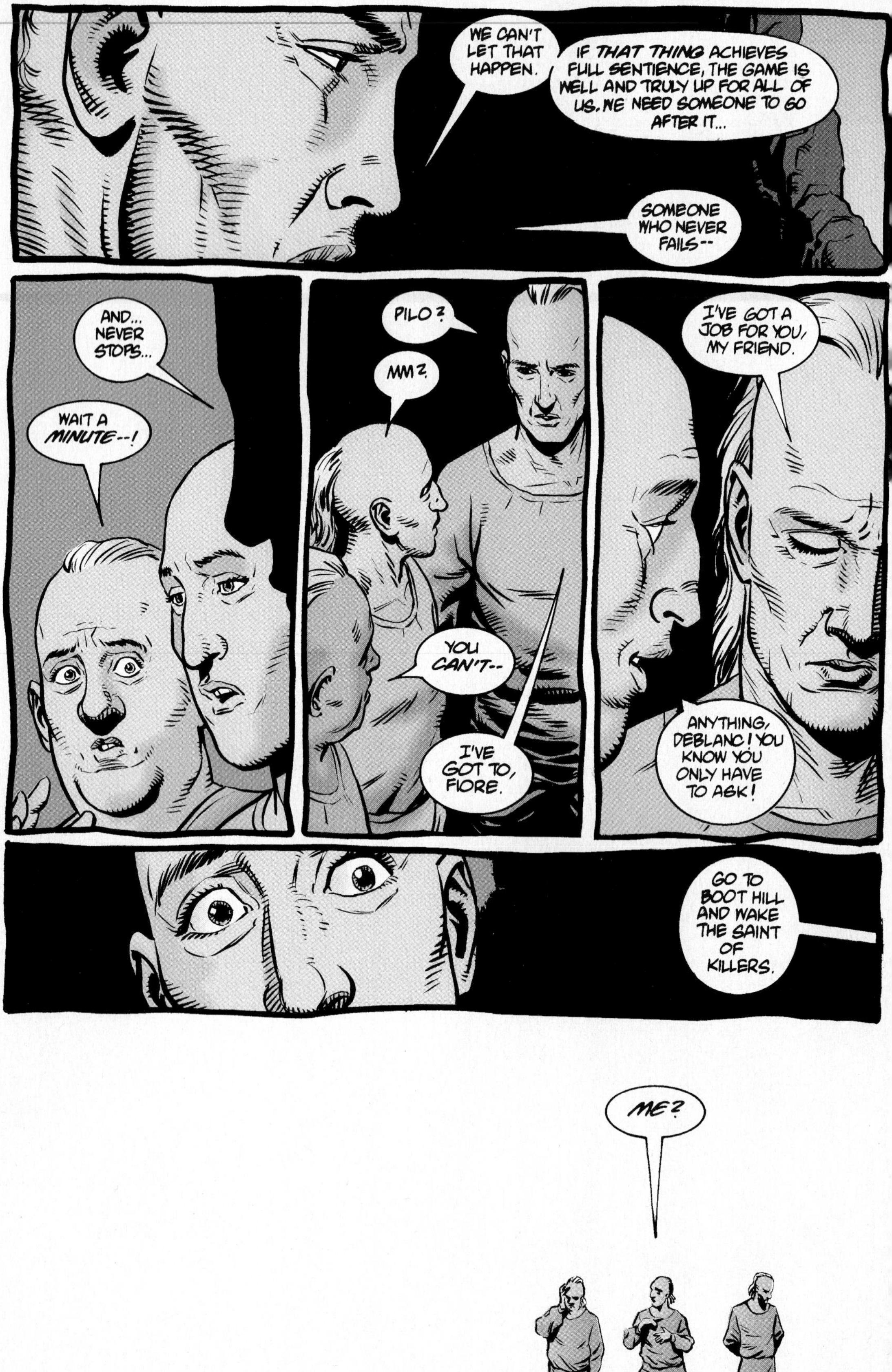
WE CAN'T LET THAT HAPPEN.
IF THAT THING ACHIEVES FULL SENTIENCE, THE GAME IS WELL AND TRULY UP FOR ALL OF US. WE NEED SOMEONE TO GO AFTER IT...
SOMEONE WHO NEVER FAILS--
AND... NEVER STOPS...
WAIT A MINUTE--!
PILO?
MM?
YOU CAN'T--
I'VE GOT TO, FIORE.
I'VE GOT A JOB FOR YOU, MY FRIEND.
ANYTHING, DEBLANC! YOU KNOW YOU ONLY HAVE TO ASK!
GO TO BOOT HILL AND WAKE THE SAINT OF KILLERS.
ME?

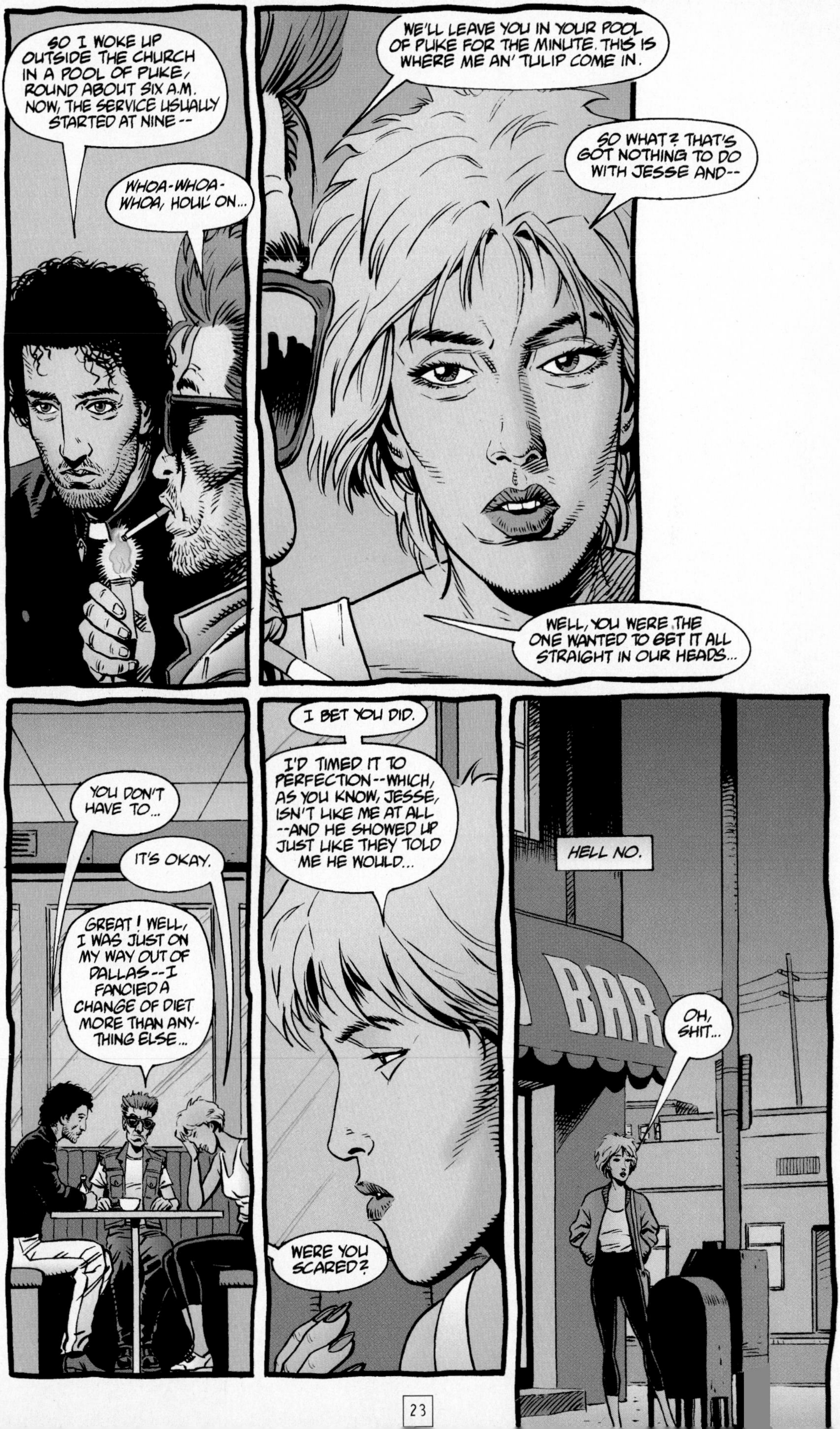

SO I WOKE UP OUTSIDE THE CHURCH IN A POOL OF PUKE, ROUND ABOUT SIX A.M. NOW, THE SERVICE USUALLY STARTED AT NINE --
WHOA-WHOA-WHOA, HOUL' ON...
WE'LL LEAVE YOU IN YOUR POOL OF PUKE FOR THE MINUTE. THIS IS WHERE ME AN' TULIP COME IN.
SO WHAT? THAT'S GOT NOTHING TO DO WITH JESSE AND--
WELL, YOU WERE THE ONE WANTED TO GET IT ALL STRAIGHT IN OUR HEADS...
YOU DON'T HAVE TO...
IT'S OKAY.
GREAT! WELL, I WAS JUST ON MY WAY OUT OF DALLAS--I FANCIED A CHANGE OF DIET MORE THAN ANYTHING ELSE...
I BET YOU DID.
I'D TIMED IT TO PERFECTION--WHICH, AS YOU KNOW, JESSE, ISN'T LIKE ME AT ALL --AND HE SHOWED UP JUST LIKE THEY TOLD ME HE WOULD...
WERE YOU SCARED?
HELL NO.
BAR
OH, SHIT...

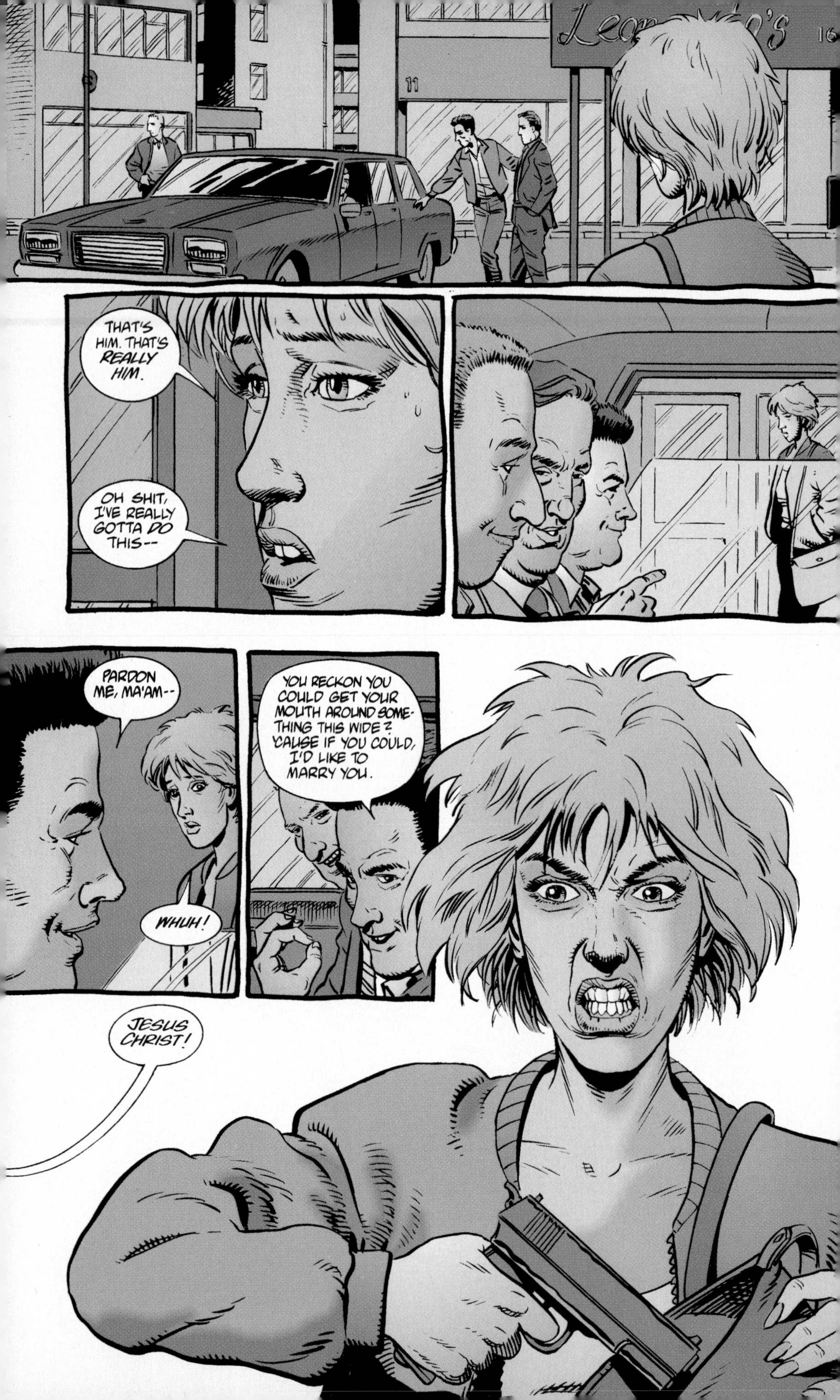
THAT'S HIM. THAT'S REALLY HIM.
OH SHIT, I'VE REALLY GOTTA DO THIS--
PARDON ME, MA'AM--
WHUH!
YOU RECKON YOU COULD GET YOUR MOUTH AROUND SOME-THING THIS WIDE? 'CAUSE IF YOU COULD, I'D LIKE TO MARRY YOU.
JESUS CHRIST!

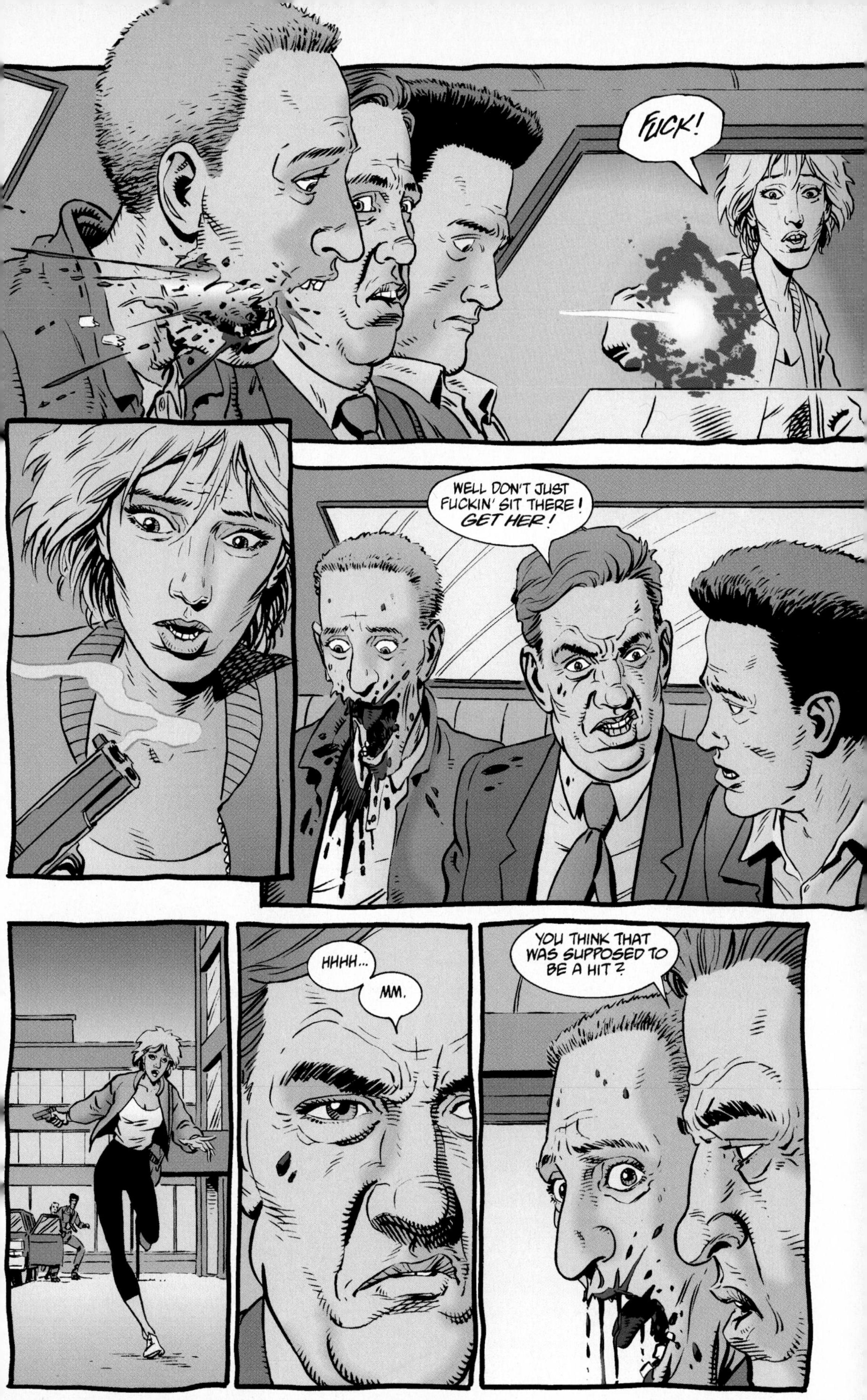
FUCK!
WELL DON'T JUST FUCKIN' SIT THERE! GET HER!
HHHH...
MM.
YOU THINK THAT WAS SUPPOSED TO BE A HIT?

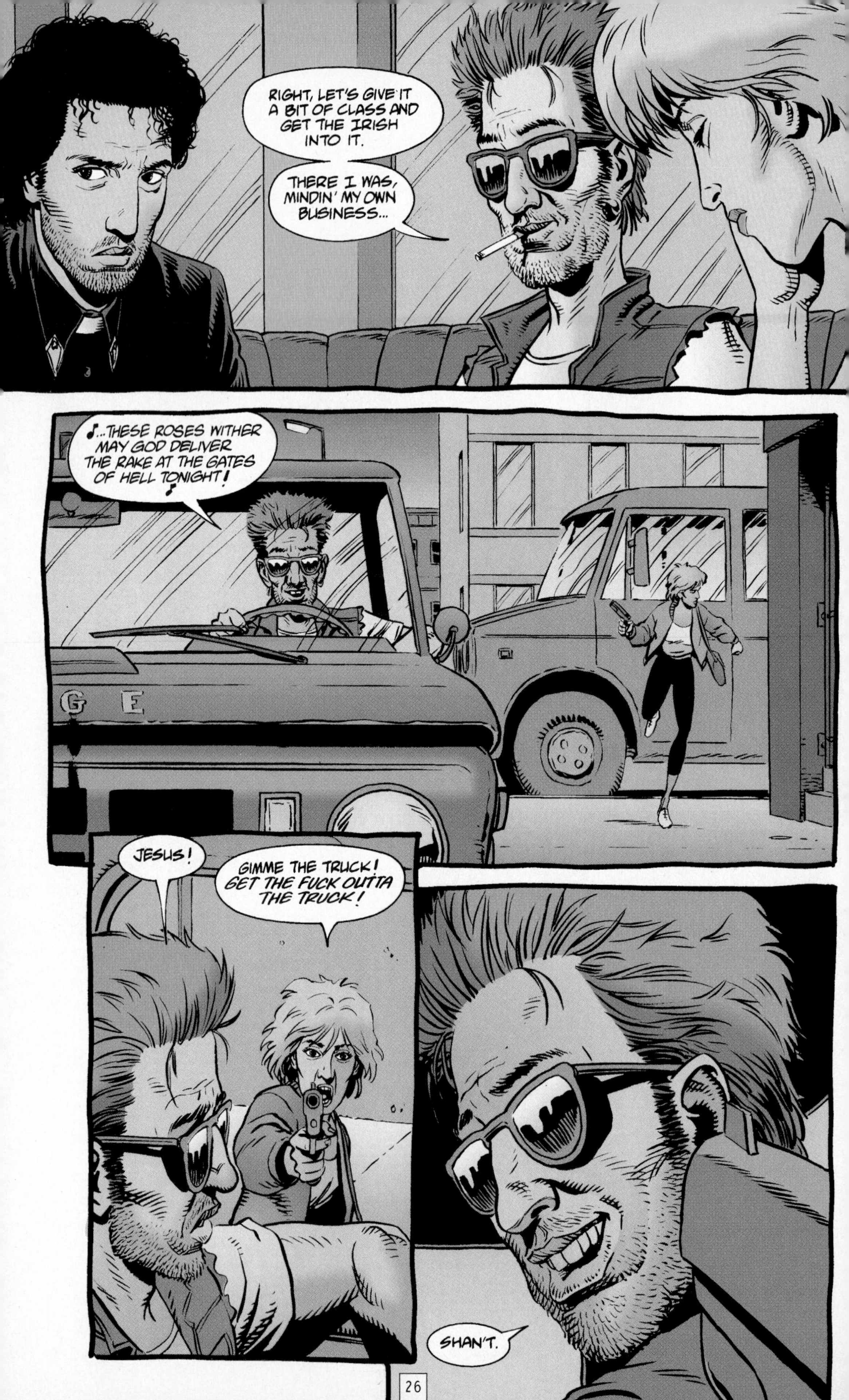
RIGHT, LET'S GIVE IT A BIT OF CLASS AND GET THE IRISH INTO IT.
THERE I WAS, MINDIN' MY OWN BUSINESS...
♪...THESE ROSES WITHER MAY GOD DELIVER THE RAKE AT THE GATES OF HELL TONIGHT! ♪
G E
JESUS!
GIMME THE TRUCK! GET THE FUCK OUTTA THE TRUCK!
SHAN'T.

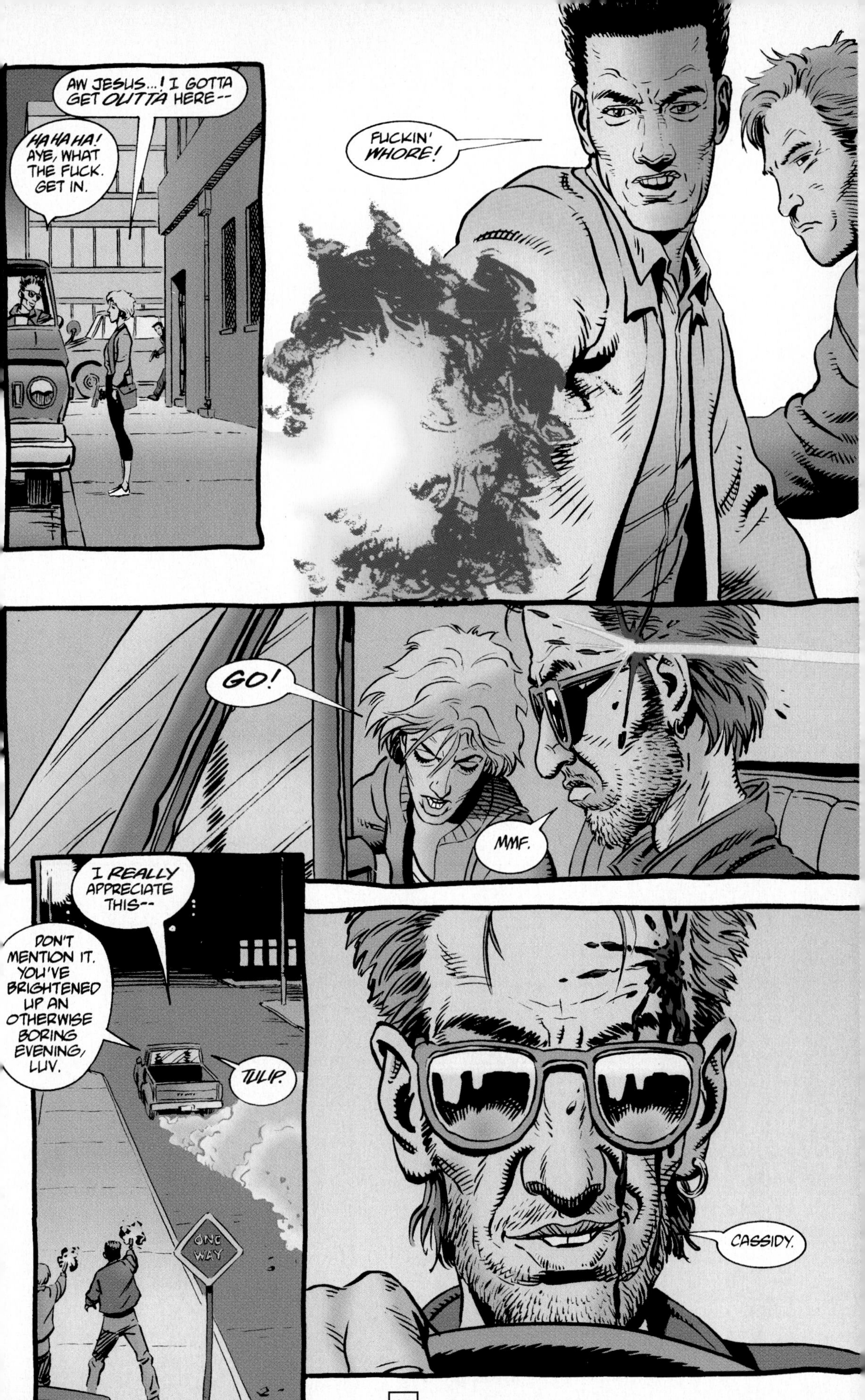
AW JESUS...! I GOTTA GET OUTTA HERE--
HAHAHA! AYE, WHAT THE FUCK. GET IN.
FUCKIN' WHORE!
GO!
MMF.
I REALLY APPRECIATE THIS--
DON'T MENTION IT. YOU'VE BRIGHTENED UP AN OTHERWISE BORING EVENING, LUV.
TULIP.
CASSIDY.
ONE WAY

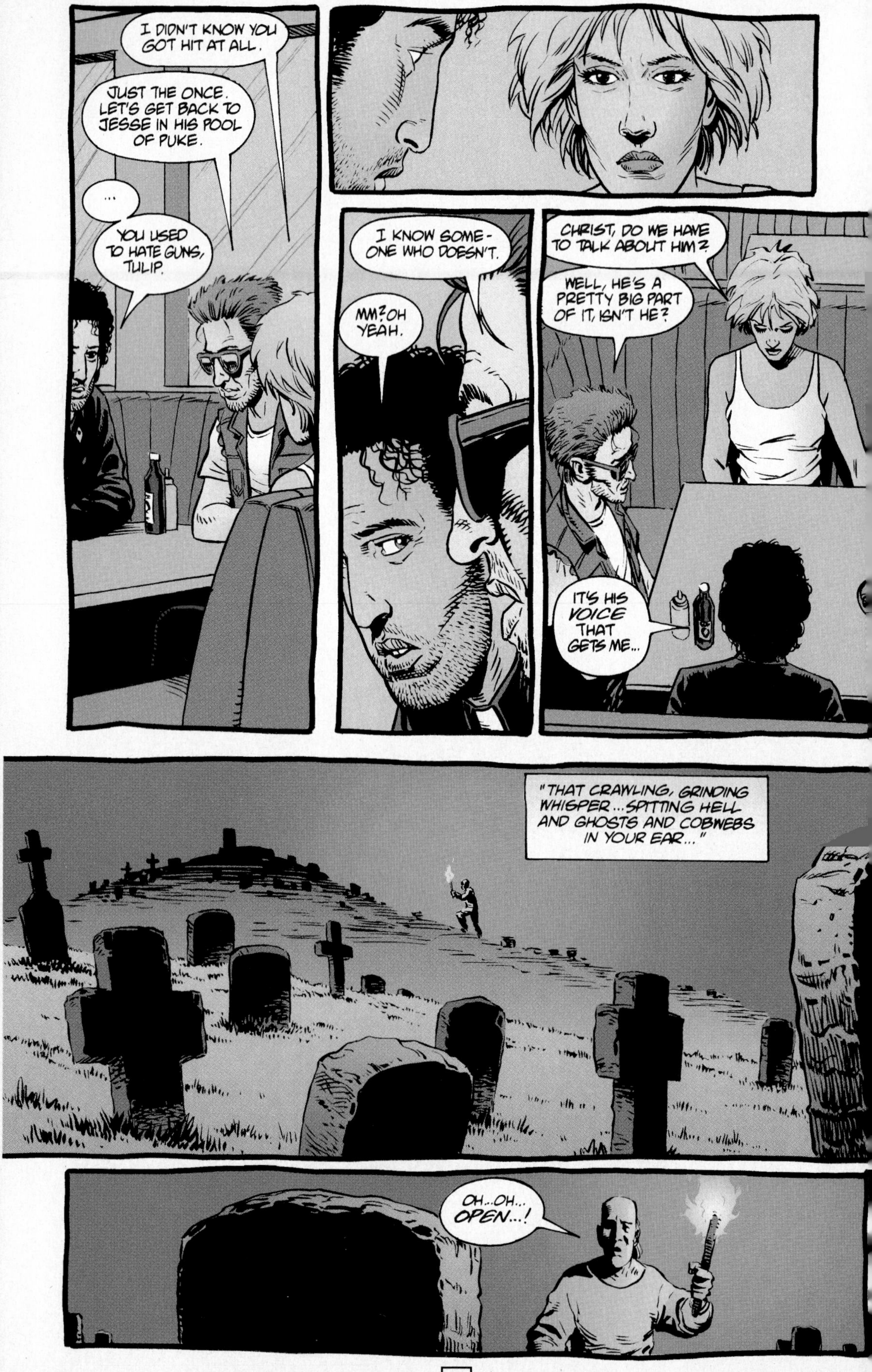
I DIDN'T KNOW YOU GOT HIT AT ALL.
JUST THE ONCE. LET'S GET BACK TO JESSE IN HIS POOL OF PUKE.
...
YOU USED TO HATE GUNS, TULIP.
I KNOW SOME-ONE WHO DOESN'T.
MM? OH YEAH.
CHRIST, DO WE HAVE TO TALK ABOUT HIM?
WELL, HE'S A PRETTY BIG PART OF IT, ISN'T HE?
IT'S HIS VOICE THAT GETS ME...
"THAT CRAWLING, GRINDING WHISPER... SPITTING HELL AND GHOSTS AND COBWEBS IN YOUR EAR..."
OH...OH... OPEN...!

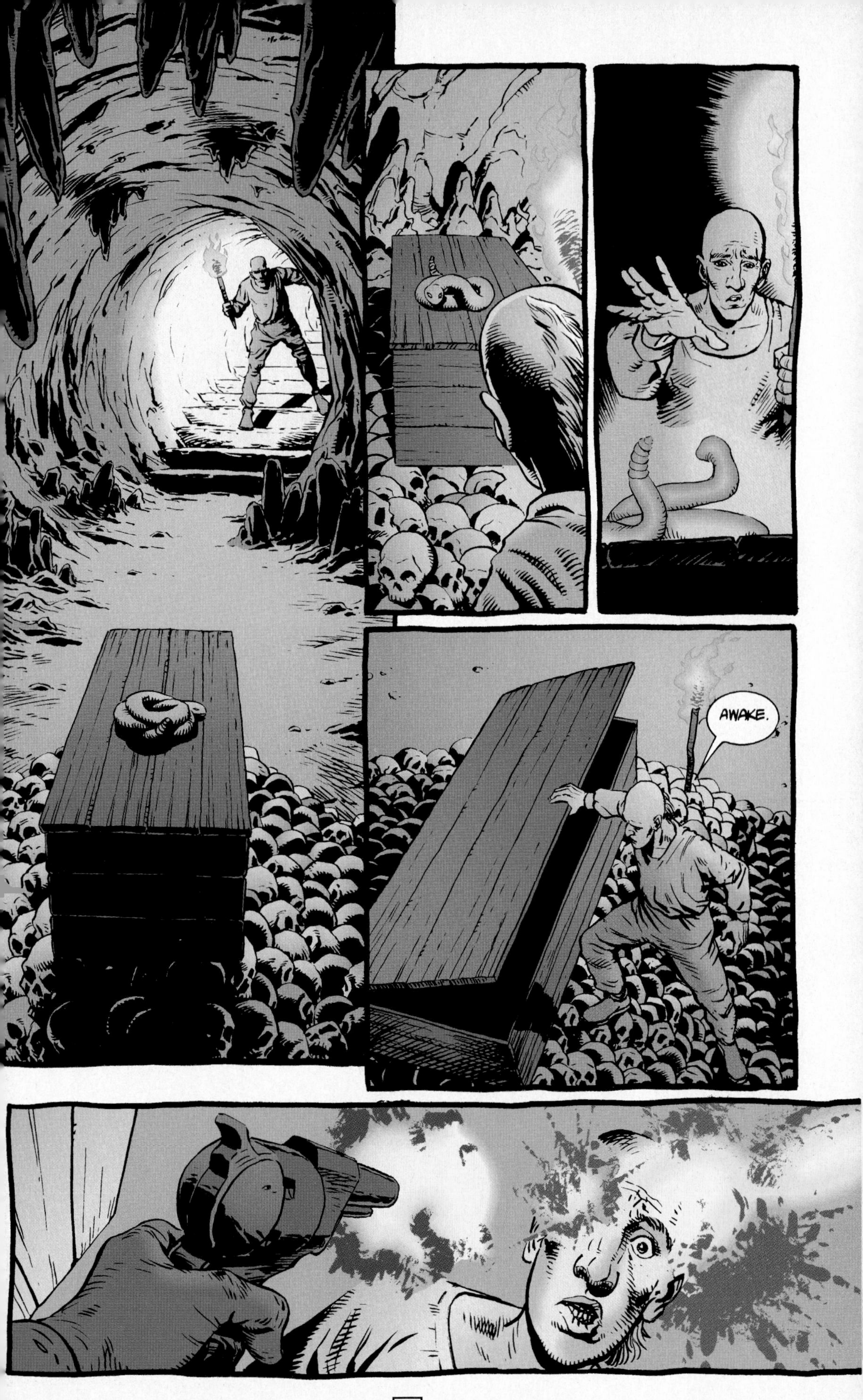
AWAKE.

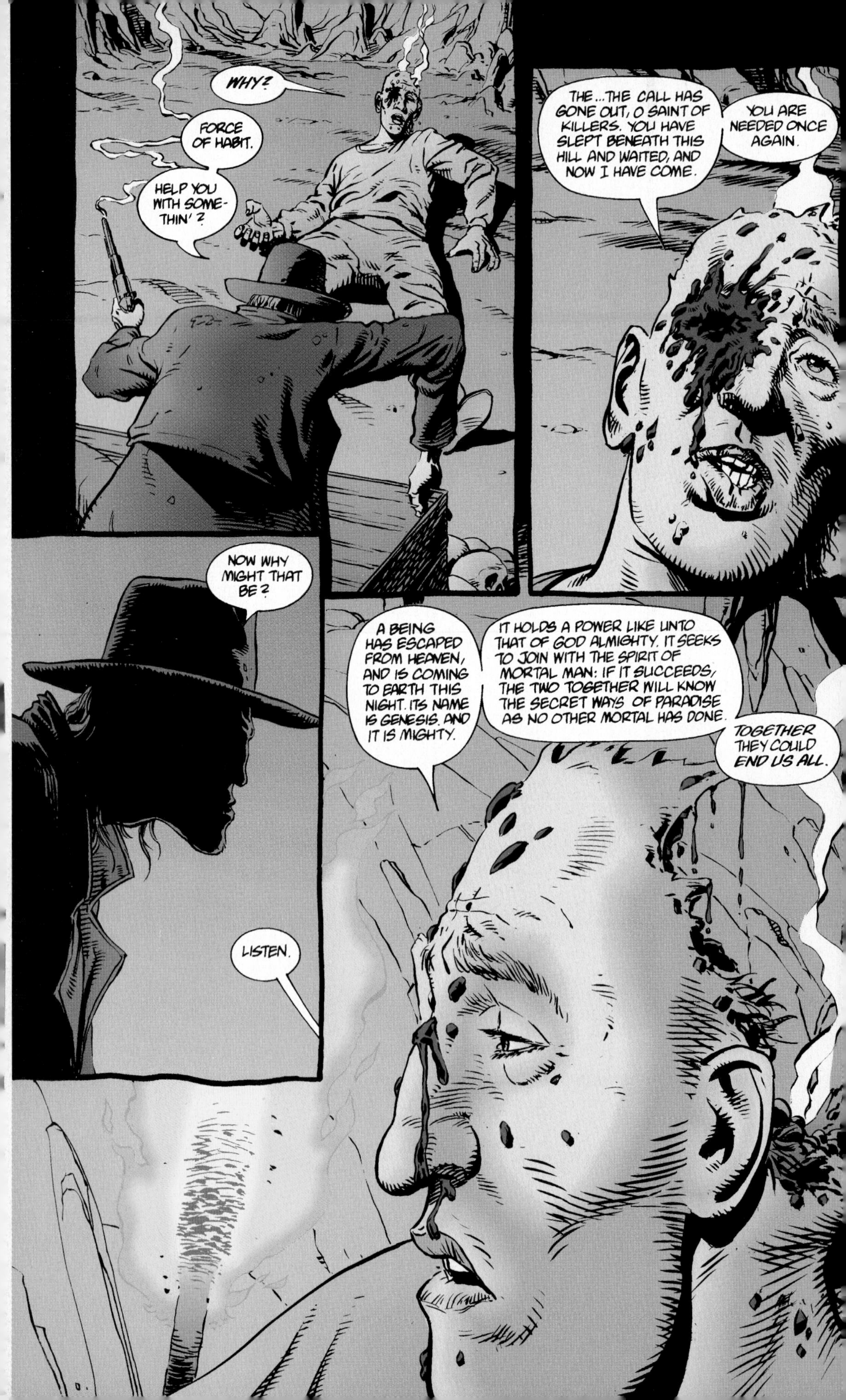
WHY?
FORCE OF HABIT.
HELP YOU WITH SOME-THIN'?
THE...THE CALL HAS GONE OUT, O SAINT OF KILLERS. YOU HAVE SLEPT BENEATH THIS HILL AND WAITED, AND NOW I HAVE COME.
YOU ARE NEEDED ONCE AGAIN.
NOW WHY MIGHT THAT BE?
LISTEN.
A BEING HAS ESCAPED FROM HEAVEN, AND IS COMING TO EARTH THIS NIGHT. ITS NAME IS GENESIS. AND IT IS MIGHTY.
IT HOLDS A POWER LIKE UNTO THAT OF GOD ALMIGHTY. IT SEEKS TO JOIN WITH THE SPIRIT OF MORTAL MAN: IF IT SUCCEEDS, THE TWO TOGETHER WILL KNOW THE SECRET WAYS OF PARADISE AS NO OTHER MORTAL HAS DONE.
TOGETHER THEY COULD END US ALL.

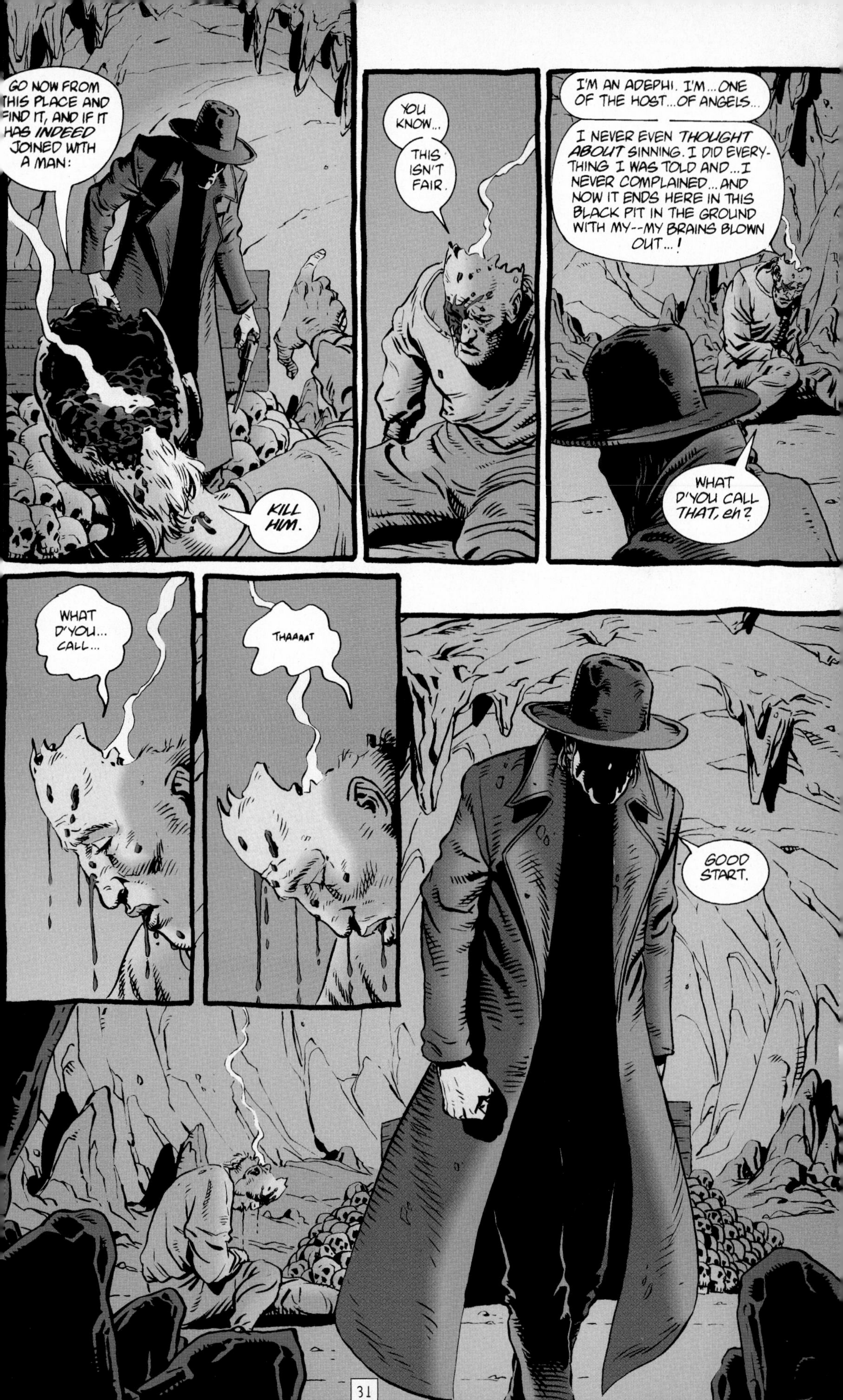
GO NOW FROM THIS PLACE AND FIND IT, AND IF IT HAS *INDEED* JOINED WITH A MAN:
KILL HIM.
YOU KNOW...
THIS ISN'T FAIR.
I'M AN ADEPHI. I'M... ONE OF THE HOST... OF ANGELS...
I NEVER EVEN *THOUGHT ABOUT* SINNING. I DID EVERYTHING I WAS TOLD AND... I NEVER COMPLAINED... AND NOW IT ENDS HERE IN THIS BLACK PIT IN THE GROUND WITH MY--MY BRAINS BLOWN OUT...!
WHAT D'YOU CALL *THAT, eh?*
WHAT D'YOU... CALL...
THAAAAT
GOOD START.

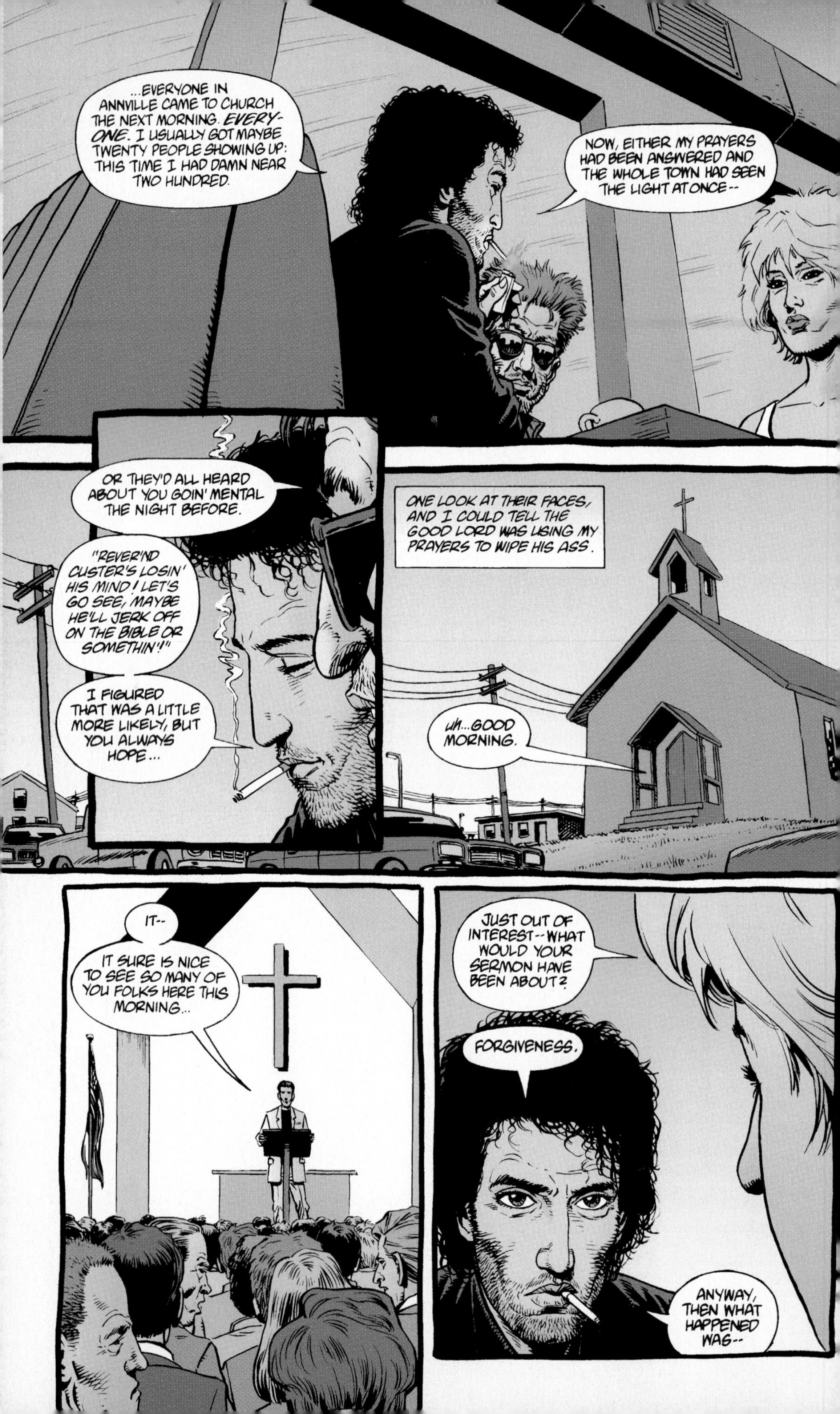
...EVERYONE IN ANNVILLE CAME TO CHURCH THE NEXT MORNING. *EVERY-ONE*. I USUALLY GOT MAYBE TWENTY PEOPLE SHOWING UP: THIS TIME I HAD DAMN NEAR TWO HUNDRED.
NOW, EITHER MY PRAYERS HAD BEEN ANSWERED AND THE WHOLE TOWN HAD SEEN THE LIGHT AT ONCE--
OR THEY'D ALL HEARD ABOUT YOU GOIN' MENTAL THE NIGHT BEFORE.
"REVER'ND CUSTER'S LOSIN' HIS MIND! LET'S GO SEE, MAYBE HE'LL JERK OFF ON THE BIBLE OR SOMETHIN'!"
I FIGURED THAT WAS A LITTLE MORE LIKELY, BUT YOU ALWAYS HOPE...
ONE LOOK AT THEIR FACES, AND I COULD TELL THE GOOD LORD WAS USING MY PRAYERS TO WIPE HIS ASS.
uh...GOOD MORNING.
IT--
IT SURE IS NICE TO SEE SO MANY OF YOU FOLKS HERE THIS MORNING...
JUST OUT OF INTEREST--WHAT WOULD YOUR SERMON HAVE BEEN ABOUT?
FORGIVENESS.
ANYWAY, THEN WHAT HAPPENED WAS--

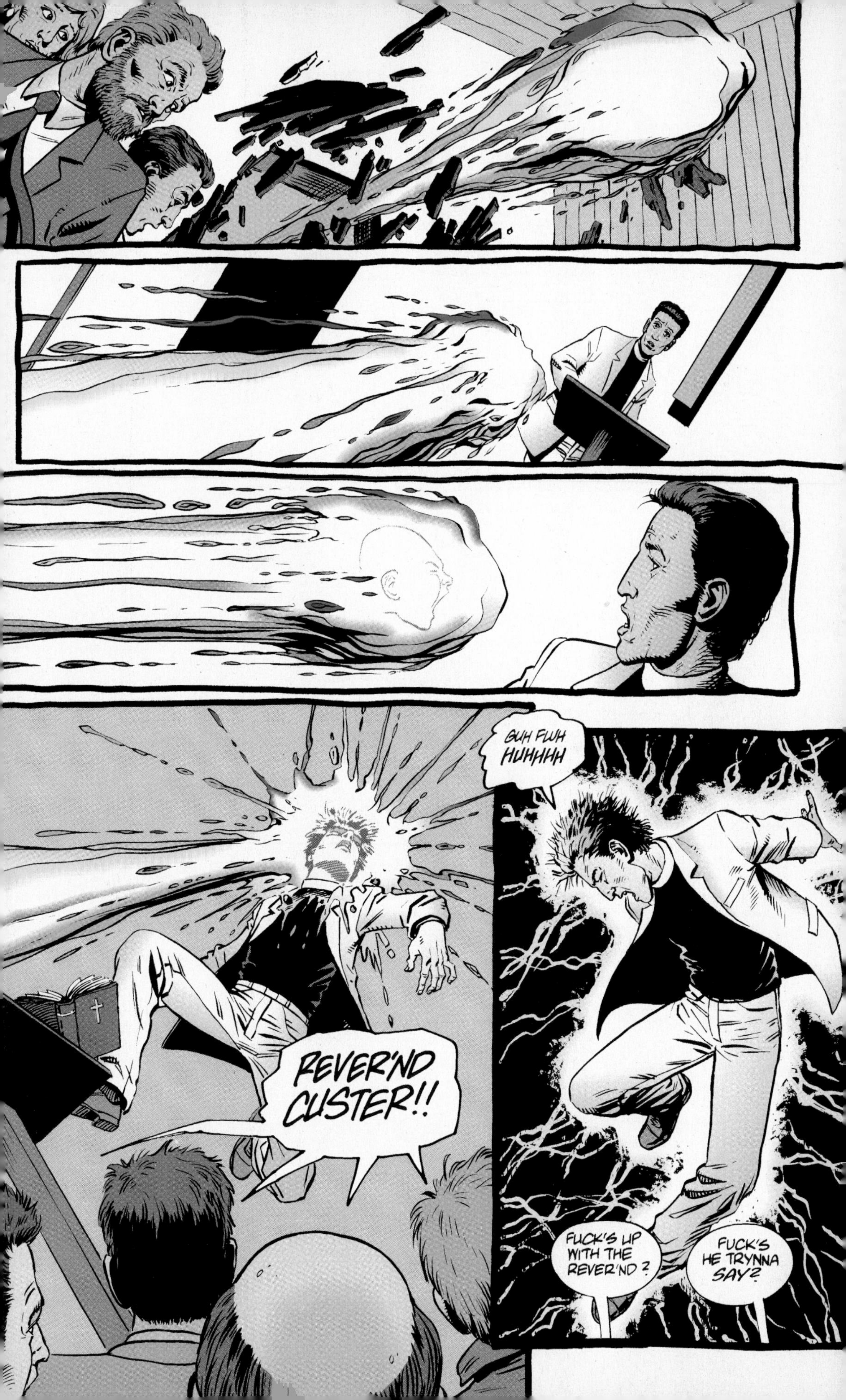
GUH FLUH HUHHHH
REVER'ND CUSTER!!
FUCK'S UP WITH THE REVER'ND?
FUCK'S HE TRYNNA SAY?

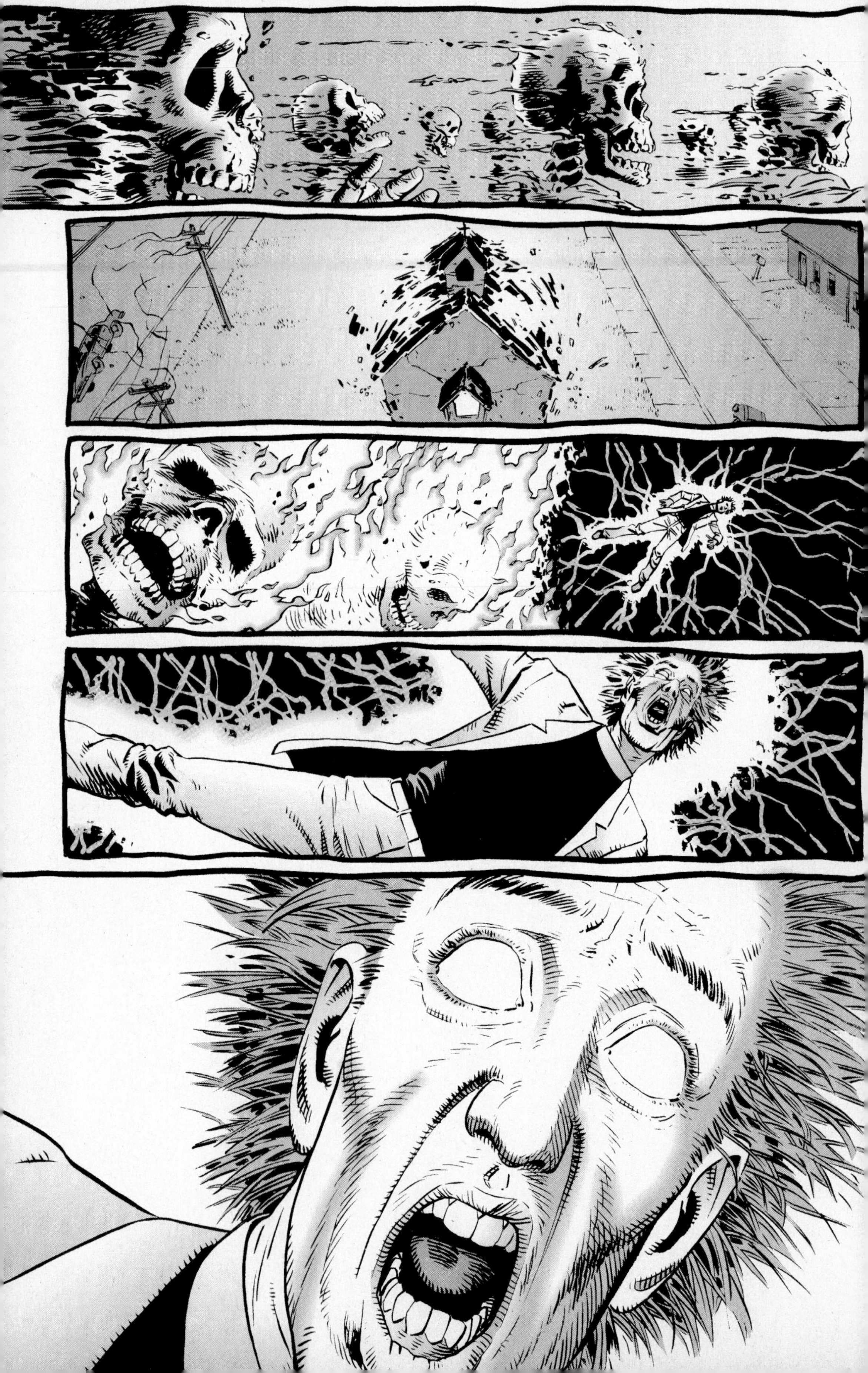

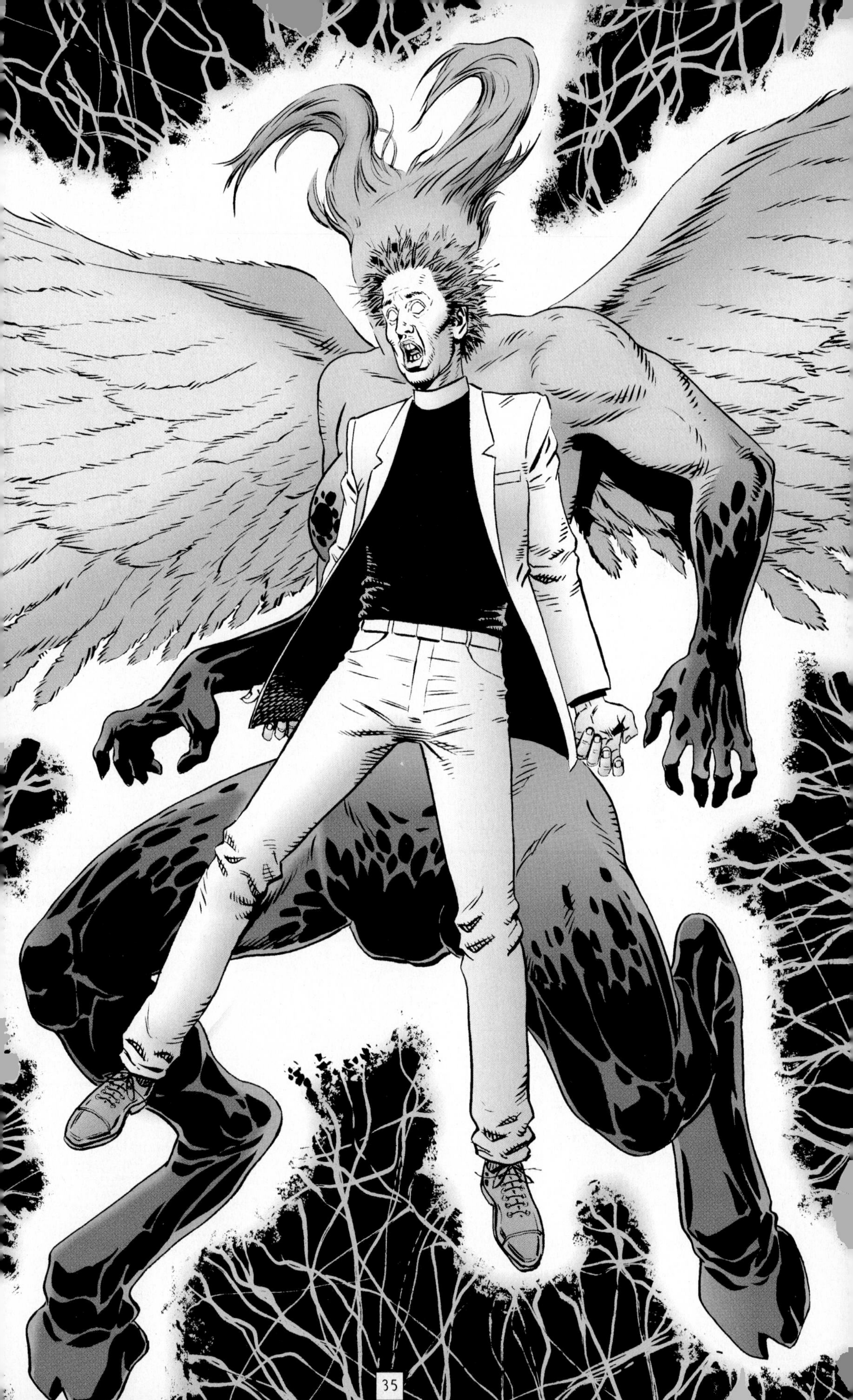

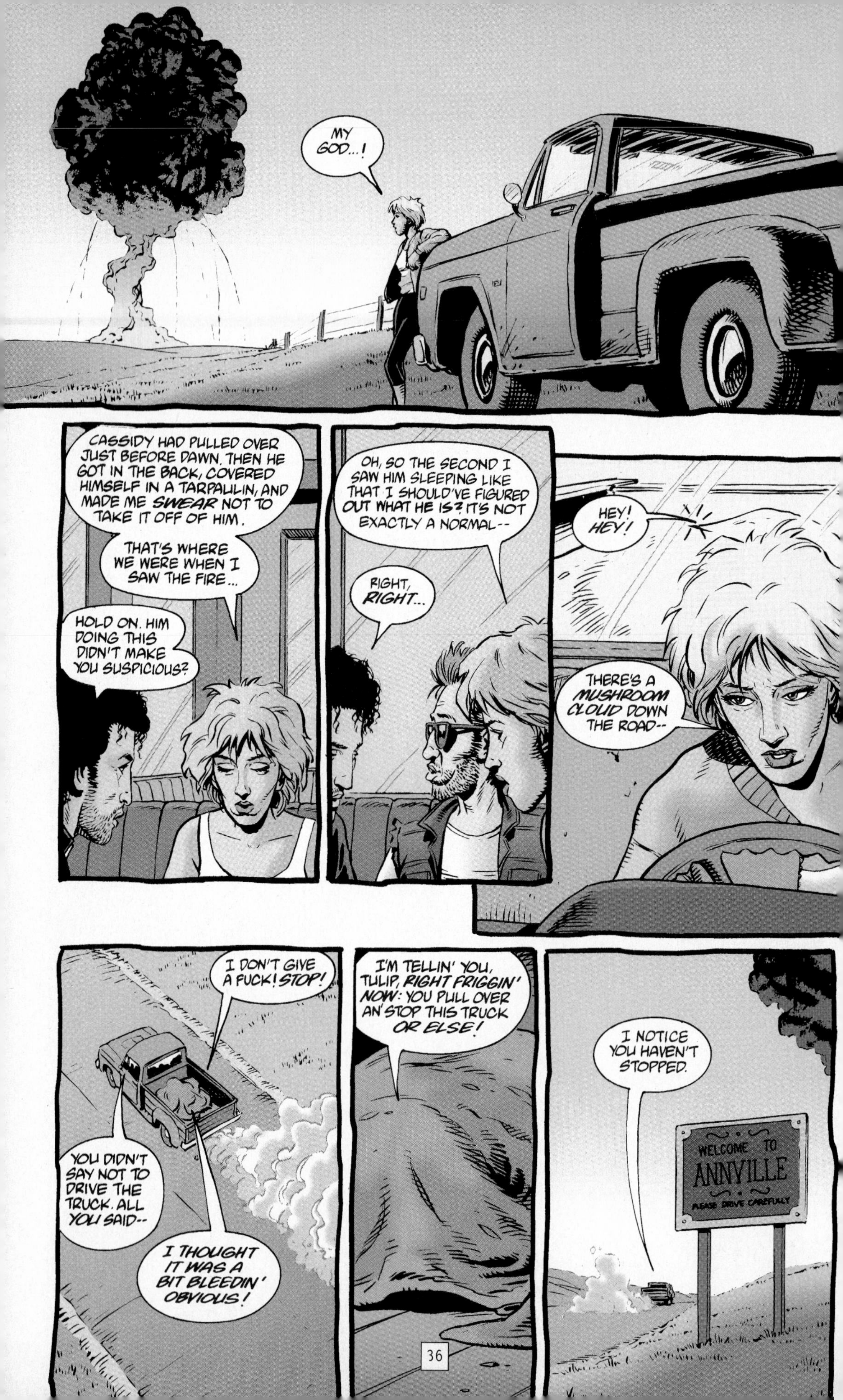
MY GOD...!
CASSIDY HAD PULLED OVER JUST BEFORE DAWN. THEN HE GOT IN THE BACK, COVERED HIMSELF IN A TARPAULIN, AND MADE ME SWEAR NOT TO TAKE IT OFF OF HIM.
THAT'S WHERE WE WERE WHEN I SAW THE FIRE...
HOLD ON. HIM DOING THIS DIDN'T MAKE YOU SUSPICIOUS?
OH, SO THE SECOND I SAW HIM SLEEPING LIKE THAT I SHOULD'VE FIGURED OUT WHAT HE IS? IT'S NOT EXACTLY A NORMAL--
RIGHT, RIGHT...
HEY! HEY!
THERE'S A MUSHROOM CLOUD DOWN THE ROAD--
I DON'T GIVE A FUCK! STOP!
YOU DIDN'T SAY NOT TO DRIVE THE TRUCK. ALL YOU SAID--
I THOUGHT IT WAS A BIT BLEEDIN' OBVIOUS!
I'M TELLIN' YOU, TULIP, RIGHT FRIGGIN' NOW: YOU PULL OVER AN' STOP THIS TRUCK OR ELSE!
I NOTICE YOU HAVEN'T STOPPED.
WELCOME TO
ANNVILLE
PLEASE DRIVE CAREFULLY

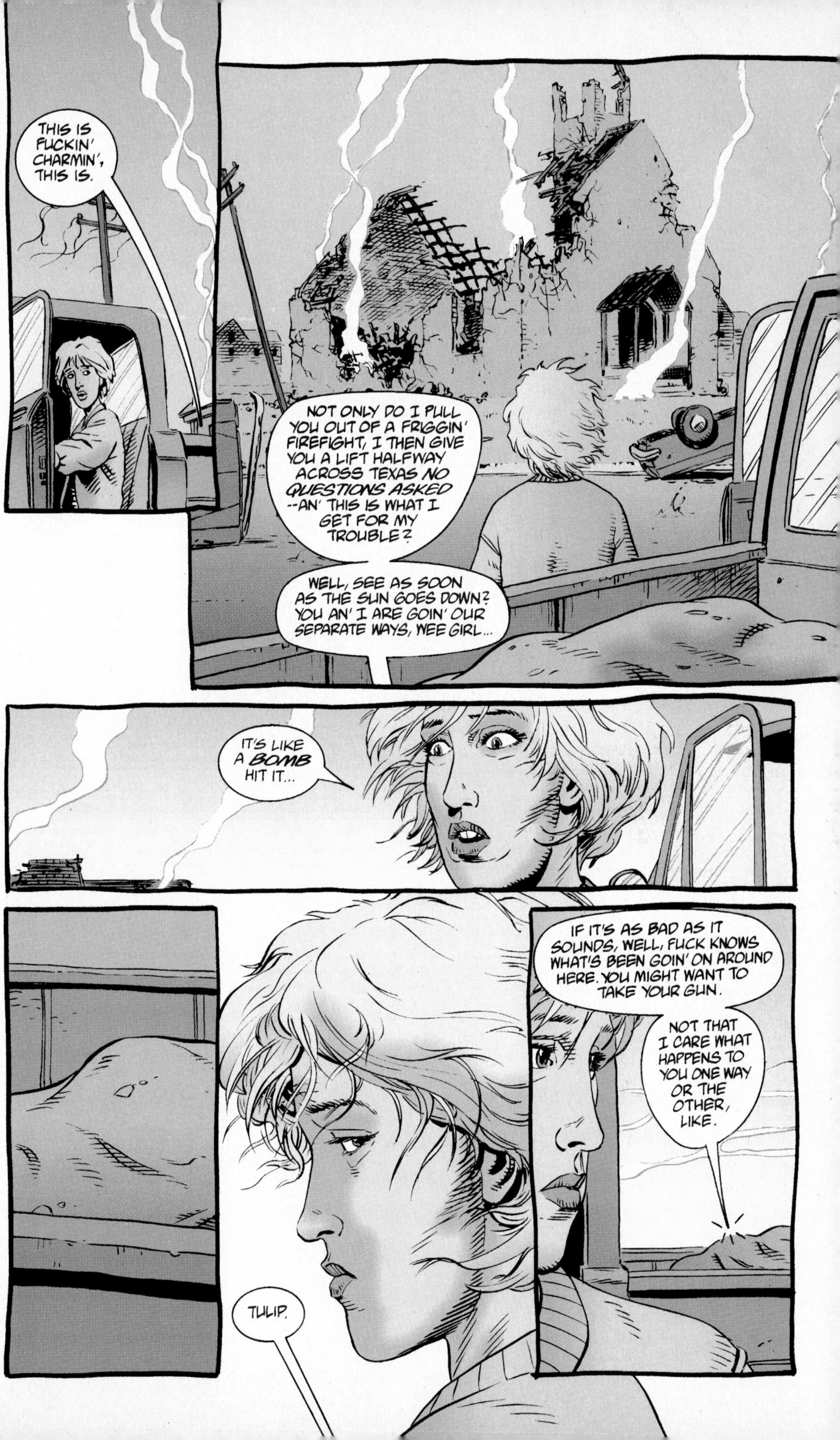
THIS IS FUCKIN' CHARMIN', THIS IS.
NOT ONLY DO I PULL YOU OUT OF A FRIGGIN' FIREFIGHT, I THEN GIVE YOU A LIFT HALFWAY ACROSS TEXAS NO QUESTIONS ASKED --AN' THIS IS WHAT I GET FOR MY TROUBLE?
WELL, SEE AS SOON AS THE SUN GOES DOWN? YOU AN' I ARE GOIN' OUR SEPARATE WAYS, WEE GIRL...
IT'S LIKE A BOMB HIT IT...
IF IT'S AS BAD AS IT SOUNDS, WELL, FUCK KNOWS WHAT'S BEEN GOIN' ON AROUND HERE. YOU MIGHT WANT TO TAKE YOUR GUN.
NOT THAT I CARE WHAT HAPPENS TO YOU ONE WAY OR THE OTHER, LIKE.
TULIP.

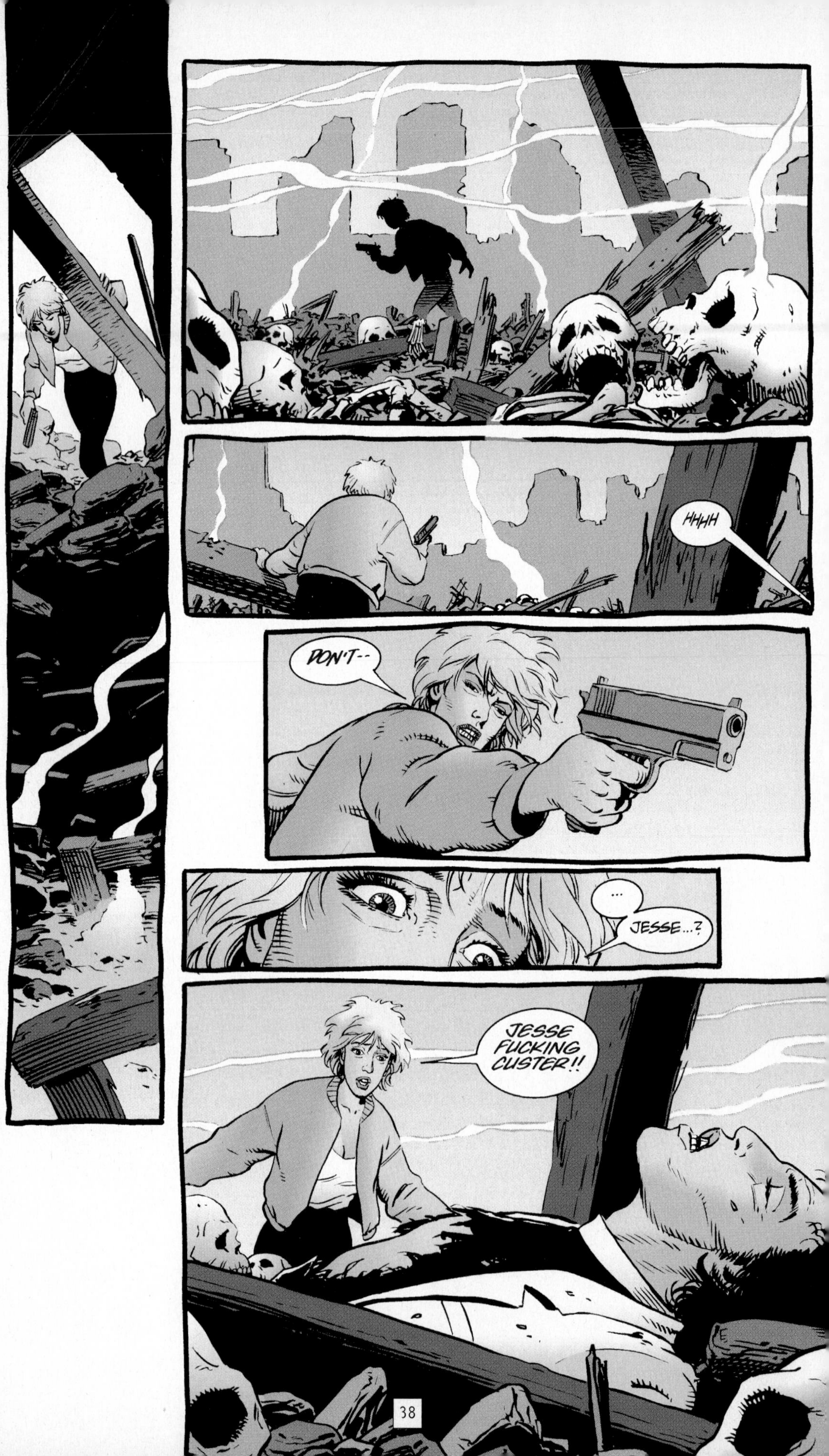
HHHH
DON'T--
...
JESSE...?
JESSE FUCKING CUSTER!!

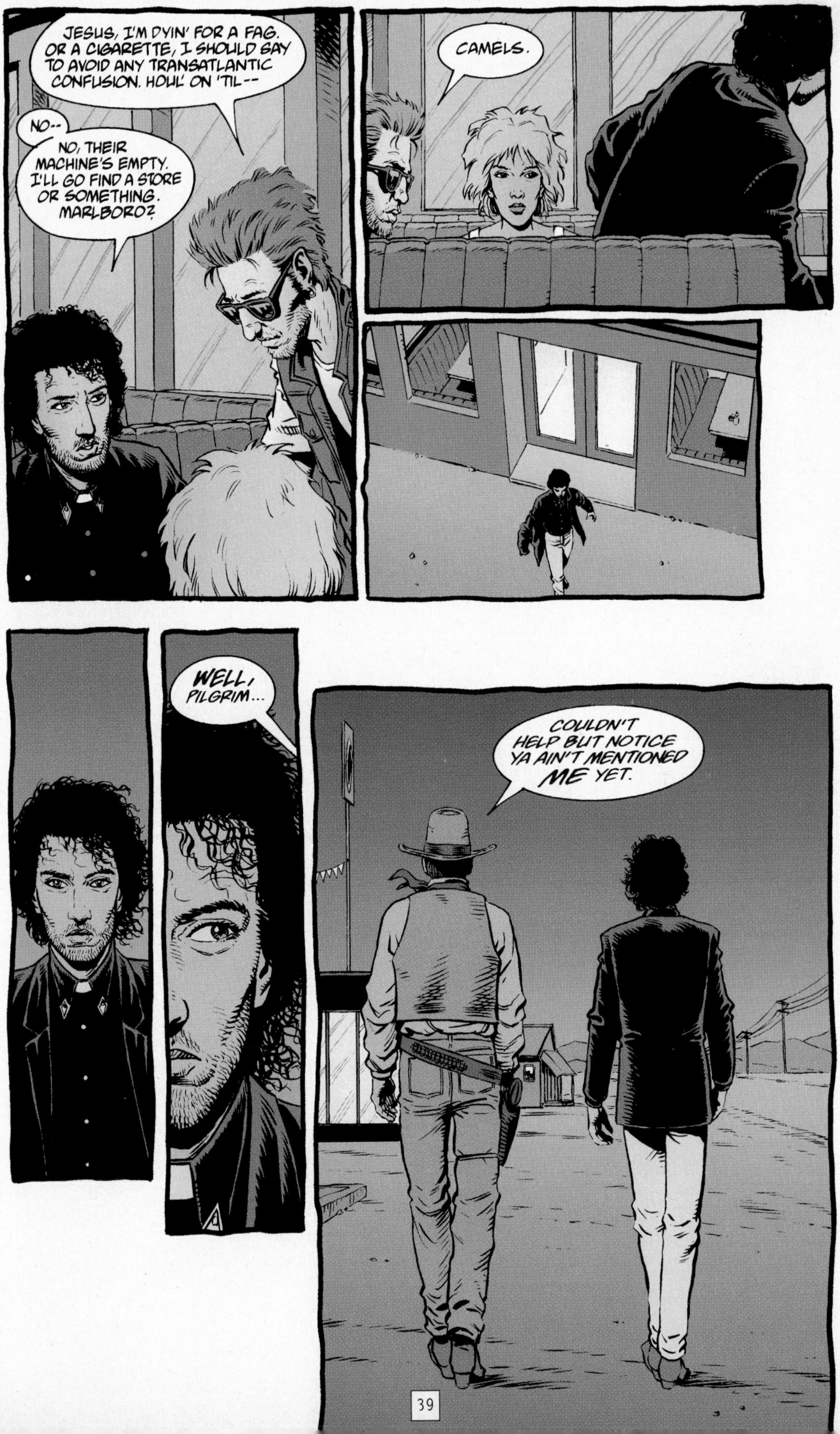
JESUS, I'M DYIN' FOR A FAG. OR A CIGARETTE, I SHOULD SAY TO AVOID ANY TRANSATLANTIC CONFUSION. HOUL' ON 'TIL--
NO--
NO, THEIR MACHINE'S EMPTY. I'LL GO FIND A STORE OR SOMETHING. MARLBORO?
CAMELS.
WELL, PILGRIM...
COULDN'T HELP BUT NOTICE YA AIN'T MENTIONED ME YET.

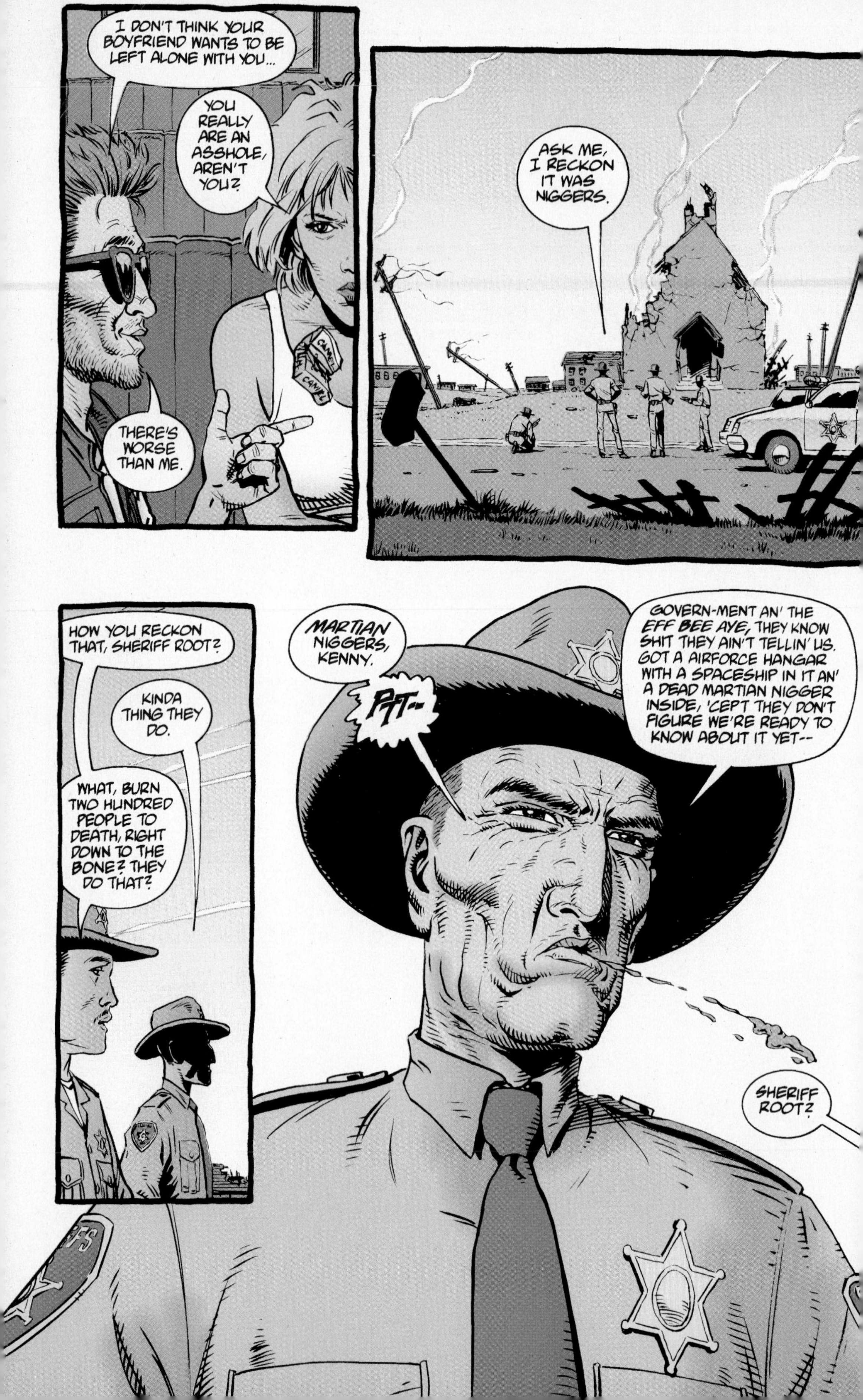
I DON'T THINK YOUR BOYFRIEND WANTS TO BE LEFT ALONE WITH YOU...
YOU REALLY ARE AN ASSHOLE, AREN'T YOU?
THERE'S WORSE THAN ME.
ASK ME, I RECKON IT WAS NIGGERS.
HOW YOU RECKON THAT, SHERIFF ROOT?
KINDA THING THEY DO.
WHAT, BURN TWO HUNDRED PEOPLE TO DEATH, RIGHT DOWN TO THE BONE? THEY DO THAT?
PTT--
MARTIAN NIGGERS, KENNY.
GOVERN-MENT AN' THE EFF BEE AYE, THEY KNOW SHIT THEY AIN'T TELLIN' US. GOT A AIRFORCE HANGAR WITH A SPACESHIP IN IT AN' A DEAD MARTIAN NIGGER INSIDE, 'CEPT THEY DON'T FIGURE WE'RE READY TO KNOW ABOUT IT YET--
SHERIFF ROOT?

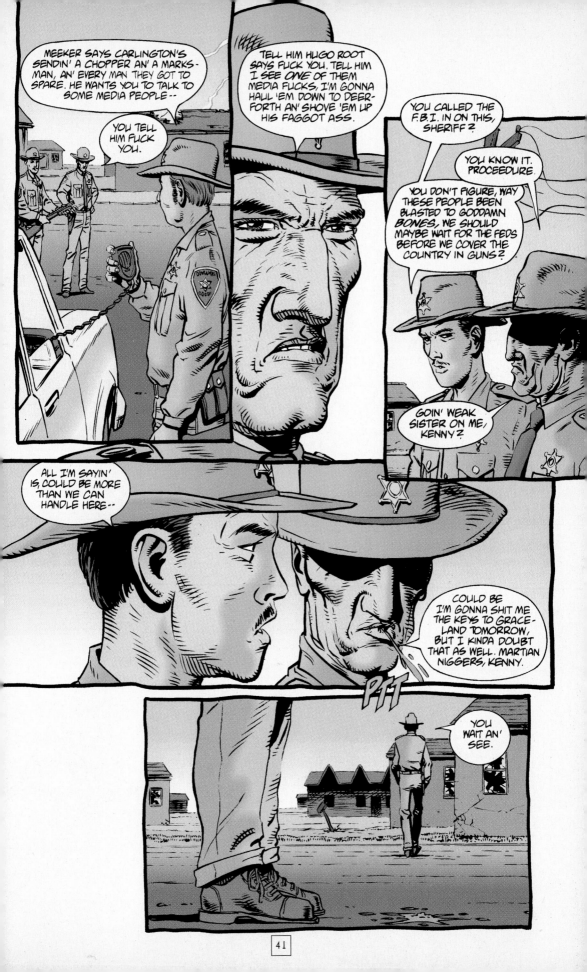

MEEKER SAYS CARLINGTON'S SENDIN' A CHOPPER AN' A MARKSMAN, AN' EVERY MAN THEY GOT TO SPARE. HE WANTS YOU TO TALK TO SOME MEDIA PEOPLE--

YOU TELL HIM FUCK YOU.

TELL HIM HUGO ROOT SAYS FUCK YOU. TELL HIM I SEE *ONE* OF THEM MEDIA FUCKS, I'M GONNA HAUL 'EM DOWN TO DEERFORTH AN' SHOVE 'EM UP HIS FAGGOT ASS.

YOU CALLED THE F.B.I. IN ON THIS, SHERIFF?

YOU KNOW IT. PROCEEDURE.

YOU DON'T FIGURE, WAY THESE PEOPLE BEEN BLASTED TO GODDAMN *BONES,* WE SHOULD MAYBE WAIT FOR THE FEDS BEFORE WE COVER THE COUNTRY IN GUNS?

GOIN' WEAK SISTER ON ME, KENNY?

ALL I'M SAYIN' IS, COULD BE MORE THAN WE CAN HANDLE HERE--

COULD BE I'M GONNA SHIT ME THE KEYS TO GRACELAND TOMORROW, BUT I KINDA DOUBT THAT AS WELL. MARTIAN NIGGERS, KENNY.

PFT

YOU WAIT AN' SEE.

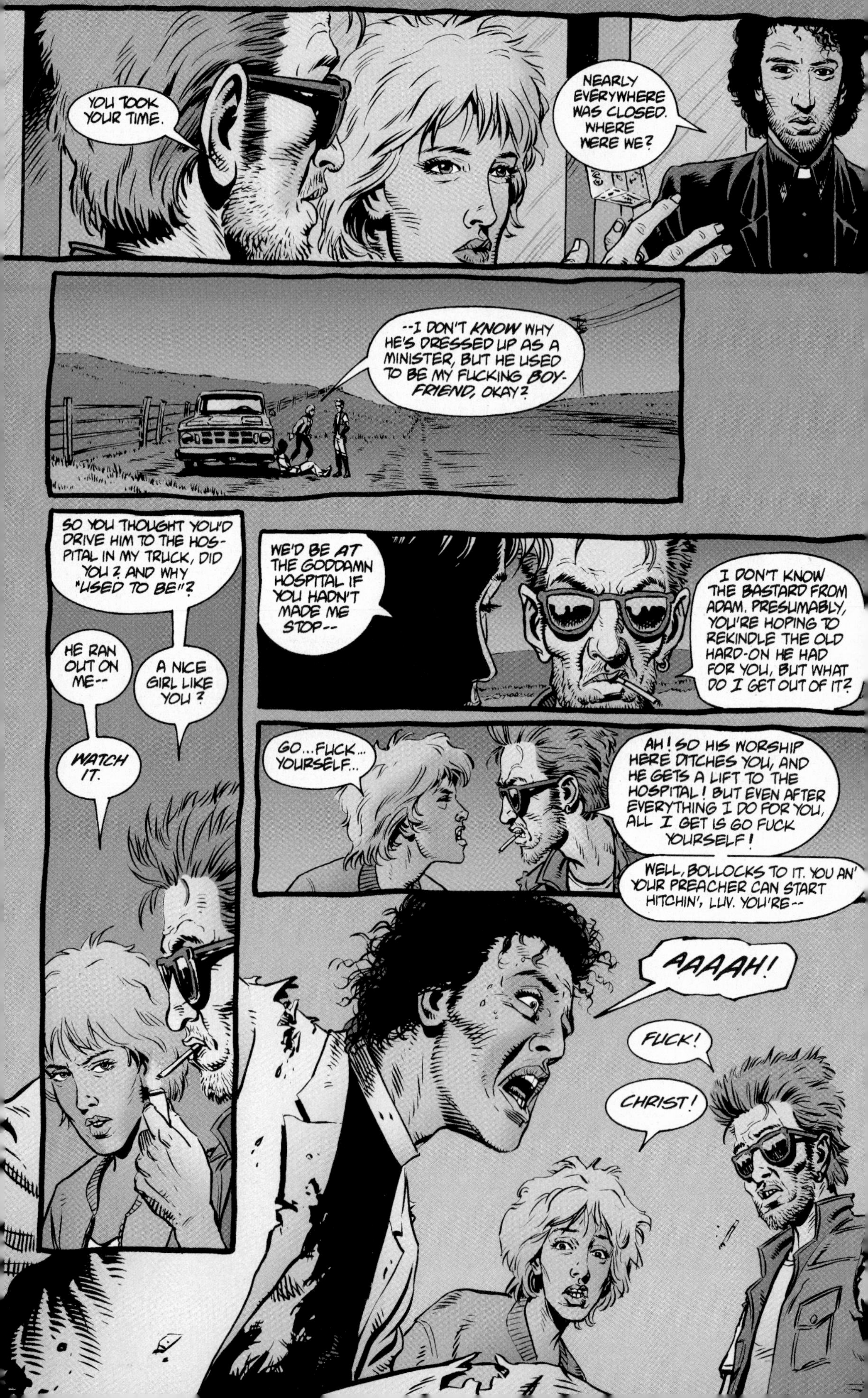
YOU TOOK YOUR TIME.
NEARLY EVERYWHERE WAS CLOSED. WHERE WERE WE?
--I DON'T KNOW WHY HE'S DRESSED UP AS A MINISTER, BUT HE USED TO BE MY FUCKING BOY-FRIEND, OKAY?
SO YOU THOUGHT YOU'D DRIVE HIM TO THE HOS-PITAL IN MY TRUCK, DID YOU? AND WHY "USED TO BE"?
HE RAN OUT ON ME--
A NICE GIRL LIKE YOU?
WATCH IT.
WE'D BE AT THE GODDAMN HOSPITAL IF YOU HADN'T MADE ME STOP--
I DON'T KNOW THE BASTARD FROM ADAM. PRESUMABLY, YOU'RE HOPING TO REKINDLE THE OLD HARD-ON HE HAD FOR YOU, BUT WHAT DO I GET OUT OF IT?
GO...FUCK... YOURSELF...
AH! SO HIS WORSHIP HERE DITCHES YOU, AND HE GETS A LIFT TO THE HOSPITAL! BUT EVEN AFTER EVERYTHING I DO FOR YOU, ALL I GET IS GO FUCK YOURSELF!
WELL, BOLLOCKS TO IT. YOU AN' YOUR PREACHER CAN START HITCHIN', LUV. YOU'RE--
AAAAH!
FUCK!
CHRIST!

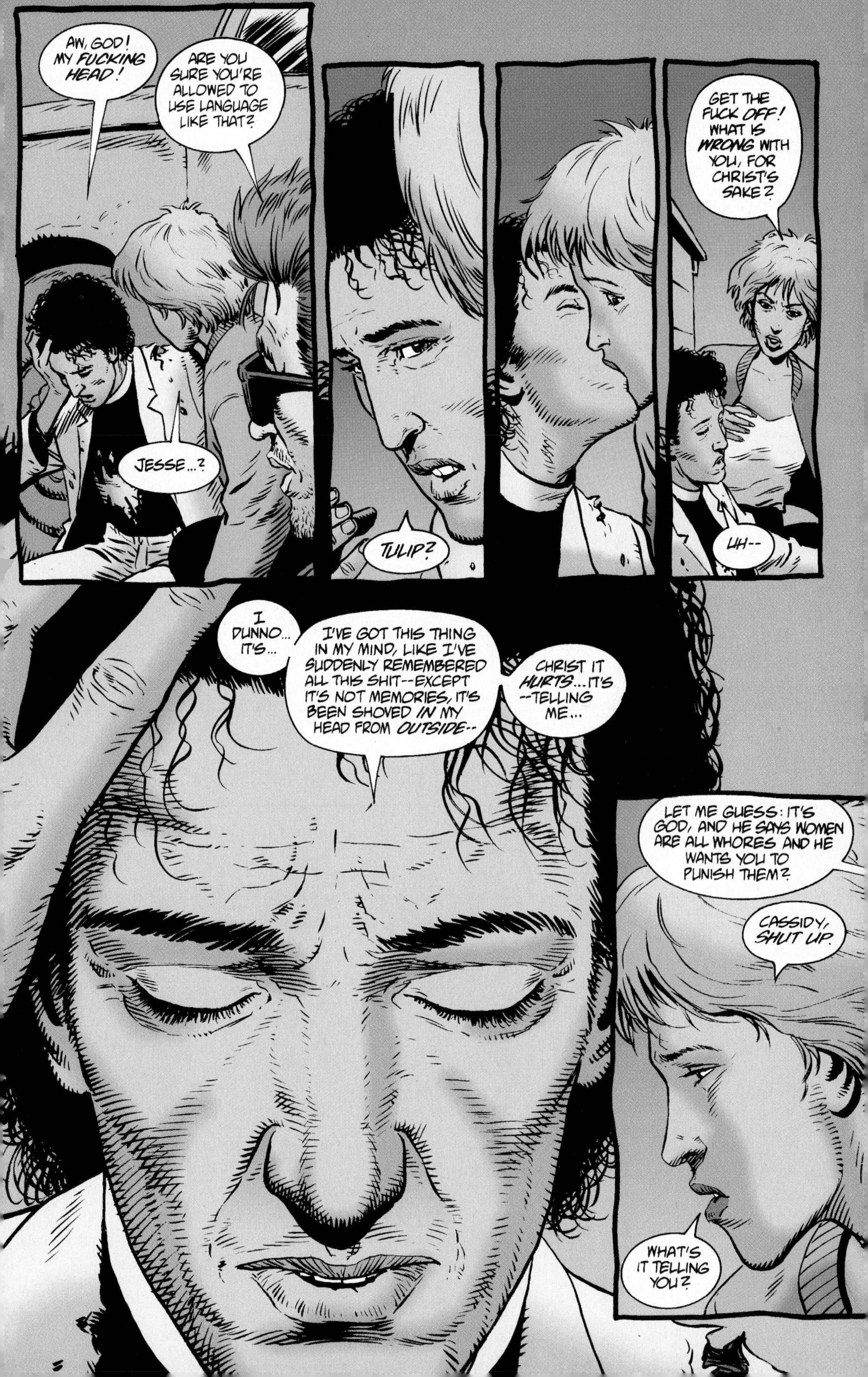

AW, GOD! MY FUCKING HEAD!
ARE YOU SURE YOU'RE ALLOWED TO USE LANGUAGE LIKE THAT?
JESSE...?
TULIP?
GET THE FUCK OFF! WHAT IS WRONG WITH YOU, FOR CHRIST'S SAKE?
UH--
I DUNNO... IT'S...
I'VE GOT THIS THING IN MY MIND, LIKE I'VE SUDDENLY REMEMBERED ALL THIS SHIT--EXCEPT IT'S NOT MEMORIES, IT'S BEEN SHOVED IN MY HEAD FROM OUTSIDE--
CHRIST IT HURTS... IT'S --TELLING ME...
LET ME GUESS: IT'S GOD, AND HE SAYS WOMEN ARE ALL WHORES AND HE WANTS YOU TO PUNISH THEM?
CASSIDY, SHUT UP.
WHAT'S IT TELLING YOU?

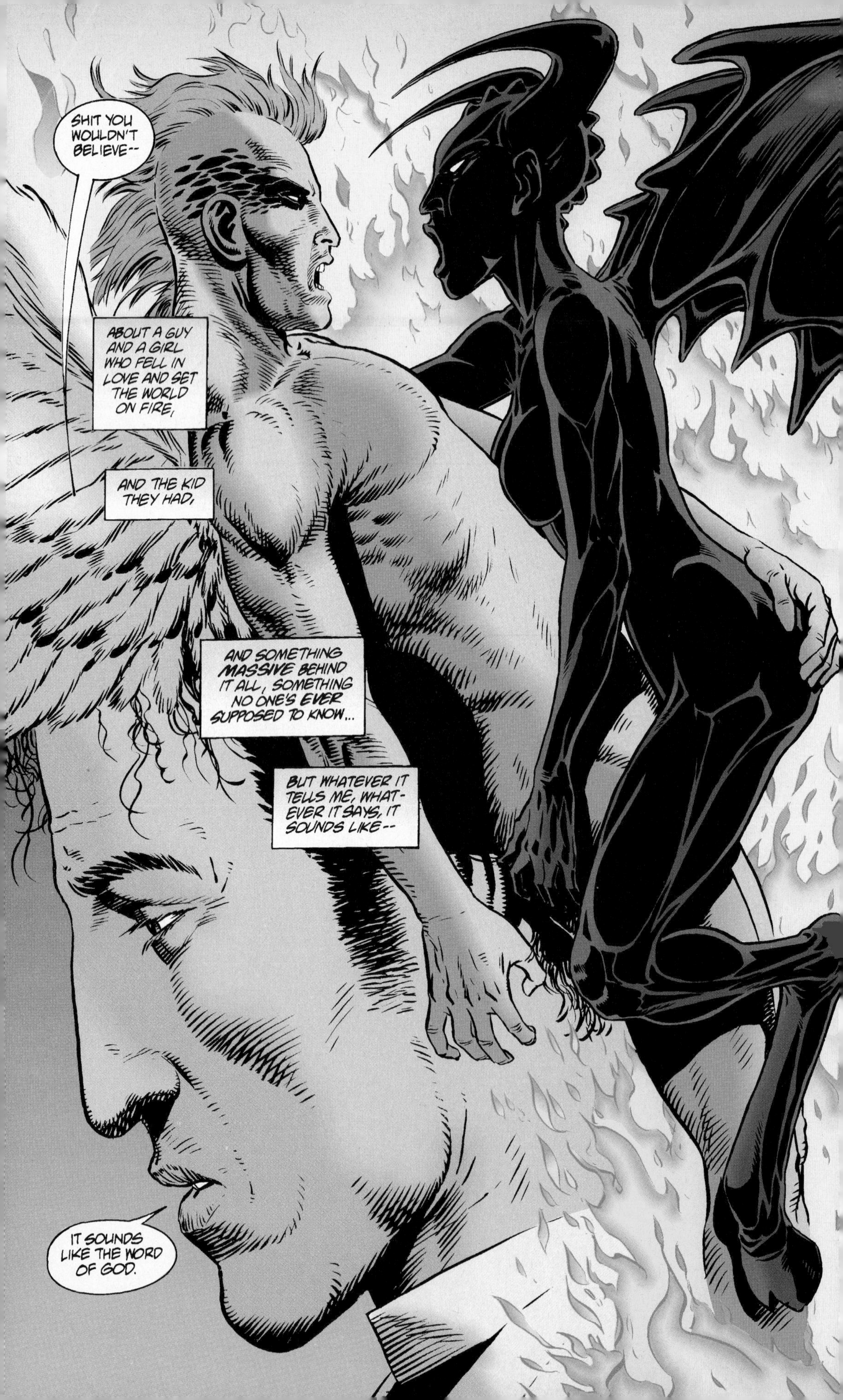

SHIT YOU WOULDN'T BELIEVE--
ABOUT A GUY AND A GIRL WHO FELL IN LOVE AND SET THE WORLD ON FIRE,
AND THE KID THEY HAD,
AND SOMETHING MASSIVE BEHIND IT ALL, SOMETHING NO ONE'S EVER SUPPOSED TO KNOW...
BUT WHATEVER IT TELLS ME, WHAT-EVER IT SAYS, IT SOUNDS LIKE--
IT SOUNDS LIKE THE WORD OF GOD.

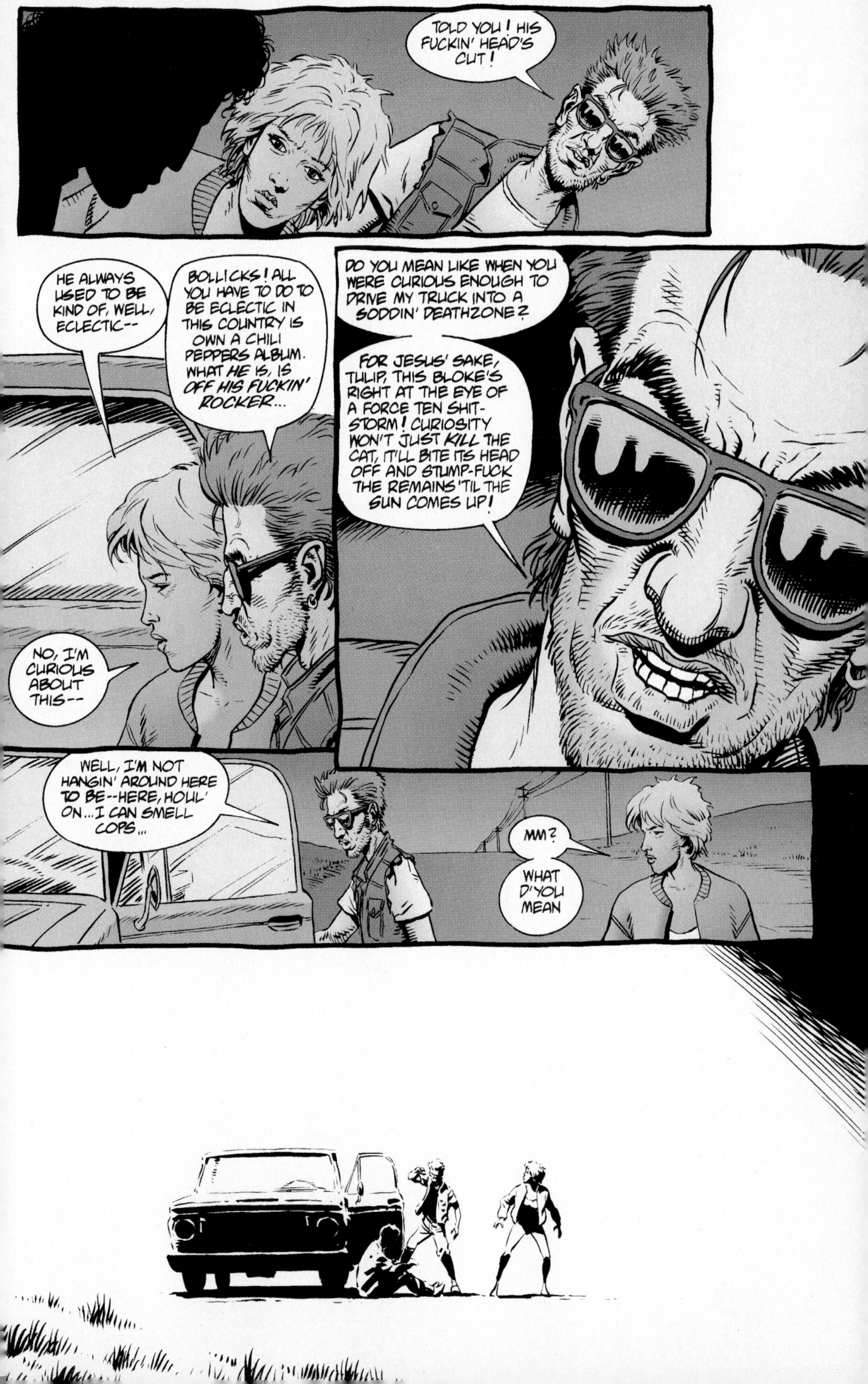

TOLD YOU! HIS FUCKIN' HEAD'S CUT!
HE ALWAYS USED TO BE KIND OF, WELL, ECLECTIC--
BOLLICKS! ALL YOU HAVE TO DO TO BE ECLECTIC IN THIS COUNTRY IS OWN A CHILI PEPPERS ALBUM. WHAT HE IS, IS OFF HIS FUCKIN' ROCKER...
NO, I'M CURIOUS ABOUT THIS--
DO YOU MEAN LIKE WHEN YOU WERE CURIOUS ENOUGH TO DRIVE MY TRUCK INTO A SODDIN' DEATHZONE?
FOR JESUS' SAKE, TULIP, THIS BLOKE'S RIGHT AT THE EYE OF A FORCE TEN SHIT-STORM! CURIOSITY WON'T JUST KILL THE CAT, IT'LL BITE ITS HEAD OFF AND STUMP-FUCK THE REMAINS 'TIL THE SUN COMES UP!
WELL, I'M NOT HANGIN' AROUND HERE TO BE--HERE, HOUL' ON...I CAN SMELL COPS...
MM?
WHAT D'YOU MEAN

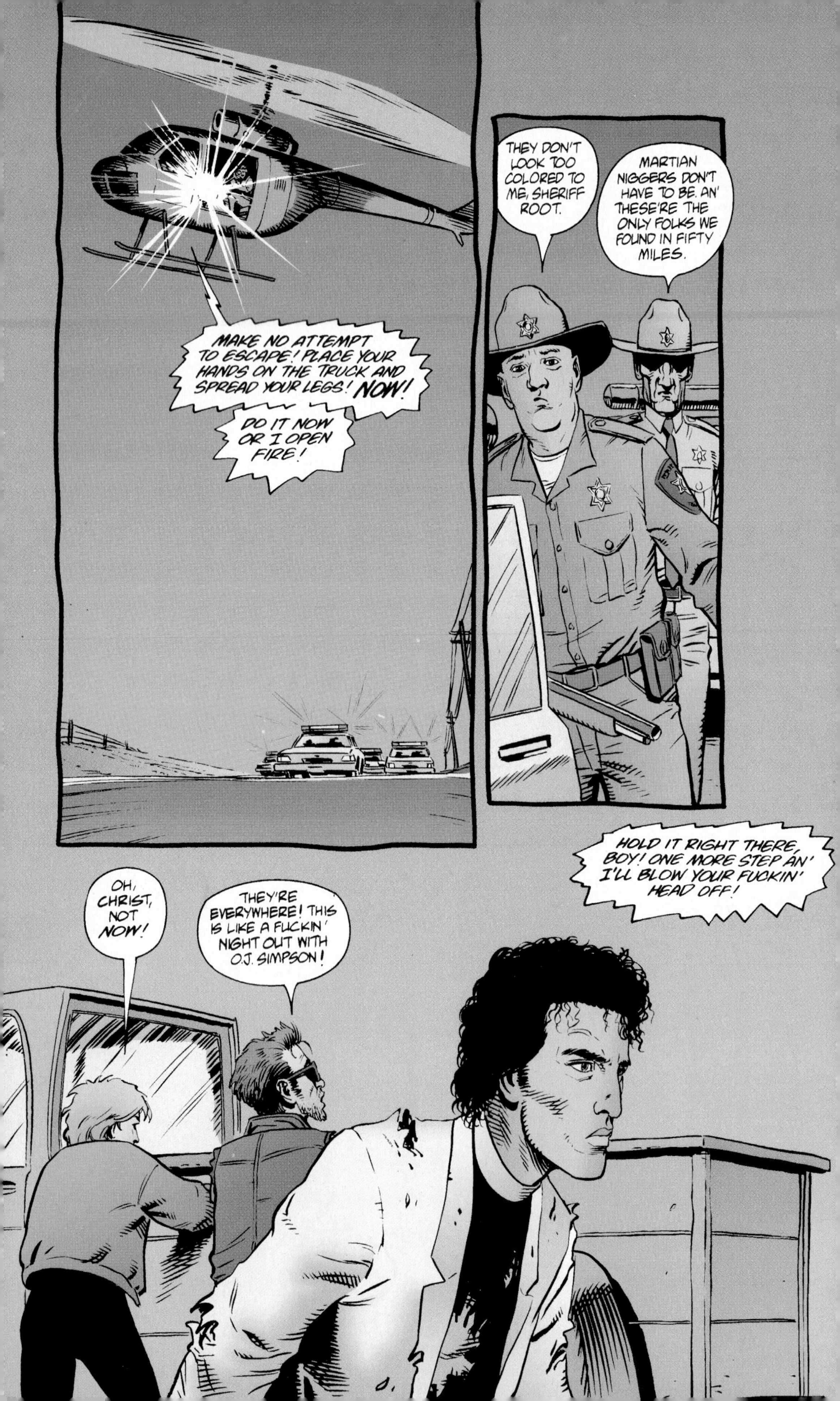

MAKE NO ATTEMPT TO ESCAPE! PLACE YOUR HANDS ON THE TRUCK AND SPREAD YOUR LEGS! NOW!
DO IT NOW OR I OPEN FIRE!
THEY DON'T LOOK TOO COLORED TO ME, SHERIFF ROOT.
MARTIAN NIGGERS DON'T HAVE TO BE. AN' THESE'RE THE ONLY FOLKS WE FOUND IN FIFTY MILES.
OH, CHRIST, NOT NOW!
THEY'RE EVERYWHERE! THIS IS LIKE A FUCKIN' NIGHT OUT WITH O.J. SIMPSON!
HOLD IT RIGHT THERE, BOY! ONE MORE STEP AN' I'LL BLOW YOUR FUCKIN' HEAD OFF!

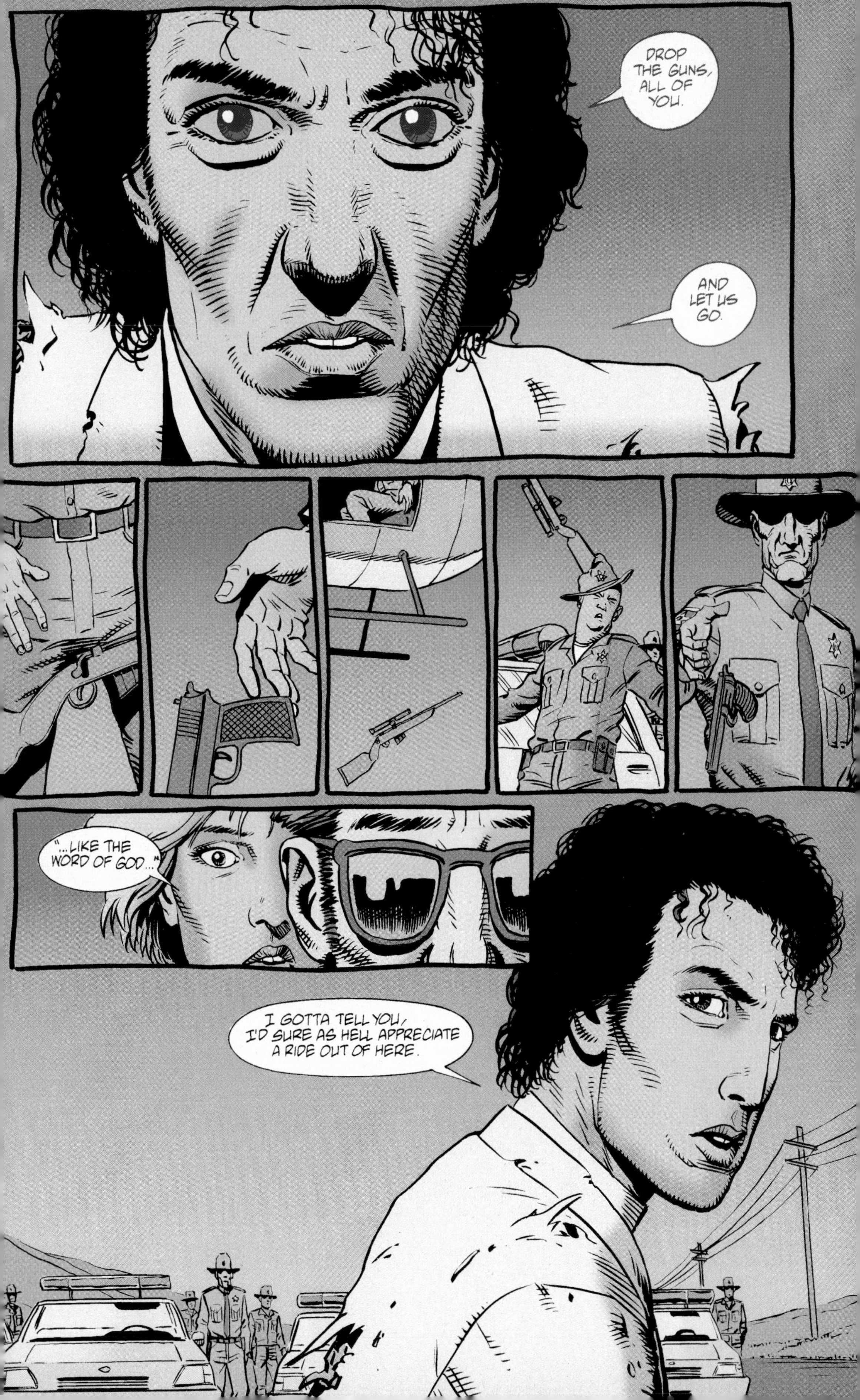

DROP THE GUNS, ALL OF YOU.
AND LET US GO.
"...LIKE THE WORD OF GOD..."
I GOTTA TELL YOU, I'D SURE AS HELL APPRECIATE A RIDE OUT OF HERE.

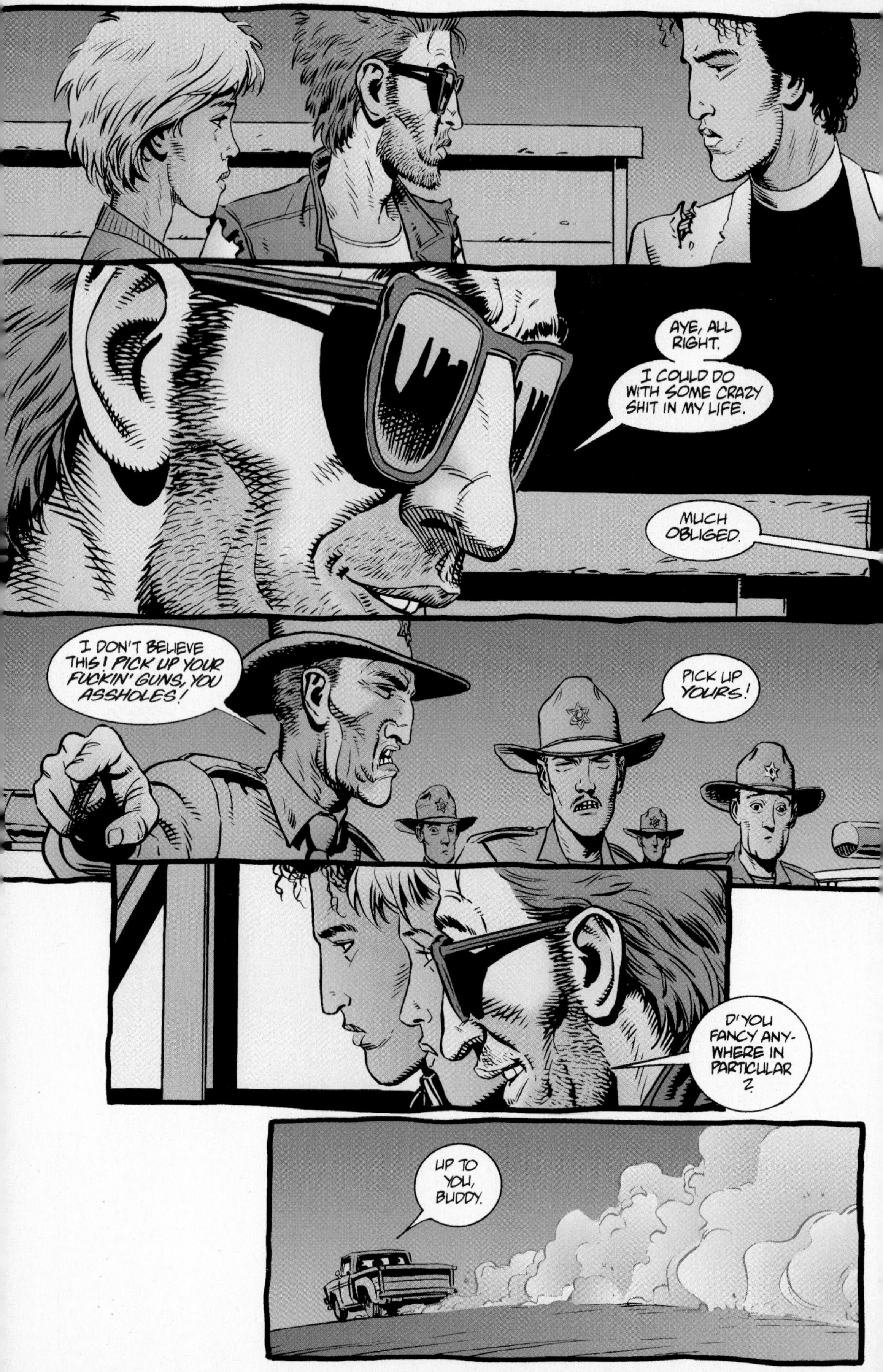
AYE, ALL RIGHT.
I COULD DO WITH SOME CRAZY SHIT IN MY LIFE.
MUCH OBLIGED.
I DON'T BELIEVE THIS! PICK UP YOUR FUCKIN' GUNS, YOU ASSHOLES!
PICK UP YOURS!
D'YOU FANCY ANY-WHERE IN PARTICULAR ?
UP TO YOU, BUDDY.

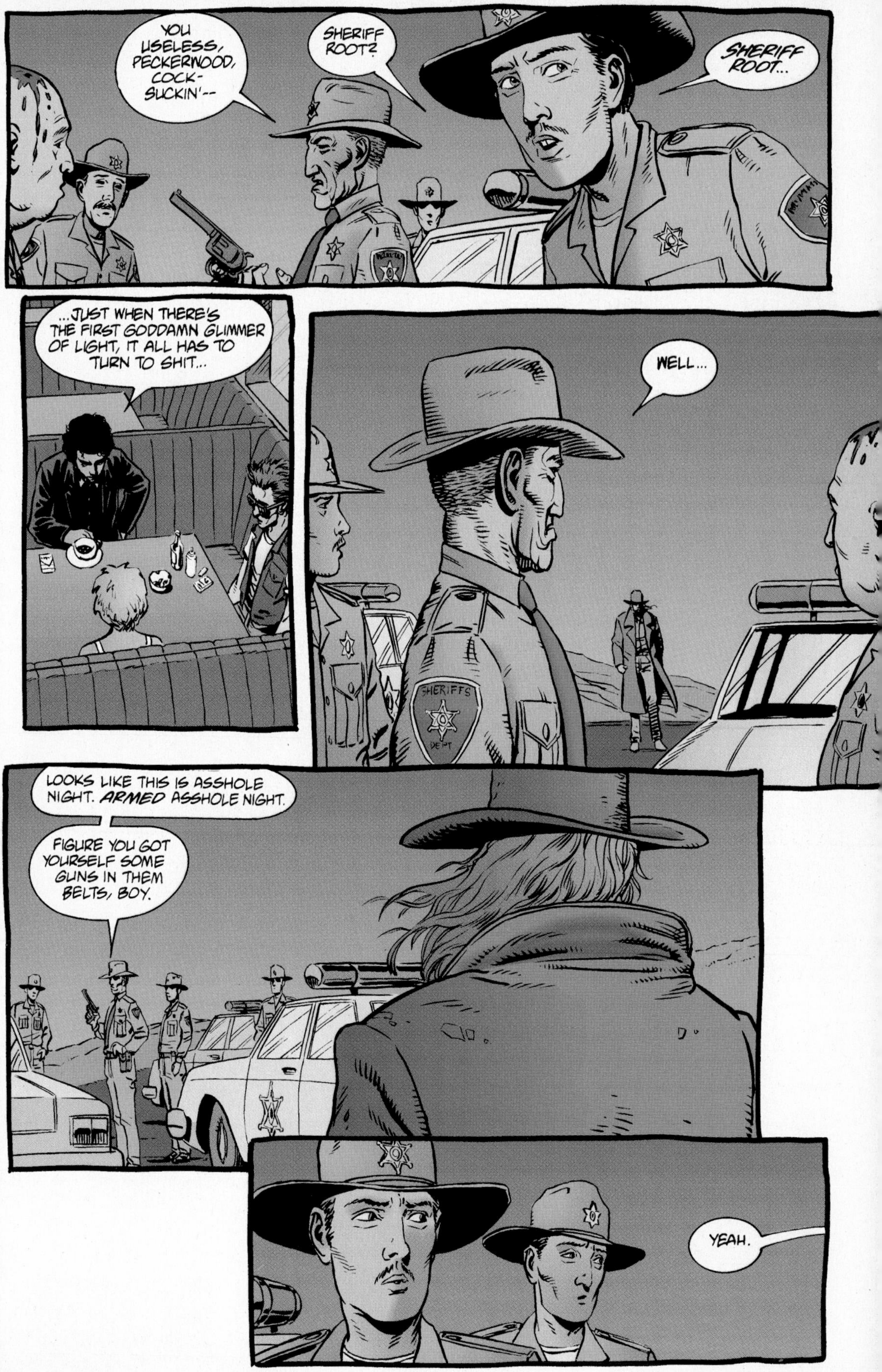
YOU USELESS, PECKERWOOD, COCK-SUCKIN'--
SHERIFF ROOT?
SHERIFF ROOT...
...JUST WHEN THERE'S THE FIRST GODDAMN GLIMMER OF LIGHT, IT ALL HAS TO TURN TO SHIT...
WELL...
SHERIFFS DEPT
LOOKS LIKE THIS IS ASSHOLE NIGHT. ARMED ASSHOLE NIGHT.
FIGURE YOU GOT YOURSELF SOME GUNS IN THEM BELTS, BOY.
YEAH.

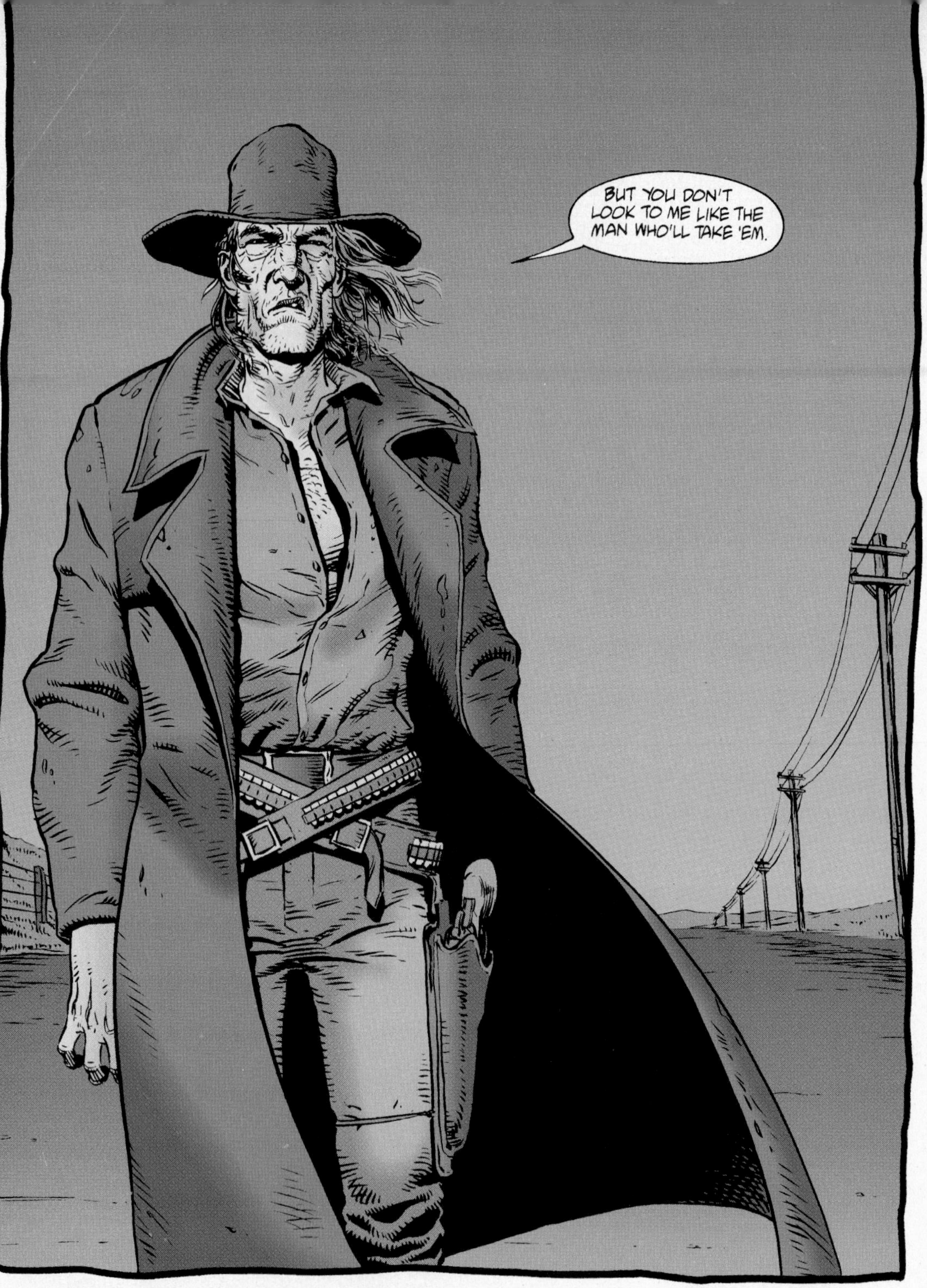
BUT YOU DON'T LOOK TO ME LIKE THE MAN WHO'LL TAKE 'EM.

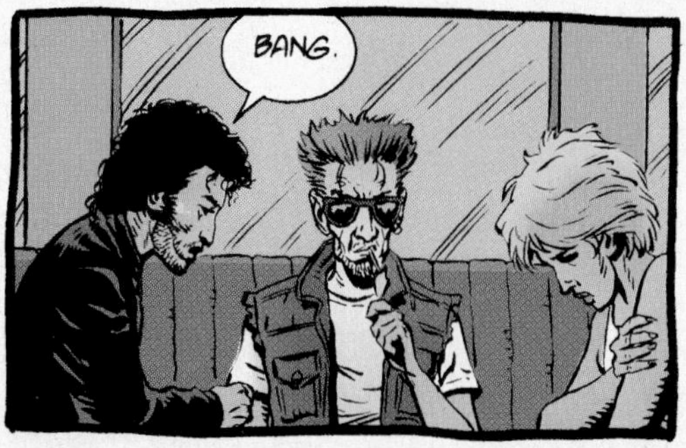
BANG.

NEXT: JUST A FEW COPS

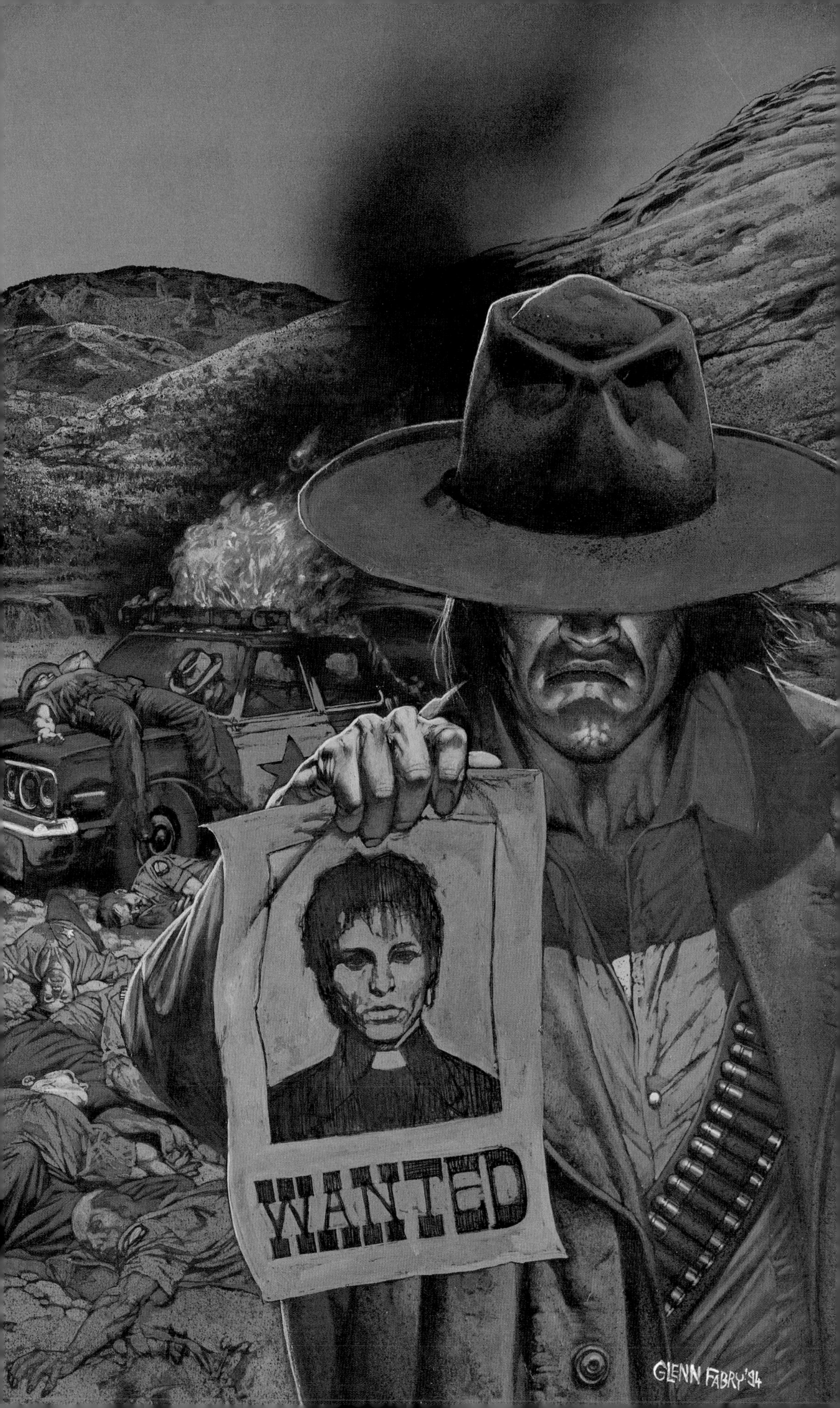

WANTED
GLENN FABRY '94

"He's got a soul so damn cold an' rattlesnake-mean,
Satan himself threw him back outta Hell."

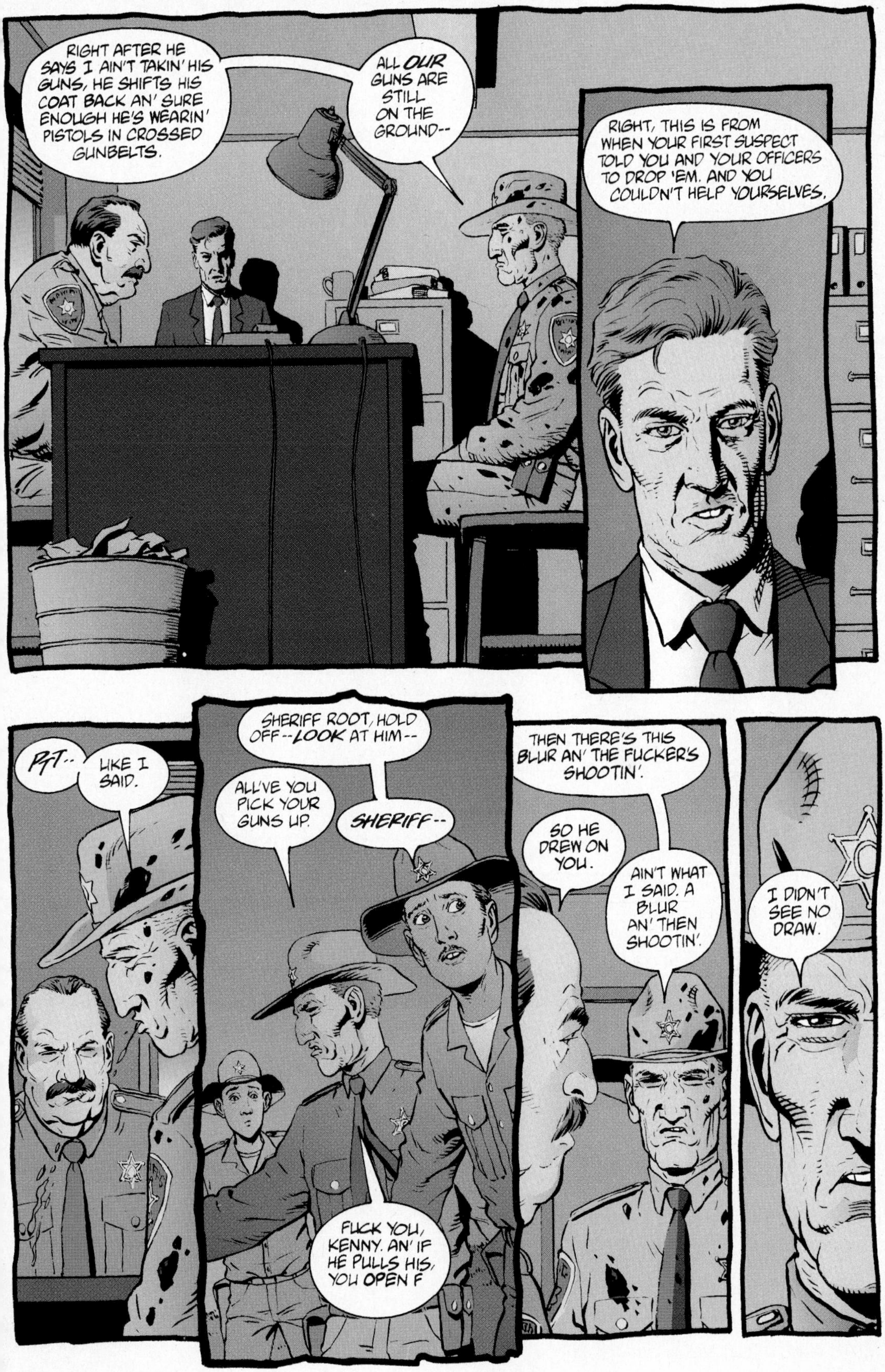
RIGHT AFTER HE SAYS I AIN'T TAKIN' HIS GUNS, HE SHIFTS HIS COAT BACK AN' SURE ENOUGH HE'S WEARIN' PISTOLS IN CROSSED GUNBELTS.
ALL *OUR* GUNS ARE STILL ON THE GROUND--
RIGHT, THIS IS FROM WHEN YOUR FIRST SUSPECT TOLD YOU AND YOUR OFFICERS TO DROP 'EM. AND YOU COULDN'T HELP YOURSELVES.
PTT..
LIKE I SAID.
SHERIFF ROOT, HOLD OFF--*LOOK* AT HIM--
ALL'VE YOU PICK YOUR GUNS UP.
SHERIFF--
FUCK YOU, KENNY. AN' IF HE PULLS HIS, YOU **OPEN** F
THEN THERE'S THIS BLUR AN' THE FUCKER'S SHOOTIN'.
SO HE DREW ON YOU.
AIN'T WHAT I SAID. A BLUR AN' THEN SHOOTIN'.
I DIDN'T SEE NO DRAW.

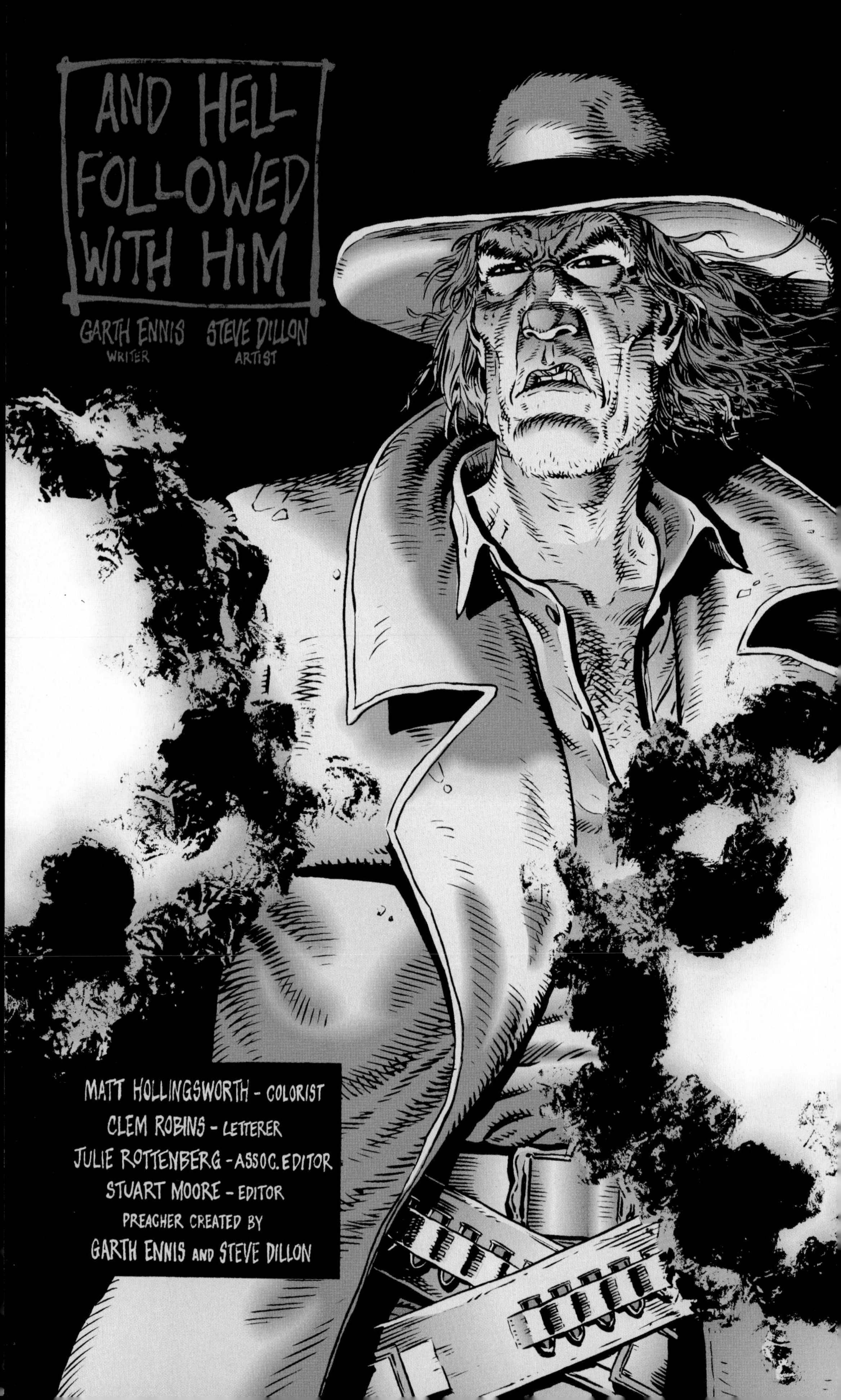

AND HELL FOLLOWED WITH HIM
GARTH ENNIS WRITER
STEVE DILLON ARTIST
MATT HOLLINGSWORTH - COLORIST
CLEM ROBINS - LETTERER
JULIE ROTTENBERG - ASSOC. EDITOR
STUART MOORE - EDITOR
PREACHER CREATED BY
GARTH ENNIS AND STEVE DILLON

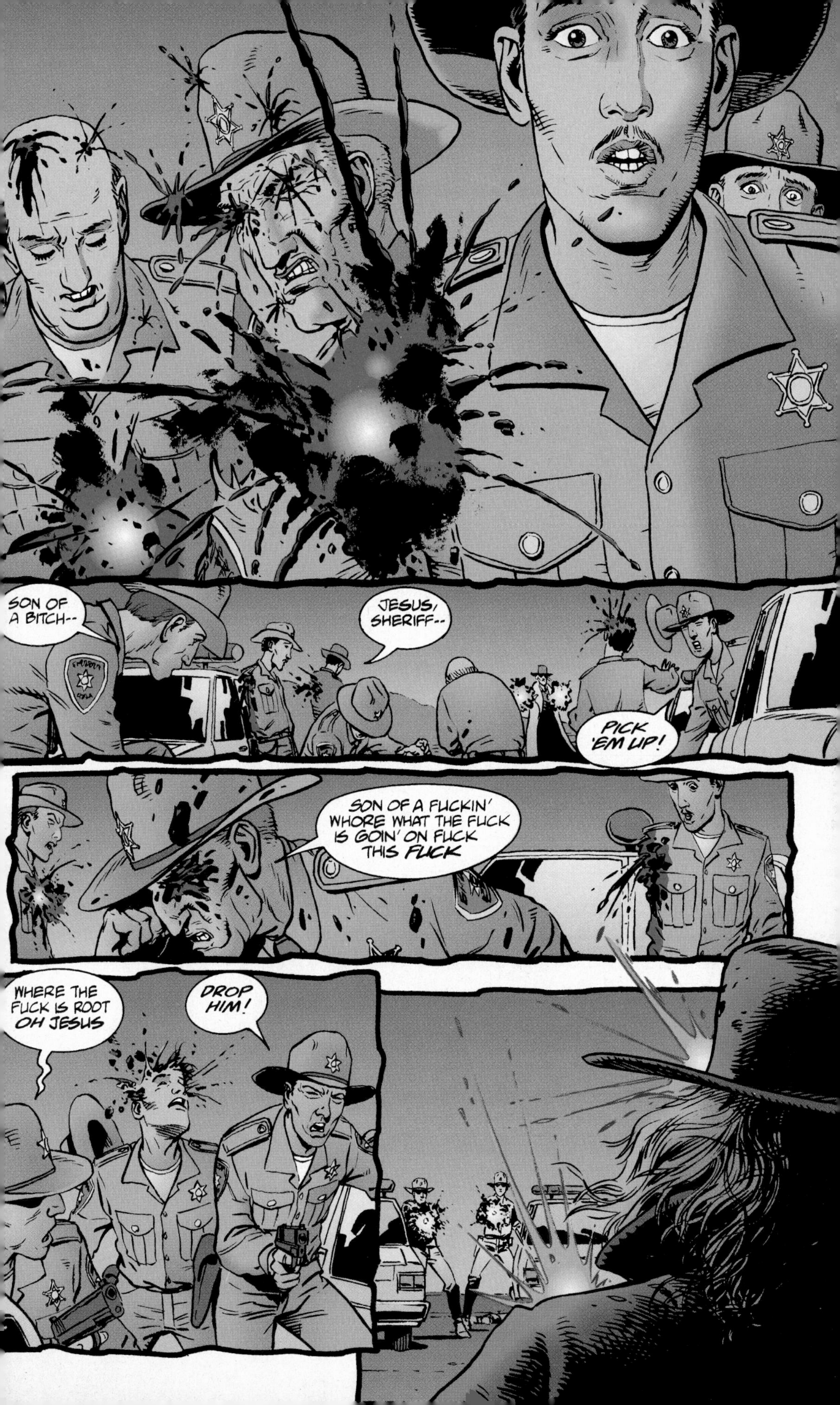
SON OF A BITCH--
JESUS, SHERIFF--
PICK 'EM UP!
SON OF A FUCKIN' WHORE WHAT THE FUCK IS GOIN' ON FUCK THIS FUCK
WHERE THE FUCK IS ROOT OH JESUS
DROP HIM!

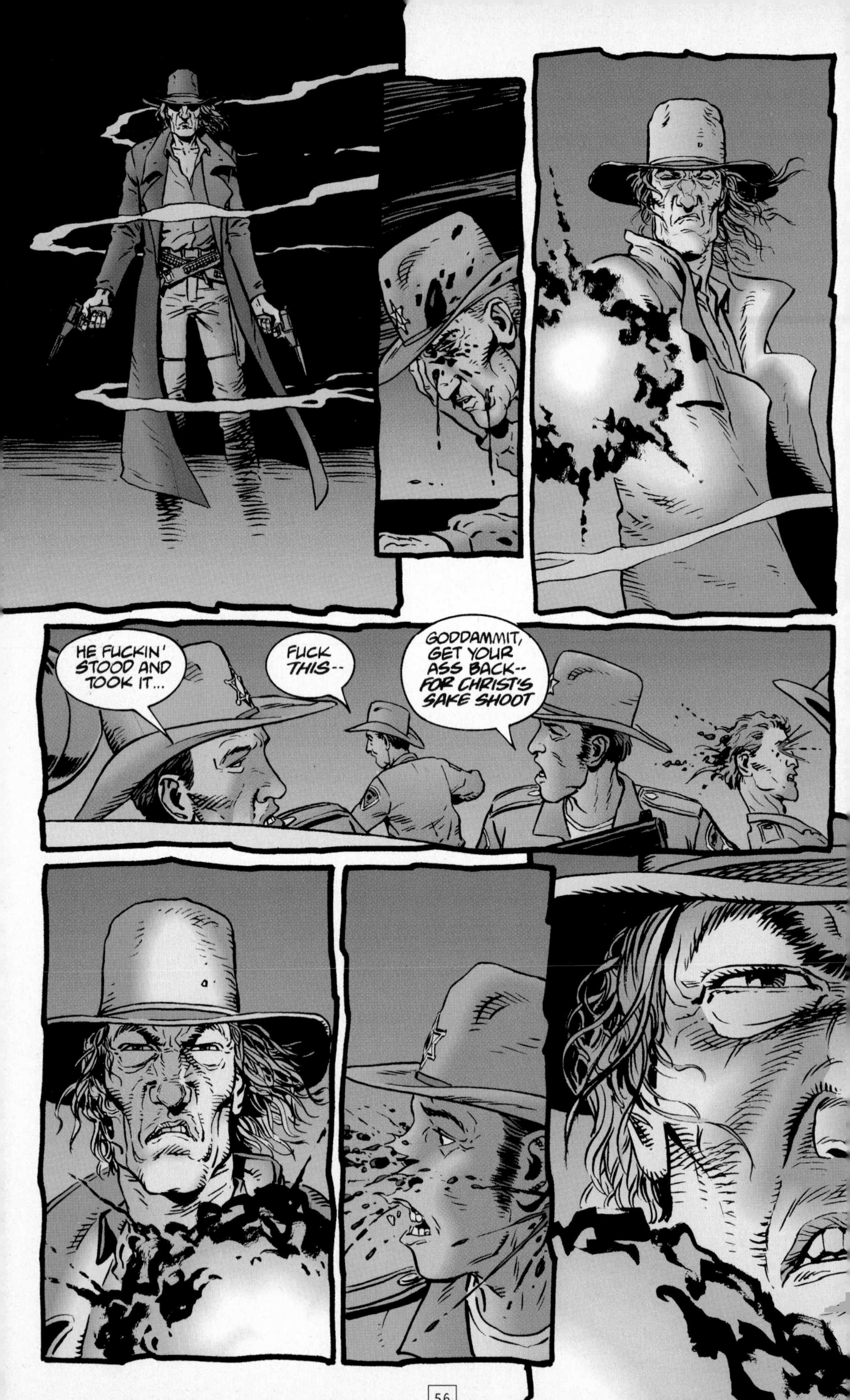

HE FUCKIN' STOOD AND TOOK IT...
FUCK THIS--
GODDAMMIT, GET YOUR ASS BACK-- FOR CHRIST'S SAKE SHOOT

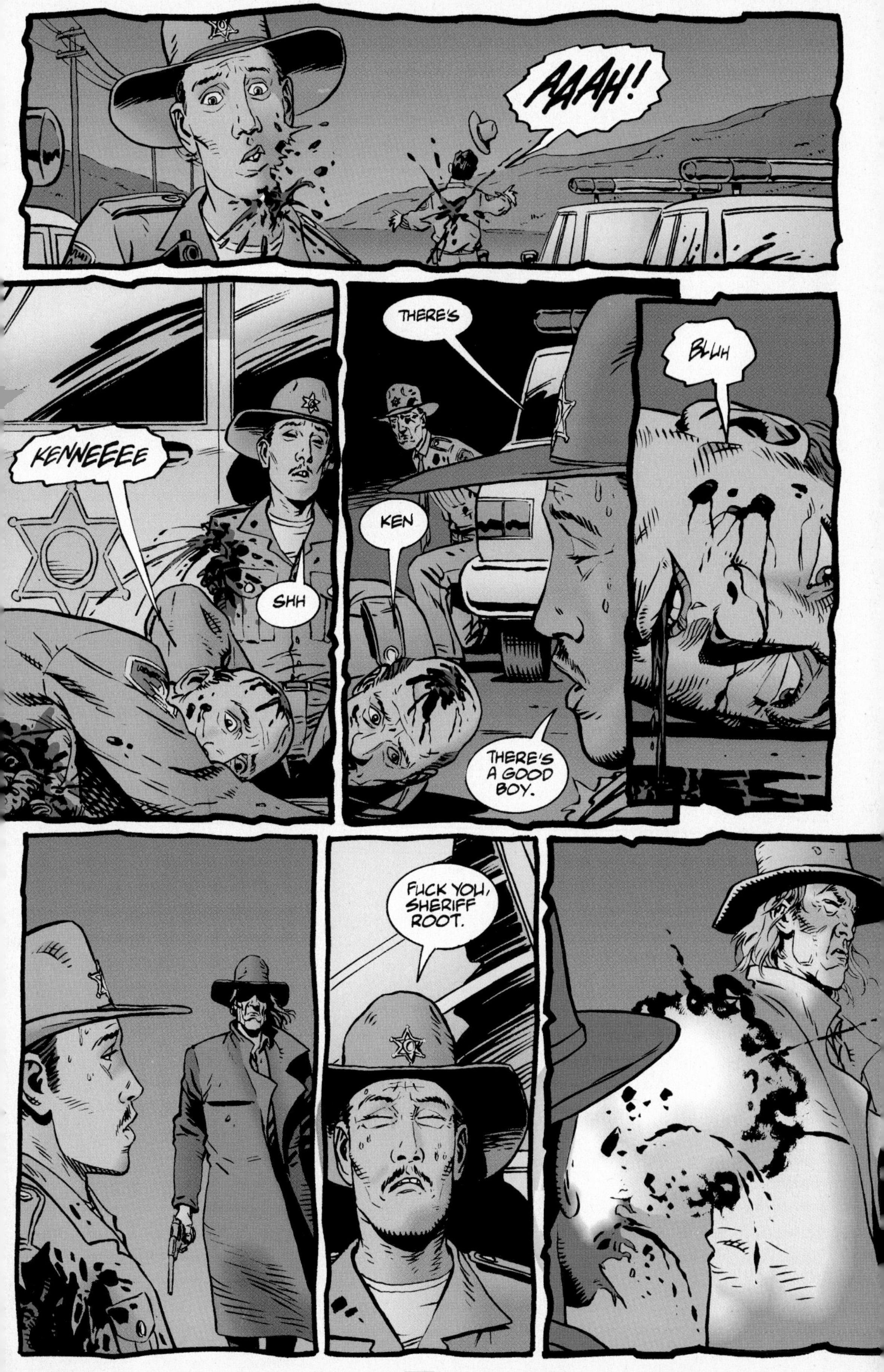

AAAH!
KENNEEEE
SHH
THERE'S
KEN
THERE'S A GOOD BOY.
BLUH
FUCK YOU, SHERIFF ROOT.

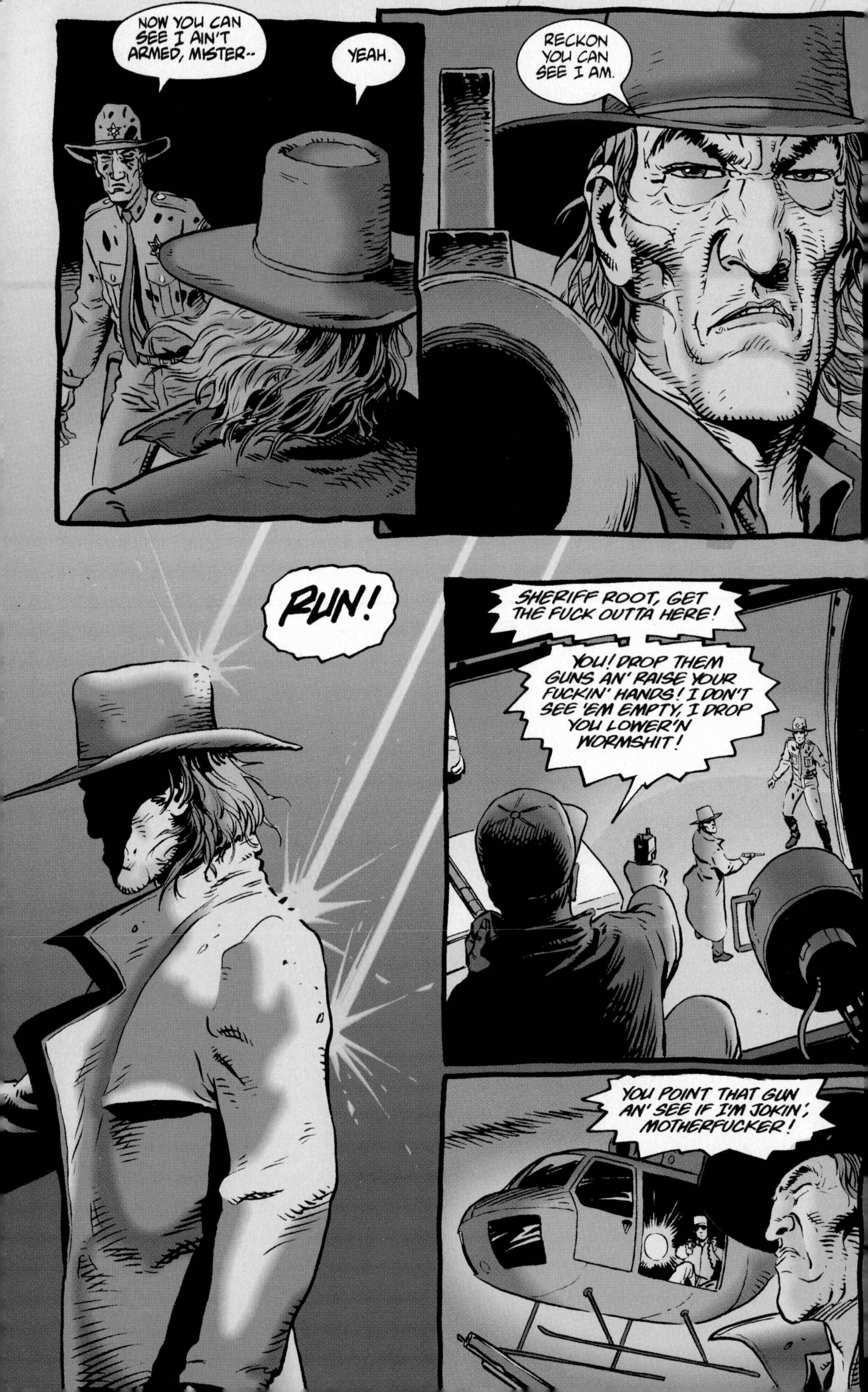
NOW YOU CAN SEE I AIN'T ARMED, MISTER--
YEAH.
RECKON YOU CAN SEE I AM.
RUN!
SHERIFF ROOT, GET THE FUCK OUTTA HERE!
YOU! DROP THEM GUNS AN' RAISE YOUR FUCKIN' HANDS! I DON'T SEE 'EM EMPTY, I DROP YOU LOWER'N WORMSHIT!
YOU POINT THAT GUN AN' SEE IF I'M JOKIN', MOTHERFUCKER!

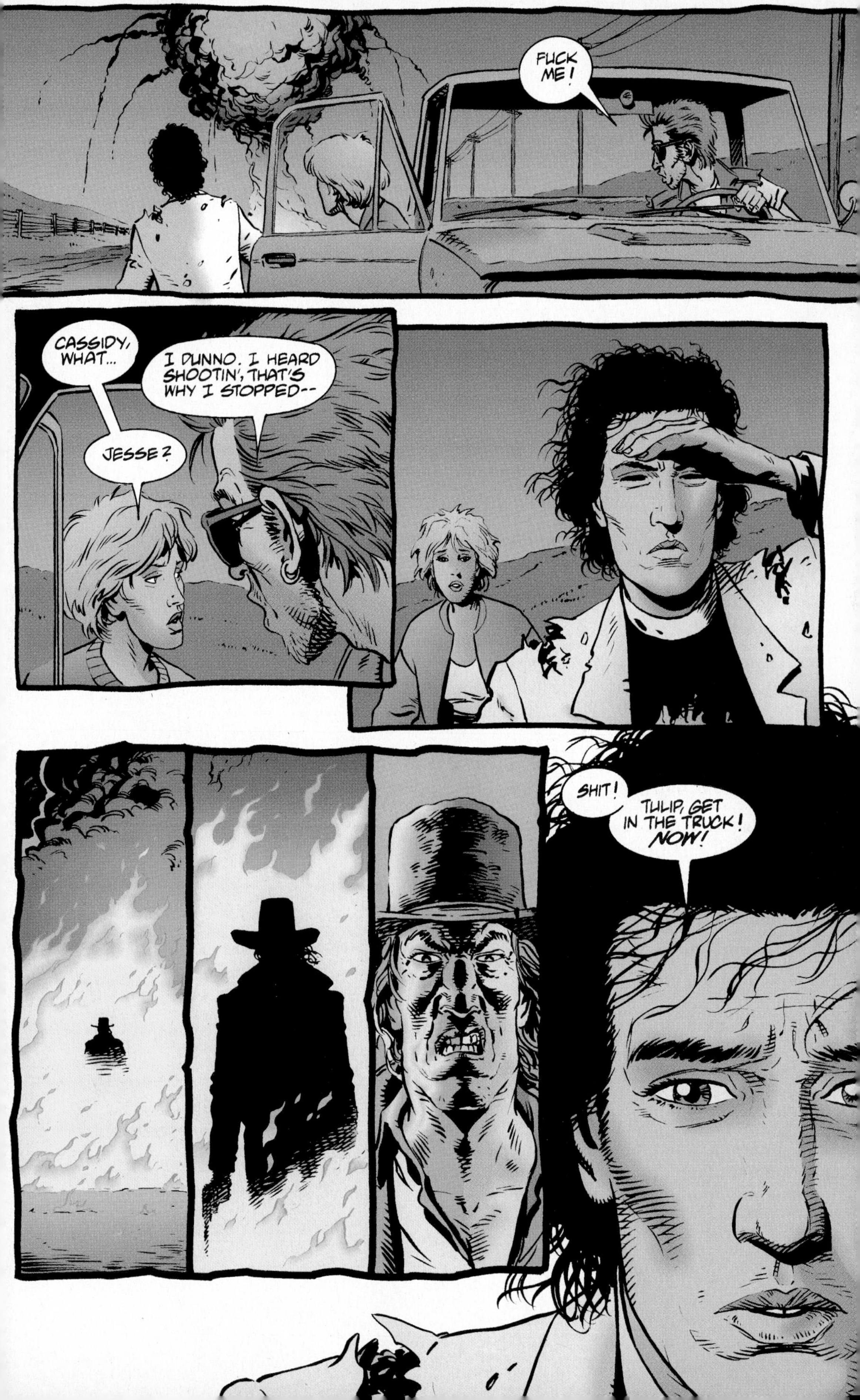
FUCK ME!
CASSIDY, WHAT...
I DUNNO. I HEARD SHOOTIN', THAT'S WHY I STOPPED--
JESSE?
SHIT!
TULIP, GET IN THE TRUCK! NOW!

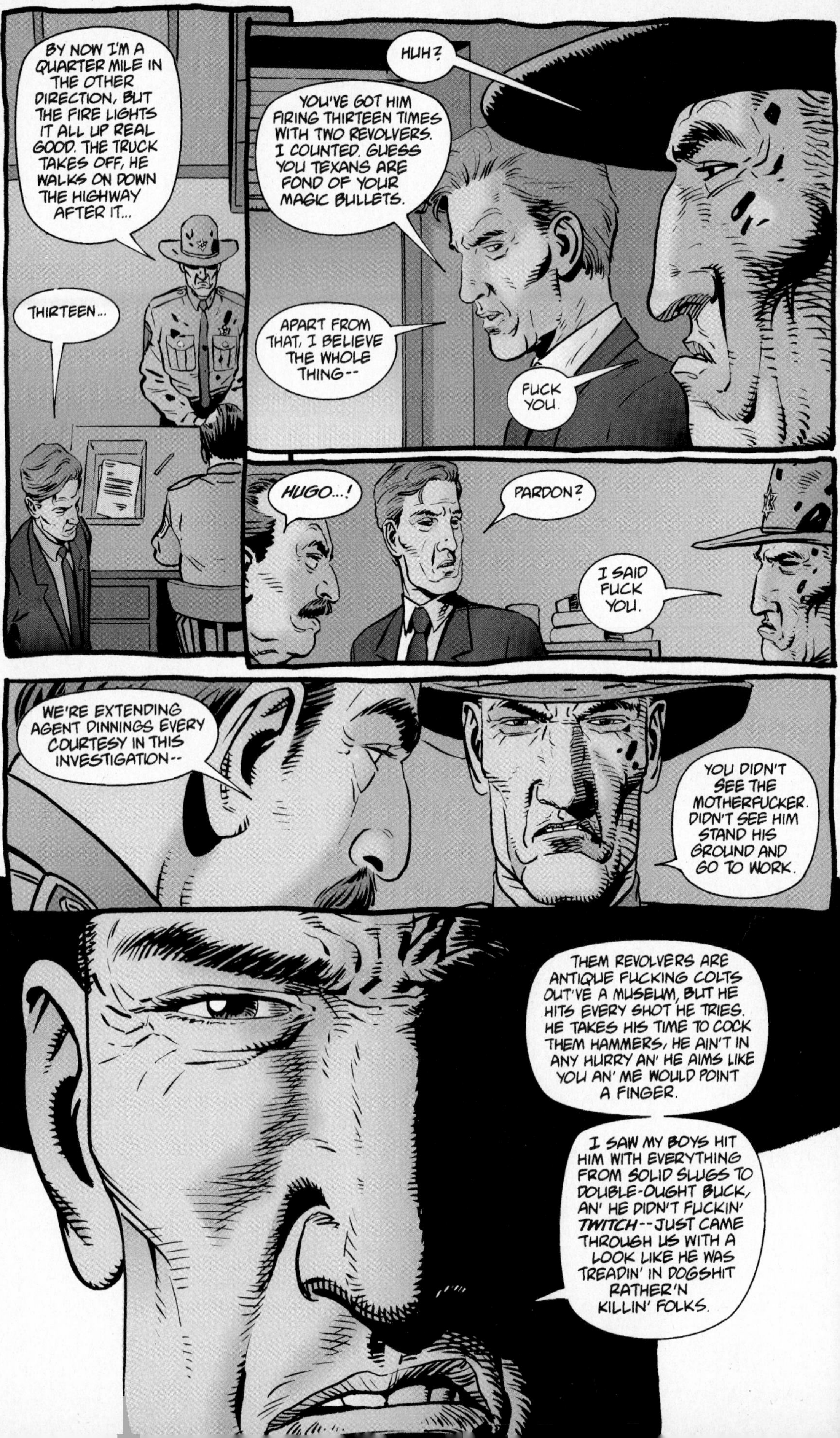
BY NOW I'M A QUARTER MILE IN THE OTHER DIRECTION, BUT THE FIRE LIGHTS IT ALL UP REAL GOOD. THE TRUCK TAKES OFF, HE WALKS ON DOWN THE HIGHWAY AFTER IT...
THIRTEEN...
HUH?
YOU'VE GOT HIM FIRING THIRTEEN TIMES WITH TWO REVOLVERS. I COUNTED. GUESS YOU TEXANS ARE FOND OF YOUR MAGIC BULLETS.
APART FROM THAT, I BELIEVE THE WHOLE THING--
FUCK YOU.
HUGO...!
PARDON?
I SAID FUCK YOU.
WE'RE EXTENDING AGENT DINNINGS EVERY COURTESY IN THIS INVESTIGATION--
YOU DIDN'T SEE THE MOTHERFUCKER. DIDN'T SEE HIM STAND HIS GROUND AND GO TO WORK.
THEM REVOLVERS ARE ANTIQUE FUCKING COLTS OUT'VE A MUSEUM, BUT HE HITS EVERY SHOT HE TRIES. HE TAKES HIS TIME TO COCK THEM HAMMERS, HE AIN'T IN ANY HURRY AN' HE AIMS LIKE YOU AN' ME WOULD POINT A FINGER.
I SAW MY BOYS HIT HIM WITH EVERYTHING FROM SOLID SLUGS TO DOUBLE-OUGHT BUCK, AN' HE DIDN'T FUCKIN' TWITCH--JUST CAME THROUGH US WITH A LOOK LIKE HE WAS TREADIN' IN DOGSHIT RATHER'N KILLIN' FOLKS.

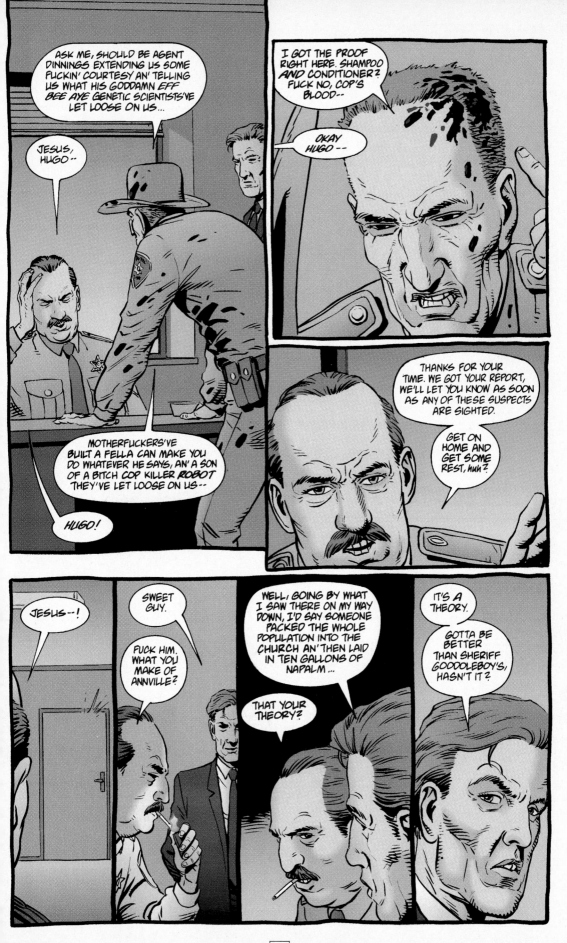

ASK ME, SHOULD BE AGENT DINNINGS EXTENDING US SOME FUCKIN' COURTESY AN' TELLING US WHAT HIS GODDAMN *EFF BEE AYE* GENETIC SCIENTISTS'VE LET LOOSE ON US...

JESUS, HUGO --

I GOT THE PROOF RIGHT HERE. SHAMPOO *AND* CONDITIONER? FUCK NO, COP'S BLOOD--

OKAY HUGO --

MOTHERFUCKERS'VE BUILT A FELLA CAN MAKE YOU DO WHATEVER HE SAYS, AN' A SON OF A BITCH COP KILLER *ROBOT* THEY'VE LET LOOSE ON US--

HUGO!

THANKS FOR YOUR TIME. WE GOT YOUR REPORT, WE'LL LET YOU KNOW AS SOON AS ANY OF THESE SUSPECTS ARE SIGHTED.

GET ON HOME AND GET SOME REST, *huh?*

JESUS--!

SWEET GUY.

FUCK HIM. WHAT YOU MAKE OF ANNVILLE?

WELL, GOING BY WHAT I SAW THERE ON MY WAY DOWN, I'D SAY SOMEONE PACKED THE WHOLE POPULATION INTO THE CHURCH AN' THEN LAID IN TEN GALLONS OF NAPALM ...

THAT YOUR THEORY?

IT'S A THEORY.

GOTTA BE BETTER THAN SHERIFF GOODOLEBOY'S, HASN'T IT?

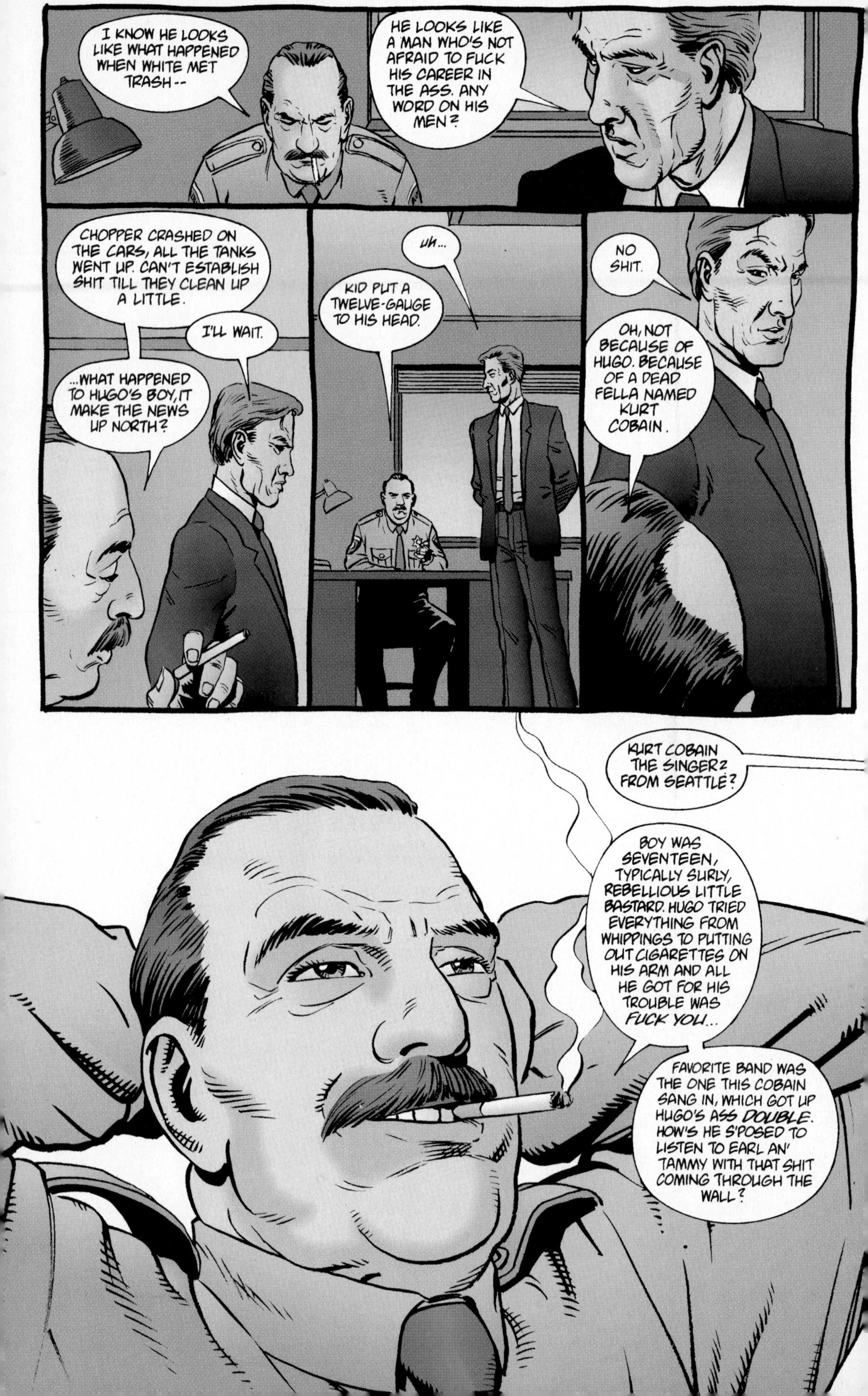
I KNOW HE LOOKS LIKE WHAT HAPPENED WHEN WHITE MET TRASH --
HE LOOKS LIKE A MAN WHO'S NOT AFRAID TO FUCK HIS CAREER IN THE ASS. ANY WORD ON HIS MEN?
CHOPPER CRASHED ON THE CARS, ALL THE TANKS WENT UP. CAN'T ESTABLISH SHIT TILL THEY CLEAN UP A LITTLE.
I'LL WAIT.
...WHAT HAPPENED TO HUGO'S BOY, IT MAKE THE NEWS UP NORTH?
uh...
KID PUT A TWELVE-GAUGE TO HIS HEAD.
NO SHIT.
OH, NOT BECAUSE OF HUGO. BECAUSE OF A DEAD FELLA NAMED KURT COBAIN.
KURT COBAIN THE SINGER? FROM SEATTLE?
BOY WAS SEVENTEEN, TYPICALLY SURLY, REBELLIOUS LITTLE BASTARD. HUGO TRIED EVERYTHING FROM WHIPPINGS TO PUTTING OUT CIGARETTES ON HIS ARM AND ALL HE GOT FOR HIS TROUBLE WAS *FUCK YOU*...
FAVORITE BAND WAS THE ONE THIS COBAIN SANG IN, WHICH GOT UP HUGO'S ASS *DOUBLE*. HOW'S HE S'POSED TO LISTEN TO EARL AN' TAMMY WITH THAT SHIT COMING THROUGH THE WALL?

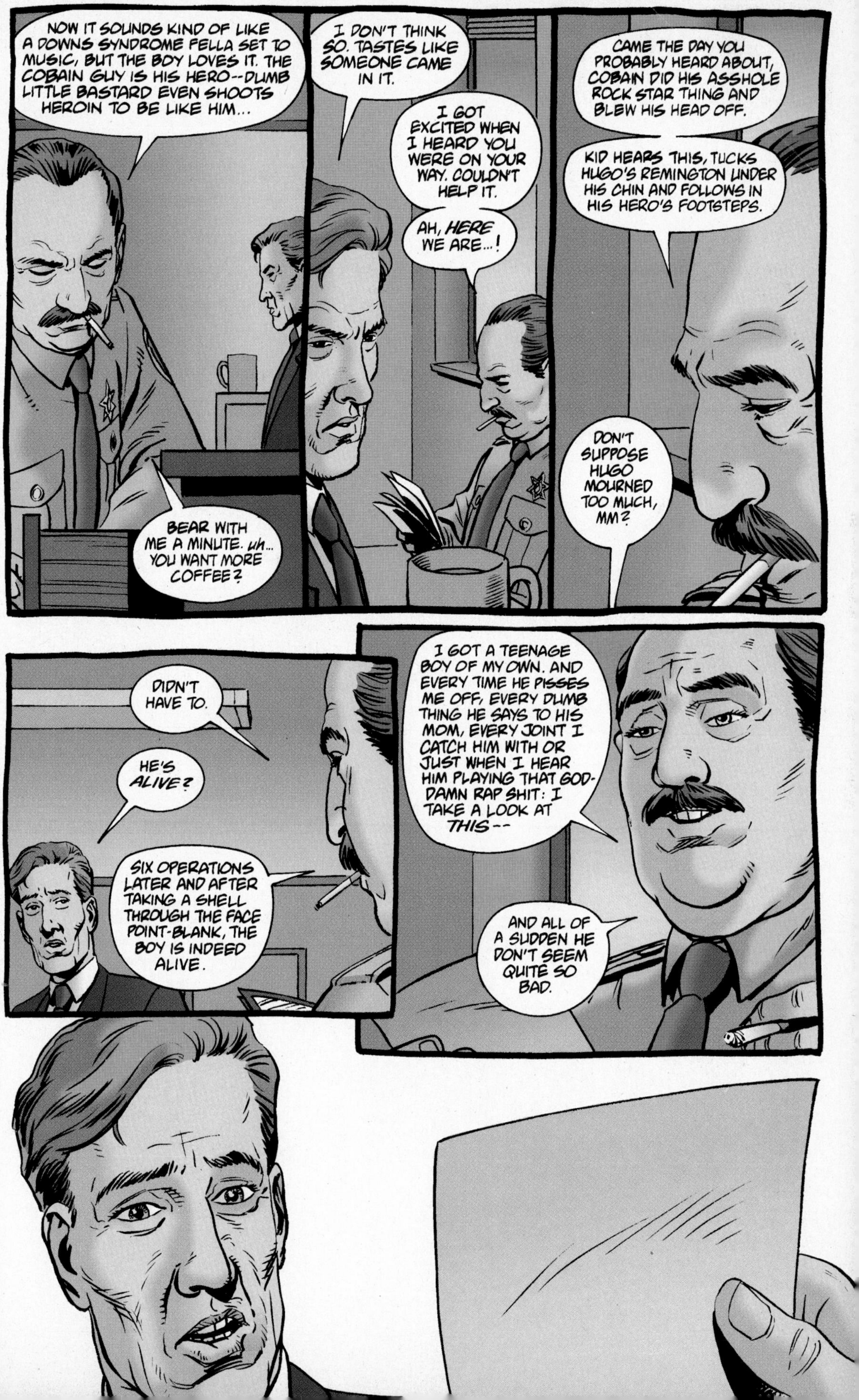
NOW IT SOUNDS KIND OF LIKE A DOWNS SYNDROME FELLA SET TO MUSIC, BUT THE BOY LOVES IT. THE COBAIN GUY IS HIS HERO--DUMB LITTLE BASTARD EVEN SHOOTS HEROIN TO BE LIKE HIM...
BEAR WITH ME A MINUTE. uh... YOU WANT MORE COFFEE?
I DON'T THINK SO. TASTES LIKE SOMEONE CAME IN IT.
I GOT EXCITED WHEN I HEARD YOU WERE ON YOUR WAY. COULDN'T HELP IT.
AH, HERE WE ARE...!
CAME THE DAY YOU PROBABLY HEARD ABOUT, COBAIN DID HIS ASSHOLE ROCK STAR THING AND BLEW HIS HEAD OFF.
KID HEARS THIS, TUCKS HUGO'S REMINGTON UNDER HIS CHIN AND FOLLOWS IN HIS HERO'S FOOTSTEPS.
DON'T SUPPOSE HUGO MOURNED TOO MUCH, MM?
DIDN'T HAVE TO.
HE'S ALIVE?
SIX OPERATIONS LATER AND AFTER TAKING A SHELL THROUGH THE FACE POINT-BLANK, THE BOY IS INDEED ALIVE.
I GOT A TEENAGE BOY OF MY OWN. AND EVERY TIME HE PISSES ME OFF, EVERY DUMB THING HE SAYS TO HIS MOM, EVERY JOINT I CATCH HIM WITH OR JUST WHEN I HEAR HIM PLAYING THAT GOD-DAMN RAP SHIT: I TAKE A LOOK AT THIS--
AND ALL OF A SUDDEN HE DON'T SEEM QUITE SO BAD.

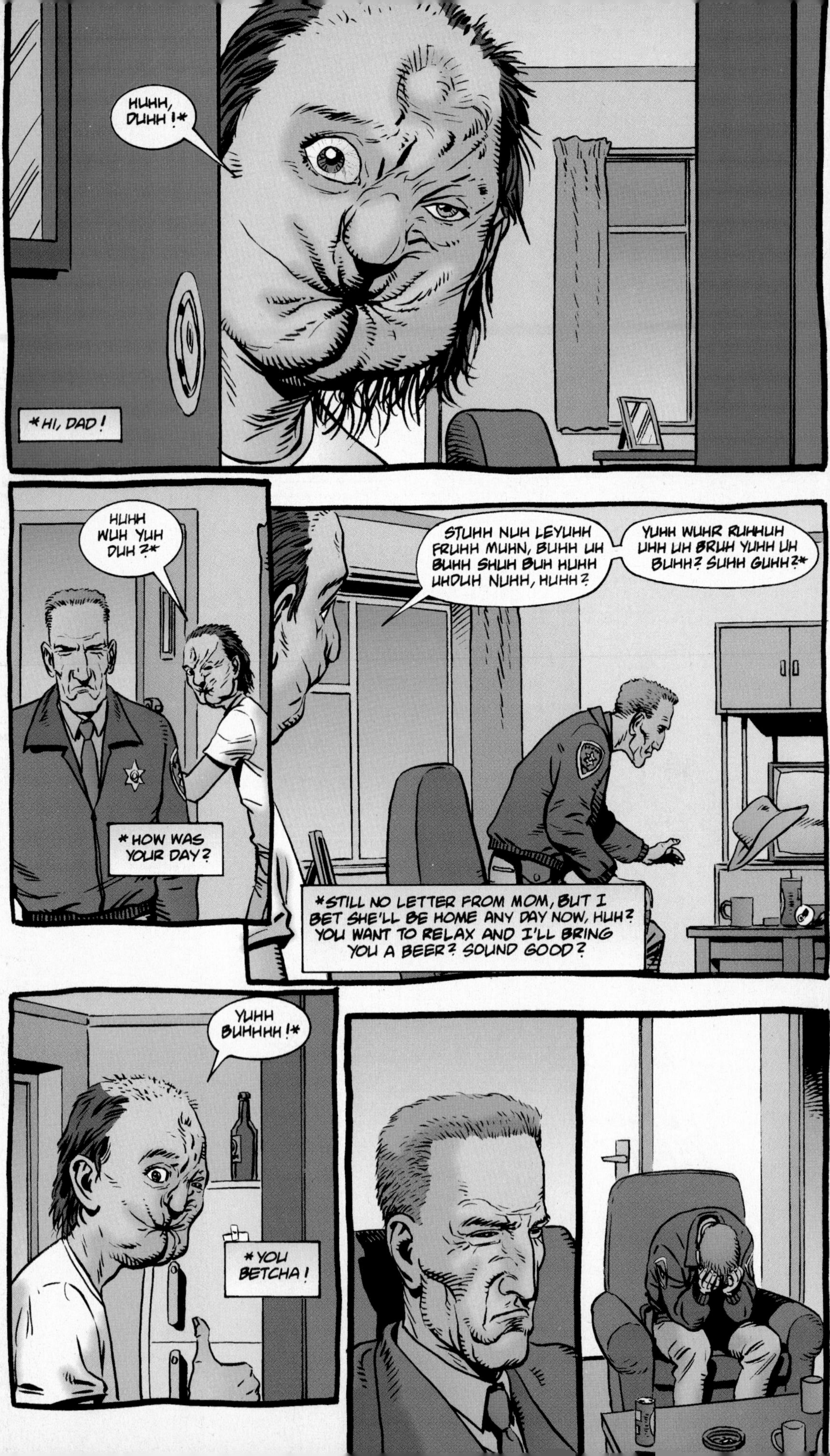
HUHH, DUHH!*
*HI, DAD!
HUHH WUH YUH DUH?*
*HOW WAS YOUR DAY?
STUHH NUH LEYUHH FRUHH MUHN, BUHH UH BUHH SHUH BUH HUHH UHDUH NUHH, HUHH?
YUHH WUHR RUHHUH UHH UH BRUH YUHH UH BUHH? SUHH GUHH?*
*STILL NO LETTER FROM MOM, BUT I BET SHE'LL BE HOME ANY DAY NOW, HUH? YOU WANT TO RELAX AND I'LL BRING YOU A BEER? SOUND GOOD?
YUHH BUHHHH!*
*YOU BETCHA!

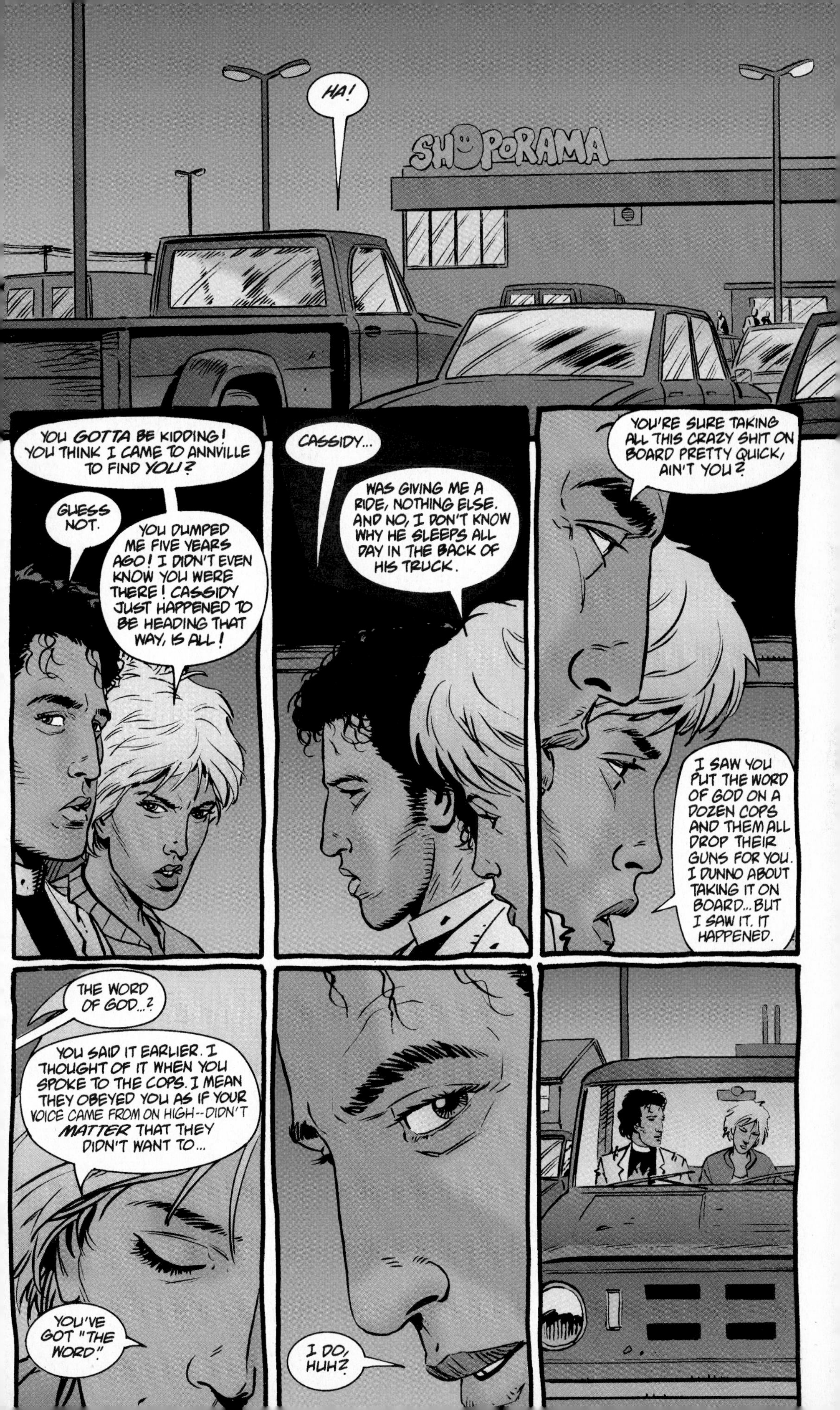

HA!
SHOPORAMA
YOU GOTTA BE KIDDING! YOU THINK I CAME TO ANNVILLE TO FIND YOU?
GUESS NOT.
YOU DUMPED ME FIVE YEARS AGO! I DIDN'T EVEN KNOW YOU WERE THERE! CASSIDY JUST HAPPENED TO BE HEADING THAT WAY, IS ALL!
CASSIDY...
WAS GIVING ME A RIDE, NOTHING ELSE. AND NO, I DON'T KNOW WHY HE SLEEPS ALL DAY IN THE BACK OF HIS TRUCK.
YOU'RE SURE TAKING ALL THIS CRAZY SHIT ON BOARD PRETTY QUICK, AIN'T YOU?
I SAW YOU PUT THE WORD OF GOD ON A DOZEN COPS AND THEM ALL DROP THEIR GUNS FOR YOU. I DUNNO ABOUT TAKING IT ON BOARD... BUT I SAW IT. IT HAPPENED.
THE WORD OF GOD...?
YOU SAID IT EARLIER. I THOUGHT OF IT WHEN YOU SPOKE TO THE COPS. I MEAN THEY OBEYED YOU AS IF YOUR VOICE CAME FROM ON HIGH--DIDN'T MATTER THAT THEY DIDN'T WANT TO...
YOU'VE GOT "THE WORD."
I DO, HUH?

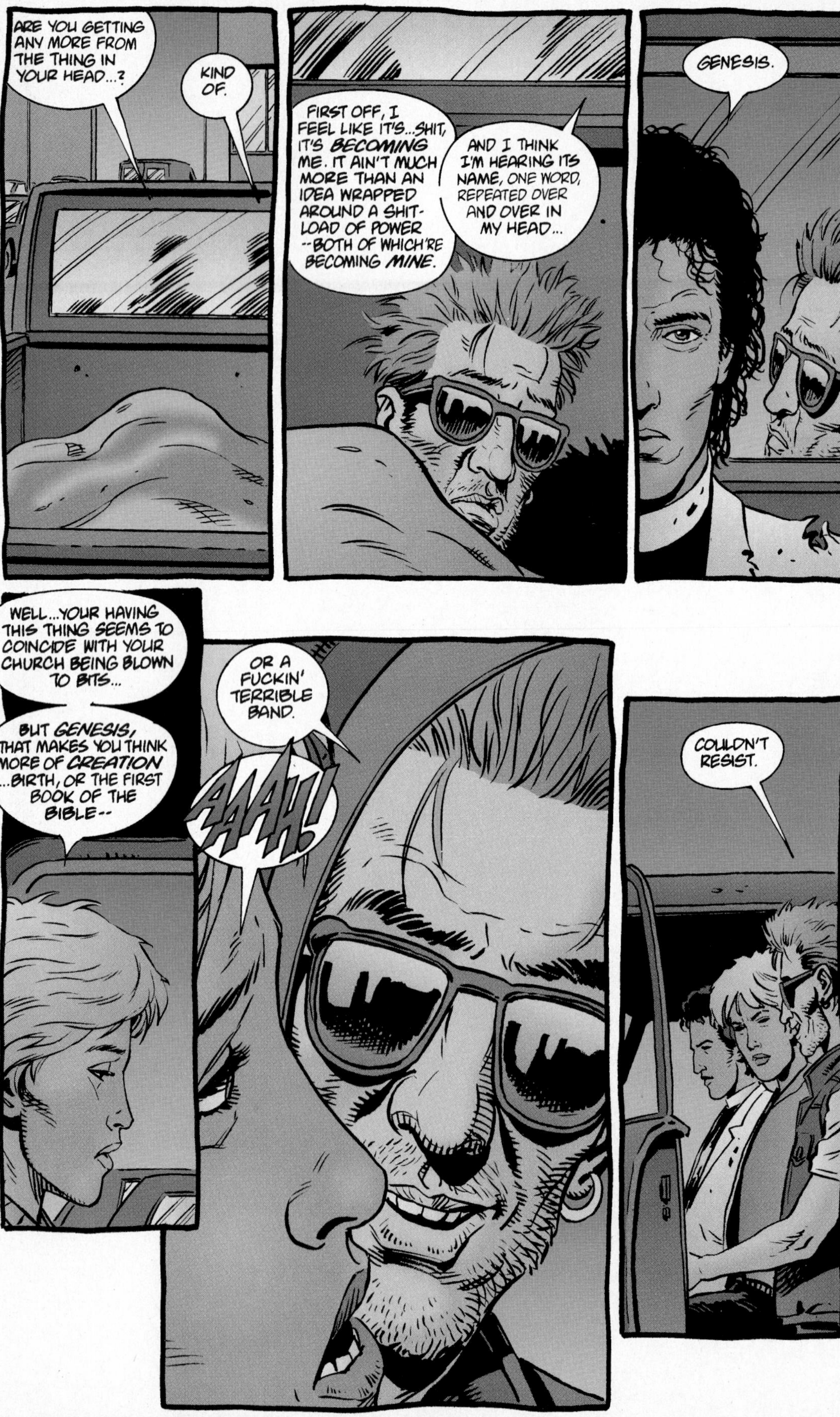

ARE YOU GETTING ANY MORE FROM THE THING IN YOUR HEAD...?
KIND OF.
FIRST OFF, I FEEL LIKE IT'S...SHIT, IT'S BECOMING ME. IT AIN'T MUCH MORE THAN AN IDEA WRAPPED AROUND A SHIT-LOAD OF POWER --BOTH OF WHICH'RE BECOMING MINE.
AND I THINK I'M HEARING ITS NAME, ONE WORD, REPEATED OVER AND OVER IN MY HEAD...
GENESIS.
WELL...YOUR HAVING THIS THING SEEMS TO COINCIDE WITH YOUR CHURCH BEING BLOWN TO BITS...
BUT GENESIS, THAT MAKES YOU THINK MORE OF CREATION ...BIRTH, OR THE FIRST BOOK OF THE BIBLE--
OR A FUCKIN' TERRIBLE BAND.
AAAH!
COULDN'T RESIST.

I THOUGHT YEZ WERE GOIN' SHOPPIN' FOR CLOTHES. YOU DROVE ALL DAY TO GET HERE, LIKE...

WE GOT TO TALKING.

IS IT LOVE?

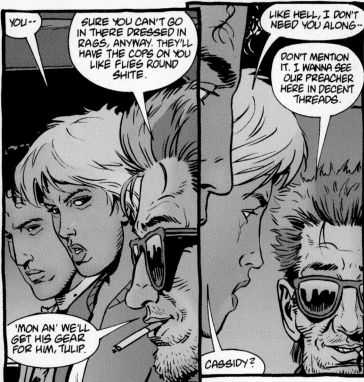

YOU--

SURE YOU CAN'T GO IN THERE DRESSED IN RAGS, ANYWAY. THEY'LL HAVE THE COPS ON YOU LIKE FLIES ROUND SHITE.

'MON AN' WE'LL GET HIS GEAR FOR HIM, TULIP.

LIKE HELL, I DON'T NEED YOU ALONG--

DON'T MENTION IT. I WANNA SEE OUR PREACHER HERE IN DECENT THREADS.

CASSIDY?

STAND ON YOUR HEAD.

THIS IS DEAD FUNNY, SO IT IS.

DON'T DO IT AGAIN.

YOU GOT IT.

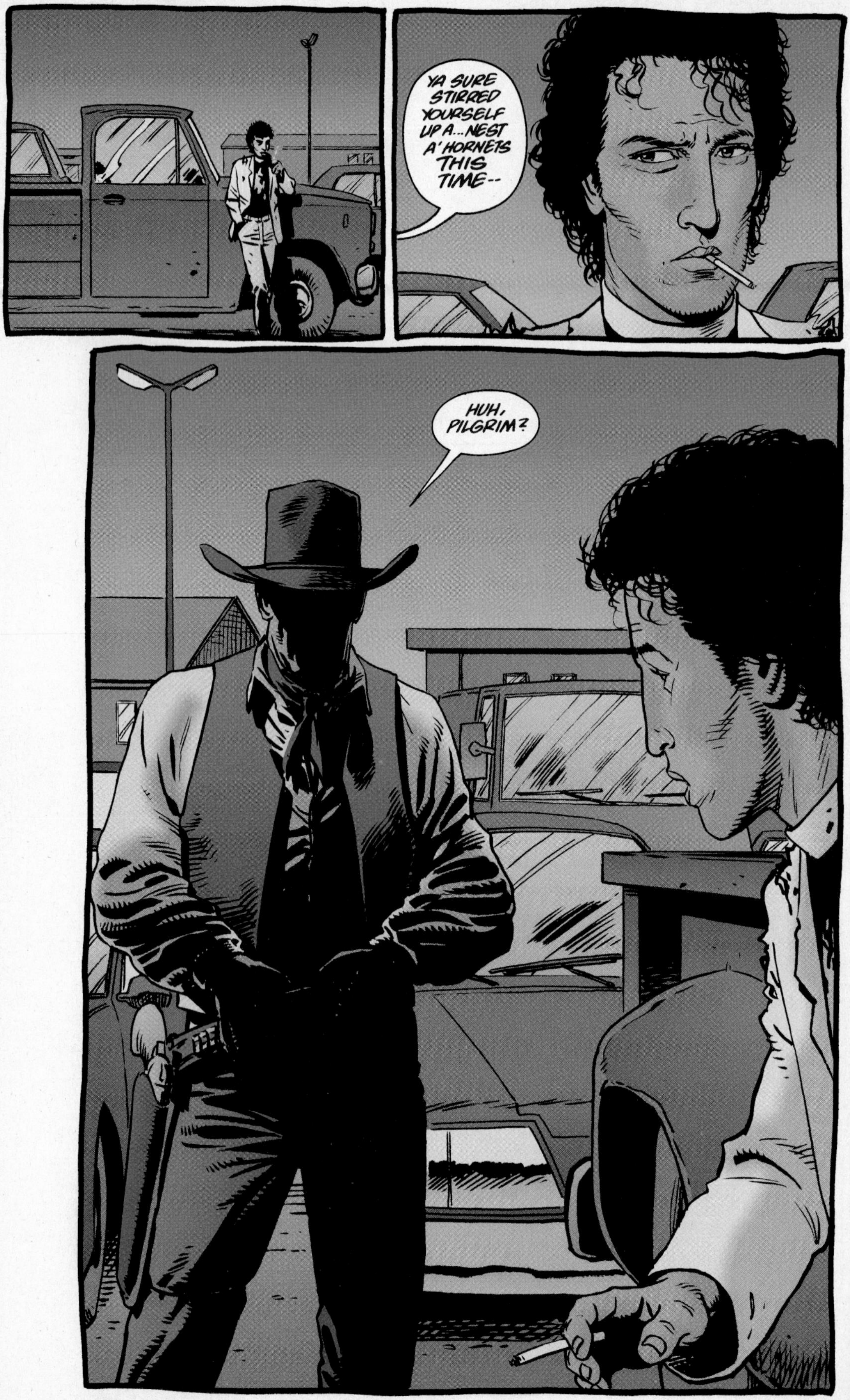
YA SURE STIRRED YOURSELF UP A...NEST A' HORNETS THIS TIME--
HUH, PILGRIM?

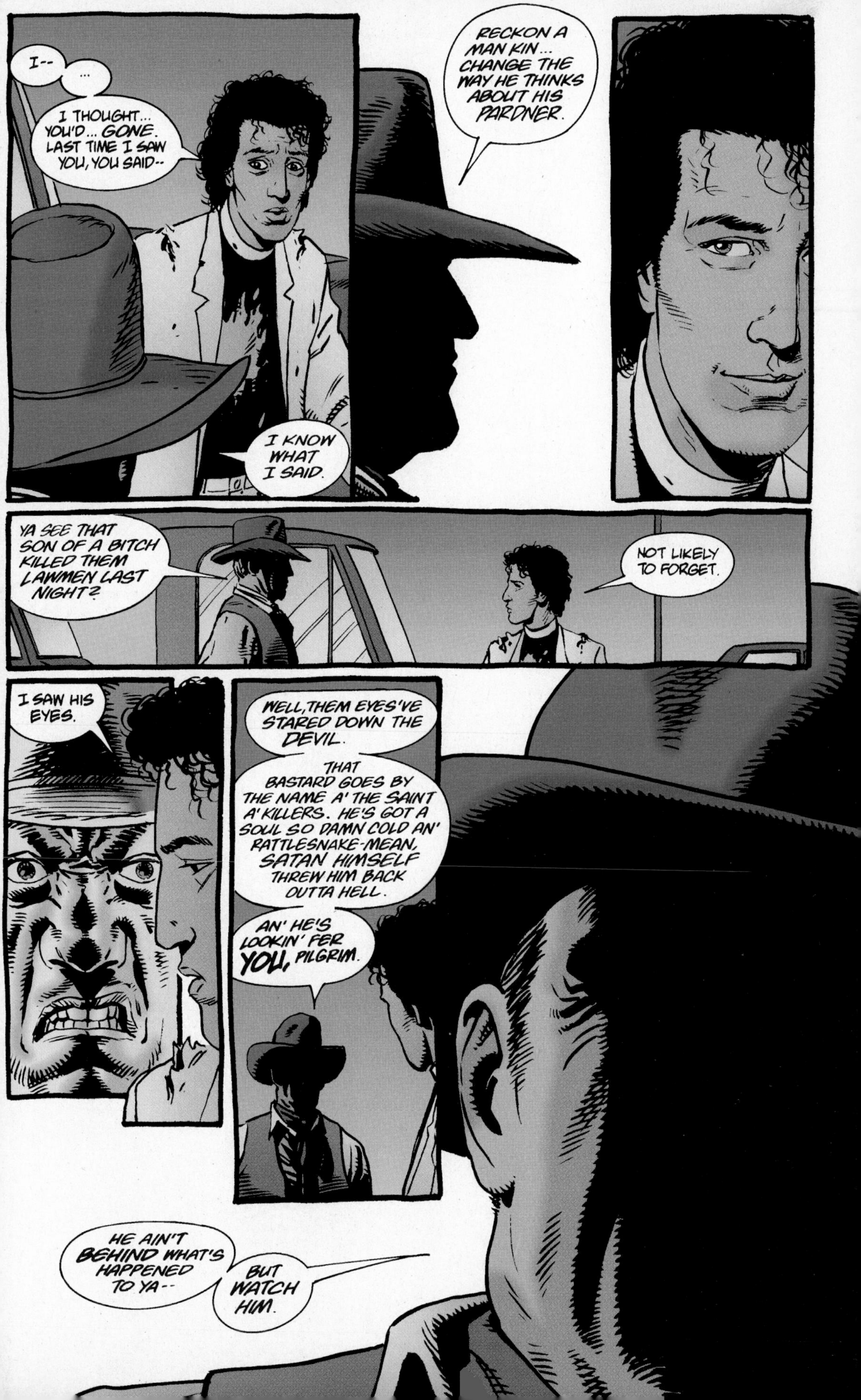
I--
...
I THOUGHT... YOU'D... GONE. LAST TIME I SAW YOU, YOU SAID--
I KNOW WHAT I SAID.
RECKON A MAN KIN... CHANGE THE WAY HE THINKS ABOUT HIS PARDNER.
YA SEE THAT SON OF A BITCH KILLED THEM LAWMEN LAST NIGHT?
NOT LIKELY TO FORGET.
I SAW HIS EYES.
WELL, THEM EYES'VE STARED DOWN THE DEVIL.
THAT BASTARD GOES BY THE NAME A' THE SAINT A' KILLERS. HE'S GOT A SOUL SO DAMN COLD AN' RATTLESNAKE-MEAN, SATAN HIMSELF THREW HIM BACK OUTTA HELL.
AN' HE'S LOOKIN' FER YOU, PILGRIM.
HE AIN'T BEHIND WHAT'S HAPPENED TO YA--
BUT WATCH HIM.

WHITE JEANS AN' A BLACK SHIRT?

IT'S WHAT HE LIKES.

YOU WOULD KNOW, I SUPPOSE.

WE WERE TOGETHER A YEAR AND A HALF. I CAN'T HELP IT, CAN I?

I'M NOT CRITICIZIN'.

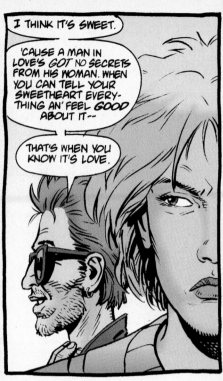

I THINK IT'S SWEET.

'CAUSE A MAN IN LOVE'S GOT NO SECRETS FROM HIS WOMAN. WHEN YOU CAN TELL YOUR SWEETHEART EVERYTHING AN' FEEL GOOD ABOUT IT--

THAT'S WHEN YOU KNOW IT'S LOVE.

I FUCKING HATE YOU, CASSIDY. I REALLY FUCKING HATE YOU--

STILL, AS I OFTEN SAY: SOMETIMES IT'S HARD TO BE A WOMAN, Y'KNOW? THE WAY YOU GIVE ALL YOUR LOVE TO ...JUST ONE MAN...

♪MM-HMM-HMM-HMM, MM-HMM-HMM...HMM-MM-HMM-HMMM, HMM-HM-MMM...

IS THERE A LEATHER GOODS STORE IN THE MALL?

UH... YEAH...

HOW ABOUT SOMEWHERE I CAN BUY MATCHES AN' GASOLINE?

'CAUSE AFTER ALL HE'S--JUST A MAN.

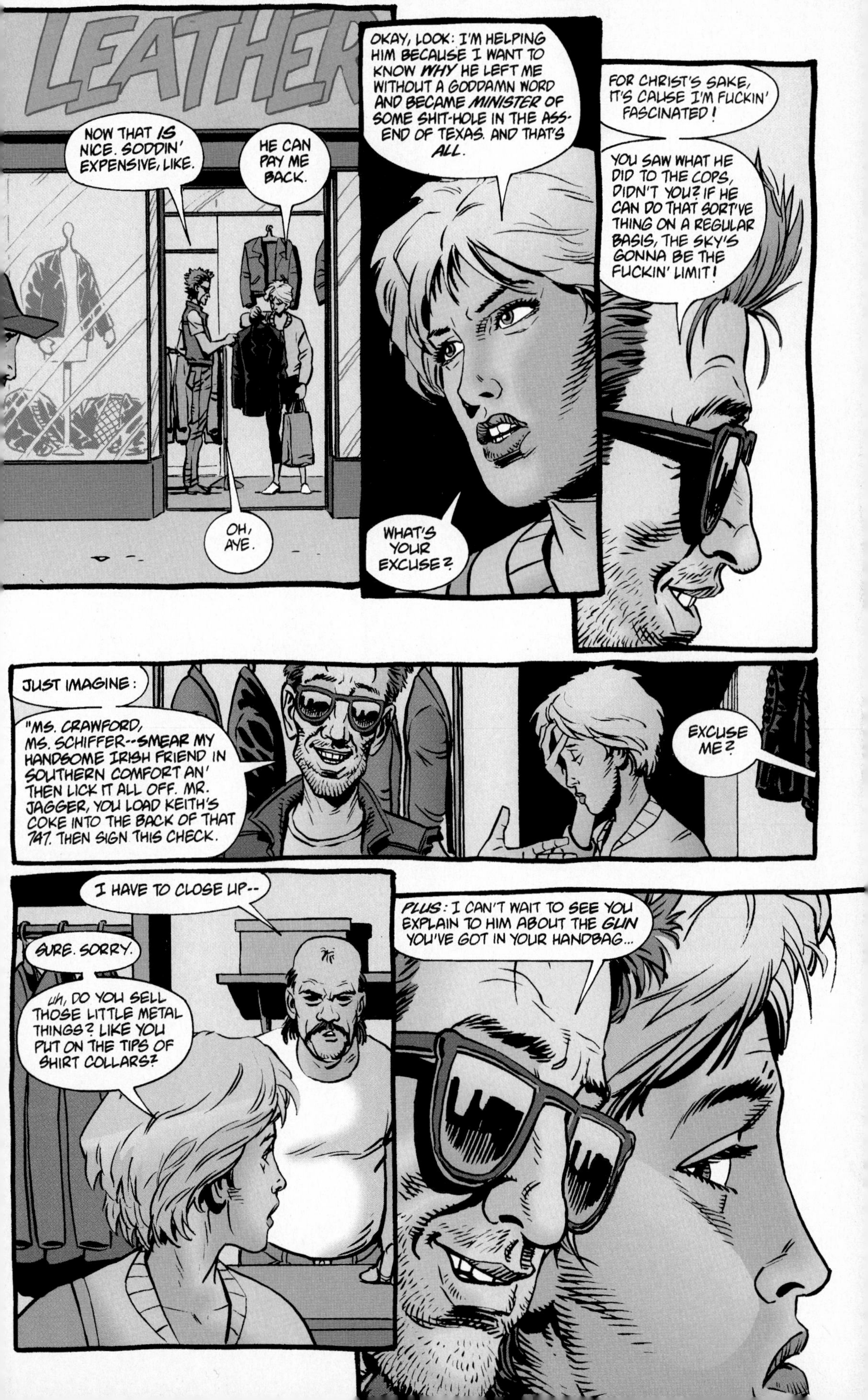
LEATHER
NOW THAT *IS* NICE. SODDIN' EXPENSIVE, LIKE.
HE CAN PAY ME BACK.
OH, AYE.
OKAY, LOOK: I'M HELPING HIM BECAUSE I WANT TO KNOW *WHY* HE LEFT ME WITHOUT A GODDAMN WORD AND BECAME *MINISTER* OF SOME SHIT-HOLE IN THE ASS-END OF TEXAS. AND THAT'S *ALL*.
WHAT'S YOUR EXCUSE?
FOR CHRIST'S SAKE, IT'S CAUSE I'M FUCKIN' FASCINATED!
YOU SAW WHAT HE DID TO THE COPS, DIDN'T YOU? IF HE CAN DO THAT SORT'VE THING ON A REGULAR BASIS, THE SKY'S GONNA BE THE FUCKIN' LIMIT!
JUST IMAGINE:
"MS. CRAWFORD, MS. SCHIFFER--SMEAR MY HANDSOME IRISH FRIEND IN SOUTHERN COMFORT AN' THEN LICK IT ALL OFF. MR. JAGGER, YOU LOAD KEITH'S COKE INTO THE BACK OF THAT 747. THEN SIGN THIS CHECK.
EXCUSE ME?
I HAVE TO CLOSE UP--
SURE. SORRY.
UH, DO YOU SELL THOSE LITTLE METAL THINGS? LIKE YOU PUT ON THE TIPS OF SHIRT COLLARS?
PLUS: I CAN'T WAIT TO SEE YOU EXPLAIN TO HIM ABOUT THE *GUN* YOU'VE GOT IN YOUR HANDBAG...

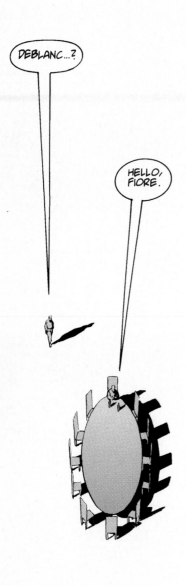

DEBLANC...?

HELLO, FIORE.

WHAT'RE YOU--ARE YOU DRUNK?

I TELL YOU WHAT: YOU GIVE ME WHATEVER MESSAGE IT IS YOU CAME TO GIVE ME, AND I'LL TELL YOU WHY I'M GETTING SO ARSEHOLED.

MM-HMMMM...

THE SAINT HAS KILLED PILO AND ABOUT A DOZEN MORTALS--

IMAGINE THAT. THE PATRON SAINT OF MURDERERS AND ASSASSINS HAS BEEN KILLING PEOPLE.

WHY?!

FIORE, I DON'T CARE IF THE BODYCOUNT REACHES TRIPLE FIGURES. WE SENT HIM BECAUSE NOTHING'LL STOP HIM GETTING GENESIS BACK.

IT'S NOT JUST THAT! HIS INVOLVEMENT PROVES OURS! HAD YOU CONSIDERED THAT?

SURE I CONSIDERED IT. BUT THAT'S NOT WHY I'M DRINKING.

I'M DRINKING BECAUSE SOONER OR LATER THE GRAIL ARE GONNA HEAR ABOUT THIS.

OH FUCK.

I THINK I NEED A DRINK.

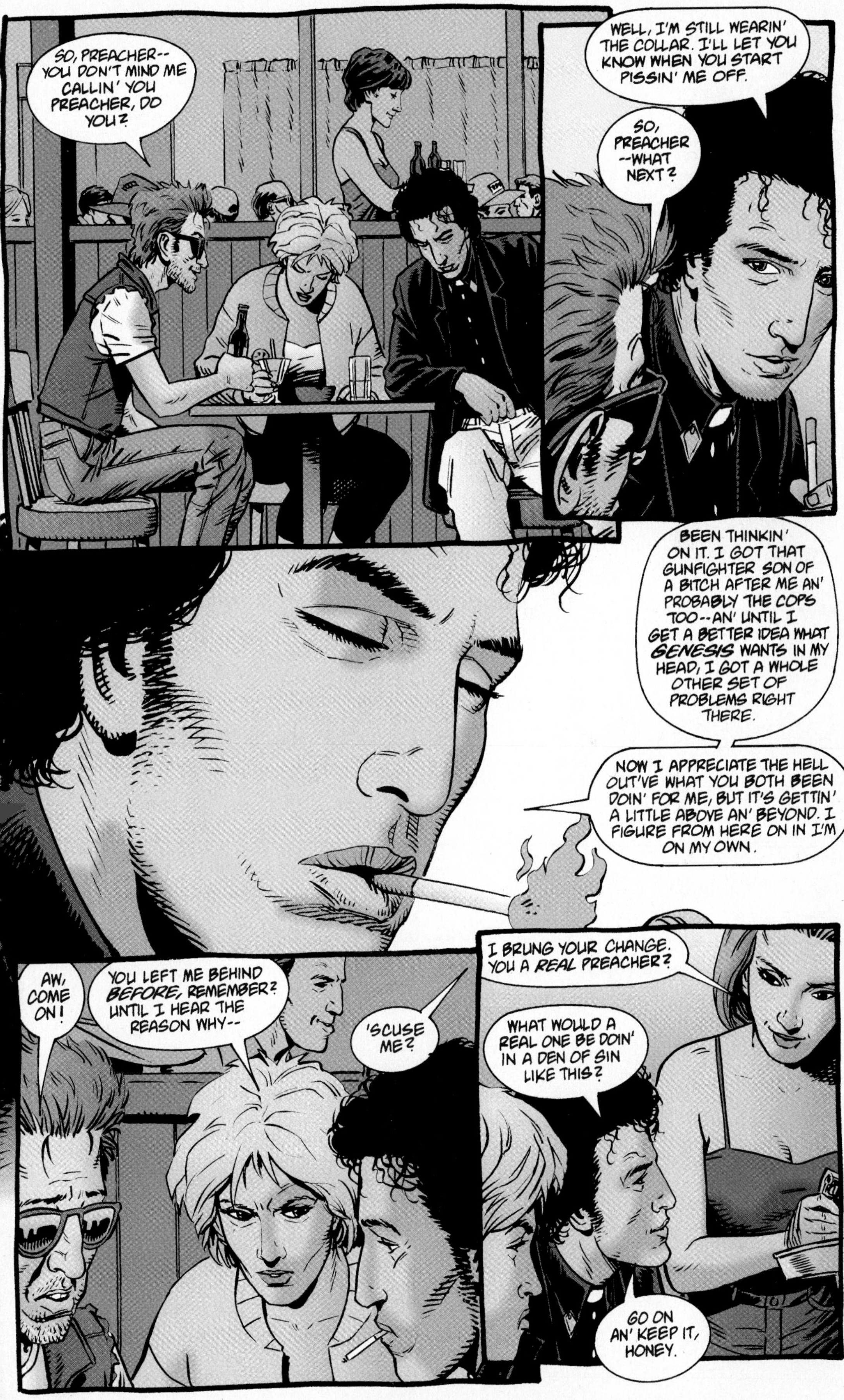
SO, PREACHER--YOU DON'T MIND ME CALLIN' YOU PREACHER, DO YOU?
WELL, I'M STILL WEARIN' THE COLLAR. I'LL LET YOU KNOW WHEN YOU START PISSIN' ME OFF.
SO, PREACHER--WHAT NEXT?
BEEN THINKIN' ON IT. I GOT THAT GUNFIGHTER SON OF A BITCH AFTER ME AN' PROBABLY THE COPS TOO--AN' UNTIL I GET A BETTER IDEA WHAT GENESIS WANTS IN MY HEAD, I GOT A WHOLE OTHER SET OF PROBLEMS RIGHT THERE.
NOW I APPRECIATE THE HELL OUT'VE WHAT YOU BOTH BEEN DOIN' FOR ME, BUT IT'S GETTIN' A LITTLE ABOVE AN' BEYOND. I FIGURE FROM HERE ON IN I'M ON MY OWN.
AW, COME ON!
YOU LEFT ME BEHIND BEFORE, REMEMBER? UNTIL I HEAR THE REASON WHY--
'SCUSE ME?
I BRUNG YOUR CHANGE. YOU A REAL PREACHER?
WHAT WOULD A REAL ONE BE DOIN' IN A DEN OF SIN LIKE THIS?
GO ON AN' KEEP IT, HONEY.

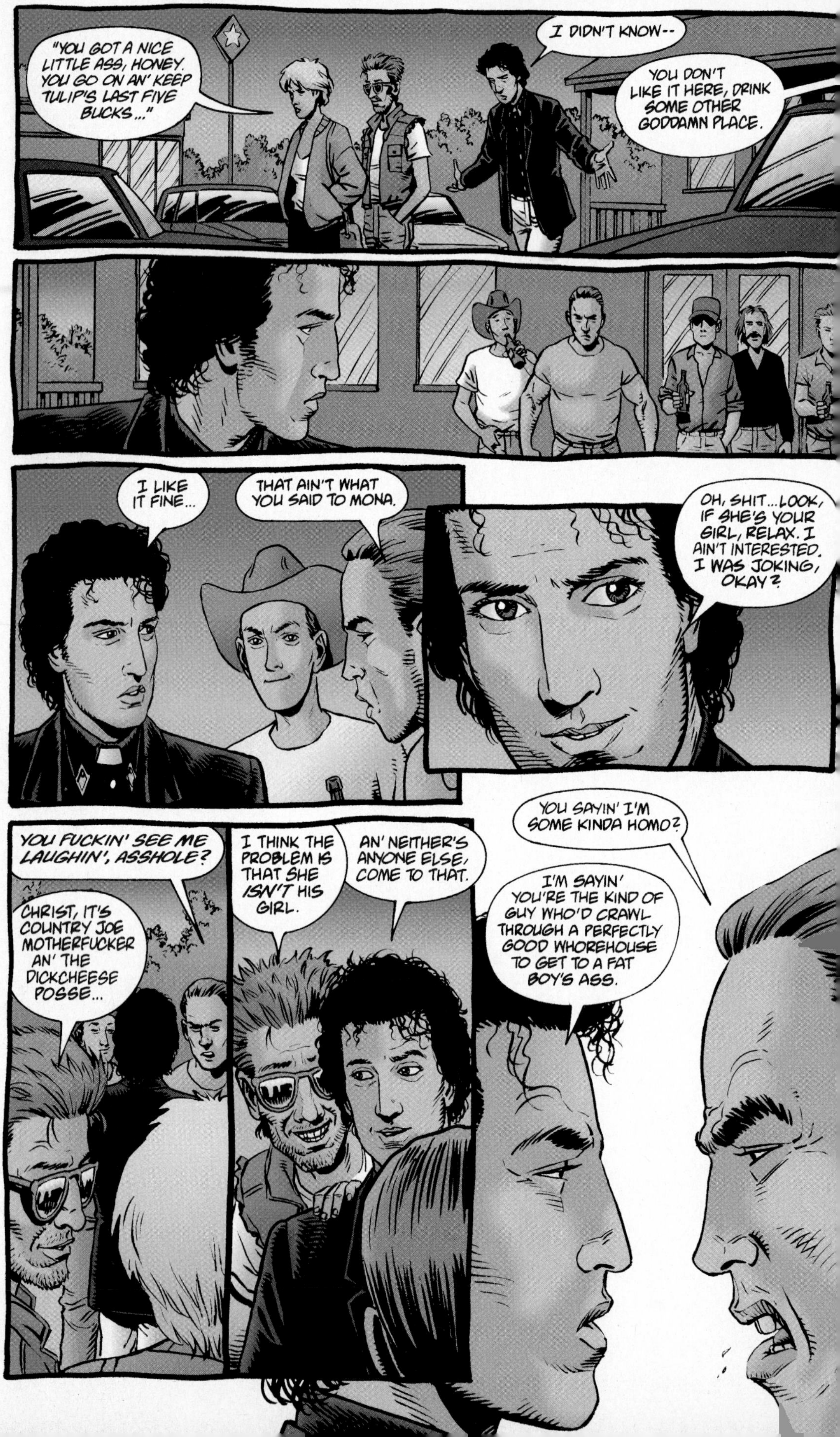
"YOU GOT A NICE LITTLE ASS, HONEY. YOU GO ON AN' KEEP TULIP'S LAST FIVE BUCKS..."
I DIDN'T KNOW--
YOU DON'T LIKE IT HERE, DRINK SOME OTHER GODDAMN PLACE.
I LIKE IT FINE...
THAT AIN'T WHAT YOU SAID TO MONA.
OH, SHIT...LOOK, IF SHE'S YOUR GIRL, RELAX. I AIN'T INTERESTED. I WAS JOKING, OKAY?
YOU FUCKIN' SEE ME LAUGHIN', ASSHOLE?
CHRIST, IT'S COUNTRY JOE MOTHERFUCKER AN' THE DICKCHEESE POSSE...
I THINK THE PROBLEM IS THAT SHE ISN'T HIS GIRL.
AN' NEITHER'S ANYONE ELSE, COME TO THAT.
YOU SAYIN' I'M SOME KINDA HOMO?
I'M SAYIN' YOU'RE THE KIND OF GUY WHO'D CRAWL THROUGH A PERFECTLY GOOD WHOREHOUSE TO GET TO A FAT BOY'S ASS.

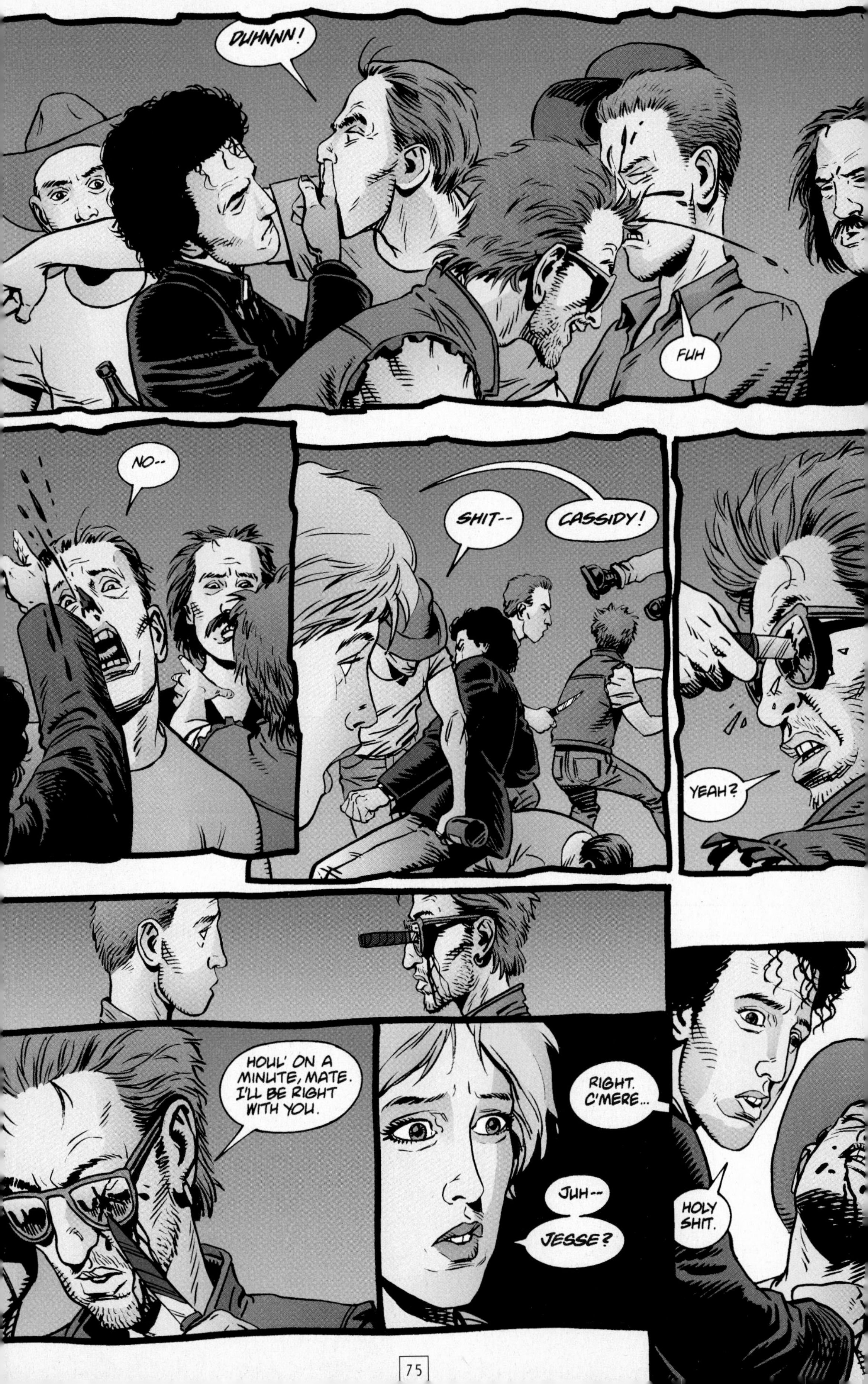
DUHNNN!
FUH
NO--
SHIT--
CASSIDY!
YEAH?
HOUL' ON A MINUTE, MATE. I'LL BE RIGHT WITH YOU.
RIGHT. C'MERE...
JUH--
JESSE?
HOLY SHIT.

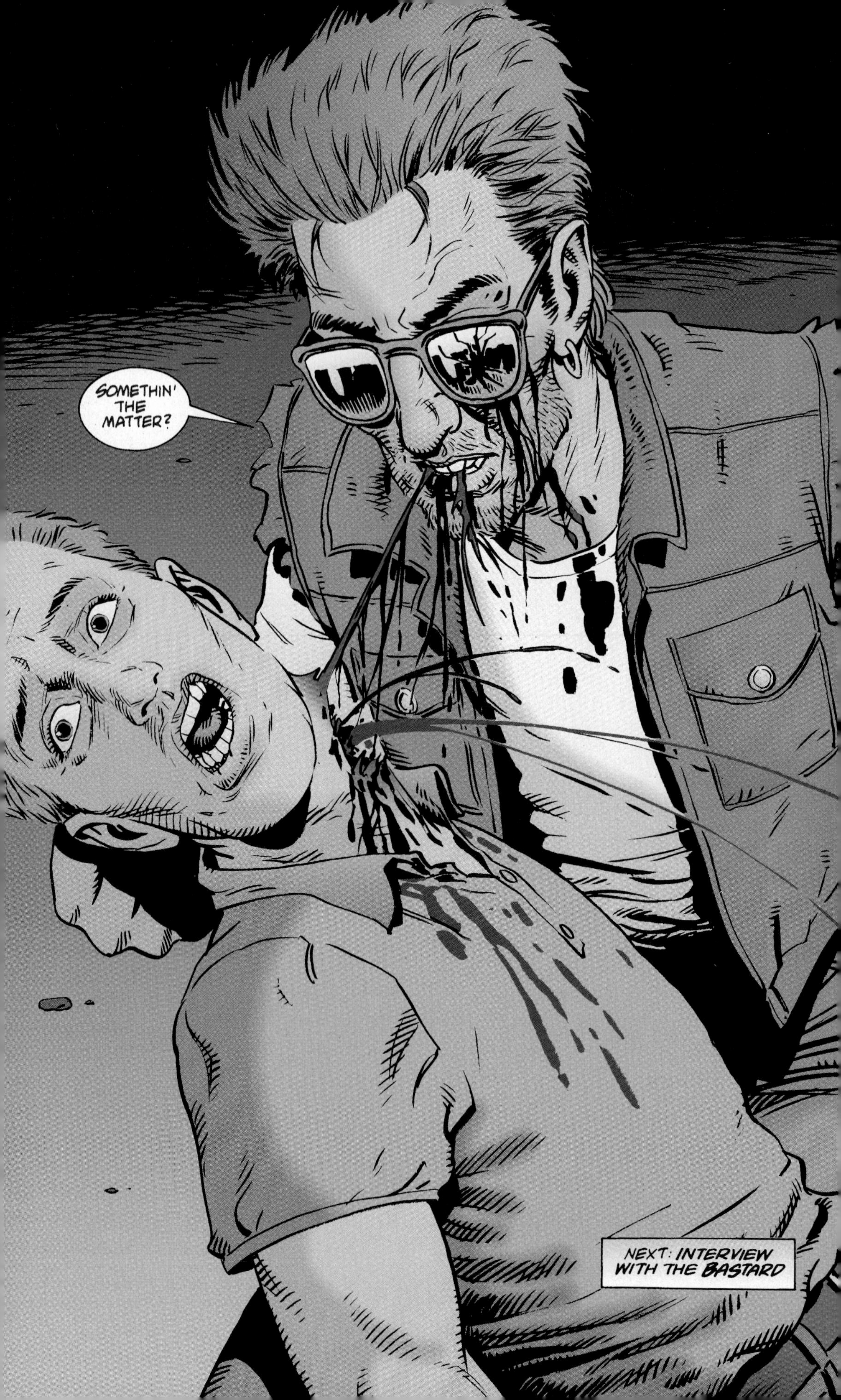
SOMETHIN' THE MATTER?
NEXT: INTERVIEW WITH THE BASTARD

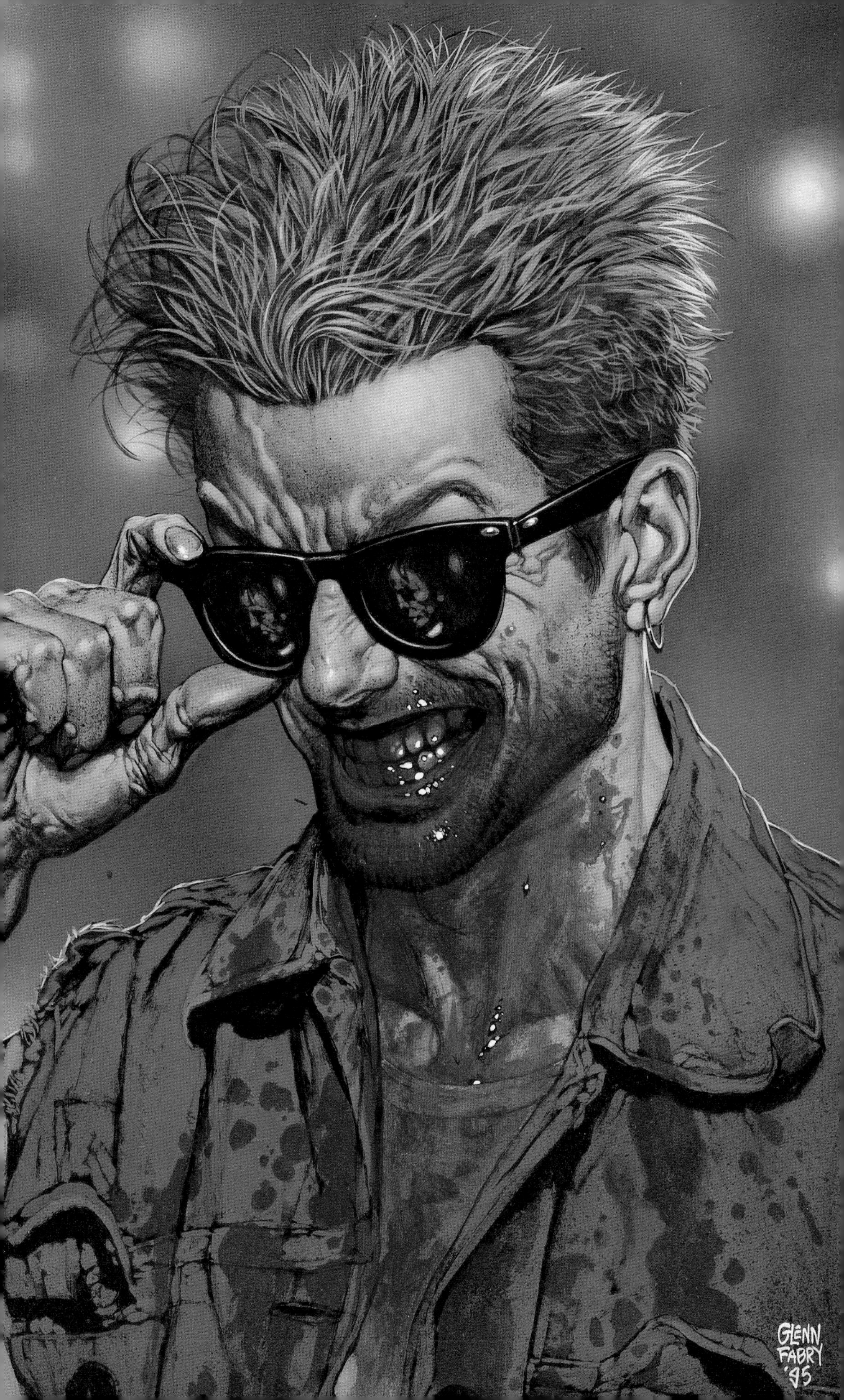
GLENN
FABRY
'95

"I won't be spoken to like that, not by any son of a bitch alive."

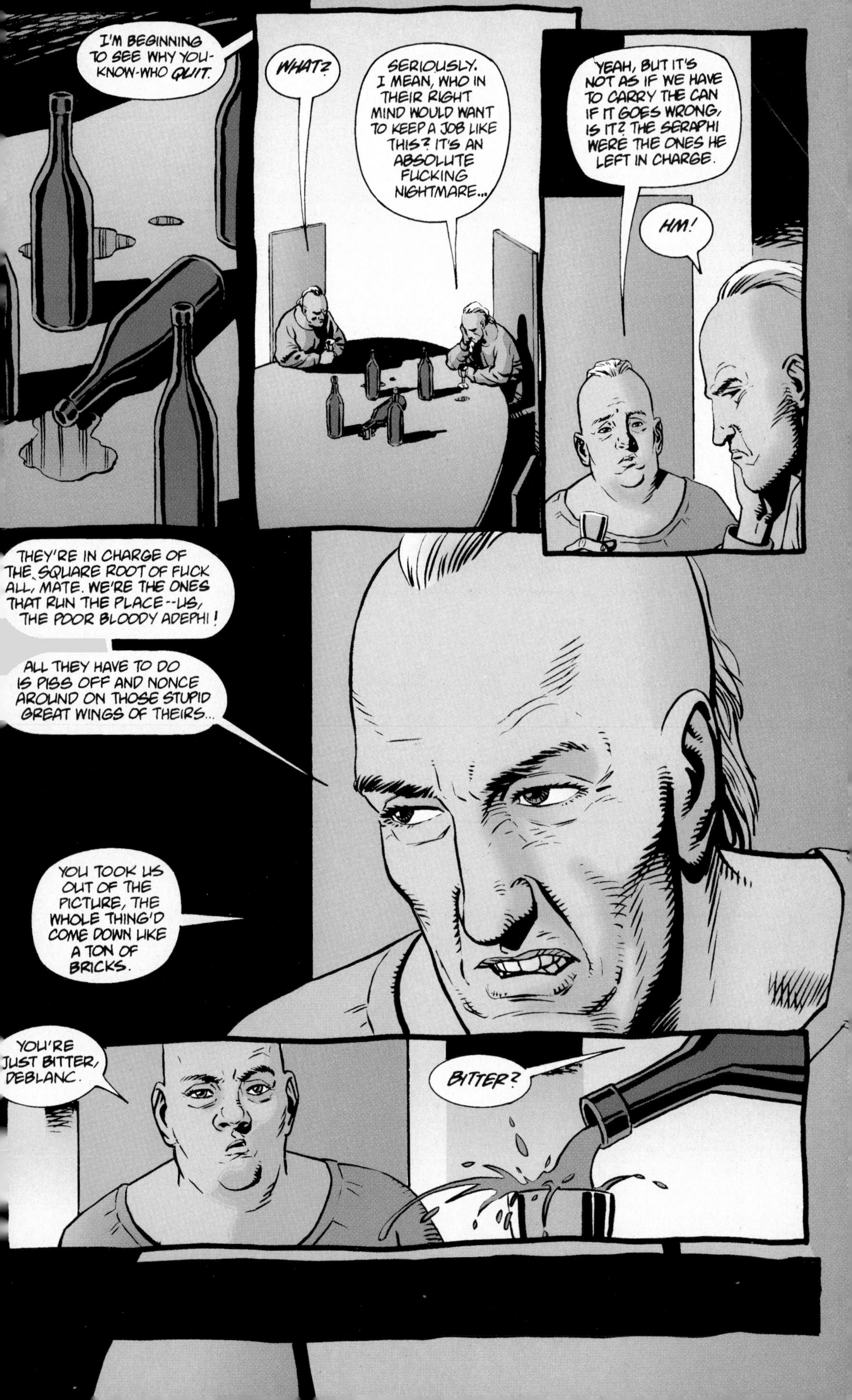

I'M BEGINNING TO SEE WHY YOU-KNOW-WHO QUIT.
WHAT?
SERIOUSLY. I MEAN, WHO IN THEIR RIGHT MIND WOULD WANT TO KEEP A JOB LIKE THIS? IT'S AN ABSOLUTE FUCKING NIGHTMARE...
YEAH, BUT IT'S NOT AS IF WE HAVE TO CARRY THE CAN IF IT GOES WRONG, IS IT? THE SERAPHI WERE THE ONES HE LEFT IN CHARGE.
HM!
THEY'RE IN CHARGE OF THE SQUARE ROOT OF FUCK ALL, MATE. WE'RE THE ONES THAT RUN THE PLACE--US, THE POOR BLOODY ADEPHI!
ALL THEY HAVE TO DO IS PISS OFF AND NONCE AROUND ON THOSE STUPID GREAT WINGS OF THEIRS...
YOU TOOK US OUT OF THE PICTURE, THE WHOLE THING'D COME DOWN LIKE A TON OF BRICKS.
YOU'RE JUST BITTER, DEBLANC.
BITTER?

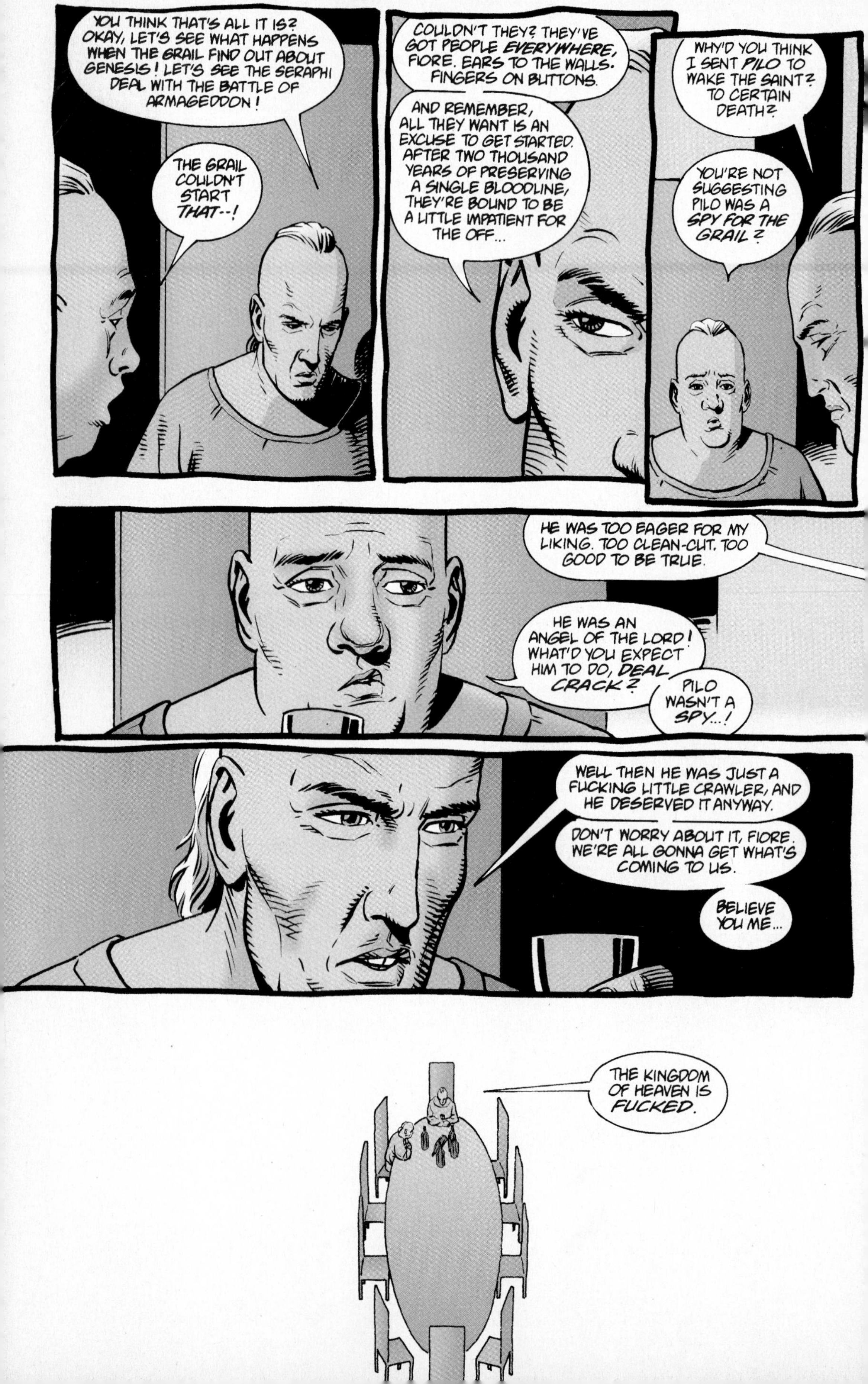
YOU THINK THAT'S ALL IT IS? OKAY, LET'S SEE WHAT HAPPENS WHEN THE GRAIL FIND OUT ABOUT GENESIS! LET'S SEE THE SERAPHI DEAL WITH THE BATTLE OF ARMAGEDDON!
THE GRAIL COULDN'T START THAT--!
COULDN'T THEY? THEY'VE GOT PEOPLE EVERYWHERE, FIORE. EARS TO THE WALLS. FINGERS ON BUTTONS.
AND REMEMBER, ALL THEY WANT IS AN EXCUSE TO GET STARTED. AFTER TWO THOUSAND YEARS OF PRESERVING A SINGLE BLOODLINE, THEY'RE BOUND TO BE A LITTLE IMPATIENT FOR THE OFF...
WHY'D YOU THINK I SENT PILO TO WAKE THE SAINT? TO CERTAIN DEATH?
YOU'RE NOT SUGGESTING PILO WAS A SPY FOR THE GRAIL?
HE WAS TOO EAGER FOR MY LIKING. TOO CLEAN-CUT. TOO GOOD TO BE TRUE.
HE WAS AN ANGEL OF THE LORD! WHAT'D YOU EXPECT HIM TO DO, DEAL CRACK?
PILO WASN'T A SPY...!
WELL THEN HE WAS JUST A FUCKING LITTLE CRAWLER, AND HE DESERVED IT ANYWAY.
DON'T WORRY ABOUT IT, FIORE. WE'RE ALL GONNA GET WHAT'S COMING TO US.
BELIEVE YOU ME...
THE KINGDOM OF HEAVEN IS FUCKED.

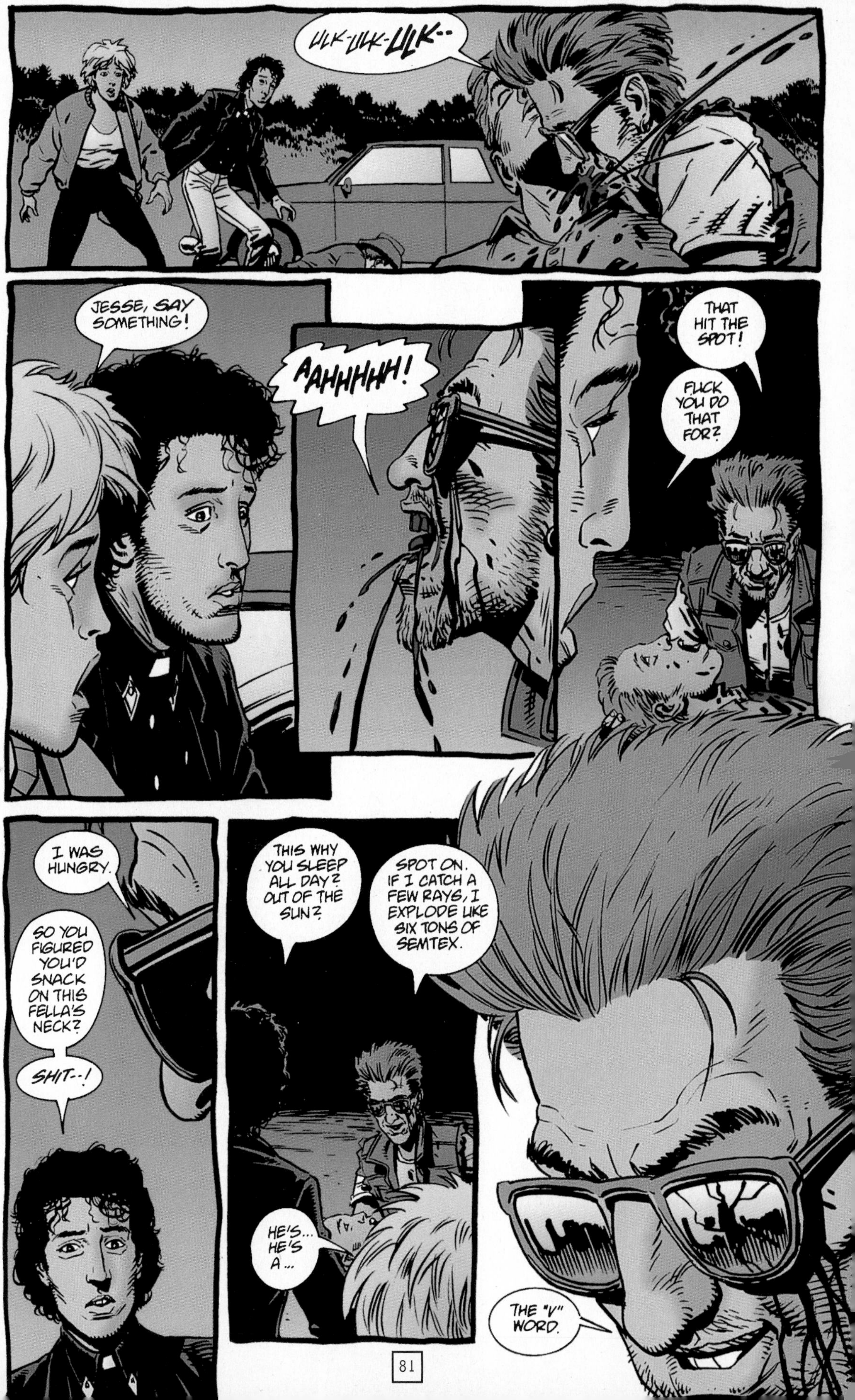

ULK-ULK-ULK--
JESSE, SAY SOMETHING!
AAHHHHH!
THAT HIT THE SPOT!
FUCK YOU DO THAT FOR?
I WAS HUNGRY.
SO YOU FIGURED YOU'D SNACK ON THIS FELLA'S NECK?
SHIT--!
THIS WHY YOU SLEEP ALL DAY? OUT OF THE SUN?
SPOT ON. IF I CATCH A FEW RAYS, I EXPLODE LIKE SIX TONS OF SEMTEX.
HE'S... HE'S A...
THE "V" WORD.

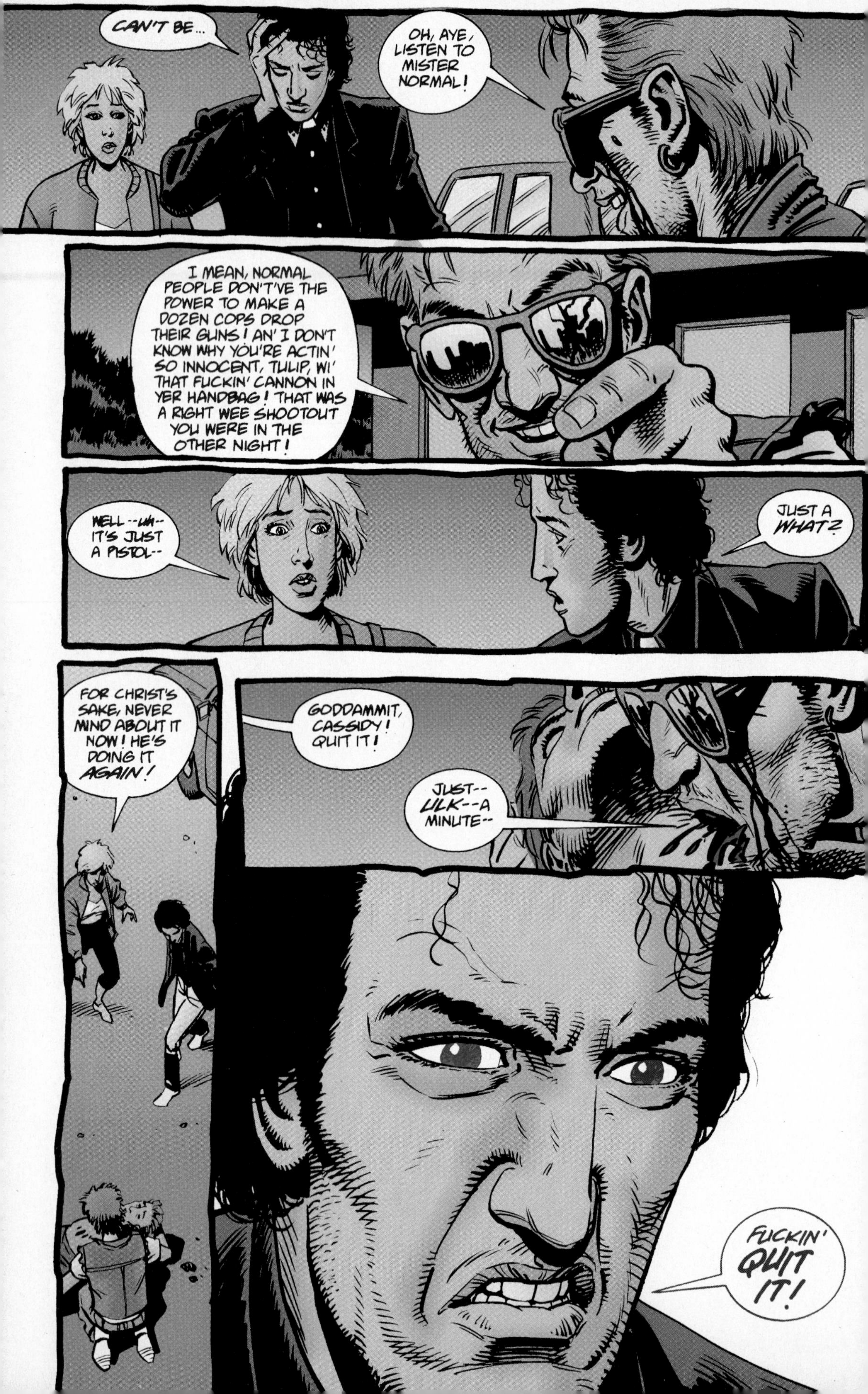
CAN'T BE...
OH, AYE, LISTEN TO MISTER NORMAL!
I MEAN, NORMAL PEOPLE DON'T'VE THE POWER TO MAKE A DOZEN COPS DROP THEIR GUNS! AN' I DON'T KNOW WHY YOU'RE ACTIN' SO INNOCENT, TULIP, WI' THAT FUCKIN' CANNON IN YER HANDBAG! THAT WAS A RIGHT WEE SHOOTOUT YOU WERE IN THE OTHER NIGHT!
WELL--UH-- IT'S JUST A PISTOL--
JUST A WHAT?
FOR CHRIST'S SAKE, NEVER MIND ABOUT IT NOW! HE'S DOING IT AGAIN!
GODDAMMIT, CASSIDY! QUIT IT!
JUST-- ULK--A MINUTE--
FUCKIN' QUIT IT!

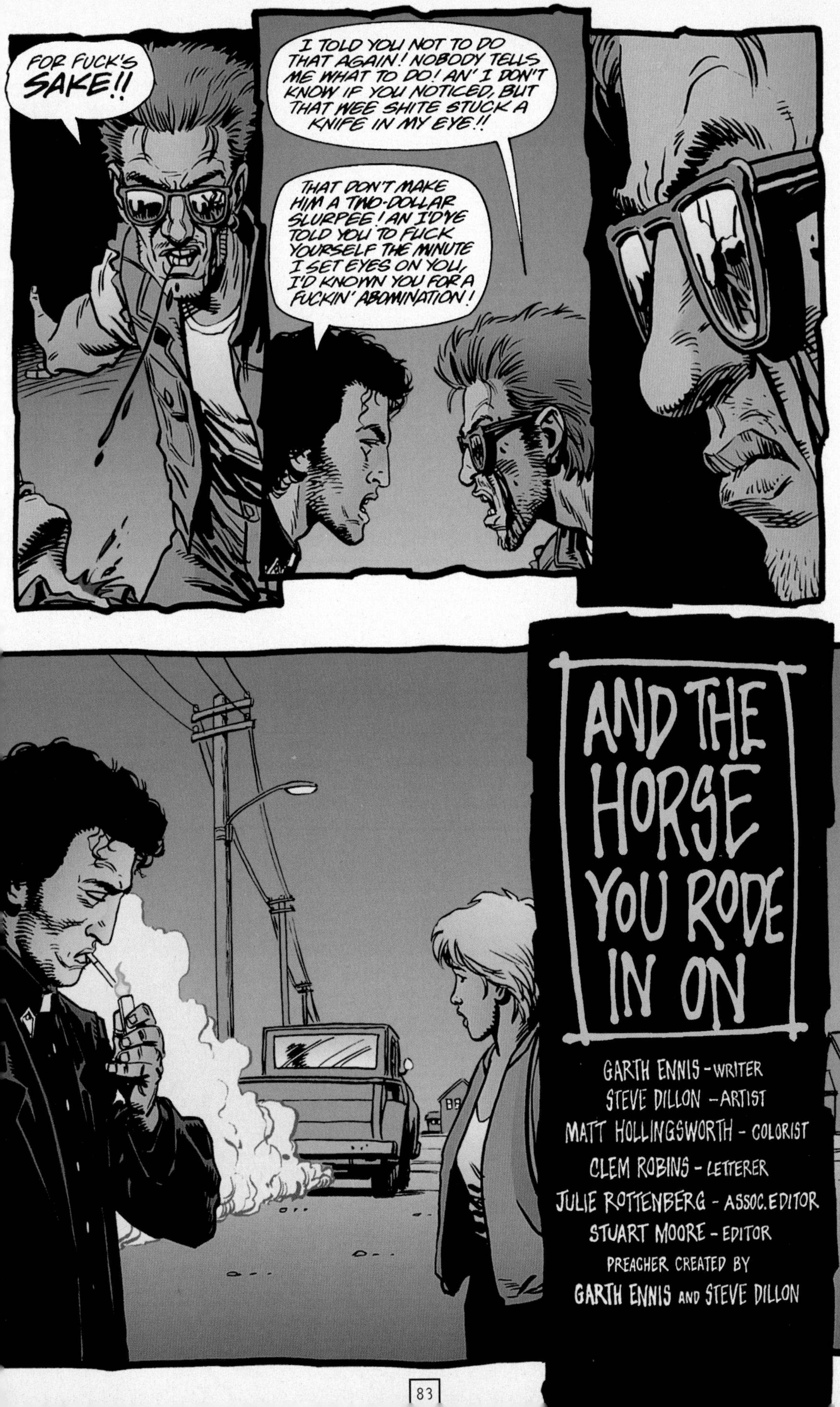
FOR FUCK'S SAKE!!
I TOLD YOU NOT TO DO THAT AGAIN! NOBODY TELLS ME WHAT TO DO! AN' I DON'T KNOW IF YOU NOTICED, BUT THAT WEE SHITE STUCK A KNIFE IN MY EYE!!
THAT DON'T MAKE HIM A TWO-DOLLAR SLURPEE! AN I'D'VE TOLD YOU TO FUCK YOURSELF THE MINUTE I SET EYES ON YOU, I'D KNOWN YOU FOR A FUCKIN' ABOMINATION!
AND THE HORSE YOU RODE IN ON
GARTH ENNIS - WRITER
STEVE DILLON - ARTIST
MATT HOLLINGSWORTH - COLORIST
CLEM ROBINS - LETTERER
JULIE ROTTENBERG - ASSOC. EDITOR
STUART MOORE - EDITOR
PREACHER CREATED BY
GARTH ENNIS AND STEVE DILLON

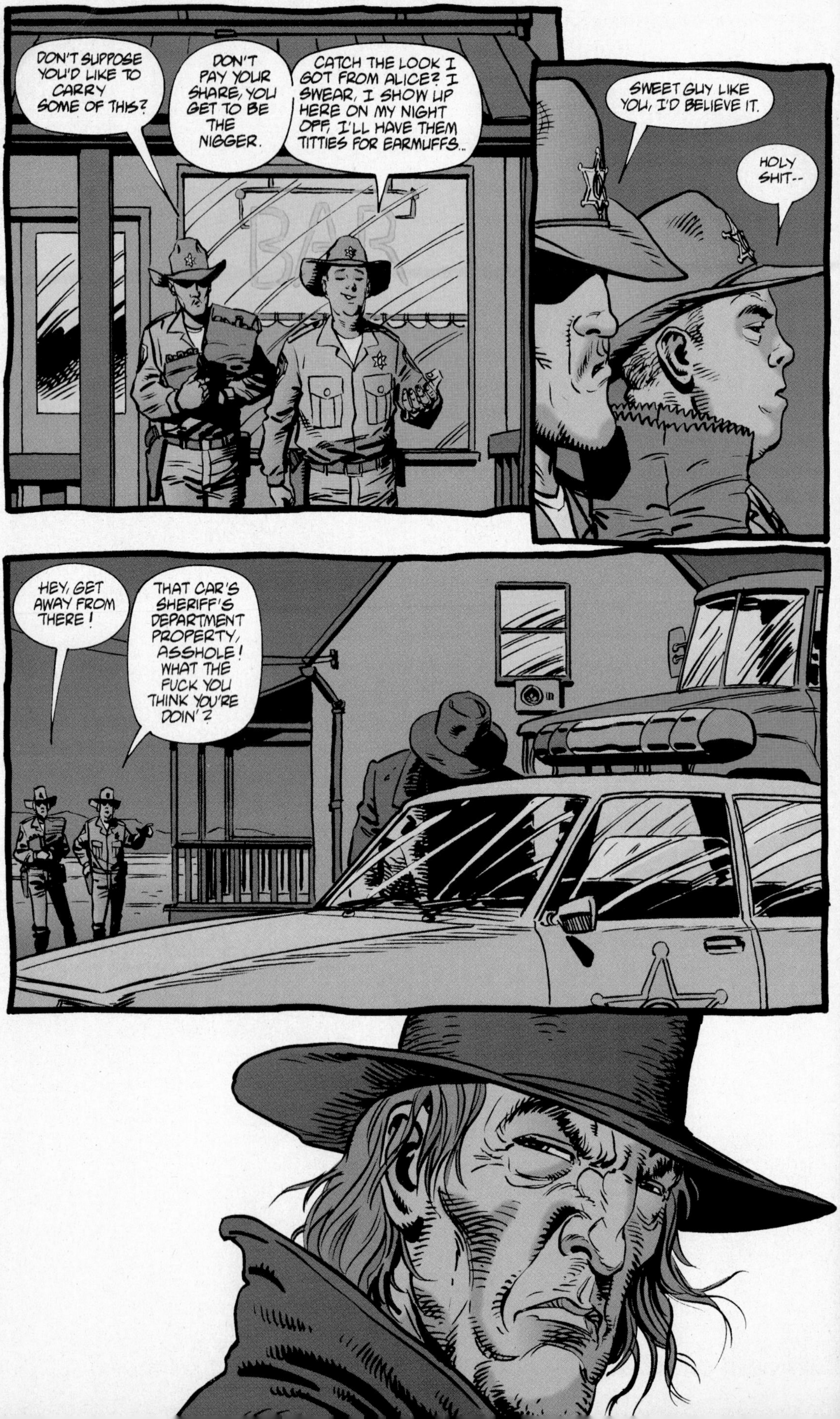
DON'T SUPPOSE YOU'D LIKE TO CARRY SOME OF THIS?
DON'T PAY YOUR SHARE, YOU GET TO BE THE NIGGER.
CATCH THE LOOK I GOT FROM ALICE? I SWEAR, I SHOW UP HERE ON MY NIGHT OFF, I'LL HAVE THEM TITTIES FOR EARMUFFS..
BAR
SWEET GUY LIKE YOU, I'D BELIEVE IT.
HOLY SHIT--
HEY, GET AWAY FROM THERE!
THAT CAR'S SHERIFF'S DEPARTMENT PROPERTY, ASSHOLE! WHAT THE FUCK YOU THINK YOU'RE DOIN'?

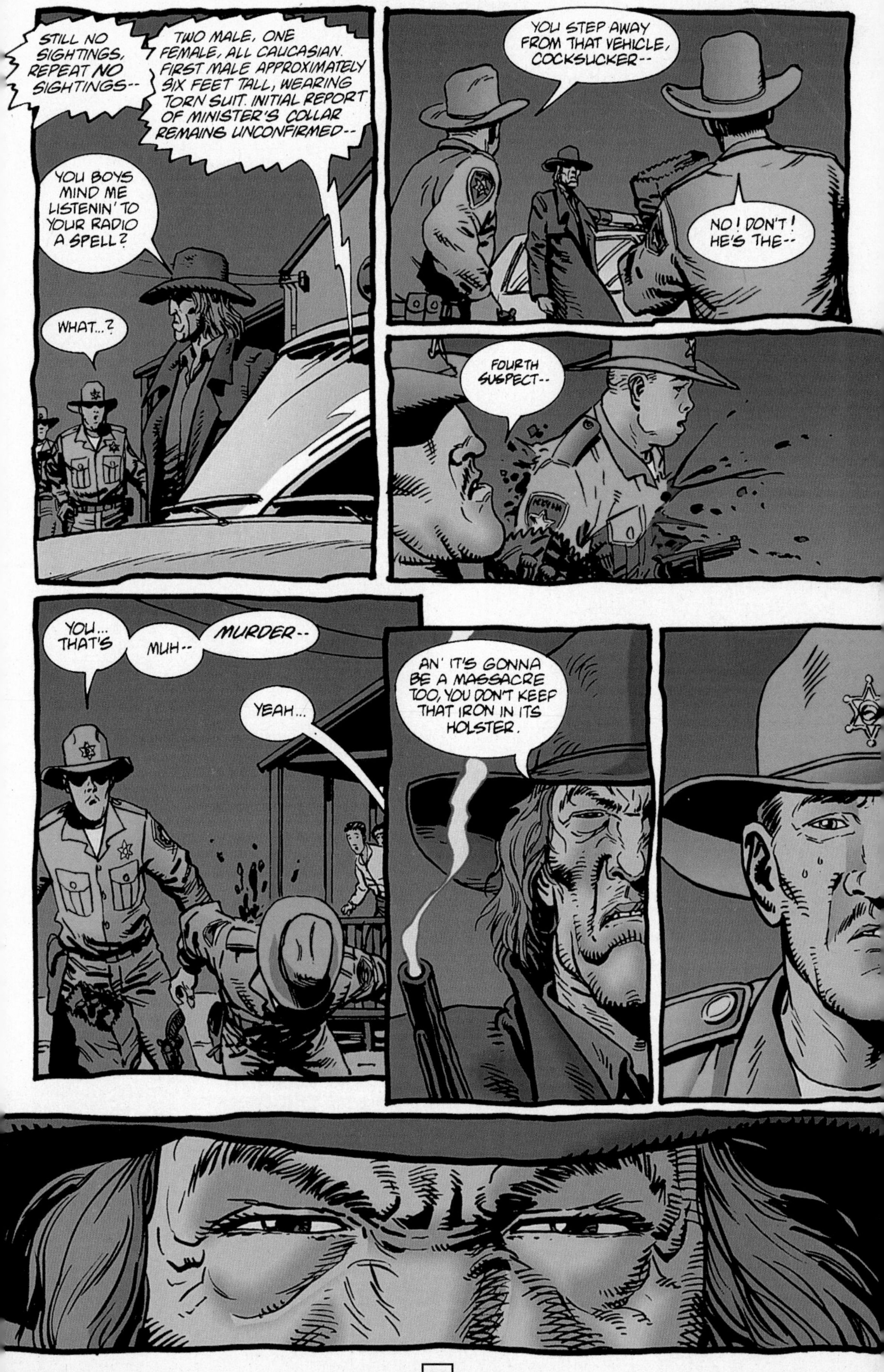

STILL NO SIGHTINGS, REPEAT NO SIGHTINGS--
TWO MALE, ONE FEMALE, ALL CAUCASIAN. FIRST MALE APPROXIMATELY SIX FEET TALL, WEARING TORN SUIT. INITIAL REPORT OF MINISTER'S COLLAR REMAINS UNCONFIRMED--
YOU BOYS MIND ME LISTENIN' TO YOUR RADIO A SPELL?
WHAT...?
YOU STEP AWAY FROM THAT VEHICLE, COCKSUCKER--
NO! DON'T! HE'S THE--
FOURTH SUSPECT--
YOU... THAT'S
MUH--
MURDER--
YEAH...
AN' IT'S GONNA BE A MASSACRE TOO, YOU DON'T KEEP THAT IRON IN ITS HOLSTER.

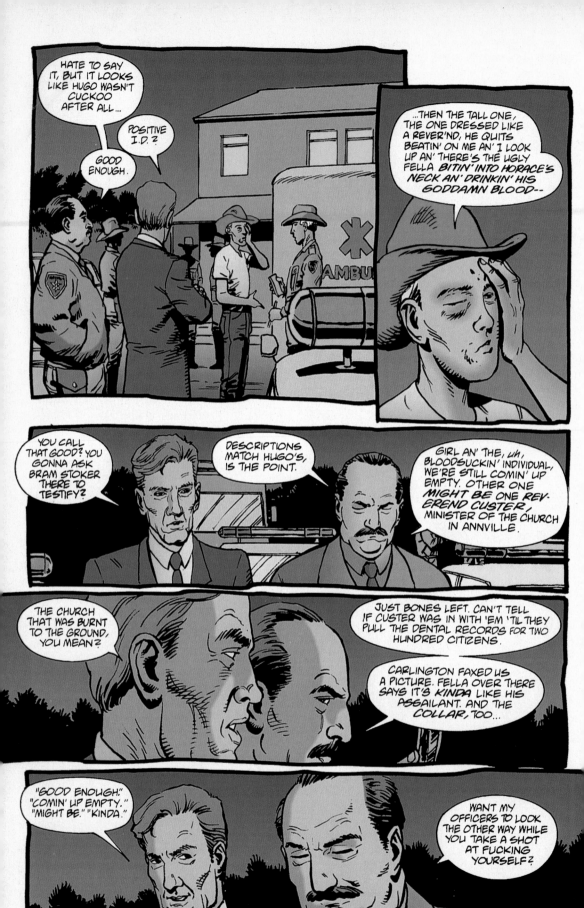

HATE TO SAY IT, BUT IT LOOKS LIKE HUGO WASN'T CUCKOO AFTER ALL...

POSITIVE I.D.?

GOOD ENOUGH.

...THEN THE TALL ONE, THE ONE DRESSED LIKE A REVER'ND, HE QUITS BEATIN' ON ME AN' I LOOK UP AN' THERE'S THE UGLY FELLA *BITIN'* INTO HORACE'S *NECK AN' DRINKIN' HIS GODDAMN BLOOD--*

YOU CALL THAT GOOD? YOU GONNA ASK BRAM STOKER THERE TO TESTIFY?

DESCRIPTIONS MATCH HUGO'S, IS THE POINT.

GIRL AN' THE, *UH,* BLOODSUCKIN' INDIVIDUAL, WE'RE STILL COMIN' UP EMPTY. OTHER ONE *MIGHT BE* ONE REVEREND CUSTER, MINISTER OF THE CHURCH IN ANNVILLE.

THE CHURCH THAT WAS BURNT TO THE GROUND, YOU MEAN?

JUST BONES LEFT. CAN'T TELL IF CUSTER WAS IN WITH 'EM 'TIL THEY PULL THE DENTAL RECORDS FOR TWO HUNDRED CITIZENS.

CARLINGTON FAXED US A PICTURE. FELLA OVER THERE SAYS IT'S *KINDA* LIKE HIS ASSAILANT. AND THE *COLLAR,* TOO...

"GOOD ENOUGH." "COMIN' UP EMPTY." "MIGHT BE." "KINDA."

WANT MY OFFICERS TO LOOK THE OTHER WAY WHILE YOU TAKE A SHOT AT FUCKING YOURSELF?

86

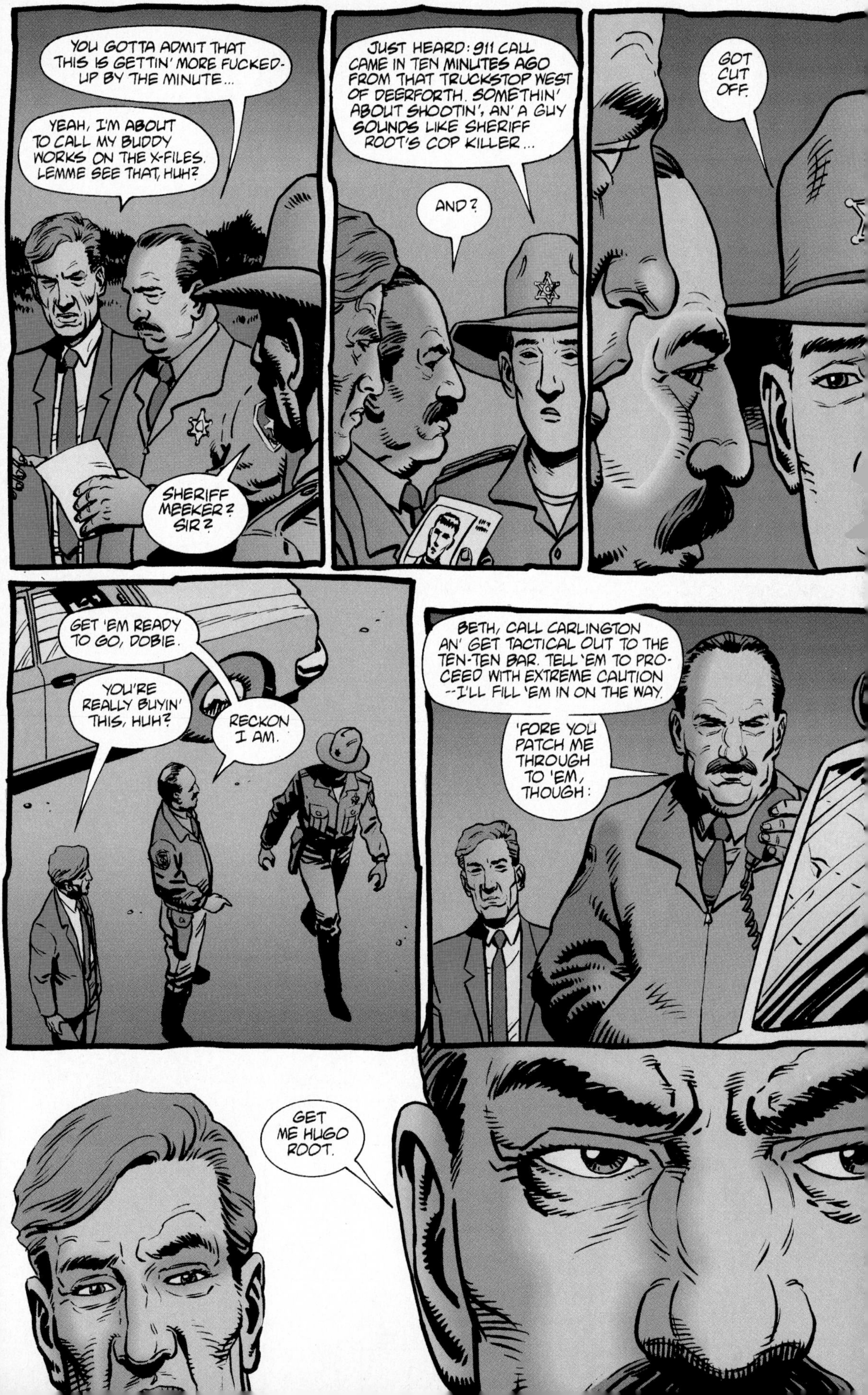
YOU GOTTA ADMIT THAT THIS IS GETTIN' MORE FUCKED-UP BY THE MINUTE...
YEAH, I'M ABOUT TO CALL MY BUDDY WORKS ON THE X-FILES. LEMME SEE THAT, HUH?
SHERIFF MEEKER? SIR?
JUST HEARD: 911 CALL CAME IN TEN MINUTES AGO FROM THAT TRUCKSTOP WEST OF DEERFORTH. SOMETHIN' ABOUT SHOOTIN', AN' A GUY SOUNDS LIKE SHERIFF ROOT'S COP KILLER...
AND?
GOT CUT OFF.
GET 'EM READY TO GO, DOBIE.
YOU'RE REALLY BUYIN' THIS, HUH?
RECKON I AM.
BETH, CALL CARLINGTON AN' GET TACTICAL OUT TO THE TEN-TEN BAR. TELL 'EM TO PROCEED WITH EXTREME CAUTION --I'LL FILL 'EM IN ON THE WAY.
'FORE YOU PATCH ME THROUGH TO 'EM, THOUGH:
GET ME HUGO ROOT.

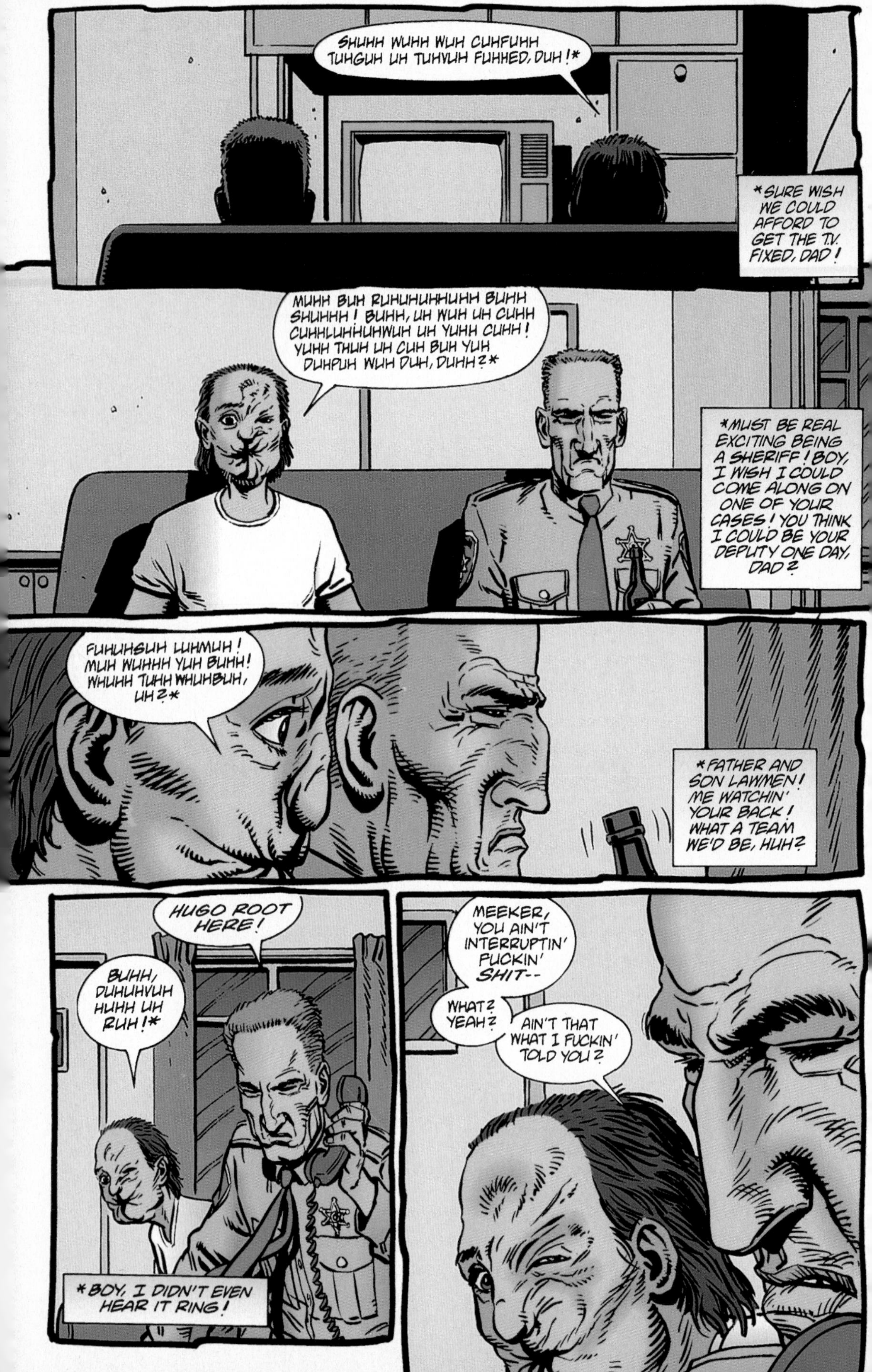
SHUHH WUHH WUH CUHFUHH TUHGUH UH TUHVUH FUHHED, DUH!*
*SURE WISH WE COULD AFFORD TO GET THE T.V. FIXED, DAD!
MUHH BUH RUHUHUHHUHH BUHH SHUHHH! BUHH, UH WUH UH CUHH CUHHLUHHUHWUH UH YUHH CUHH! YUHH THUH UH CUH BUH YUH DUHPUH WUH DUH, DUHH?*
*MUST BE REAL EXCITING BEING A SHERIFF! BOY, I WISH I COULD COME ALONG ON ONE OF YOUR CASES! YOU THINK I COULD BE YOUR DEPUTY ONE DAY, DAD?
FUHUHSUH LUHMUH! MUH WUHHH YUH BUHH! WHUHH TUHH WHUHBUH, UH?*
*FATHER AND SON LAWMEN! ME WATCHIN' YOUR BACK! WHAT A TEAM WE'D BE, HUH?
HUGO ROOT HERE!
BUHH, DUHUHVUH HUHH UH RUH!*
*BOY, I DIDN'T EVEN HEAR IT RING!
MEEKER, YOU AIN'T INTERRUPTIN' FUCKIN' SHIT--
WHAT? YEAH?
AIN'T THAT WHAT I FUCKIN' TOLD YOU?

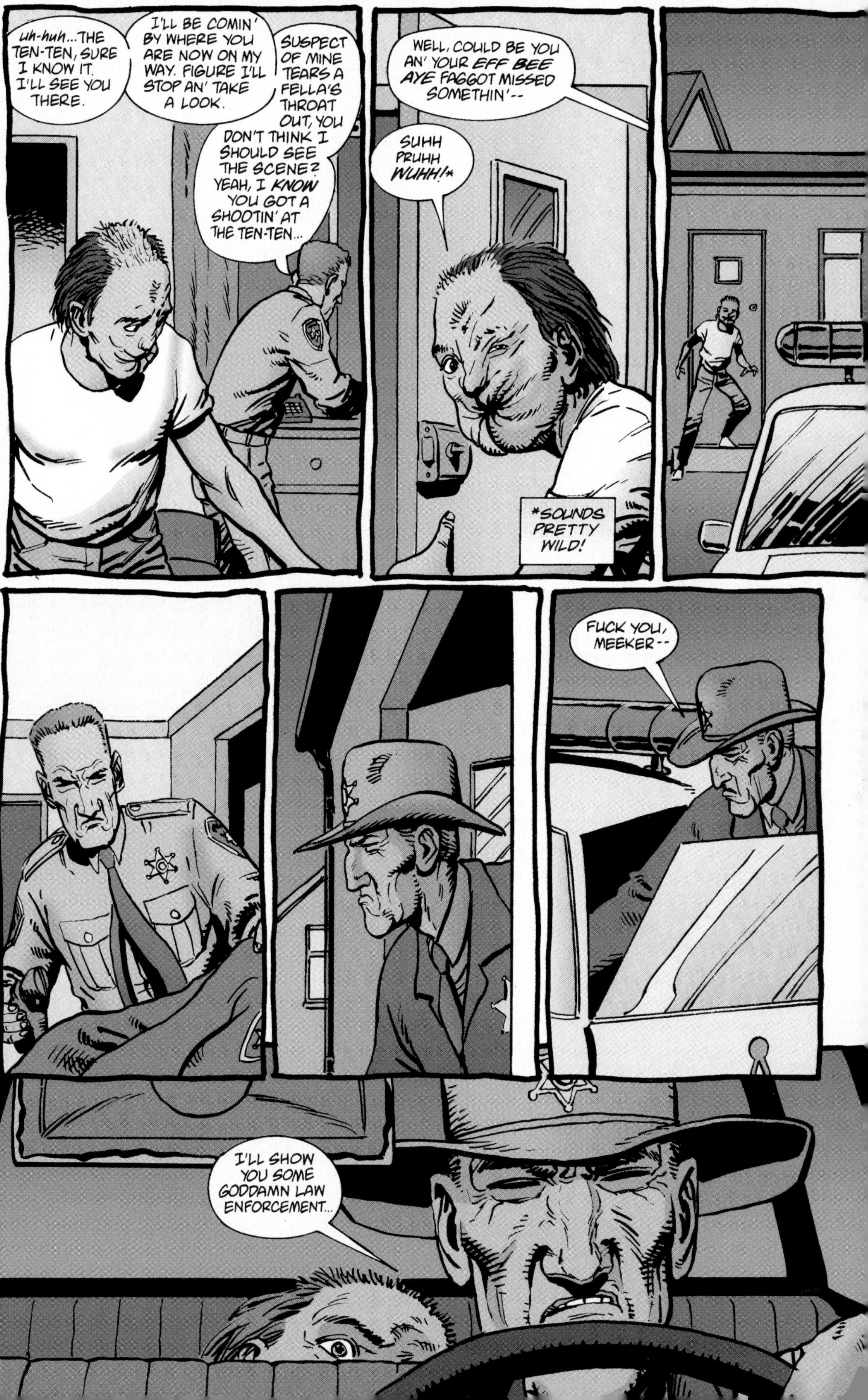
uh-huh... THE TEN-TEN, SURE I KNOW IT. I'LL SEE YOU THERE.
I'LL BE COMIN' BY WHERE YOU ARE NOW ON MY WAY. FIGURE I'LL STOP AN' TAKE A LOOK.
SUSPECT OF MINE TEARS A FELLA'S THROAT OUT, YOU DON'T THINK I SHOULD SEE THE SCENE? YEAH, I KNOW YOU GOT A SHOOTIN' AT THE TEN-TEN...
WELL, COULD BE YOU AN' YOUR EFF BEE AYE FAGGOT MISSED SOMETHIN'--
SUHH PRUHH WUHH!*
*SOUNDS PRETTY WILD!
FUCK YOU, MEEKER--
I'LL SHOW YOU SOME GODDAMN LAW ENFORCEMENT...

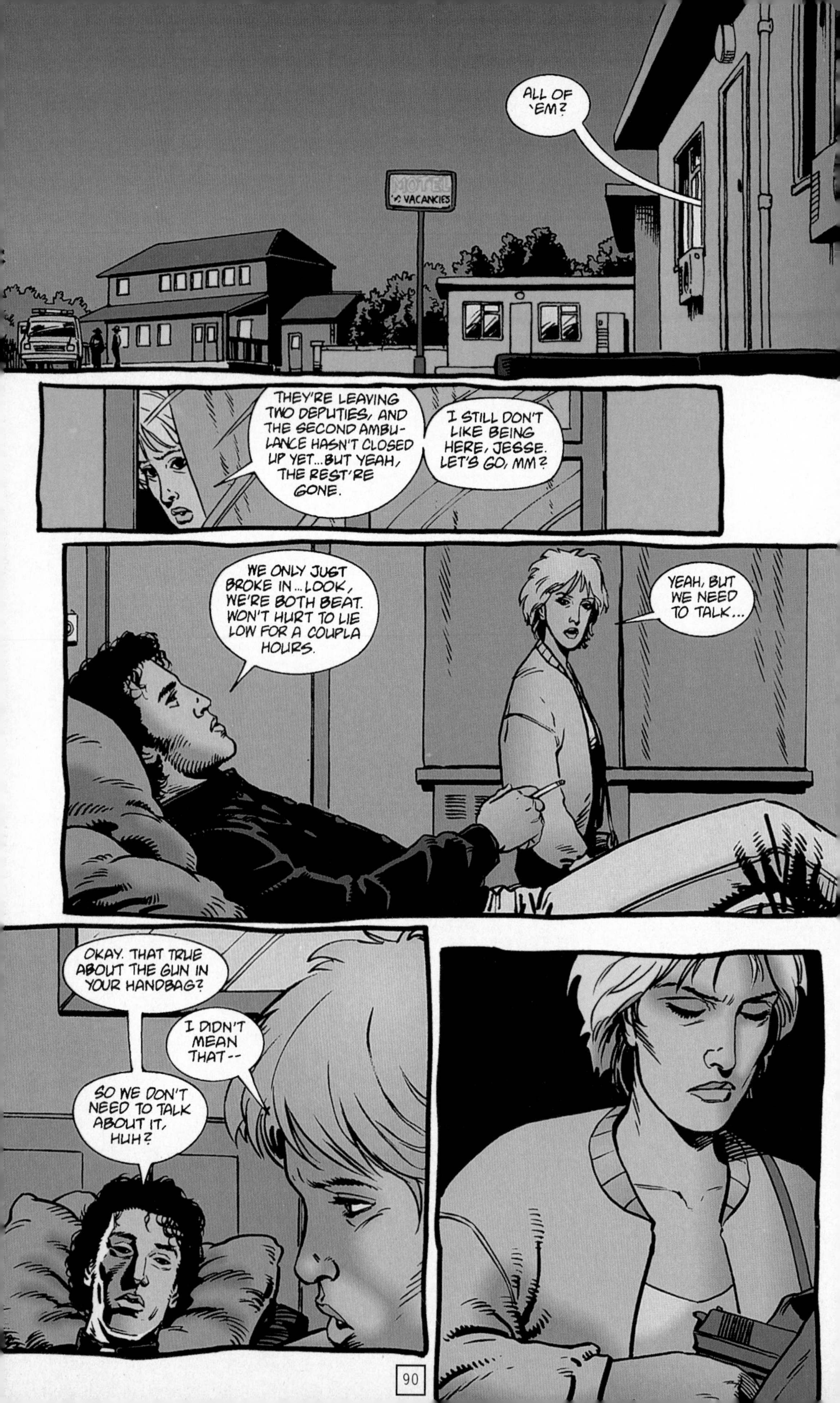
MOTEL
VACANCIES
ALL OF 'EM?
THEY'RE LEAVING TWO DEPUTIES, AND THE SECOND AMBU-LANCE HASN'T CLOSED UP YET...BUT YEAH, THE REST'RE GONE.
I STILL DON'T LIKE BEING HERE, JESSE. LET'S GO, MM?
WE ONLY JUST BROKE IN...LOOK, WE'RE BOTH BEAT. WON'T HURT TO LIE LOW FOR A COUPLA HOURS.
YEAH, BUT WE NEED TO TALK...
OKAY. THAT TRUE ABOUT THE GUN IN YOUR HANDBAG?
I DIDN'T MEAN THAT--
SO WE DON'T NEED TO TALK ABOUT IT, HUH?

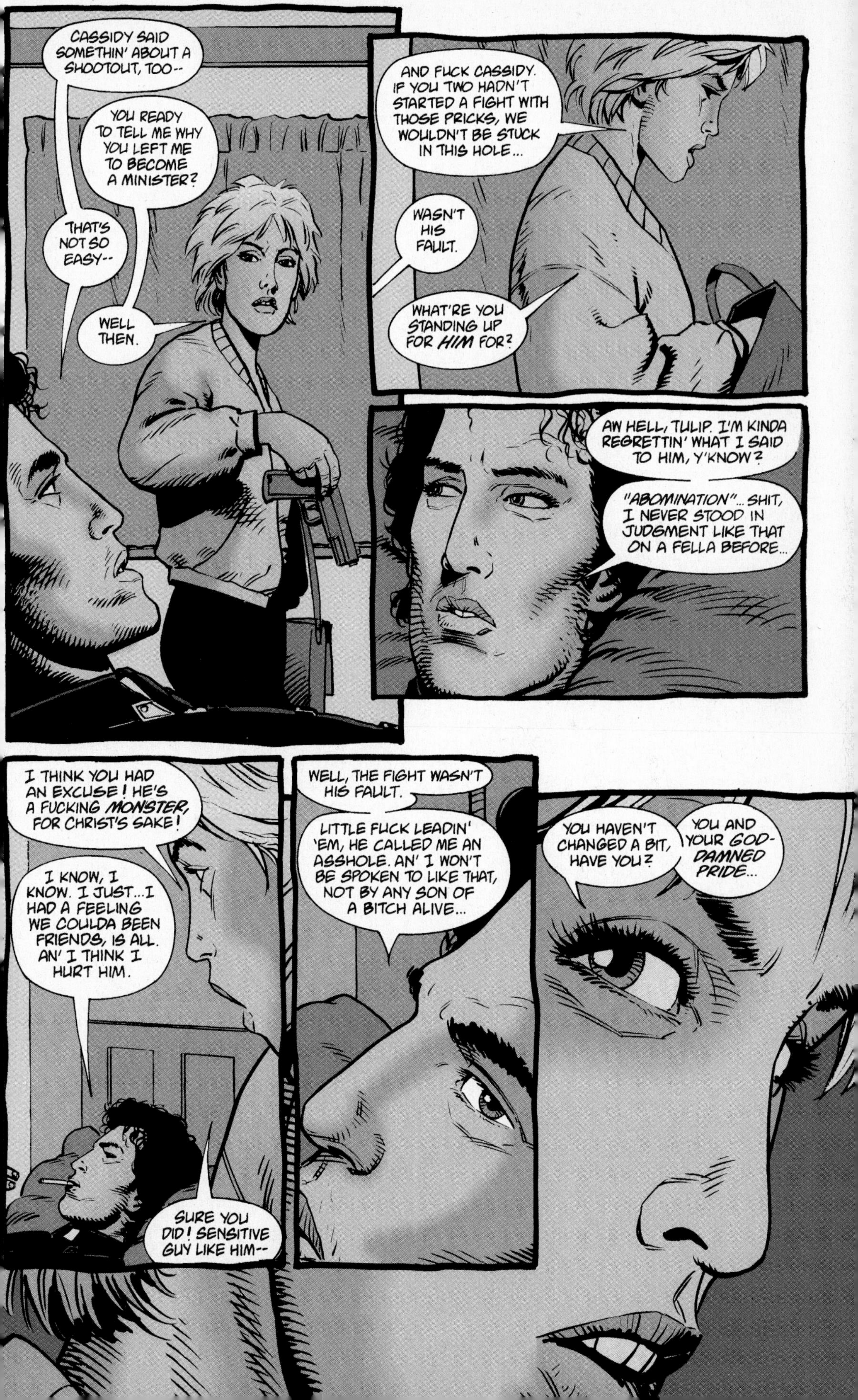
CASSIDY SAID SOMETHIN' ABOUT A SHOOTOUT, TOO--
YOU READY TO TELL ME WHY YOU LEFT ME TO BECOME A MINISTER?
THAT'S NOT SO EASY--
WELL THEN.
AND FUCK CASSIDY. IF YOU TWO HADN'T STARTED A FIGHT WITH THOSE PRICKS, WE WOULDN'T BE STUCK IN THIS HOLE...
WASN'T HIS FAULT.
WHAT'RE YOU STANDING UP FOR HIM FOR?
AW HELL, TULIP. I'M KINDA REGRETTIN' WHAT I SAID TO HIM, Y'KNOW?
"ABOMINATION"... SHIT, I NEVER STOOD IN JUDGMENT LIKE THAT ON A FELLA BEFORE...
I THINK YOU HAD AN EXCUSE! HE'S A FUCKING MONSTER, FOR CHRIST'S SAKE!
I KNOW, I KNOW. I JUST...I HAD A FEELING WE COULDA BEEN FRIENDS, IS ALL. AN' I THINK I HURT HIM.
SURE YOU DID! SENSITIVE GUY LIKE HIM--
WELL, THE FIGHT WASN'T HIS FAULT.
LITTLE FUCK LEADIN' 'EM, HE CALLED ME AN ASSHOLE. AN' I WON'T BE SPOKEN TO LIKE THAT, NOT BY ANY SON OF A BITCH ALIVE...
YOU HAVEN'T CHANGED A BIT, HAVE YOU?
YOU AND YOUR GOD-DAMNED PRIDE...

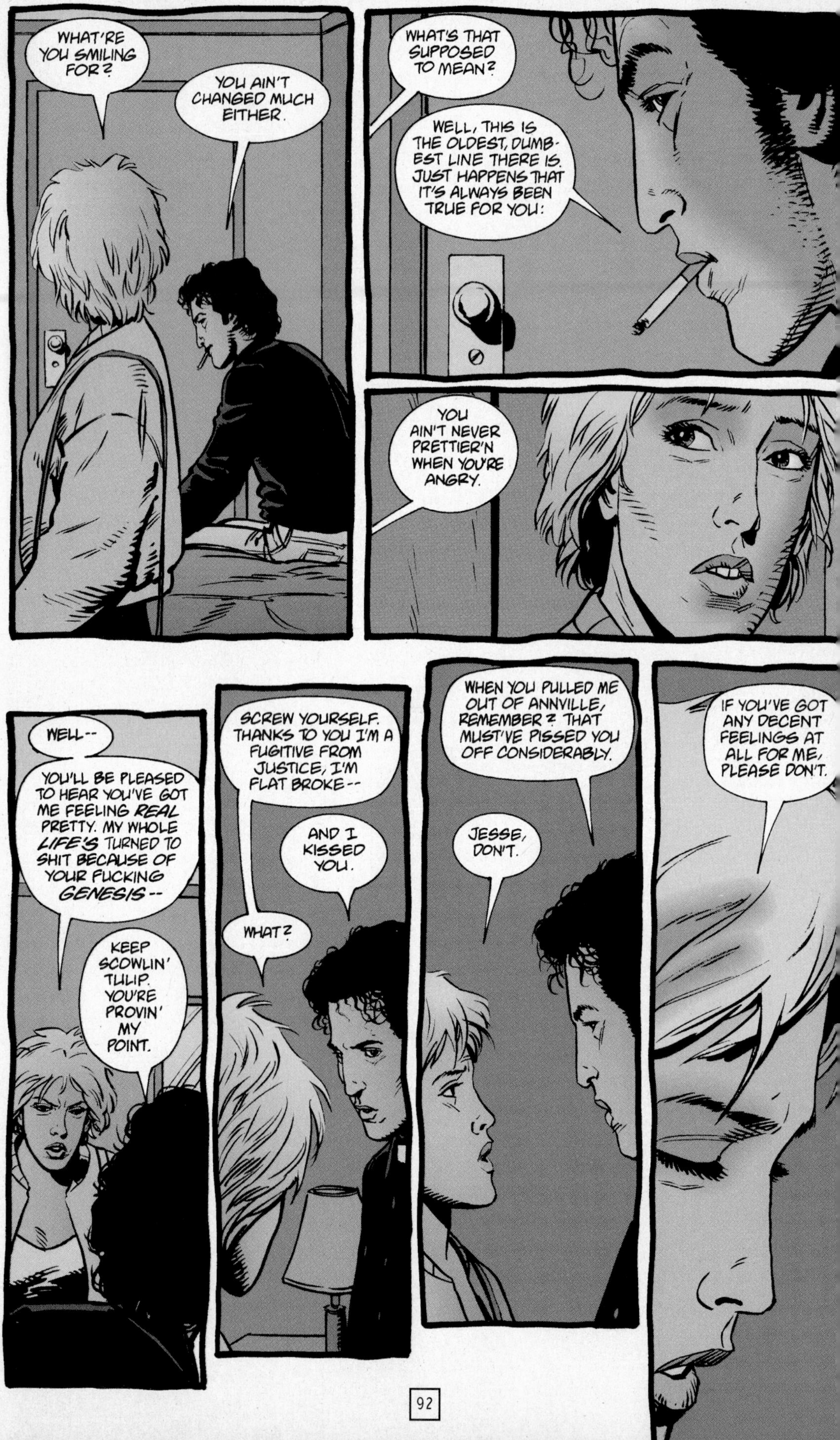
WHAT'RE YOU SMILING FOR?
YOU AIN'T CHANGED MUCH EITHER.
WHAT'S THAT SUPPOSED TO MEAN?
WELL, THIS IS THE OLDEST, DUMB-EST LINE THERE IS. JUST HAPPENS THAT IT'S ALWAYS BEEN TRUE FOR YOU:
YOU AIN'T NEVER PRETTIER'N WHEN YOU'RE ANGRY.
WELL--
YOU'LL BE PLEASED TO HEAR YOU'VE GOT ME FEELING REAL PRETTY. MY WHOLE LIFE'S TURNED TO SHIT BECAUSE OF YOUR FUCKING GENESIS--
KEEP SCOWLIN' TULIP. YOU'RE PROVIN' MY POINT.
SCREW YOURSELF. THANKS TO YOU I'M A FUGITIVE FROM JUSTICE, I'M FLAT BROKE--
AND I KISSED YOU.
WHAT?
WHEN YOU PULLED ME OUT OF ANNVILLE, REMEMBER? THAT MUST'VE PISSED YOU OFF CONSIDERABLY.
JESSE, DON'T.
IF YOU'VE GOT ANY DECENT FEELINGS AT ALL FOR ME, PLEASE DON'T.

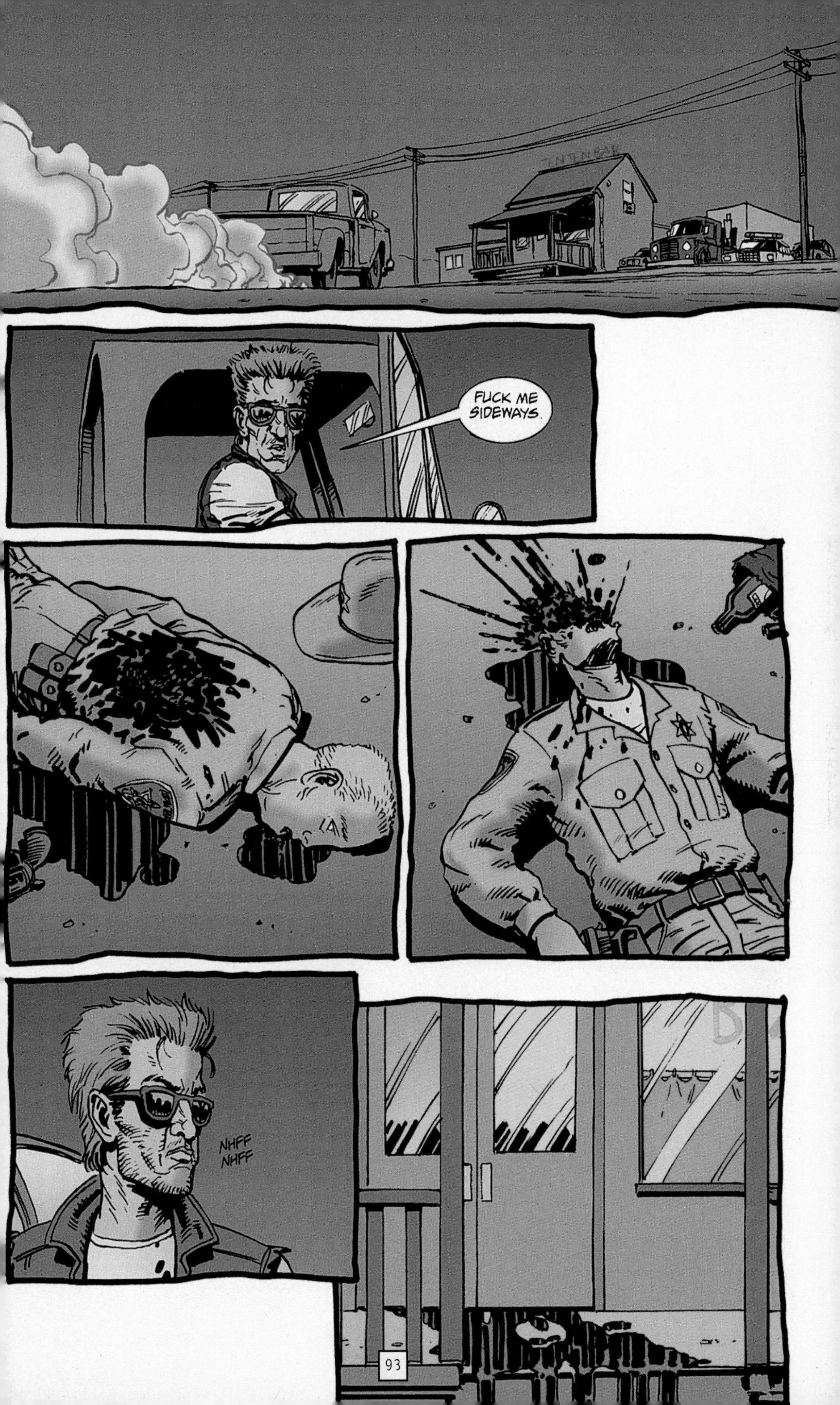
TEN TEN BAR
FUCK ME SIDEWAYS.
NHFF NHFF

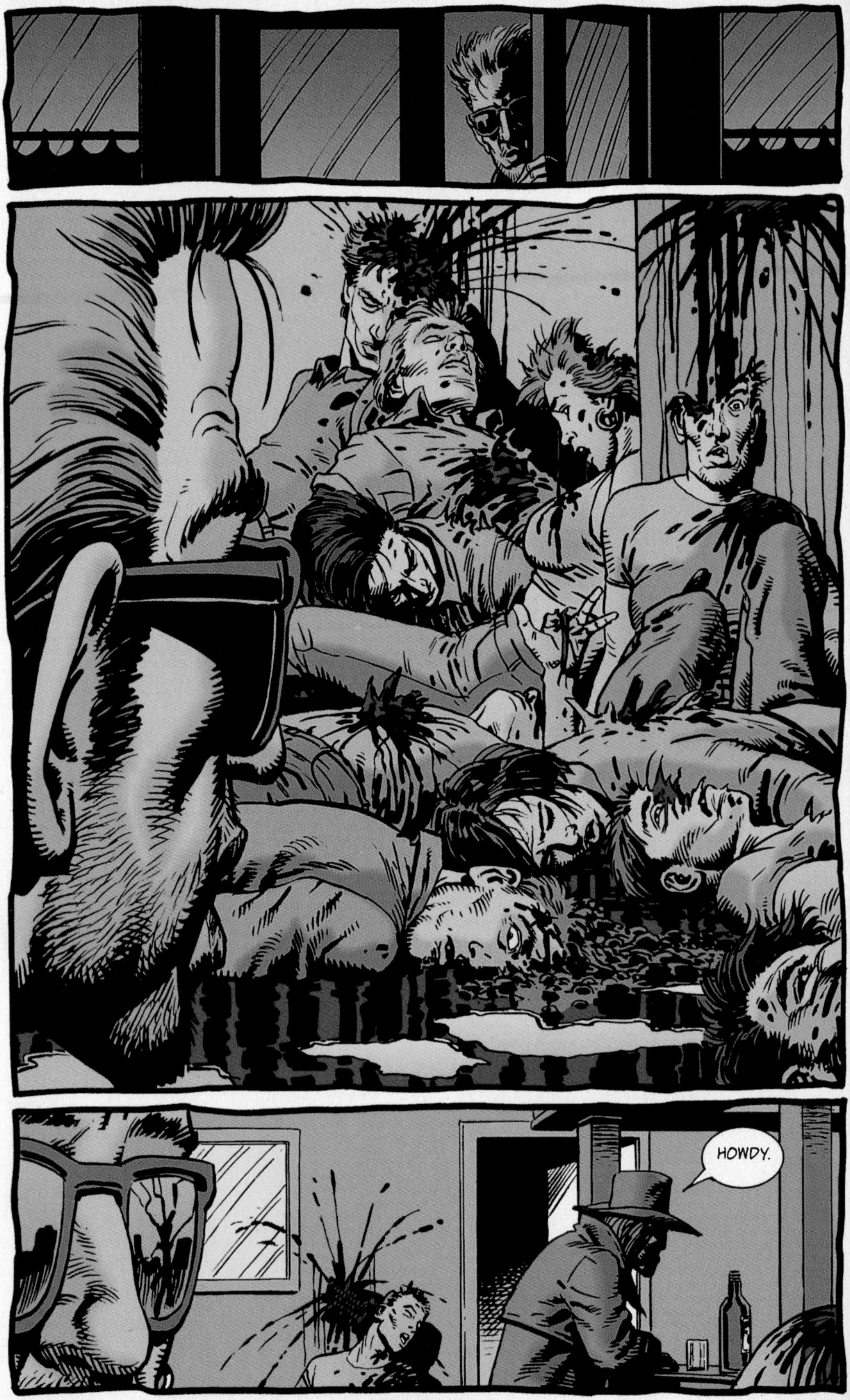
HOWDY.

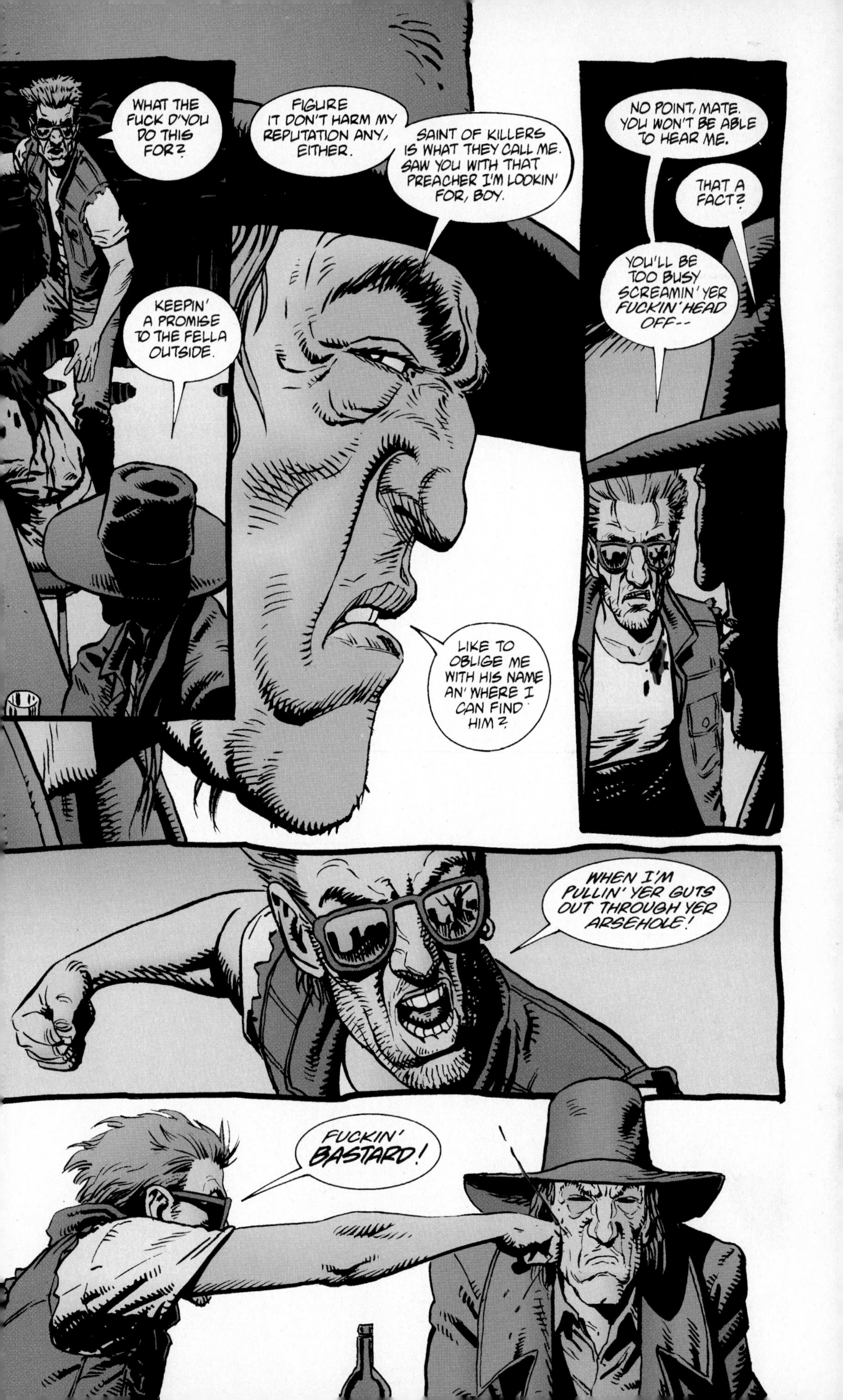
WHAT THE FUCK D'YOU DO THIS FOR?
FIGURE IT DON'T HARM MY REPUTATION ANY, EITHER.
SAINT OF KILLERS IS WHAT THEY CALL ME. SAW YOU WITH THAT PREACHER I'M LOOKIN' FOR, BOY.
KEEPIN' A PROMISE TO THE FELLA OUTSIDE.
LIKE TO OBLIGE ME WITH HIS NAME AN' WHERE I CAN FIND HIM?
NO POINT, MATE. YOU WON'T BE ABLE TO HEAR ME.
THAT A FACT?
YOU'LL BE TOO BUSY SCREAMIN' YER FUCKIN' HEAD OFF--
WHEN I'M PULLIN' YER GUTS OUT THROUGH YER ARSEHOLE!
FUCKIN' BASTARD!

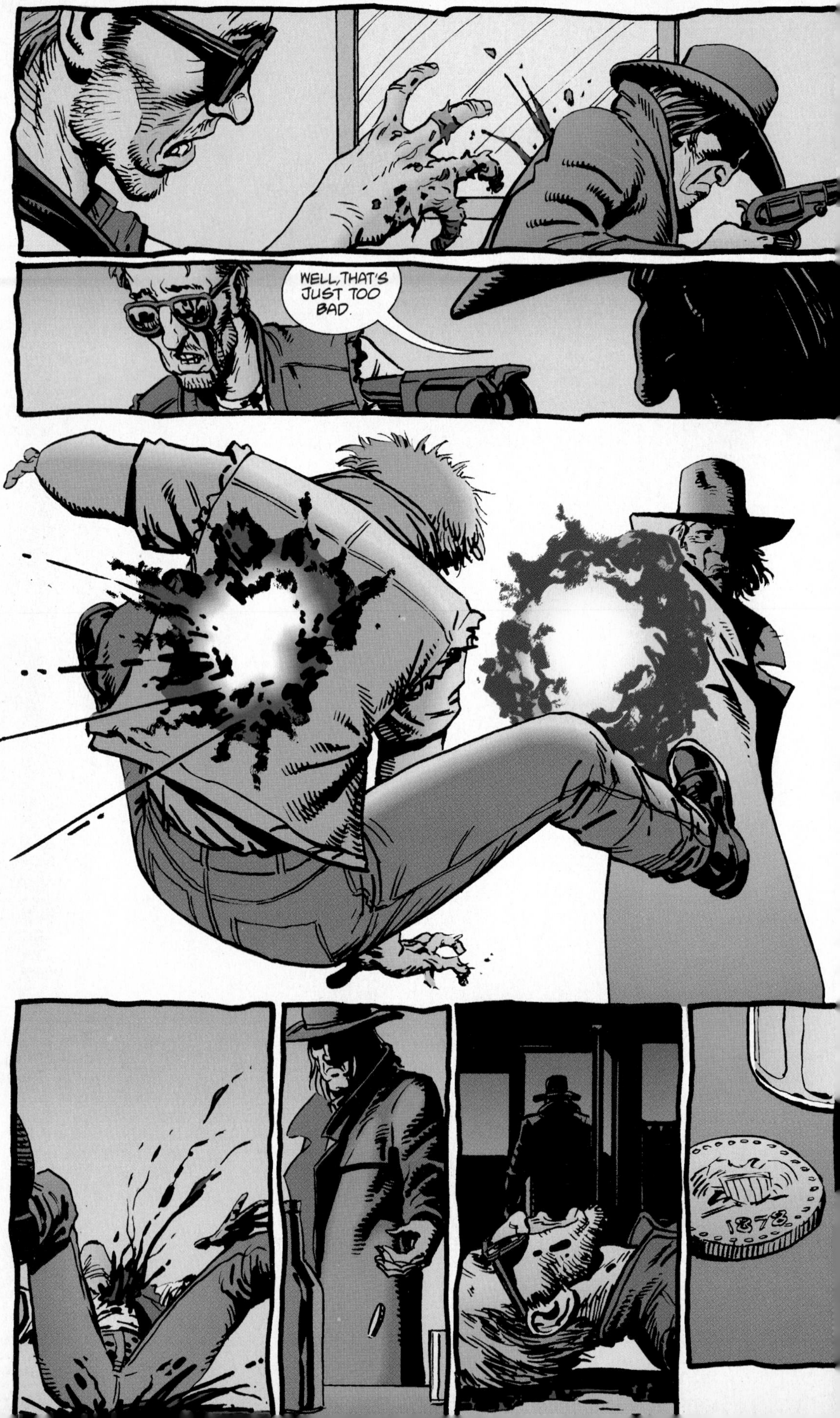
WELL, THAT'S JUST TOO BAD.
1878

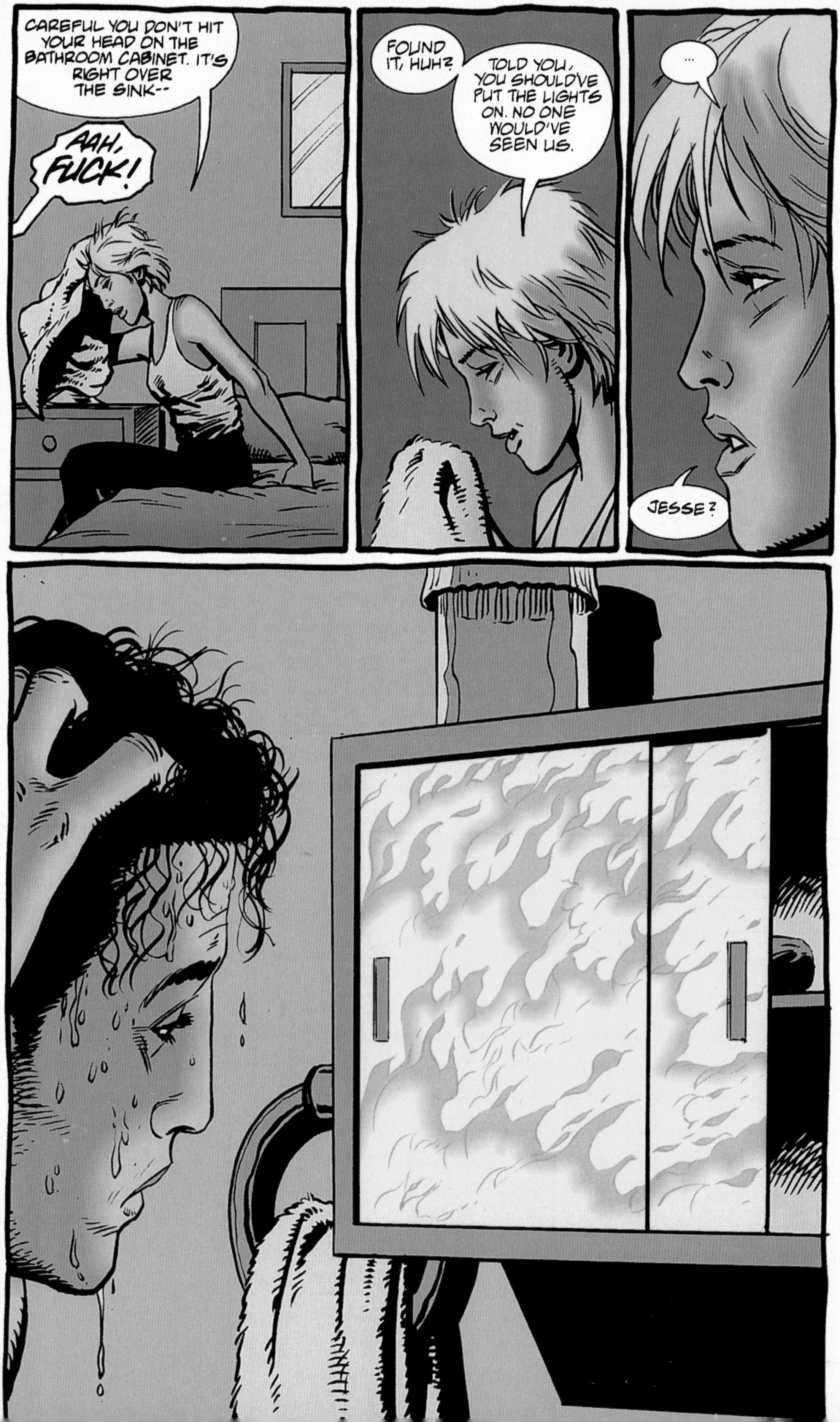
CAREFUL YOU DON'T HIT YOUR HEAD ON THE BATHROOM CABINET. IT'S RIGHT OVER THE SINK--
AAH, FUCK!
FOUND IT, HUH?
TOLD YOU, YOU SHOULD'VE PUT THE LIGHTS ON. NO ONE WOULD'VE SEEN US.
...
JESSE?

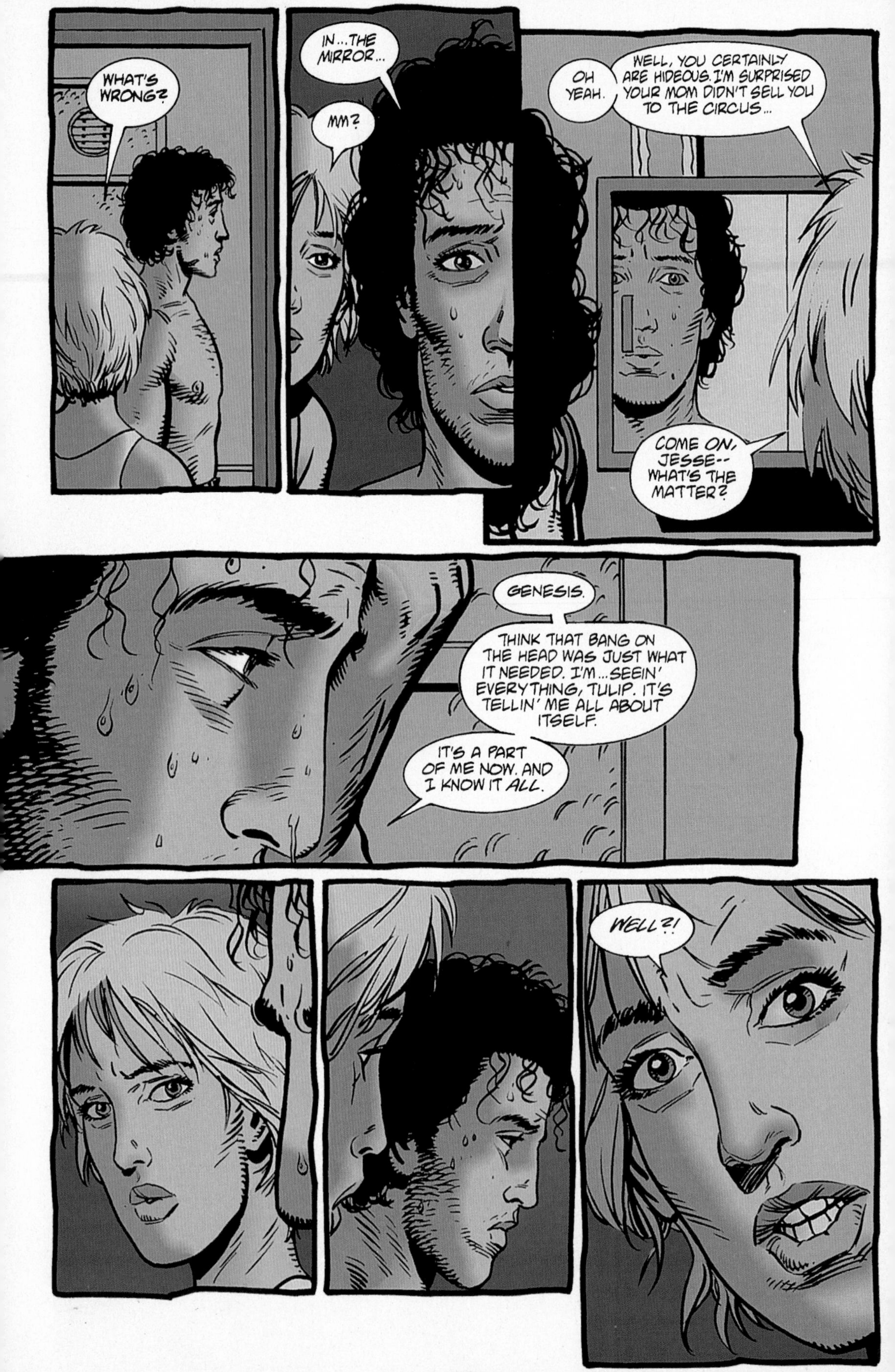
WHAT'S WRONG?
IN... THE MIRROR...
MM?
OH YEAH.
WELL, YOU CERTAINLY ARE HIDEOUS. I'M SURPRISED YOUR MOM DIDN'T SELL YOU TO THE CIRCUS...
COME ON, JESSE-- WHAT'S THE MATTER?
GENESIS.
THINK THAT BANG ON THE HEAD WAS JUST WHAT IT NEEDED. I'M... SEEIN' EVERYTHING, TULIP. IT'S TELLIN' ME ALL ABOUT ITSELF.
IT'S A PART OF ME NOW. AND I KNOW IT *ALL*.
WELL?!

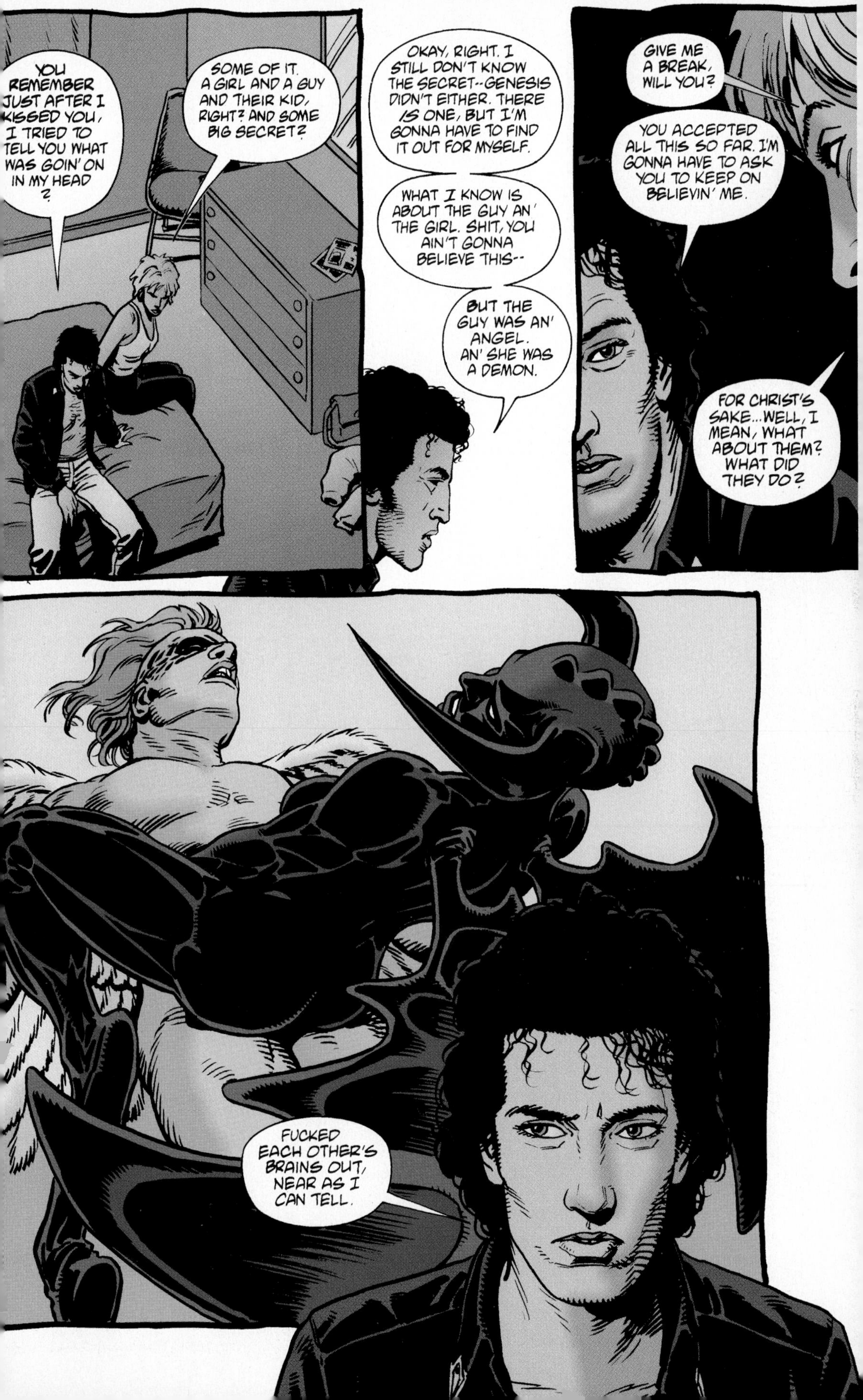
YOU REMEMBER JUST AFTER I KISSED YOU, I TRIED TO TELL YOU WHAT WAS GOIN' ON IN MY HEAD?
SOME OF IT. A GIRL AND A GUY AND THEIR KID, RIGHT? AND SOME BIG SECRET?
OKAY, RIGHT. I STILL DON'T KNOW THE SECRET--GENESIS DIDN'T EITHER. THERE IS ONE, BUT I'M GONNA HAVE TO FIND IT OUT FOR MYSELF.
WHAT I KNOW IS ABOUT THE GUY AN' THE GIRL. SHIT, YOU AIN'T GONNA BELIEVE THIS--
BUT THE GUY WAS AN' ANGEL. AN' SHE WAS A DEMON.
GIVE ME A BREAK, WILL YOU?
YOU ACCEPTED ALL THIS SO FAR. I'M GONNA HAVE TO ASK YOU TO KEEP ON BELIEVIN' ME.
FOR CHRIST'S SAKE...WELL, I MEAN, WHAT ABOUT THEM? WHAT DID THEY DO?
FUCKED EACH OTHER'S BRAINS OUT, NEAR AS I CAN TELL.

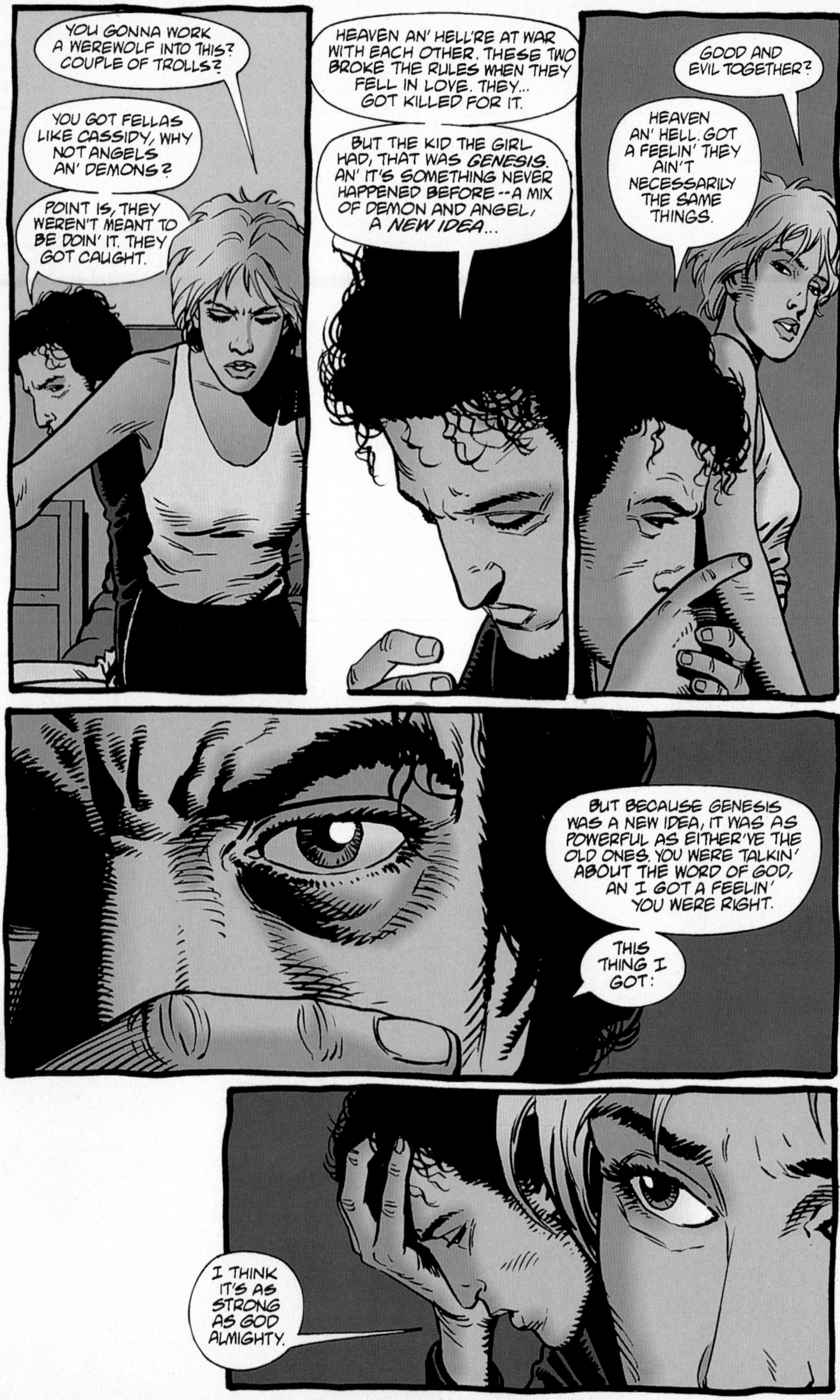
YOU GONNA WORK A WEREWOLF INTO THIS? COUPLE OF TROLLS?
YOU GOT FELLAS LIKE CASSIDY, WHY NOT ANGELS AN' DEMONS?
POINT IS, THEY WEREN'T MEANT TO BE DOIN' IT. THEY GOT CAUGHT.
HEAVEN AN' HELL'RE AT WAR WITH EACH OTHER. THESE TWO BROKE THE RULES WHEN THEY FELL IN LOVE. THEY... GOT KILLED FOR IT.
BUT THE KID THE GIRL HAD, THAT WAS GENESIS. AN' IT'S SOMETHING NEVER HAPPENED BEFORE--A MIX OF DEMON AND ANGEL, A NEW IDEA...
GOOD AND EVIL TOGETHER?
HEAVEN AN' HELL. GOT A FEELIN' THEY AIN'T NECESSARILY THE SAME THINGS.
BUT BECAUSE GENESIS WAS A NEW IDEA, IT WAS AS POWERFUL AS EITHER'VE THE OLD ONES. YOU WERE TALKIN' ABOUT THE WORD OF GOD, AN I GOT A FEELIN' YOU WERE RIGHT.
THIS THING I GOT:
I THINK IT'S AS STRONG AS GOD ALMIGHTY.

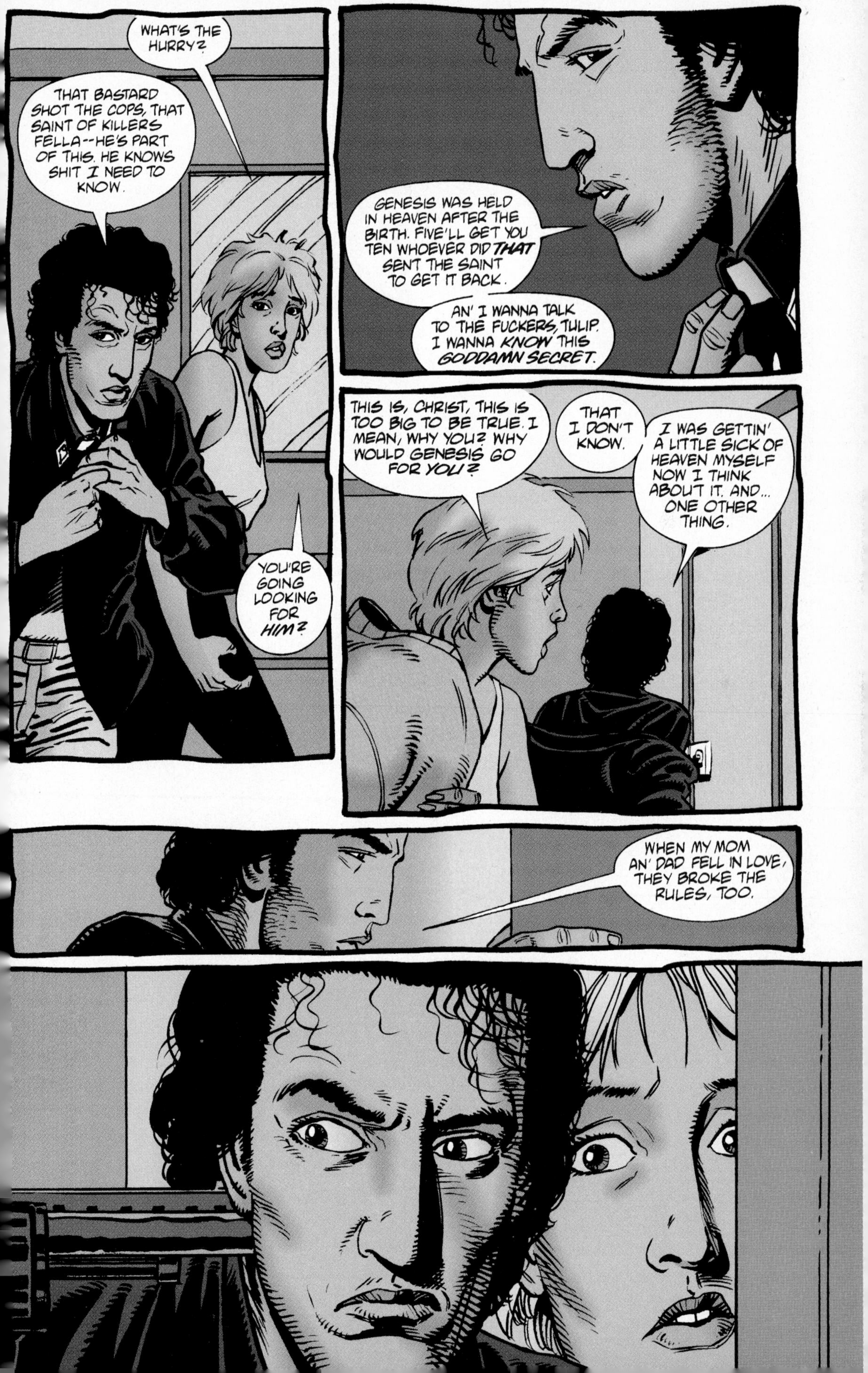
WHAT'S THE HURRY?
THAT BASTARD SHOT THE COPS, THAT SAINT OF KILLERS FELLA--HE'S PART OF THIS. HE KNOWS SHIT I NEED TO KNOW.
YOU'RE GOING LOOKING FOR HIM?
GENESIS WAS HELD IN HEAVEN AFTER THE BIRTH. FIVE'LL GET YOU TEN WHOEVER DID THAT SENT THE SAINT TO GET IT BACK.
AN' I WANNA TALK TO THE FUCKERS, TULIP. I WANNA KNOW THIS GODDAMN SECRET.
THIS IS, CHRIST, THIS IS TOO BIG TO BE TRUE. I MEAN, WHY YOU? WHY WOULD GENESIS GO FOR YOU?
THAT I DON'T KNOW.
I WAS GETTIN' A LITTLE SICK OF HEAVEN MYSELF NOW I THINK ABOUT IT. AND... ONE OTHER THING.
WHEN MY MOM AN' DAD FELL IN LOVE, THEY BROKE THE RULES, TOO.

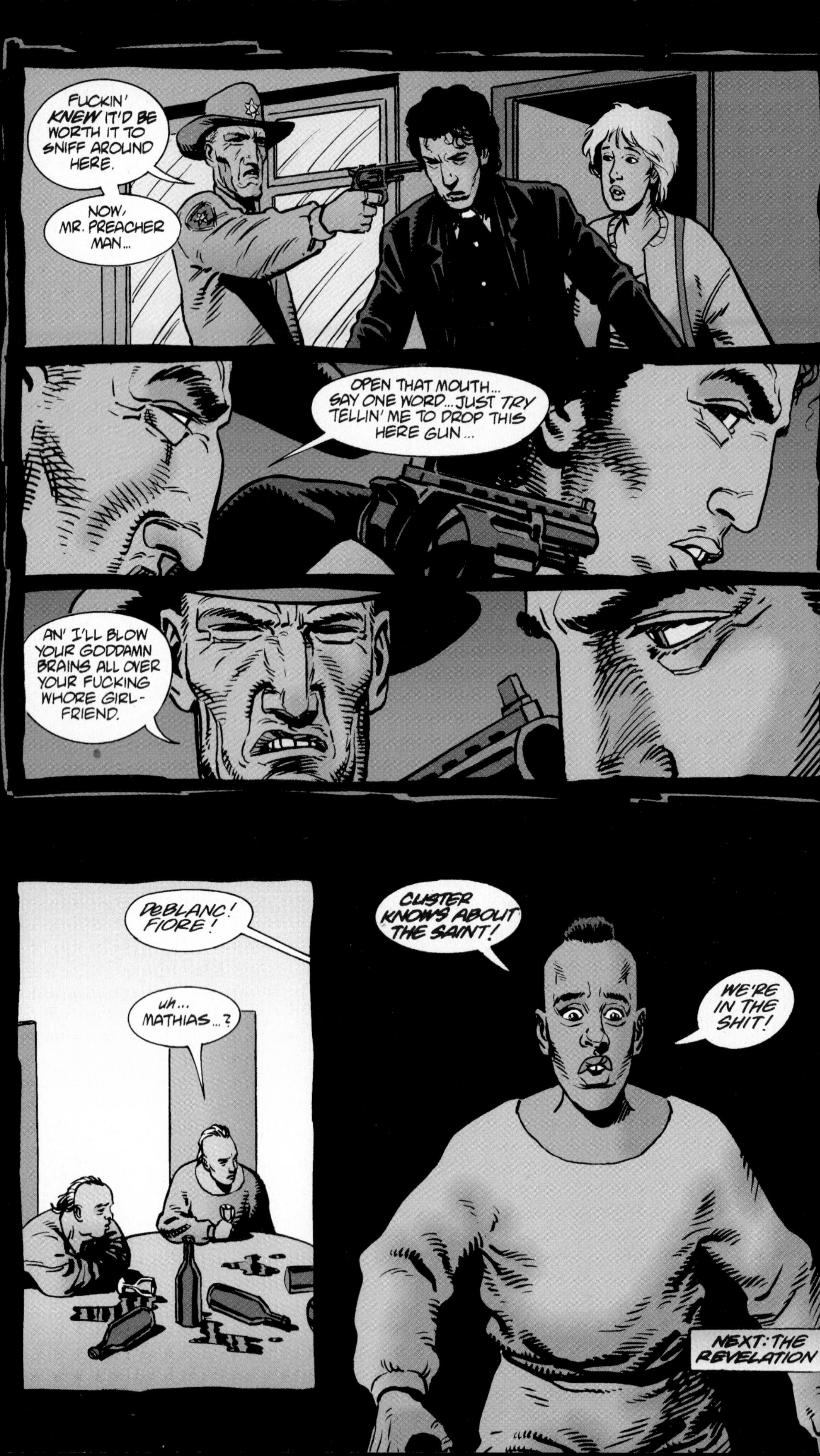
FUCKIN' KNEW IT'D BE WORTH IT TO SNIFF AROUND HERE.
NOW, MR. PREACHER MAN...
OPEN THAT MOUTH... SAY ONE WORD... JUST TRY TELLIN' ME TO DROP THIS HERE GUN...
AN' I'LL BLOW YOUR GODDAMN BRAINS ALL OVER YOUR FUCKING WHORE GIRL-FRIEND.
DeBLANC! FIORE!
CUSTER KNOWS ABOUT THE SAINT!
uh... MATHIAS...?
WE'RE IN THE SHIT!
NEXT: THE REVELATION

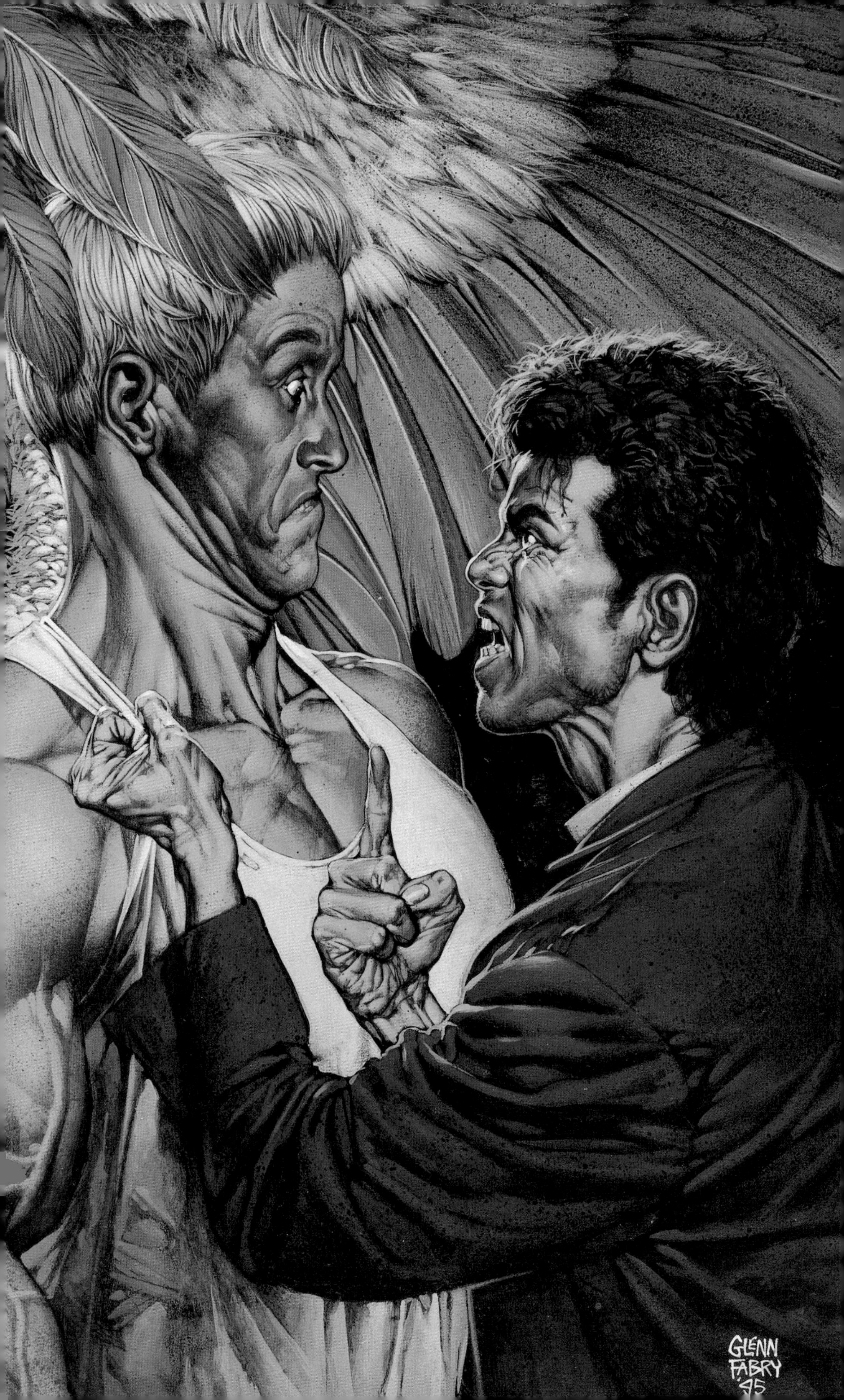
GLENN
FABRY
'95

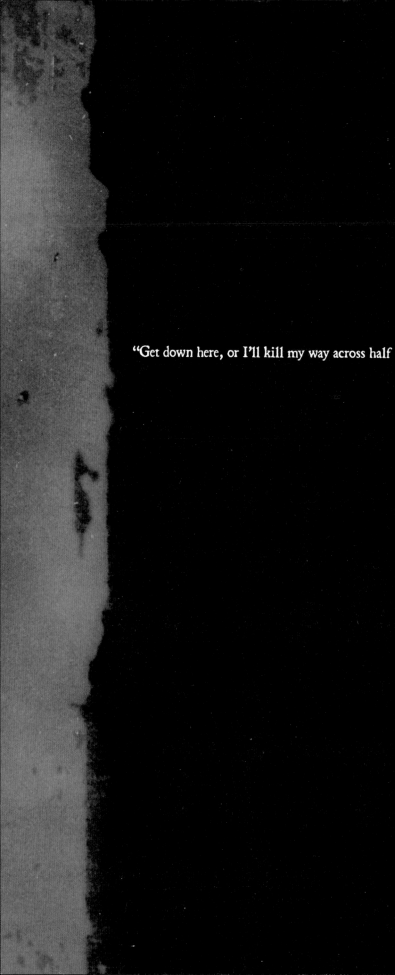

"Get down here, or I'll kill my way across half

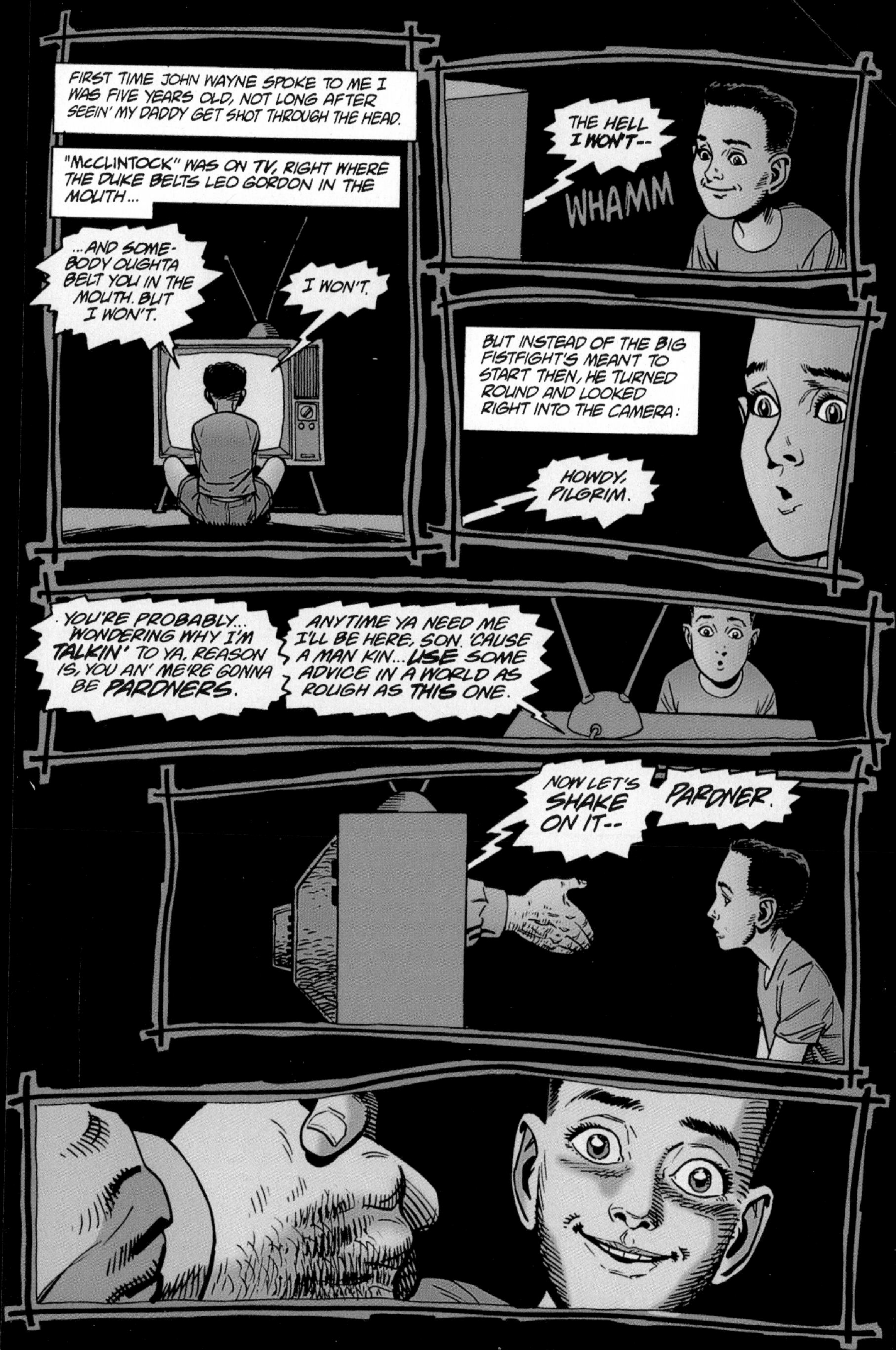

FIRST TIME JOHN WAYNE SPOKE TO ME I WAS FIVE YEARS OLD, NOT LONG AFTER SEEIN' MY DADDY GET SHOT THROUGH THE HEAD.
"McCLINTOCK" WAS ON TV, RIGHT WHERE THE DUKE BELTS LEO GORDON IN THE MOUTH...
...AND SOME-BODY OUGHTA BELT YOU IN THE MOUTH. BUT I WON'T.
I WON'T.
THE HELL I WON'T--
WHAMM
BUT INSTEAD OF THE BIG FISTFIGHT'S MEANT TO START THEN, HE TURNED ROUND AND LOOKED RIGHT INTO THE CAMERA:
HOWDY, PILGRIM.
YOU'RE PROBABLY... WONDERING WHY I'M TALKIN' TO YA. REASON IS, YOU AN' ME'RE GONNA BE PARDNERS.
ANYTIME YA NEED ME I'LL BE HERE, SON. 'CAUSE A MAN KIN... USE SOME ADVICE IN A WORLD AS ROUGH AS THIS ONE.
NOW LET'S SHAKE ON IT--
PARDNER.

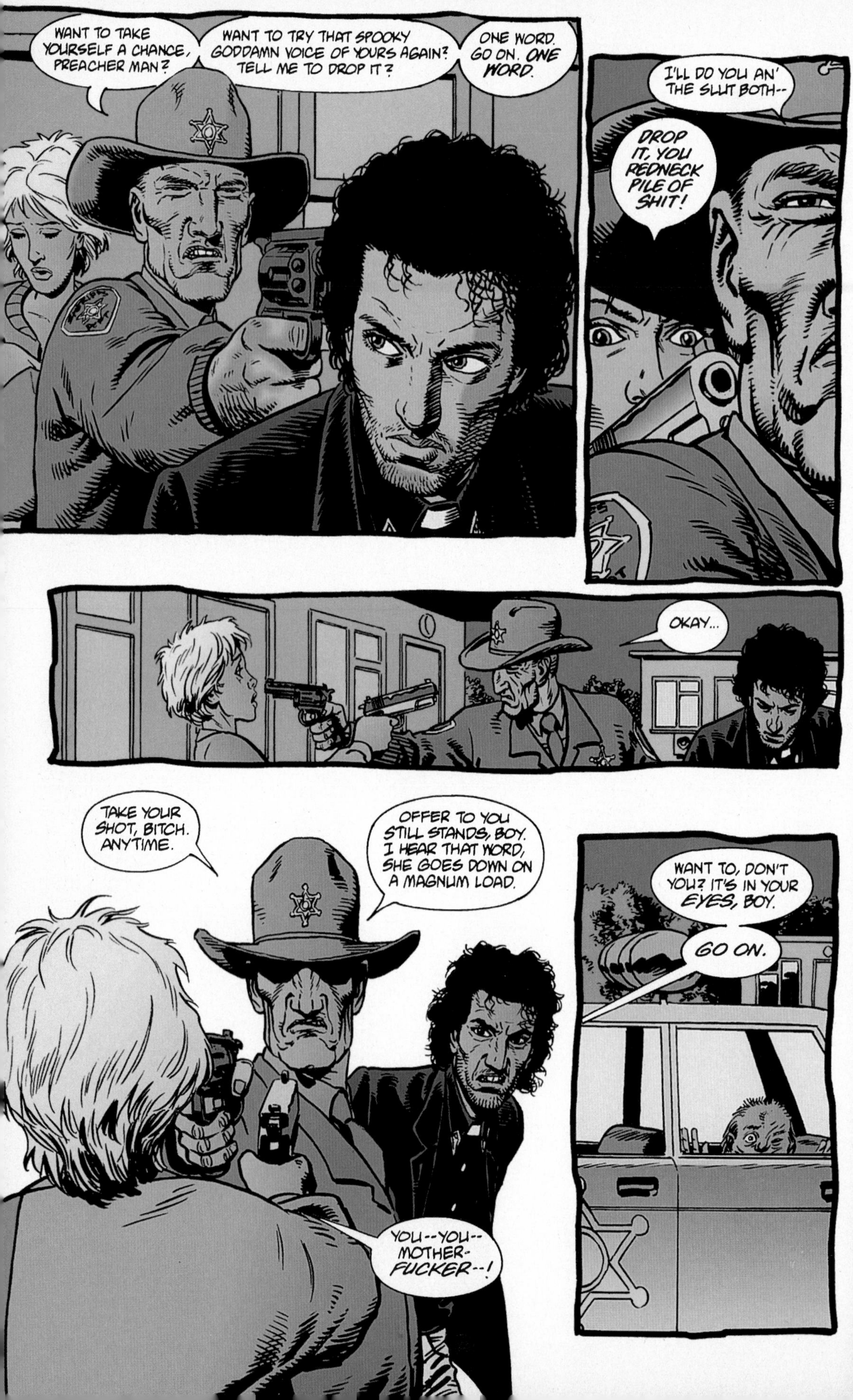
WANT TO TAKE YOURSELF A CHANCE, PREACHER MAN?
WANT TO TRY THAT SPOOKY GODDAMN VOICE OF YOURS AGAIN? TELL ME TO DROP IT?
ONE WORD. GO ON. ONE WORD.
I'LL DO YOU AN' THE SLUT BOTH--
DROP IT, YOU REDNECK PILE OF SHIT!
OKAY...
TAKE YOUR SHOT, BITCH. ANYTIME.
OFFER TO YOU STILL STANDS, BOY. I HEAR THAT WORD, SHE GOES DOWN ON A MAGNUM LOAD.
YOU--YOU--MOTHER-FUCKER--!
WANT TO, DON'T YOU? IT'S IN YOUR EYES, BOY.
GO ON.

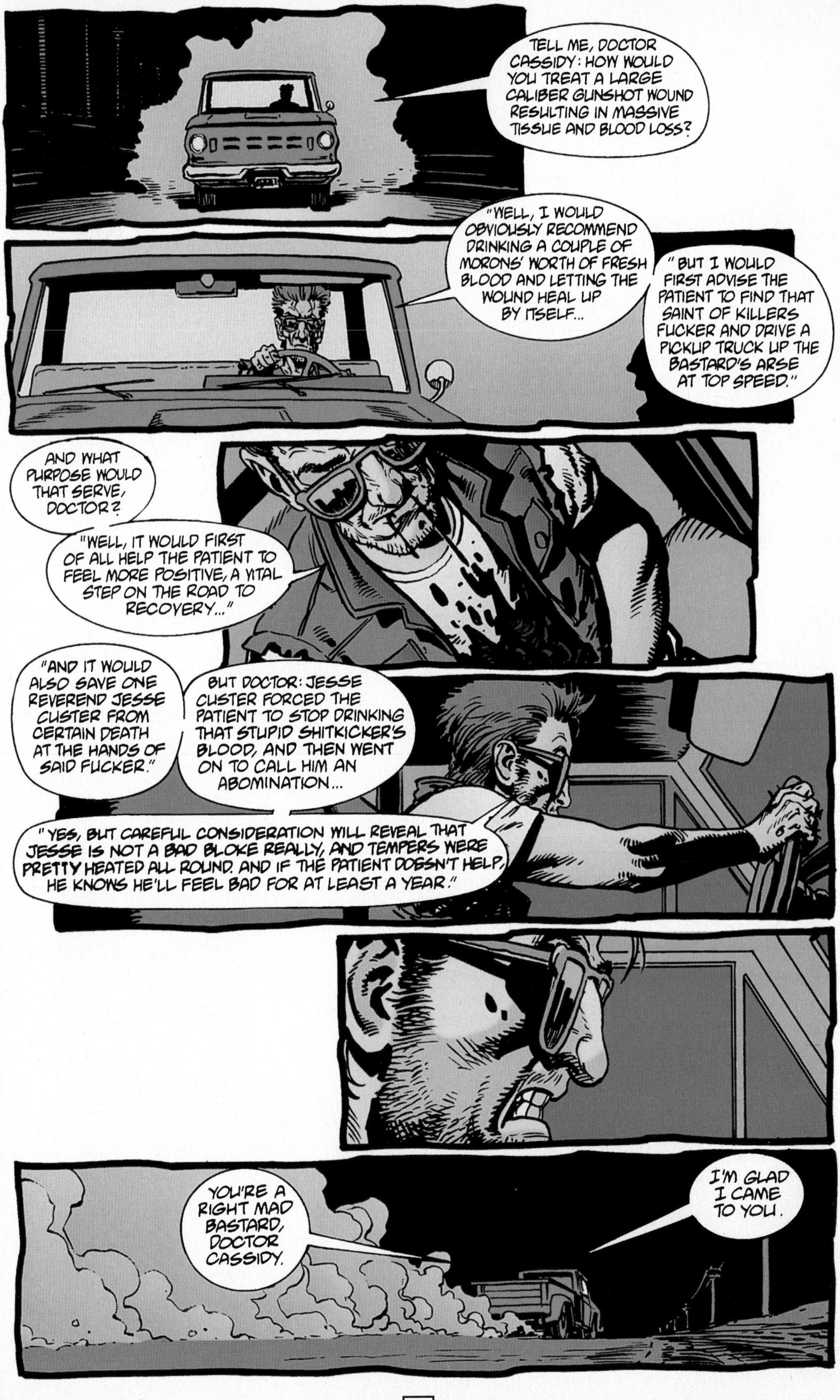
TELL ME, DOCTOR CASSIDY: HOW WOULD YOU TREAT A LARGE CALIBER GUNSHOT WOUND RESULTING IN MASSIVE TISSUE AND BLOOD LOSS?
"WELL, I WOULD OBVIOUSLY RECOMMEND DRINKING A COUPLE OF MORONS' WORTH OF FRESH BLOOD AND LETTING THE WOUND HEAL UP BY ITSELF...
" BUT I WOULD FIRST ADVISE THE PATIENT TO FIND THAT SAINT OF KILLERS FUCKER AND DRIVE A PICKUP TRUCK UP THE BASTARD'S ARSE AT TOP SPEED."
AND WHAT PURPOSE WOULD THAT SERVE, DOCTOR?
"WELL, IT WOULD FIRST OF ALL HELP THE PATIENT TO FEEL MORE POSITIVE, A VITAL STEP ON THE ROAD TO RECOVERY..."
"AND IT WOULD ALSO SAVE ONE REVEREND JESSE CUSTER FROM CERTAIN DEATH AT THE HANDS OF SAID FUCKER."
BUT DOCTOR: JESSE CUSTER FORCED THE PATIENT TO STOP DRINKING THAT STUPID SHITKICKER'S BLOOD, AND THEN WENT ON TO CALL HIM AN ABOMINATION...
" YES, BUT CAREFUL CONSIDERATION WILL REVEAL THAT JESSE IS NOT A BAD BLOKE REALLY, AND TEMPERS WERE PRETTY HEATED ALL ROUND. AND IF THE PATIENT DOESN'T HELP, HE KNOWS HE'LL FEEL BAD FOR AT LEAST A YEAR."
YOU'RE A RIGHT MAD BASTARD, DOCTOR CASSIDY.
I'M GLAD I CAME TO YOU.

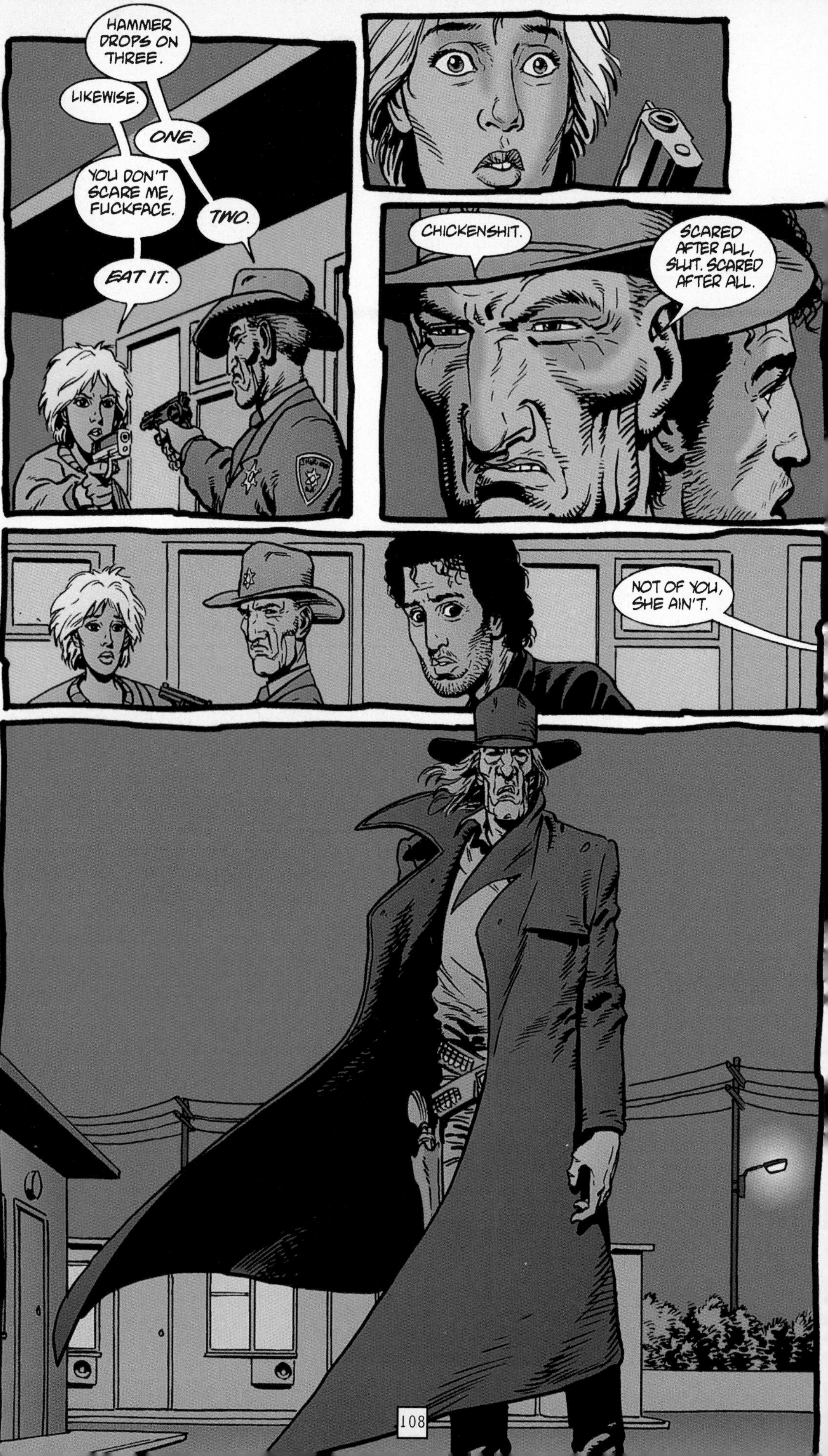
HAMMER DROPS ON THREE.
LIKEWISE.
ONE.
YOU DON'T SCARE ME, FUCKFACE.
TWO.
EAT IT.
CHICKENSHIT.
SCARED AFTER ALL, SLUT. SCARED AFTER ALL.
NOT OF YOU, SHE AIN'T.

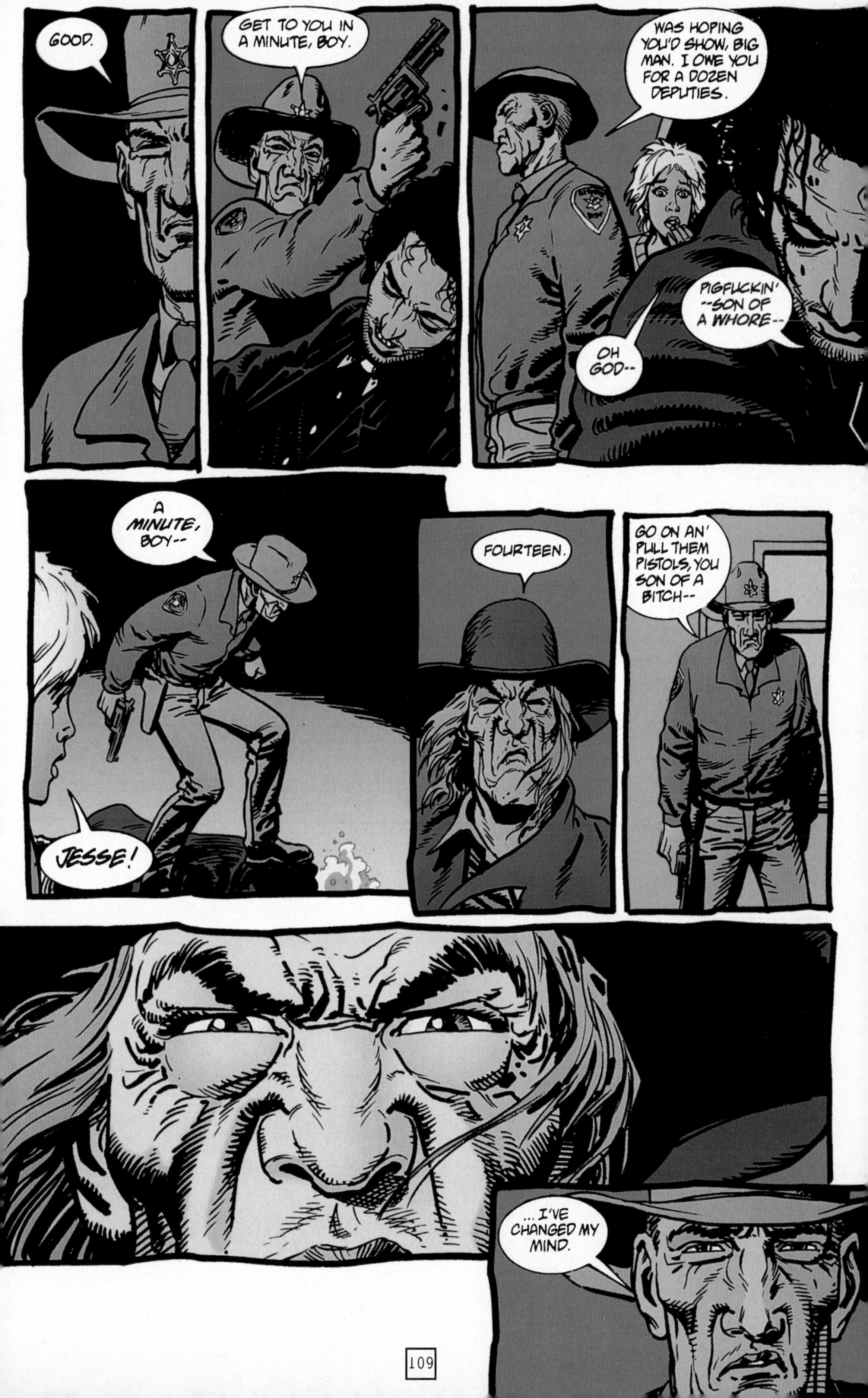
GOOD.
GET TO YOU IN A MINUTE, BOY.
WAS HOPING YOU'D SHOW, BIG MAN. I OWE YOU FOR A DOZEN DEPUTIES.
PIGFUCKIN' --SON OF A WHORE--
OH GOD--
A MINUTE, BOY--
JESSE!
FOURTEEN.
GO ON AN' PULL THEM PISTOLS, YOU SON OF A BITCH--
...I'VE CHANGED MY MIND.

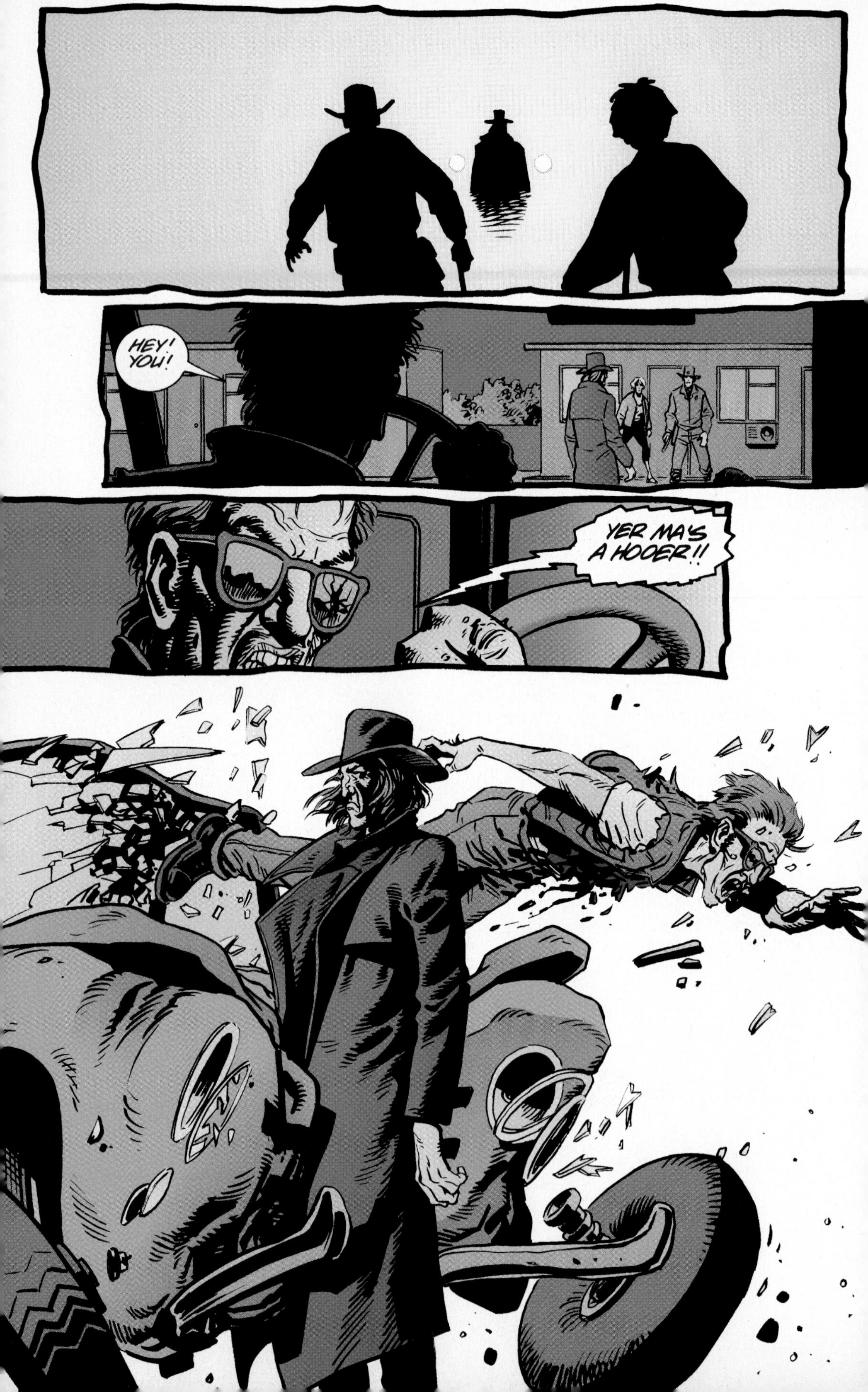
HEY! YOU!
YER MA'S A HOOER!!

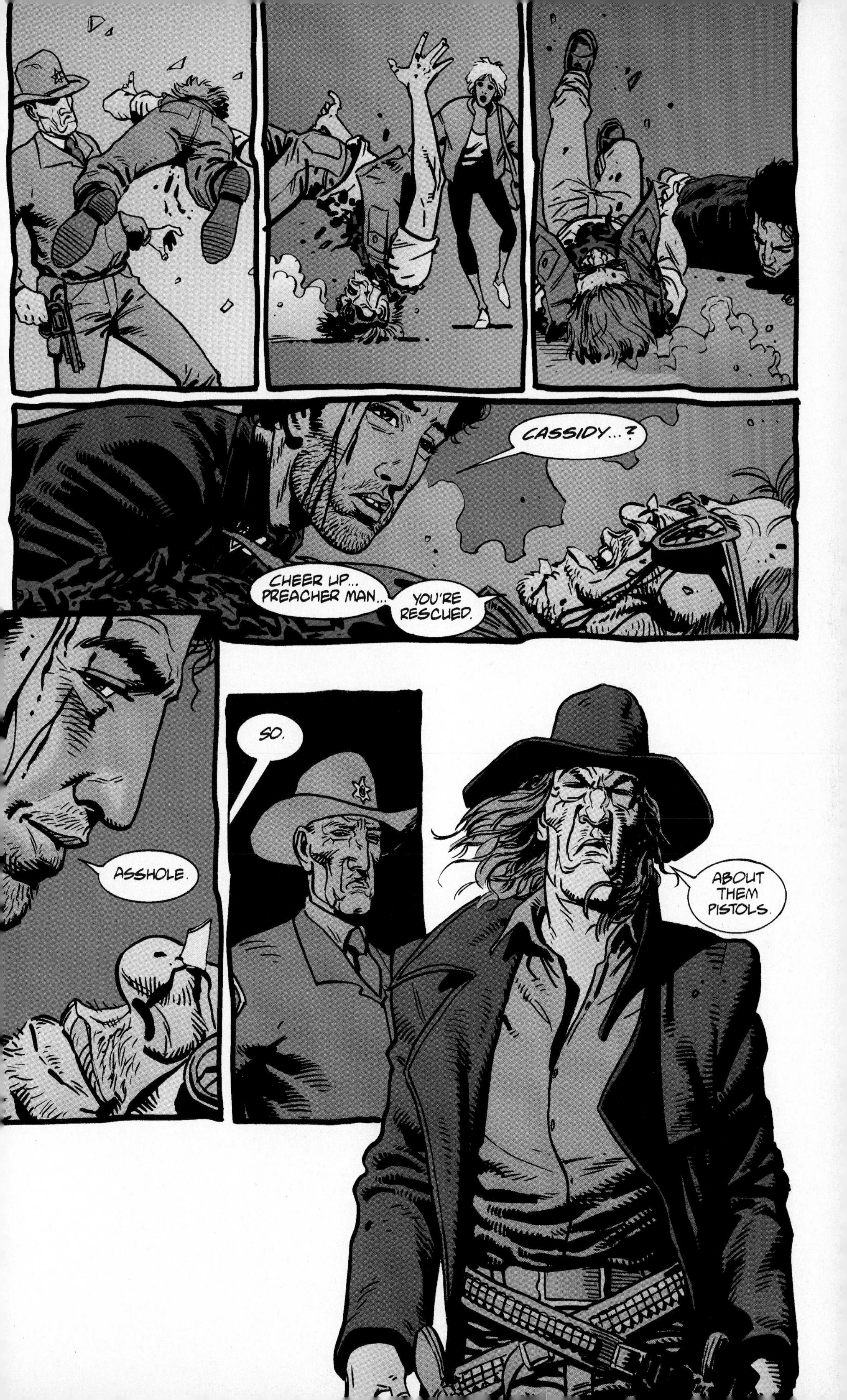
CASSIDY...?
CHEER UP... PREACHER MAN...
YOU'RE RESCUED.
ASSHOLE.
SO.
ABOUT THEM PISTOLS.

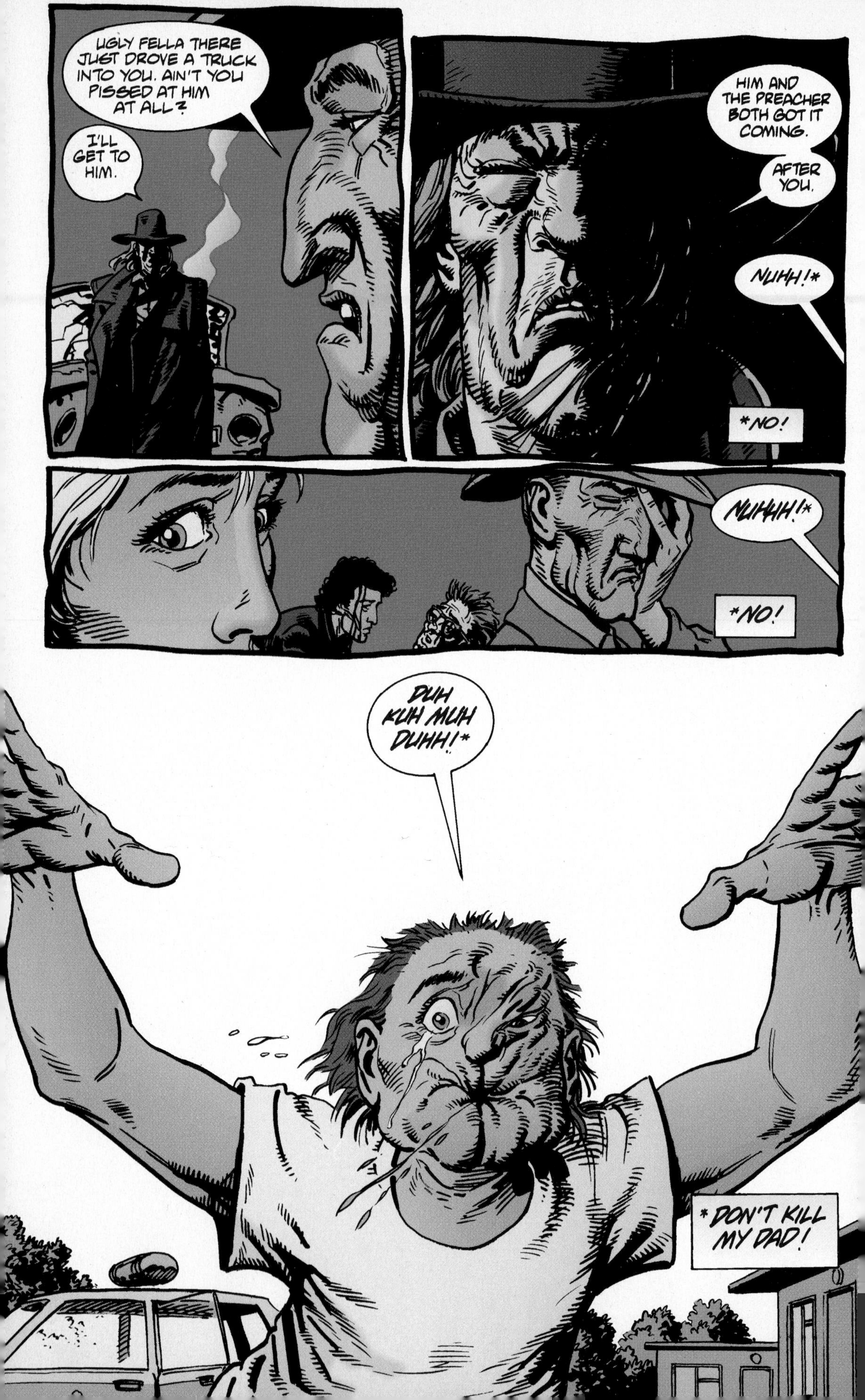
UGLY FELLA THERE JUST DROVE A TRUCK INTO YOU. AIN'T YOU PISSED AT HIM AT ALL?
I'LL GET TO HIM.
HIM AND THE PREACHER BOTH GOT IT COMING.
AFTER YOU.
NUHH!*
*NO!
NUHHH!*
*NO!
DUH KUH MUH DUHH!*
*DON'T KILL MY DAD!

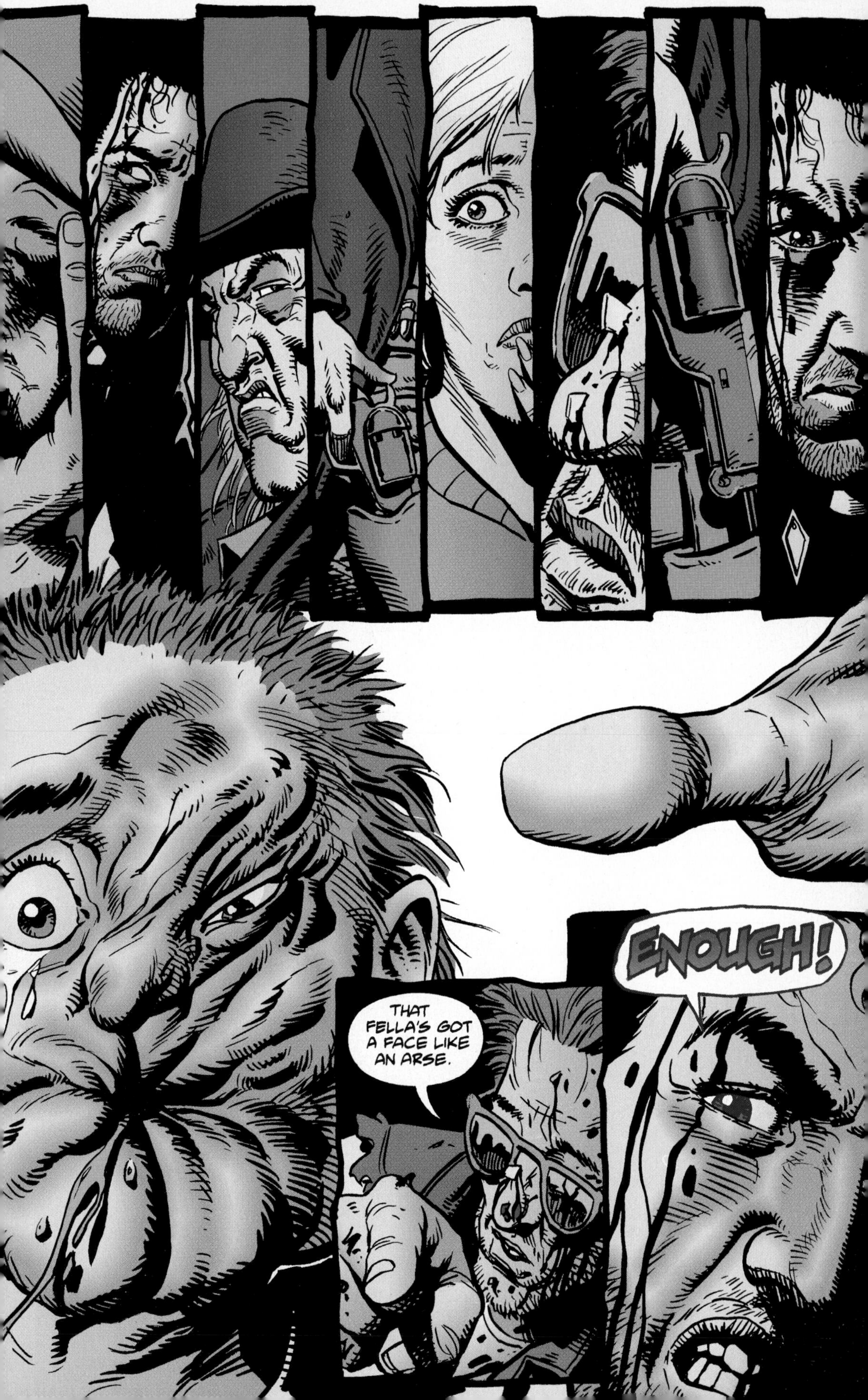
THAT FELLA'S GOT A FACE LIKE AN ARSE.
ENOUGH!

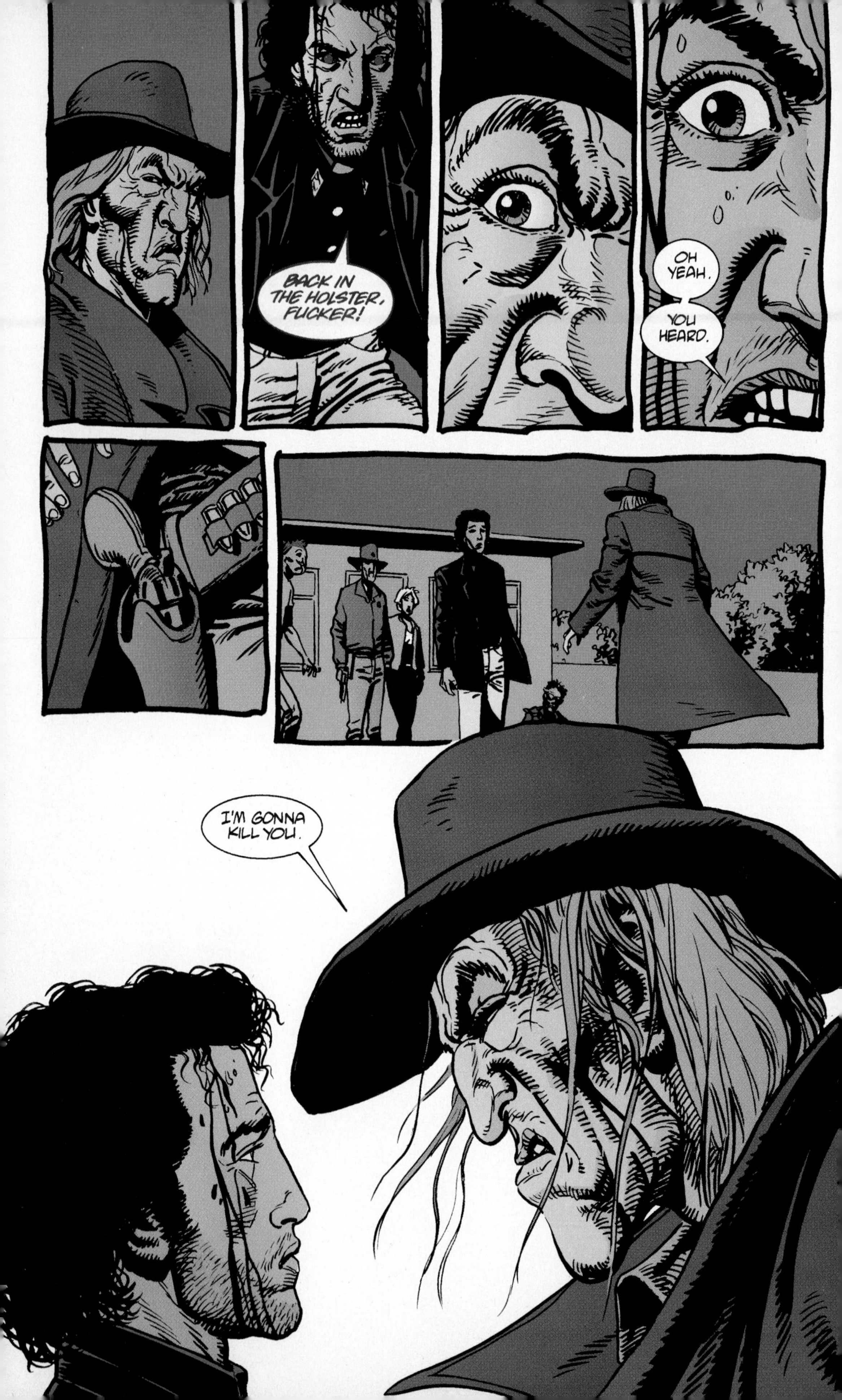
BACK IN THE HOLSTER, FUCKER!
OH YEAH.
YOU HEARD.
I'M GONNA KILL YOU.

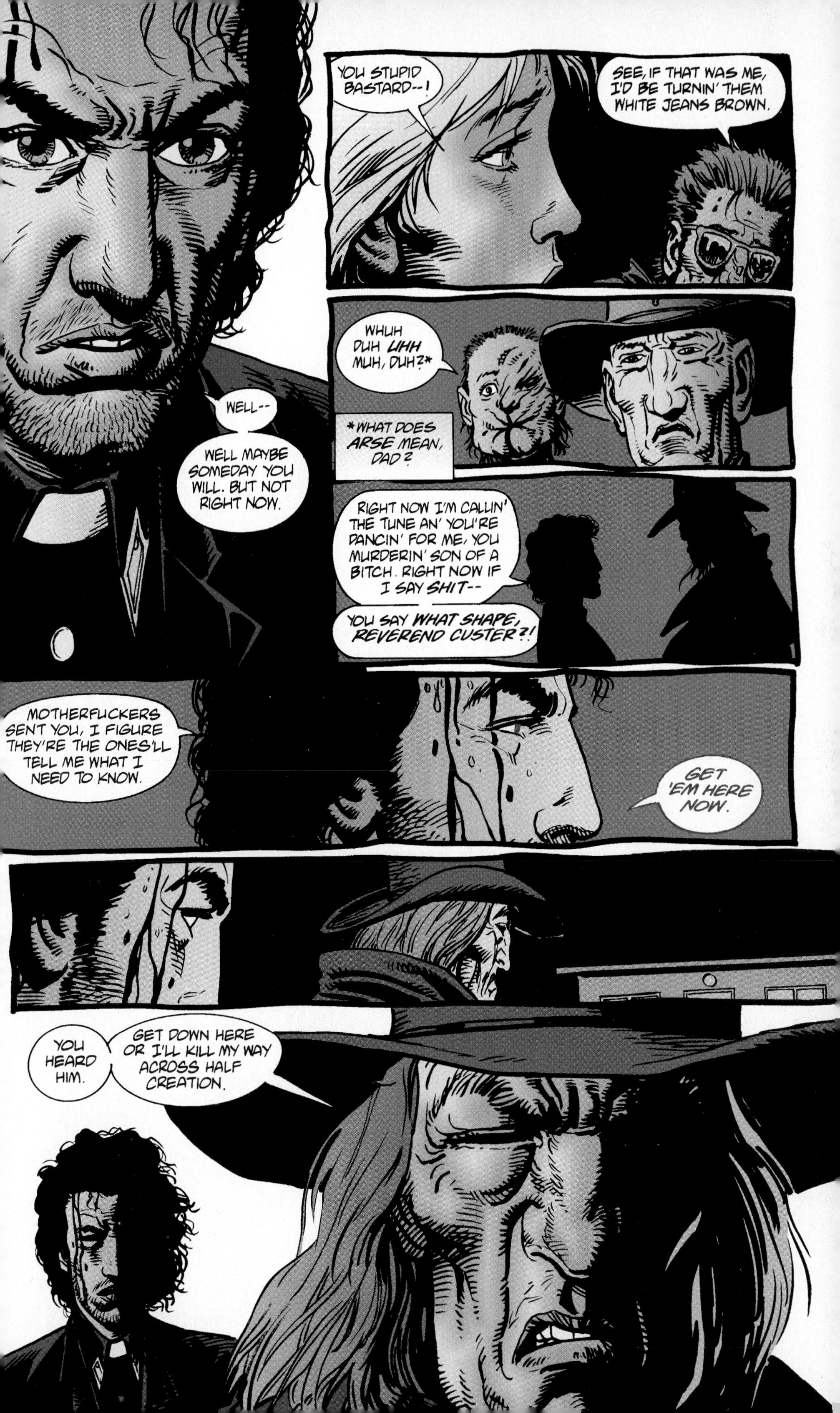

YOU STUPID BASTARD--!
SEE, IF THAT WAS ME, I'D BE TURNIN' THEM WHITE JEANS BROWN.
WELL--
WELL MAYBE SOMEDAY YOU WILL. BUT NOT RIGHT NOW.
WHUH DUH UHH MUH, DUH?*
*WHAT DOES ARSE MEAN, DAD?
RIGHT NOW I'M CALLIN' THE TUNE AN' YOU'RE DANCIN' FOR ME, YOU MURDERIN' SON OF A BITCH. RIGHT NOW IF I SAY SHIT--
YOU SAY WHAT SHAPE, REVEREND CUSTER?!
MOTHERFUCKERS SENT YOU, I FIGURE THEY'RE THE ONES'LL TELL ME WHAT I NEED TO KNOW.
GET 'EM HERE NOW.
YOU HEARD HIM.
GET DOWN HERE OR I'LL KILL MY WAY ACROSS HALF CREATION.

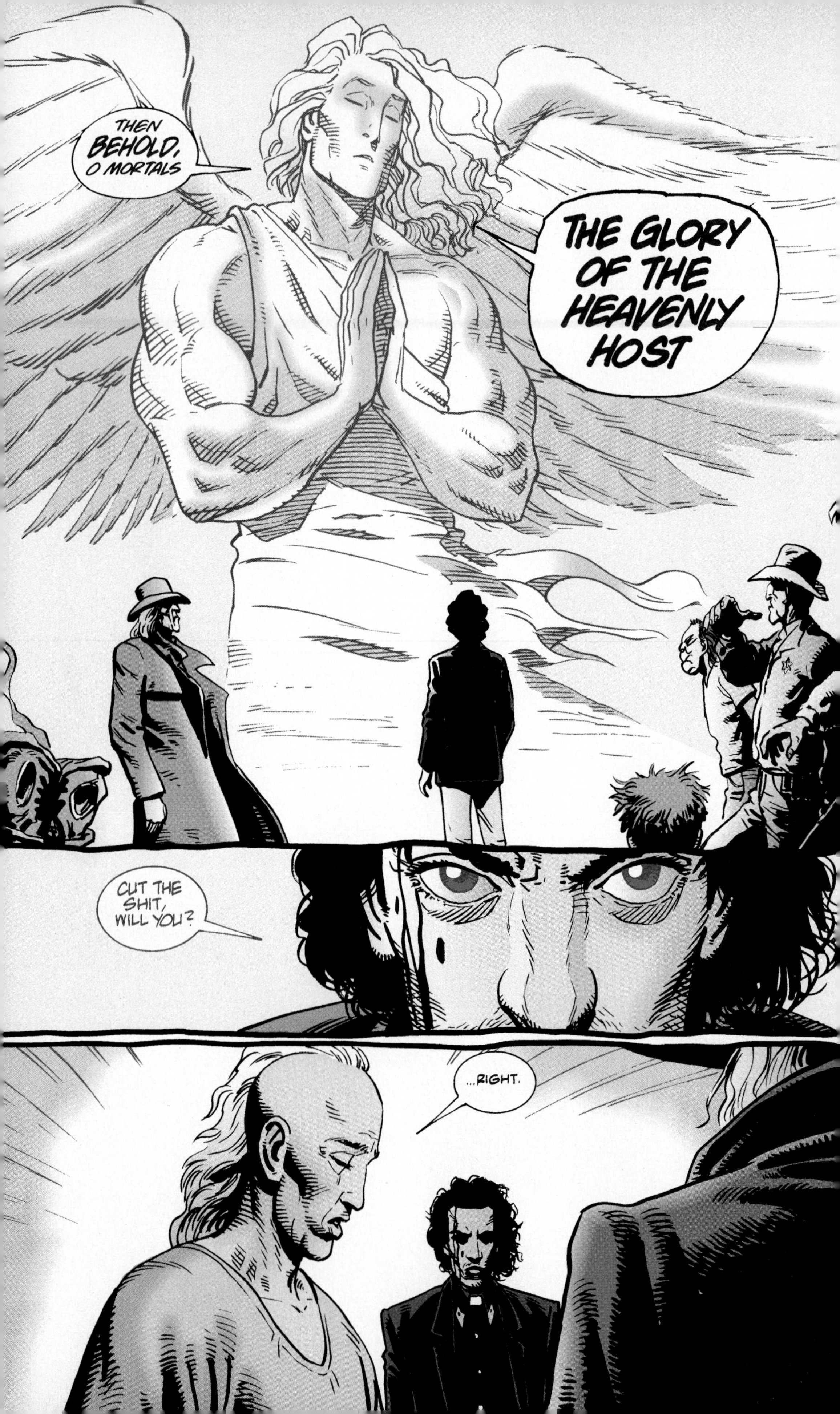
THEN BEHOLD, O MORTALS
THE GLORY OF THE HEAVENLY HOST
CUT THE SHIT, WILL YOU?
...RIGHT.

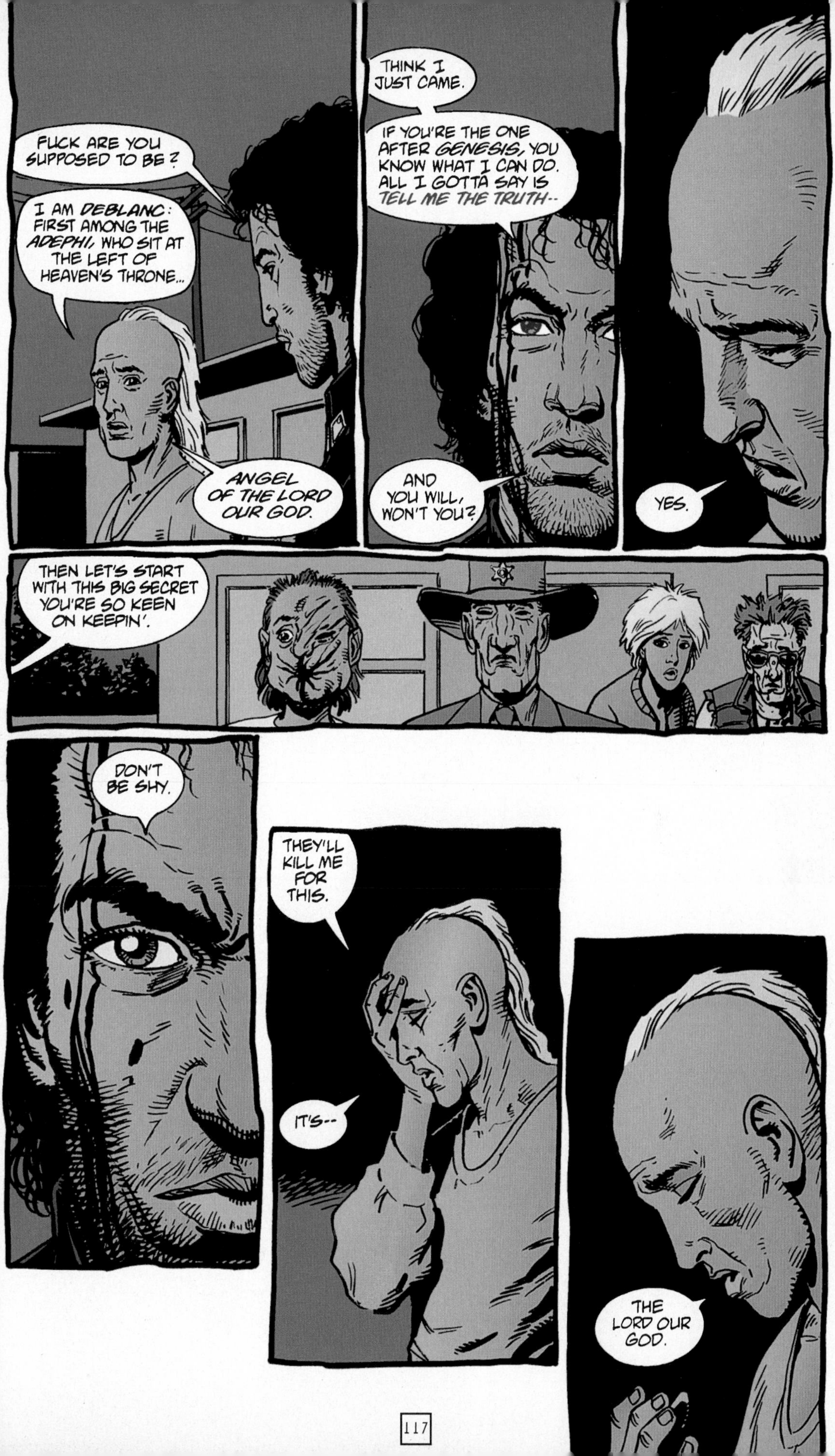
FUCK ARE YOU SUPPOSED TO BE?
I AM DEBLANC: FIRST AMONG THE ADEPHI, WHO SIT AT THE LEFT OF HEAVEN'S THRONE...
ANGEL OF THE LORD OUR GOD.
THINK I JUST CAME.
IF YOU'RE THE ONE AFTER GENESIS, YOU KNOW WHAT I CAN DO. ALL I GOTTA SAY IS TELL ME THE TRUTH--
AND YOU WILL, WON'T YOU?
YES.
THEN LET'S START WITH THIS BIG SECRET YOU'RE SO KEEN ON KEEPIN'.
DON'T BE SHY.
THEY'LL KILL ME FOR THIS.
IT'S--
THE LORD OUR GOD.

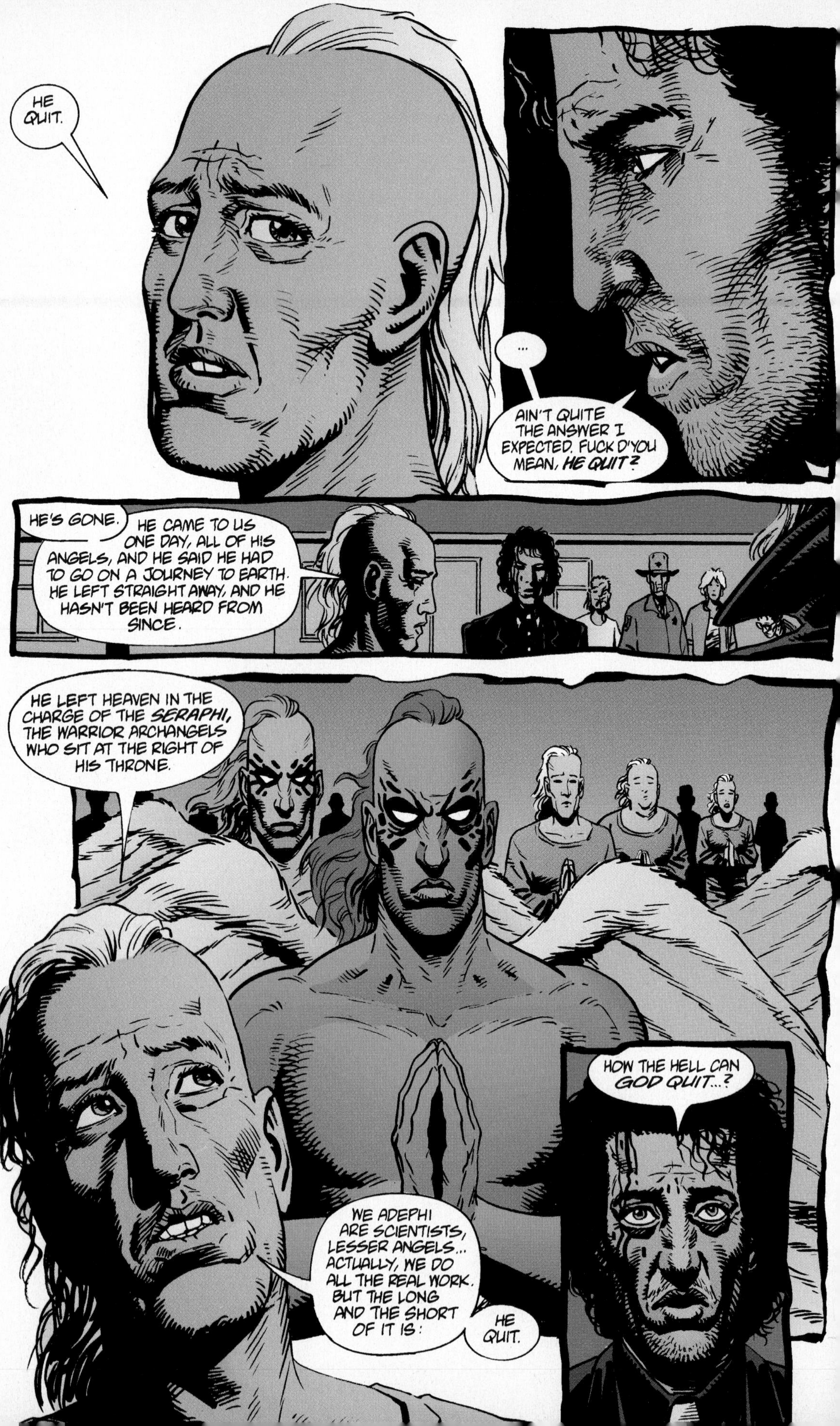
HE QUIT.
...
AIN'T QUITE THE ANSWER I EXPECTED. FUCK D'YOU MEAN, HE QUIT?
HE'S GONE.
HE CAME TO US ONE DAY, ALL OF HIS ANGELS, AND HE SAID HE HAD TO GO ON A JOURNEY TO EARTH. HE LEFT STRAIGHT AWAY, AND HE HASN'T BEEN HEARD FROM SINCE.
HE LEFT HEAVEN IN THE CHARGE OF THE SERAPHI, THE WARRIOR ARCHANGELS WHO SIT AT THE RIGHT OF HIS THRONE.
HOW THE HELL CAN GOD QUIT...?
WE ADEPHI ARE SCIENTISTS, LESSER ANGELS... ACTUALLY, WE DO ALL THE REAL WORK. BUT THE LONG AND THE SHORT OF IT IS:
HE QUIT.

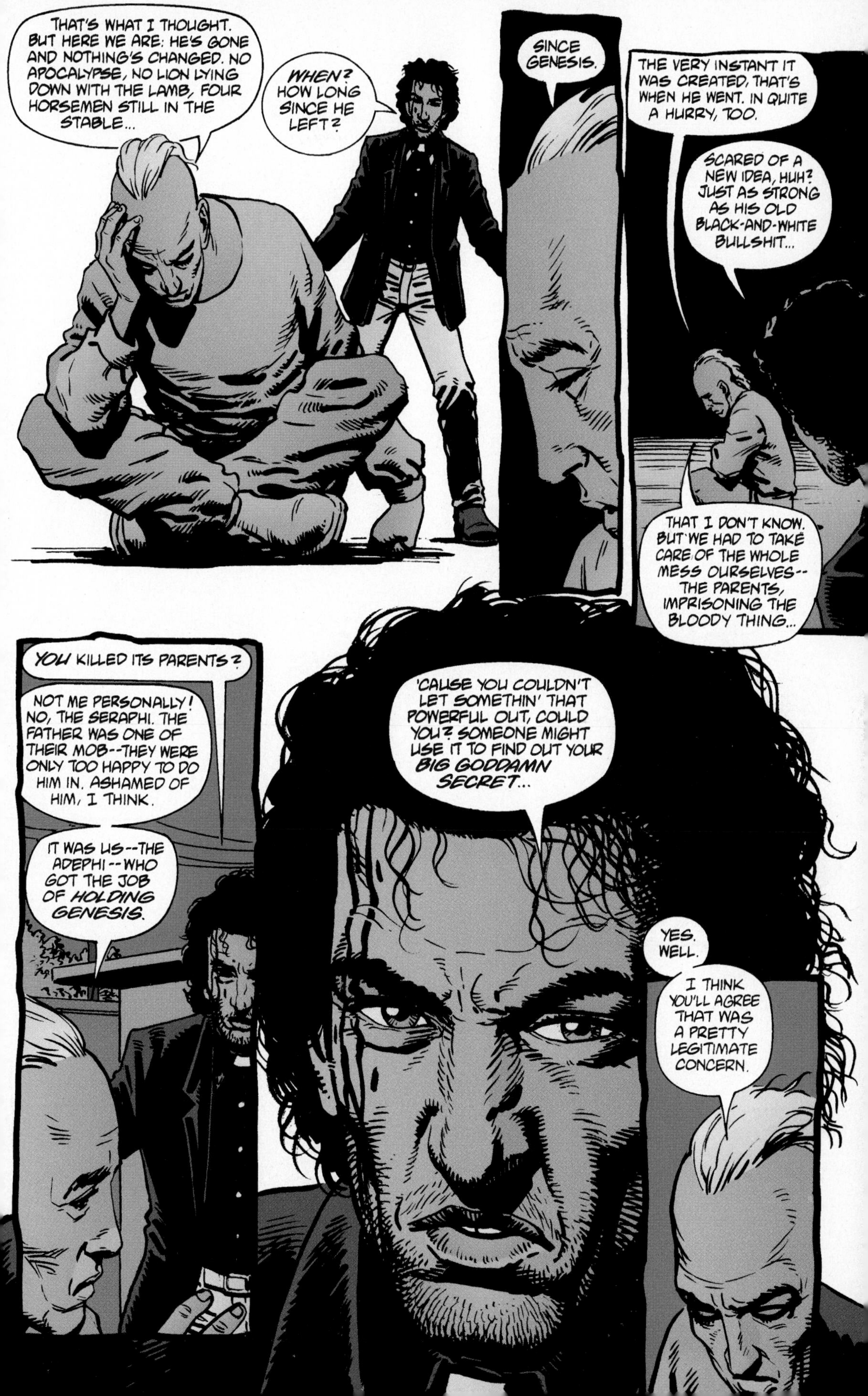

THAT'S WHAT I THOUGHT. BUT HERE WE ARE: HE'S GONE AND NOTHING'S CHANGED. NO APOCALYPSE, NO LION LYING DOWN WITH THE LAMB, FOUR HORSEMEN STILL IN THE STABLE...
WHEN? HOW LONG SINCE HE LEFT?
SINCE GENESIS.
THE VERY INSTANT IT WAS CREATED, THAT'S WHEN HE WENT. IN QUITE A HURRY, TOO.
SCARED OF A NEW IDEA, HUH? JUST AS STRONG AS HIS OLD BLACK-AND-WHITE BULLSHIT...
THAT I DON'T KNOW. BUT WE HAD TO TAKE CARE OF THE WHOLE MESS OURSELVES-- THE PARENTS, IMPRISONING THE BLOODY THING...
YOU KILLED ITS PARENTS?
NOT ME PERSONALLY! NO, THE SERAPHI. THE FATHER WAS ONE OF THEIR MOB--THEY WERE ONLY TOO HAPPY TO DO HIM IN. ASHAMED OF HIM, I THINK.
IT WAS US--THE ADEPHI--WHO GOT THE JOB OF HOLDING GENESIS.
'CAUSE YOU COULDN'T LET SOMETHIN' THAT POWERFUL OUT, COULD YOU? SOMEONE MIGHT USE IT TO FIND OUT YOUR BIG GODDAMN SECRET...
YES. WELL.
I THINK YOU'LL AGREE THAT WAS A PRETTY LEGITIMATE CONCERN.

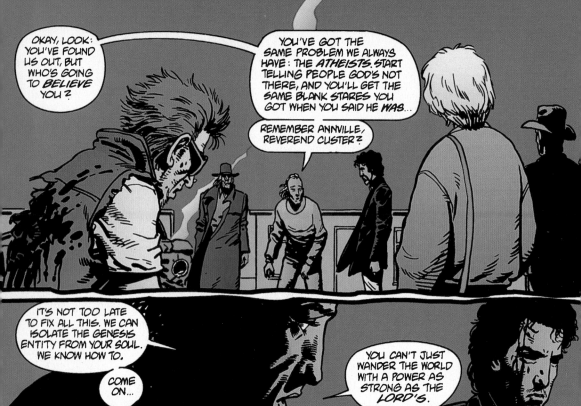

OKAY, LOOK: YOU'VE FOUND US OUT, BUT WHO'S GOING TO *BELIEVE* YOU?

YOU'VE GOT THE SAME PROBLEM WE ALWAYS HAVE: THE *ATHEISTS*. START TELLING PEOPLE GOD'S NOT THERE, AND YOU'LL GET THE SAME BLANK STARES YOU GOT WHEN YOU SAID HE *WAS*...

REMEMBER ANNVILLE, REVEREND CUSTER?

IT'S NOT TOO LATE TO FIX ALL THIS. WE CAN ISOLATE THE GENESIS ENTITY FROM YOUR SOUL. WE KNOW HOW TO.

COME ON...

YOU CAN'T JUST WANDER THE WORLD WITH A POWER AS STRONG AS THE *LORD'S*.

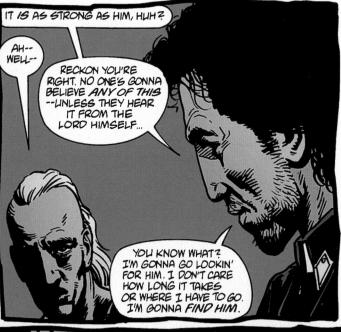

IT *IS* AS STRONG AS HIM, HUH?

AH-- WELL--

RECKON YOU'RE RIGHT. NO ONE'S GONNA BELIEVE *ANY* OF THIS --UNLESS THEY HEAR IT FROM THE LORD HIMSELF...

YOU KNOW WHAT? I'M GONNA GO LOOKIN' FOR HIM. I DON'T CARE HOW LONG IT TAKES OR WHERE I HAVE TO GO. I'M GONNA *FIND HIM*.

AN' I'M GONNA *MAKE HIM* TELL HIS PEOPLE WHAT HE'S DONE.

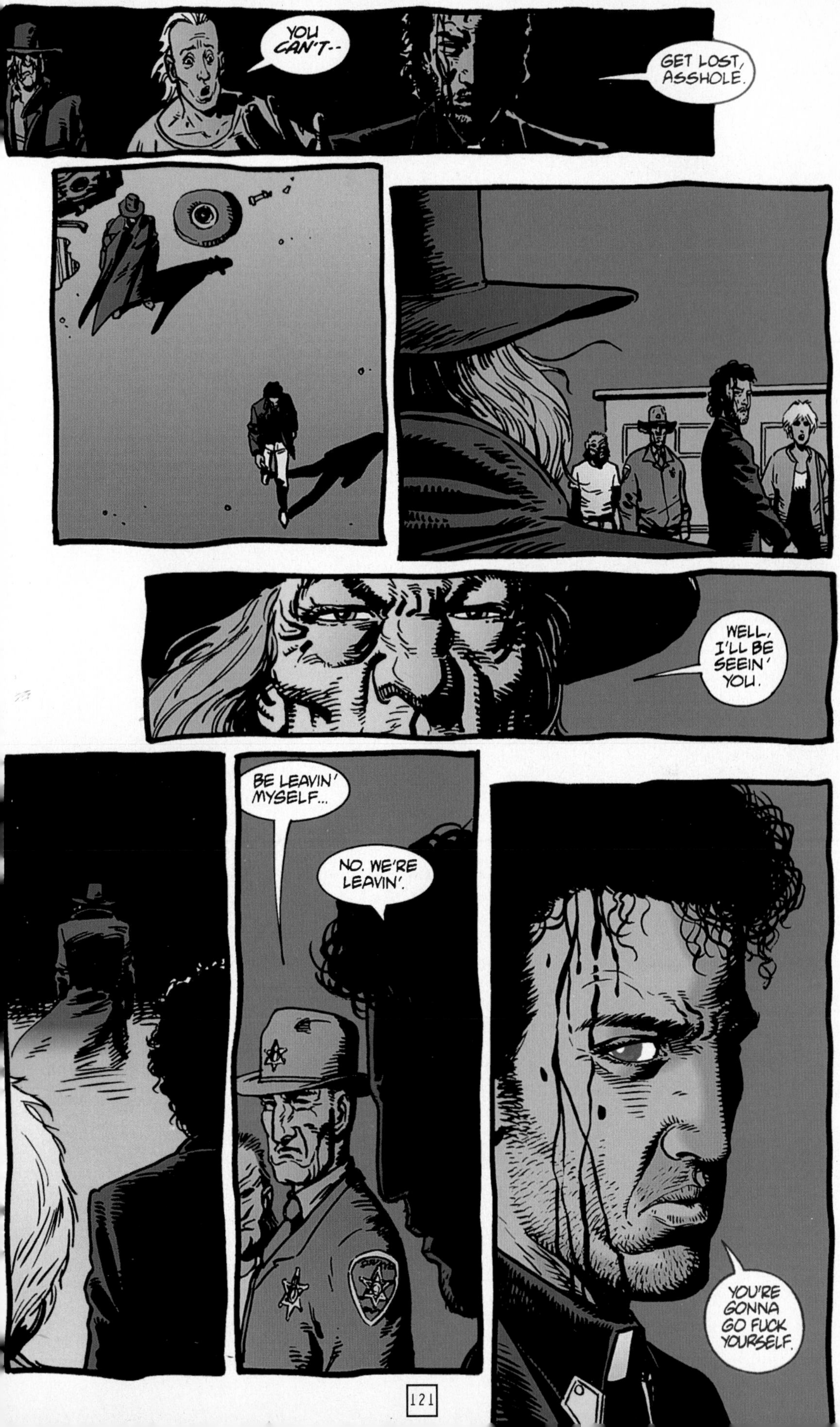
YOU CAN'T--
GET LOST, ASSHOLE.
WELL, I'LL BE SEEIN' YOU.
BE LEAVIN' MYSELF...
NO. WE'RE LEAVIN'.
YOU'RE GONNA GO FUCK YOURSELF.

FIGURE WE MISSED ALL THE ACTION HERE, TOO.

IF IT WAS ANYTHING LIKE THE ACTION AT THE TEN-TEN, I'M NOT TOO UNHAPPY ABOUT THAT.

YOU KNOW, EVER SINCE I CROSSED THE MASON-DIXON I'VE BEEN DRINKING UNIFORMLY SHITTY COFFEE. OR DID YOU GET ALL EXCITED AGAIN?

BLOW ME. HEY, THIS OUGHTA BE TOUCHING...

UH MUH DUH GUHBUH UKAH?*

*IS MY DAD GONNA BE OKAY?

WELL, UH--

LOOK, NO OFFENSE, BUT IS THERE ANY CHANCE YOU COULD FACE THE OTHER WAY WHILE I'M TALKING TO YOU? YOUR FACE IS MAKING ME NAUSEOUS, IS ALL.

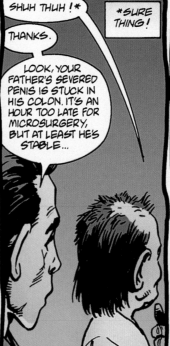

SHUH THUH!*

*SURE THING!

THANKS.

LOOK, YOUR FATHER'S SEVERED PENIS IS STUCK IN HIS COLON. IT'S AN HOUR TOO LATE FOR MICROSURGERY, BUT AT LEAST HE'S STABLE...

WE'RE TAKING HIM TO THE HOSPITAL NOW--

S...SON...?

DUHH!*

*DAD!

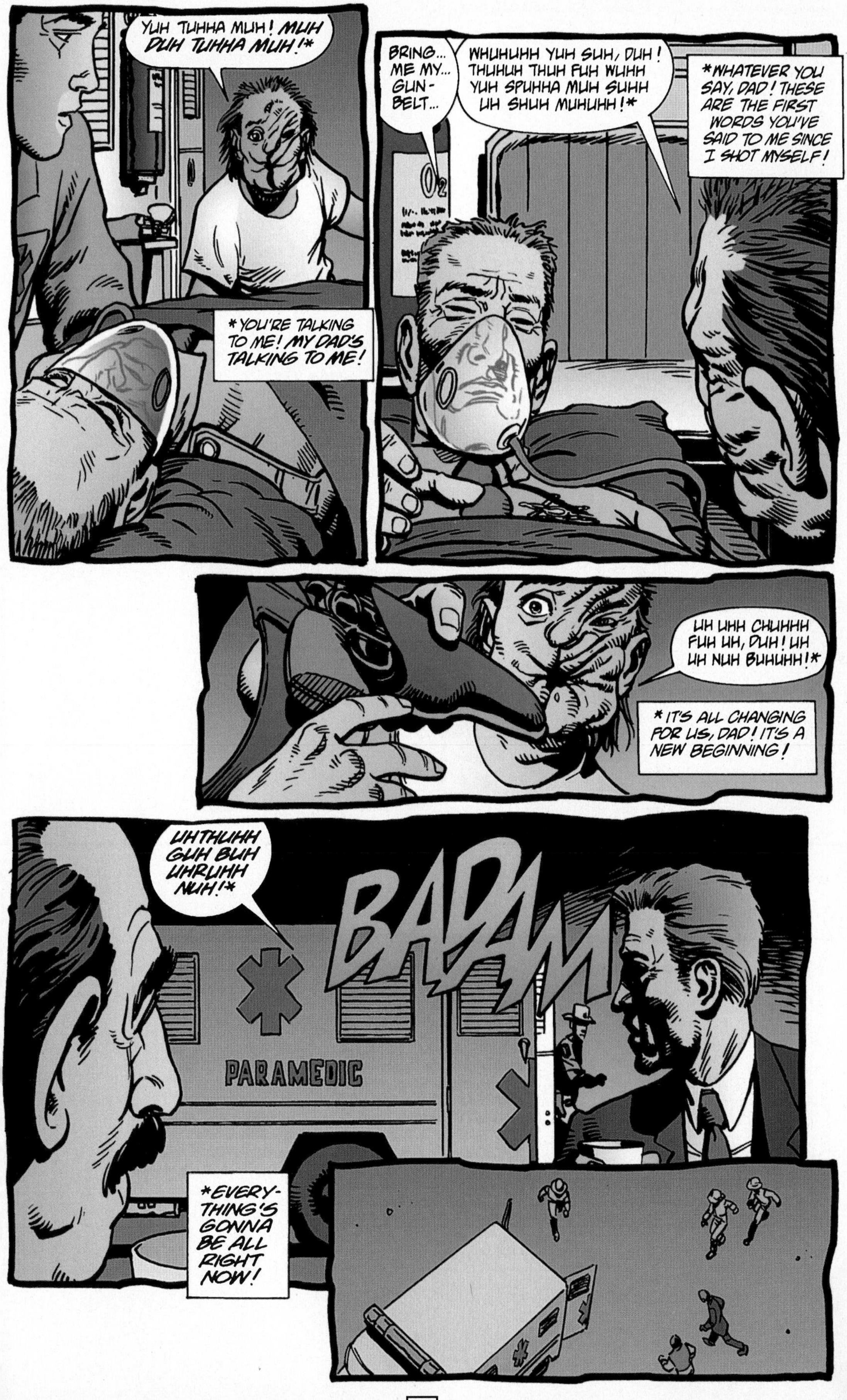
YUH TUHHA MUH! MUH DUH TUHHA MUH!*
*YOU'RE TALKING TO ME! MY DAD'S TALKING TO ME!
BRING... ME MY... GUN-BELT...
WHUHUHH YUH SUH, DUH! THUHUH THUH FUH WUHH YUH SPUHHA MUH SUHH UH SHUH MUHUHH!*
*WHATEVER YOU SAY, DAD! THESE ARE THE FIRST WORDS YOU'VE SAID TO ME SINCE I SHOT MYSELF!
O_2
UH UHH CHUHHH FUH UH, DUH! UH UH NUH BUHUHH!*
*IT'S ALL CHANGING FOR US, DAD! IT'S A NEW BEGINNING!
UHTHUHH GUH BUH UHRUHH NUH!*
BADAM
PARAMEDIC
*EVERY-THING'S GONNA BE ALL RIGHT NOW!

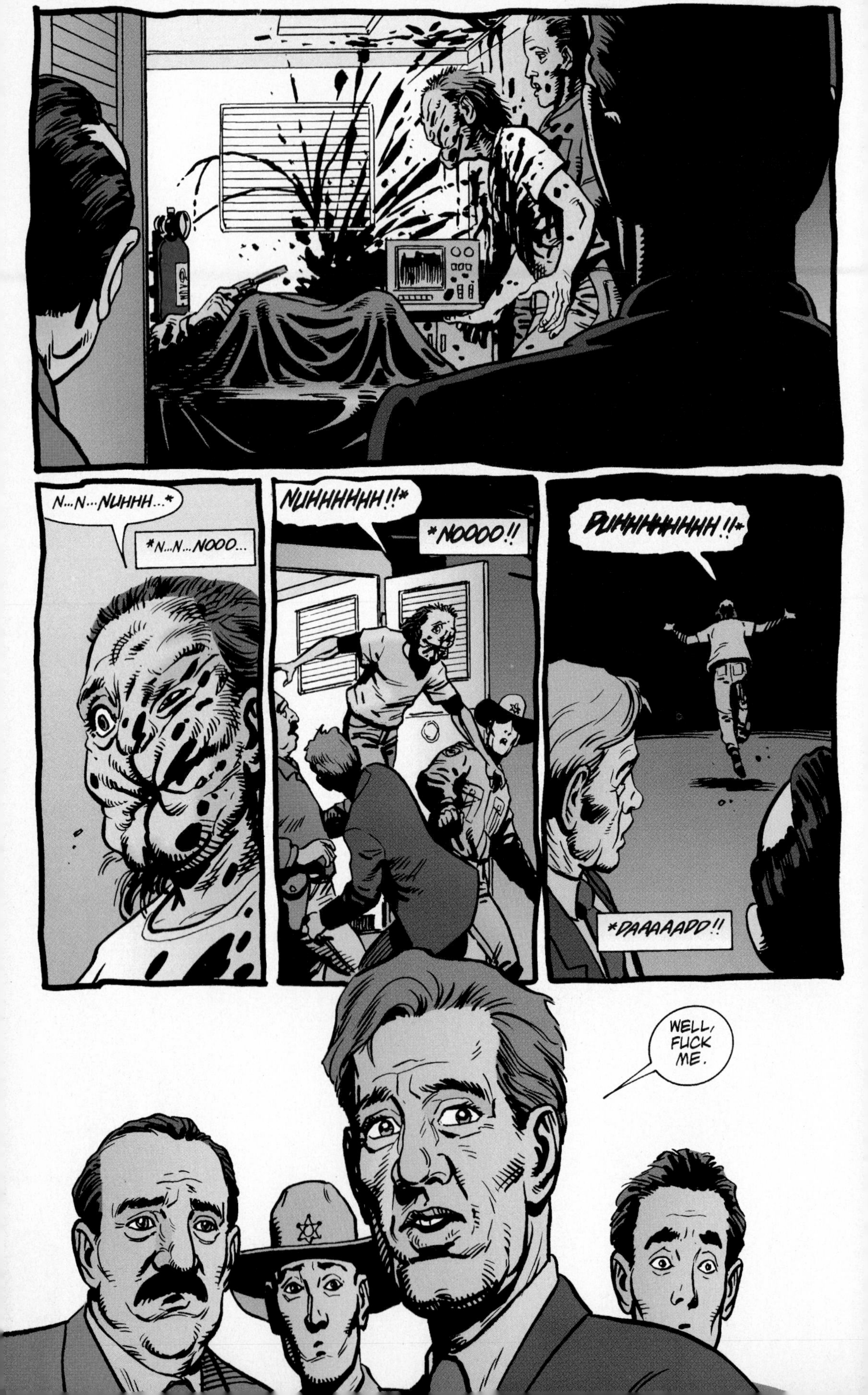
N...N...NUHHH...*
*N...N...NOOO...
NUHHHHHH!!*
*NOOOO!!
DUHHHHHHHH!!*
*DAAAAADD!!
WELL, FUCK ME.

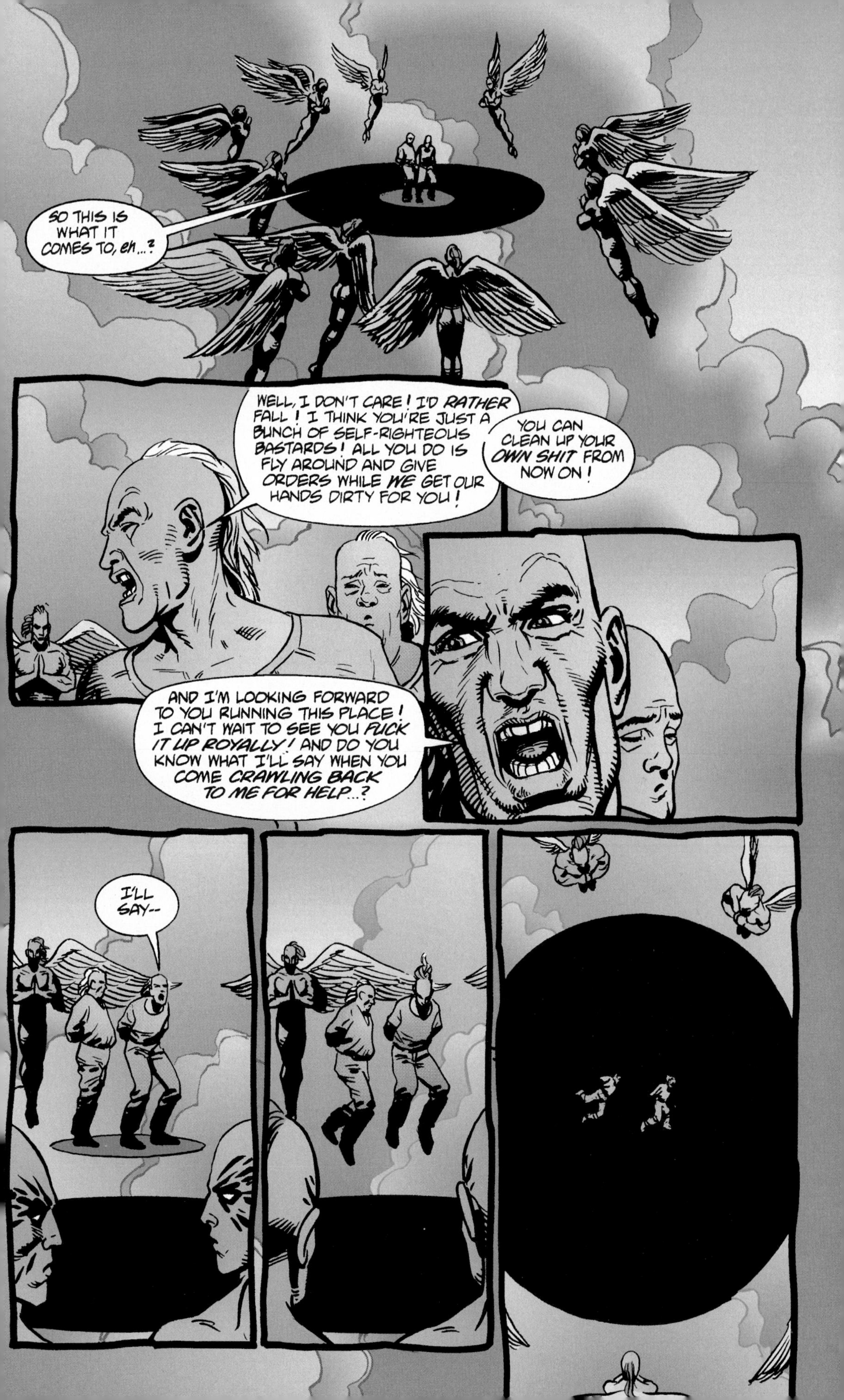

SO THIS IS WHAT IT COMES TO, eh...?
WELL, I DON'T CARE! I'D RATHER FALL! I THINK YOU'RE JUST A BUNCH OF SELF-RIGHTEOUS BASTARDS! ALL YOU DO IS FLY AROUND AND GIVE ORDERS WHILE WE GET OUR HANDS DIRTY FOR YOU!
YOU CAN CLEAN UP YOUR OWN SHIT FROM NOW ON!
AND I'M LOOKING FORWARD TO YOU RUNNING THIS PLACE! I CAN'T WAIT TO SEE YOU FUCK IT UP ROYALLY! AND DO YOU KNOW WHAT I'LL SAY WHEN YOU COME CRAWLING BACK TO ME FOR HELP...?
I'LL SAY--

HINTS

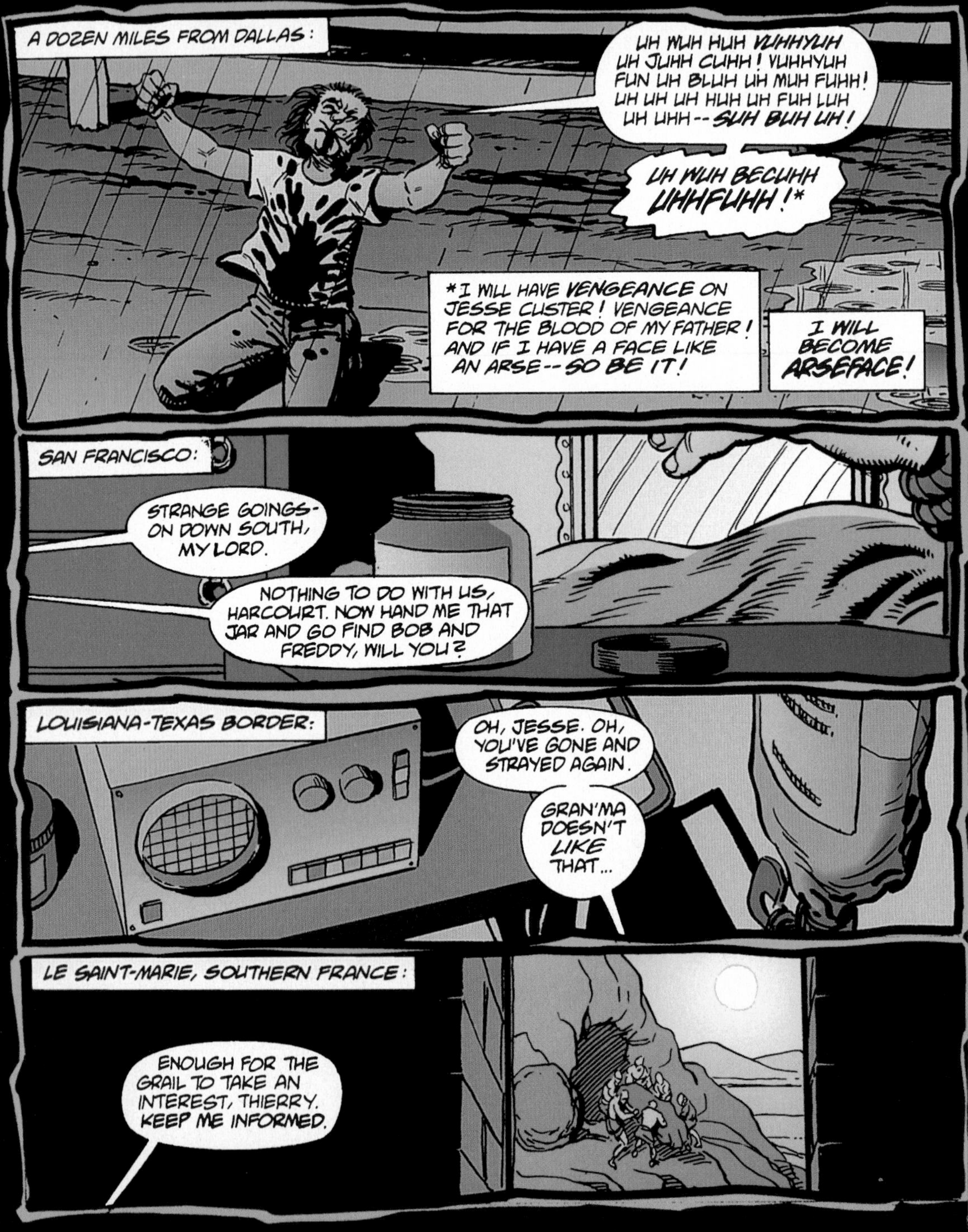
A DOZEN MILES FROM DALLAS:
UH WUH HUH VUHHYUH UH JUHH CUHH! VUHHYUH FUN UH BLUH UH MUH FUHH! UH UH UH HUH UH FUH LUH UH UHH-- SUH BUH UH!
UH WUH BECUHH UHHFUHH!*
*I WILL HAVE VENGEANCE ON JESSE CUSTER! VENGEANCE FOR THE BLOOD OF MY FATHER! AND IF I HAVE A FACE LIKE AN ARSE-- SO BE IT!
I WILL BECOME ARSEFACE!
SAN FRANCISCO:
STRANGE GOINGS-ON DOWN SOUTH, MY LORD.
NOTHING TO DO WITH US, HARCOURT. NOW HAND ME THAT JAR AND GO FIND BOB AND FREDDY, WILL YOU?
LOUISIANA-TEXAS BORDER:
OH, JESSE. OH, YOU'VE GONE AND STRAYED AGAIN.
GRAN'MA DOESN'T LIKE THAT...
LE SAINT-MARIE, SOUTHERN FRANCE:
ENOUGH FOR THE GRAIL TO TAKE AN INTEREST, THIERRY. KEEP ME INFORMED.

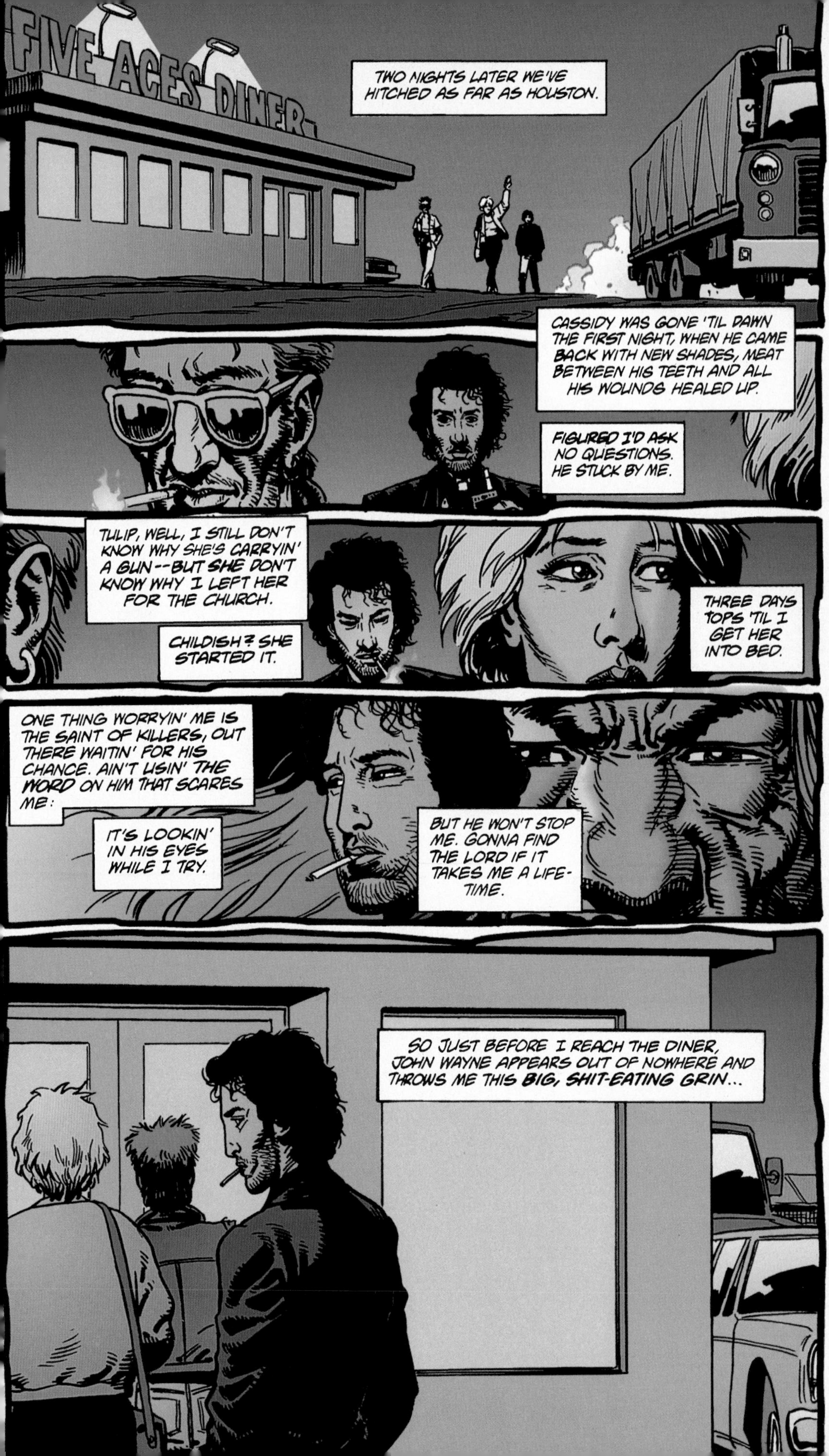
FIVE ACES DINER
TWO NIGHTS LATER WE'VE HITCHED AS FAR AS HOUSTON.
CASSIDY WAS GONE 'TIL DAWN THE FIRST NIGHT, WHEN HE CAME BACK WITH NEW SHADES, MEAT BETWEEN HIS TEETH AND ALL HIS WOUNDS HEALED UP.
FIGURED I'D ASK NO QUESTIONS. HE STUCK BY ME.
TULIP, WELL, I STILL DON'T KNOW WHY SHE'S CARRYIN' A GUN--BUT SHE DON'T KNOW WHY I LEFT HER FOR THE CHURCH.
CHILDISH? SHE STARTED IT.
THREE DAYS TOPS 'TIL I GET HER INTO BED.
ONE THING WORRYIN' ME IS THE SAINT OF KILLERS, OUT THERE WAITIN' FOR HIS CHANCE. AIN'T USIN' THE WORD ON HIM THAT SCARES ME:
IT'S LOOKIN' IN HIS EYES WHILE I TRY.
BUT HE WON'T STOP ME. GONNA FIND THE LORD IF IT TAKES ME A LIFE-TIME.
SO JUST BEFORE I REACH THE DINER, JOHN WAYNE APPEARS OUT OF NOWHERE AND THROWS ME THIS BIG, SHIT-EATING GRIN...

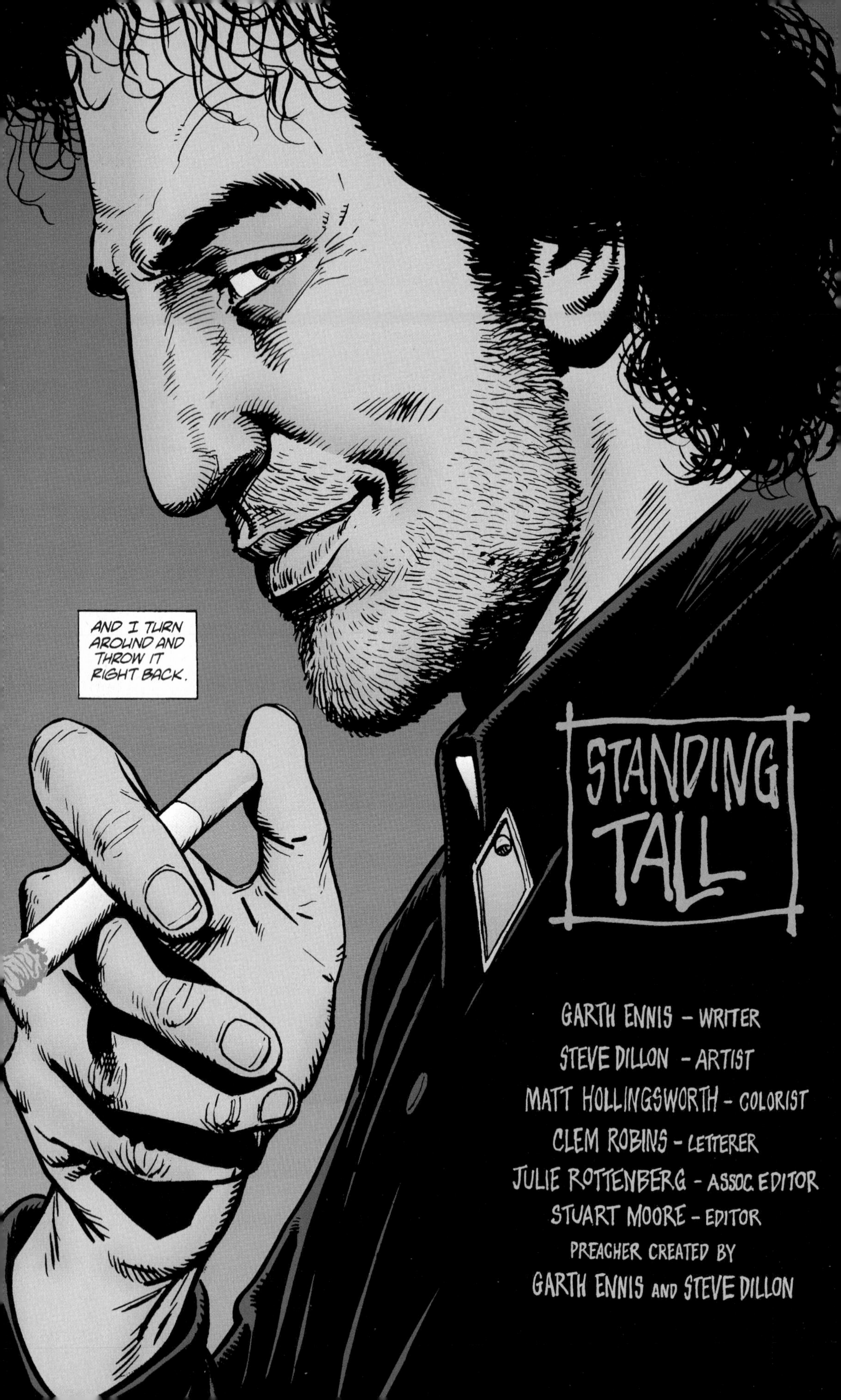
AND I TURN AROUND AND THROW IT RIGHT BACK.
STANDING TALL
GARTH ENNIS - WRITER
STEVE DILLON - ARTIST
MATT HOLLINGSWORTH - COLORIST
CLEM ROBINS - LETTERER
JULIE ROTTENBERG - ASSOC. EDITOR
STUART MOORE - EDITOR
PREACHER CREATED BY
GARTH ENNIS AND STEVE DILLON

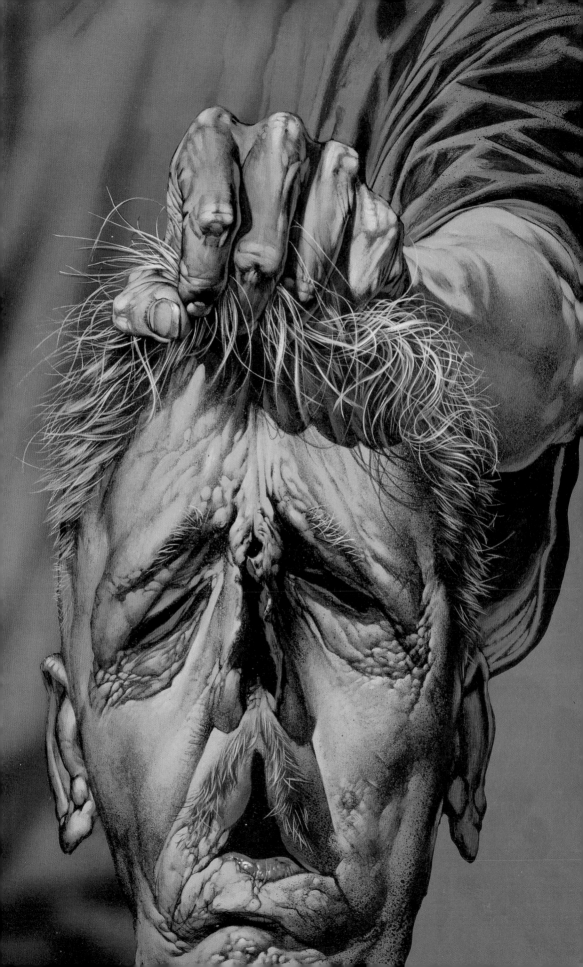

"Standin' up here, view like this...
you get a feelin' like you could do anything."

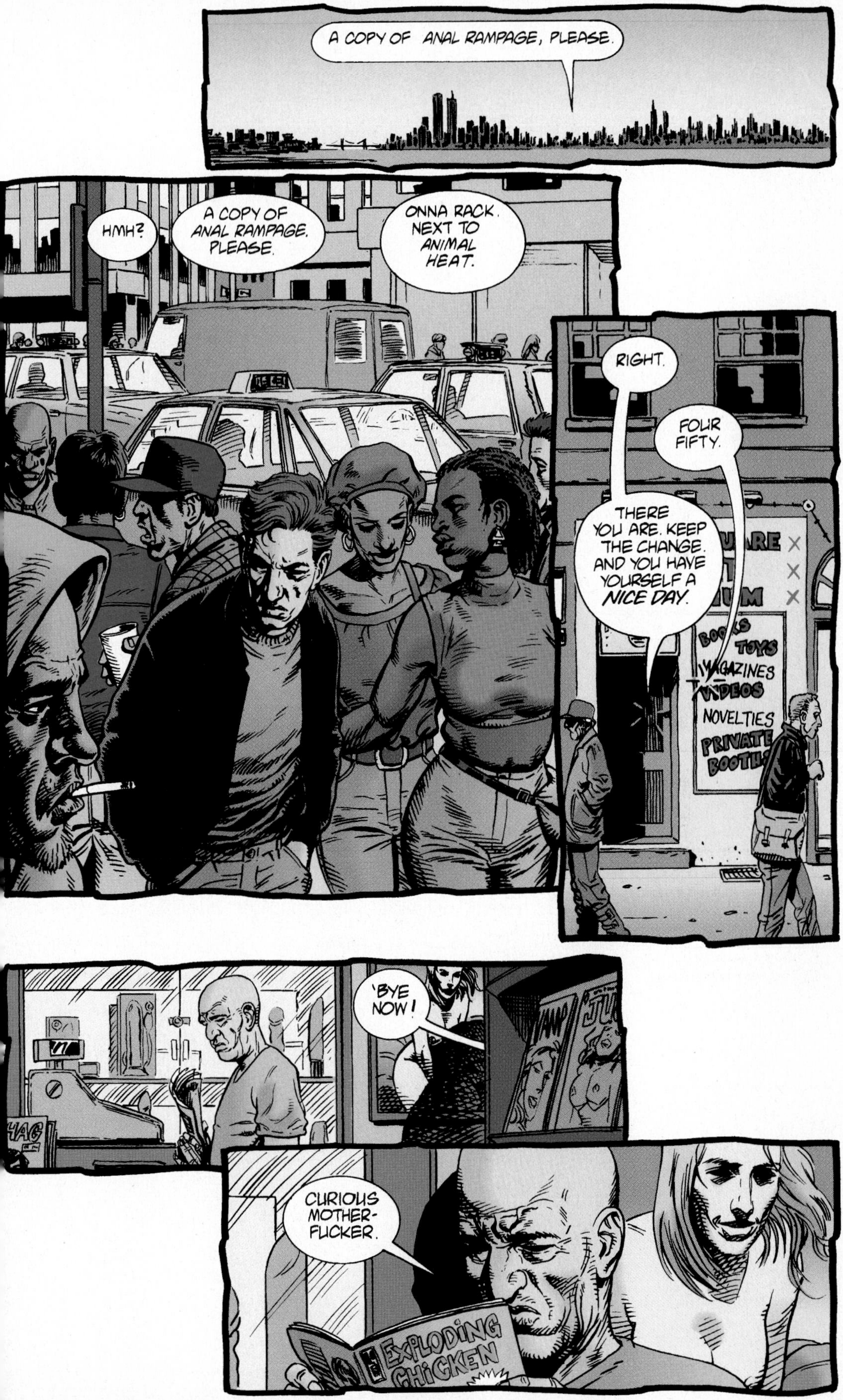
A COPY OF ANAL RAMPAGE, PLEASE.
HMH?
A COPY OF ANAL RAMPAGE. PLEASE.
ONNA RACK. NEXT TO ANIMAL HEAT.
RIGHT.
FOUR FIFTY.
THERE YOU ARE. KEEP THE CHANGE. AND YOU HAVE YOURSELF A NICE DAY.
BOOKS
TOYS
MAGAZINES
VIDEOS
NOVELTIES
PRIVATE BOOTHS
'BYE NOW!
CURIOUS MOTHER-FUCKER.
EXPLODING CHICKEN

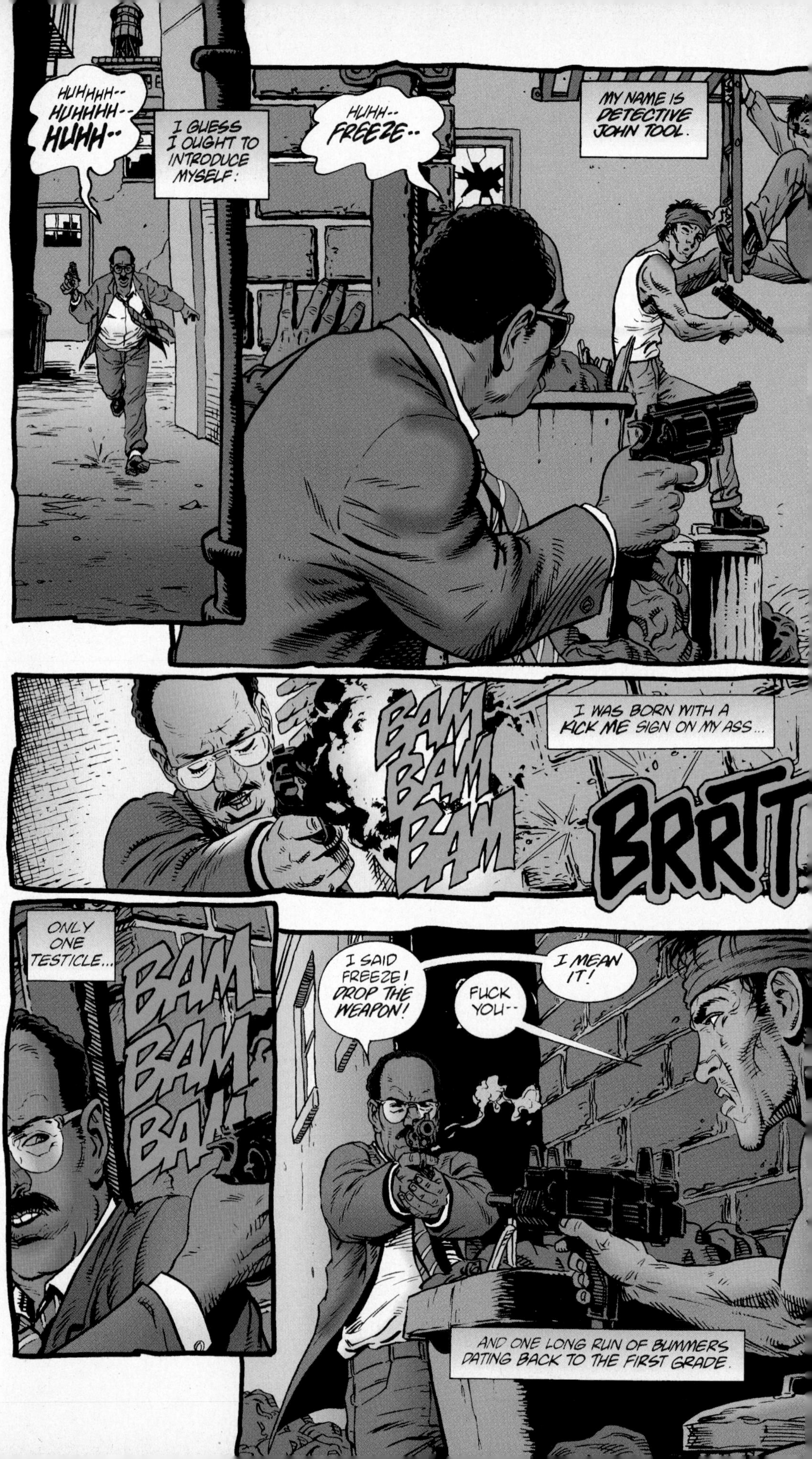
HUHHHH--
HUHHHH--
HUHH--
I GUESS I OUGHT TO INTRODUCE MYSELF:
HUHH--
FREEZE--
MY NAME IS DETECTIVE JOHN TOOL.
BAM BAM BAM
I WAS BORN WITH A KICK ME SIGN ON MY ASS...
BRRTT
ONLY ONE TESTICLE...
BAM BAM BA
I SAID FREEZE! DROP THE WEAPON!
I MEAN IT!
FUCK YOU--
AND ONE LONG RUN OF BUMMERS DATING BACK TO THE FIRST GRADE.

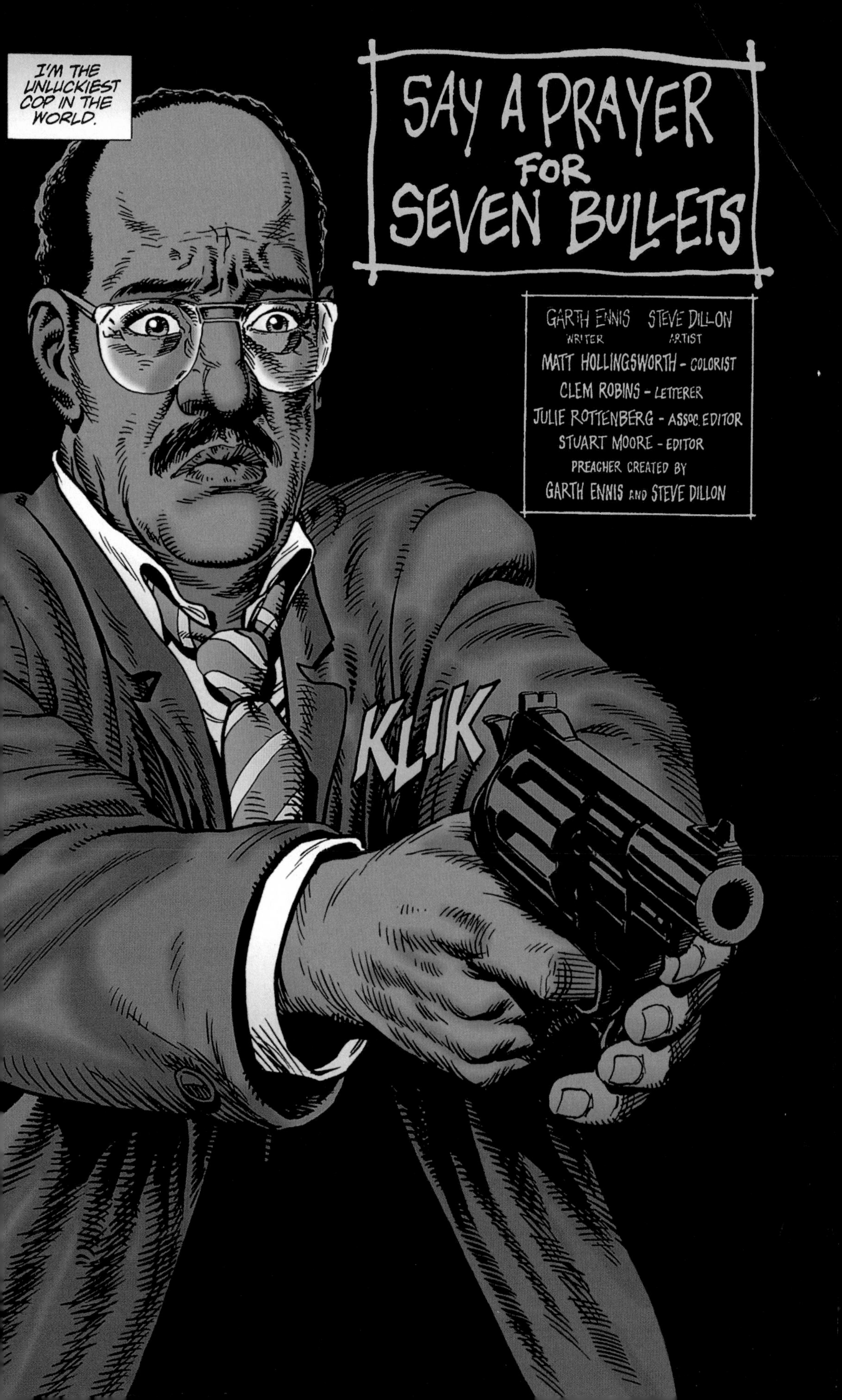

I'M THE UNLUCKIEST COP IN THE WORLD.
SAY A PRAYER FOR SEVEN BULLETS
GARTH ENNIS WRITER
STEVE DILLON ARTIST
MATT HOLLINGSWORTH - COLORIST
CLEM ROBINS - LETTERER
JULIE ROTTENBERG - ASSOC. EDITOR
STUART MOORE - EDITOR
PREACHER CREATED BY GARTH ENNIS AND STEVE DILLON
KLIK

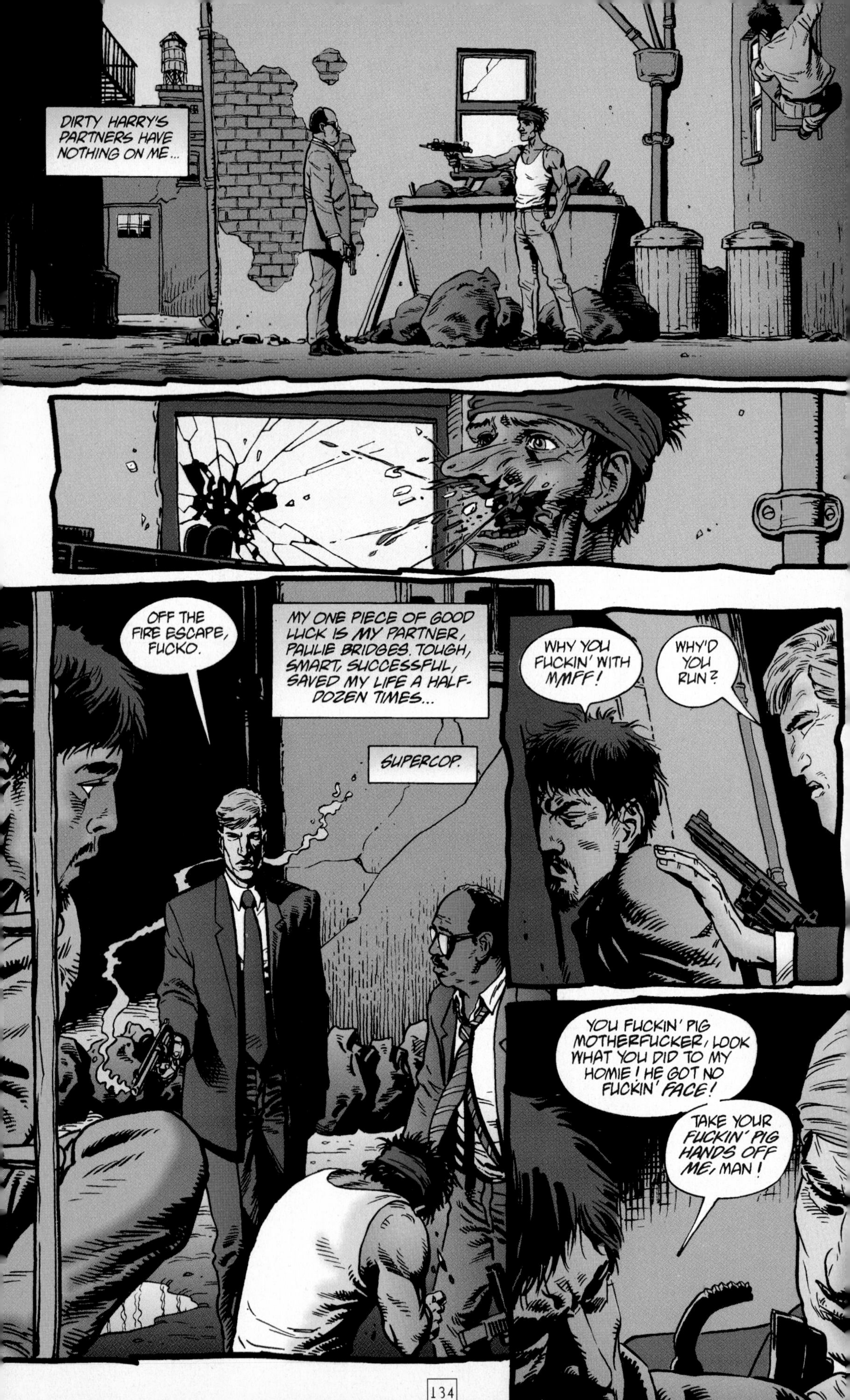
DIRTY HARRY'S PARTNERS HAVE NOTHING ON ME...
OFF THE FIRE ESCAPE, FUCKO.
MY ONE PIECE OF GOOD LUCK IS MY PARTNER, PAULIE BRIDGES. TOUGH, SMART, SUCCESSFUL, SAVED MY LIFE A HALF-DOZEN TIMES...
SUPERCOP.
WHY YOU FUCKIN' WITH M/MFF!
WHY'D YOU RUN?
YOU FUCKIN' PIG MOTHERFUCKER, LOOK WHAT YOU DID TO MY HOMIE! HE GOT NO FUCKIN' FACE!
TAKE YOUR FUCKIN' PIG HANDS OFF ME, MAN!

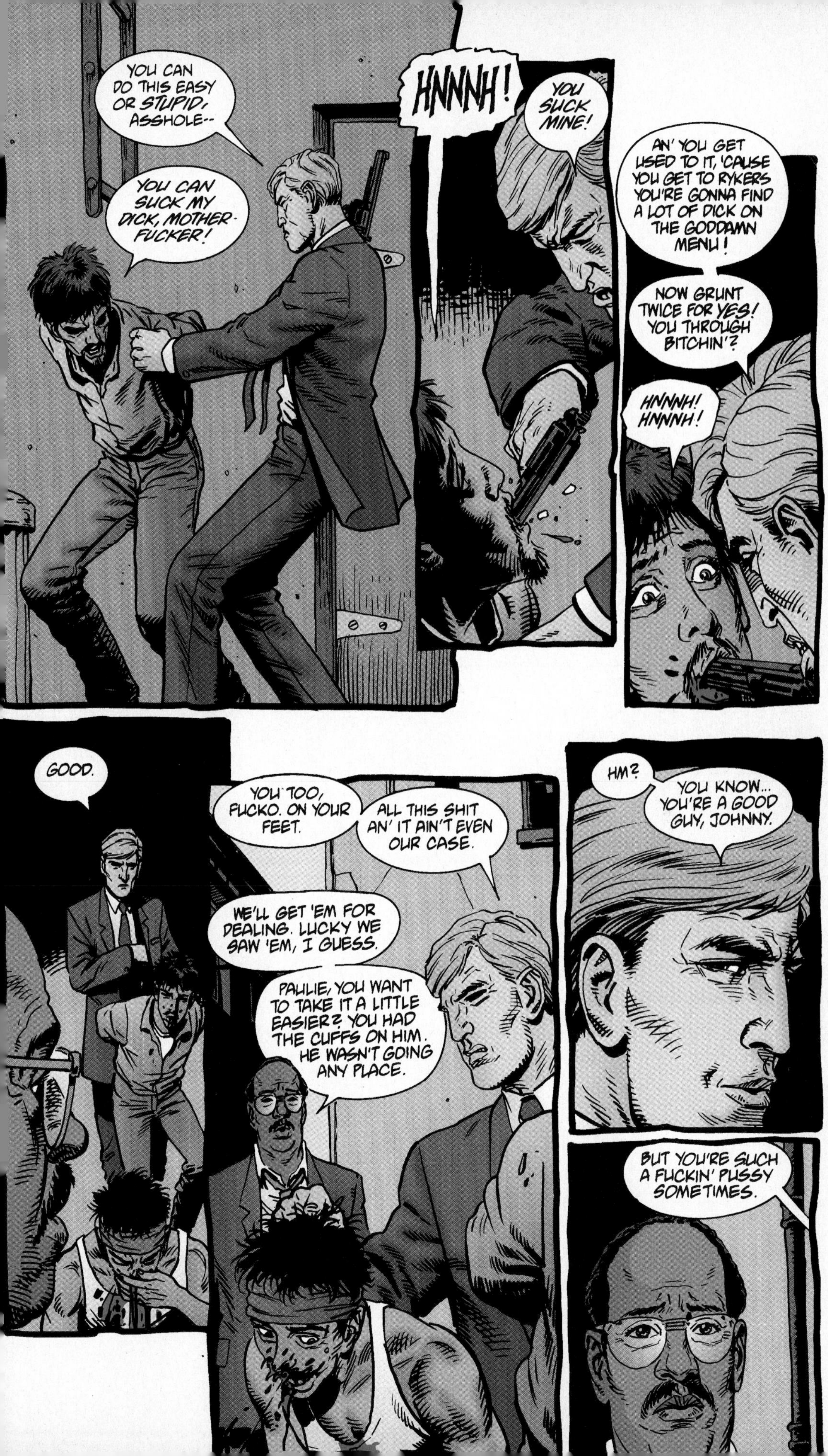
YOU CAN DO THIS EASY OR STUPID, ASSHOLE--
YOU CAN SUCK MY DICK, MOTHER-FUCKER!
HNNNH!
YOU SUCK MINE!
AN' YOU GET USED TO IT, 'CAUSE YOU GET TO RYKERS YOU'RE GONNA FIND A LOT OF DICK ON THE GODDAMN MENU!
NOW GRUNT TWICE FOR YES! YOU THROUGH BITCHIN'?
HNNNH! HNNNH!
GOOD.
YOU TOO, FUCKO. ON YOUR FEET.
ALL THIS SHIT AN' IT AIN'T EVEN OUR CASE.
WE'LL GET 'EM FOR DEALING. LUCKY WE SAW 'EM, I GUESS.
PAULIE, YOU WANT TO TAKE IT A LITTLE EASIER? YOU HAD THE CUFFS ON HIM. HE WASN'T GOING ANY PLACE.
HM?
YOU KNOW... YOU'RE A GOOD GUY, JOHNNY.
BUT YOU'RE SUCH A FUCKIN' PUSSY SOMETIMES.

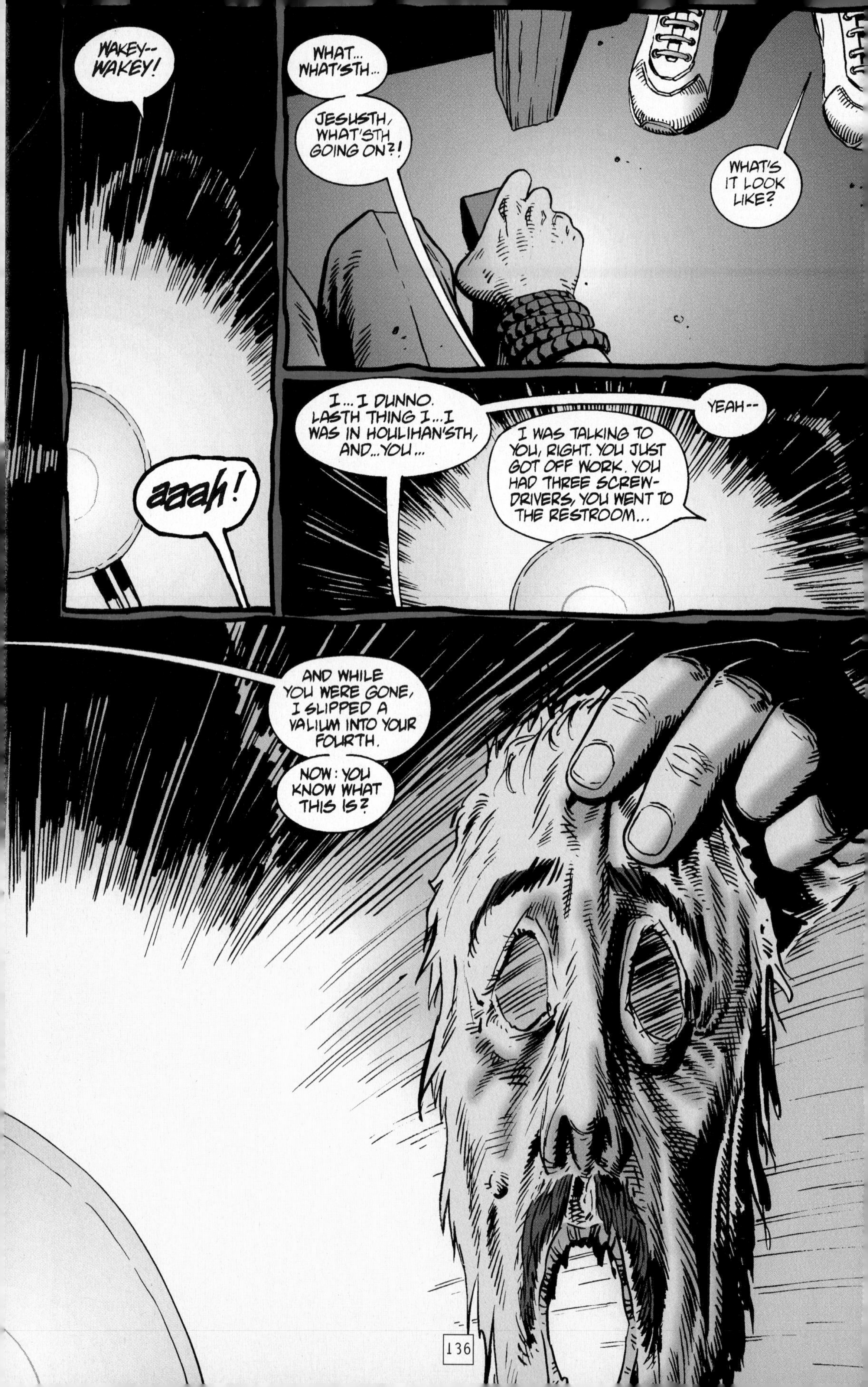
WAKEY--
WAKEY!
WHAT... WHAT'STH...
JESUSTH, WHAT'STH GOING ON?!
WHAT'S IT LOOK LIKE?
aaah!
I... I DUNNO. LASTH THING I...I WAS IN HOULIHAN'STH, AND...YOU...
YEAH--
I WAS TALKING TO YOU, RIGHT. YOU JUST GOT OFF WORK. YOU HAD THREE SCREW-DRIVERS, YOU WENT TO THE RESTROOM...
AND WHILE YOU WERE GONE, I SLIPPED A VALIUM INTO YOUR FOURTH.
NOW: YOU KNOW WHAT THIS IS?

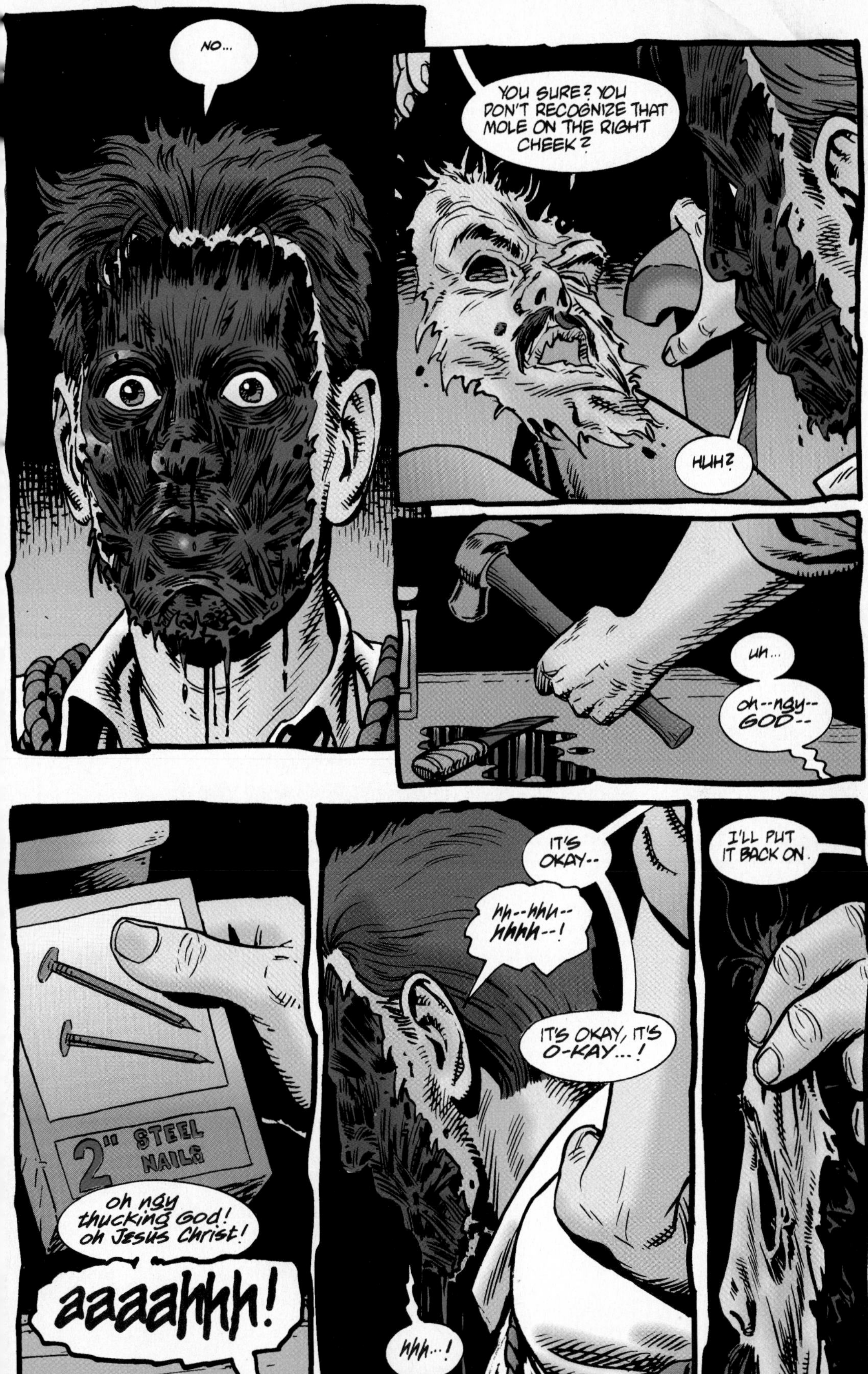
NO...
YOU SURE? YOU DON'T RECOGNIZE THAT MOLE ON THE RIGHT CHEEK?
HUH?
uh...
oh--ngy--GOD--
2" STEEL NAILS
oh ngy thucking God! oh Jesus Christ!
aaaahhh!
IT'S OKAY--
hh--hhh--hhhh--!
IT'S OKAY, IT'S O-KAY...!
hhh...!
I'LL PUT IT BACK ON.

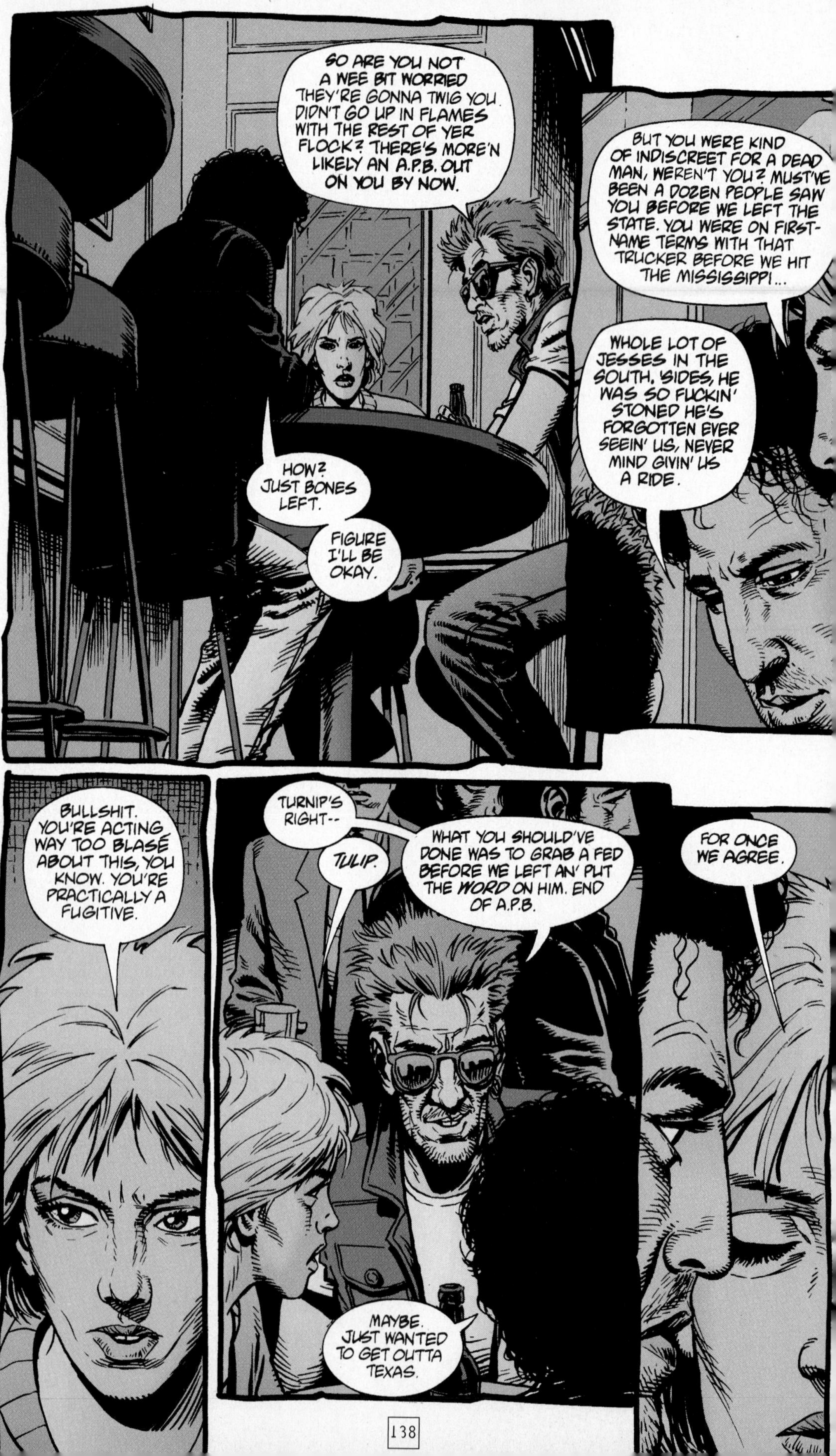

SO ARE YOU NOT A WEE BIT WORRIED THEY'RE GONNA TWIG YOU DIDN'T GO UP IN FLAMES WITH THE REST OF YER FLOCK? THERE'S MORE'N LIKELY AN A.P.B. OUT ON YOU BY NOW.
HOW? JUST BONES LEFT.
FIGURE I'LL BE OKAY.
BUT YOU WERE KIND OF INDISCREET FOR A DEAD MAN, WEREN'T YOU? MUST'VE BEEN A DOZEN PEOPLE SAW YOU BEFORE WE LEFT THE STATE. YOU WERE ON FIRST-NAME TERMS WITH THAT TRUCKER BEFORE WE HIT THE MISSISSIPPI...
WHOLE LOT OF JESSES IN THE SOUTH. 'SIDES, HE WAS SO FUCKIN' STONED HE'S FORGOTTEN EVER SEEIN' US, NEVER MIND GIVIN' US A RIDE.
BULLSHIT. YOU'RE ACTING WAY TOO BLASÉ ABOUT THIS, YOU KNOW. YOU'RE PRACTICALLY A FUGITIVE.
TURNIP'S RIGHT--
TULIP.
WHAT YOU SHOULD'VE DONE WAS TO GRAB A FED BEFORE WE LEFT AN' PUT THE WORD ON HIM. END OF A.P.B.
FOR ONCE WE AGREE.
MAYBE. JUST WANTED TO GET OUTTA TEXAS.

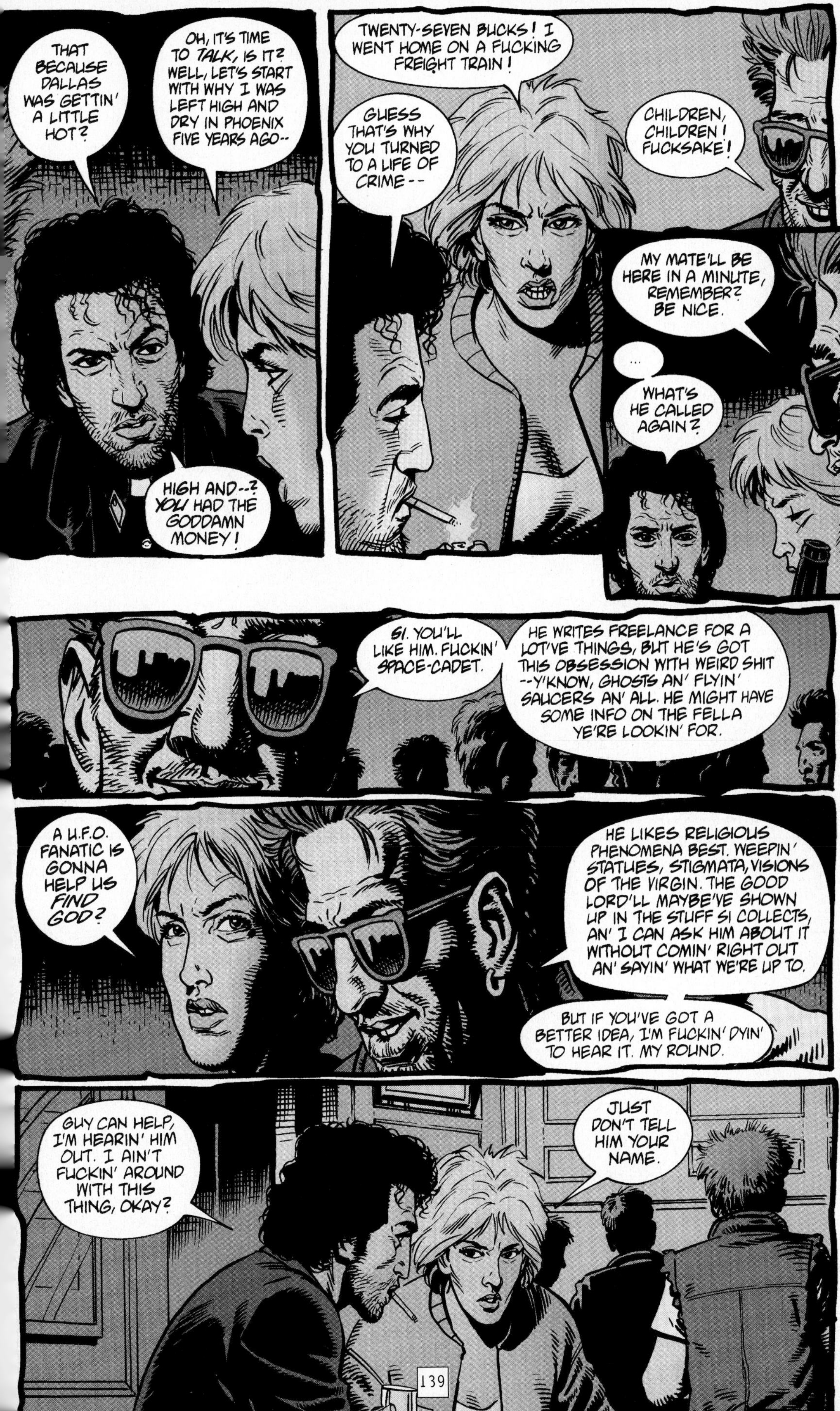
THAT BECAUSE DALLAS WAS GETTIN' A LITTLE HOT?
OH, IT'S TIME TO TALK, IS IT? WELL, LET'S START WITH WHY I WAS LEFT HIGH AND DRY IN PHOENIX FIVE YEARS AGO--
HIGH AND--? YOU HAD THE GODDAMN MONEY!
TWENTY-SEVEN BUCKS! I WENT HOME ON A FUCKING FREIGHT TRAIN!
GUESS THAT'S WHY YOU TURNED TO A LIFE OF CRIME--
CHILDREN, CHILDREN! FUCKSAKE!
MY MATE'LL BE HERE IN A MINUTE, REMEMBER? BE NICE.
...
WHAT'S HE CALLED AGAIN?
SI. YOU'LL LIKE HIM. FUCKIN' SPACE-CADET.
HE WRITES FREELANCE FOR A LOT'VE THINGS, BUT HE'S GOT THIS OBSESSION WITH WEIRD SHIT --Y'KNOW, GHOSTS AN' FLYIN' SAUCERS AN' ALL. HE MIGHT HAVE SOME INFO ON THE FELLA YE'RE LOOKIN' FOR.
A U.F.O. FANATIC IS GONNA HELP US FIND GOD?
HE LIKES RELIGIOUS PHENOMENA BEST. WEEPIN' STATUES, STIGMATA, VISIONS OF THE VIRGIN. THE GOOD LORD'LL MAYBE'VE SHOWN UP IN THE STUFF SI COLLECTS, AN' I CAN ASK HIM ABOUT IT WITHOUT COMIN' RIGHT OUT AN' SAYIN' WHAT WE'RE UP TO.
BUT IF YOU'VE GOT A BETTER IDEA, I'M FUCKIN' DYIN' TO HEAR IT. MY ROUND.
GUY CAN HELP, I'M HEARIN' HIM OUT. I AIN'T FUCKIN' AROUND WITH THIS THING, OKAY?
JUST DON'T TELL HIM YOUR NAME.

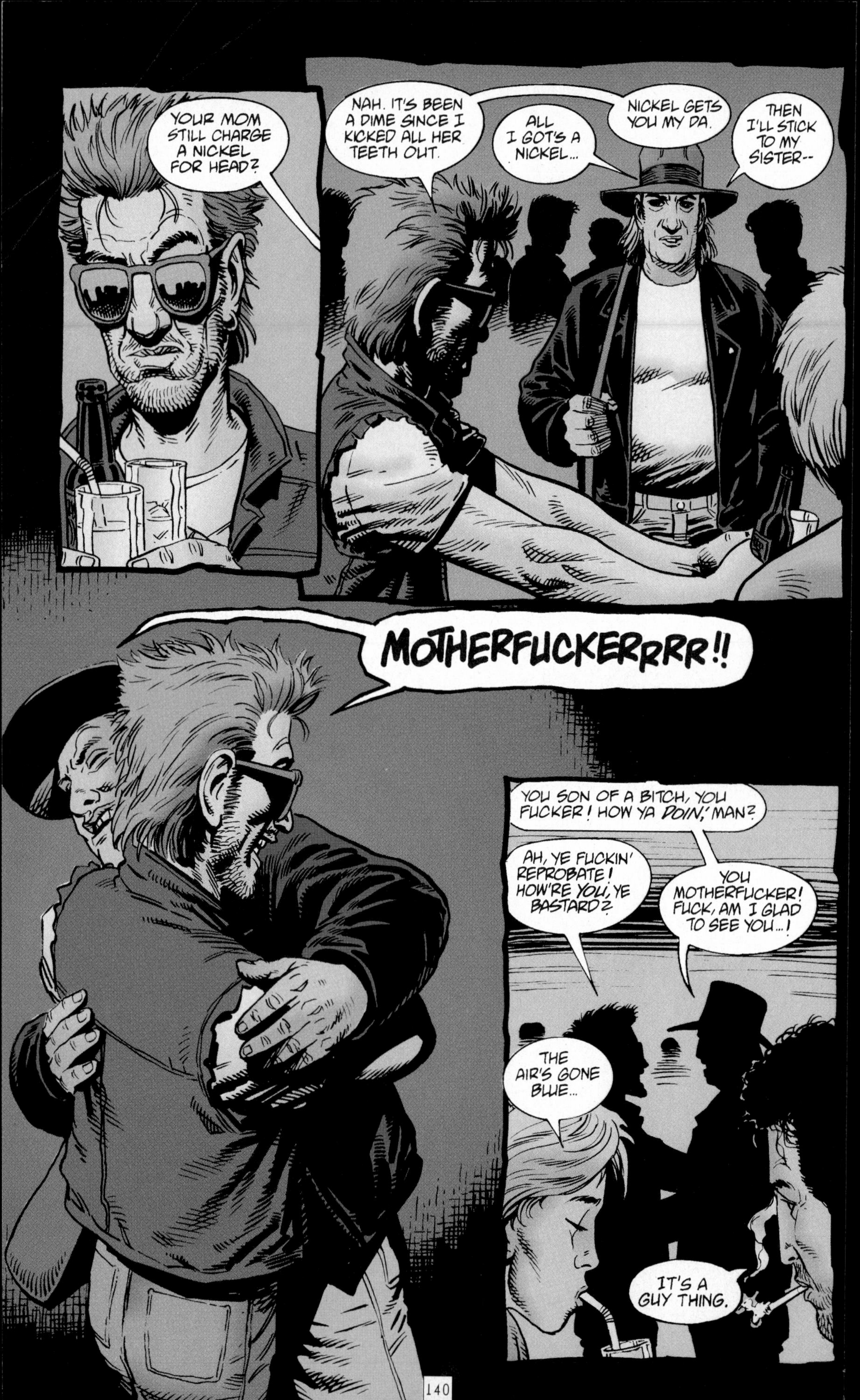
YOUR MOM STILL CHARGE A NICKEL FOR HEAD?
NAH. IT'S BEEN A DIME SINCE I KICKED ALL HER TEETH OUT.
ALL I GOT'S A NICKEL...
NICKEL GETS YOU MY DA.
THEN I'LL STICK TO MY SISTER--
MOTHERFUCKERRRR!!
YOU SON OF A BITCH, YOU FUCKER! HOW YA DOIN,' MAN?
AH, YE FUCKIN' REPROBATE! HOW'RE YOU, YE BASTARD?
YOU MOTHERFUCKER! FUCK, AM I GLAD TO SEE YOU...!
THE AIR'S GONE BLUE...
IT'S A GUY THING.

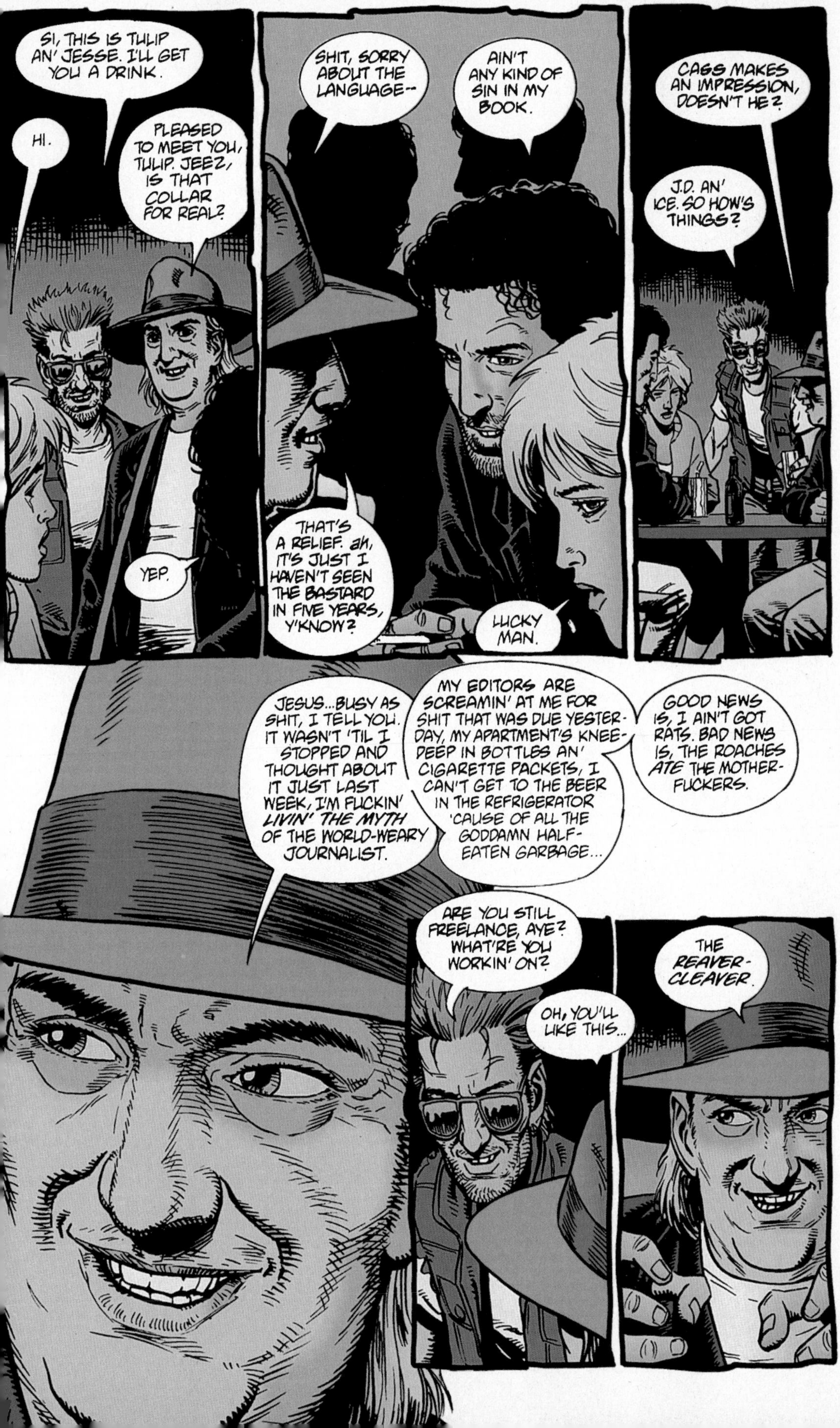

SI, THIS IS TULIP AN' JESSE. I'LL GET YOU A DRINK.
HI.
PLEASED TO MEET YOU, TULIP. JEEZ, IS THAT COLLAR FOR REAL?
YEP.
SHIT, SORRY ABOUT THE LANGUAGE--
AIN'T ANY KIND OF SIN IN MY BOOK.
THAT'S A RELIEF. AH, IT'S JUST I HAVEN'T SEEN THE BASTARD IN FIVE YEARS, Y'KNOW?
LUCKY MAN.
CASS MAKES AN IMPRESSION, DOESN'T HE?
J.D. AN' ICE. SO HOW'S THINGS?
JESUS...BUSY AS SHIT, I TELL YOU. IT WASN'T 'TIL I STOPPED AND THOUGHT ABOUT IT JUST LAST WEEK, I'M FUCKIN' LIVIN' THE MYTH OF THE WORLD-WEARY JOURNALIST.
MY EDITORS ARE SCREAMIN' AT ME FOR SHIT THAT WAS DUE YESTERDAY, MY APARTMENT'S KNEE-DEEP IN BOTTLES AN' CIGARETTE PACKETS, I CAN'T GET TO THE BEER IN THE REFRIGERATOR 'CAUSE OF ALL THE GODDAMN HALF-EATEN GARBAGE...
GOOD NEWS IS, I AIN'T GOT RATS. BAD NEWS IS, THE ROACHES ATE THE MOTHERFUCKERS.
ARE YOU STILL FREELANCE, AYE? WHAT'RE YOU WORKIN' ON?
OH, YOU'LL LIKE THIS...
THE REAVER-CLEAVER.

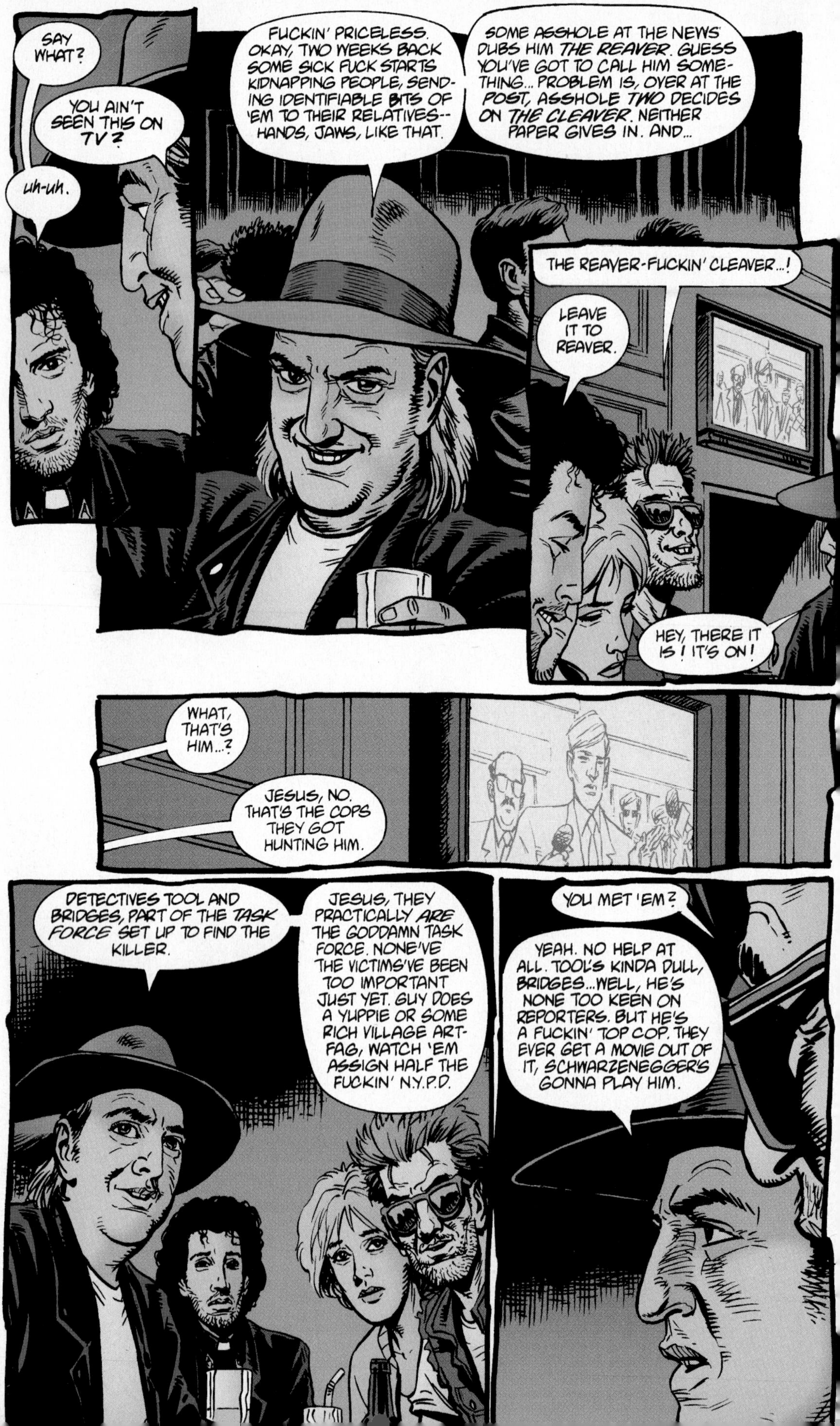
SAY WHAT?
YOU AIN'T SEEN THIS ON TV?
uh-uh.
FUCKIN' PRICELESS. OKAY, TWO WEEKS BACK SOME SICK FUCK STARTS KIDNAPPING PEOPLE, SENDING IDENTIFIABLE BITS OF 'EM TO THEIR RELATIVES-- HANDS, JAWS, LIKE THAT.
SOME ASSHOLE AT THE NEWS DUBS HIM THE REAVER. GUESS YOU'VE GOT TO CALL HIM SOMETHING... PROBLEM IS, OVER AT THE POST, ASSHOLE TWO DECIDES ON THE CLEAVER. NEITHER PAPER GIVES IN. AND...
THE REAVER-FUCKIN' CLEAVER...!
LEAVE IT TO REAVER.
HEY, THERE IT IS! IT'S ON!
WHAT, THAT'S HIM...?
JESUS, NO. THAT'S THE COPS THEY GOT HUNTING HIM.
DETECTIVES TOOL AND BRIDGES, PART OF THE TASK FORCE SET UP TO FIND THE KILLER.
JESUS, THEY PRACTICALLY ARE THE GODDAMN TASK FORCE. NONE'VE THE VICTIMS'VE BEEN TOO IMPORTANT JUST YET. GUY DOES A YUPPIE OR SOME RICH VILLAGE ART-FAG, WATCH 'EM ASSIGN HALF THE FUCKIN' N.Y.P.D.
YOU MET 'EM?
YEAH. NO HELP AT ALL. TOOL'S KINDA DULL, BRIDGES...WELL, HE'S NONE TOO KEEN ON REPORTERS. BUT HE'S A FUCKIN' TOP COP. THEY EVER GET A MOVIE OUT OF IT, SCHWARZENEGGER'S GONNA PLAY HIM.

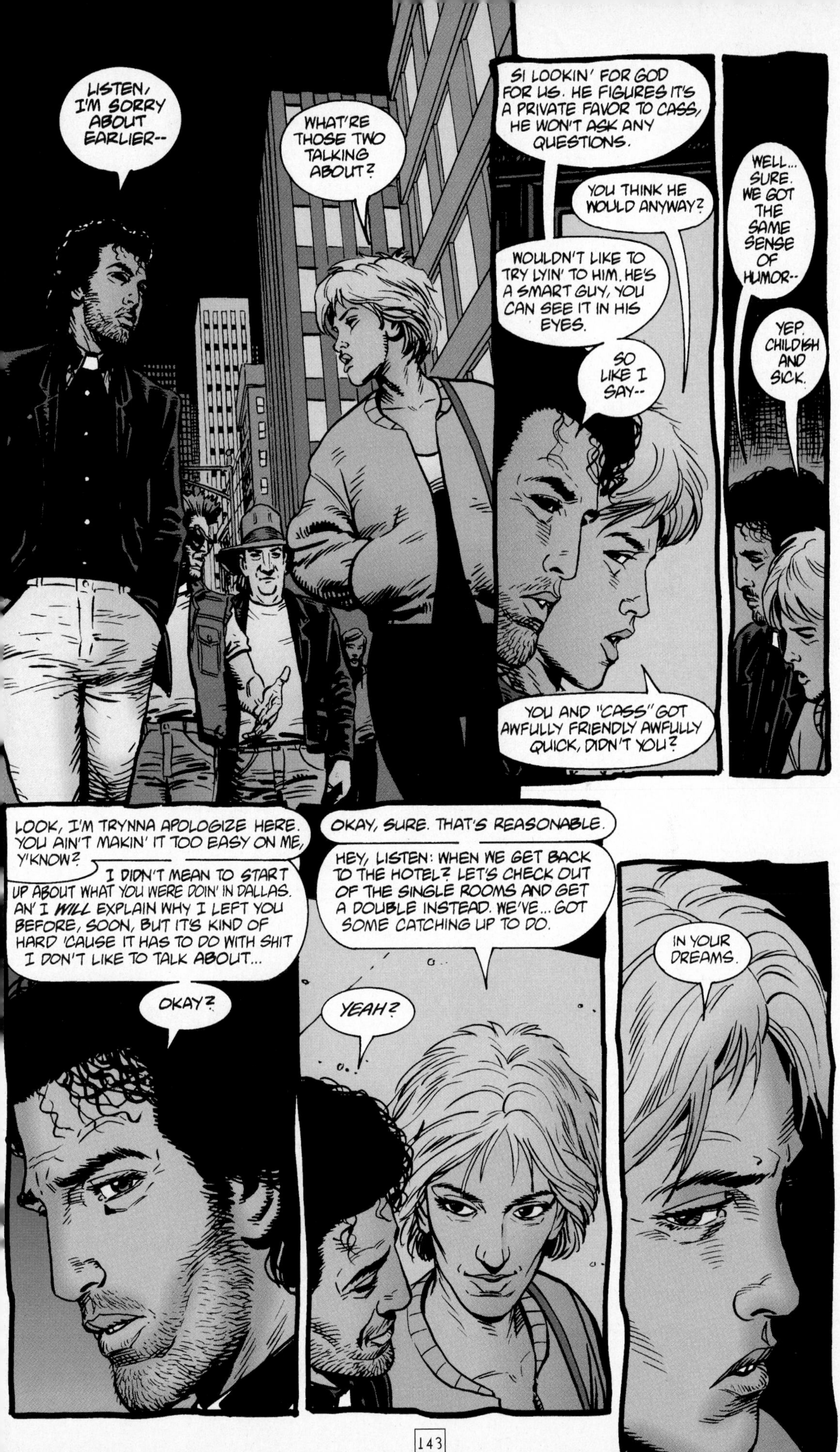

LISTEN, I'M SORRY ABOUT EARLIER--
WHAT'RE THOSE TWO TALKING ABOUT?
SI LOOKIN' FOR GOD FOR US. HE FIGURES IT'S A PRIVATE FAVOR TO CASS, HE WON'T ASK ANY QUESTIONS.
YOU THINK HE WOULD ANYWAY?
WOULDN'T LIKE TO TRY LYIN' TO HIM. HE'S A SMART GUY, YOU CAN SEE IT IN HIS EYES.
SO LIKE I SAY--
YOU AND "CASS" GOT AWFULLY FRIENDLY AWFULLY QUICK, DIDN'T YOU?
WELL... SURE. WE GOT THE SAME SENSE OF HUMOR--
YEP. CHILDISH AND SICK.
LOOK, I'M TRYNNA APOLOGIZE HERE. YOU AIN'T MAKIN' IT TOO EASY ON ME, Y'KNOW?
I DIDN'T MEAN TO START UP ABOUT WHAT YOU WERE DOIN' IN DALLAS. AN' I WILL EXPLAIN WHY I LEFT YOU BEFORE, SOON, BUT IT'S KIND OF HARD 'CAUSE IT HAS TO DO WITH SHIT I DON'T LIKE TO TALK ABOUT...
OKAY?
OKAY, SURE. THAT'S REASONABLE.
HEY, LISTEN: WHEN WE GET BACK TO THE HOTEL? LET'S CHECK OUT OF THE SINGLE ROOMS AND GET A DOUBLE INSTEAD. WE'VE... GOT SOME CATCHING UP TO DO.
YEAH?
IN YOUR DREAMS.

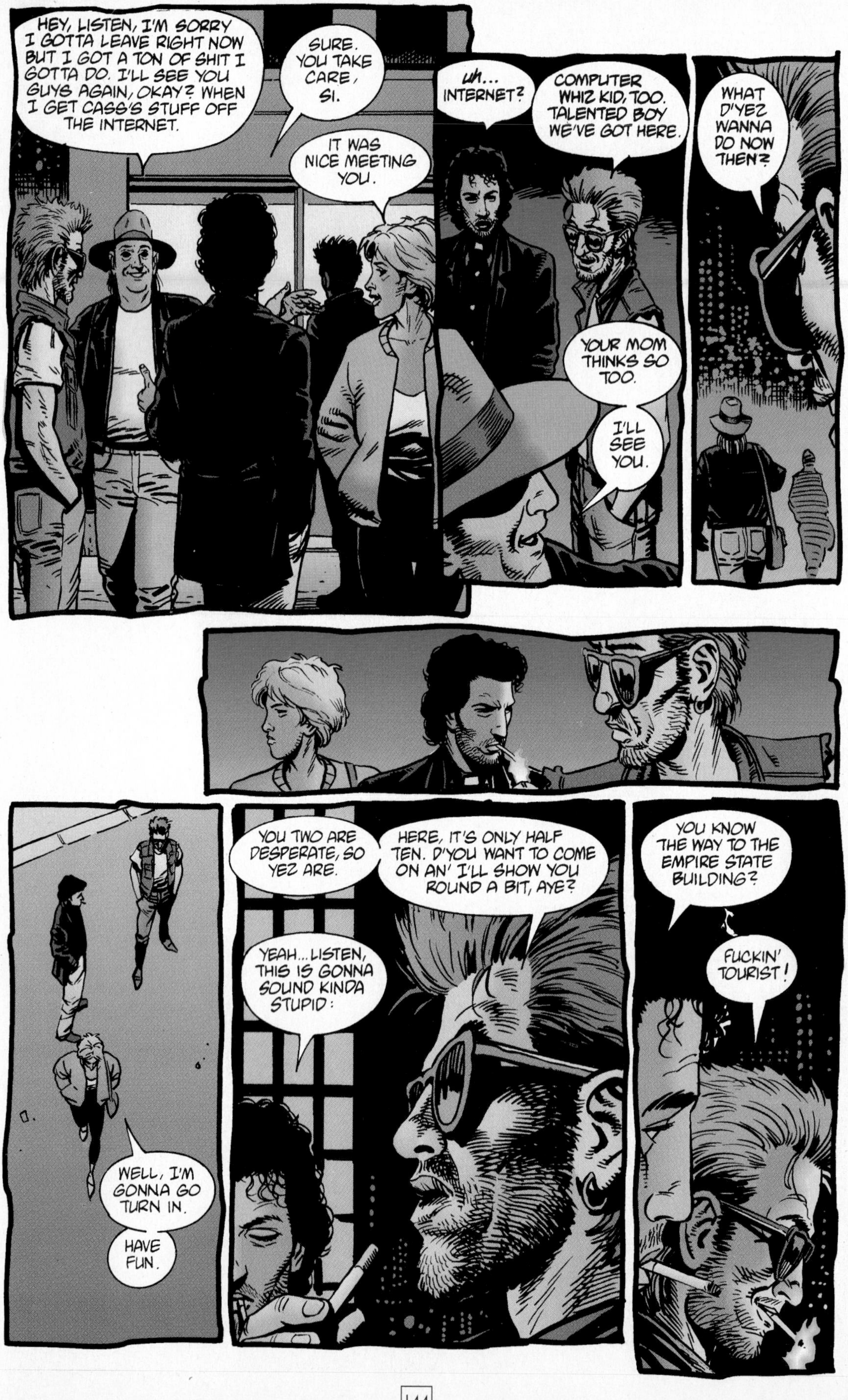
HEY, LISTEN, I'M SORRY I GOTTA LEAVE RIGHT NOW BUT I GOT A TON OF SHIT I GOTTA DO. I'LL SEE YOU GUYS AGAIN, OKAY? WHEN I GET CASS'S STUFF OFF THE INTERNET.
SURE. YOU TAKE CARE, SI.
IT WAS NICE MEETING YOU.
uh... INTERNET?
COMPUTER WHIZ KID, TOO. TALENTED BOY WE'VE GOT HERE.
YOUR MOM THINKS SO TOO.
I'LL SEE YOU.
WHAT D'YEZ WANNA DO NOW THEN?
WELL, I'M GONNA GO TURN IN.
HAVE FUN.
YOU TWO ARE DESPERATE, SO YEZ ARE.
HERE, IT'S ONLY HALF TEN. D'YOU WANT TO COME ON AN' I'LL SHOW YOU ROUND A BIT, AYE?
YEAH... LISTEN, THIS IS GONNA SOUND KINDA STUPID:
YOU KNOW THE WAY TO THE EMPIRE STATE BUILDING?
FUCKIN' TOURIST!

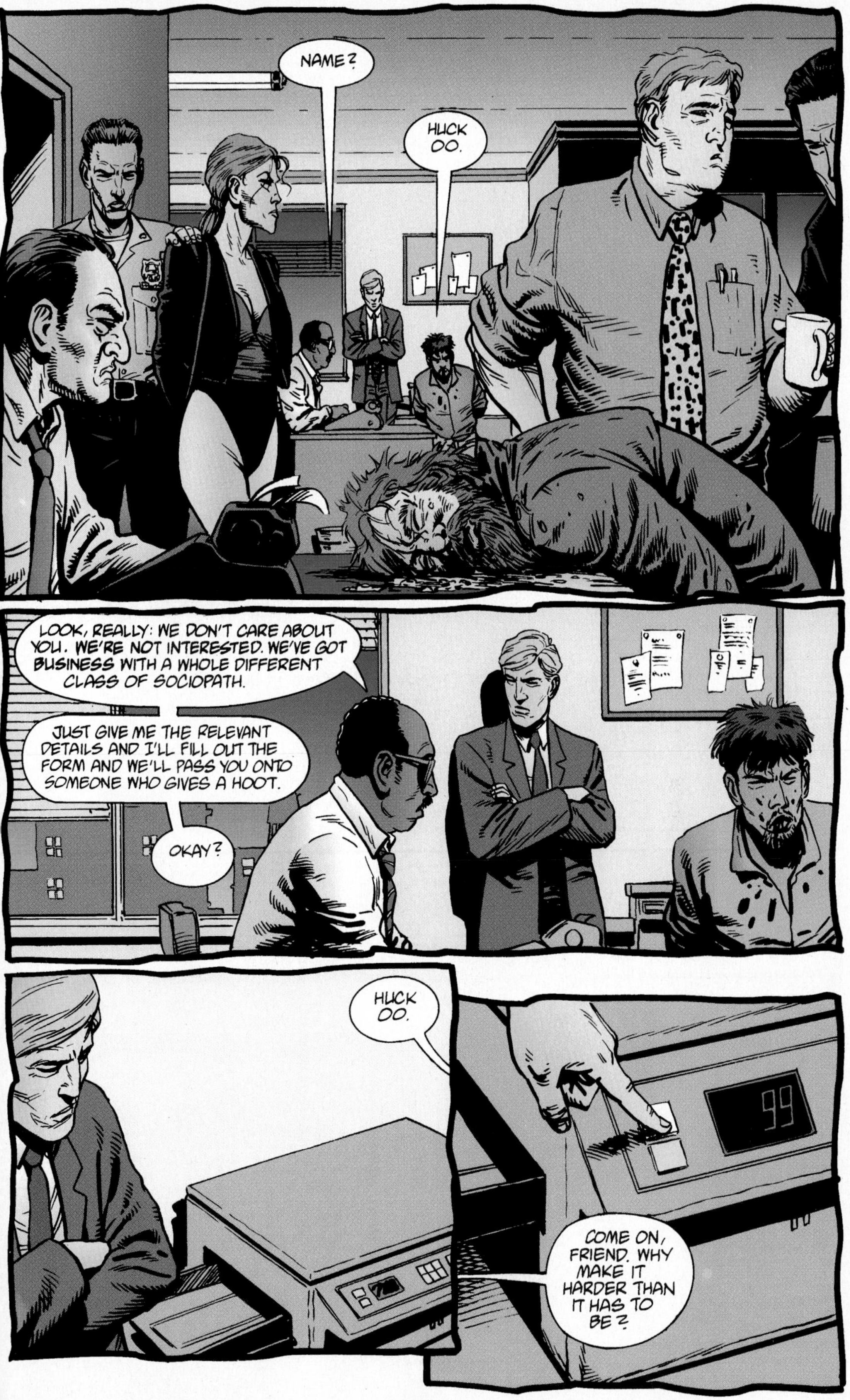

NAME?
HUCK OO.
LOOK, REALLY: WE DON'T CARE ABOUT YOU. WE'RE NOT INTERESTED. WE'VE GOT BUSINESS WITH A WHOLE DIFFERENT CLASS OF SOCIOPATH.
JUST GIVE ME THE RELEVANT DETAILS AND I'LL FILL OUT THE FORM AND WE'LL PASS YOU ONTO SOMEONE WHO GIVES A HOOT.
OKAY?
HUCK OO.
99
COME ON, FRIEND. WHY MAKE IT HARDER THAN IT HAS TO BE?

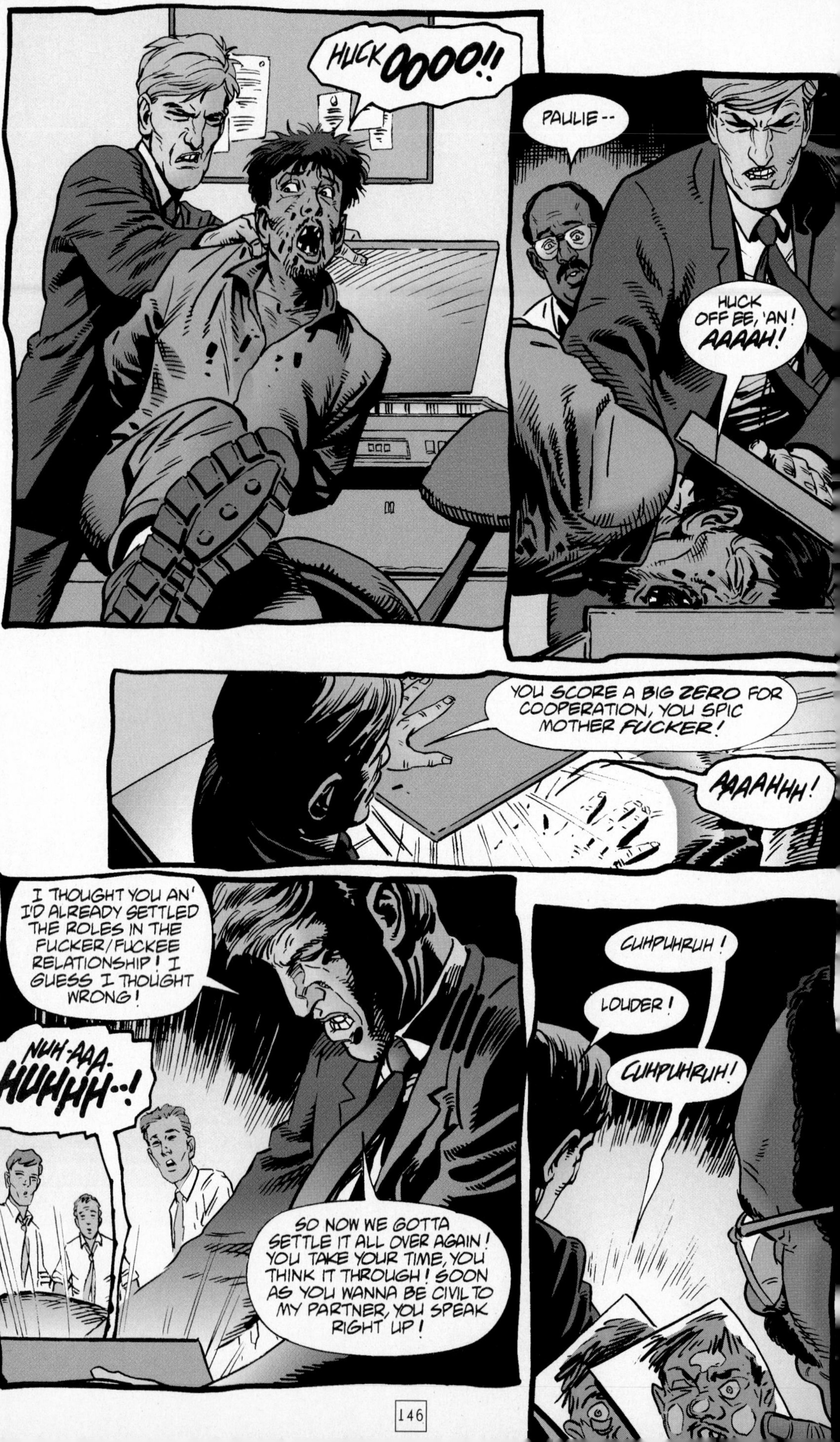
HUCK OOOO!!
PAULIE --
HUCK OFF EE, 'AN! AAAAH!
YOU SCORE A BIG ZERO FOR COOPERATION, YOU SPIC MOTHER FUCKER!
AAAAHHH!
I THOUGHT YOU AN' I'D ALREADY SETTLED THE ROLES IN THE FUCKER/FUCKEE RELATIONSHIP! I GUESS I THOUGHT WRONG!
NUH-AAA-HUHHH--!
SO NOW WE GOTTA SETTLE IT ALL OVER AGAIN! YOU TAKE YOUR TIME, YOU THINK IT THROUGH! SOON AS YOU WANNA BE CIVIL TO MY PARTNER, YOU SPEAK RIGHT UP!
CUHPUHRUH!
LOUDER!
CUHPUHRUH!

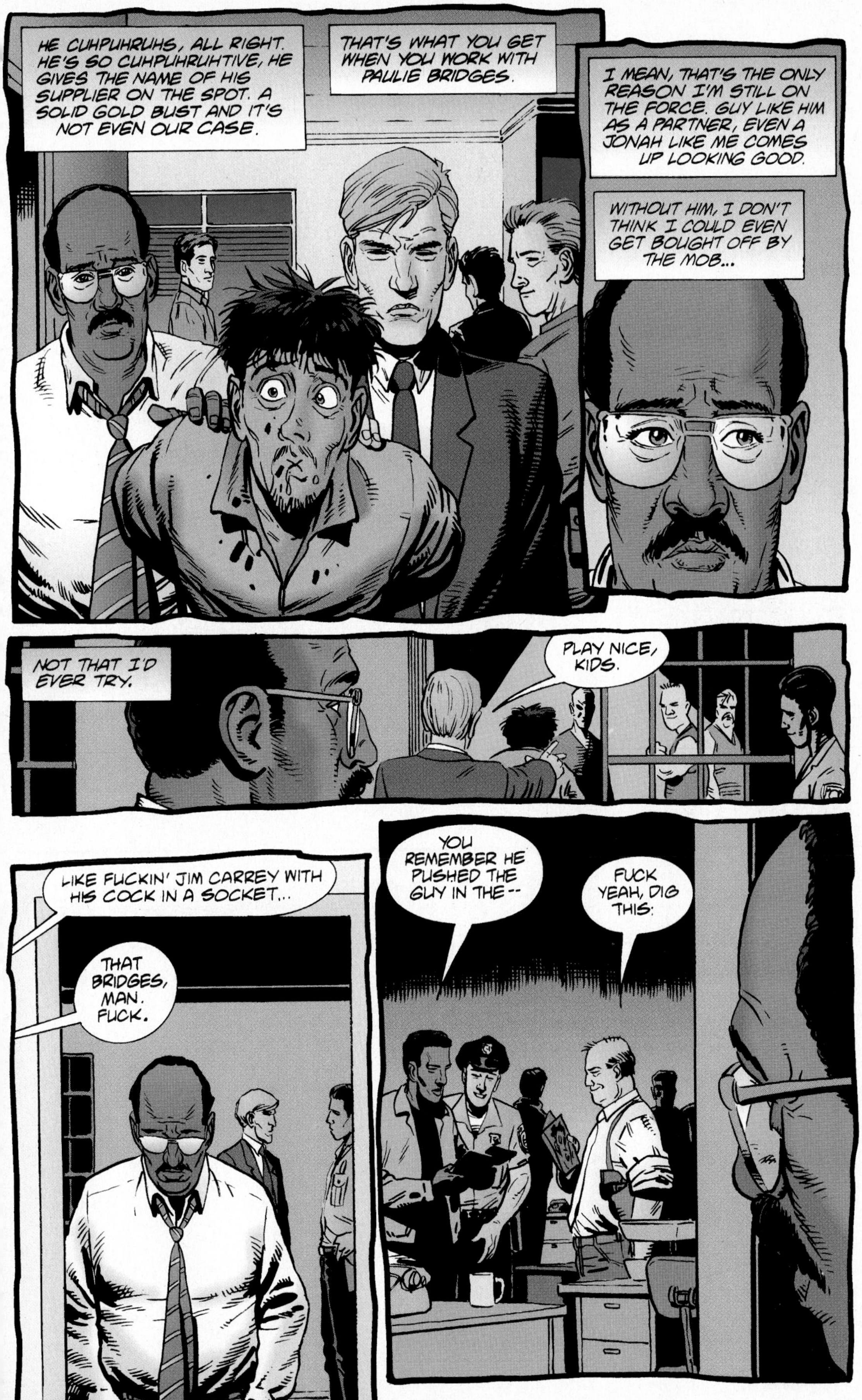
HE CUHPUHRUHS, ALL RIGHT. HE'S SO CUHPUHRUHTIVE, HE GIVES THE NAME OF HIS SUPPLIER ON THE SPOT. A SOLID GOLD BUST AND IT'S NOT EVEN OUR CASE.
THAT'S WHAT YOU GET WHEN YOU WORK WITH PAULIE BRIDGES.
I MEAN, THAT'S THE ONLY REASON I'M STILL ON THE FORCE. GUY LIKE HIM AS A PARTNER, EVEN A JONAH LIKE ME COMES UP LOOKING GOOD.
WITHOUT HIM, I DON'T THINK I COULD EVEN GET BOUGHT OFF BY THE MOB...
NOT THAT I'D EVER TRY.
PLAY NICE, KIDS.
LIKE FUCKIN' JIM CARREY WITH HIS COCK IN A SOCKET...
THAT BRIDGES, MAN. FUCK.
YOU REMEMBER HE PUSHED THE GUY IN THE --
FUCK YEAH, DIG THIS:

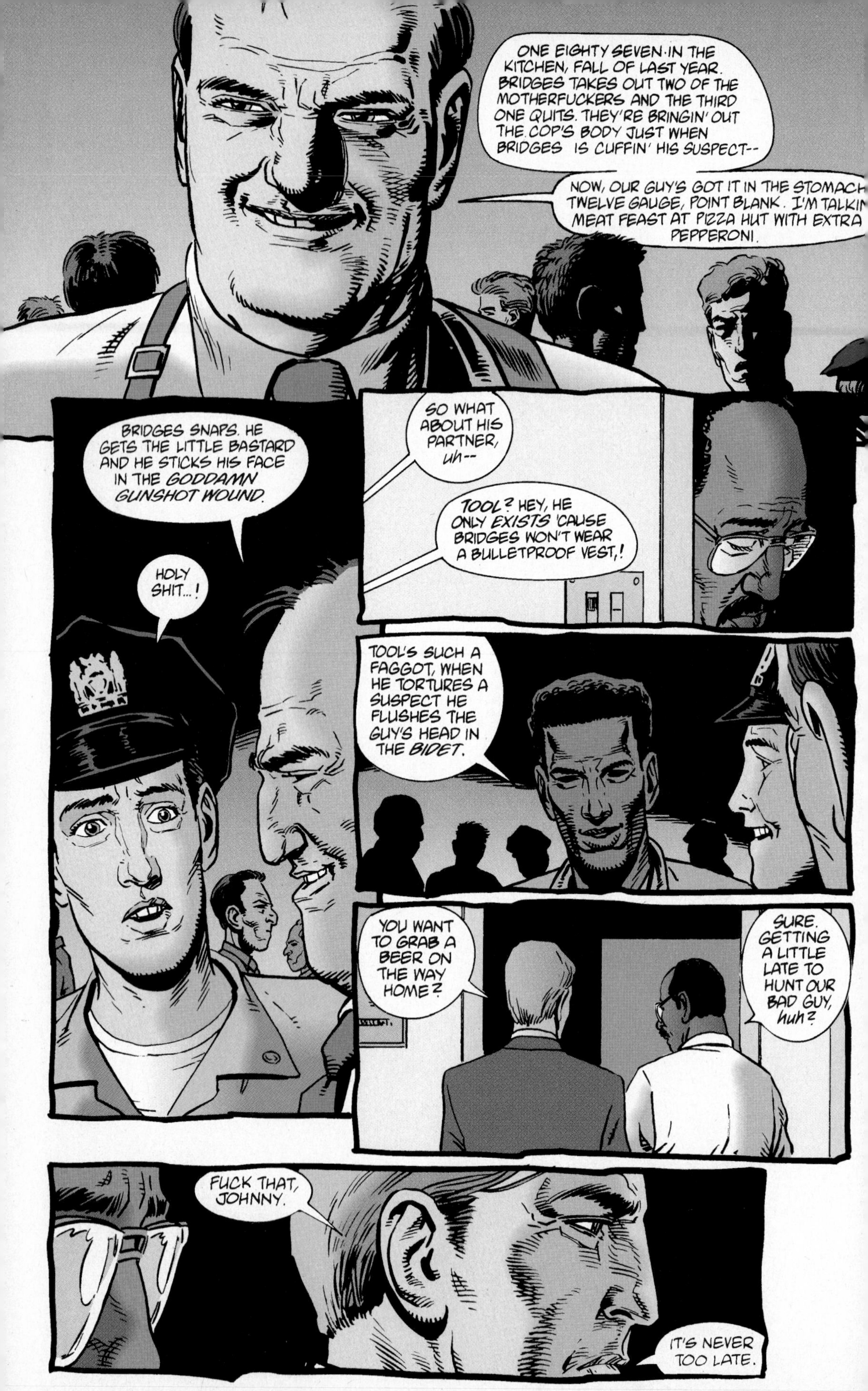
ONE EIGHTY SEVEN IN THE KITCHEN, FALL OF LAST YEAR. BRIDGES TAKES OUT TWO OF THE MOTHERFUCKERS AND THE THIRD ONE QUITS. THEY'RE BRINGIN' OUT THE COP'S BODY JUST WHEN BRIDGES IS CUFFIN' HIS SUSPECT--
NOW, OUR GUY'S GOT IT IN THE STOMACH TWELVE GAUGE, POINT BLANK. I'M TALKIN MEAT FEAST AT PIZZA HUT WITH EXTRA PEPPERONI.
BRIDGES SNAPS. HE GETS THE LITTLE BASTARD AND HE STICKS HIS FACE IN THE GODDAMN GUNSHOT WOUND.
HOLY SHIT...!
SO WHAT ABOUT HIS PARTNER, uh--
TOOL? HEY, HE ONLY EXISTS 'CAUSE BRIDGES WON'T WEAR A BULLETPROOF VEST,!
TOOL'S SUCH A FAGGOT, WHEN HE TORTURES A SUSPECT HE FLUSHES THE GUY'S HEAD IN THE BIDET.
YOU WANT TO GRAB A BEER ON THE WAY HOME?
SURE. GETTING A LITTLE LATE TO HUNT OUR BAD GUY, huh?
FUCK THAT, JOHNNY.
IT'S NEVER TOO LATE.

ALL THEY HAD WAS BUD.

'COURSE, YOU COULD NIP IN THERE AN' ORDER THEM TO GO OUT AN' GET US A MAGNUM OF KRUG AN' THEY'D HAVE TO OBEY YOU, Y'KNOW.

MM.

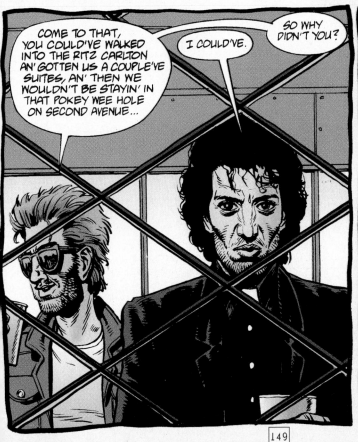

COME TO THAT, YOU COULD'VE WALKED INTO THE RITZ CARLTON AN' GOTTEN US A COUPLE'VE SUITES, AN' THEN WE WOULDN'T BE STAYIN' IN THAT POKEY WEE HOLE ON SECOND AVENUE...

I COULD'VE.

SO WHY DIDN'T YOU?

'CAUSE THAT JUST AIN'T THE WAY IT WORKS.

149

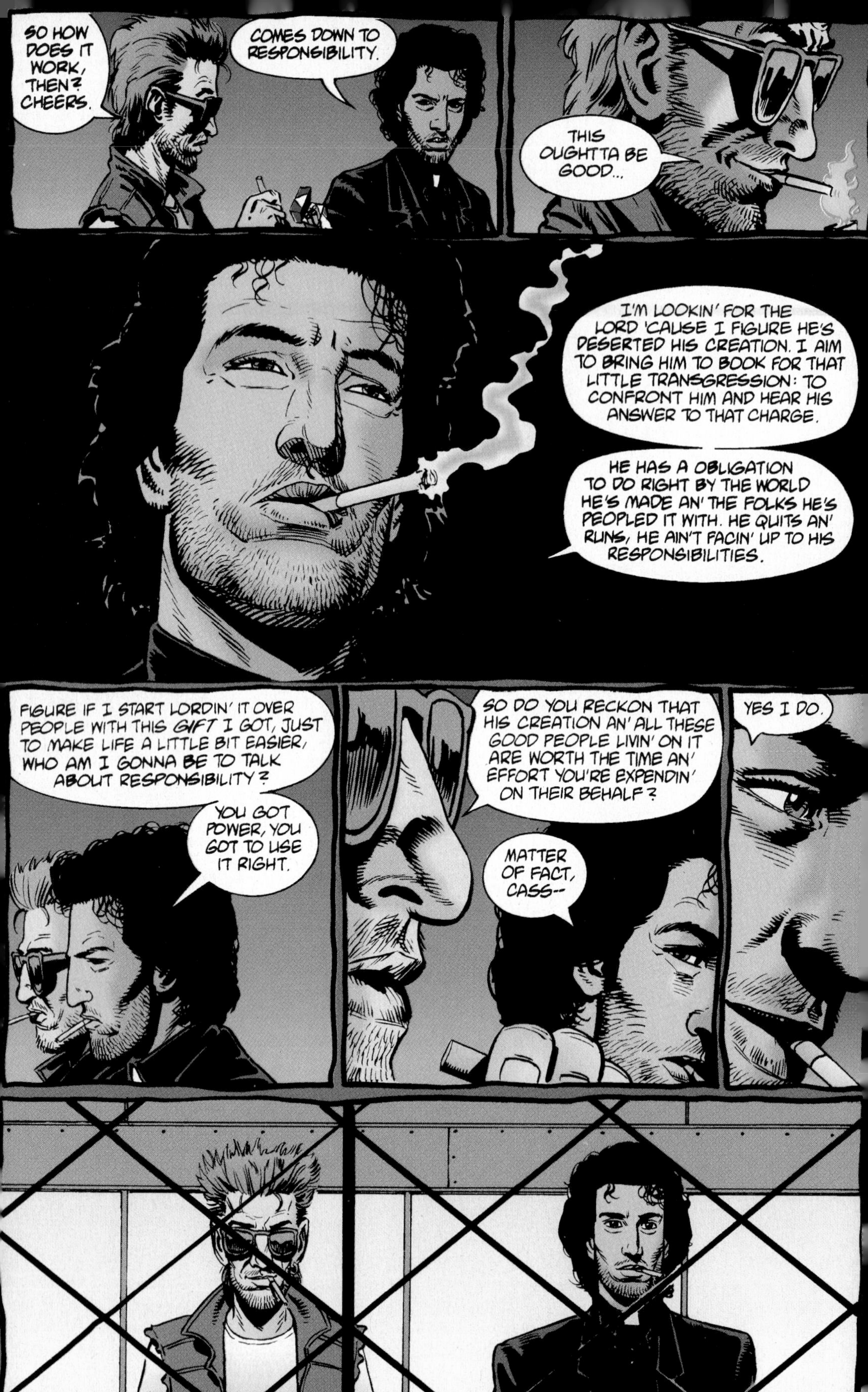
SO HOW DOES IT WORK, THEN? CHEERS.
COMES DOWN TO RESPONSIBILITY.
THIS OUGHTTA BE GOOD...
I'M LOOKIN' FOR THE LORD 'CAUSE I FIGURE HE'S DESERTED HIS CREATION. I AIM TO BRING HIM TO BOOK FOR THAT LITTLE TRANSGRESSION: TO CONFRONT HIM AND HEAR HIS ANSWER TO THAT CHARGE.
HE HAS A OBLIGATION TO DO RIGHT BY THE WORLD HE'S MADE AN' THE FOLKS HE'S PEOPLED IT WITH. HE QUITS AN' RUNS, HE AIN'T FACIN' UP TO HIS RESPONSIBILITIES.
FIGURE IF I START LORDIN' IT OVER PEOPLE WITH THIS *GIFT* I GOT, JUST TO MAKE LIFE A LITTLE BIT EASIER, WHO AM I GONNA BE TO TALK ABOUT RESPONSIBILITY?
YOU GOT POWER, YOU GOT TO USE IT RIGHT.
SO DO YOU RECKON THAT HIS CREATION AN' ALL THESE GOOD PEOPLE LIVIN' ON IT ARE WORTH THE TIME AN' EFFORT YOU'RE EXPENDIN' ON THEIR BEHALF?
MATTER OF FACT, CASS--
YES I DO.

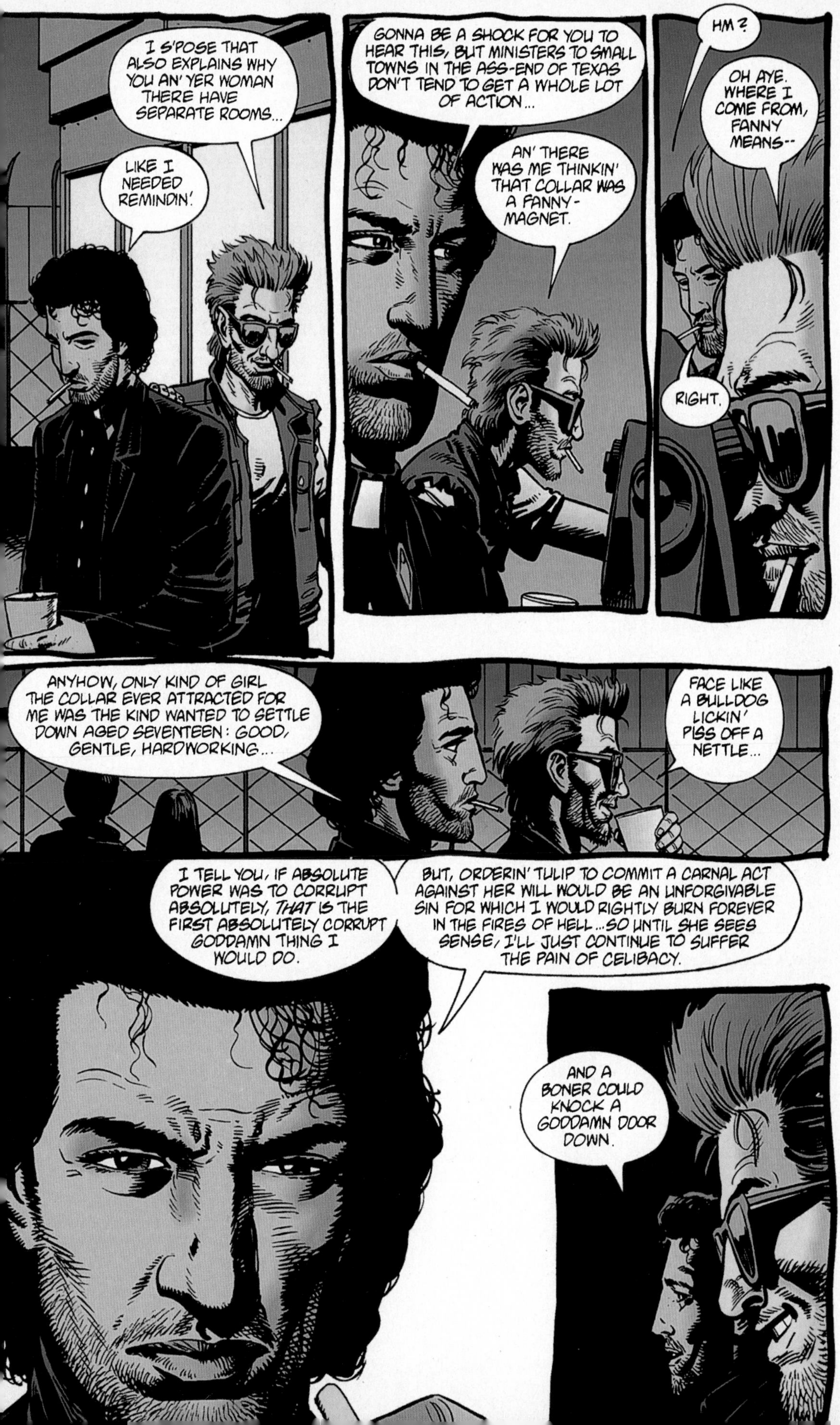
I S'POSE THAT ALSO EXPLAINS WHY YOU AN' YER WOMAN THERE HAVE SEPARATE ROOMS...
LIKE I NEEDED REMINDIN'.
GONNA BE A SHOCK FOR YOU TO HEAR THIS, BUT MINISTERS TO SMALL TOWNS IN THE ASS-END OF TEXAS DON'T TEND TO GET A WHOLE LOT OF ACTION...
AN' THERE WAS ME THINKIN' THAT COLLAR WAS A FANNY-MAGNET.
HM?
OH AYE. WHERE I COME FROM, FANNY MEANS--
RIGHT.
ANYHOW, ONLY KIND OF GIRL THE COLLAR EVER ATTRACTED FOR ME WAS THE KIND WANTED TO SETTLE DOWN AGED SEVENTEEN: GOOD, GENTLE, HARDWORKING...
FACE LIKE A BULLDOG LICKIN' PISS OFF A NETTLE...
I TELL YOU, IF ABSOLUTE POWER WAS TO CORRUPT ABSOLUTELY, THAT IS THE FIRST ABSOLUTELY CORRUPT GODDAMN THING I WOULD DO.
BUT, ORDERIN' TULIP TO COMMIT A CARNAL ACT AGAINST HER WILL WOULD BE AN UNFORGIVABLE SIN FOR WHICH I WOULD RIGHTLY BURN FOREVER IN THE FIRES OF HELL...SO UNTIL SHE SEES SENSE, I'LL JUST CONTINUE TO SUFFER THE PAIN OF CELIBACY.
AND A BONER COULD KNOCK A GODDAMN DOOR DOWN.

THAT TRULY IS SOMETHIN'!

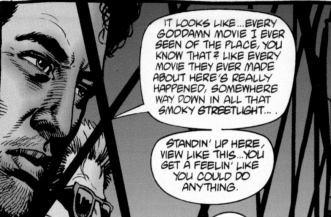

IT LOOKS LIKE...EVERY GODDAMN MOVIE I EVER SEEN OF THE PLACE, YOU KNOW THAT? LIKE EVERY MOVIE THEY EVER MADE ABOUT HERE'S REALLY HAPPENED, SOMEWHERE WAY DOWN IN ALL THAT SMOKY STREETLIGHT... .

STANDIN' UP HERE, VIEW LIKE THIS...YOU GET A FEELIN' LIKE YOU COULD DO ANYTHING.

AYE.

THAT'S THE FEELIN' I HAD, THE FIRST NIGHT I WAS UP HERE.

THE NIGHT THEY OPENED THE BUILDING.

NO SHIT?

NO SHIT. I WAS IN SOME PLACE OVER IN QUEENS DRINKIN' WITH A COUPLE'VE FELLAS, AN' THE BARMAN SAID THEY WERE OPENIN' THE EMPIRE STATE TO THE PUBLIC.

TOOK US AGES TO GET THROUGH ALL THE CROWDS, BUT BY CHRIST IT WAS FUCKIN' WELL WORTH IT...

HOW THE HELL OLD ARE YOU...?

SAME AGE AS THE CENTURY, MATE.

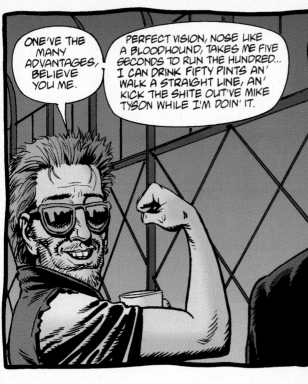

ONE'VE THE MANY ADVANTAGES, BELIEVE YOU ME.

PERFECT VISION, NOSE LIKE A BLOODHOUND, TAKES ME FIVE SECONDS TO RUN THE HUNDRED... I CAN DRINK FIFTY PINTS AN' WALK A STRAIGHT LINE, AN' KICK THE SHITE OUT'VE MIKE TYSON WHILE I'M DOIN' IT.

AN' I'LL SHOW YOU SOMETHIN' ELSE:

HUH?

QUICKER'N TAKIN' THE LIFT, PREACHER-MAN! SEE YOU AT THE BOTTOM!

WHAT THE FUCK ARE YOU DOIN'? GET DOWN!

OH GOD, I CAN'T STAND IT ANY LONGER! THE BLOOD! THE KILLING! THE POINTLESS BUTCHERY! LET IT END HERE!

CASSIDY, FOR FUCK'S SAKE!

AAAAAAAAHHHHH

CASSIDYY!!

... COCK.

SUCKER.

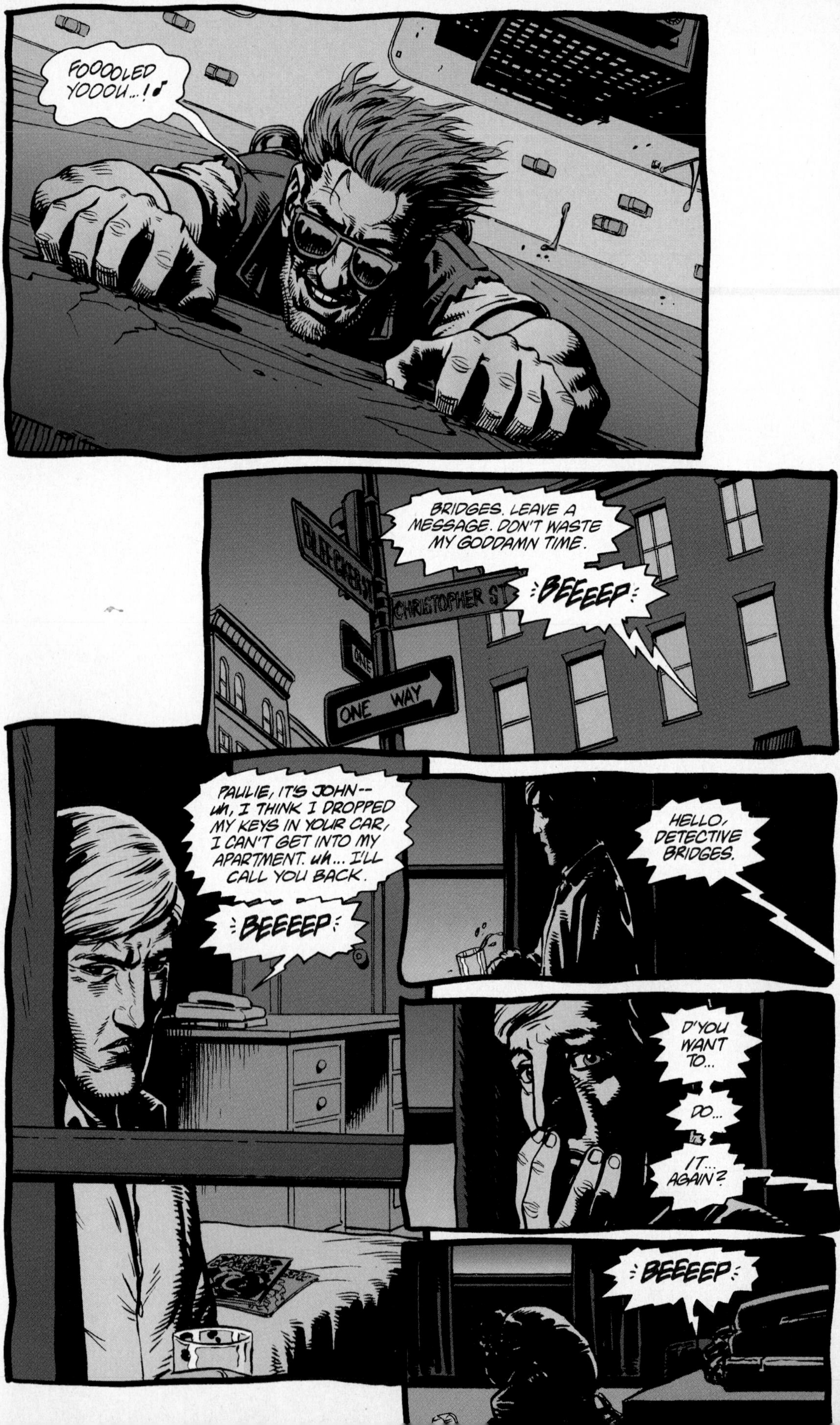
FOOOOLED YOOOU...!♪
BRIDGES. LEAVE A MESSAGE. DON'T WASTE MY GODDAMN TIME.
CHRISTOPHER ST
ONE
ONE WAY
BEEEEP
PAULIE, IT'S JOHN-- uh, I THINK I DROPPED MY KEYS IN YOUR CAR, I CAN'T GET INTO MY APARTMENT. uh... I'LL CALL YOU BACK.
BEEEEP
HELLO, DETECTIVE BRIDGES.
D'YOU WANT TO...
DO...
IT... AGAIN?
BEEEEP

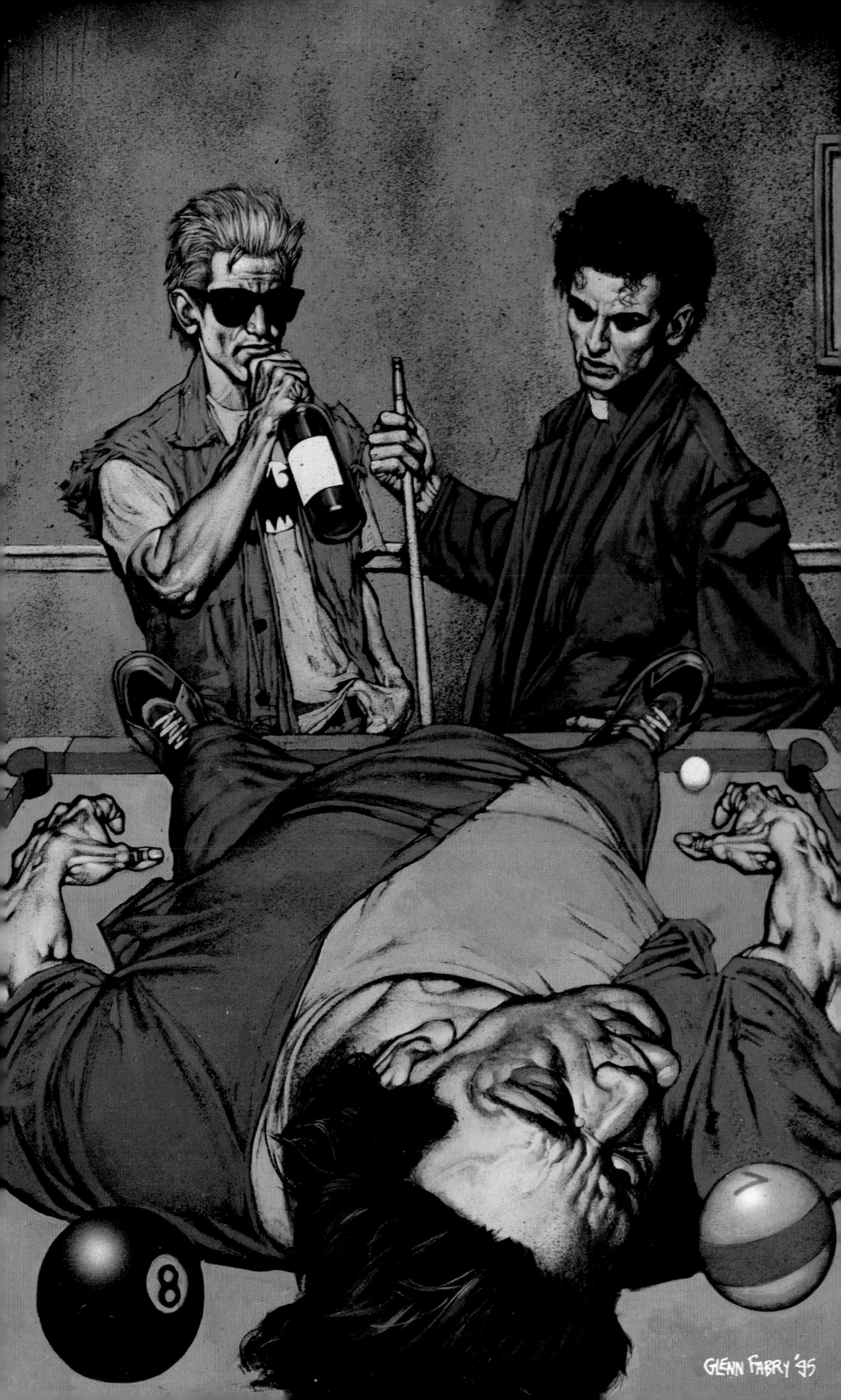
GLENN FABRY '95

"You're lookin' for God —
where the hell're you supposed to start?"

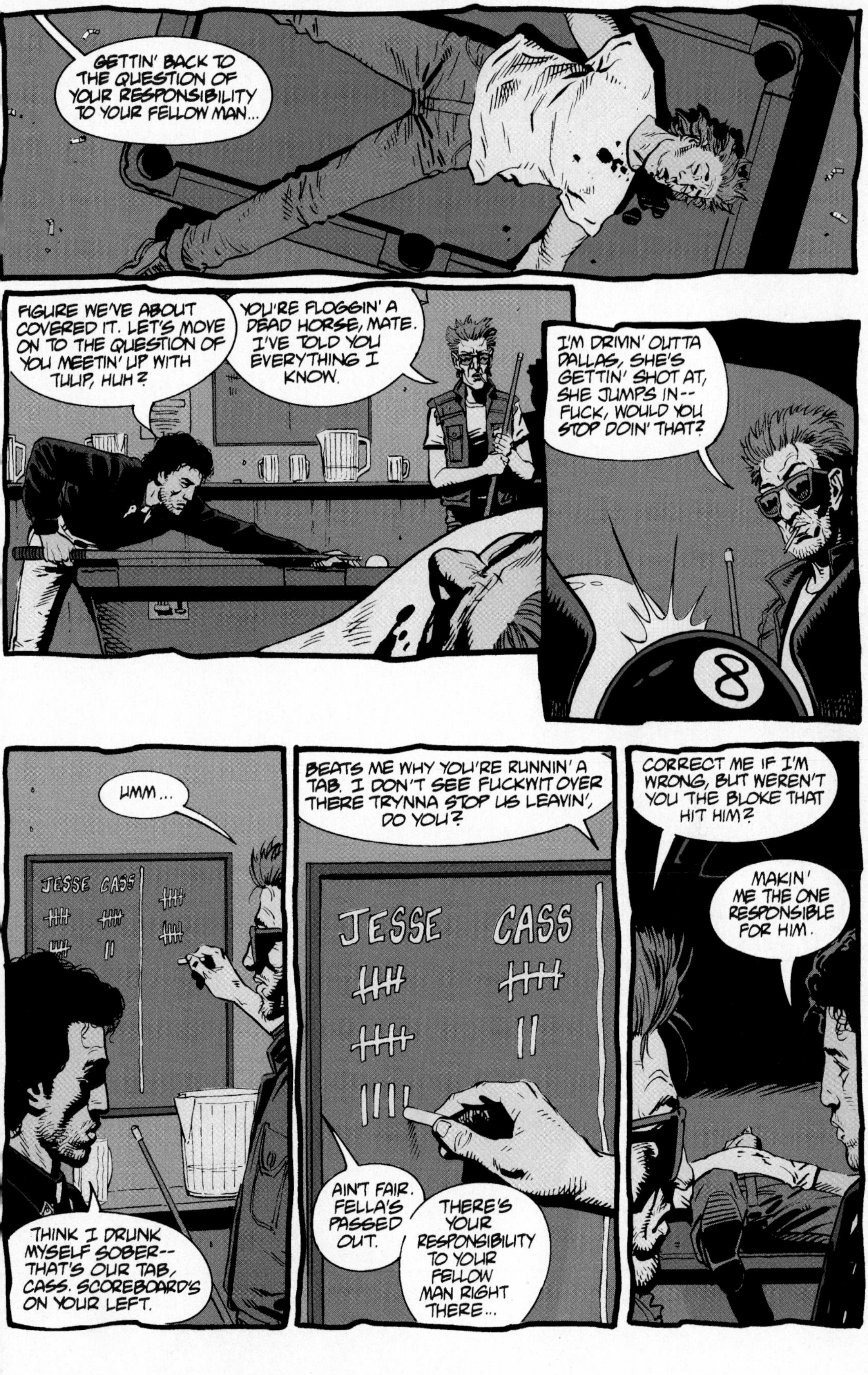
GETTIN' BACK TO THE QUESTION OF YOUR RESPONSIBILITY TO YOUR FELLOW MAN...
FIGURE WE'VE ABOUT COVERED IT. LET'S MOVE ON TO THE QUESTION OF YOU MEETIN' UP WITH TULIP, HUH?
YOU'RE FLOGGIN' A DEAD HORSE, MATE. I'VE TOLD YOU EVERYTHING I KNOW.
I'M DRIVIN' OUTTA DALLAS, SHE'S GETTIN' SHOT AT, SHE JUMPS IN-- FUCK, WOULD YOU STOP DOIN' THAT?
8
UMM...
JESSE CASS
THINK I DRUNK MYSELF SOBER-- THAT'S OUR TAB, CASS. SCOREBOARD'S ON YOUR LEFT.
BEATS ME WHY YOU'RE RUNNIN' A TAB. I DON'T SEE FUCKWIT OVER THERE TRYNNA STOP US LEAVIN', DO YOU?
JESSE CASS
AIN'T FAIR. FELLA'S PASSED OUT.
THERE'S YOUR RESPONSIBILITY TO YOUR FELLOW MAN RIGHT THERE...
CORRECT ME IF I'M WRONG, BUT WEREN'T YOU THE BLOKE THAT HIT HIM?
MAKIN' ME THE ONE RESPONSIBLE FOR HIM.

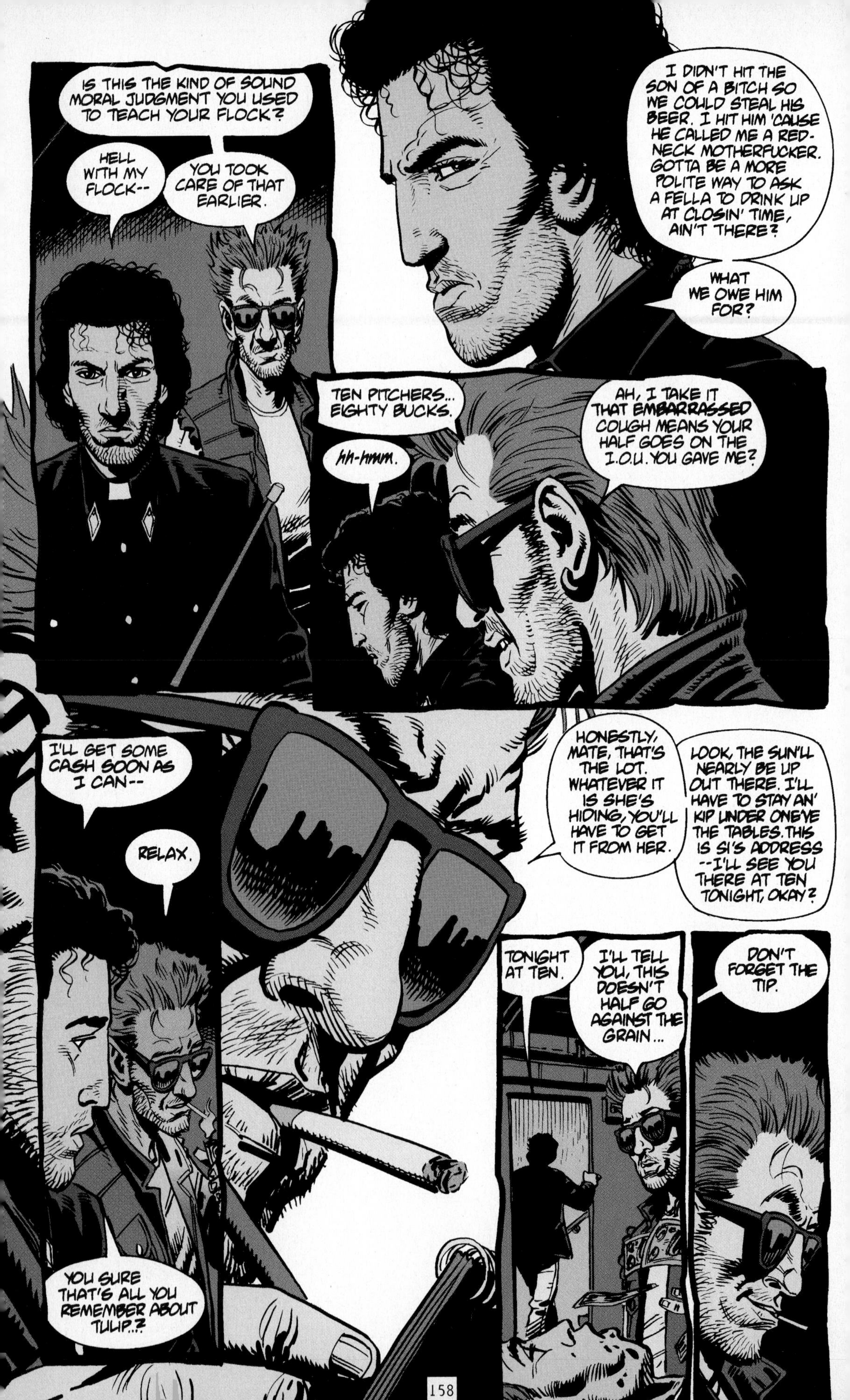
IS THIS THE KIND OF SOUND MORAL JUDGMENT YOU USED TO TEACH YOUR FLOCK?
HELL WITH MY FLOCK--
YOU TOOK CARE OF THAT EARLIER.
I DIDN'T HIT THE SON OF A BITCH SO WE COULD STEAL HIS BEER. I HIT HIM 'CAUSE HE CALLED ME A RED-NECK MOTHERFUCKER. GOTTA BE A MORE POLITE WAY TO ASK A FELLA TO DRINK UP AT CLOSIN' TIME, AIN'T THERE?
WHAT WE OWE HIM FOR?
TEN PITCHERS... EIGHTY BUCKS.
hh-hmm.
AH, I TAKE IT THAT EMBARRASSED COUGH MEANS YOUR HALF GOES ON THE I.O.U. YOU GAVE ME?
I'LL GET SOME CASH SOON AS I CAN--
RELAX.
YOU SURE THAT'S ALL YOU REMEMBER ABOUT TULIP...?
HONESTLY, MATE, THAT'S THE LOT. WHATEVER IT IS SHE'S HIDING, YOU'LL HAVE TO GET IT FROM HER.
LOOK, THE SUN'LL NEARLY BE UP OUT THERE. I'LL HAVE TO STAY AN' KIP UNDER ONE'VE THE TABLES. THIS IS SI'S ADDRESS --I'LL SEE YOU THERE AT TEN TONIGHT, OKAY?
TONIGHT AT TEN.
I'LL TELL YOU, THIS DOESN'T HALF GO AGAINST THE GRAIN...
DON'T FORGET THE TIP.

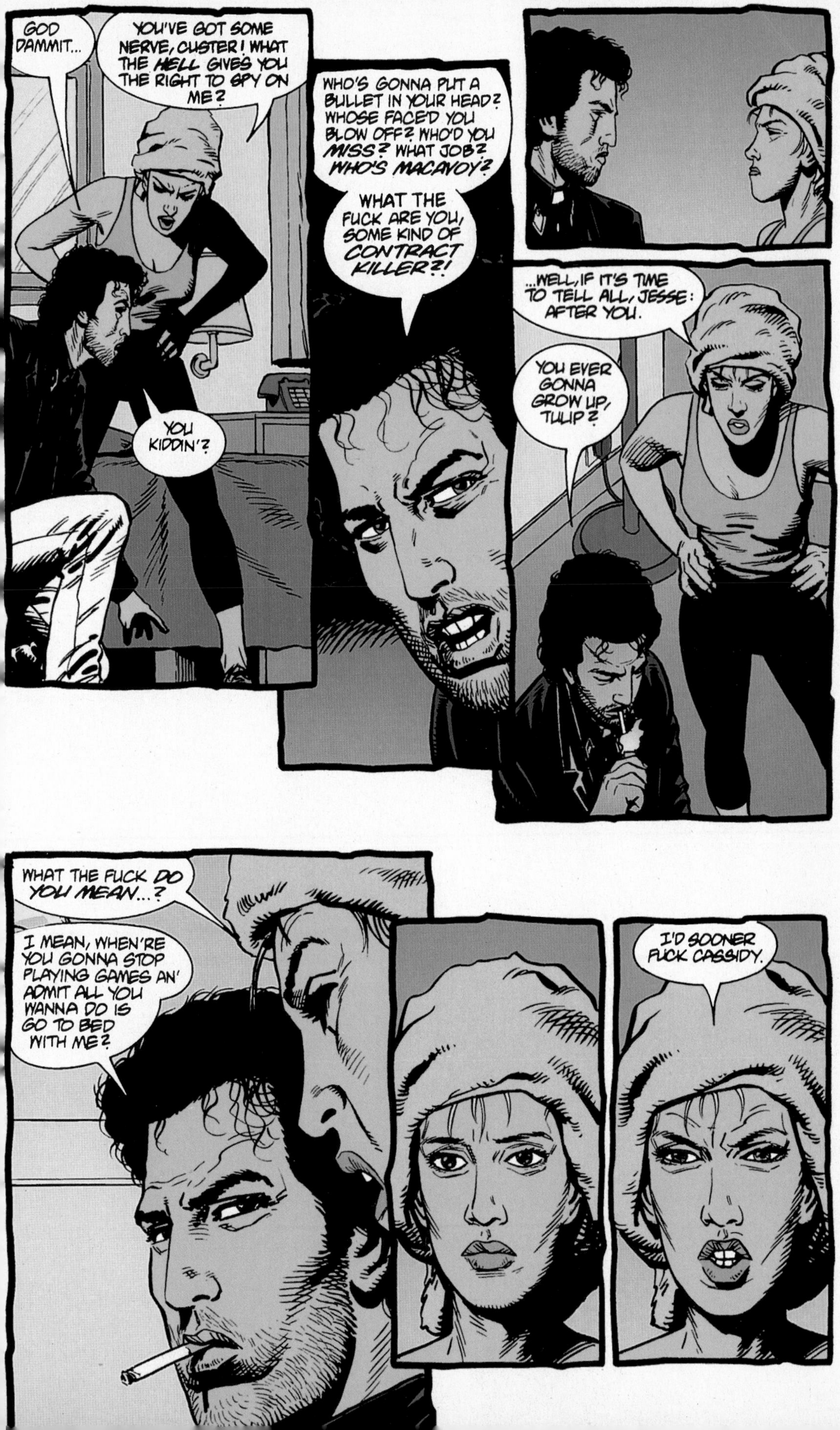
GOD DAMMIT...
YOU'VE GOT SOME NERVE, CUSTER! WHAT THE HELL GIVES YOU THE RIGHT TO SPY ON ME?
YOU KIDDIN'?
WHO'S GONNA PUT A BULLET IN YOUR HEAD? WHOSE FACE'D YOU BLOW OFF? WHO'D YOU MISS? WHAT JOB? WHO'S MACAVOY?
WHAT THE FUCK ARE YOU, SOME KIND OF CONTRACT KILLER?!
...WELL, IF IT'S TIME TO TELL ALL, JESSE: AFTER YOU.
YOU EVER GONNA GROW UP, TULIP?
WHAT THE FUCK DO YOU MEAN...?
I MEAN, WHEN'RE YOU GONNA STOP PLAYING GAMES AN' ADMIT ALL YOU WANNA DO IS GO TO BED WITH ME?
I'D SOONER FUCK CASSIDY.

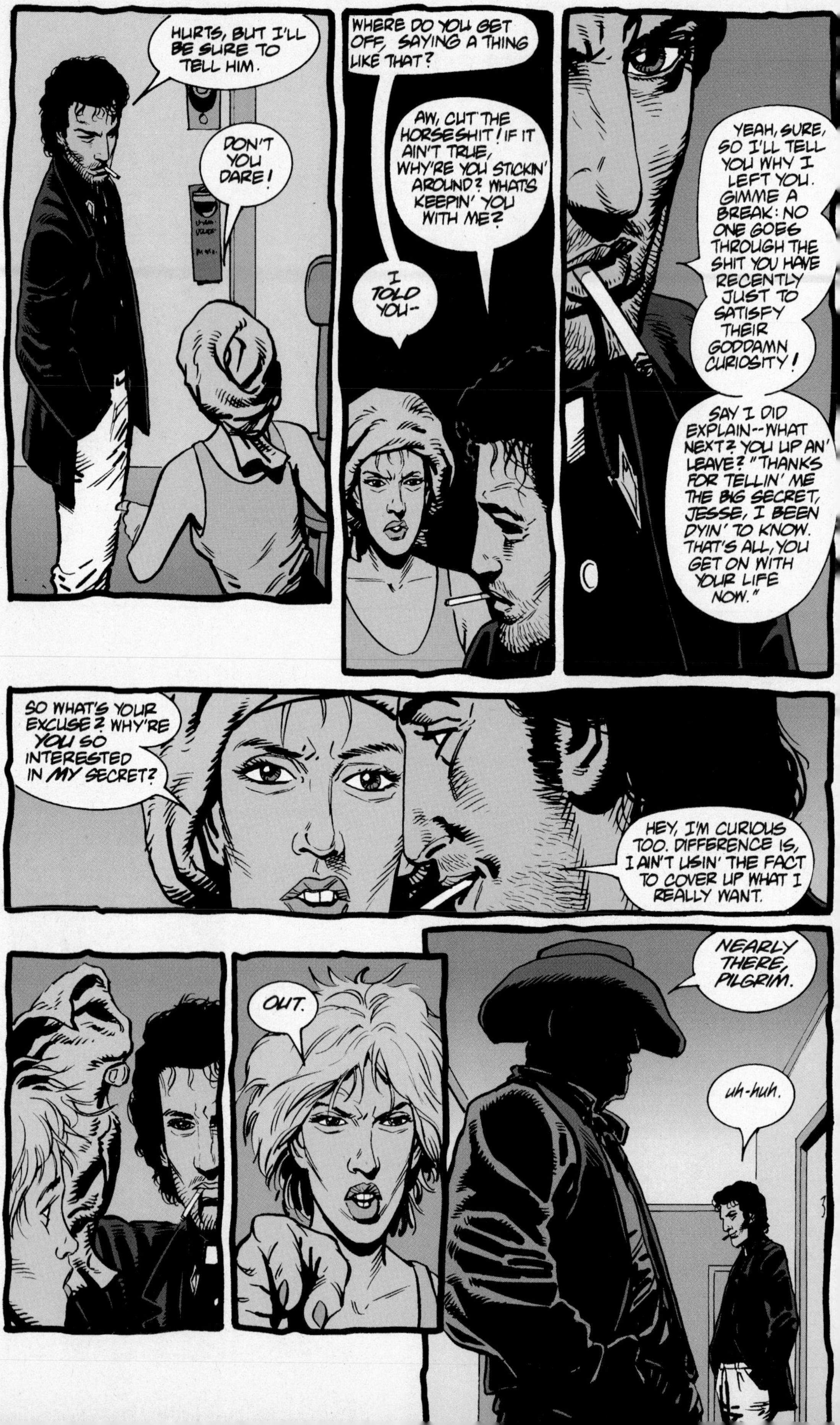

HURTS, BUT I'LL BE SURE TO TELL HIM.
DON'T YOU DARE!
WHERE DO YOU GET OFF, SAYING A THING LIKE THAT?
I TOLD YOU--
AW, CUT THE HORSESHIT! IF IT AIN'T TRUE, WHY'RE YOU STICKIN' AROUND? WHAT'S KEEPIN' YOU WITH ME?
YEAH, SURE, SO I'LL TELL YOU WHY I LEFT YOU. GIMME A BREAK: NO ONE GOES THROUGH THE SHIT YOU HAVE RECENTLY JUST TO SATISFY THEIR GODDAMN CURIOSITY!
SAY I DID EXPLAIN--WHAT NEXT? YOU UP AN' LEAVE? "THANKS FOR TELLIN' ME THE BIG SECRET, JESSE, I BEEN DYIN' TO KNOW. THAT'S ALL, YOU GET ON WITH YOUR LIFE NOW."
SO WHAT'S YOUR EXCUSE? WHY'RE YOU SO INTERESTED IN MY SECRET?
HEY, I'M CURIOUS TOO. DIFFERENCE IS, I AIN'T USIN' THE FACT TO COVER UP WHAT I REALLY WANT.
OUT.
NEARLY THERE, PILGRIM.
uh-huh.

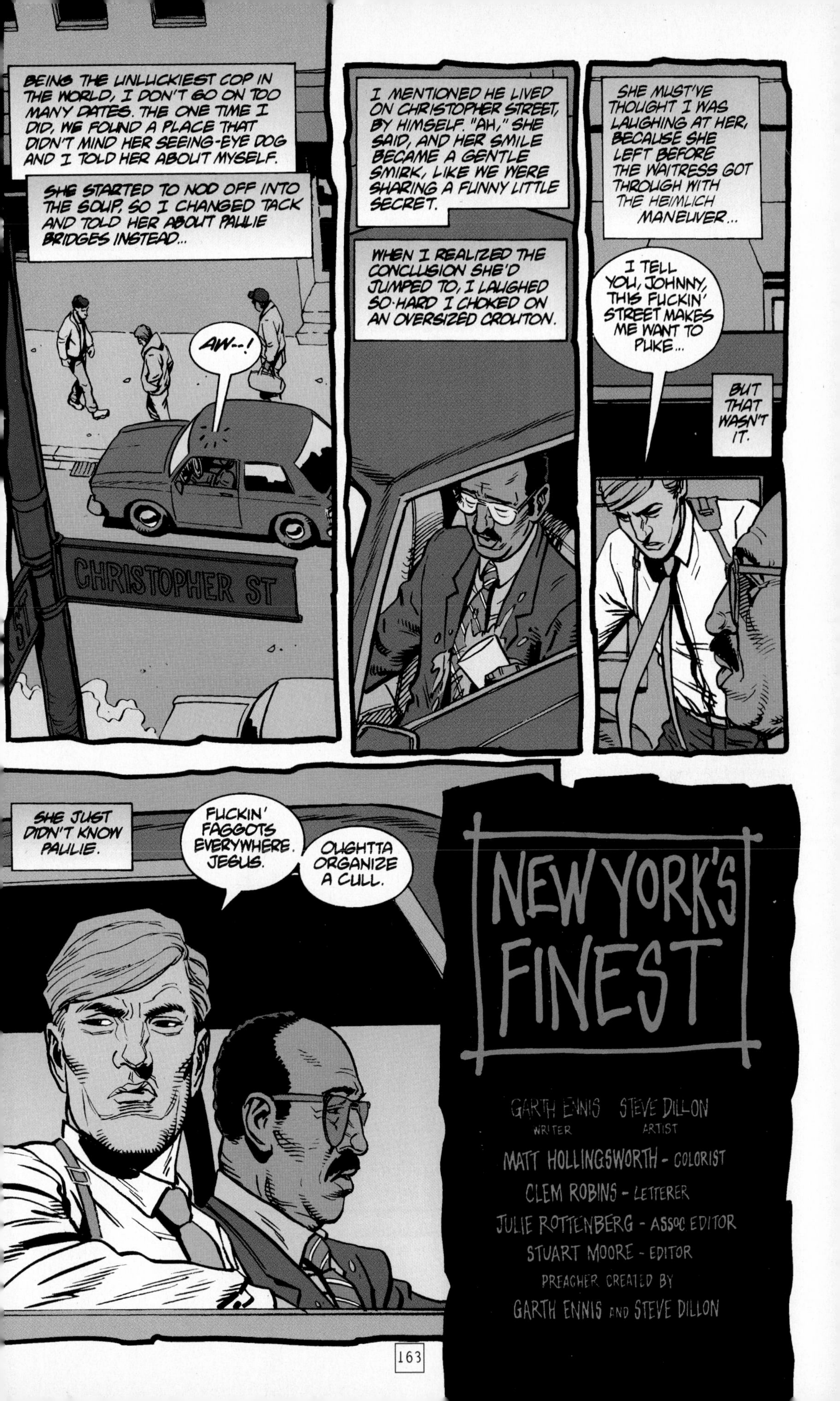

BEING THE UNLUCKIEST COP IN THE WORLD, I DON'T GO ON TOO MANY DATES. THE ONE TIME I DID, WE FOUND A PLACE THAT DIDN'T MIND HER SEEING-EYE DOG AND I TOLD HER ABOUT MYSELF.
SHE STARTED TO NOD OFF INTO THE SOUP, SO I CHANGED TACK AND TOLD HER ABOUT PAULIE BRIDGES INSTEAD...
AW--!
CHRISTOPHER ST
I MENTIONED HE LIVED ON CHRISTOPHER STREET, BY HIMSELF. "AH," SHE SAID, AND HER SMILE BECAME A GENTLE SMIRK, LIKE WE WERE SHARING A FUNNY LITTLE SECRET.
WHEN I REALIZED THE CONCLUSION SHE'D JUMPED TO, I LAUGHED SO HARD I CHOKED ON AN OVERSIZED CROUTON.
SHE MUST'VE THOUGHT I WAS LAUGHING AT HER, BECAUSE SHE LEFT BEFORE THE WAITRESS GOT THROUGH WITH THE HEIMLICH MANEUVER...
I TELL YOU, JOHNNY, THIS FUCKIN' STREET MAKES ME WANT TO PUKE...
BUT THAT WASN'T IT.
SHE JUST DIDN'T KNOW PAULIE.
FUCKIN' FAGGOTS EVERYWHERE. JESUS.
OUGHTTA ORGANIZE A CULL.
NEW YORK'S FINEST
GARTH ENNIS WRITER
STEVE DILLON ARTIST
MATT HOLLINGSWORTH - COLORIST
CLEM ROBINS - LETTERER
JULIE ROTTENBERG - ASSOC EDITOR
STUART MOORE - EDITOR
PREACHER CREATED BY GARTH ENNIS AND STEVE DILLON

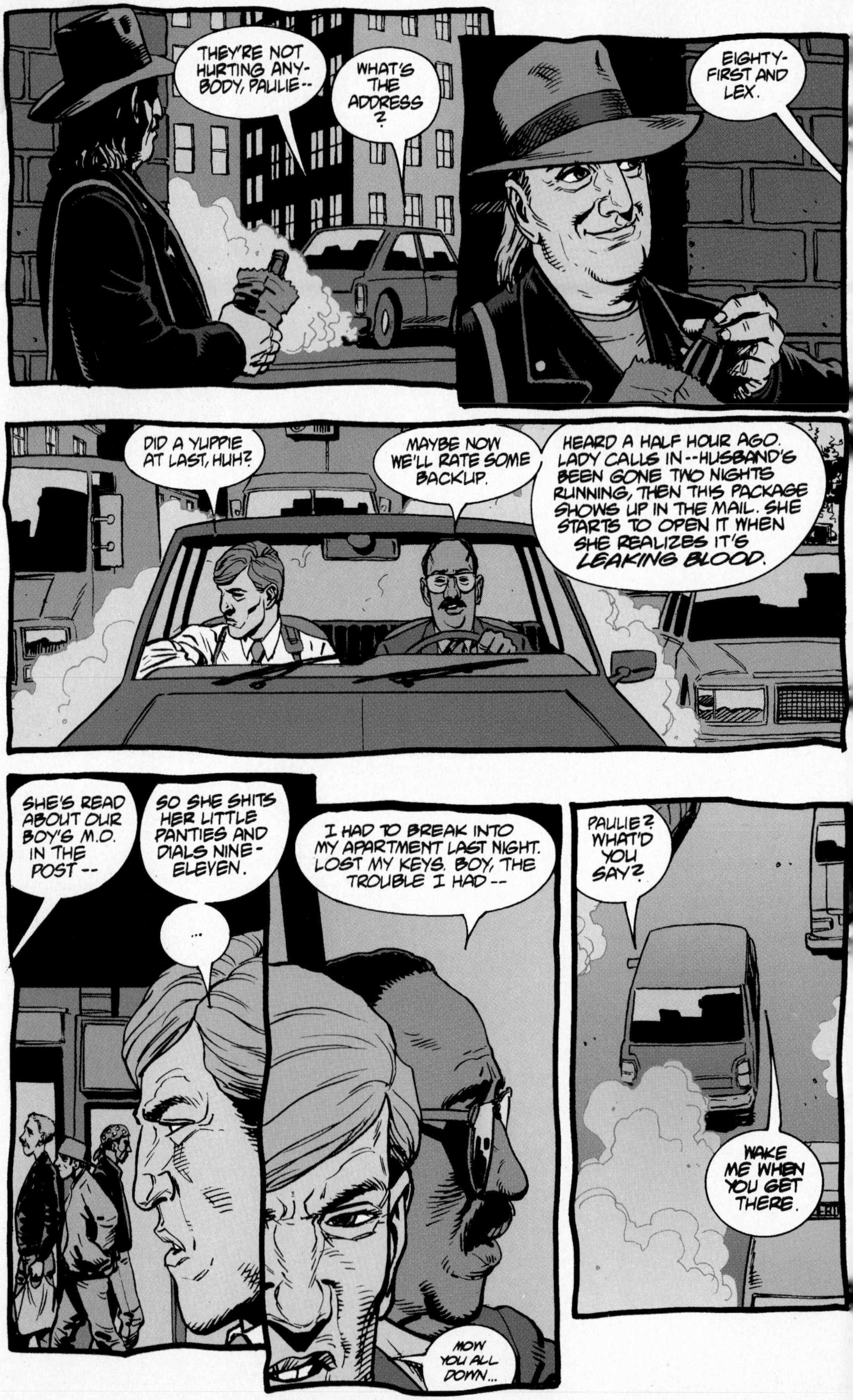
THEY'RE NOT HURTING ANYBODY, PAULIE--
WHAT'S THE ADDRESS?
EIGHTY-FIRST AND LEX.
DID A YUPPIE AT LAST, HUH?
MAYBE NOW WE'LL RATE SOME BACKUP.
HEARD A HALF HOUR AGO. LADY CALLS IN--HUSBAND'S BEEN GONE TWO NIGHTS RUNNING, THEN THIS PACKAGE SHOWS UP IN THE MAIL. SHE STARTS TO OPEN IT WHEN SHE REALIZES IT'S LEAKING BLOOD.
SHE'S READ ABOUT OUR BOY'S M.O. IN THE POST--
SO SHE SHITS HER LITTLE PANTIES AND DIALS NINE-ELEVEN.
...
I HAD TO BREAK INTO MY APARTMENT LAST NIGHT. LOST MY KEYS. BOY, THE TROUBLE I HAD--
MOW YOU ALL DOWN...
PAULIE? WHAT'D YOU SAY?
WAKE ME WHEN YOU GET THERE.

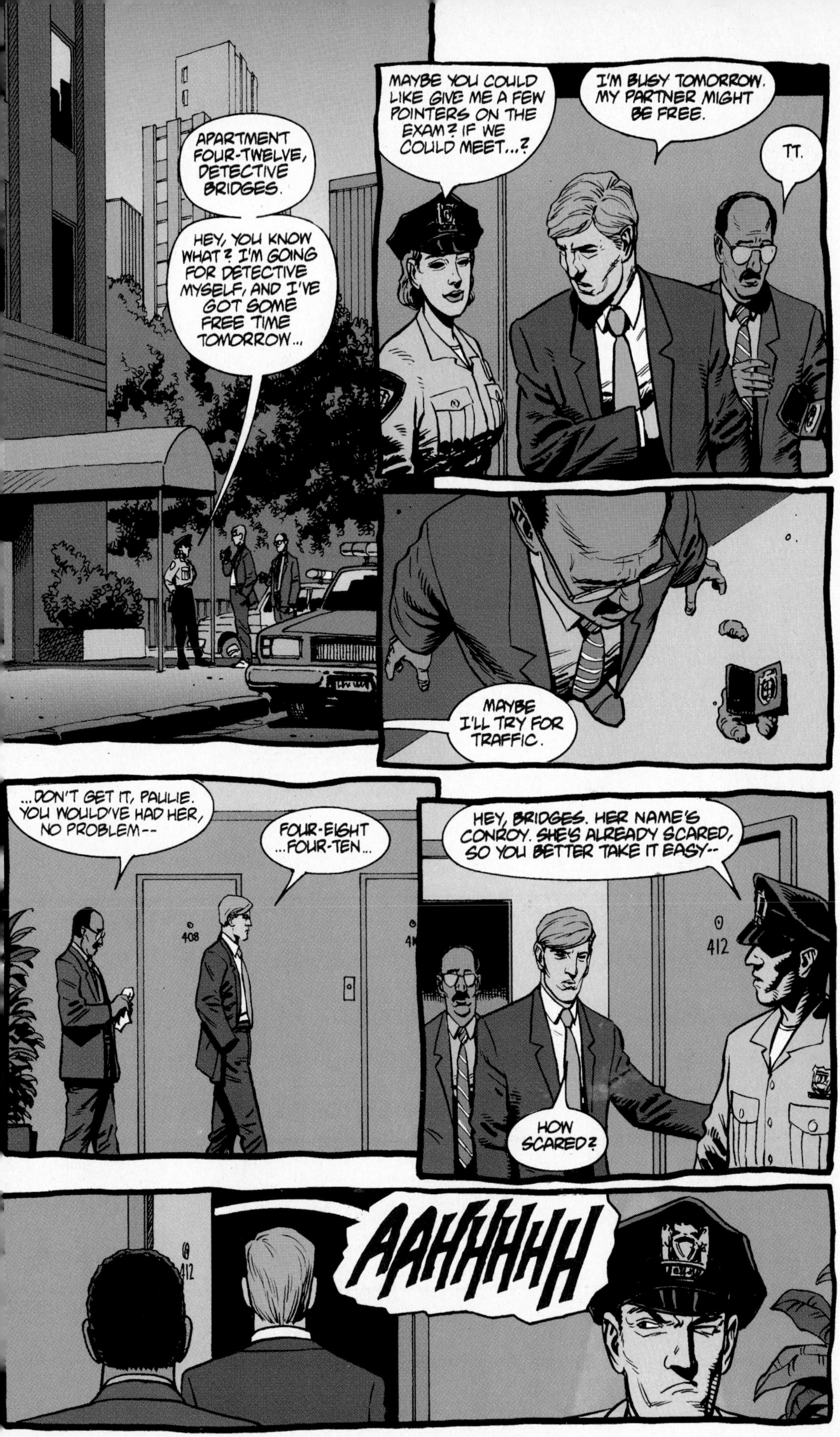
APARTMENT FOUR-TWELVE, DETECTIVE BRIDGES.
HEY, YOU KNOW WHAT? I'M GOING FOR DETECTIVE MYSELF, AND I'VE GOT SOME FREE TIME TOMORROW...
MAYBE YOU COULD LIKE GIVE ME A FEW POINTERS ON THE EXAM? IF WE COULD MEET...?
I'M BUSY TOMORROW. MY PARTNER MIGHT BE FREE.
TT.
MAYBE I'LL TRY FOR TRAFFIC.
...DON'T GET IT, PAULIE. YOU WOULD'VE HAD HER, NO PROBLEM--
FOUR-EIGHT ...FOUR-TEN...
408
HEY, BRIDGES. HER NAME'S CONROY. SHE'S ALREADY SCARED, SO YOU BETTER TAKE IT EASY--
412
HOW SCARED?
412
AAHHHHHH

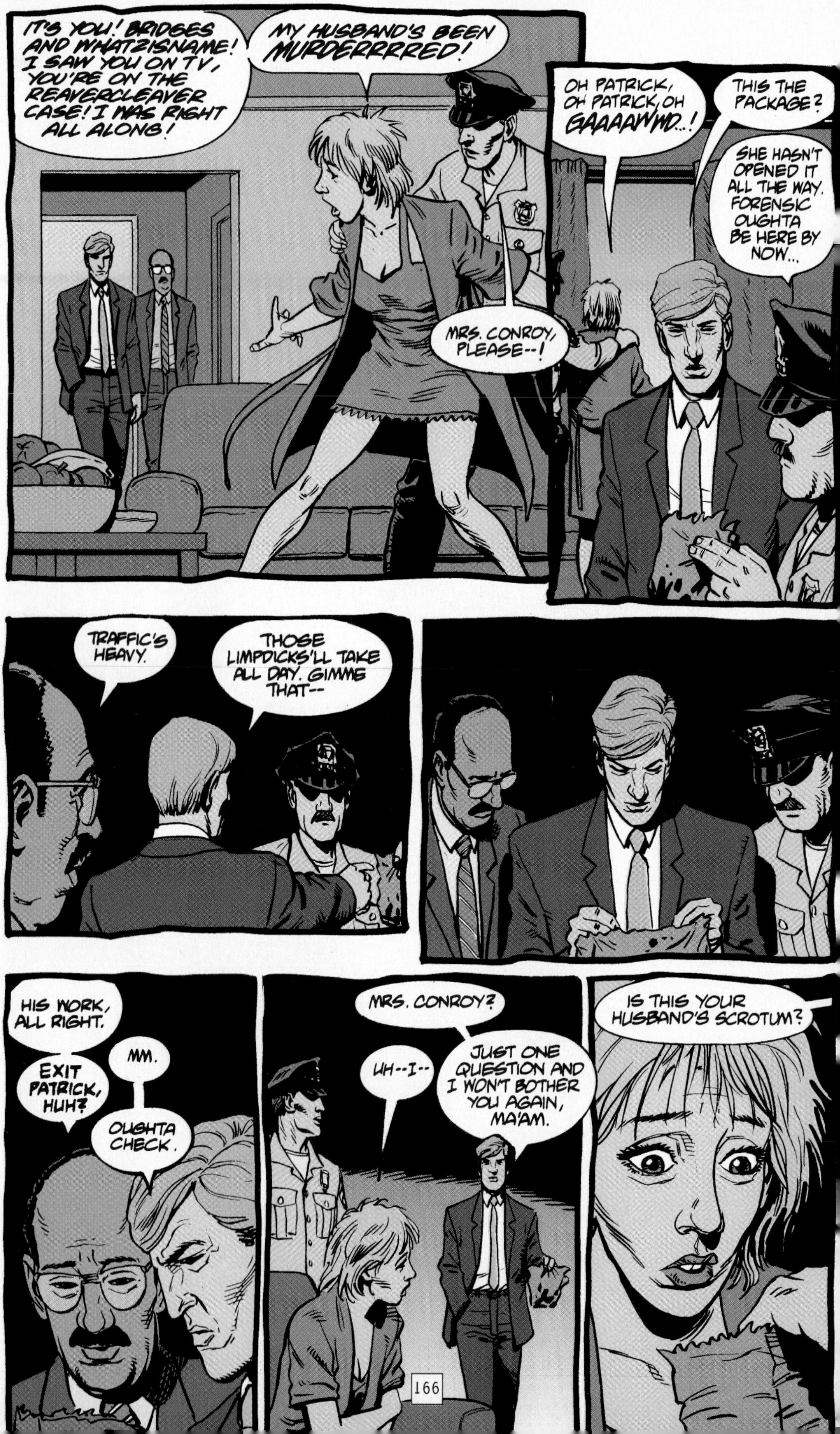
IT'S YOU! BRIDGES AND WHATZISNAME! I SAW YOU ON TV, YOU'RE ON THE REAVERCLEAVER CASE! I WAS RIGHT ALL ALONG!
MY HUSBAND'S BEEN MURDERRRRED!
MRS. CONROY, PLEASE--!
OH PATRICK, OH PATRICK, OH GAAAAWWD..!
THIS THE PACKAGE?
SHE HASN'T OPENED IT ALL THE WAY. FORENSIC OUGHTA BE HERE BY NOW...
TRAFFIC'S HEAVY.
THOSE LIMPDICKS'LL TAKE ALL DAY. GIMME THAT--
HIS WORK, ALL RIGHT.
MM.
EXIT PATRICK, HUH?
OUGHTA CHECK.
MRS. CONROY?
UH--I--
JUST ONE QUESTION AND I WON'T BOTHER YOU AGAIN, MA'AM.
IS THIS YOUR HUSBAND'S SCROTUM?

KNOCK IT OFF, WILL YOU?

AW, YOU GOTTA ADMIT IT'S A HELL OF A SIGHT...

NO, I DON'T. BUT THEN, I'M NOT A YOKEL ON HIS FIRST TRIP OUT OF THE BOONIES.

FOR CHRIST'S SAKE *STOP IT*, JESSE.. IT'S A DAMN GOOD WAY TO GET MUGGED.

CASS SAYS THAT'S MOSTLY BULLSHIT. ANYHOW, SOME PRICK TRIES IT, I'LL JUST TELL HIM GO FUCK YOURSELF.

NOT A GOOD IDEA. REMEMBER ROOT?

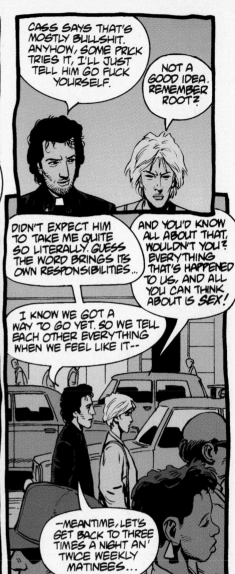

DIDN'T EXPECT HIM TO TAKE ME QUITE SO LITERALLY. GUESS THE WORD BRINGS ITS OWN RESPONSIBILITIES...

AND YOU'D KNOW ALL ABOUT THAT, WOULDN'T YOU? EVERYTHING THAT'S HAPPENED TO US, AND ALL YOU CAN THINK ABOUT IS *SEX!*

I KNOW WE GOT A WAY TO GO YET, SO WE TELL EACH OTHER EVERYTHING WHEN WE FEEL LIKE IT--

--MEANTIME, LET'S GET BACK TO THREE TIMES A NIGHT AN' TWICE WEEKLY MATINEES...

YOU WALKED OUT ON THAT FIVE YEARS AGO--

HEY, YOU KNOW SOMETHIN'?

YOU AIN'T SMILED ALL DAY, YOU KNOW THAT? HOW ABOUT SMILIN' FOR ME, JUST ONCE. JUST TO REMIND ME WHAT IT LOOKS LIKE.

YOU--

BASTARD...

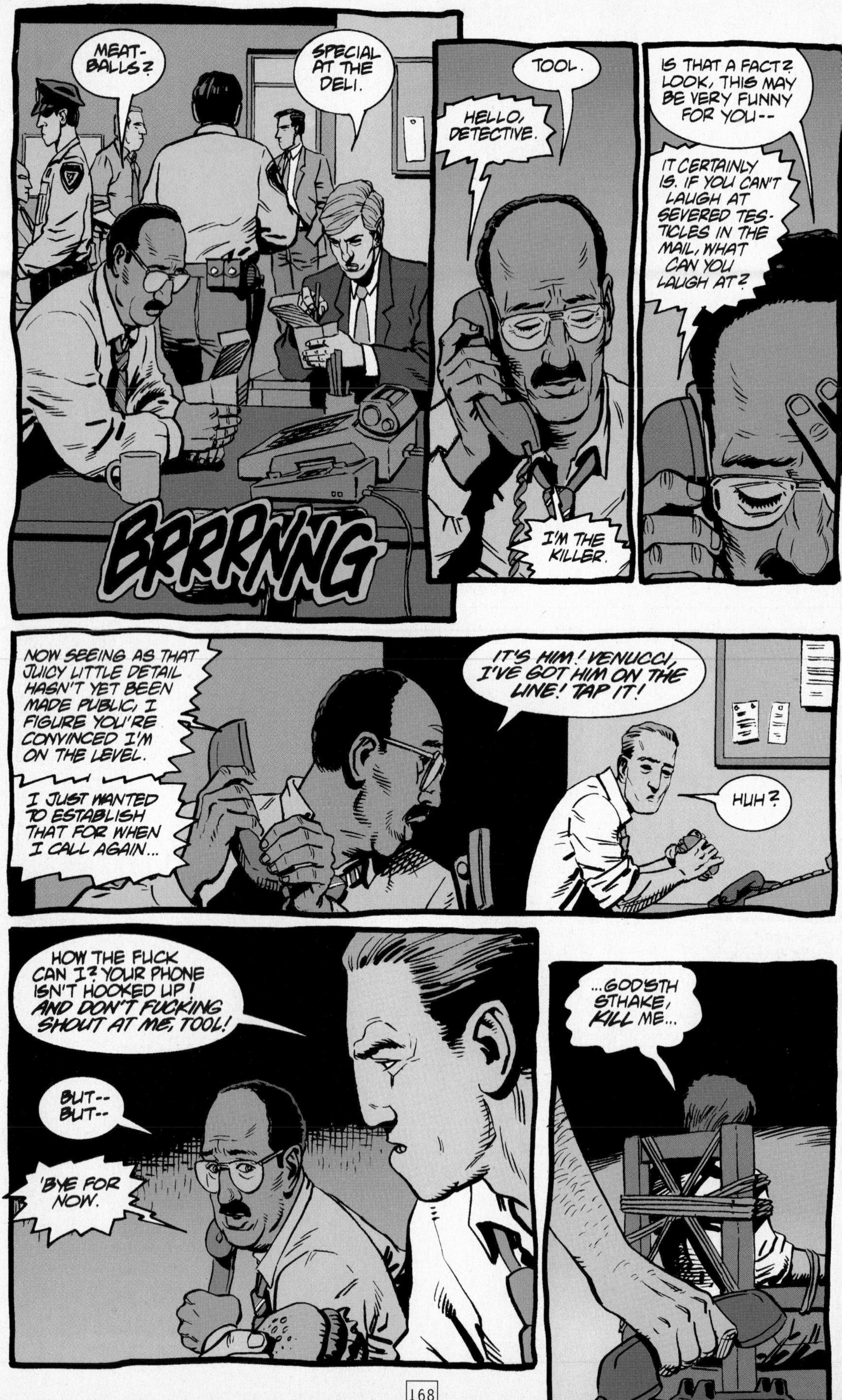
MEAT-BALLS?
SPECIAL AT THE DELI.
BRRRNNG
TOOL.
HELLO, DETECTIVE.
I'M THE KILLER.
IS THAT A FACT? LOOK, THIS MAY BE VERY FUNNY FOR YOU--
IT CERTAINLY IS. IF YOU CAN'T LAUGH AT SEVERED TES-TICLES IN THE MAIL, WHAT CAN YOU LAUGH AT?
NOW SEEING AS THAT JUICY LITTLE DETAIL HASN'T YET BEEN MADE PUBLIC, I FIGURE YOU'RE CONVINCED I'M ON THE LEVEL.
I JUST WANTED TO ESTABLISH THAT FOR WHEN I CALL AGAIN...
IT'S HIM! VENUCCI, I'VE GOT HIM ON THE LINE! TAP IT!
HUH?
HOW THE FUCK CAN I? YOUR PHONE ISN'T HOOKED UP! AND DON'T FUCKING SHOUT AT ME, TOOL!
BUT-- BUT--
'BYE FOR NOW.
...GOD'STH STHAKE, KILL ME...

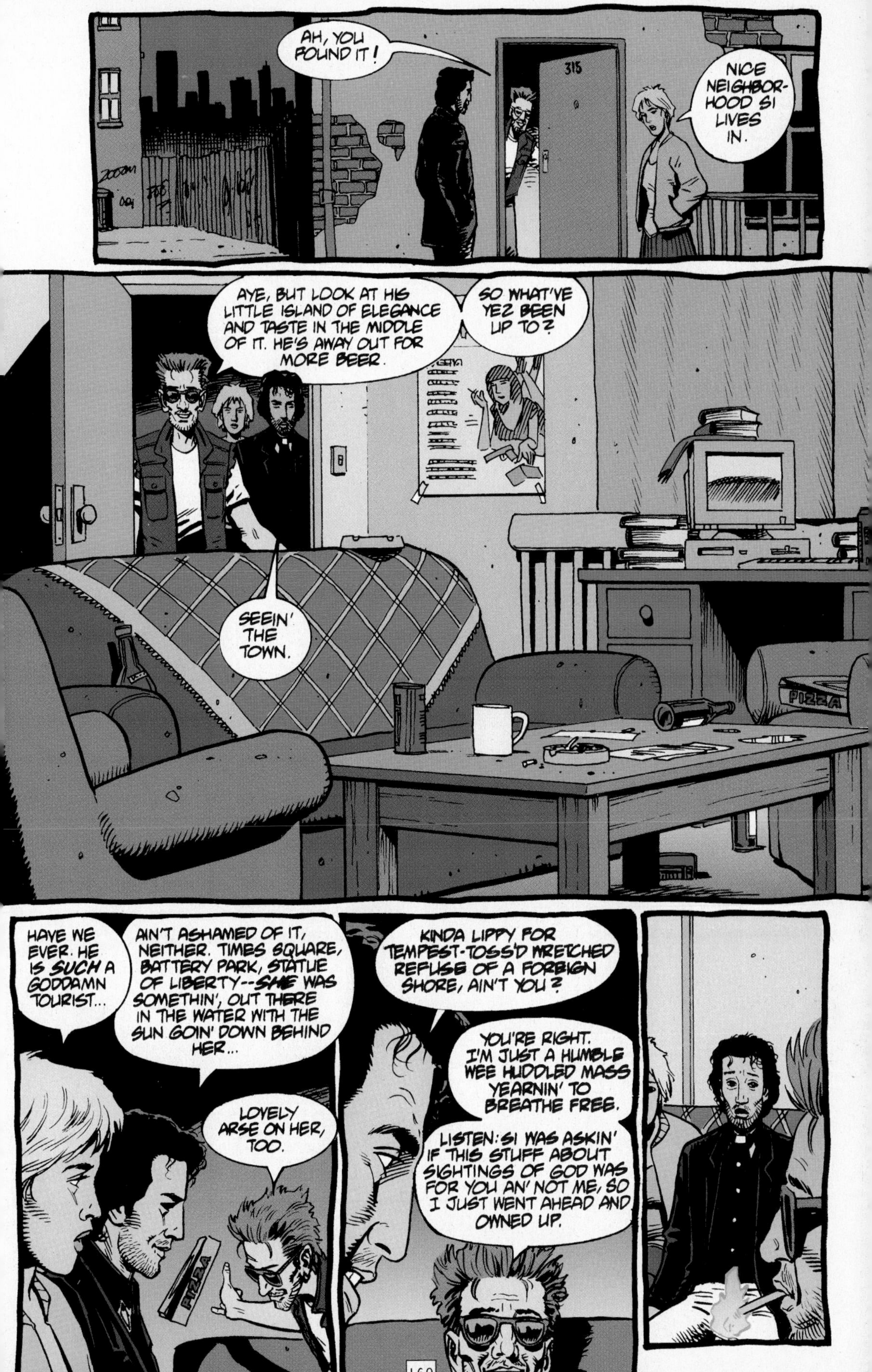
AH, YOU FOUND IT!
315
NICE NEIGHBOR-HOOD SI LIVES IN.
AYE, BUT LOOK AT HIS LITTLE ISLAND OF ELEGANCE AND TASTE IN THE MIDDLE OF IT. HE'S AWAY OUT FOR MORE BEER.
SO WHAT'VE YEZ BEEN UP TO?
SEEIN' THE TOWN.
PIZZA
HAVE WE EVER. HE IS *SUCH* A GODDAMN TOURIST...
AIN'T ASHAMED OF IT, NEITHER. TIMES SQUARE, BATTERY PARK, STATUE OF LIBERTY--*SHE* WAS SOMETHIN', OUT THERE IN THE WATER WITH THE SUN GOIN' DOWN BEHIND HER...
LOVELY ARSE ON HER, TOO.
KINDA LIPPY FOR TEMPEST-TOSS'D WRETCHED REFUSE OF A FOREIGN SHORE, AIN'T YOU?
YOU'RE RIGHT. I'M JUST A HUMBLE WEE HUDDLED MASS YEARNIN' TO BREATHE FREE.
LISTEN: SI WAS ASKIN' IF THIS STUFF ABOUT SIGHTINGS OF GOD WAS FOR YOU AN' NOT ME, SO I JUST WENT AHEAD AND OWNED UP.
PIZZA

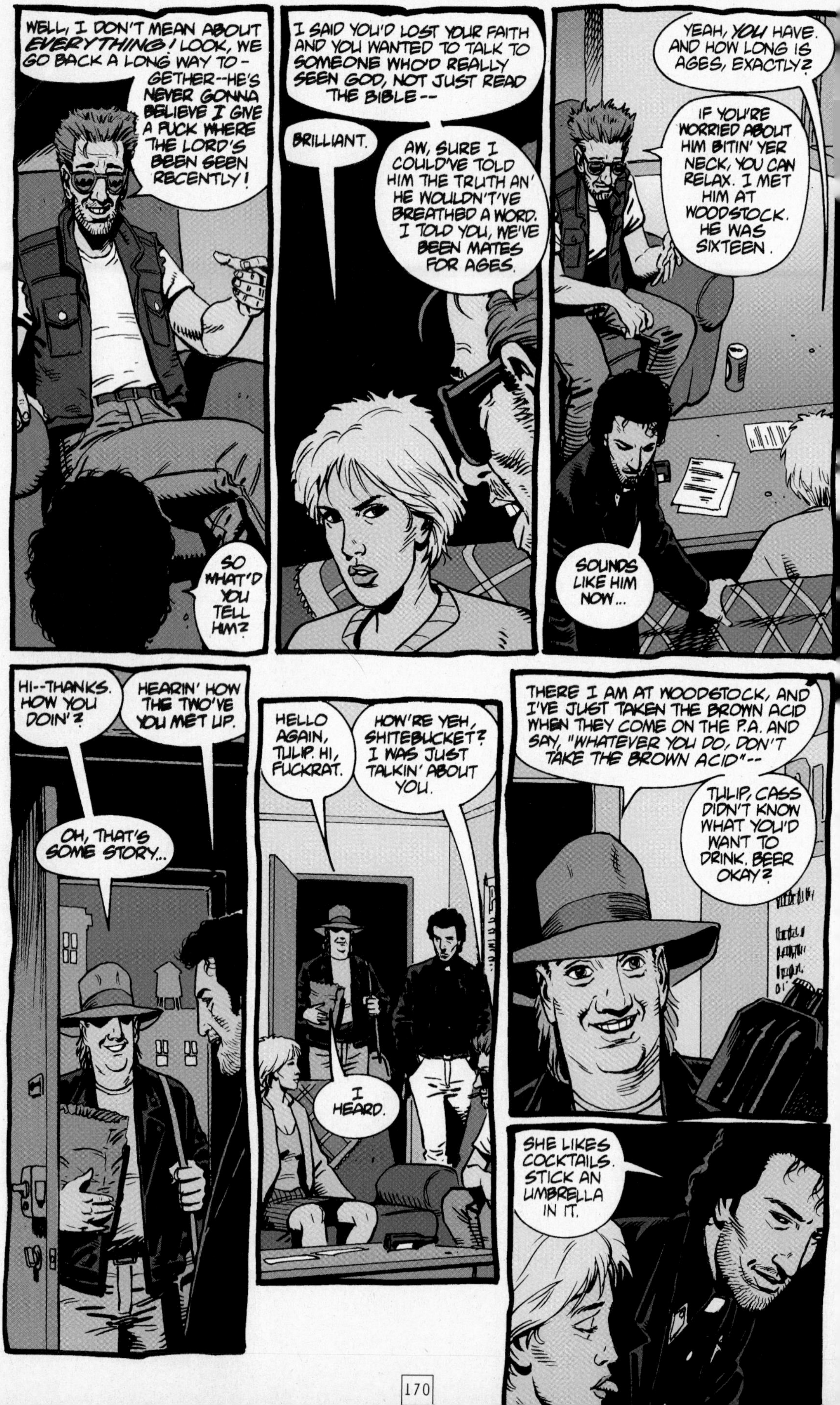
WELL, I DON'T MEAN ABOUT *EVERYTHING!* LOOK, WE GO BACK A LONG WAY TO-GETHER--HE'S NEVER GONNA BELIEVE I GIVE A FUCK WHERE THE LORD'S BEEN SEEN RECENTLY!
SO WHAT'D YOU TELL HIM?
I SAID YOU'D LOST YOUR FAITH AND YOU WANTED TO TALK TO SOMEONE WHO'D REALLY SEEN GOD, NOT JUST READ THE BIBLE--
BRILLIANT.
AW, SURE I COULD'VE TOLD HIM THE TRUTH AN' HE WOULDN'T'VE BREATHED A WORD. I TOLD YOU, WE'VE BEEN MATES FOR AGES.
YEAH, *YOU* HAVE. AND HOW LONG IS AGES, EXACTLY?
IF YOU'RE WORRIED ABOUT HIM BITIN' YER NECK, YOU CAN RELAX. I MET HIM AT WOODSTOCK. HE WAS SIXTEEN.
SOUNDS LIKE HIM NOW...
HI--THANKS. HOW YOU DOIN'?
HEARIN' HOW THE TWO'VE YOU MET UP.
OH, THAT'S SOME STORY...
HELLO AGAIN, TULIP. HI, FUCKRAT.
HOW'RE YEH, SHITEBUCKET? I WAS JUST TALKIN' ABOUT YOU.
I HEARD.
THERE I AM AT WOODSTOCK, AND I'VE JUST TAKEN THE BROWN ACID WHEN THEY COME ON THE P.A. AND SAY, "WHATEVER YOU DO, DON'T TAKE THE BROWN ACID"--
TULIP, CASS DIDN'T KNOW WHAT YOU'D WANT TO DRINK. BEER OKAY?
SHE LIKES COCKTAILS. STICK AN UMBRELLA IN IT.

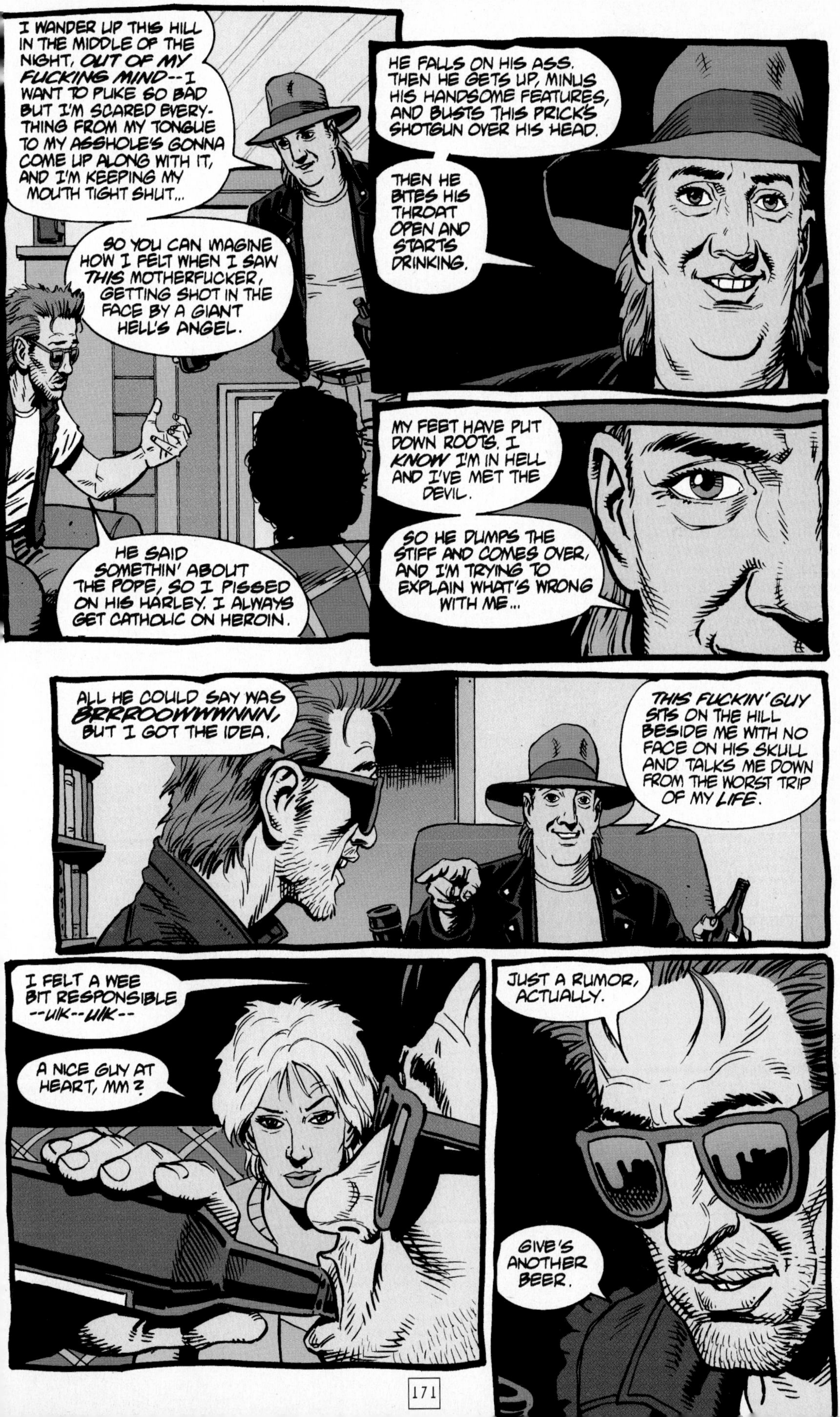
I WANDER UP THIS HILL IN THE MIDDLE OF THE NIGHT, OUT OF MY FUCKING MIND--I WANT TO PUKE SO BAD BUT I'M SCARED EVERYTHING FROM MY TONGUE TO MY ASSHOLE'S GONNA COME UP ALONG WITH IT, AND I'M KEEPING MY MOUTH TIGHT SHUT...
SO YOU CAN IMAGINE HOW I FELT WHEN I SAW THIS MOTHERFUCKER, GETTING SHOT IN THE FACE BY A GIANT HELL'S ANGEL.
HE SAID SOMETHIN' ABOUT THE POPE, SO I PISSED ON HIS HARLEY. I ALWAYS GET CATHOLIC ON HEROIN.
HE FALLS ON HIS ASS. THEN HE GETS UP, MINUS HIS HANDSOME FEATURES, AND BUSTS THIS PRICK'S SHOTGUN OVER HIS HEAD.
THEN HE BITES HIS THROAT OPEN AND STARTS DRINKING.
MY FEET HAVE PUT DOWN ROOTS. I KNOW I'M IN HELL AND I'VE MET THE DEVIL.
SO HE DUMPS THE STIFF AND COMES OVER, AND I'M TRYING TO EXPLAIN WHAT'S WRONG WITH ME...
ALL HE COULD SAY WAS BRRROOWWWNNN, BUT I GOT THE IDEA.
THIS FUCKIN' GUY SITS ON THE HILL BESIDE ME WITH NO FACE ON HIS SKULL AND TALKS ME DOWN FROM THE WORST TRIP OF MY LIFE.
I FELT A WEE BIT RESPONSIBLE --UIK--UIK--
A NICE GUY AT HEART, MM?
JUST A RUMOR, ACTUALLY.
GIVE'S ANOTHER BEER.

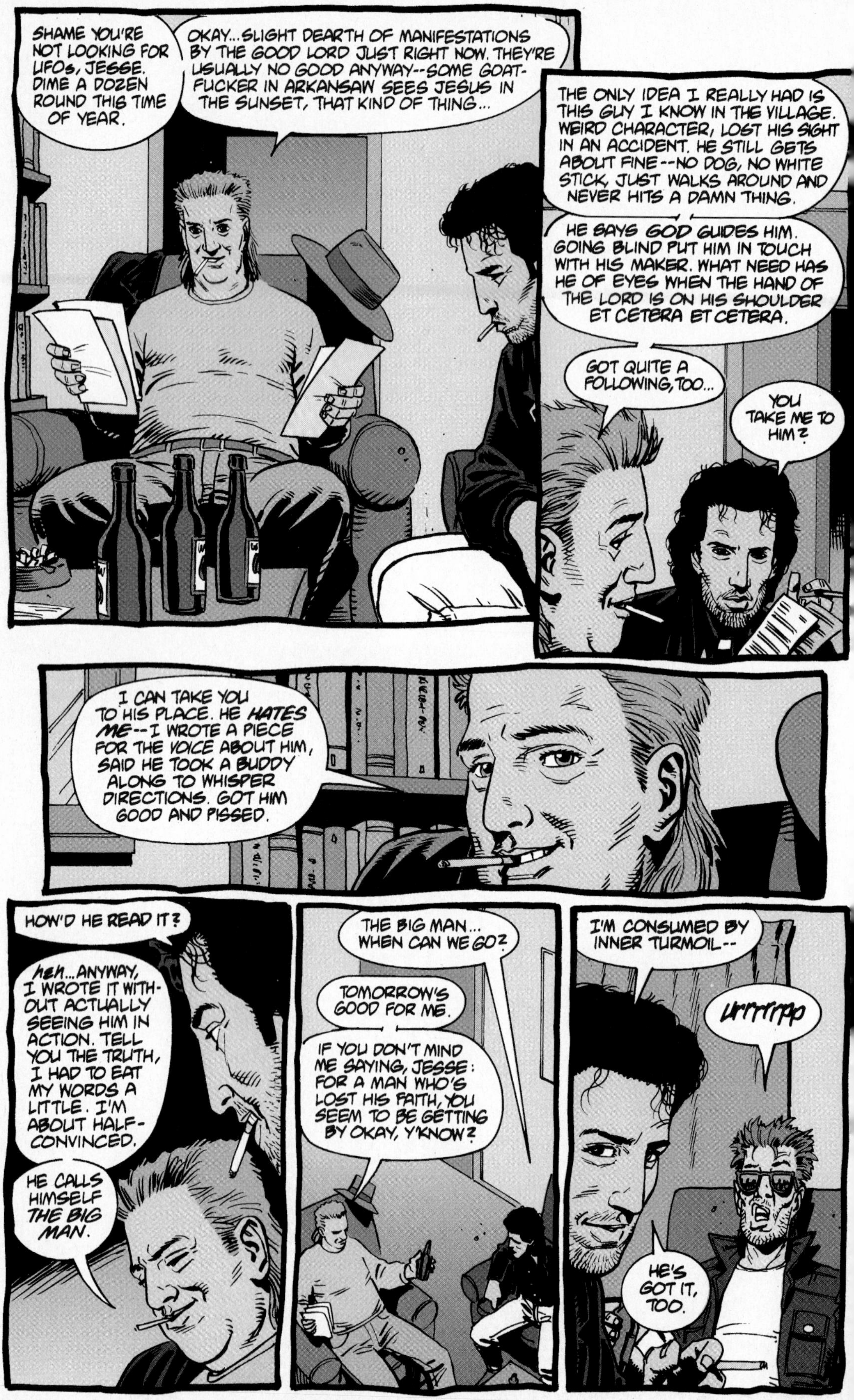
SHAME YOU'RE NOT LOOKING FOR UFOs, JESSE. DIME A DOZEN ROUND THIS TIME OF YEAR.
OKAY... SLIGHT DEARTH OF MANIFESTATIONS BY THE GOOD LORD JUST RIGHT NOW. THEY'RE USUALLY NO GOOD ANYWAY--SOME GOAT-FUCKER IN ARKANSAW SEES JESUS IN THE SUNSET, THAT KIND OF THING...
THE ONLY IDEA I REALLY HAD IS THIS GUY I KNOW IN THE VILLAGE. WEIRD CHARACTER, LOST HIS SIGHT IN AN ACCIDENT. HE STILL GETS ABOUT FINE--NO DOG, NO WHITE STICK, JUST WALKS AROUND AND NEVER HITS A DAMN THING.
HE SAYS GOD GUIDES HIM. GOING BLIND PUT HIM IN TOUCH WITH HIS MAKER. WHAT NEED HAS HE OF EYES WHEN THE HAND OF THE LORD IS ON HIS SHOULDER ET CETERA ET CETERA.
GOT QUITE A FOLLOWING, TOO...
YOU TAKE ME TO HIM?
I CAN TAKE YOU TO HIS PLACE. HE HATES ME--I WROTE A PIECE FOR THE VOICE ABOUT HIM, SAID HE TOOK A BUDDY ALONG TO WHISPER DIRECTIONS. GOT HIM GOOD AND PISSED.
HOW'D HE READ IT?
heh... ANYWAY, I WROTE IT WITHOUT ACTUALLY SEEING HIM IN ACTION. TELL YOU THE TRUTH, I HAD TO EAT MY WORDS A LITTLE. I'M ABOUT HALF-CONVINCED.
HE CALLS HIMSELF THE BIG MAN.
THE BIG MAN... WHEN CAN WE GO?
TOMORROW'S GOOD FOR ME.
IF YOU DON'T MIND ME SAYING, JESSE: FOR A MAN WHO'S LOST HIS FAITH, YOU SEEM TO BE GETTING BY OKAY, Y'KNOW?
I'M CONSUMED BY INNER TURMOIL--
Urrrrrpp
HE'S GOT IT, TOO.

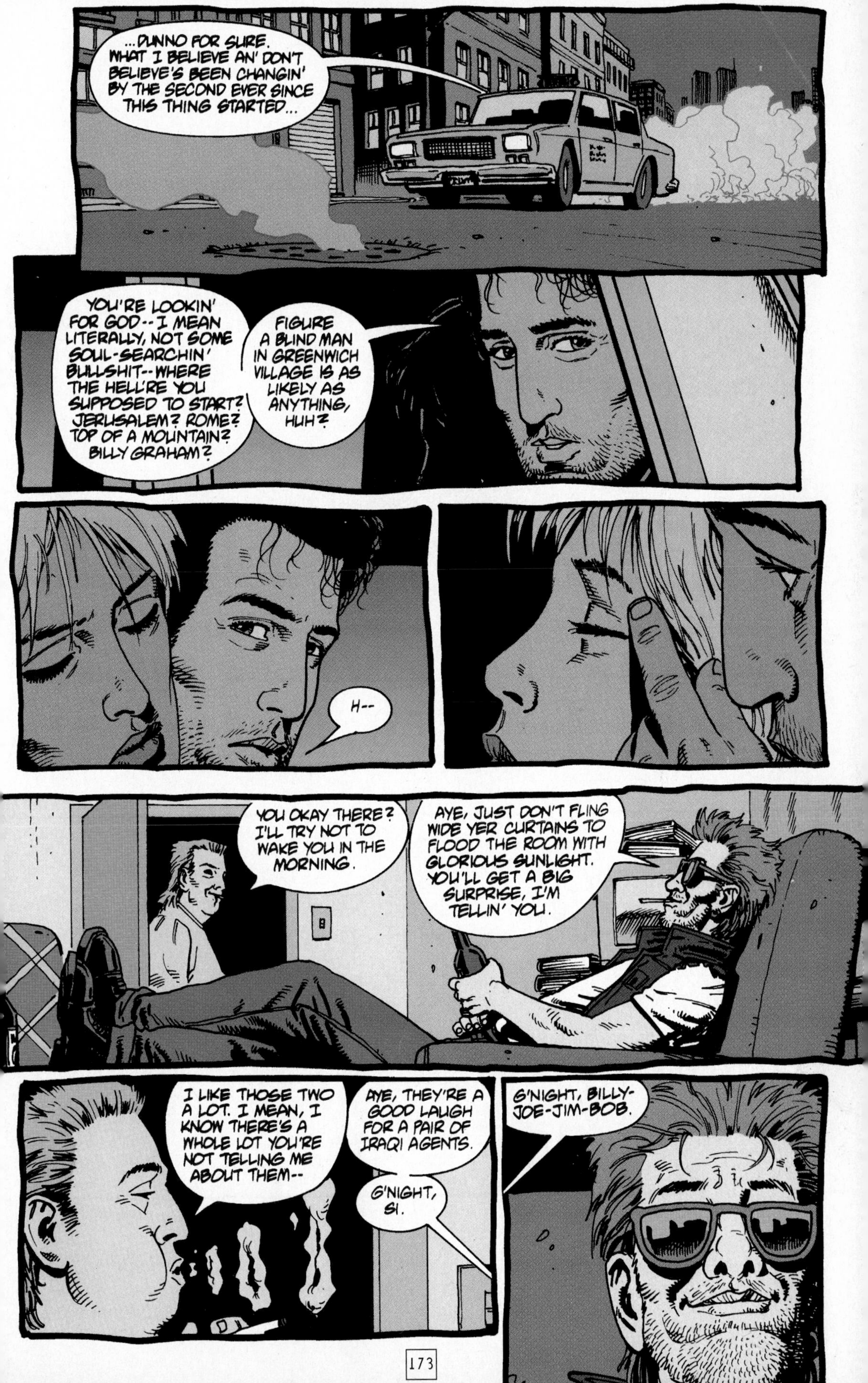
...DUNNO FOR SURE. WHAT I BELIEVE AN' DON'T BELIEVE'S BEEN CHANGIN' BY THE SECOND EVER SINCE THIS THING STARTED...
YOU'RE LOOKIN' FOR GOD--I MEAN LITERALLY, NOT SOME SOUL-SEARCHIN' BULLSHIT--WHERE THE HELL'RE YOU SUPPOSED TO START? JERUSALEM? ROME? TOP OF A MOUNTAIN? BILLY GRAHAM?
FIGURE A BLIND MAN IN GREENWICH VILLAGE IS AS LIKELY AS ANYTHING, HUH?
H--
YOU OKAY THERE? I'LL TRY NOT TO WAKE YOU IN THE MORNING.
AYE, JUST DON'T FLING WIDE YER CURTAINS TO FLOOD THE ROOM WITH GLORIOUS SUNLIGHT. YOU'LL GET A BIG SURPRISE, I'M TELLIN' YOU.
I LIKE THOSE TWO A LOT. I MEAN, I KNOW THERE'S A WHOLE LOT YOU'RE NOT TELLING ME ABOUT THEM--
AYE, THEY'RE A GOOD LAUGH FOR A PAIR OF IRAQI AGENTS.
G'NIGHT, SI.
G'NIGHT, BILLY-JOE-JIM-BOB.

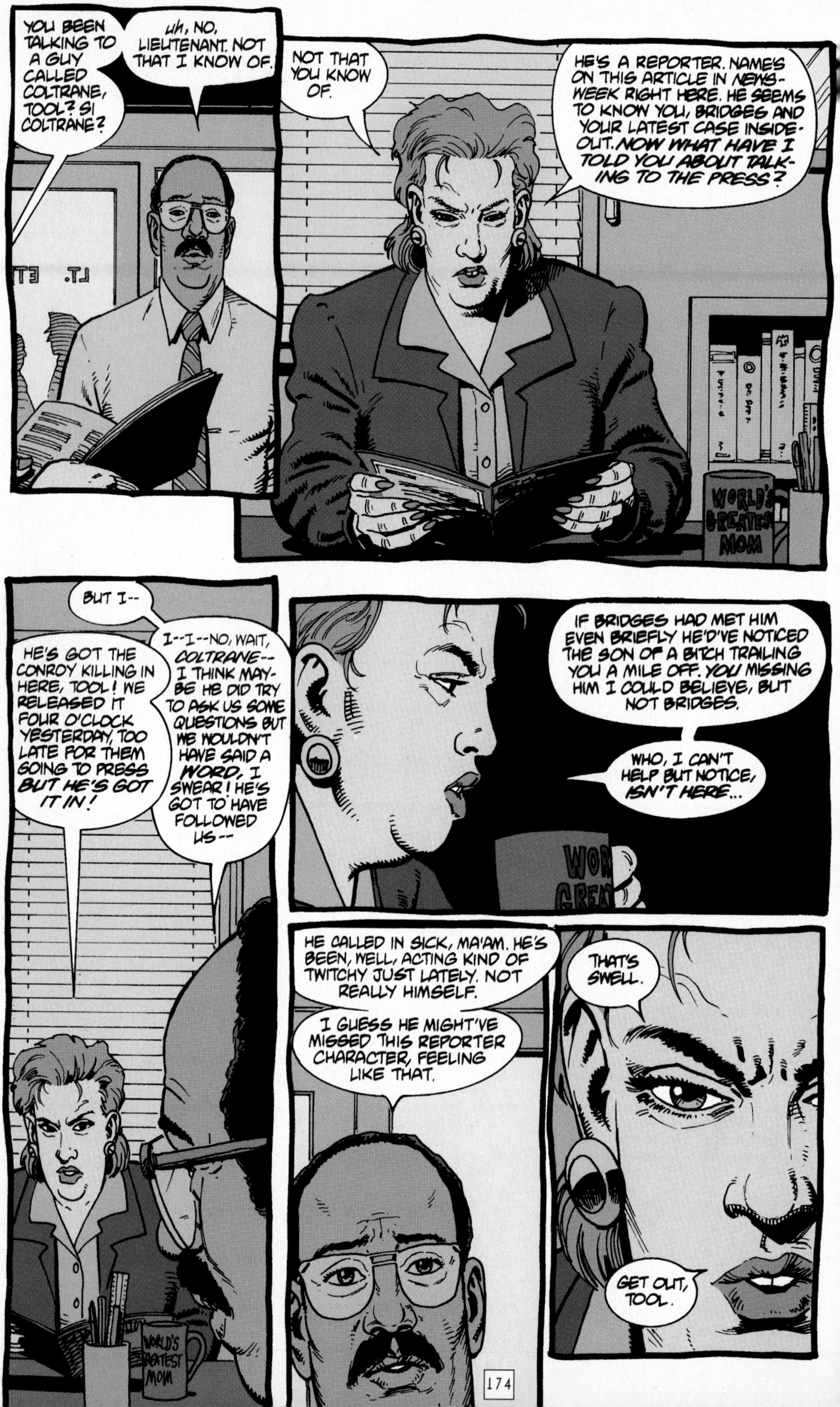

YOU BEEN TALKING TO A GUY CALLED COLTRANE, TOOL? SI COLTRANE?
UH, NO, LIEUTENANT. NOT THAT I KNOW OF.
NOT THAT YOU KNOW OF.
HE'S A REPORTER. NAME'S ON THIS ARTICLE IN NEWSWEEK RIGHT HERE. HE SEEMS TO KNOW YOU, BRIDGES AND YOUR LATEST CASE INSIDE-OUT. NOW WHAT HAVE I TOLD YOU ABOUT TALKING TO THE PRESS?
LT. ET
WORLD'S GREATEST MOM
BUT I--
HE'S GOT THE CONROY KILLING IN HERE, TOOL! WE RELEASED IT FOUR O'CLOCK YESTERDAY, TOO LATE FOR THEM GOING TO PRESS BUT HE'S GOT IT IN!
I--I--NO, WAIT, COLTRANE-- I THINK MAYBE HE DID TRY TO ASK US SOME QUESTIONS BUT WE WOULDN'T HAVE SAID A WORD, I SWEAR! HE'S GOT TO HAVE FOLLOWED US--
IF BRIDGES HAD MET HIM EVEN BRIEFLY HE'D'VE NOTICED THE SON OF A BITCH TRAILING YOU A MILE OFF. YOU MISSING HIM I COULD BELIEVE, BUT NOT BRIDGES.
WHO, I CAN'T HELP BUT NOTICE, ISN'T HERE...
HE CALLED IN SICK, MA'AM. HE'S BEEN, WELL, ACTING KIND OF TWITCHY JUST LATELY. NOT REALLY HIMSELF.
I GUESS HE MIGHT'VE MISSED THIS REPORTER CHARACTER, FEELING LIKE THAT.
THAT'S SWELL.
GET OUT, TOOL.
WORLD'S GREATEST MOM

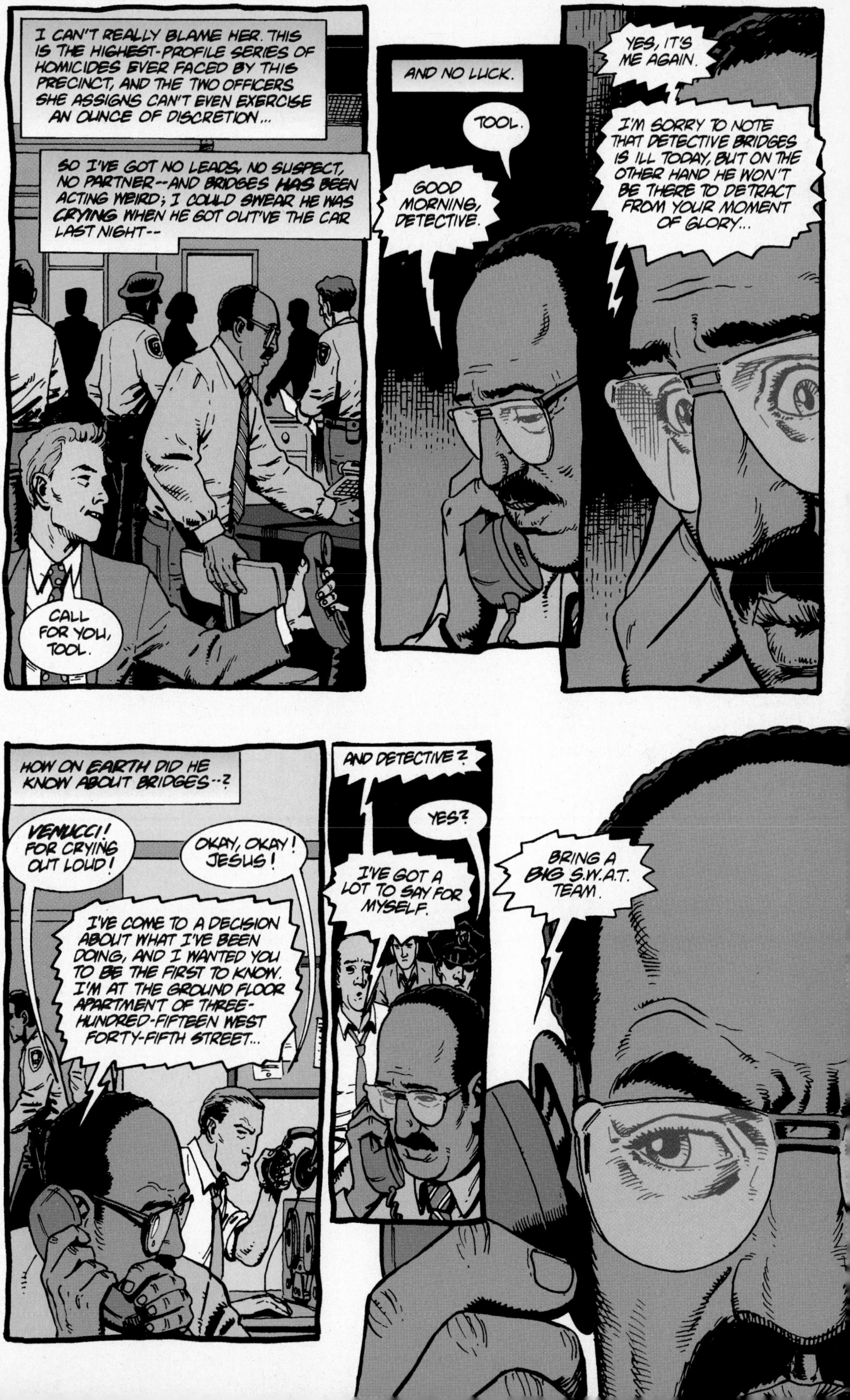

I CAN'T REALLY BLAME HER. THIS IS THE HIGHEST-PROFILE SERIES OF HOMICIDES EVER FACED BY THIS PRECINCT, AND THE TWO OFFICERS SHE ASSIGNS CAN'T EVEN EXERCISE AN OUNCE OF DISCRETION...
SO I'VE GOT NO LEADS, NO SUSPECT, NO PARTNER--AND BRIDGES HAS BEEN ACTING WEIRD; I COULD SWEAR HE WAS CRYING WHEN HE GOT OUT'VE THE CAR LAST NIGHT--
CALL FOR YOU, TOOL.
AND NO LUCK.
TOOL.
GOOD MORNING, DETECTIVE.
YES, IT'S ME AGAIN.
I'M SORRY TO NOTE THAT DETECTIVE BRIDGES IS ILL TODAY, BUT ON THE OTHER HAND HE WON'T BE THERE TO DETRACT FROM YOUR MOMENT OF GLORY...
HOW ON EARTH DID HE KNOW ABOUT BRIDGES--?
VENUCCI! FOR CRYING OUT LOUD!
OKAY, OKAY! JESUS!
I'VE COME TO A DECISION ABOUT WHAT I'VE BEEN DOING, AND I WANTED YOU TO BE THE FIRST TO KNOW. I'M AT THE GROUND FLOOR APARTMENT OF THREE-HUNDRED-FIFTEEN WEST FORTY-FIFTH STREET...
AND DETECTIVE?
YES?
I'VE GOT A LOT TO SAY FOR MYSELF.
BRING A BIG S.W.A.T. TEAM.

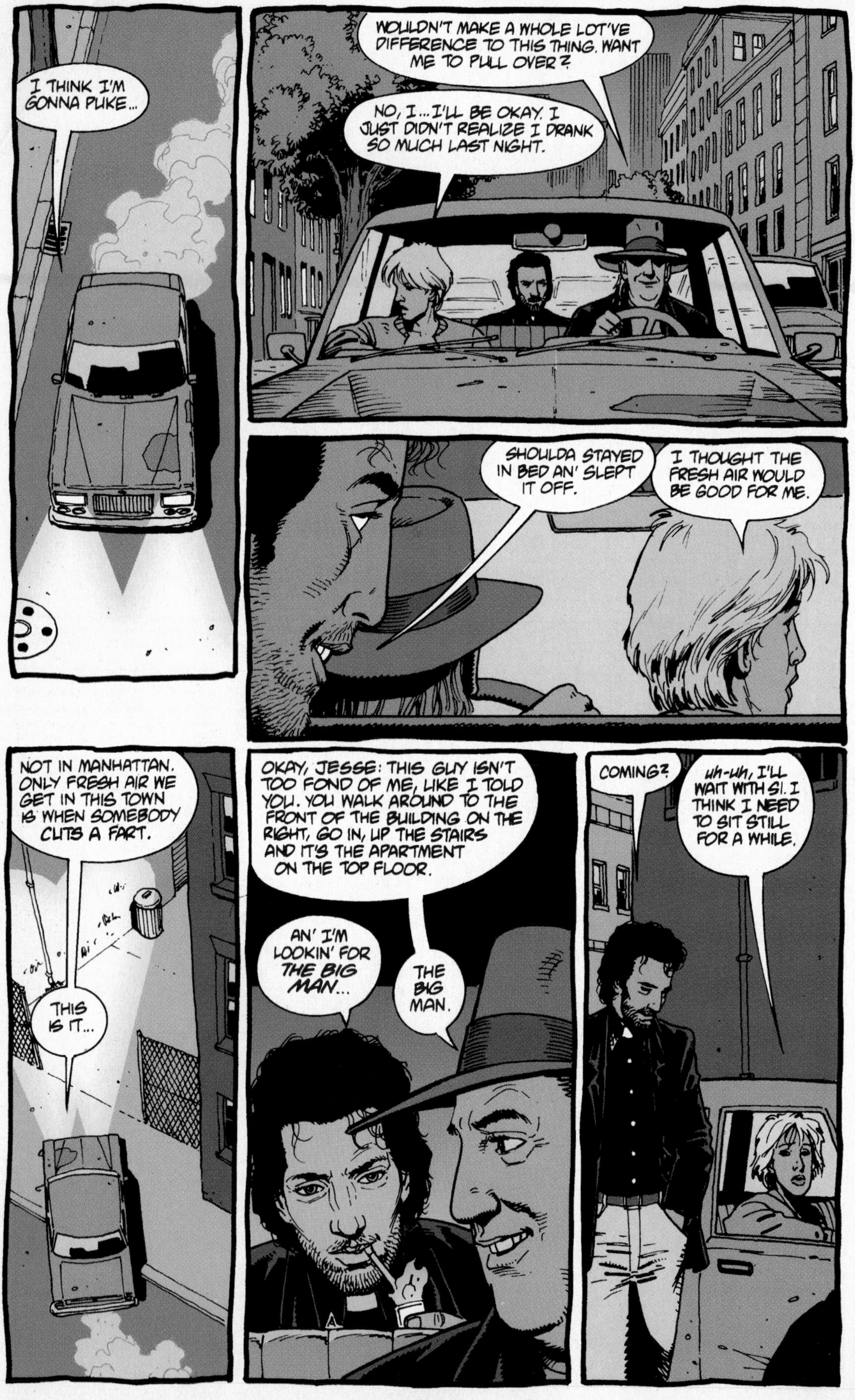
I THINK I'M GONNA PUKE...
WOULDN'T MAKE A WHOLE LOT'VE DIFFERENCE TO THIS THING. WANT ME TO PULL OVER?
NO, I... I'LL BE OKAY. I JUST DIDN'T REALIZE I DRANK SO MUCH LAST NIGHT.
SHOULDA STAYED IN BED AN' SLEPT IT OFF.
I THOUGHT THE FRESH AIR WOULD BE GOOD FOR ME.
NOT IN MANHATTAN. ONLY FRESH AIR WE GET IN THIS TOWN IS WHEN SOMEBODY CUTS A FART.
THIS IS IT...
OKAY, JESSE: THIS GUY ISN'T TOO FOND OF ME, LIKE I TOLD YOU. YOU WALK AROUND TO THE FRONT OF THE BUILDING ON THE RIGHT, GO IN, UP THE STAIRS AND IT'S THE APARTMENT ON THE TOP FLOOR.
AN' I'M LOOKIN' FOR THE BIG MAN...
THE BIG MAN.
COMING?
UH-UH, I'LL WAIT WITH SI. I THINK I NEED TO SIT STILL FOR A WHILE.

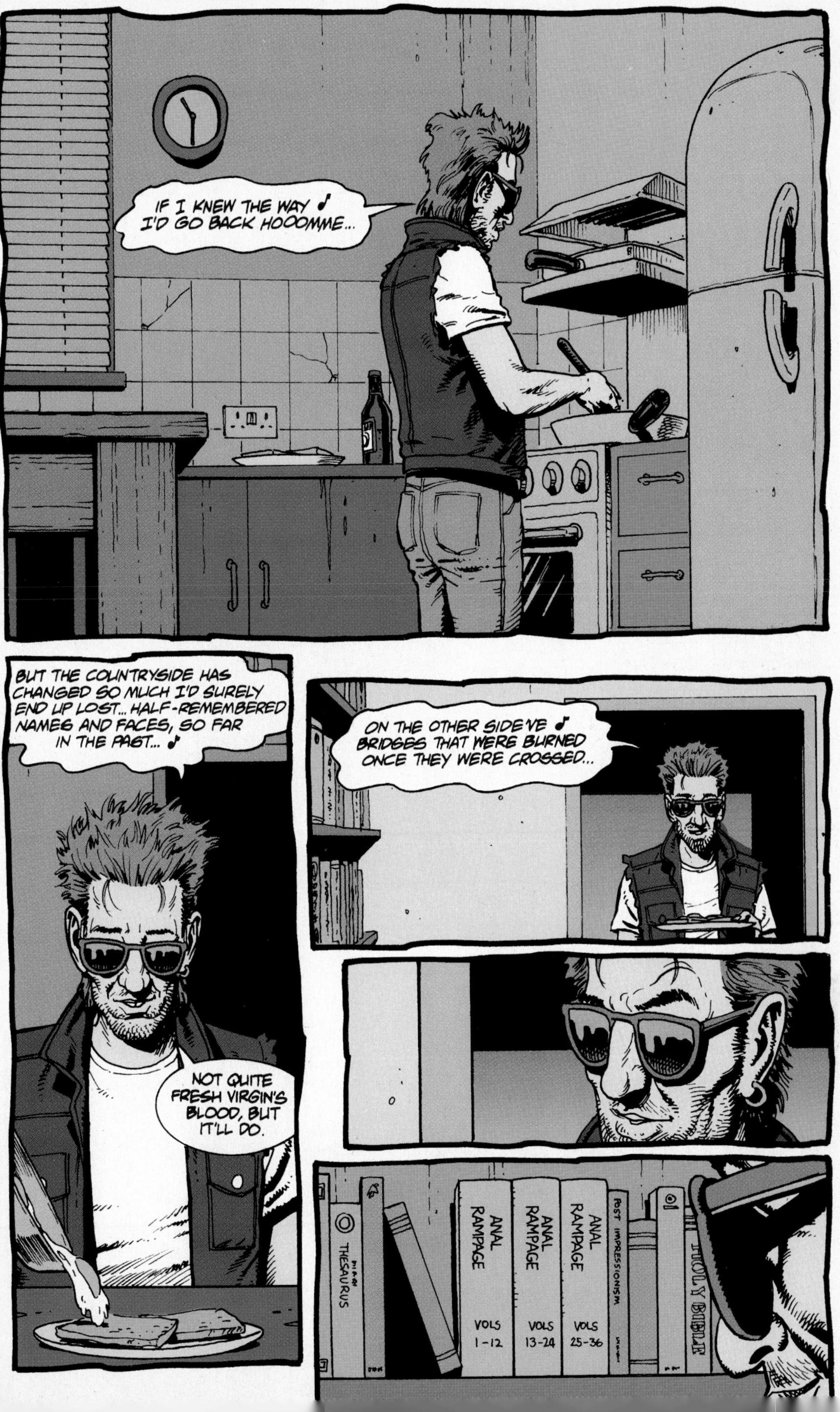
IF I KNEW THE WAY ♪ I'D GO BACK HOOOMME...
BUT THE COUNTRYSIDE HAS CHANGED SO MUCH I'D SURELY END UP LOST... HALF-REMEMBERED NAMES AND FACES, SO FAR IN THE PAST... ♪
ON THE OTHER SIDE'VE ♪ BRIDGES THAT WERE BURNED ONCE THEY WERE CROSSED...
NOT QUITE FRESH VIRGIN'S BLOOD, BUT IT'LL DO.
THESAURUS
ANAL RAMPAGE VOLS 1-12
ANAL RAMPAGE VOLS 13-24
ANAL RAMPAGE VOLS 25-36
POST IMPRESSIONISM
HOLY BIBLE

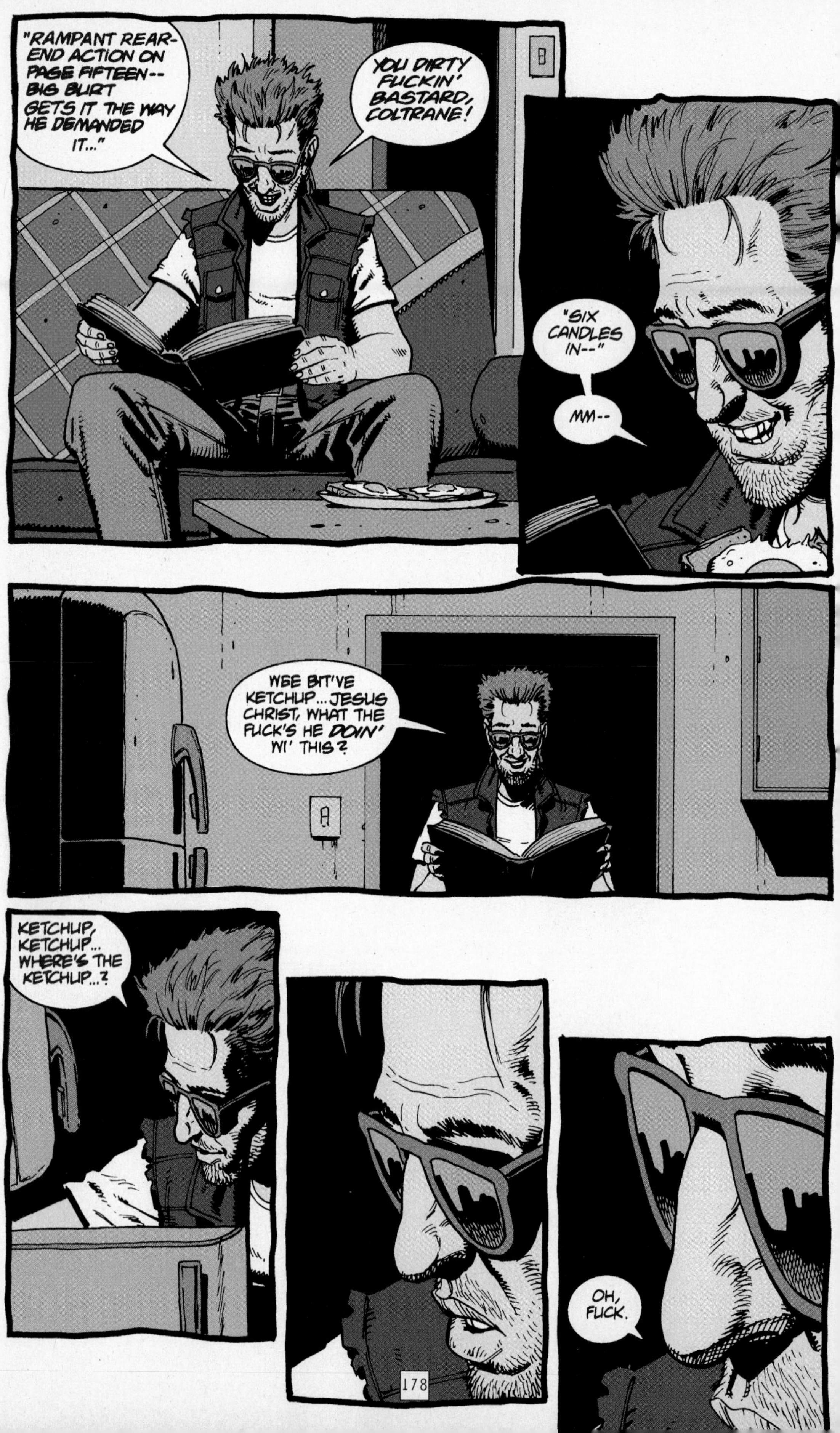
"RAMPANT REAR-END ACTION ON PAGE FIFTEEN-- BIG BURT GETS IT THE WAY HE DEMANDED IT..."
YOU DIRTY FUCKIN' BASTARD, COLTRANE!
"SIX CANDLES IN--"
MM--
WEE BIT'VE KETCHUP... JESUS CHRIST, WHAT THE FUCK'S HE DOIN' WI' THIS?
KETCHUP, KETCHUP... WHERE'S THE KETCHUP...?
OH, FUCK.

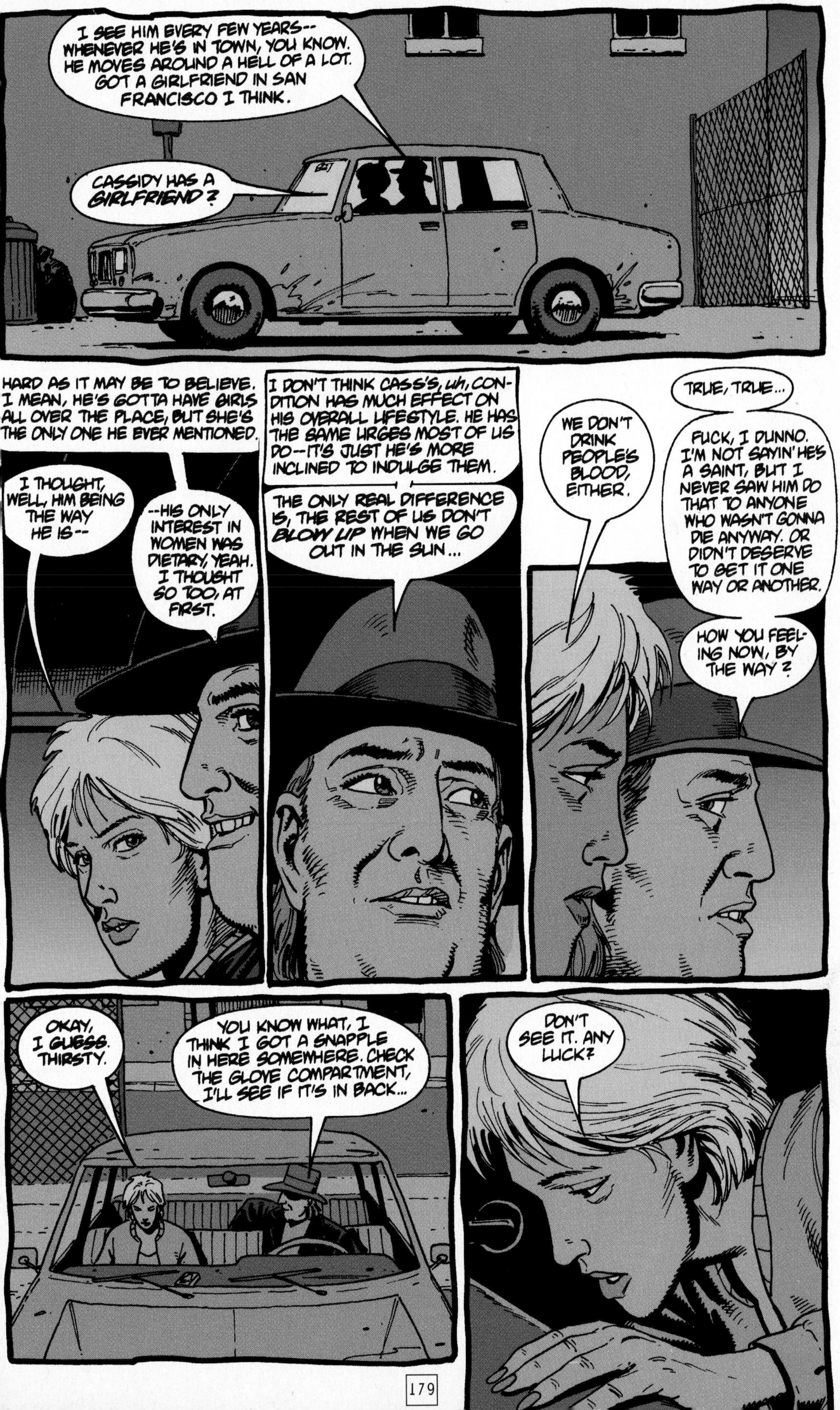
I SEE HIM EVERY FEW YEARS-- WHENEVER HE'S IN TOWN, YOU KNOW. HE MOVES AROUND A HELL OF A LOT. GOT A GIRLFRIEND IN SAN FRANCISCO I THINK.
CASSIDY HAS A GIRLFRIEND?
HARD AS IT MAY BE TO BELIEVE. I MEAN, HE'S GOTTA HAVE GIRLS ALL OVER THE PLACE, BUT SHE'S THE ONLY ONE HE EVER MENTIONED.
I THOUGHT, WELL, HIM BEING THE WAY HE IS--
--HIS ONLY INTEREST IN WOMEN WAS DIETARY, YEAH. I THOUGHT SO TOO, AT FIRST.
I DON'T THINK CASS'S, uh, CONDITION HAS MUCH EFFECT ON HIS OVERALL LIFESTYLE. HE HAS THE SAME URGES MOST OF US DO--IT'S JUST HE'S MORE INCLINED TO INDULGE THEM.
THE ONLY REAL DIFFERENCE IS, THE REST OF US DON'T BLOW UP WHEN WE GO OUT IN THE SUN...
WE DON'T DRINK PEOPLE'S BLOOD, EITHER.
TRUE, TRUE...
FUCK, I DUNNO. I'M NOT SAYIN' HE'S A SAINT, BUT I NEVER SAW HIM DO THAT TO ANYONE WHO WASN'T GONNA DIE ANYWAY. OR DIDN'T DESERVE TO GET IT ONE WAY OR ANOTHER.
HOW YOU FEELING NOW, BY THE WAY?
OKAY, I GUESS. THIRSTY.
YOU KNOW WHAT, I THINK I GOT A SNAPPLE IN HERE SOMEWHERE. CHECK THE GLOVE COMPARTMENT, I'LL SEE IF IT'S IN BACK...
DON'T SEE IT. ANY LUCK?

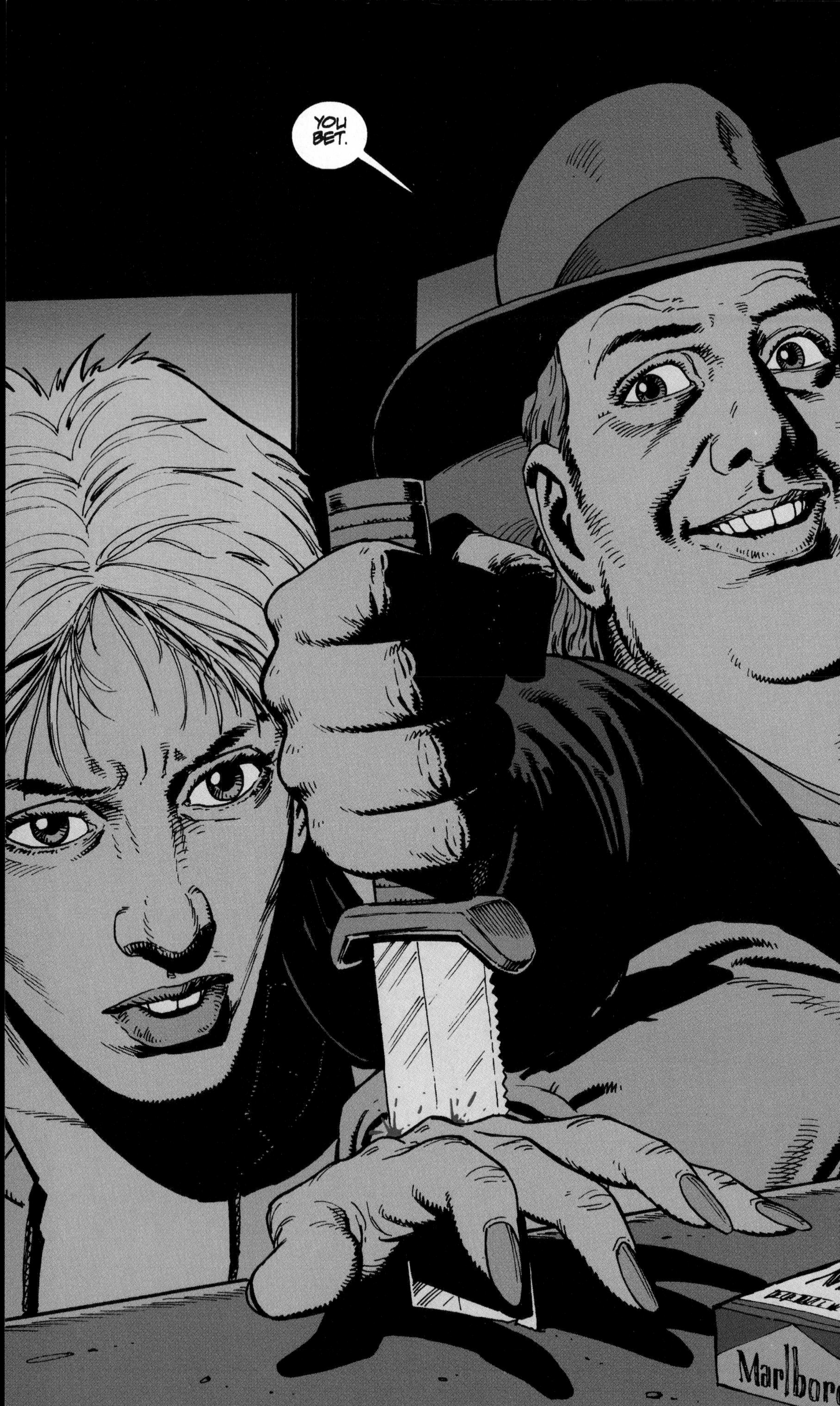

YOU BET.
Marlboro

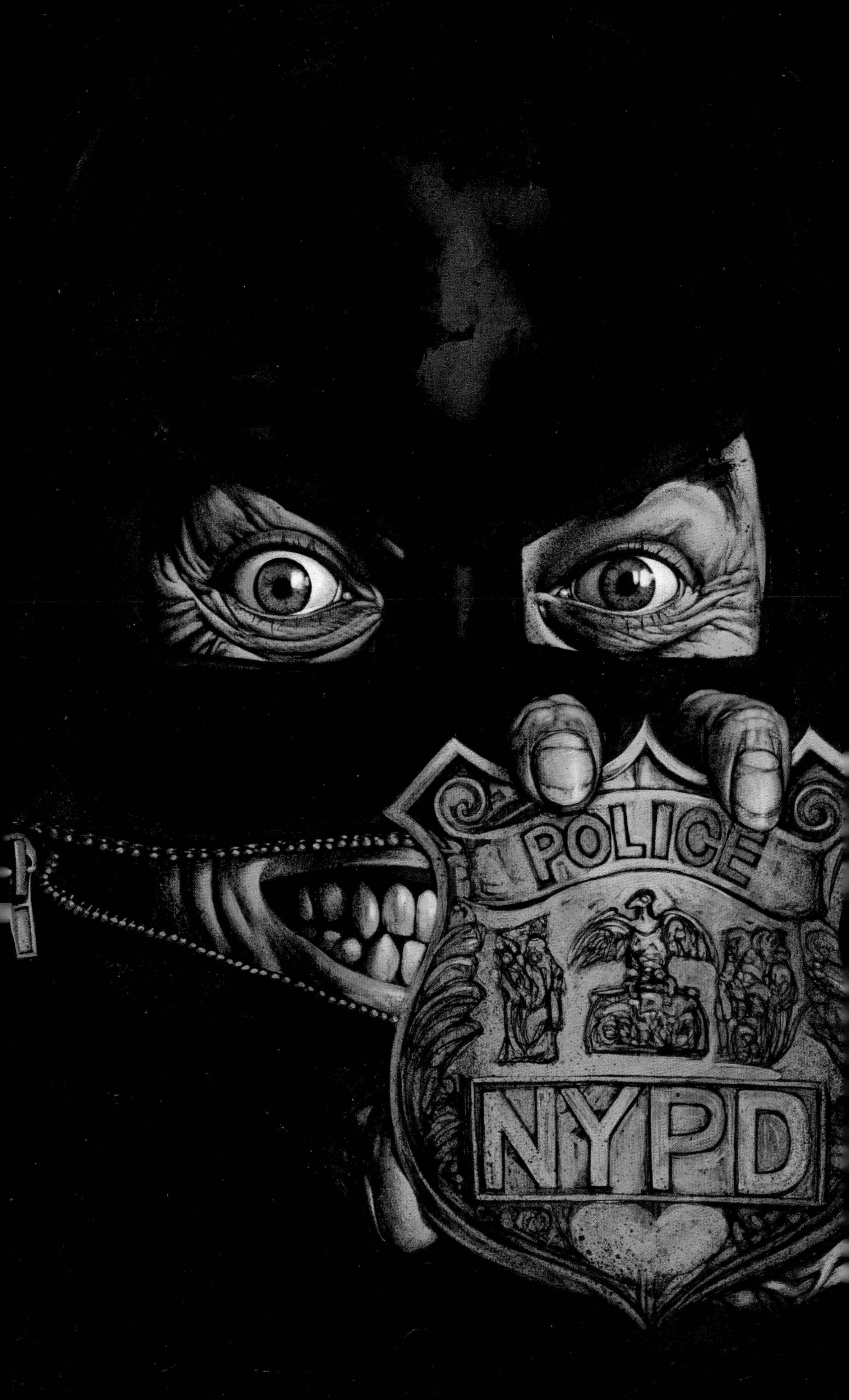
POLICE
NYPD

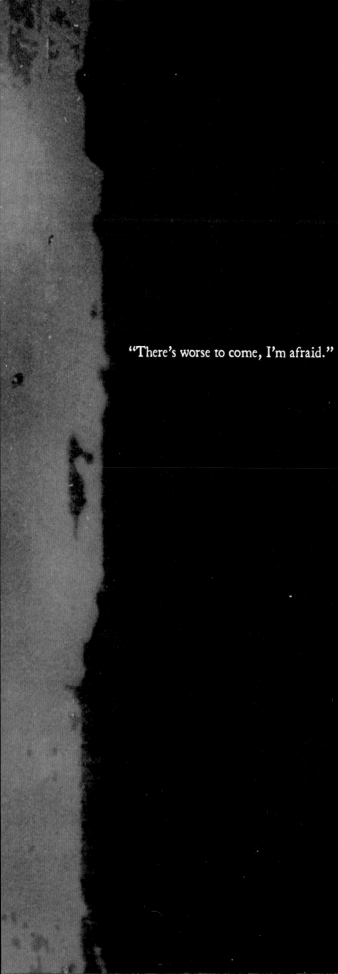

"There's worse to come, I'm afraid."

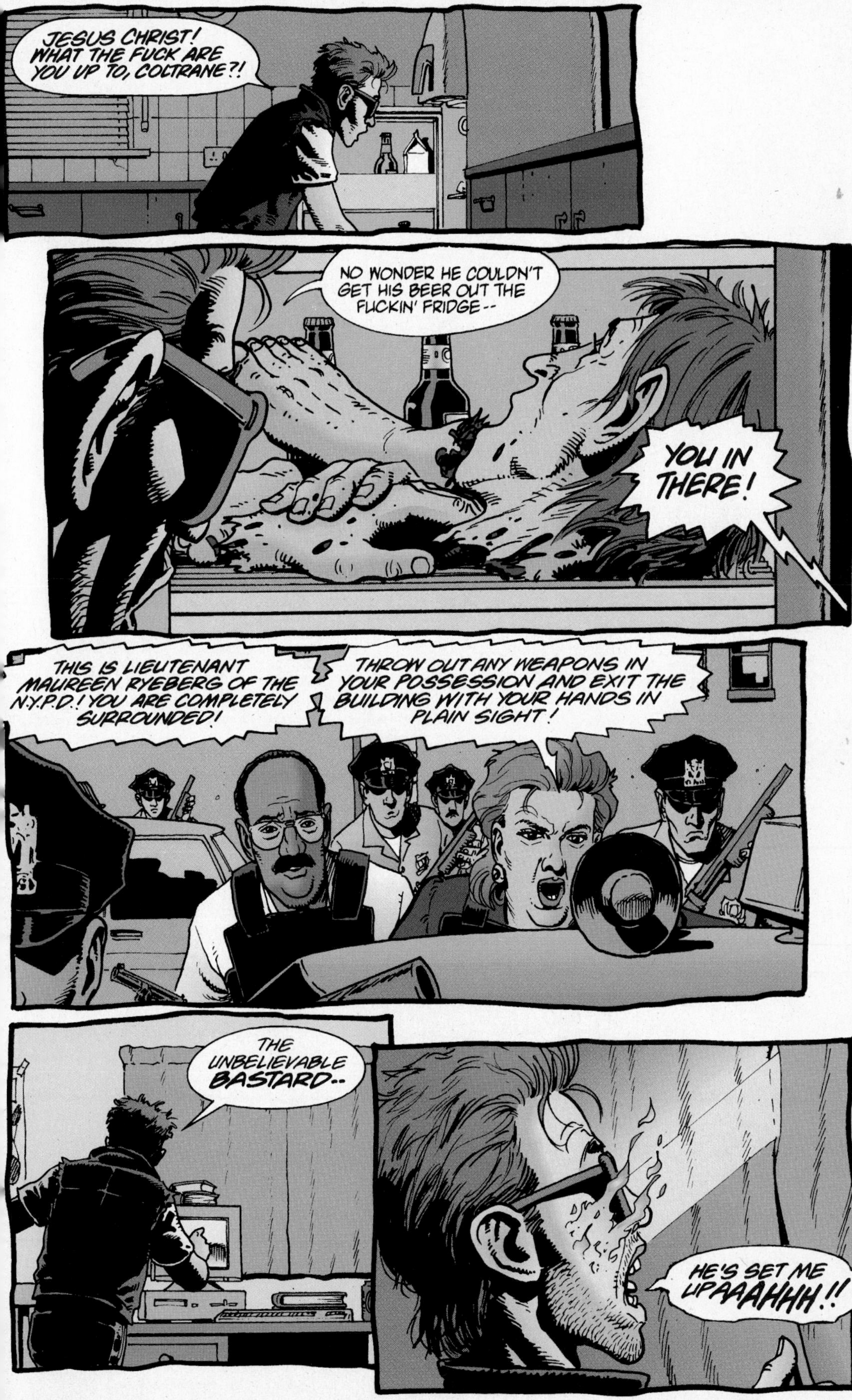
JESUS CHRIST! WHAT THE FUCK ARE YOU UP TO, COLTRANE?!
NO WONDER HE COULDN'T GET HIS BEER OUT THE FUCKIN' FRIDGE--
YOU IN THERE!
THIS IS LIEUTENANT MAUREEN RYEBERG OF THE N.Y.P.D.! YOU ARE COMPLETELY SURROUNDED!
THROW OUT ANY WEAPONS IN YOUR POSSESSION AND EXIT THE BUILDING WITH YOUR HANDS IN PLAIN SIGHT!
THE UNBELIEVABLE BASTARD--
HE'S SET ME UPAAAHHH!!

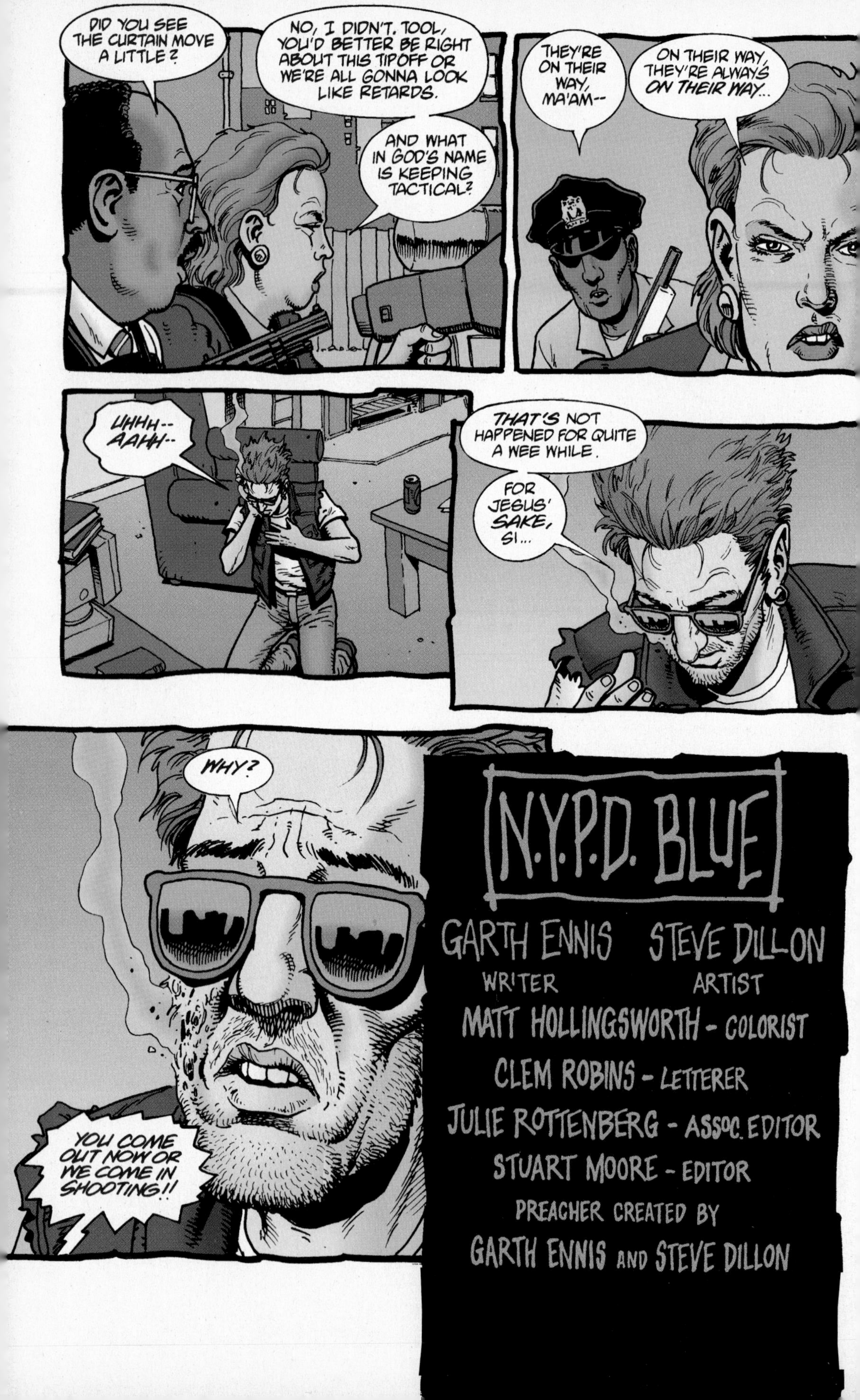

DID YOU SEE THE CURTAIN MOVE A LITTLE?
NO, I DIDN'T. TOOL, YOU'D BETTER BE RIGHT ABOUT THIS TIPOFF OR WE'RE ALL GONNA LOOK LIKE RETARDS.
AND WHAT IN GOD'S NAME IS KEEPING TACTICAL?
THEY'RE ON THEIR WAY, MA'AM--
ON THEIR WAY, THEY'RE ALWAYS ON THEIR WAY...
UHHH-- AAHH--
THAT'S NOT HAPPENED FOR QUITE A WEE WHILE.
FOR JESUS' SAKE, SI...
WHY?
YOU COME OUT NOW OR WE COME IN SHOOTING!!
N.Y.P.D. BLUE
GARTH ENNIS WRITER
STEVE DILLON ARTIST
MATT HOLLINGSWORTH - COLORIST
CLEM ROBINS - LETTERER
JULIE ROTTENBERG - ASSOC. EDITOR
STUART MOORE - EDITOR
PREACHER CREATED BY GARTH ENNIS AND STEVE DILLON

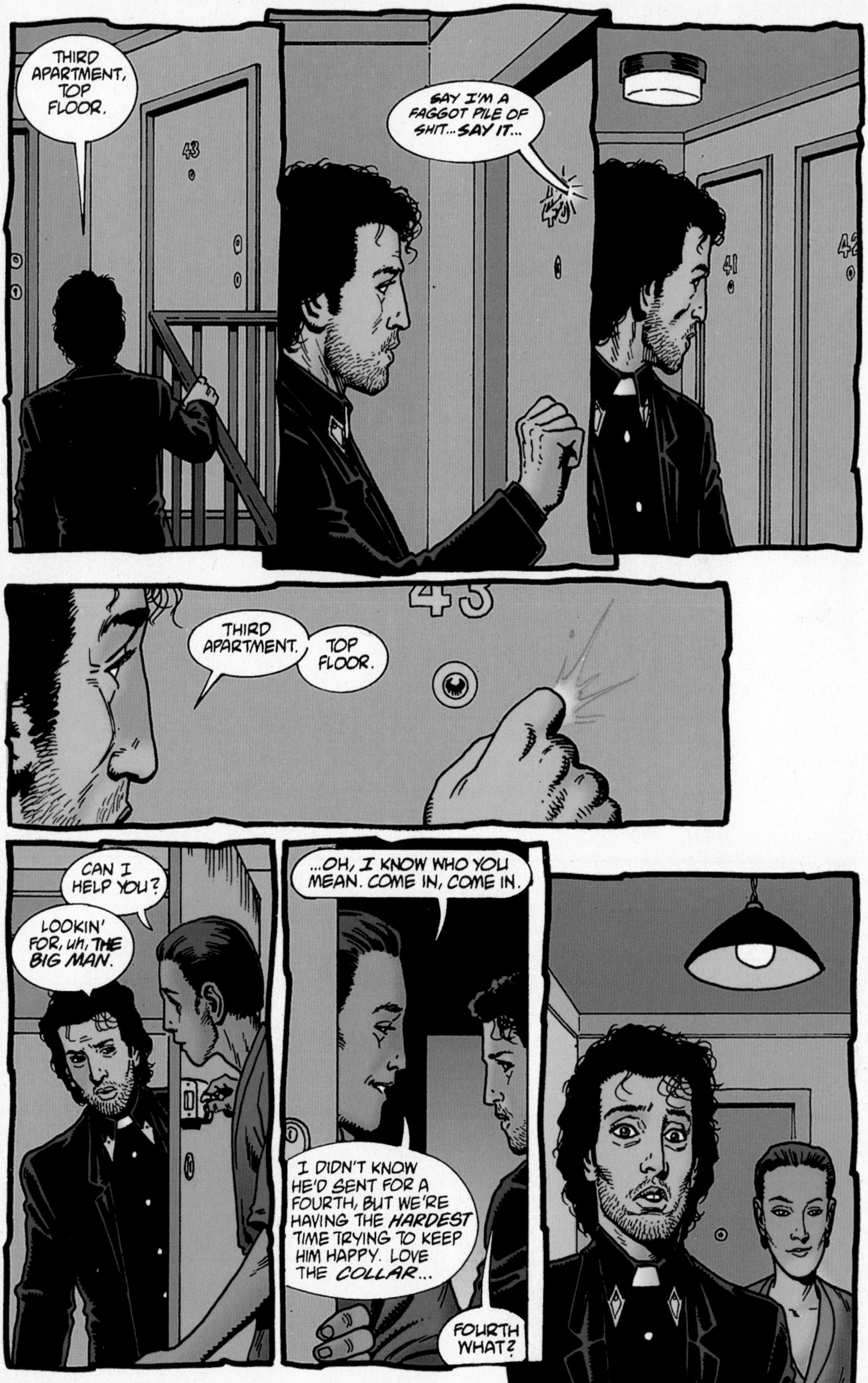
THIRD APARTMENT, TOP FLOOR.
SAY I'M A FAGGOT PILE OF SHIT... SAY IT...
43
41
THIRD APARTMENT.
TOP FLOOR.
43
CAN I HELP YOU?
LOOKIN' FOR, uh, THE BIG MAN.
...OH, I KNOW WHO YOU MEAN. COME IN, COME IN.
I DIDN'T KNOW HE'D SENT FOR A FOURTH, BUT WE'RE HAVING THE HARDEST TIME TRYING TO KEEP HIM HAPPY. LOVE THE COLLAR...
FOURTH WHAT?

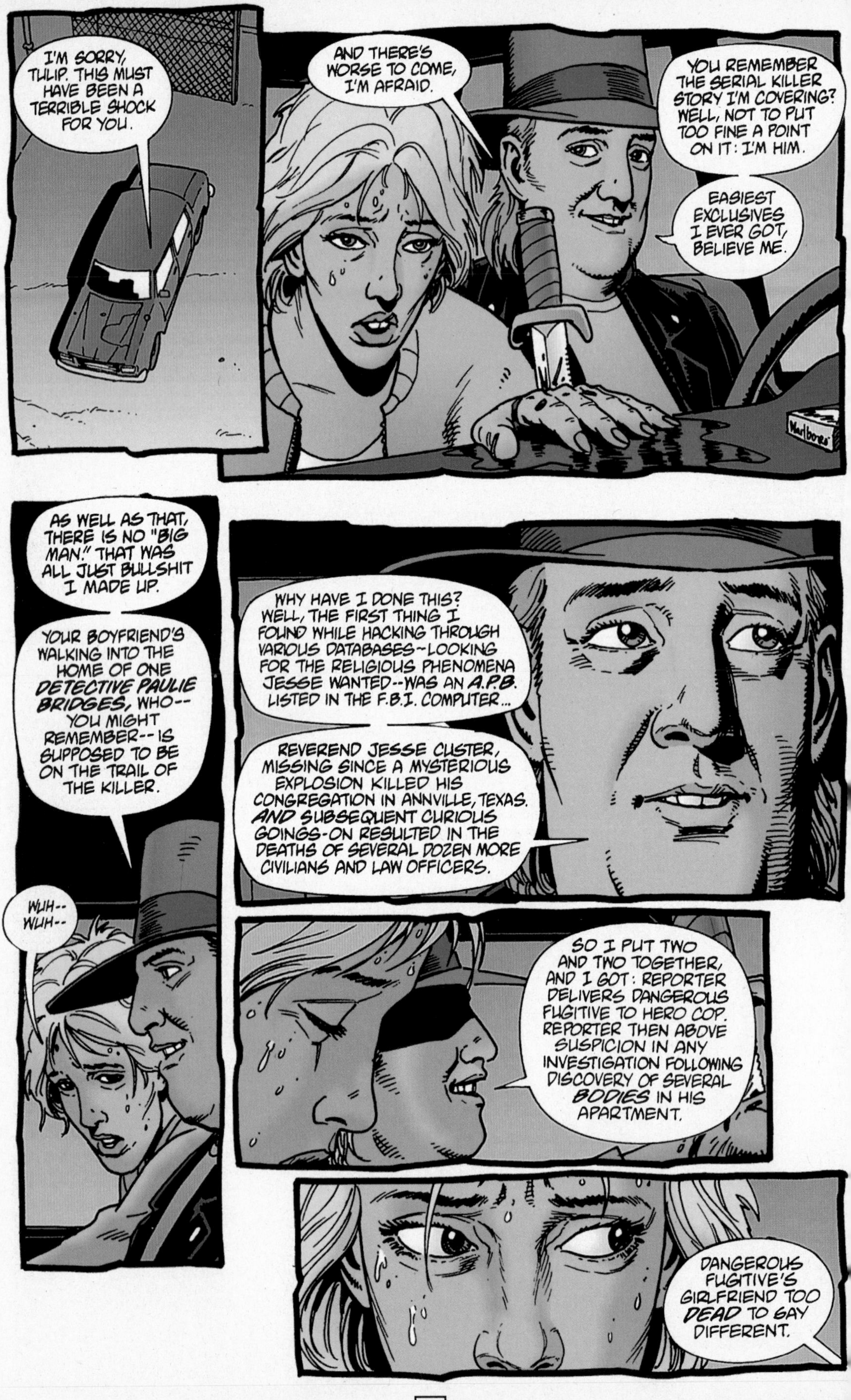
I'M SORRY, TULIP. THIS MUST HAVE BEEN A TERRIBLE SHOCK FOR YOU.
AND THERE'S WORSE TO COME, I'M AFRAID.
YOU REMEMBER THE SERIAL KILLER STORY I'M COVERING? WELL, NOT TO PUT TOO FINE A POINT ON IT: I'M HIM.
EASIEST EXCLUSIVES I EVER GOT, BELIEVE ME.
AS WELL AS THAT, THERE IS NO "BIG MAN." THAT WAS ALL JUST BULLSHIT I MADE UP.
YOUR BOYFRIEND'S WALKING INTO THE HOME OF ONE DETECTIVE PAULIE BRIDGES, WHO--YOU MIGHT REMEMBER--IS SUPPOSED TO BE ON THE TRAIL OF THE KILLER.
WUH--WUH--
WHY HAVE I DONE THIS? WELL, THE FIRST THING I FOUND WHILE HACKING THROUGH VARIOUS DATABASES~LOOKING FOR THE RELIGIOUS PHENOMENA JESSE WANTED--WAS AN A.P.B. LISTED IN THE F.B.I. COMPUTER...
REVEREND JESSE CUSTER, MISSING SINCE A MYSTERIOUS EXPLOSION KILLED HIS CONGREGATION IN ANNVILLE, TEXAS. AND SUBSEQUENT CURIOUS GOINGS-ON RESULTED IN THE DEATHS OF SEVERAL DOZEN MORE CIVILIANS AND LAW OFFICERS.
SO I PUT TWO AND TWO TOGETHER, AND I GOT: REPORTER DELIVERS DANGEROUS FUGITIVE TO HERO COP. REPORTER THEN ABOVE SUSPICION IN ANY INVESTIGATION FOLLOWING DISCOVERY OF SEVERAL BODIES IN HIS APARTMENT.
DANGEROUS FUGITIVE'S GIRLFRIEND TOO DEAD TO SAY DIFFERENT.

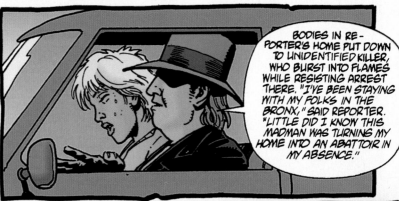

CAH... SUH...

CASSIDY IS THE ICING ON THE CAKE.

BODIES IN REPORTER'S HOME PUT DOWN TO UNIDENTIFIED KILLER, WHO BURST INTO FLAMES WHILE RESISTING ARREST THERE. "I'VE BEEN STAYING WITH MY FOLKS IN THE BRONX," SAID REPORTER. "LITTLE DID I KNOW THIS MADMAN WAS TURNING MY HOME INTO AN ABATTOIR IN MY ABSENCE."

WHYYY...?

BECAUSE IT'S FUN.

TWO YEARS BACK I WAS DRIVING HOME DRUNK WHEN I RAN A GUY OVER. I GOT OUT TO HELP, SAW I'D KILLED HIM. IT WAS FOUR A.M.: NO ONE AROUND. I GOT BACK IN THE CAR AND DROVE LIKE HELL, AND IT WAS FIVE MINUTES BEFORE I REALIZED I WAS LAUGHING FIT TO BUST--

'CAUSE I'D GOTTEN CLEAN AWAY WITH IT.

SO I BEGAN SEEING WHAT ELSE I COULD GET AWAY WITH, AND IT JUST GOT FUNNIER EACH TIME.

WHY? YOU EXPECTING SOME CRAP ABOUT GETTING RAPED BY MY DAD? OR BEING A WOLF THAT PREYS ON SHEEPLIKE HUMANITY, BLAH-BLAH-BLAH?

AND THEN I'LL SHOW YOU JUST HOW MUCH FUN SERIAL KILLING CAN BE.

ANYWAY, DON'T SCREAM, OR THE COPS'LL COME AND THEY'LL GET JESSE ANYWAY. I'M GONNA GO TELL BRIDGES ABOUT HIS LUCKY BREAK.

THEN WE'LL HEAD UP TO MY FOLKS' PLACE, AND I'LL GET 'EM OUT OF THE FREEZER...

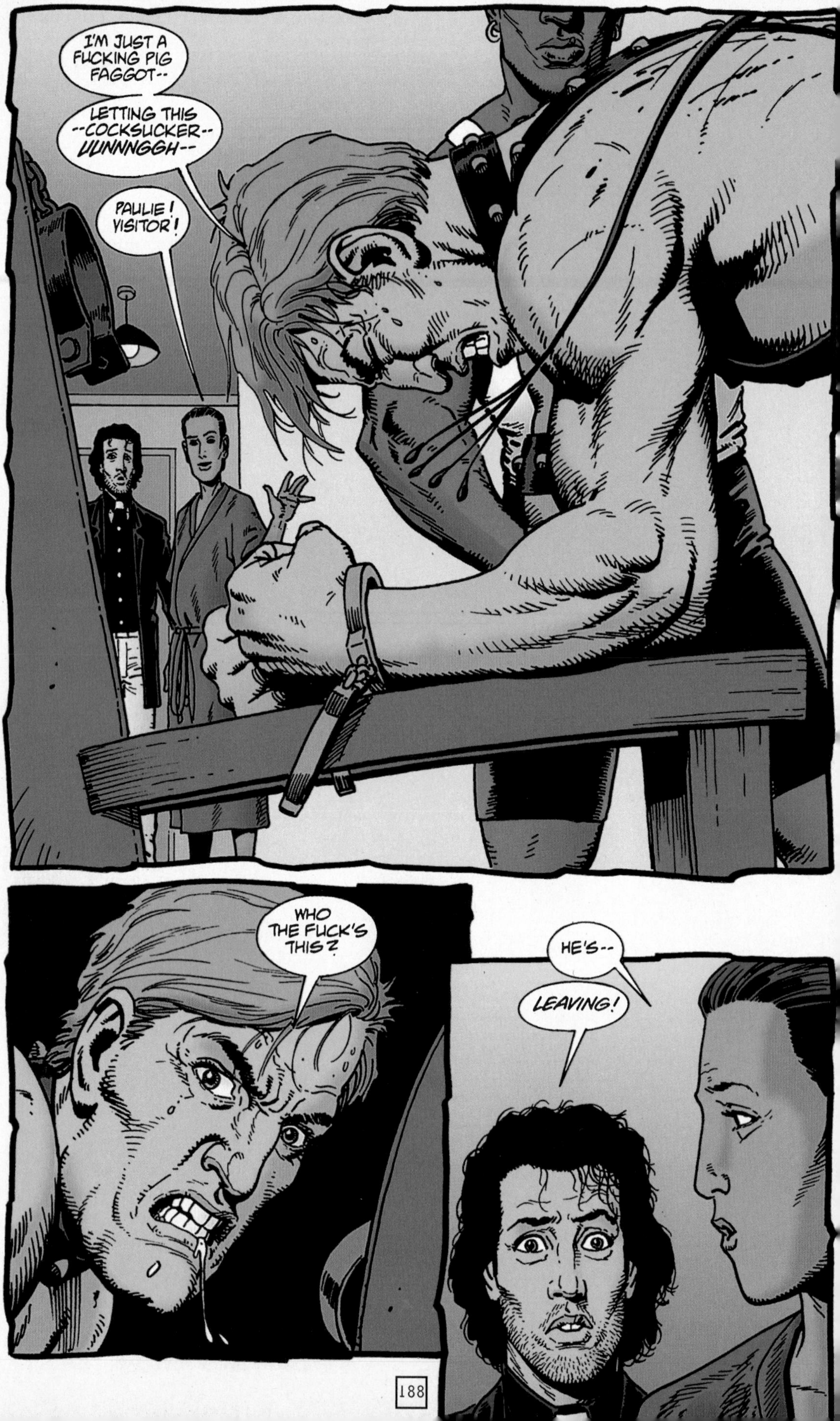
I'M JUST A FUCKING PIG FAGGOT--
LETTING THIS --COCKSUCKER-- UUNNNGGH--
PAULIE! VISITOR!
WHO THE FUCK'S THIS?
HE'S--
LEAVING!

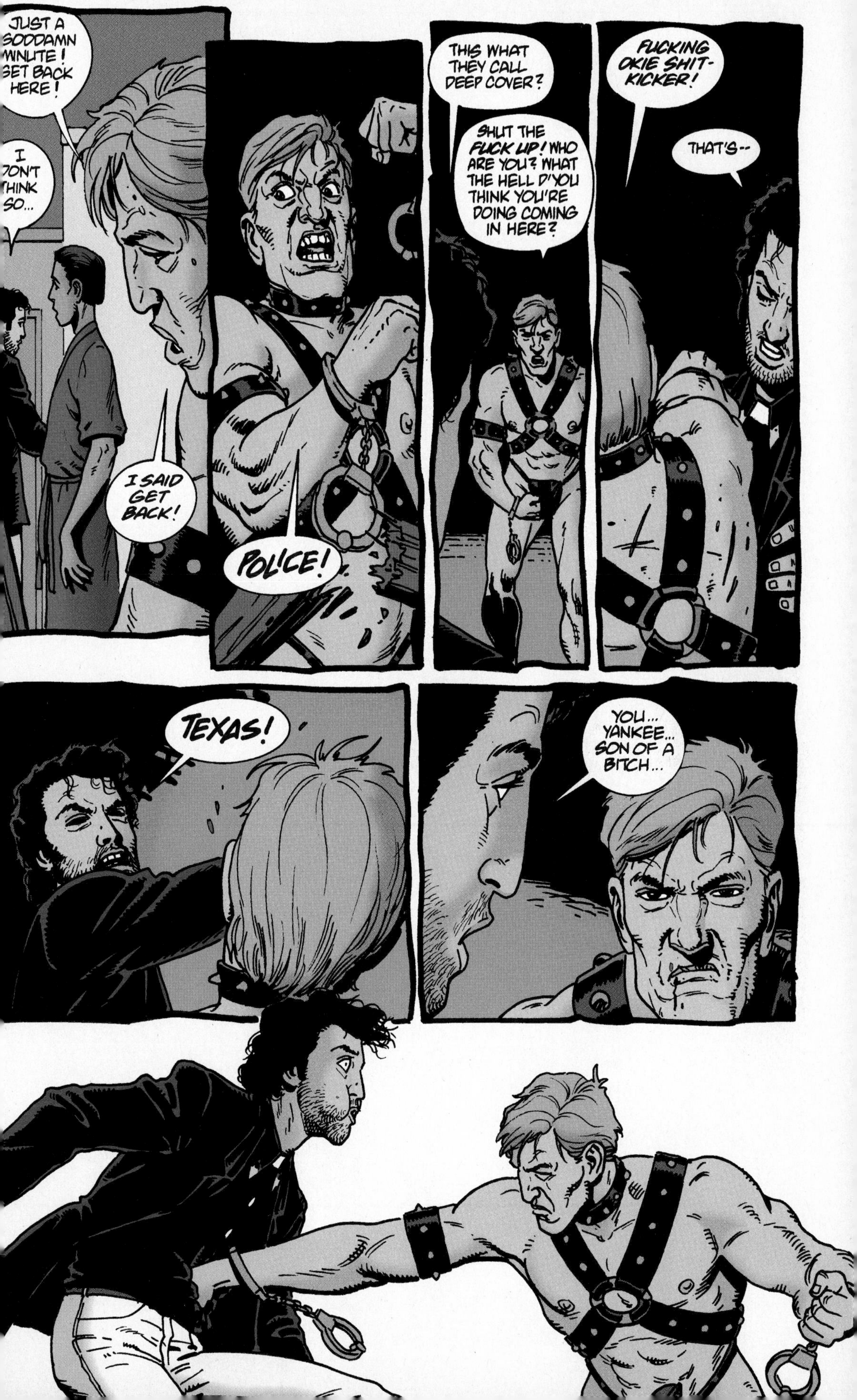
JUST A GODDAMN MINUTE! GET BACK HERE!
I DON'T THINK SO...
I SAID GET BACK!
POLICE!
THIS WHAT THEY CALL DEEP COVER?
SHUT THE FUCK UP! WHO ARE YOU? WHAT THE HELL D'YOU THINK YOU'RE DOING COMING IN HERE?
FUCKING OKIE SHIT-KICKER!
THAT'S--
TEXAS!
YOU... YANKEE... SON OF A BITCH...

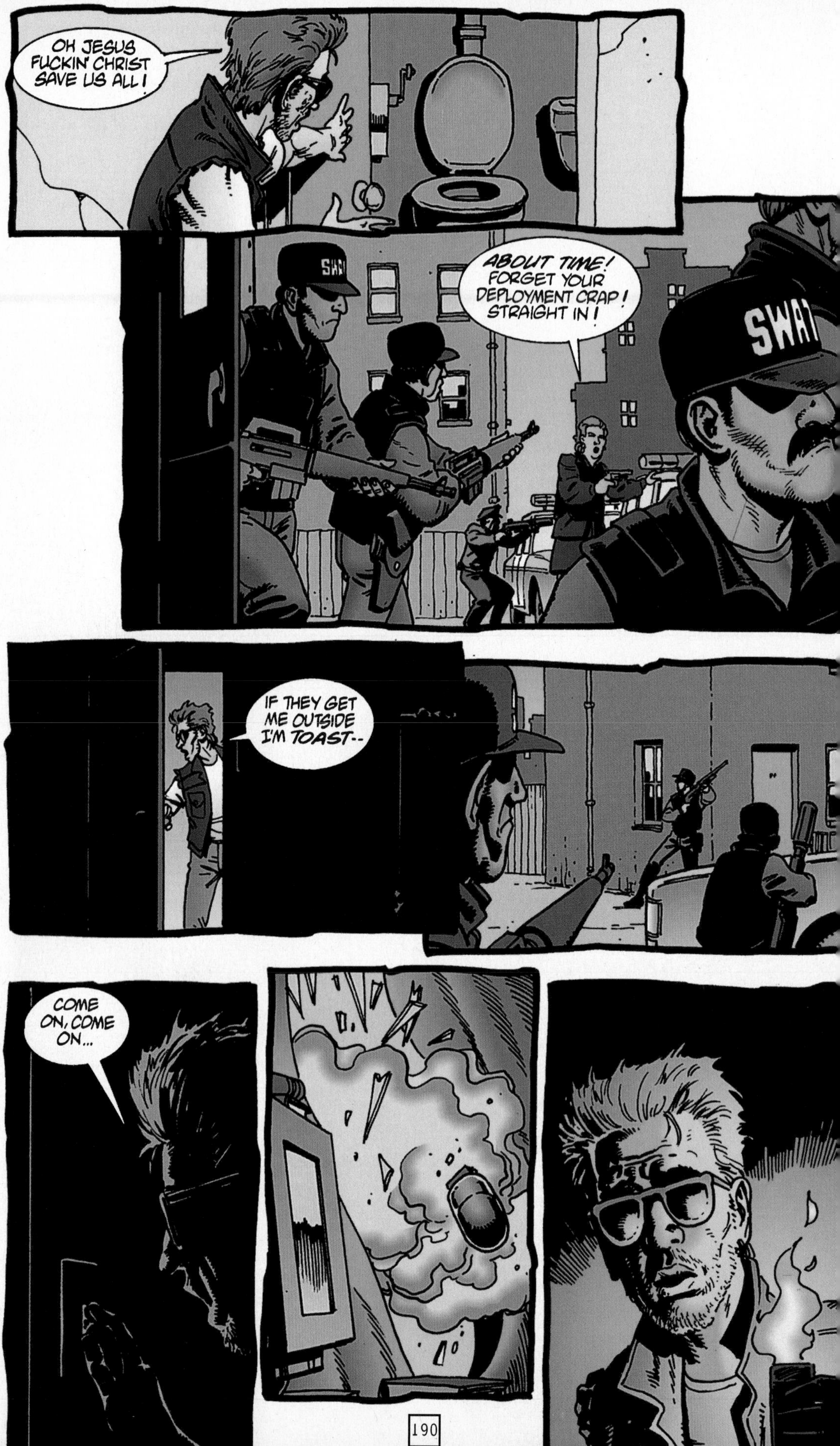
OH JESUS FUCKIN' CHRIST SAVE US ALL!
ABOUT TIME! FORGET YOUR DEPLOYMENT CRAP! STRAIGHT IN!
SWAT
SWAT
IF THEY GET ME OUTSIDE I'M TOAST--
COME ON, COME ON...

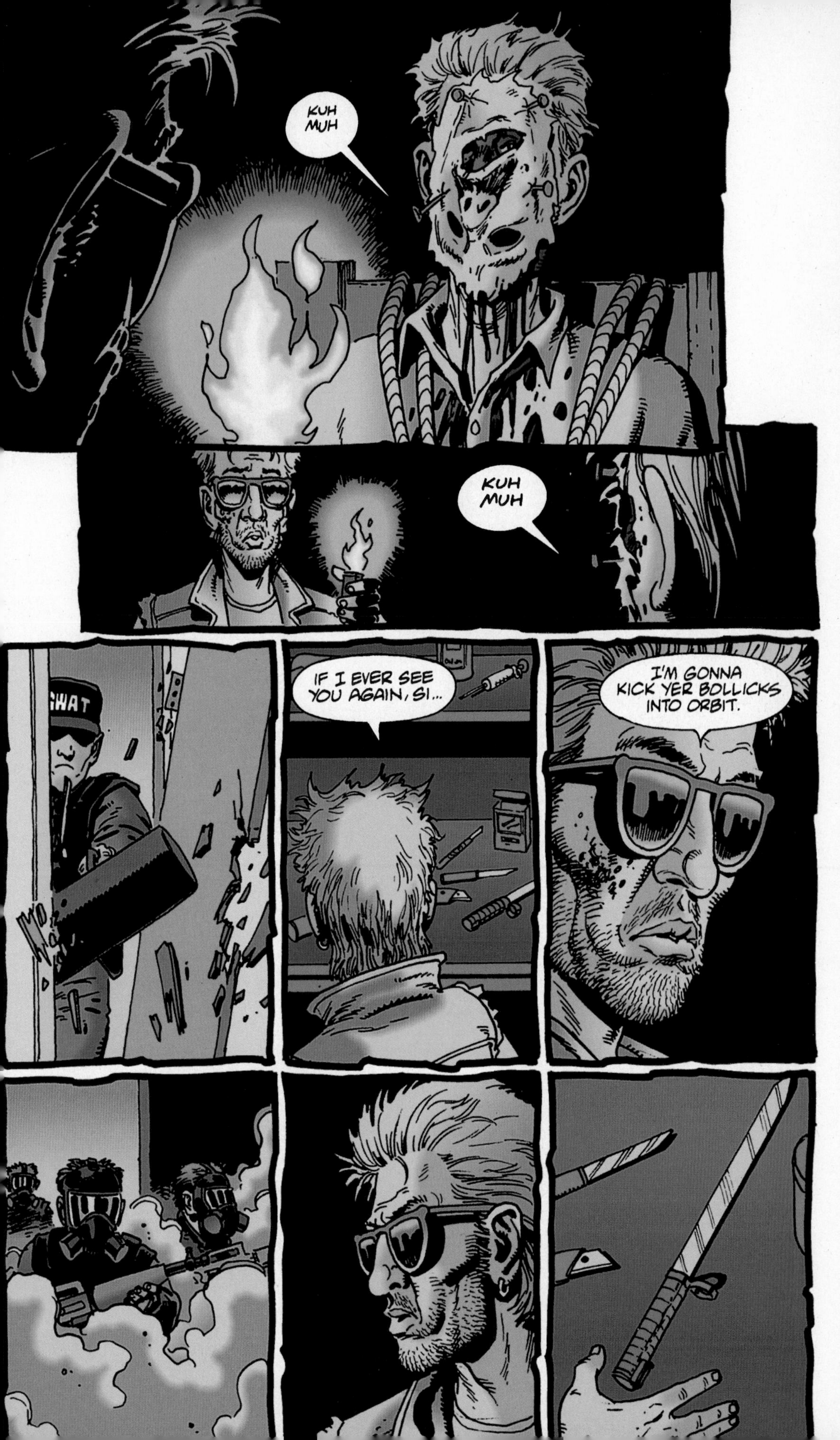
KUH MUH
KUH MUH
SWAT
IF I EVER SEE YOU AGAIN, SI...
I'M GONNA KICK YER BOLLICKS INTO ORBIT.

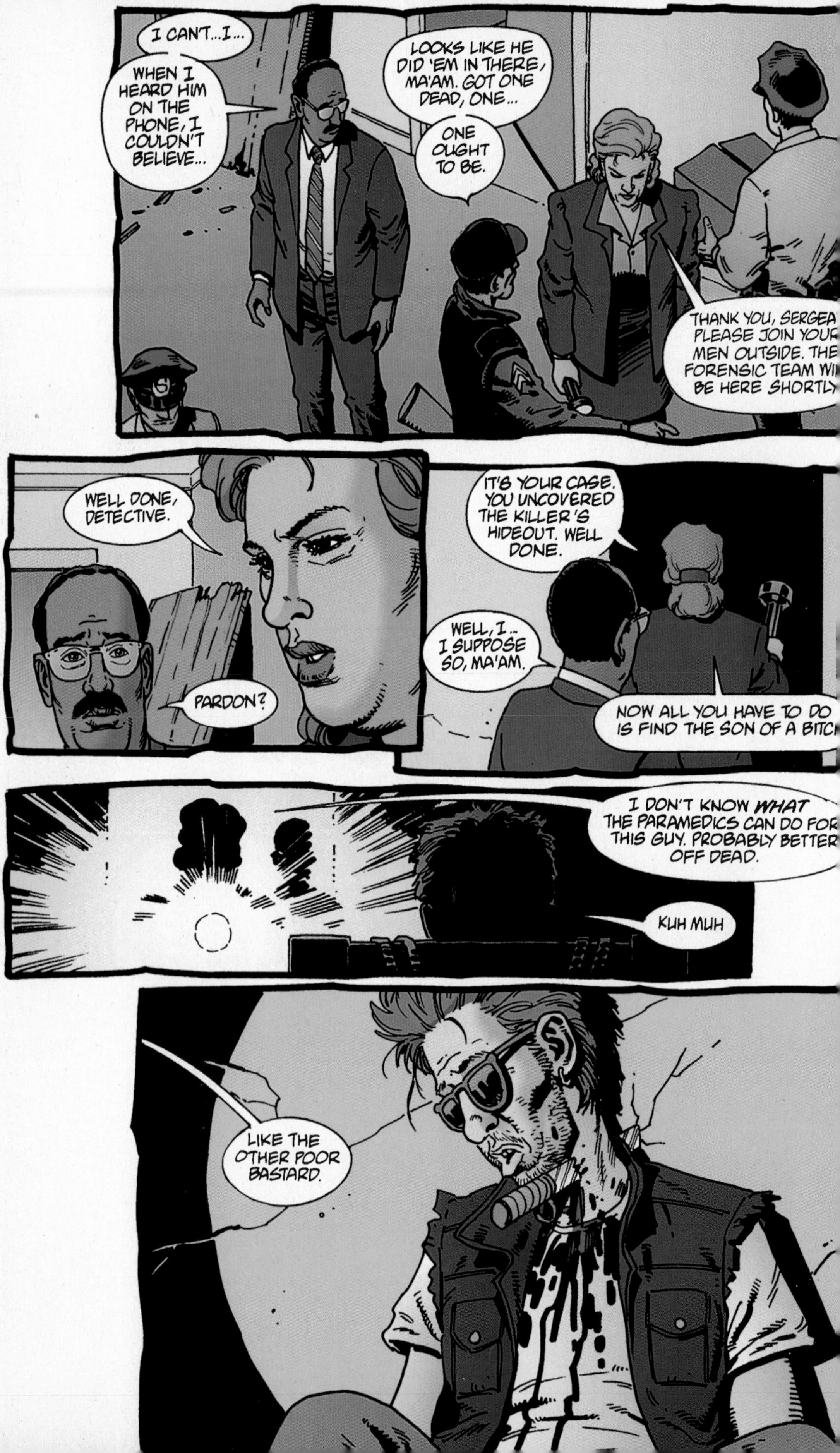

I CAN'T...I...
WHEN I HEARD HIM ON THE PHONE, I COULDN'T BELIEVE...
LOOKS LIKE HE DID 'EM IN THERE, MA'AM. GOT ONE DEAD, ONE...
ONE OUGHT TO BE.
THANK YOU, SERGEA PLEASE JOIN YOUR MEN OUTSIDE. THE FORENSIC TEAM WI BE HERE SHORTLY
WELL DONE, DETECTIVE.
PARDON?
IT'S YOUR CASE. YOU UNCOVERED THE KILLER'S HIDEOUT. WELL DONE.
WELL, I... I SUPPOSE SO, MA'AM.
NOW ALL YOU HAVE TO DO IS FIND THE SON OF A BITC
I DON'T KNOW *WHAT* THE PARAMEDICS CAN DO FOR THIS GUY. PROBABLY BETTER OFF DEAD.
KUH MUH
LIKE THE OTHER POOR BASTARD.

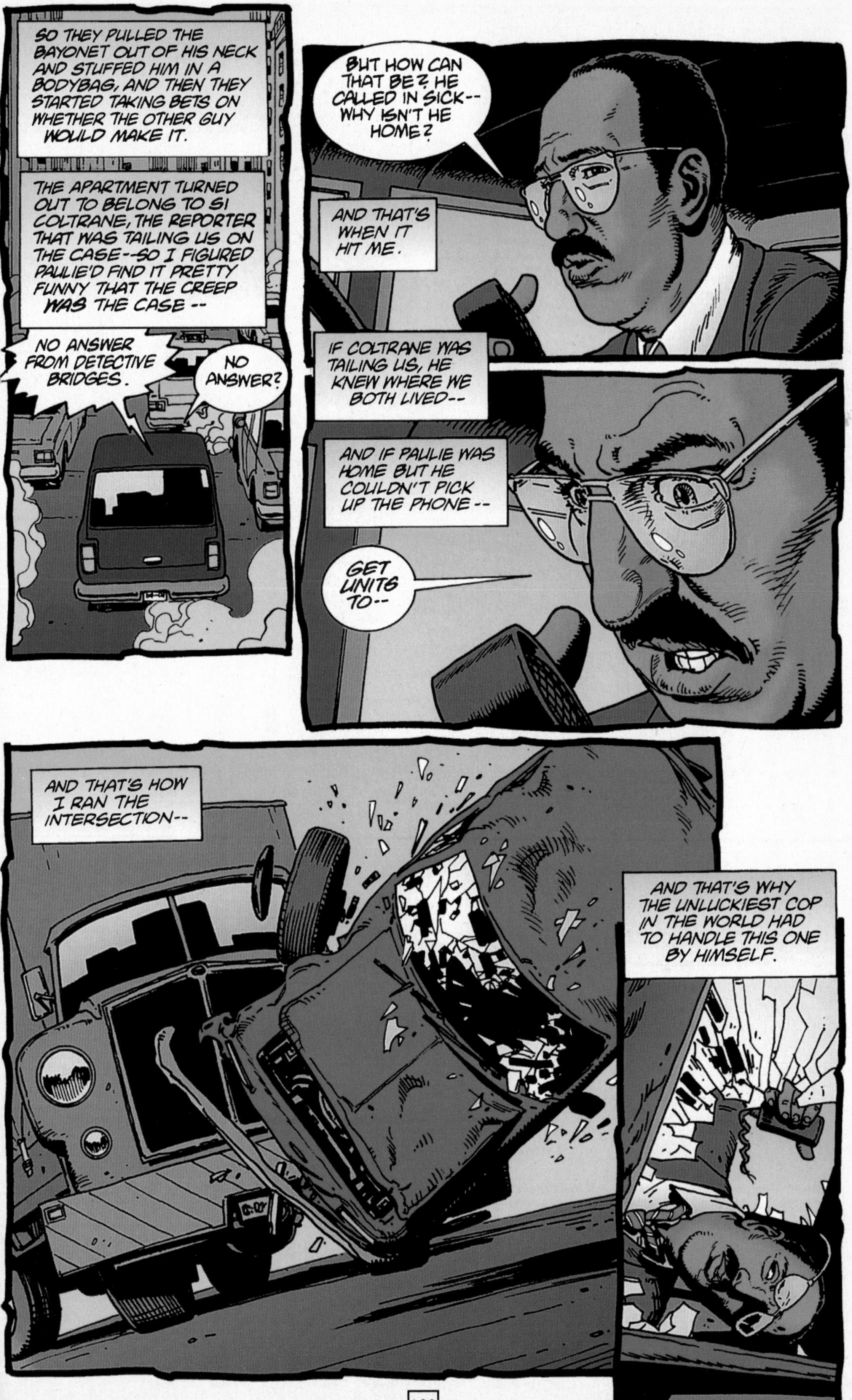
SO THEY PULLED THE BAYONET OUT OF HIS NECK AND STUFFED HIM IN A BODYBAG, AND THEN THEY STARTED TAKING BETS ON WHETHER THE OTHER GUY WOULD MAKE IT.
THE APARTMENT TURNED OUT TO BELONG TO SI COLTRANE, THE REPORTER THAT WAS TAILING US ON THE CASE--SO I FIGURED PAULIE'D FIND IT PRETTY FUNNY THAT THE CREEP WAS THE CASE --
NO ANSWER FROM DETECTIVE BRIDGES.
NO ANSWER?
BUT HOW CAN THAT BE? HE CALLED IN SICK-- WHY ISN'T HE HOME?
AND THAT'S WHEN IT HIT ME.
IF COLTRANE WAS TAILING US, HE KNEW WHERE WE BOTH LIVED--
AND IF PAULIE WAS HOME BUT HE COULDN'T PICK UP THE PHONE --
GET UNITS TO--
AND THAT'S HOW I RAN THE INTERSECTION--
AND THAT'S WHY THE UNLUCKIEST COP IN THE WORLD HAD TO HANDLE THIS ONE BY HIMSELF.

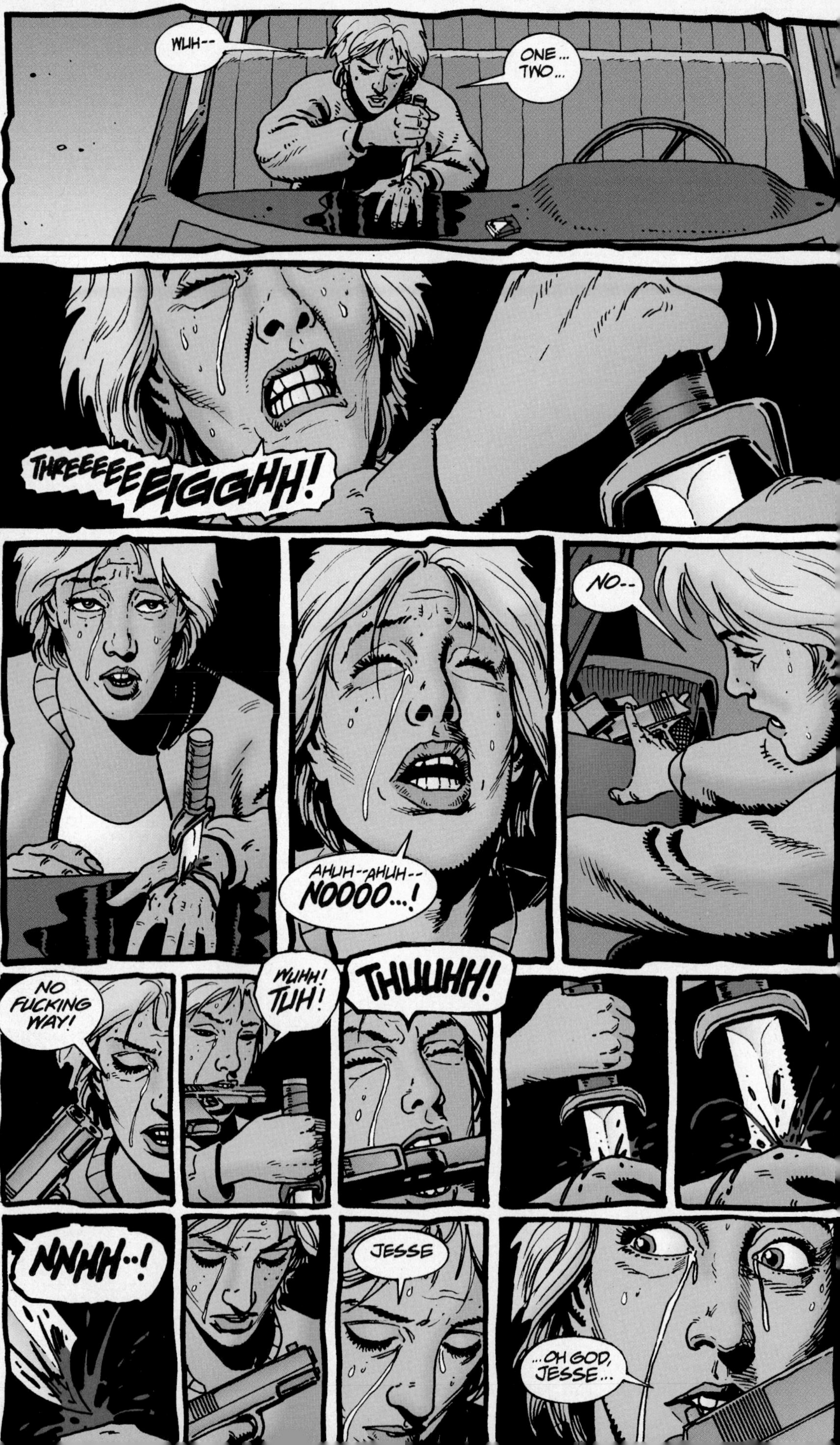

WUH--
ONE... TWO...
THREEEEEEEIGGHH!
AHUH--AHUH-- NOOOO...!
NO--
NO FUCKING WAY!
WUHH! TUH!
THUUHH!
NNHH..!
JESSE
...OH GOD, JESSE...

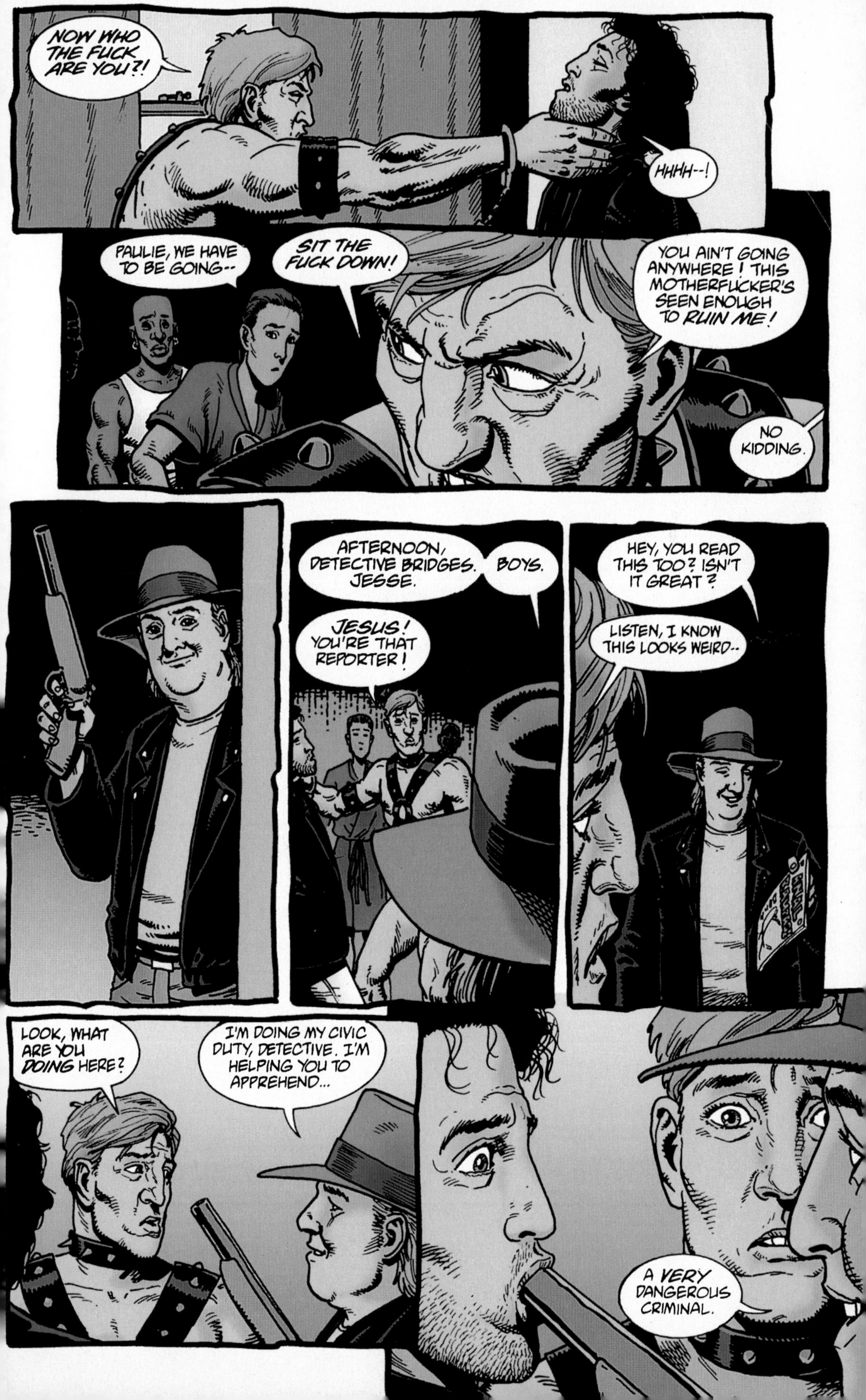

NOW WHO THE FUCK ARE YOU?!
HHHH--!
PAULIE, WE HAVE TO BE GOING--
SIT THE FUCK DOWN!
YOU AIN'T GOING ANYWHERE! THIS MOTHERFUCKER'S SEEN ENOUGH TO RUIN ME!
NO KIDDING.
AFTERNOON, DETECTIVE BRIDGES. JESSE.
BOYS.
JESUS! YOU'RE THAT REPORTER!
HEY, YOU READ THIS TOO? ISN'T IT GREAT?
LISTEN, I KNOW THIS LOOKS WEIRD--
LOOK, WHAT ARE YOU DOING HERE?
I'M DOING MY CIVIC DUTY, DETECTIVE. I'M HELPING YOU TO APPREHEND...
A VERY DANGEROUS CRIMINAL.

FREEZE!

I CALLED BACK-UP FROM A PAYPHONE, BUT I KNEW THEY'D NEVER MAKE IT IN TIME. I WAS READY FOR A **SLAUGHTERHOUSE** WHEN I KICKED OPEN THE DOOR --

PAULIE...?

JOHNNY, I... LISTEN, IT'S NOT WHAT IT LOOKS LIKE...

BUT IT WAS.

OH GOD...!

PAULIE? PAULIE?!

PAULIE, THIS GUY'S THE KILLER! YOU SHOULD'VE SEEN HIS *APARTMENT*--

COLTRANE, PUT THE GUN THE FLOOR AN

YOU DON'T WANT TO KNOW WHAT IT WAS I SLIPPED ON. SUFFICE IT TO SAY I'D SCREWED UP FOR THE LAST TIME. COLTRANE HELD ALL THE CARDS.

WHUP!

THE UNLUCKIEST COP IN THE WORLD GOT HIMSELF AND HIS PARTNER KILLED.

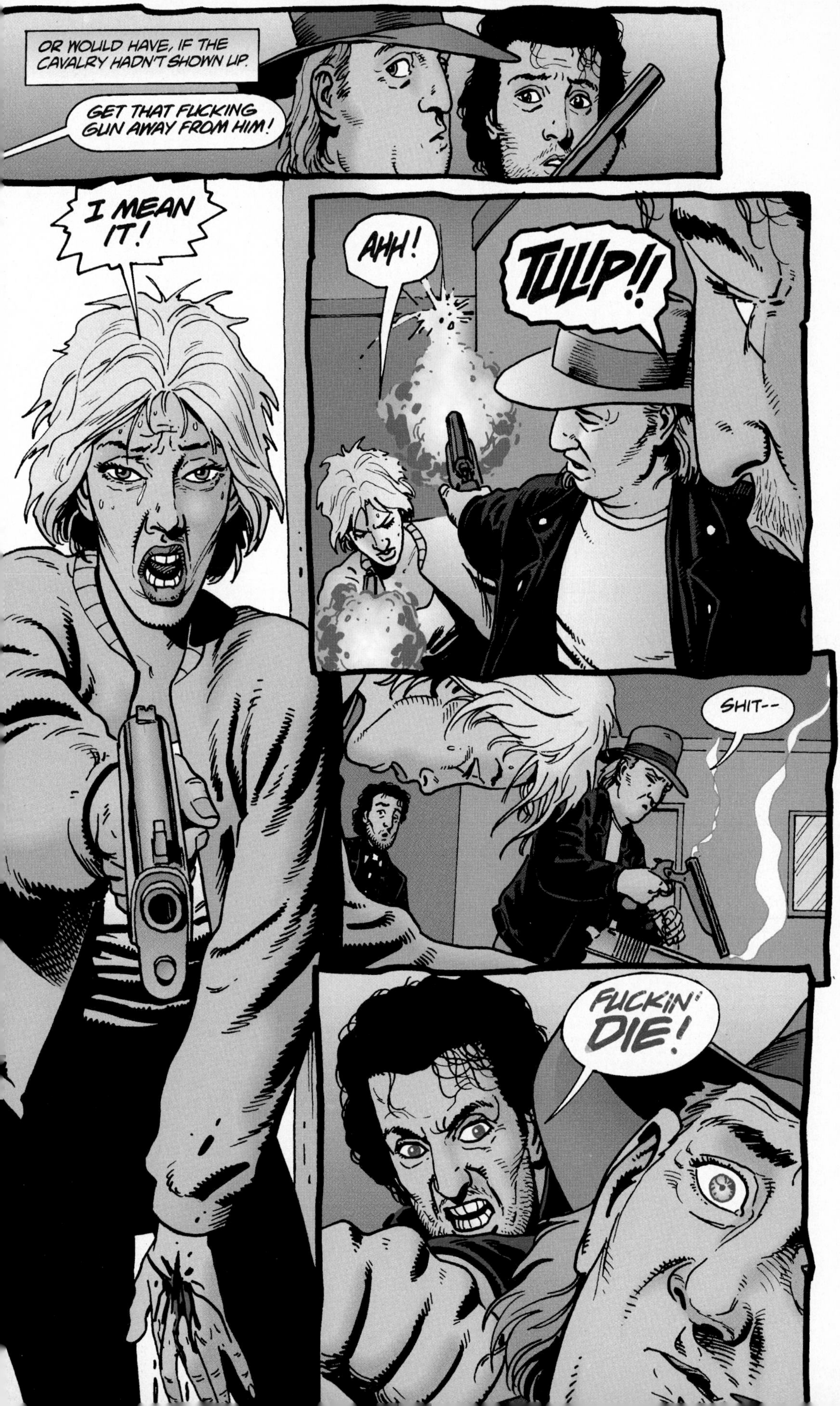
OR WOULD HAVE, IF THE CAVALRY HADN'T SHOWN UP.
GET THAT FUCKING GUN AWAY FROM HIM!
I MEAN IT!
AHH!
TULIP!!
SHIT--
FUCKIN' DIE!

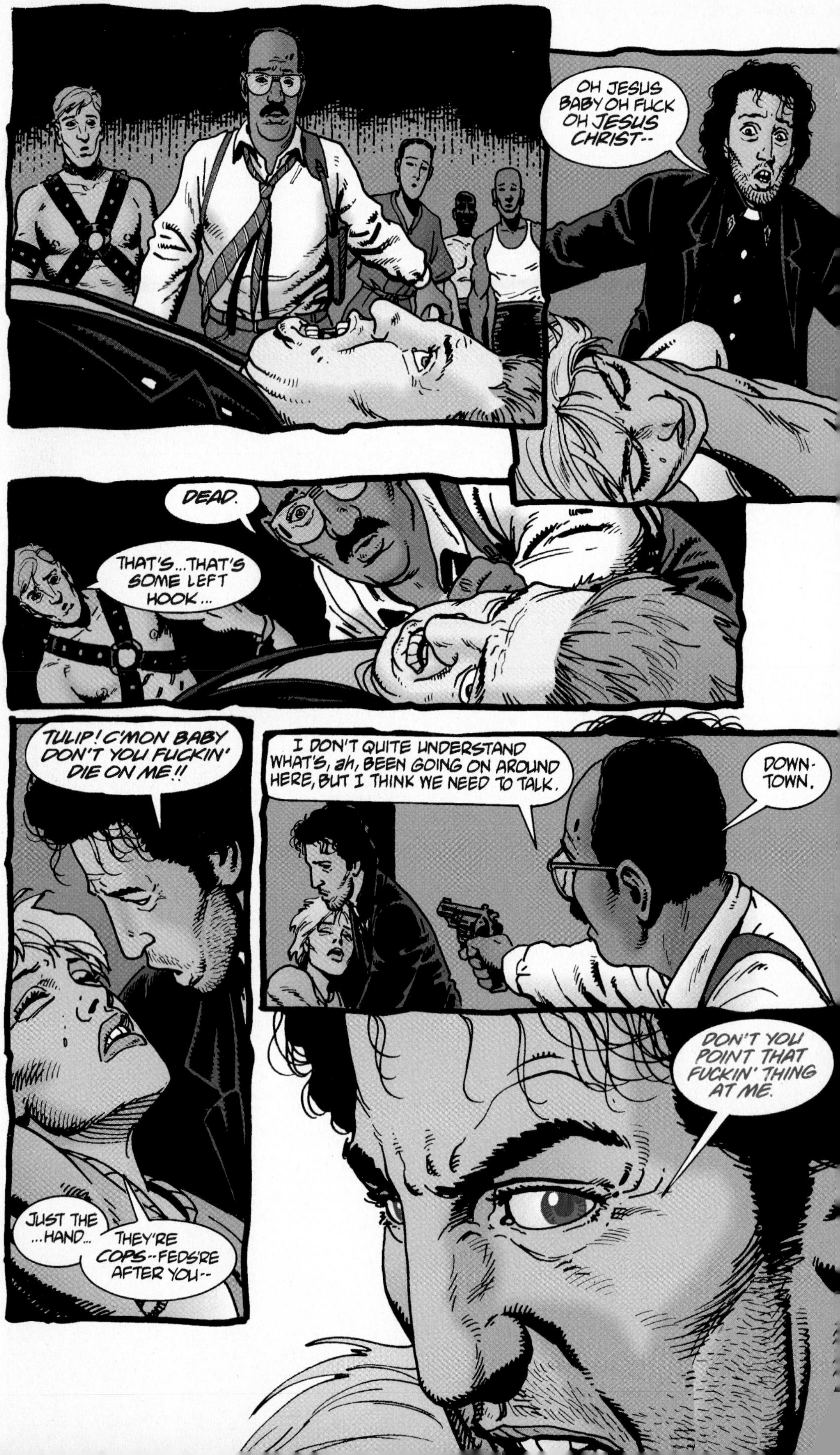
OH JESUS BABY OH FUCK OH JESUS CHRIST--
DEAD.
THAT'S...THAT'S SOME LEFT HOOK...
TULIP! C'MON BABY DON'T YOU FUCKIN' DIE ON ME!!
JUST THE ...HAND...
THEY'RE COPS--FEDS'RE AFTER YOU--
I DON'T QUITE UNDERSTAND WHAT'S, ah, BEEN GOING ON AROUND HERE, BUT I THINK WE NEED TO TALK.
DOWN-TOWN.
DON'T YOU POINT THAT FUCKIN' THING AT ME.

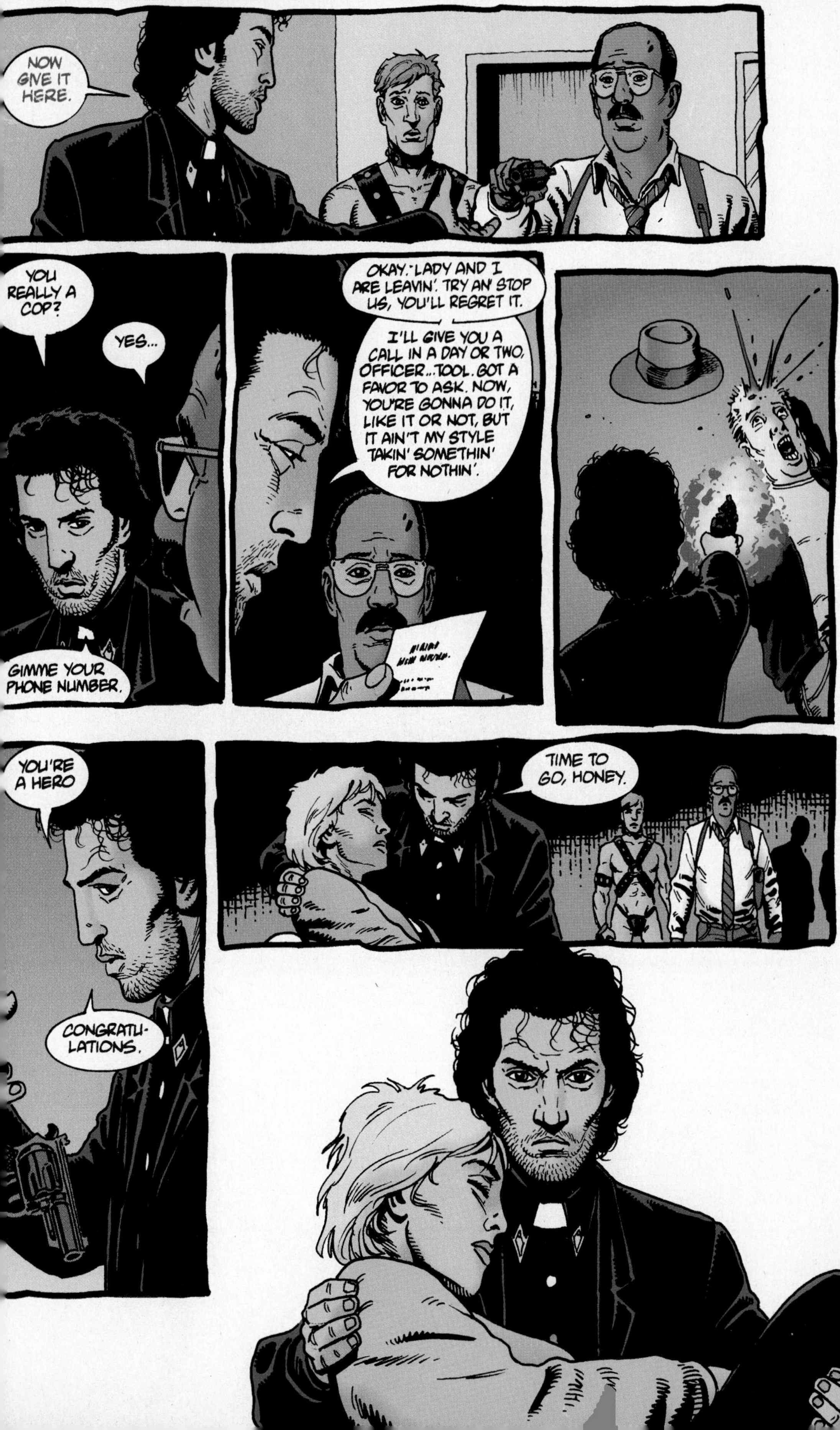
NOW GIVE IT HERE.
YOU REALLY A COP?
YES...
GIMME YOUR PHONE NUMBER.
OKAY: "LADY AND I ARE LEAVIN'. TRY AN' STOP US, YOU'LL REGRET IT.
I'LL GIVE YOU A CALL IN A DAY OR TWO, OFFICER...TOOL. GOT A FAVOR TO ASK. NOW, YOU'RE GONNA DO IT, LIKE IT OR NOT, BUT IT AIN'T MY STYLE TAKIN' SOMETHIN' FOR NOTHIN'.
YOU'RE A HERO
CONGRATULATIONS.
TIME TO GO, HONEY.

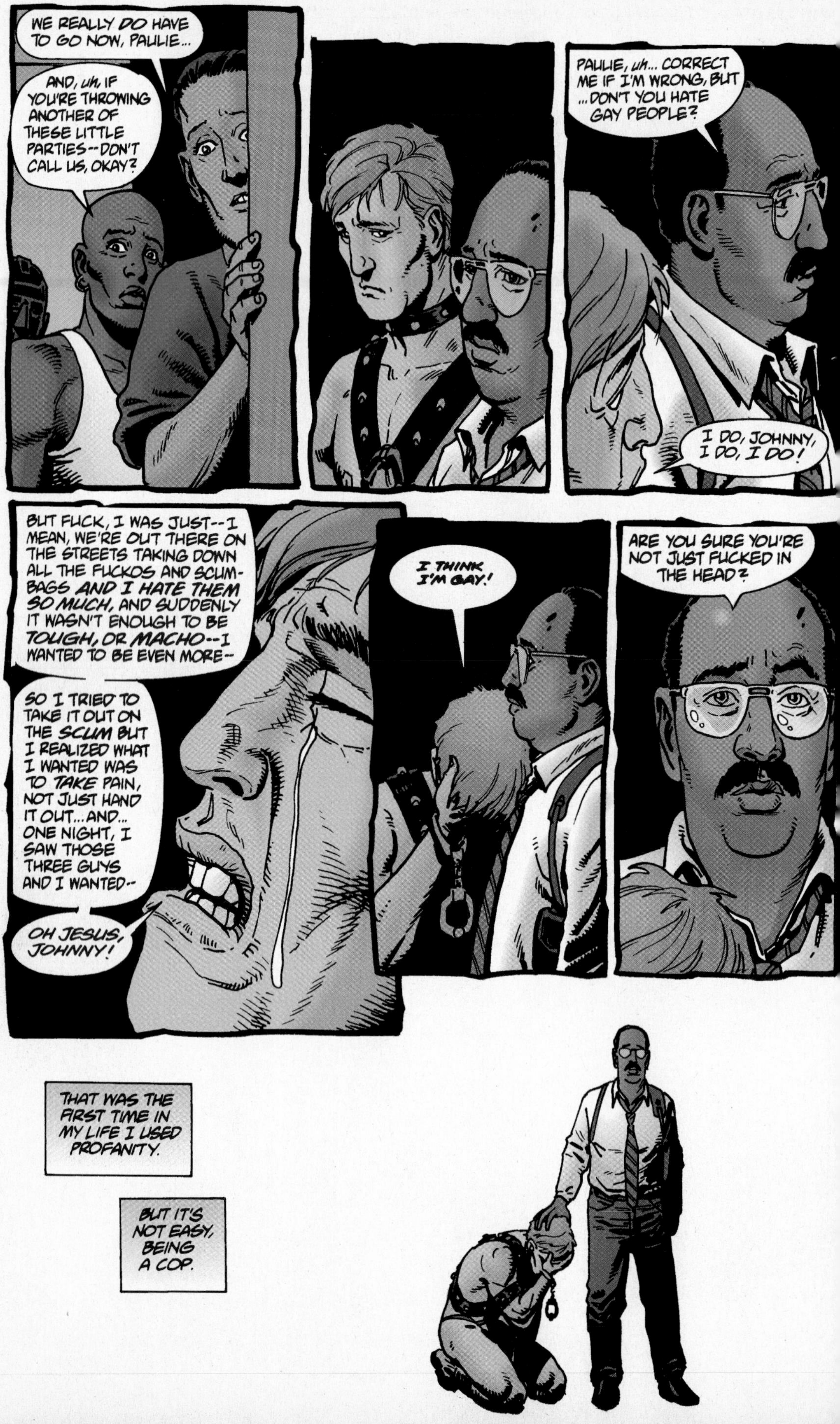

WE REALLY DO HAVE TO GO NOW, PAULIE...
AND, uh, IF YOU'RE THROWING ANOTHER OF THESE LITTLE PARTIES--DON'T CALL US, OKAY?
PAULIE, uh... CORRECT ME IF I'M WRONG, BUT ...DON'T YOU HATE GAY PEOPLE?
I DO, JOHNNY, I DO, I DO!
BUT FUCK, I WAS JUST--I MEAN, WE'RE OUT THERE ON THE STREETS TAKING DOWN ALL THE FUCKOS AND SCUMBAGS AND I HATE THEM SO MUCH, AND SUDDENLY IT WASN'T ENOUGH TO BE TOUGH, OR MACHO--I WANTED TO BE EVEN MORE--
SO I TRIED TO TAKE IT OUT ON THE SCUM BUT I REALIZED WHAT I WANTED WAS TO TAKE PAIN, NOT JUST HAND IT OUT...AND... ONE NIGHT, I SAW THOSE THREE GUYS AND I WANTED--
OH JESUS, JOHNNY!
I THINK I'M GAY!
ARE YOU SURE YOU'RE NOT JUST FUCKED IN THE HEAD?
THAT WAS THE FIRST TIME IN MY LIFE I USED PROFANITY.
BUT IT'S NOT EASY, BEING A COP.

DOC BENDER'S ON HER WAY DOWN, LIEUTENANT.

I CAN'T STAY. LOOK, THE CLOTHES ARE EVIDENCE, OKAY? BE SURE TO BAG 'EM.

YOU GOT IT.

OKAY, EVERY-ONE. SAY HI TO THE NEW GUY.

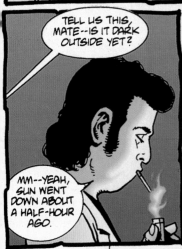

TELL US THIS, MATE--IS IT DARK OUTSIDE YET?

MM--YEAH, SUN WENT DOWN ABOUT A HALF-HOUR AGO.

AY LISTEN, I'VE GOTTA GO NOW BUT I'M DYIN' FOR A CIGARETTE. YOU COULDN'T, uh...

NICE ONE, MATE.

CHEERS.

SEE YA.

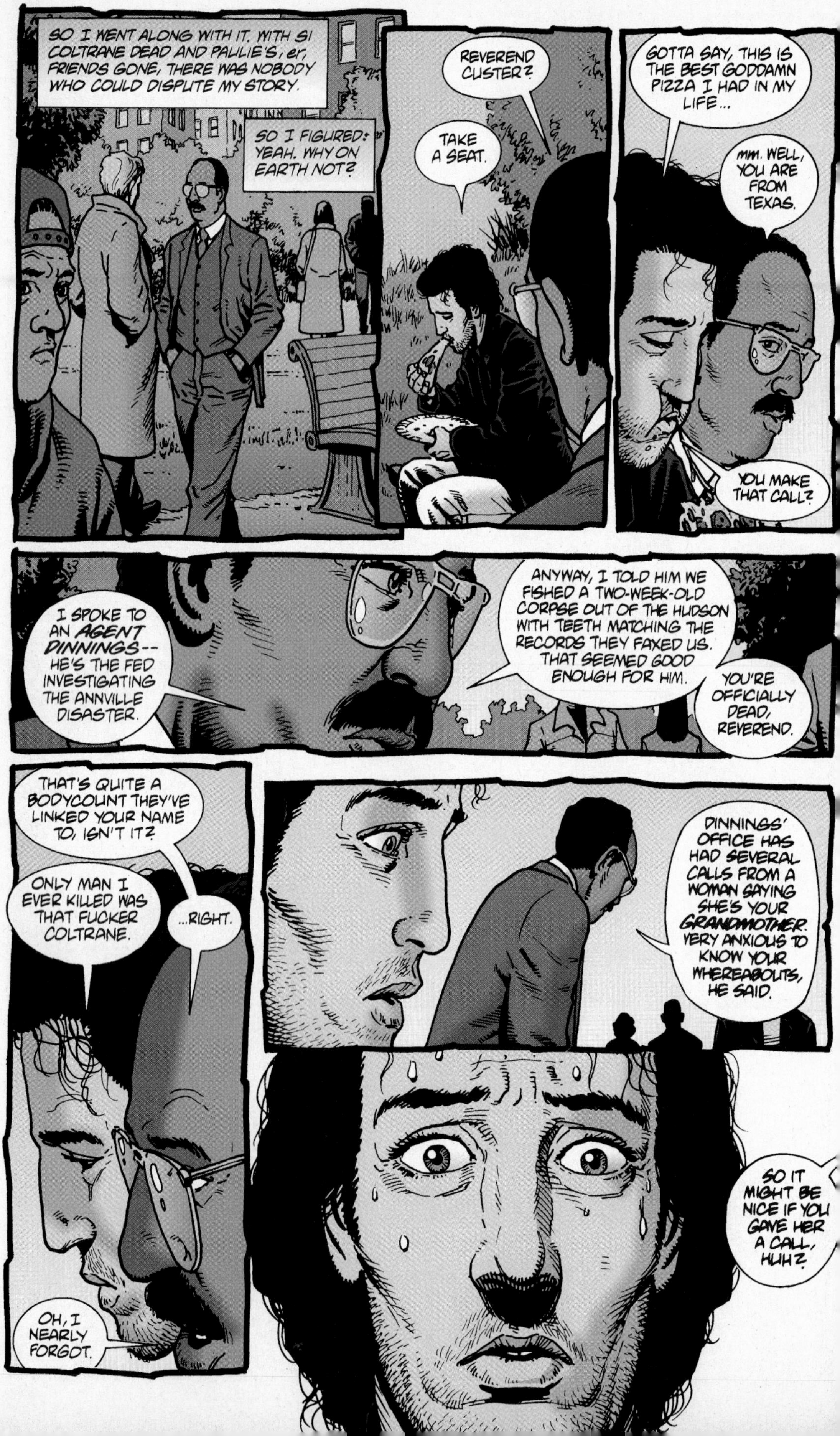

SO I WENT ALONG WITH IT. WITH SI COLTRANE DEAD AND PAULIE'S, er, FRIENDS GONE, THERE WAS NOBODY WHO COULD DISPUTE MY STORY.
SO I FIGURED: YEAH. WHY ON EARTH NOT?
REVEREND CUSTER?
TAKE A SEAT.
GOTTA SAY, THIS IS THE BEST GODDAMN PIZZA I HAD IN MY LIFE...
MM. WELL, YOU ARE FROM TEXAS.
YOU MAKE THAT CALL?
I SPOKE TO AN AGENT DINNINGS-- HE'S THE FED INVESTIGATING THE ANNVILLE DISASTER.
ANYWAY, I TOLD HIM WE FISHED A TWO-WEEK-OLD CORPSE OUT OF THE HUDSON WITH TEETH MATCHING THE RECORDS THEY FAXED US. THAT SEEMED GOOD ENOUGH FOR HIM.
YOU'RE OFFICIALLY DEAD, REVEREND.
THAT'S QUITE A BODYCOUNT THEY'VE LINKED YOUR NAME TO, ISN'T IT?
ONLY MAN I EVER KILLED WAS THAT FUCKER COLTRANE.
...RIGHT.
OH, I NEARLY FORGOT.
DINNINGS' OFFICE HAS HAD SEVERAL CALLS FROM A WOMAN SAYING SHE'S YOUR GRANDMOTHER. VERY ANXIOUS TO KNOW YOUR WHEREABOUTS, HE SAID.
SO IT MIGHT BE NICE IF YOU GAVE HER A CALL, HUH?

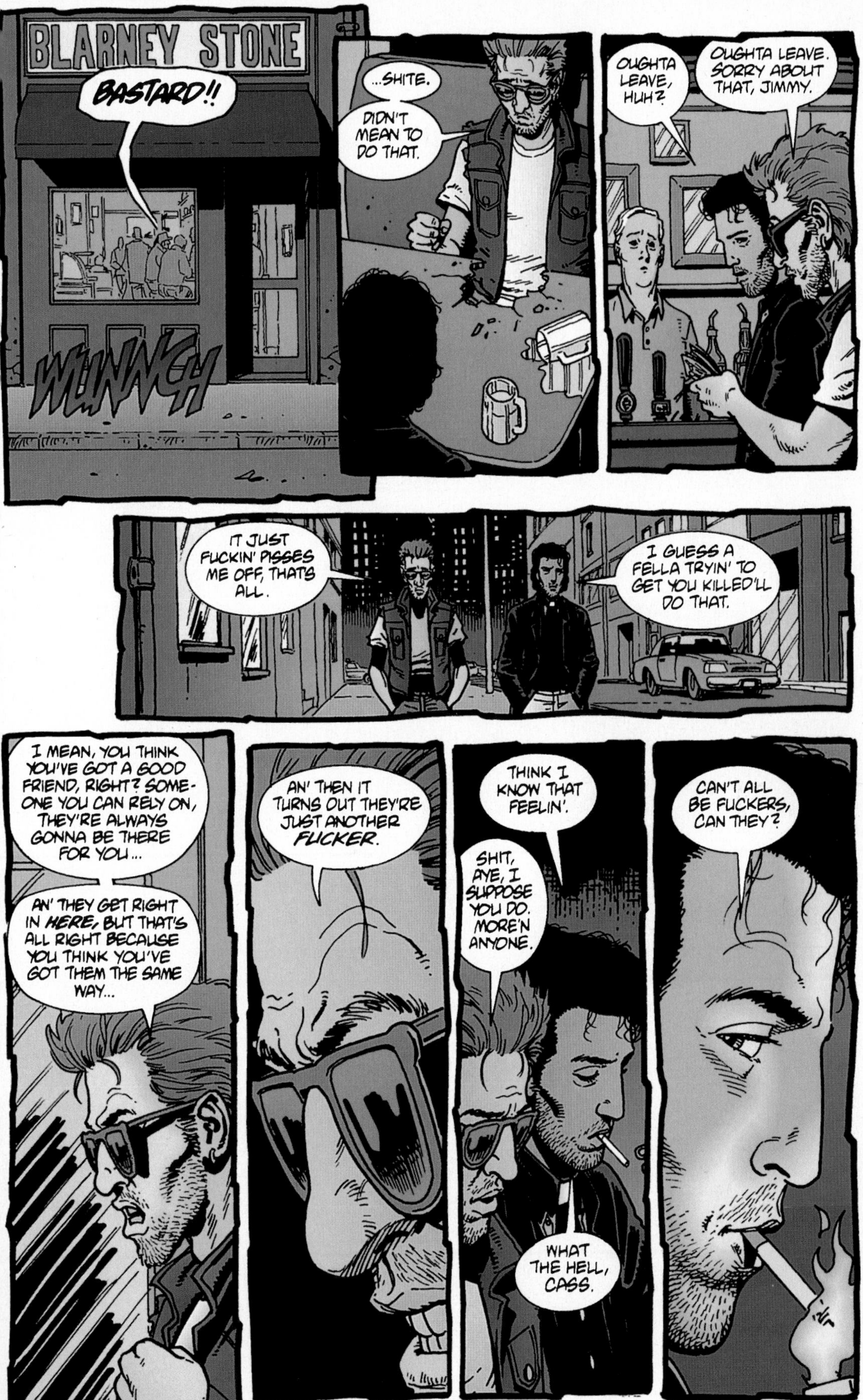
BLARNEY STONE
BASTARD!!
WUNNCH
...SHITE.
DIDN'T MEAN TO DO THAT.
OUGHTA LEAVE, HUH?
OUGHTA LEAVE. SORRY ABOUT THAT, JIMMY.
IT JUST FUCKIN' PISSES ME OFF, THAT'S ALL.
I GUESS A FELLA TRYIN' TO GET YOU KILLED'LL DO THAT.
I MEAN, YOU THINK YOU'VE GOT A GOOD FRIEND, RIGHT? SOME-ONE YOU CAN RELY ON, THEY'RE ALWAYS GONNA BE THERE FOR YOU...
AN' THEY GET RIGHT IN HERE, BUT THAT'S ALL RIGHT BECAUSE YOU THINK YOU'VE GOT THEM THE SAME WAY...
AN' THEN IT TURNS OUT THEY'RE JUST ANOTHER FUCKER.
THINK I KNOW THAT FEELIN'.
SHIT, AYE, I SUPPOSE YOU DO. MORE'N ANYONE.
WHAT THE HELL, CASS.
CAN'T ALL BE FUCKERS, CAN THEY?

S'POSE NOT.

HOW'S TULIP DOIN'?

ONE MORE NIGHT IN THE HOSPITAL. LOST A LOT'VE BLOOD.

REAL GOOD'VE YOU TO PAY HER BILL...

NO PROBS, MATE. THAT'S THE THING THAT WINDS ME UP THE MOST, Y'KNOW? BAD ENOUGH HE NEARLY DOES FOR ME, BUT TRYIN' TO KILL THE PAIR'VE YOU WHILE HE'S AT IT...

AN' I'M THE ARSE-HOLE INTRODUCED HIM TO YOU.

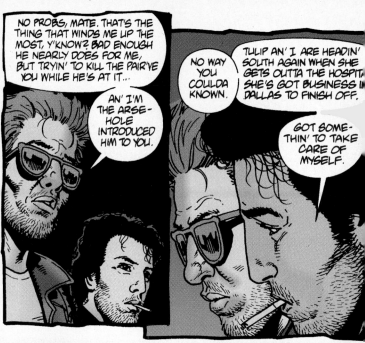

NO WAY YOU COULDA KNOWN.

TULIP AN' I ARE HEADIN' SOUTH AGAIN WHEN SHE GETS OUTTA THE HOSPITAL. SHE'S GOT BUSINESS IN DALLAS TO FINISH OFF.

GOT SOMETHIN' TO TAKE CARE OF MYSELF.

I WON'T, *uh*, I WON'T BE GOIN' WITH YOU, MATE. THINK I'M GONNA TAKE IT EASY FOR A WHILE.

LISTEN, HERE'S THE NUMBER I'LL BE AT IF YOU NEED TO GET IN TOUCH...

FOUR-ONE-FIVE ...SAN FRANCISCO, RIGHT?

AYE.

TAKE CARE'VE YERSELF, PREACHER MAN.

YOU TOO. YOU INSANE SON OF A BITCH.

NAH.

CAN'T ALL BE FUCKERS.

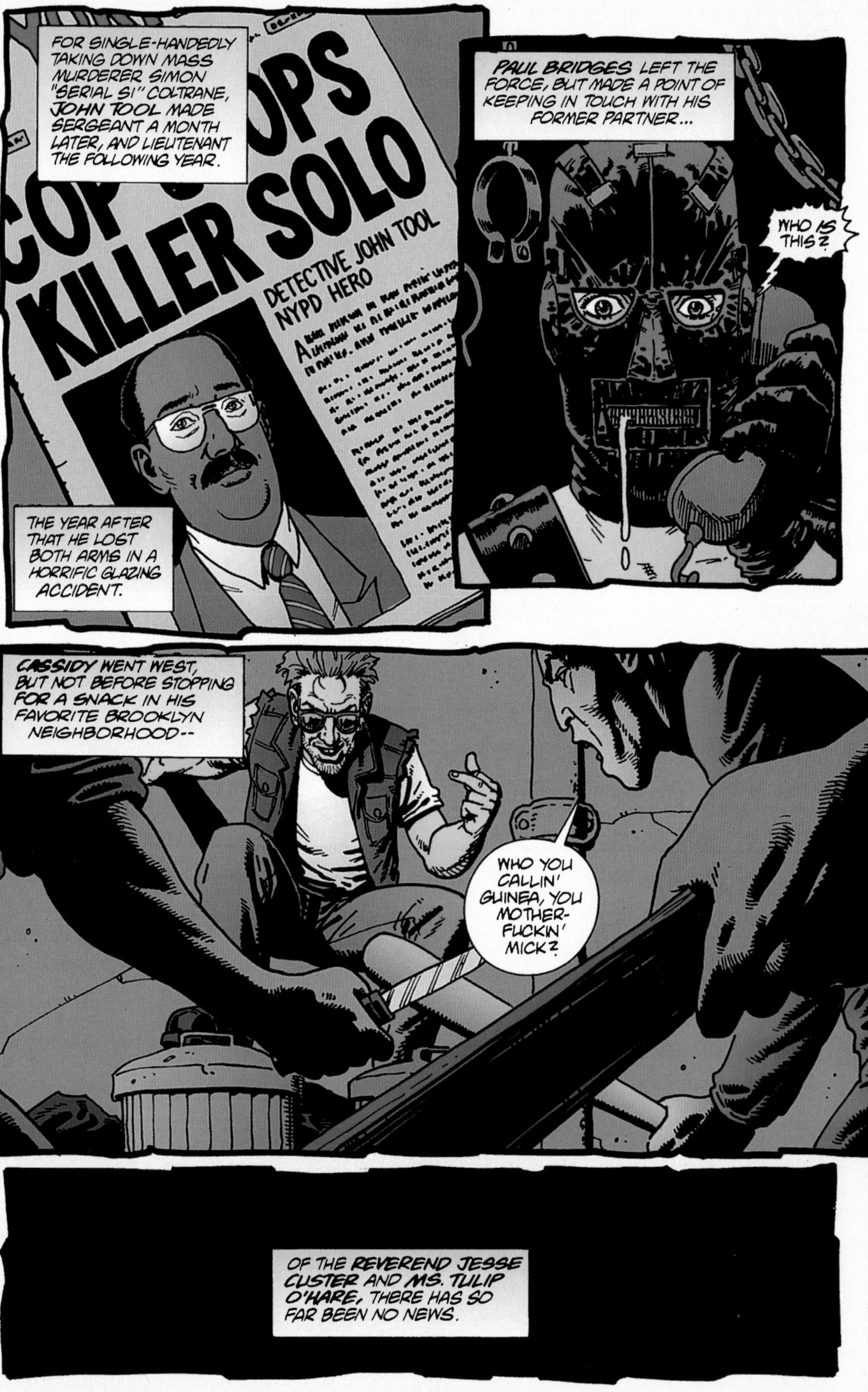
FOR SINGLE-HANDEDLY TAKING DOWN MASS MURDERER SIMON "SERIAL SI" COLTRANE, JOHN TOOL MADE SERGEANT A MONTH LATER, AND LIEUTENANT THE FOLLOWING YEAR.
KILLER SOLO
DETECTIVE JOHN TOOL
NYPD HERO
THE YEAR AFTER THAT HE LOST BOTH ARMS IN A HORRIFIC GLAZING ACCIDENT.
PAUL BRIDGES LEFT THE FORCE, BUT MADE A POINT OF KEEPING IN TOUCH WITH HIS FORMER PARTNER...
WHO IS THIS?
CASSIDY WENT WEST, BUT NOT BEFORE STOPPING FOR A SNACK IN HIS FAVORITE BROOKLYN NEIGHBORHOOD--
WHO YOU CALLIN' GUINEA, YOU MOTHER-FUCKIN' MICK?
OF THE REVEREND JESSE CUSTER AND MS. TULIP O'HARE, THERE HAS SO FAR BEEN NO NEWS.

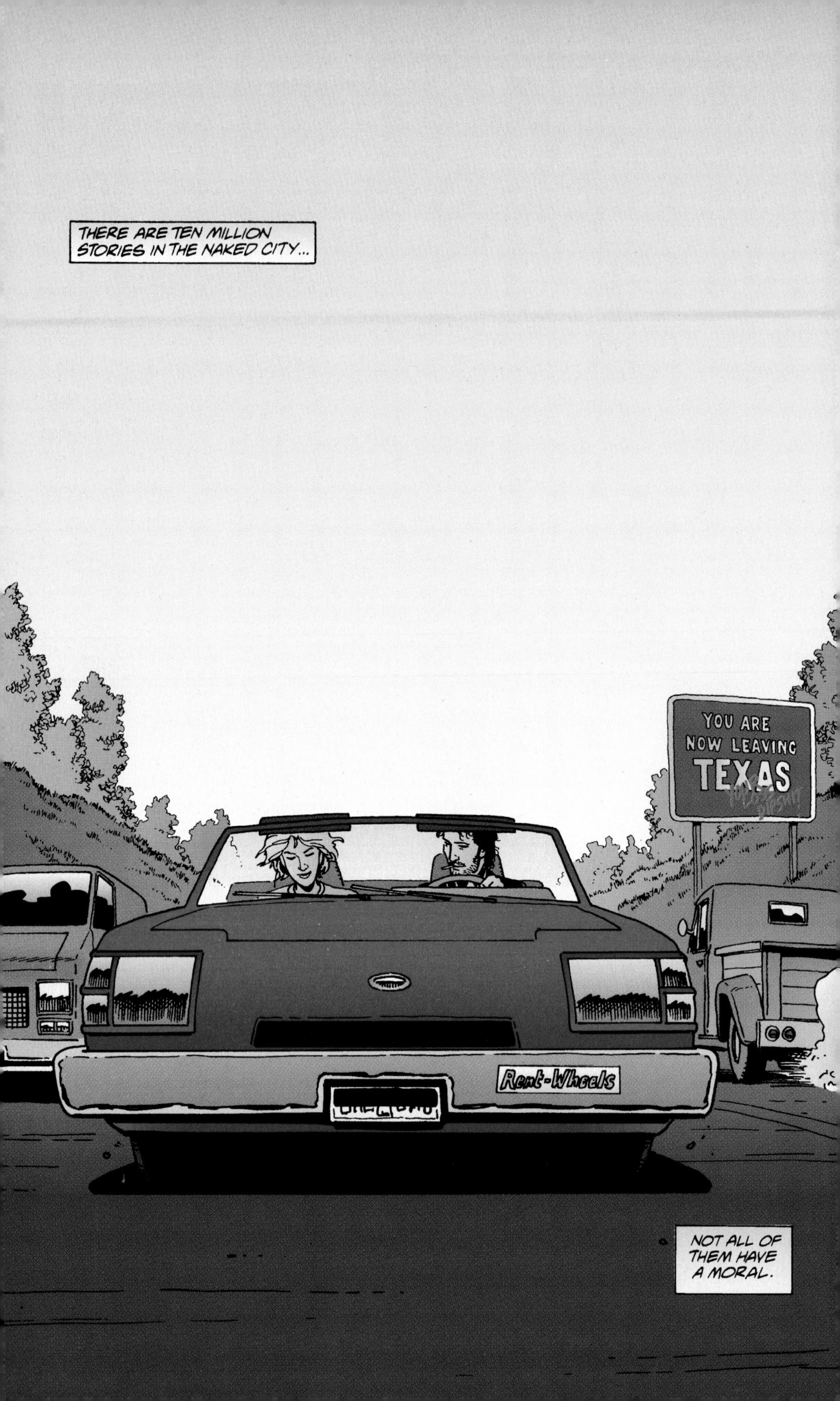
THERE ARE TEN MILLION STORIES IN THE NAKED CITY...
YOU ARE NOW LEAVING TEXAS
Rent-Wheels
NOT ALL OF THEM HAVE A MORAL.

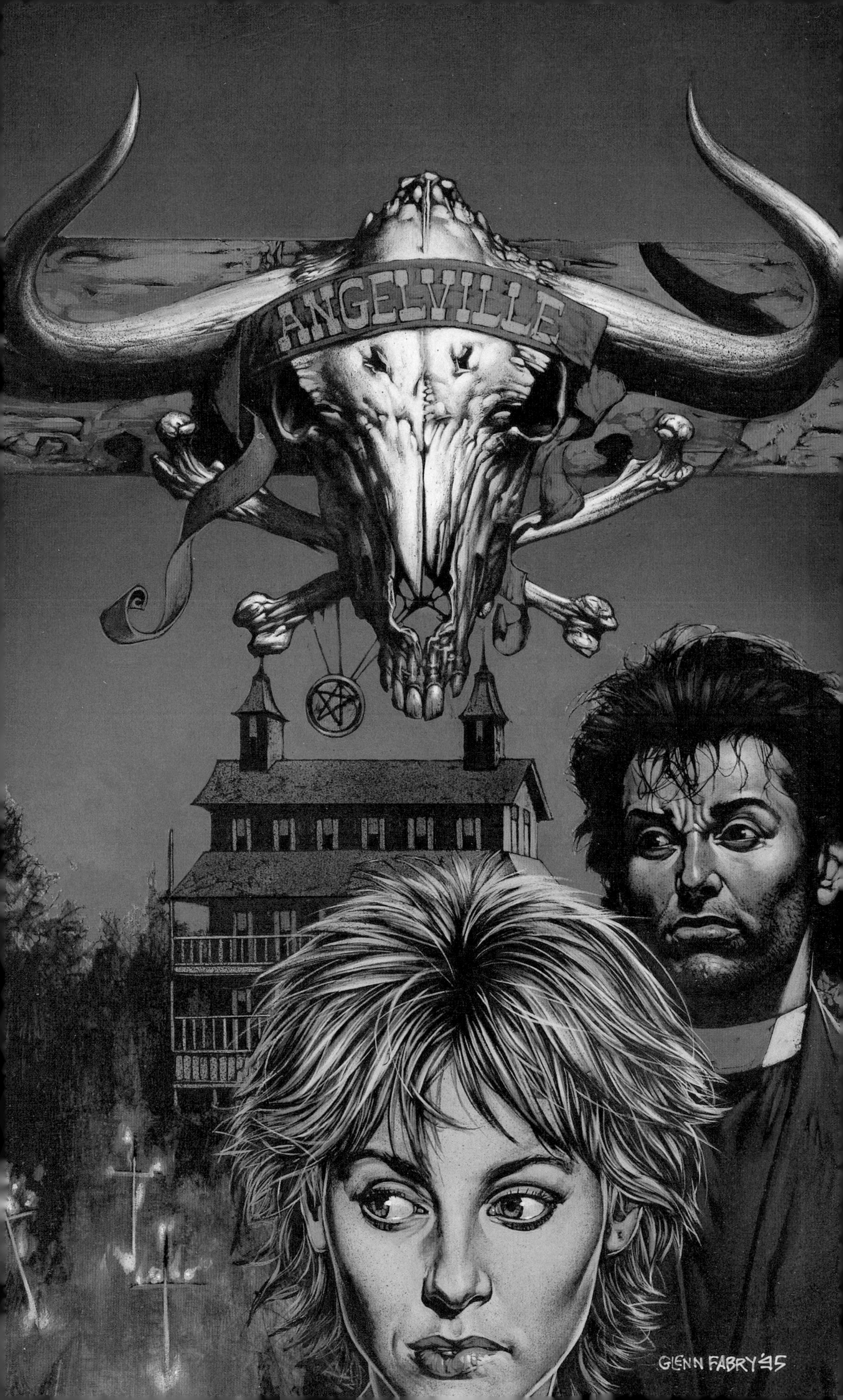
ANGELVILLE
GLENN FABRY '95

"If the Devil created Texas like some folks say he did,
this is where he rested on the seventh day."

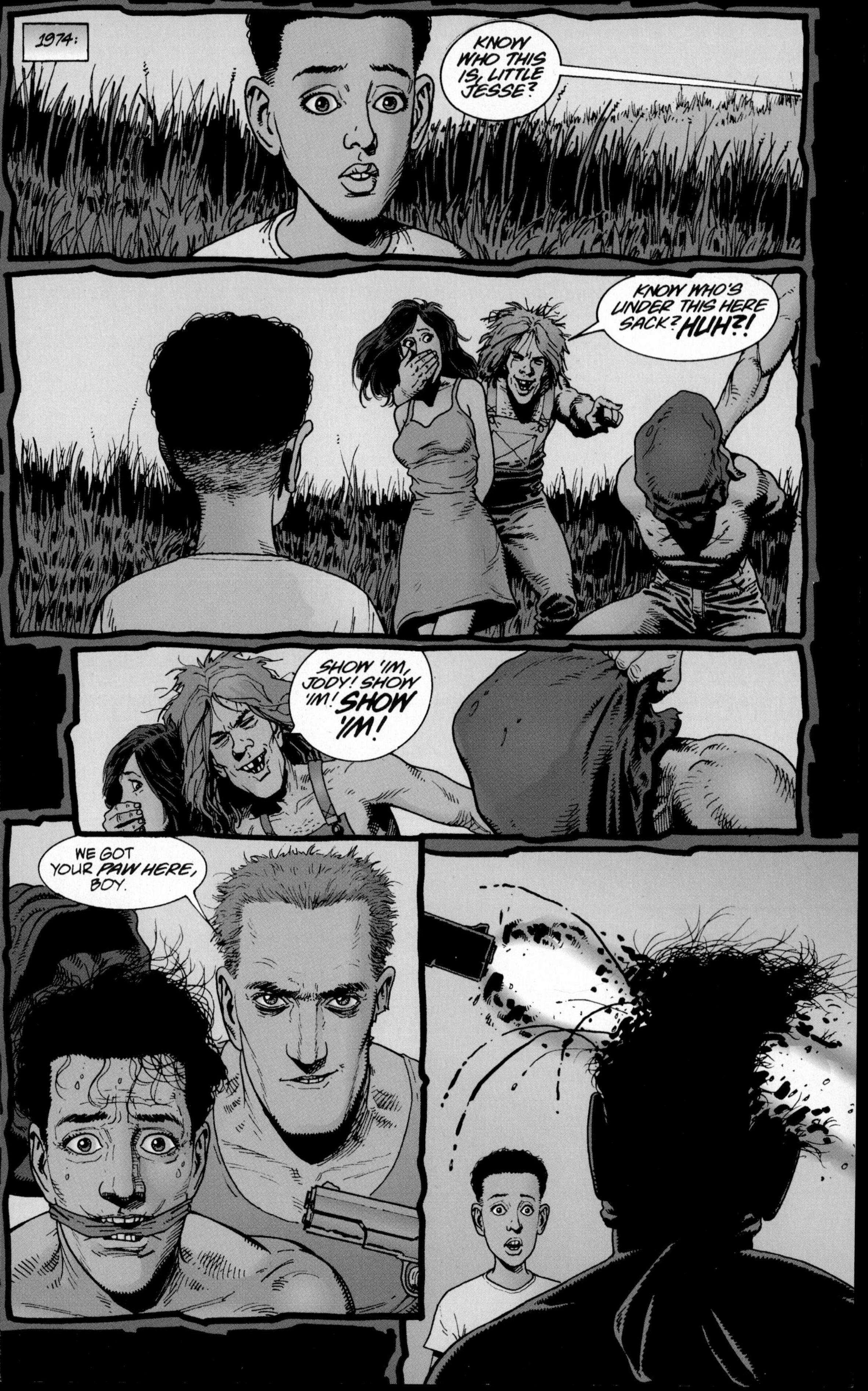

1974:
KNOW WHO THIS IS, LITTLE JESSE?
KNOW WHO'S UNDER THIS HERE SACK? HUH?!
SHOW 'IM, JODY! SHOW 'IM! SHOW 'IM!
WE GOT YOUR PAW HERE, BOY.

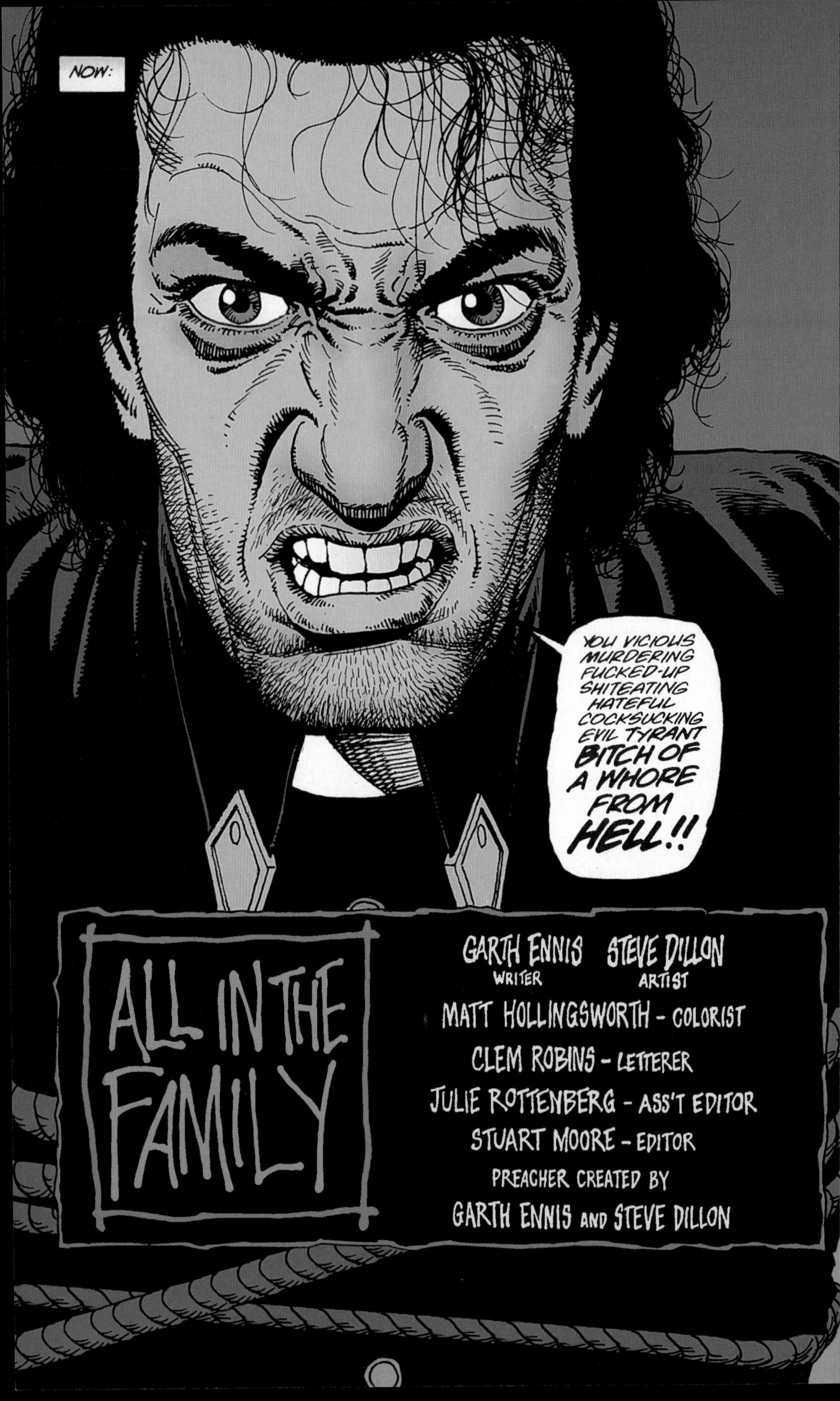
NOW:
YOU VICIOUS MURDERING FUCKED-UP SHITEATING HATEFUL COCKSUCKING EVIL TYRANT BITCH OF A WHORE FROM HELL!!
ALL IN THE FAMILY
GARTH ENNIS WRITER STEVE DILLON ARTIST
MATT HOLLINGSWORTH - COLORIST
CLEM ROBINS - LETTERER
JULIE ROTTENBERG - ASS'T EDITOR
STUART MOORE - EDITOR
PREACHER CREATED BY GARTH ENNIS AND STEVE DILLON

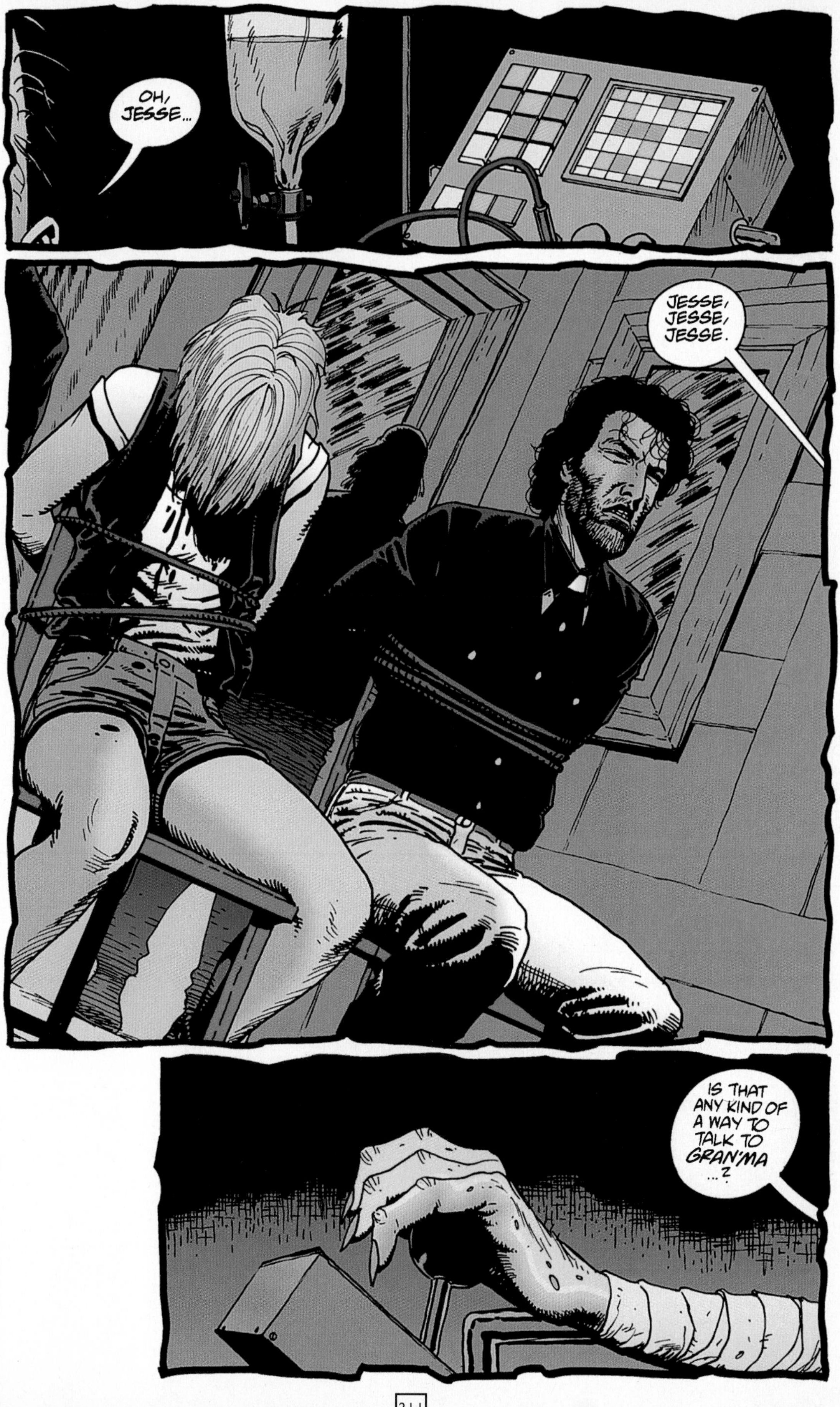
OH, JESSE...
JESSE, JESSE, JESSE.
IS THAT ANY KIND OF A WAY TO TALK TO GRAN'MA ...?

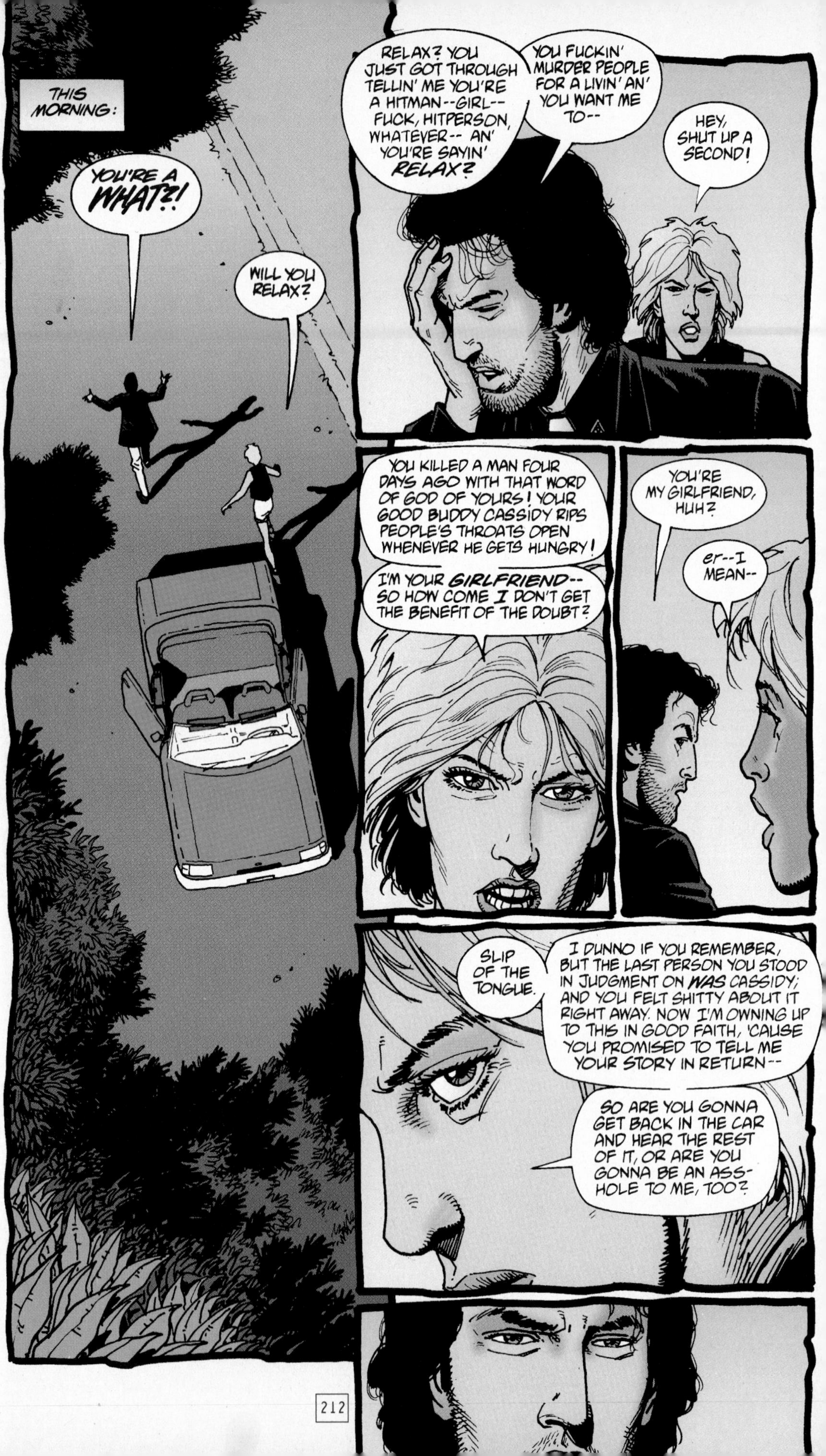
THIS MORNING:
YOU'RE A WHAT?!
WILL YOU RELAX?
RELAX? YOU JUST GOT THROUGH TELLIN' ME YOU'RE A HITMAN--GIRL--FUCK, HITPERSON, WHATEVER-- AN' YOU'RE SAYIN' RELAX?
YOU FUCKIN' MURDER PEOPLE FOR A LIVIN' AN' YOU WANT ME TO--
HEY, SHUT UP A SECOND!
YOU KILLED A MAN FOUR DAYS AGO WITH THAT WORD OF GOD OF YOURS! YOUR GOOD BUDDY CASSIDY RIPS PEOPLE'S THROATS OPEN WHENEVER HE GETS HUNGRY!
I'M YOUR GIRLFRIEND-- SO HOW COME I DON'T GET THE BENEFIT OF THE DOUBT?
YOU'RE MY GIRLFRIEND, HUH?
er--I MEAN--
SLIP OF THE TONGUE.
I DUNNO IF YOU REMEMBER, BUT THE LAST PERSON YOU STOOD IN JUDGMENT ON WAS CASSIDY; AND YOU FELT SHITTY ABOUT IT RIGHT AWAY. NOW I'M OWNING UP TO THIS IN GOOD FAITH, 'CAUSE YOU PROMISED TO TELL ME YOUR STORY IN RETURN--
SO ARE YOU GONNA GET BACK IN THE CAR AND HEAR THE REST OF IT, OR ARE YOU GONNA BE AN ASS-HOLE TO ME, TOO?

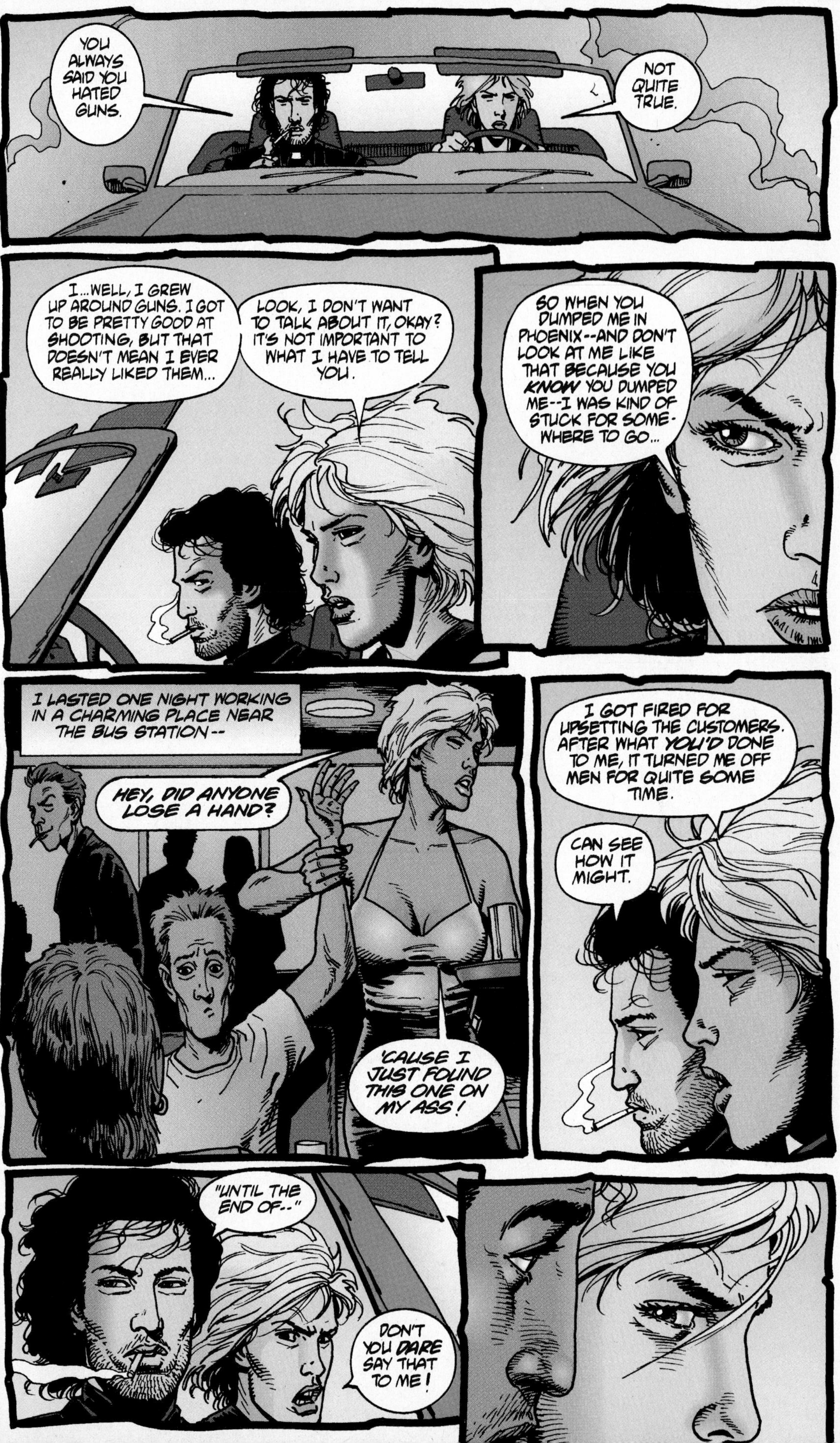
YOU ALWAYS SAID YOU HATED GUNS.
NOT QUITE TRUE.
I...WELL, I GREW UP AROUND GUNS. I GOT TO BE PRETTY GOOD AT SHOOTING, BUT THAT DOESN'T MEAN I EVER REALLY LIKED THEM...
LOOK, I DON'T WANT TO TALK ABOUT IT, OKAY? IT'S NOT IMPORTANT TO WHAT I HAVE TO TELL YOU.
SO WHEN YOU DUMPED ME IN PHOENIX--AND DON'T LOOK AT ME LIKE THAT BECAUSE YOU KNOW YOU DUMPED ME--I WAS KIND OF STUCK FOR SOME-WHERE TO GO...
I LASTED ONE NIGHT WORKING IN A CHARMING PLACE NEAR THE BUS STATION--
HEY, DID ANYONE LOSE A HAND?
'CAUSE I JUST FOUND THIS ONE ON MY ASS!
I GOT FIRED FOR UPSETTING THE CUSTOMERS. AFTER WHAT YOU'D DONE TO ME, IT TURNED ME OFF MEN FOR QUITE SOME TIME.
CAN SEE HOW IT MIGHT.
"UNTIL THE END OF--"
DON'T YOU DARE SAY THAT TO ME!

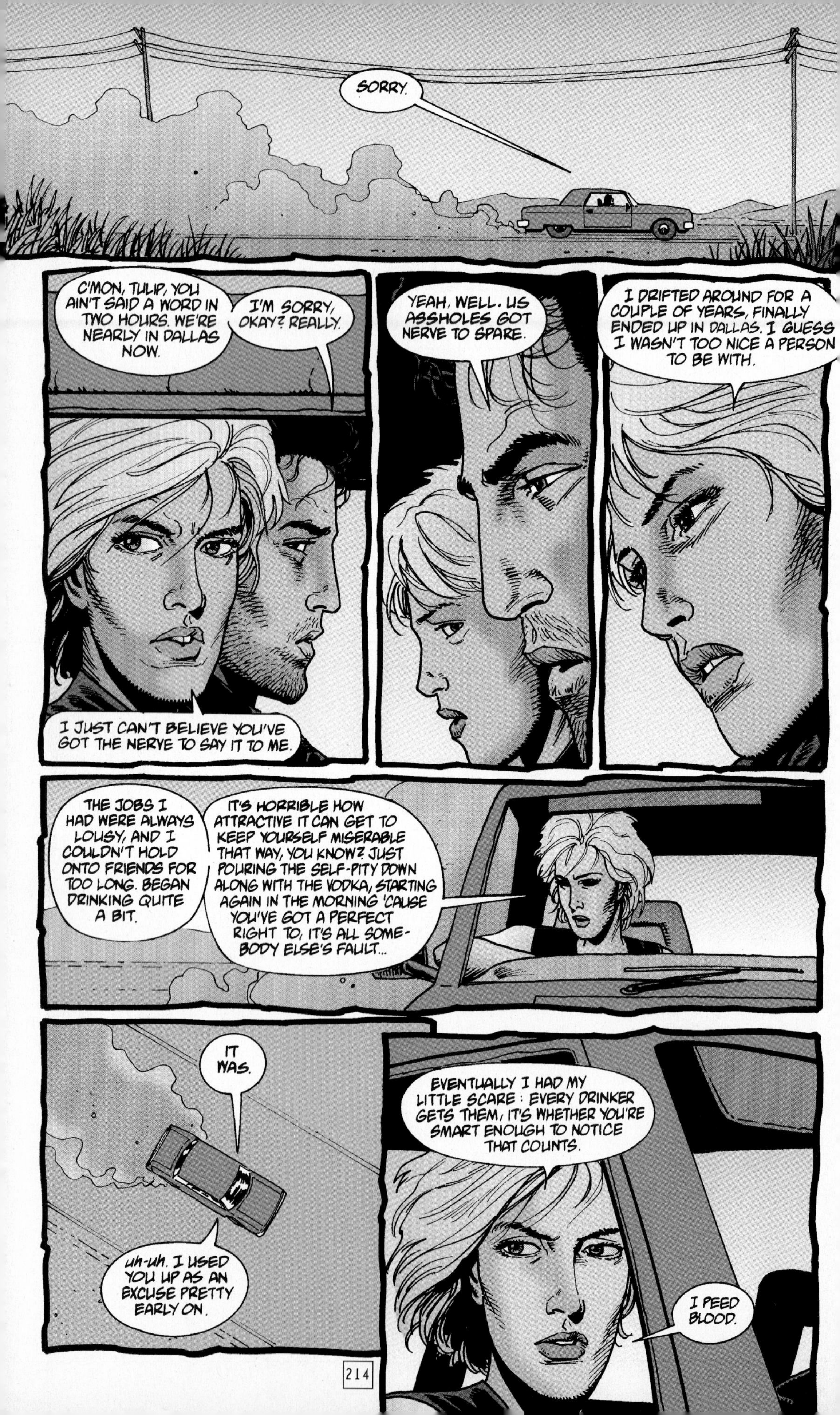
SORRY.
C'MON, TULIP, YOU AIN'T SAID A WORD IN TWO HOURS. WE'RE NEARLY IN DALLAS NOW.
I'M SORRY, OKAY? REALLY.
I JUST CAN'T BELIEVE YOU'VE GOT THE NERVE TO SAY IT TO ME.
YEAH. WELL. US ASSHOLES GOT NERVE TO SPARE.
I DRIFTED AROUND FOR A COUPLE OF YEARS, FINALLY ENDED UP IN DALLAS. I GUESS I WASN'T TOO NICE A PERSON TO BE WITH.
THE JOBS I HAD WERE ALWAYS LOUSY, AND I COULDN'T HOLD ONTO FRIENDS FOR TOO LONG. BEGAN DRINKING QUITE A BIT.
IT'S HORRIBLE HOW ATTRACTIVE IT CAN GET TO KEEP YOURSELF MISERABLE THAT WAY, YOU KNOW? JUST POURING THE SELF-PITY DOWN ALONG WITH THE VODKA, STARTING AGAIN IN THE MORNING 'CAUSE YOU'VE GOT A PERFECT RIGHT TO, IT'S ALL SOMEBODY ELSE'S FAULT...
IT WAS.
uh-uh. I USED YOU UP AS AN EXCUSE PRETTY EARLY ON.
EVENTUALLY I HAD MY LITTLE SCARE : EVERY DRINKER GETS THEM, IT'S WHETHER YOU'RE SMART ENOUGH TO NOTICE THAT COUNTS.
I PEED BLOOD.

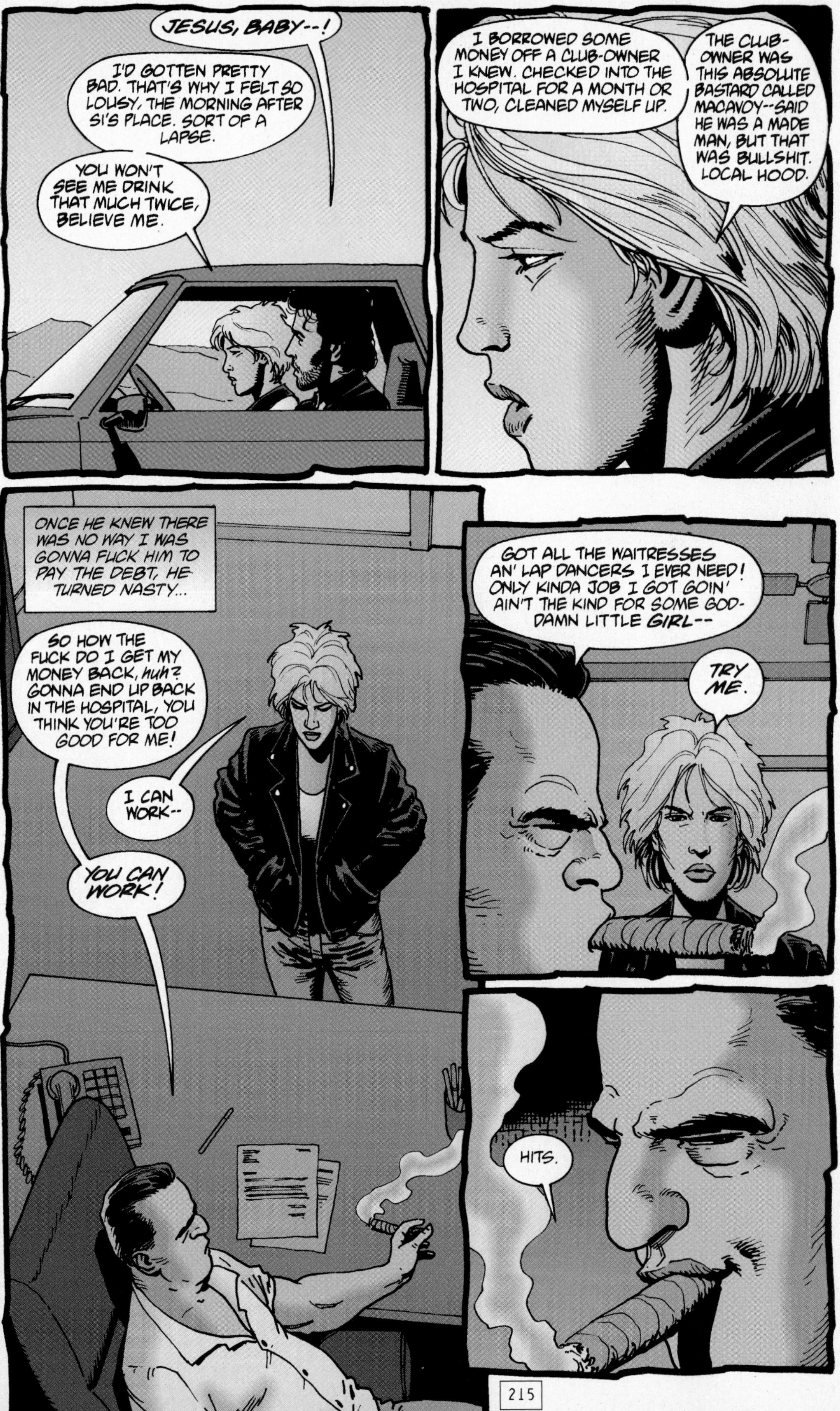

I'D GOTTEN PRETTY BAD. THAT'S WHY I FELT SO LOUSY, THE MORNING AFTER SI'S PLACE. SORT OF A LAPSE.
JESUS, BABY--!
YOU WON'T SEE ME DRINK THAT MUCH TWICE, BELIEVE ME.
I BORROWED SOME MONEY OFF A CLUB-OWNER I KNEW. CHECKED INTO THE HOSPITAL FOR A MONTH OR TWO, CLEANED MYSELF UP.
THE CLUB-OWNER WAS THIS ABSOLUTE BASTARD CALLED MACAVOY--SAID HE WAS A MADE MAN, BUT THAT WAS BULLSHIT. LOCAL HOOD.
ONCE HE KNEW THERE WAS NO WAY I WAS GONNA FUCK HIM TO PAY THE DEBT, HE TURNED NASTY...
SO HOW THE FUCK DO I GET MY MONEY BACK, *huh*? GONNA END UP BACK IN THE HOSPITAL, YOU THINK YOU'RE TOO GOOD FOR ME!
I CAN WORK--
YOU CAN WORK!
GOT ALL THE WAITRESSES AN' LAP DANCERS I EVER NEED! ONLY KINDA JOB I GOT GOIN' AIN'T THE KIND FOR SOME GOD-DAMN LITTLE *GIRL*--
TRY ME.
HITS.

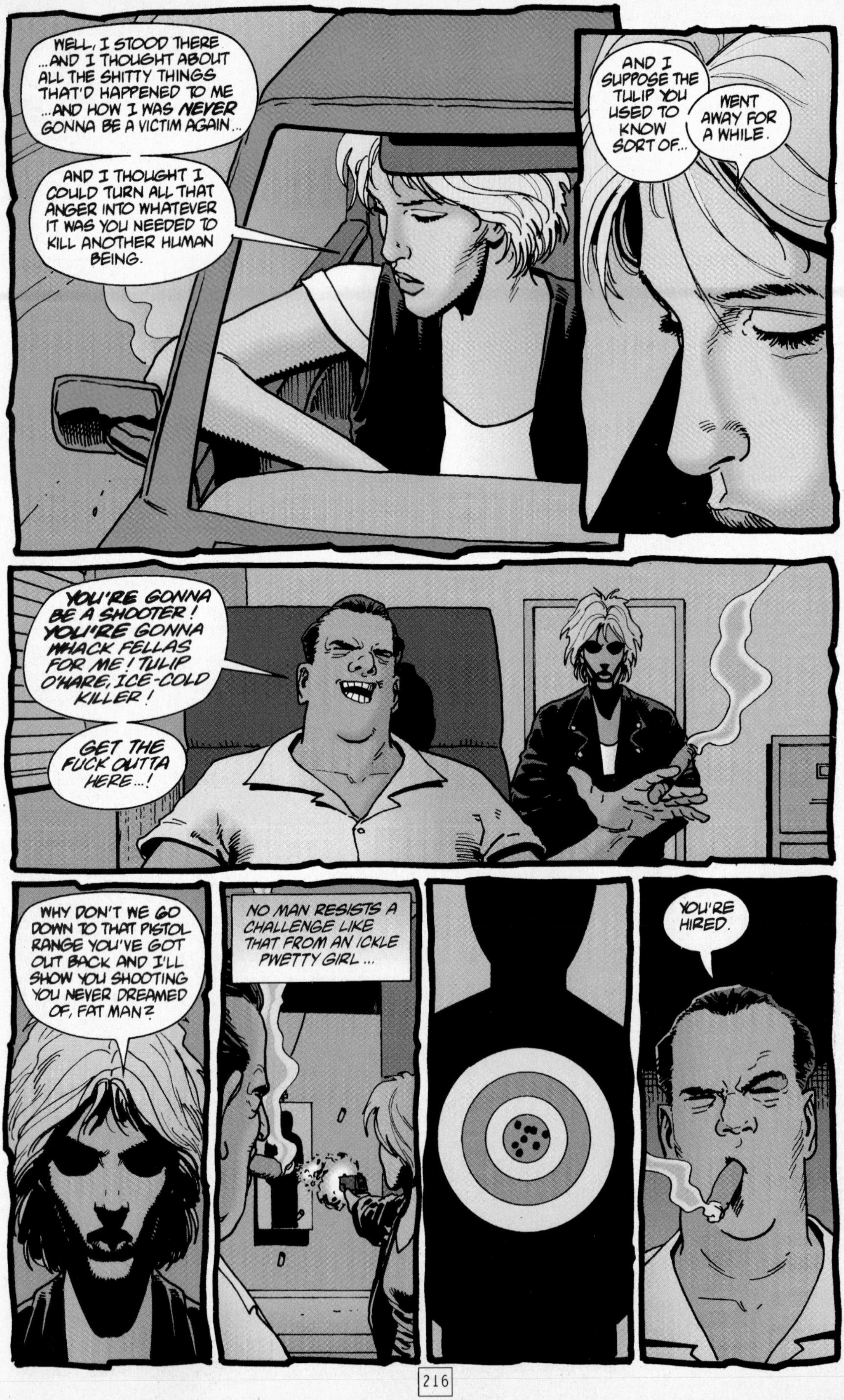
WELL, I STOOD THERE ...AND I THOUGHT ABOUT ALL THE SHITTY THINGS THAT'D HAPPENED TO ME ...AND HOW I WAS NEVER GONNA BE A VICTIM AGAIN...
AND I THOUGHT I COULD TURN ALL THAT ANGER INTO WHATEVER IT WAS YOU NEEDED TO KILL ANOTHER HUMAN BEING.
AND I SUPPOSE THE TULIP YOU USED TO KNOW SORT OF...
WENT AWAY FOR A WHILE.
YOU'RE GONNA BE A SHOOTER! YOU'RE GONNA WHACK FELLAS FOR ME! TULIP O'HARE, ICE-COLD KILLER!
GET THE FUCK OUTTA HERE...!
WHY DON'T WE GO DOWN TO THAT PISTOL RANGE YOU'VE GOT OUT BACK AND I'LL SHOW YOU SHOOTING YOU NEVER DREAMED OF, FAT MAN?
NO MAN RESISTS A CHALLENGE LIKE THAT FROM AN ICKLE PWETTY GIRL...
YOU'RE HIRED.

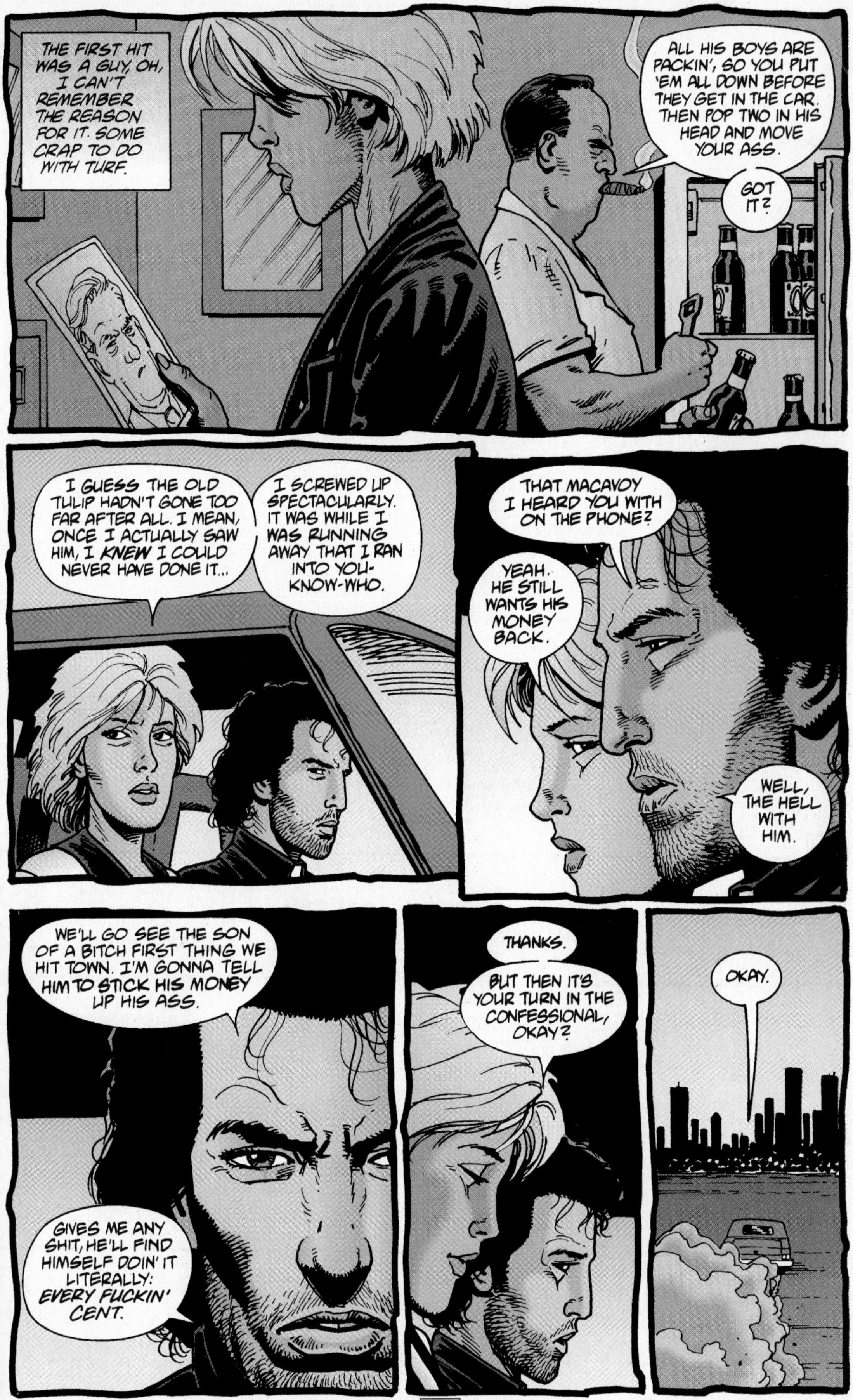

THE FIRST HIT WAS A GUY, OH, I CAN'T REMEMBER THE REASON FOR IT. SOME CRAP TO DO WITH TURF.
ALL HIS BOYS ARE PACKIN', SO YOU PUT 'EM ALL DOWN BEFORE THEY GET IN THE CAR. THEN POP TWO IN HIS HEAD AND MOVE YOUR ASS.
GOT IT?
I GUESS THE OLD TULIP HADN'T GONE TOO FAR AFTER ALL. I MEAN, ONCE I ACTUALLY SAW HIM, I *KNEW* I COULD NEVER HAVE DONE IT...
I SCREWED UP SPECTACULARLY. IT WAS WHILE I WAS RUNNING AWAY THAT I RAN INTO YOU-KNOW-WHO.
THAT MACAVOY I HEARD YOU WITH ON THE PHONE?
YEAH. HE STILL WANTS HIS MONEY BACK.
WELL, THE HELL WITH HIM.
WE'LL GO SEE THE SON OF A BITCH FIRST THING WE HIT TOWN. I'M GONNA TELL HIM TO STICK HIS MONEY UP HIS ASS.
GIVES ME ANY SHIT, HE'LL FIND HIMSELF DOIN' IT LITERALLY: *EVERY FUCKIN' CENT.*
THANKS.
BUT THEN IT'S YOUR TURN IN THE CONFESSIONAL, OKAY?
OKAY.

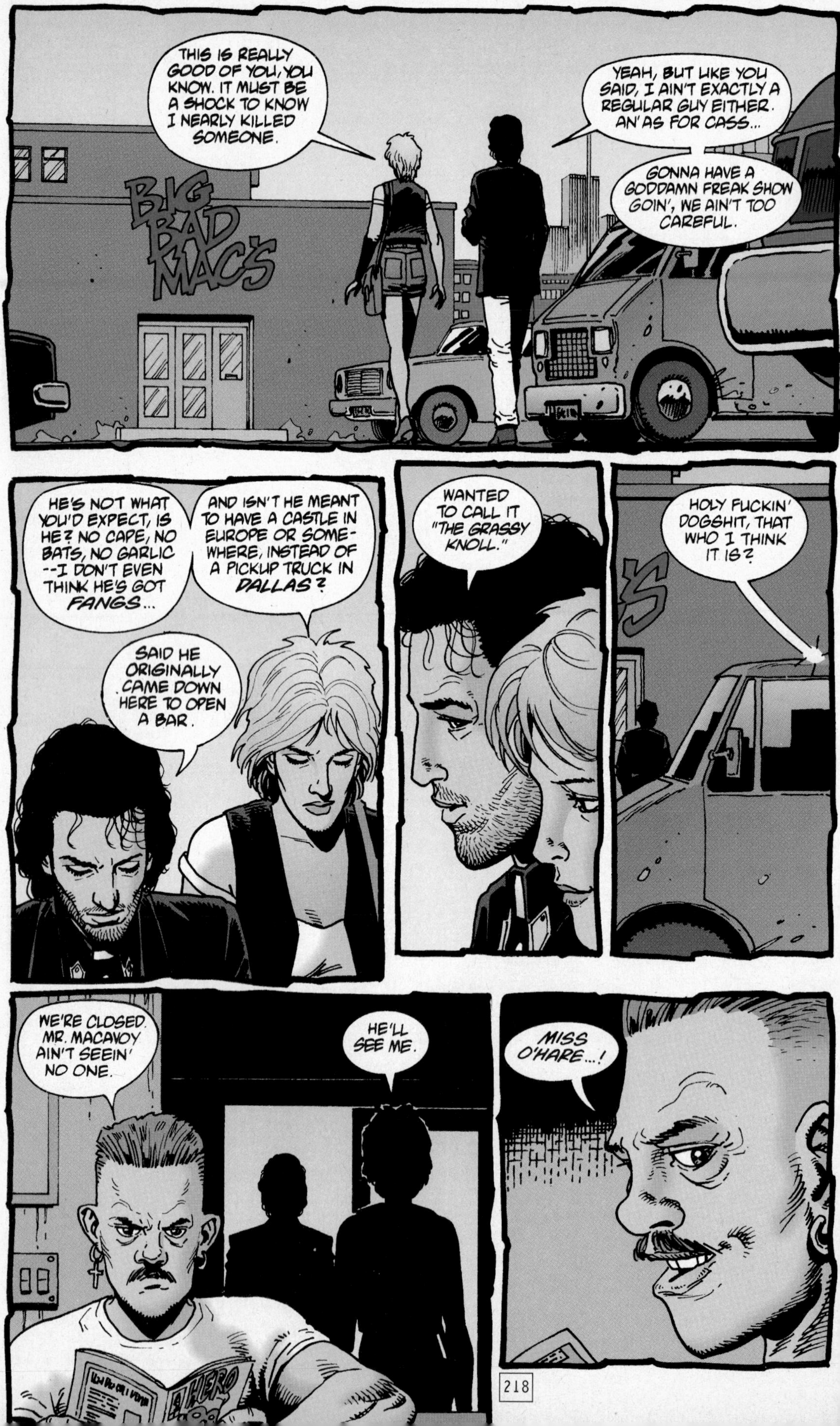

BIG BAD MAC'S
THIS IS REALLY GOOD OF YOU, YOU KNOW. IT MUST BE A SHOCK TO KNOW I NEARLY KILLED SOMEONE.
YEAH, BUT LIKE YOU SAID, I AIN'T EXACTLY A REGULAR GUY EITHER. AN' AS FOR CASS...
GONNA HAVE A GODDAMN FREAK SHOW GOIN', WE AIN'T TOO CAREFUL.
HE'S NOT WHAT YOU'D EXPECT, IS HE? NO CAPE, NO BATS, NO GARLIC --I DON'T EVEN THINK HE'S GOT *FANGS*...
AND ISN'T HE MEANT TO HAVE A CASTLE IN EUROPE OR SOME-WHERE, INSTEAD OF A PICKUP TRUCK IN *DALLAS*?
SAID HE ORIGINALLY CAME DOWN HERE TO OPEN A BAR.
WANTED TO CALL IT "THE GRASSY KNOLL."
HOLY FUCKIN' DOGSHIT, THAT WHO I THINK IT IS?
WE'RE CLOSED. MR. MACAVOY AIN'T SEEIN' NO ONE.
HE'LL SEE ME.
MISS O'HARE...!

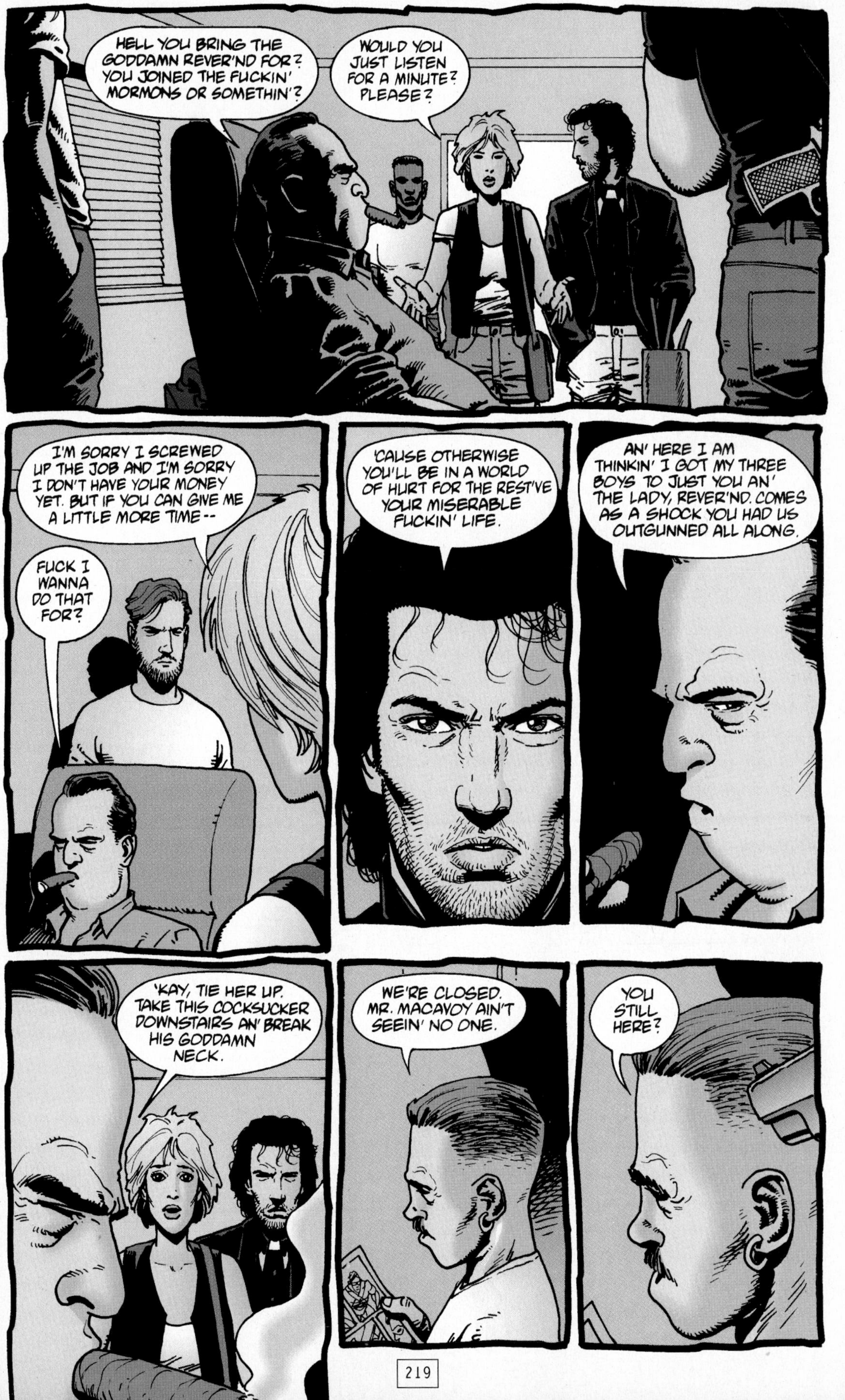

HELL YOU BRING THE GODDAMN REVER'ND FOR? YOU JOINED THE FUCKIN' MORMONS OR SOMETHIN'?
WOULD YOU JUST LISTEN FOR A MINUTE? PLEASE?
I'M SORRY I SCREWED UP THE JOB AND I'M SORRY I DON'T HAVE YOUR MONEY YET. BUT IF YOU CAN GIVE ME A LITTLE MORE TIME--
FUCK I WANNA DO THAT FOR?
'CAUSE OTHERWISE YOU'LL BE IN A WORLD OF HURT FOR THE REST'VE YOUR MISERABLE FUCKIN' LIFE.
AN' HERE I AM THINKIN' I GOT MY THREE BOYS TO JUST YOU AN' THE LADY, REVER'ND. COMES AS A SHOCK YOU HAD US OUTGUNNED ALL ALONG.
'KAY, TIE HER UP. TAKE THIS COCKSUCKER DOWNSTAIRS AN' BREAK HIS GODDAMN NECK.
WE'RE CLOSED. MR. MACAVOY AIN'T SEEIN' NO ONE.
YOU STILL HERE?

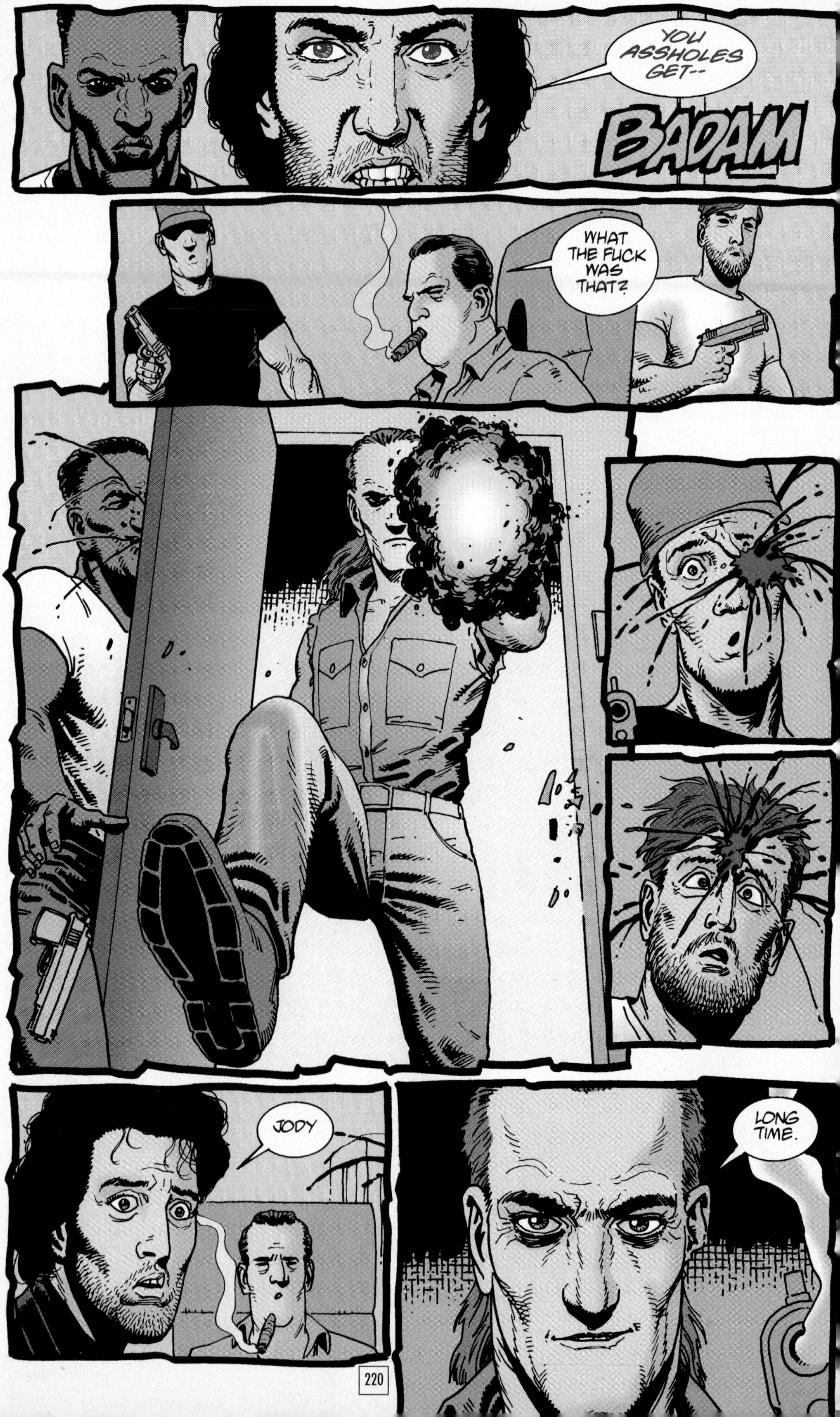
YOU ASSHOLES GET--
BADAM
WHAT THE FUCK WAS THAT?
JODY
LONG TIME.

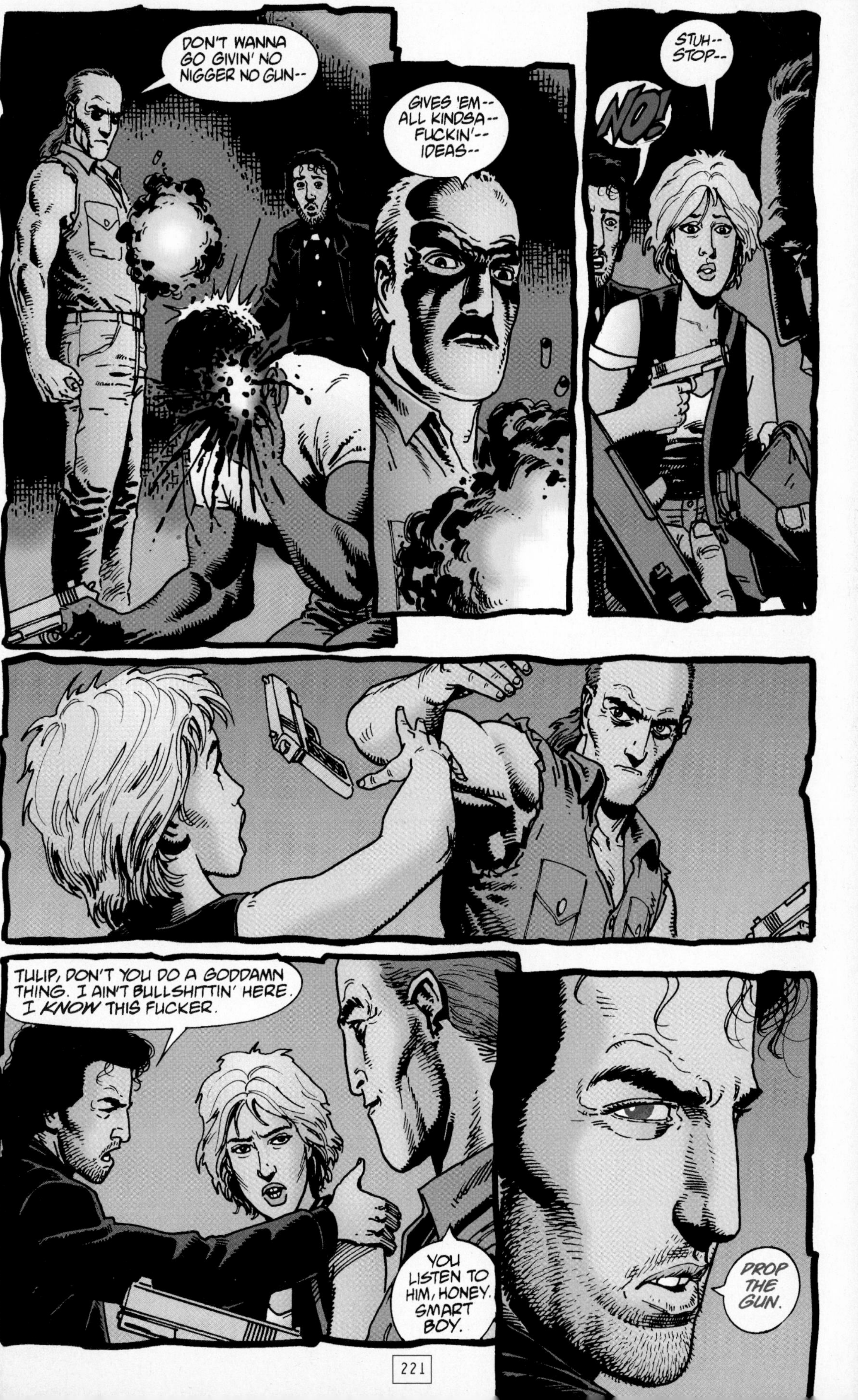
DON'T WANNA GO GIVIN' NO NIGGER NO GUN--
GIVES 'EM-- ALL KINDSA-- FUCKIN'-- IDEAS--
NO!
STUH-- STOP--
TULIP, DON'T YOU DO A GODDAMN THING. I AIN'T BULLSHITTIN' HERE. I *KNOW* THIS FUCKER.
YOU LISTEN TO HIM, HONEY. SMART BOY.
DROP THE GUN.

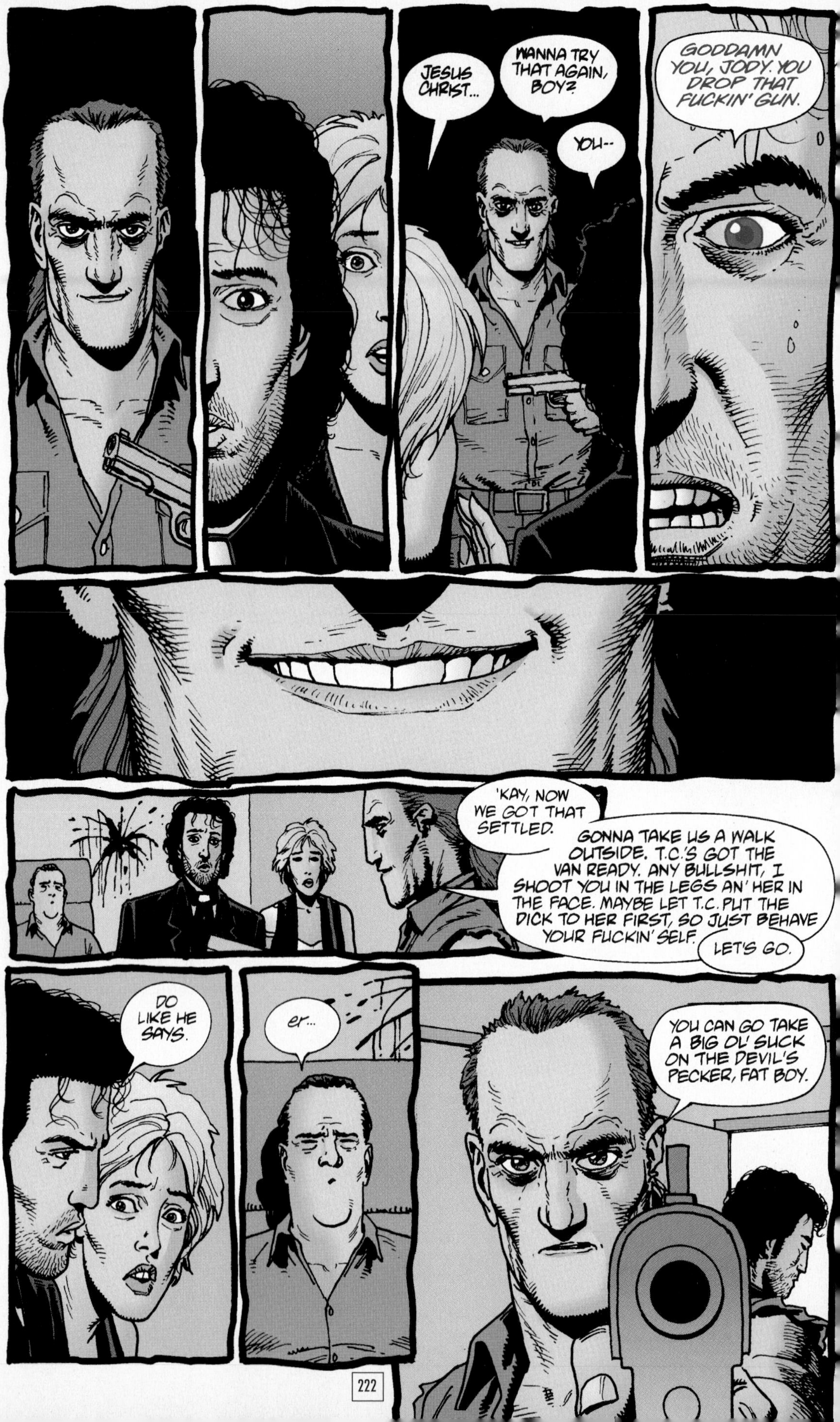

JESUS CHRIST...
WANNA TRY THAT AGAIN, BOY?
YOU--
GODDAMN YOU, JODY. YOU DROP THAT FUCKIN' GUN.
'KAY, NOW WE GOT THAT SETTLED.
GONNA TAKE US A WALK OUTSIDE. T.C.'S GOT THE VAN READY. ANY BULLSHIT, I SHOOT YOU IN THE LEGS AN' HER IN THE FACE. MAYBE LET T.C. PUT THE DICK TO HER FIRST, SO JUST BEHAVE YOUR FUCKIN' SELF.
LET'S GO.
DO LIKE HE SAYS.
er...
YOU CAN GO TAKE A BIG OL' SUCK ON THE DEVIL'S PECKER, FAT BOY.

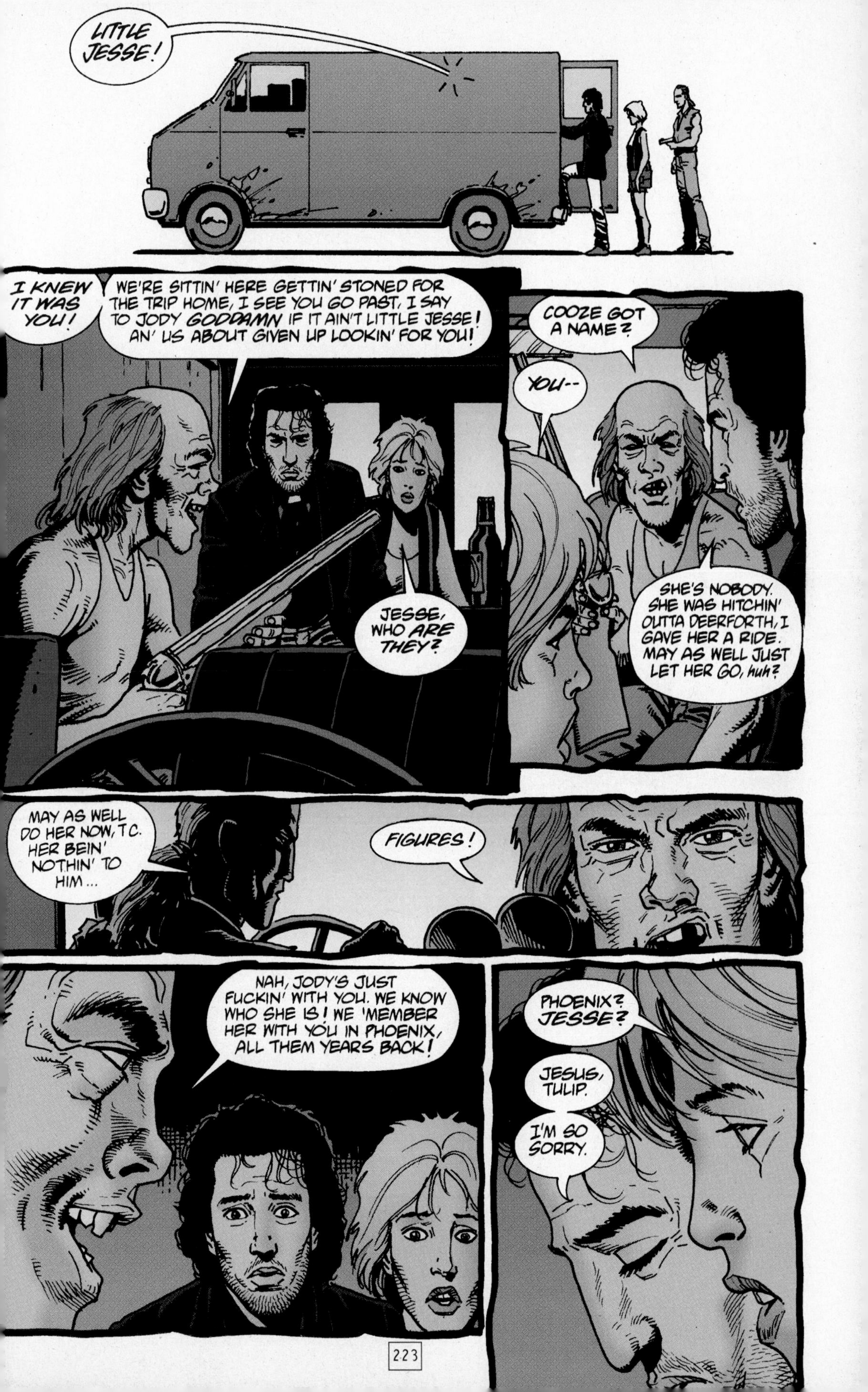
LITTLE JESSE!
I KNEW IT WAS YOU!
WE'RE SITTIN' HERE GETTIN' STONED FOR THE TRIP HOME, I SEE YOU GO PAST, I SAY TO JODY GODDAMN IF IT AIN'T LITTLE JESSE! AN' US ABOUT GIVEN UP LOOKIN' FOR YOU!
JESSE, WHO ARE THEY?
COOZE GOT A NAME?
YOU--
SHE'S NOBODY. SHE WAS HITCHIN' OUTTA DEERFORTH, I GAVE HER A RIDE. MAY AS WELL JUST LET HER GO, huh?
MAY AS WELL DO HER NOW, T.C. HER BEIN' NOTHIN' TO HIM...
FIGURES!
NAH, JODY'S JUST FUCKIN' WITH YOU. WE KNOW WHO SHE IS! WE 'MEMBER HER WITH YOU IN PHOENIX, ALL THEM YEARS BACK!
PHOENIX? JESSE?
JESUS, TULIP.
I'M SO SORRY.

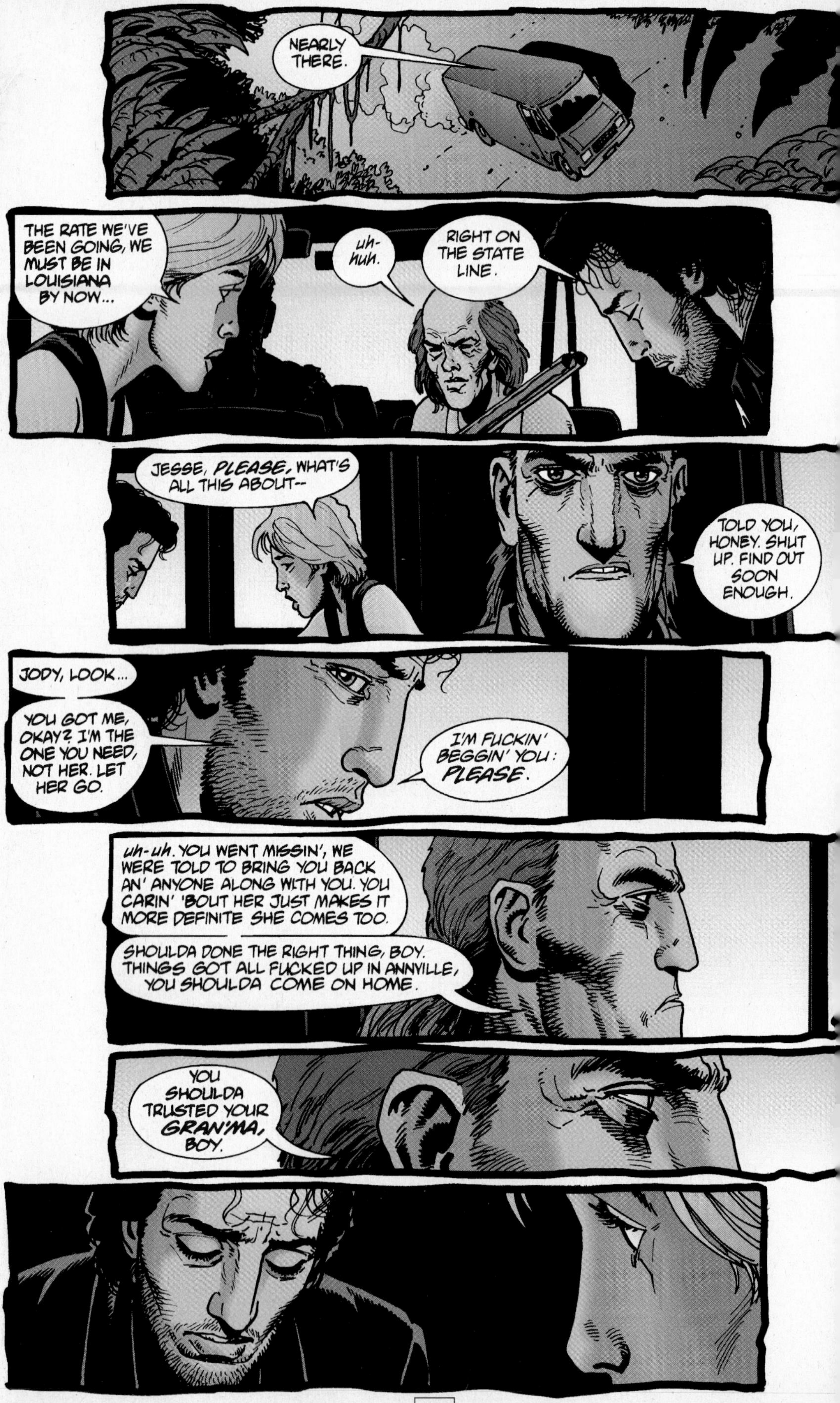
NEARLY THERE.
THE RATE WE'VE BEEN GOING, WE MUST BE IN LOUISIANA BY NOW...
uh-huh.
RIGHT ON THE STATE LINE.
JESSE, PLEASE, WHAT'S ALL THIS ABOUT--
TOLD YOU, HONEY. SHUT UP. FIND OUT SOON ENOUGH.
JODY, LOOK...
YOU GOT ME, OKAY? I'M THE ONE YOU NEED, NOT HER. LET HER GO.
I'M FUCKIN' BEGGIN' YOU: PLEASE.
uh-uh. YOU WENT MISSIN', WE WERE TOLD TO BRING YOU BACK AN' ANYONE ALONG WITH YOU. YOU CARIN' 'BOUT HER JUST MAKES IT MORE DEFINITE SHE COMES TOO.
SHOULDA DONE THE RIGHT THING, BOY. THINGS GOT ALL FUCKED UP IN ANNVILLE, YOU SHOULDA COME ON HOME.
YOU SHOULDA TRUSTED YOUR GRAN'MA, BOY.

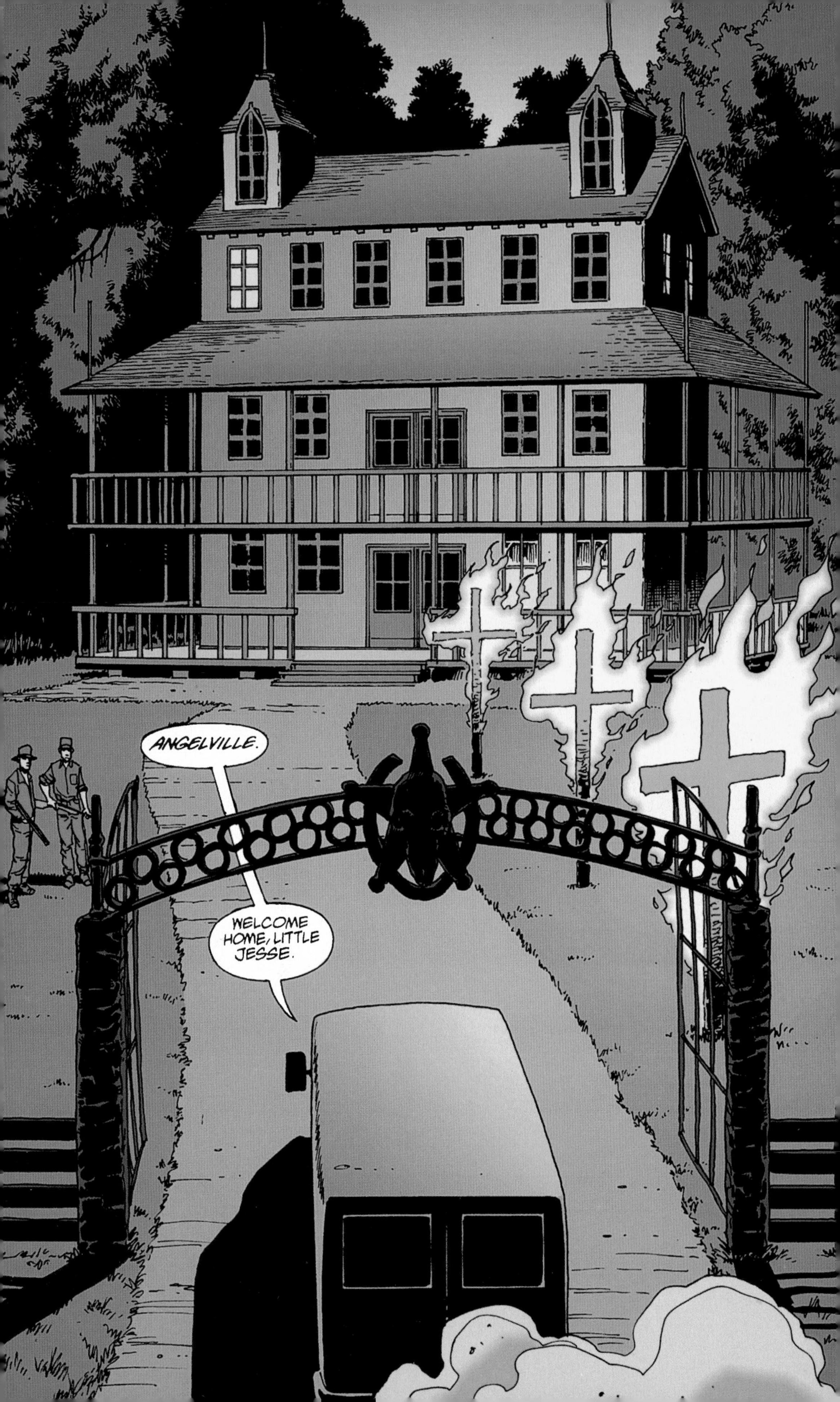
ANGELVILLE.
WELCOME HOME, LITTLE JESSE.

HOLY SHIT...!

JESSE, WHERE *ARE* WE?

MOST GODDAMNED AWFUL PLACE THERE IS.

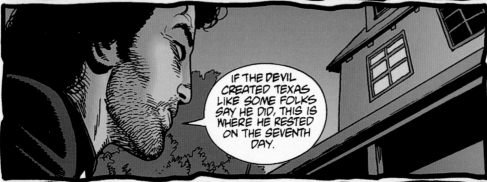

IF THE DEVIL CREATED TEXAS LIKE SOME FOLKS SAY HE DID, THIS IS WHERE HE RESTED ON THE SEVENTH DAY.

THIS IS WHERE I GREW UP, TULIP.

THIS IS WHERE THE STORY BEGAN.

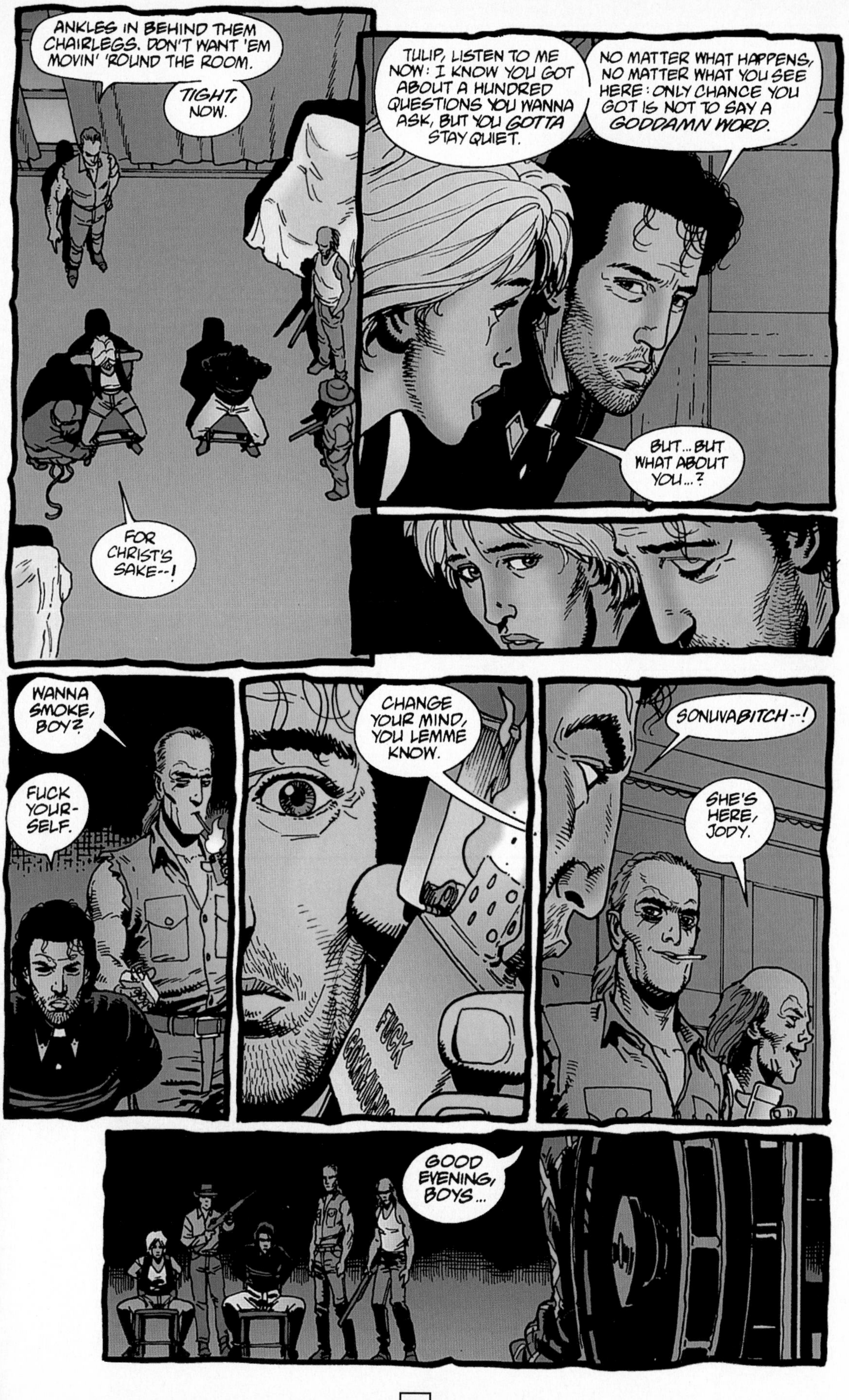
ANKLES IN BEHIND THEM CHAIRLEGS. DON'T WANT 'EM MOVIN' 'ROUND THE ROOM.
TIGHT, NOW.
FOR CHRIST'S SAKE--!
TULIP, LISTEN TO ME NOW: I KNOW YOU GOT ABOUT A HUNDRED QUESTIONS YOU WANNA ASK, BUT YOU GOTTA STAY QUIET.
NO MATTER WHAT HAPPENS, NO MATTER WHAT YOU SEE HERE: ONLY CHANCE YOU GOT IS NOT TO SAY A GODDAMN WORD.
BUT... BUT WHAT ABOUT YOU...?
WANNA SMOKE, BOY?
FUCK YOURSELF.
CHANGE YOUR MIND, YOU LEMME KNOW.
FUCK
SONUVABITCH--!
SHE'S HERE, JODY.
GOOD EVENING, BOYS...

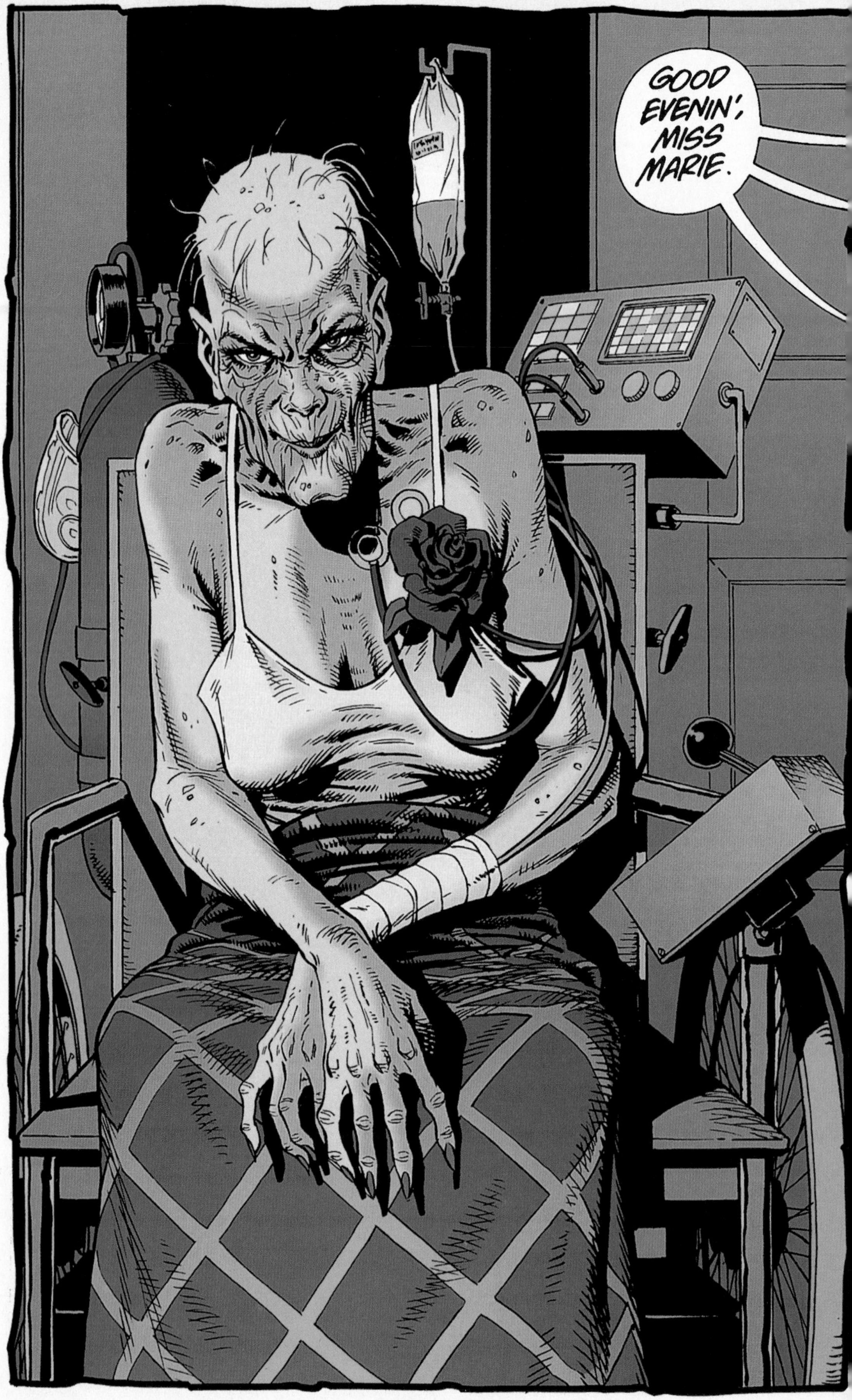
GOOD EVENIN', MISS MARIE.

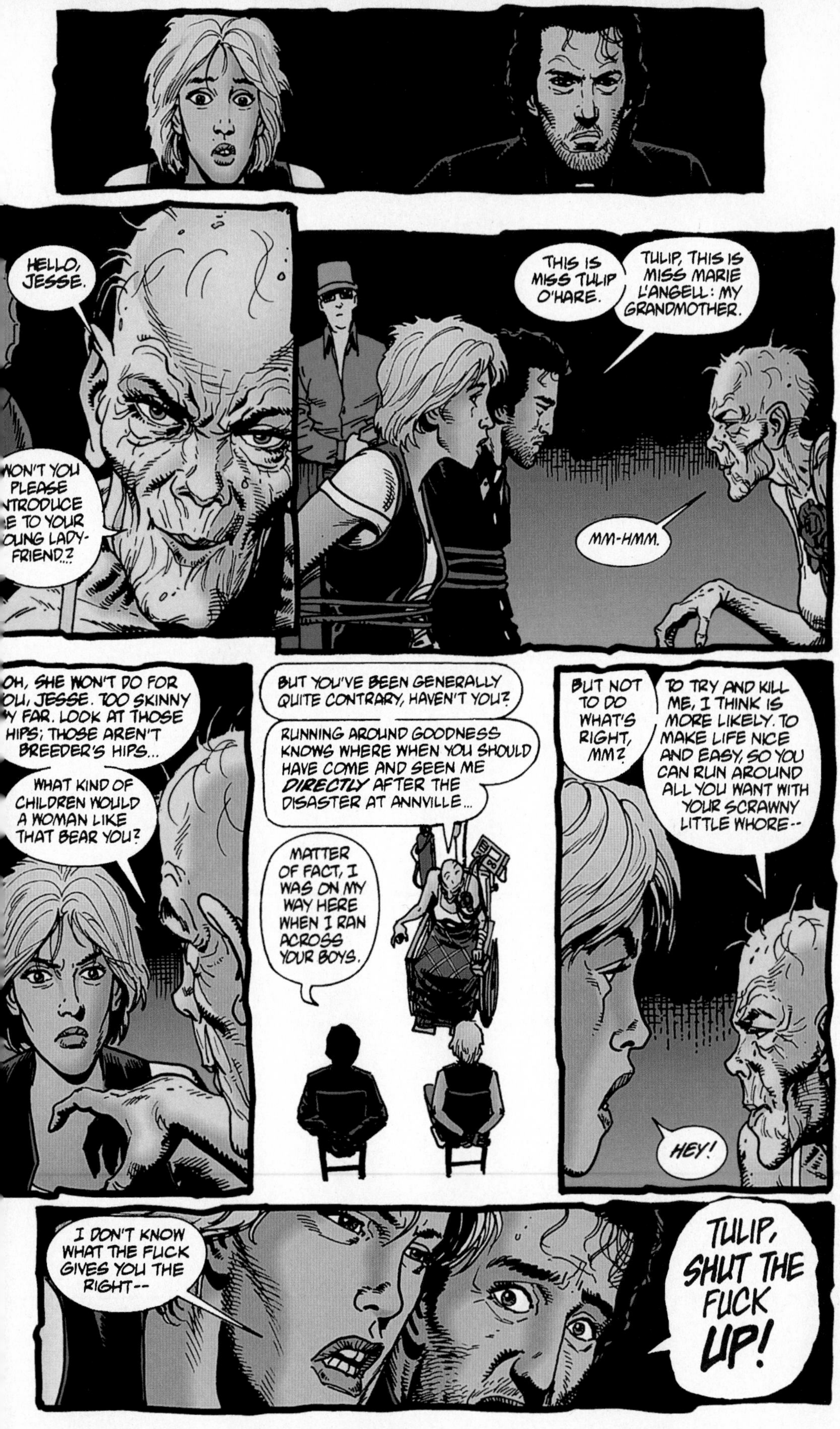

HELLO, JESSE.
WON'T YOU PLEASE INTRODUCE ME TO YOUR YOUNG LADY-FRIEND?
THIS IS MISS TULIP O'HARE.
TULIP, THIS IS MISS MARIE L'ANGELL: MY GRANDMOTHER.
MM-HMM.
OH, SHE WON'T DO FOR YOU, JESSE. TOO SKINNY BY FAR. LOOK AT THOSE HIPS; THOSE AREN'T BREEDER'S HIPS...
WHAT KIND OF CHILDREN WOULD A WOMAN LIKE THAT BEAR YOU?
BUT YOU'VE BEEN GENERALLY QUITE CONTRARY, HAVEN'T YOU?
RUNNING AROUND GOODNESS KNOWS WHERE WHEN YOU SHOULD HAVE COME AND SEEN ME DIRECTLY AFTER THE DISASTER AT ANNVILLE...
MATTER OF FACT, I WAS ON MY WAY HERE WHEN I RAN ACROSS YOUR BOYS.
BUT NOT TO DO WHAT'S RIGHT, MM?
TO TRY AND KILL ME, I THINK IS MORE LIKELY. TO MAKE LIFE NICE AND EASY, SO YOU CAN RUN AROUND ALL YOU WANT WITH YOUR SCRAWNY LITTLE WHORE--
HEY!
I DON'T KNOW WHAT THE FUCK GIVES YOU THE RIGHT--
TULIP, SHUT THE FUCK UP!

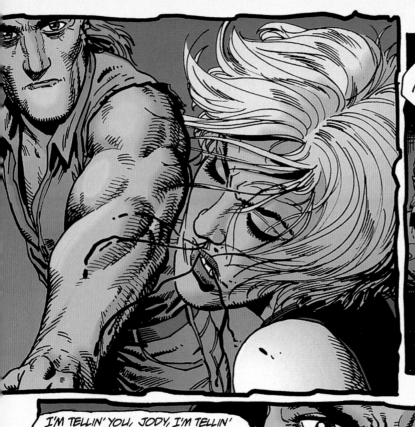

MOTHER-FUCKER!!

I'M TELLIN' YOU, JODY, I'M TELLIN' YOU RIGHT FUCKIN' NOW, **I'M GONNA KILL YOU!**

I'M GONNA CHOKE THE FUCKIN' BLACK SOUL FROM YOUR WORTHLESS CORPSE AN' I'M GONNA DO IT WITH MY OWN TWO HANDS, I SWEAR TO GOD!

I SWEAR TO FUCKIN' GOD, **YOU ARE DEAD!**

TRIED IT BEFORE, BOY.

'MEMBER?

MY, BUT DON'T YOU HAVE A HEAD OF STEAM WORKED UP, JESSE?

YOU'VE STILL GOT PLENTY OF THAT TEXAS WHITE TRASH FATHER OF YOURS IN YOU, HAVEN'T YOU? THAT WORTHLESS WASTE OF LIFE WHO LEFT YOU NOTHING BUT HIS NAME...

THAT'S ALL I'LL EVER NEED.

WELL, PERHAPS I'LL TAKE THAT FROM YOU TOO, JESSE. I'M TAKING EVERY-THING ELSE.

PERHAPS I'LL CHANGE YOUR NAME LIKE I CHANGED MY OWN, WHEN THAT USELESS CRETIN I MARRIED WENT AND FELL IN THE GUMBO.

JESSE L'ANGELL. *HIM.*

AIN'T NO WAY YOU CAN DO THAT, NOT SO IT MEANS A DAMN THING TO ME.

OH, JESSE, DON'T YOU UNDER-STAND...?

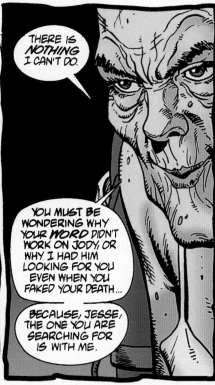

THERE IS *NOTHING* I CAN'T DO.

YOU MUST BE WONDERING WHY YOUR *WORD* DIDN'T WORK ON JODY, OR WHY I HAD HIM LOOKING FOR YOU EVEN WHEN YOU FAKED YOUR DEATH...

BECAUSE, JESSE, THE ONE YOU ARE SEARCHING FOR IS WITH ME.

I HAVE *THE LORD* ON MY SIDE.

I *KNOW* WHAT BECAME OF YOU IN ANNVILLE. I *KNOW* ABOUT GENESIS, AND THE ANGELS, AND THE SAINT OF KILLERS.

YOU'RE *MINE AGAIN,* LIKE YOU ALWAYS WERE. YOU'RE GOING TO BE A *MINISTER* AGAIN, AS GOD INTENDED...

AND AS I WILL GUIDE YOU.

YOUR WHORE IS THE PROOF: YOU'LL BE LEFT ALONE WITH HER TILL DAWN, BECAUSE GRAN'MA LOVES YOU AND WANTS YOU TO KNOW TRUE HAPPINESS...

AND THEN, BECAUSE GRAN'MA WANTS YOU TO KNOW THAT *SHE'S IN CHARGE FOREVER...*

JODY WILL BLOW THE LITTLE BITCH'S BRAINS OUT.

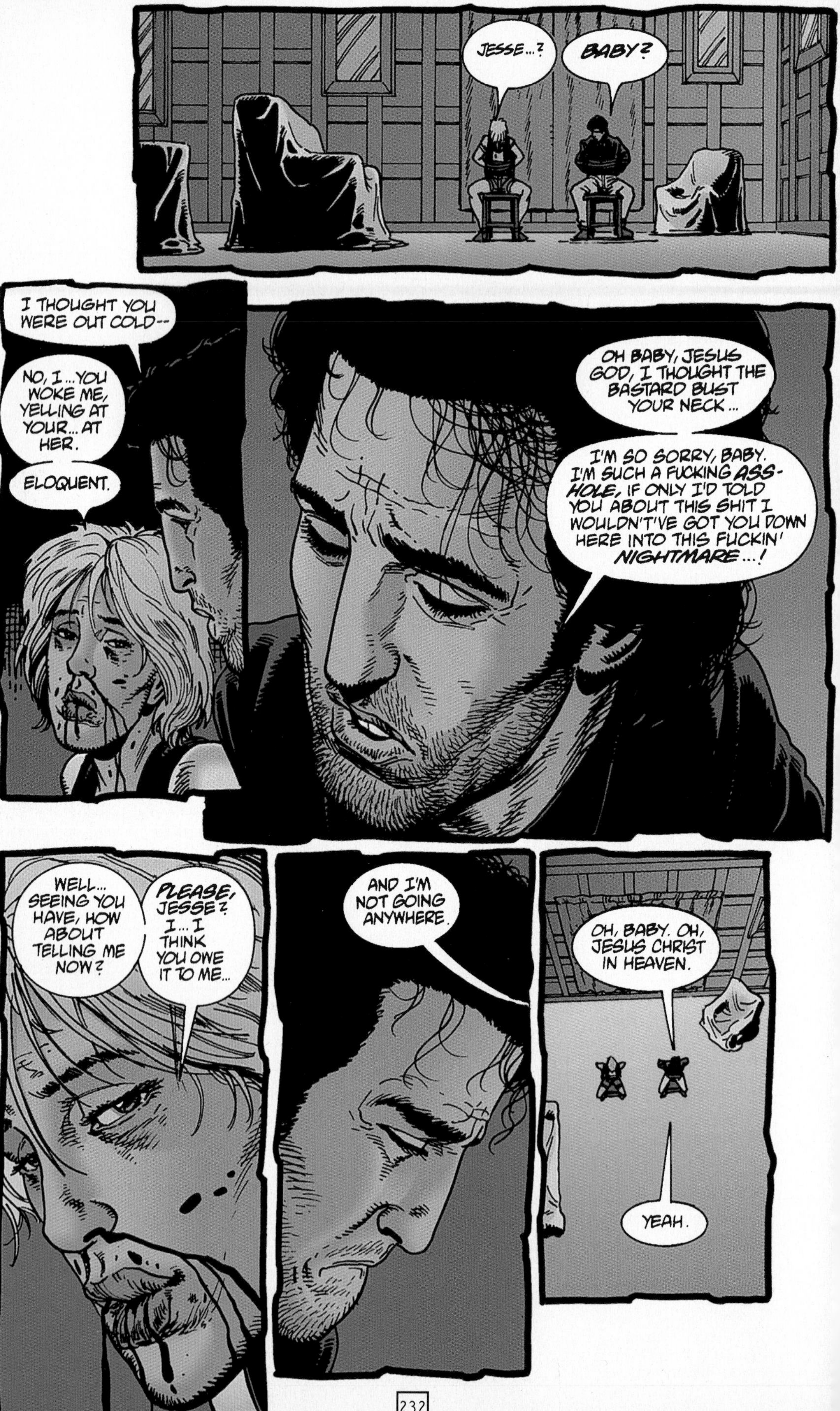
JESSE...?
BABY?
I THOUGHT YOU WERE OUT COLD--
NO, I...YOU WOKE ME, YELLING AT YOUR... AT HER.
ELOQUENT.
OH BABY, JESUS GOD, I THOUGHT THE BASTARD BUST YOUR NECK...
I'M SO SORRY, BABY. I'M SUCH A FUCKING ASS-HOLE, IF ONLY I'D TOLD YOU ABOUT THIS SHIT I WOULDN'T'VE GOT YOU DOWN HERE INTO THIS FUCKIN' NIGHTMARE...!
WELL... SEEING YOU HAVE, HOW ABOUT TELLING ME NOW?
PLEASE, JESSE? I... I THINK YOU OWE IT TO ME...
AND I'M NOT GOING ANYWHERE.
OH, BABY. OH, JESUS CHRIST IN HEAVEN.
YEAH.

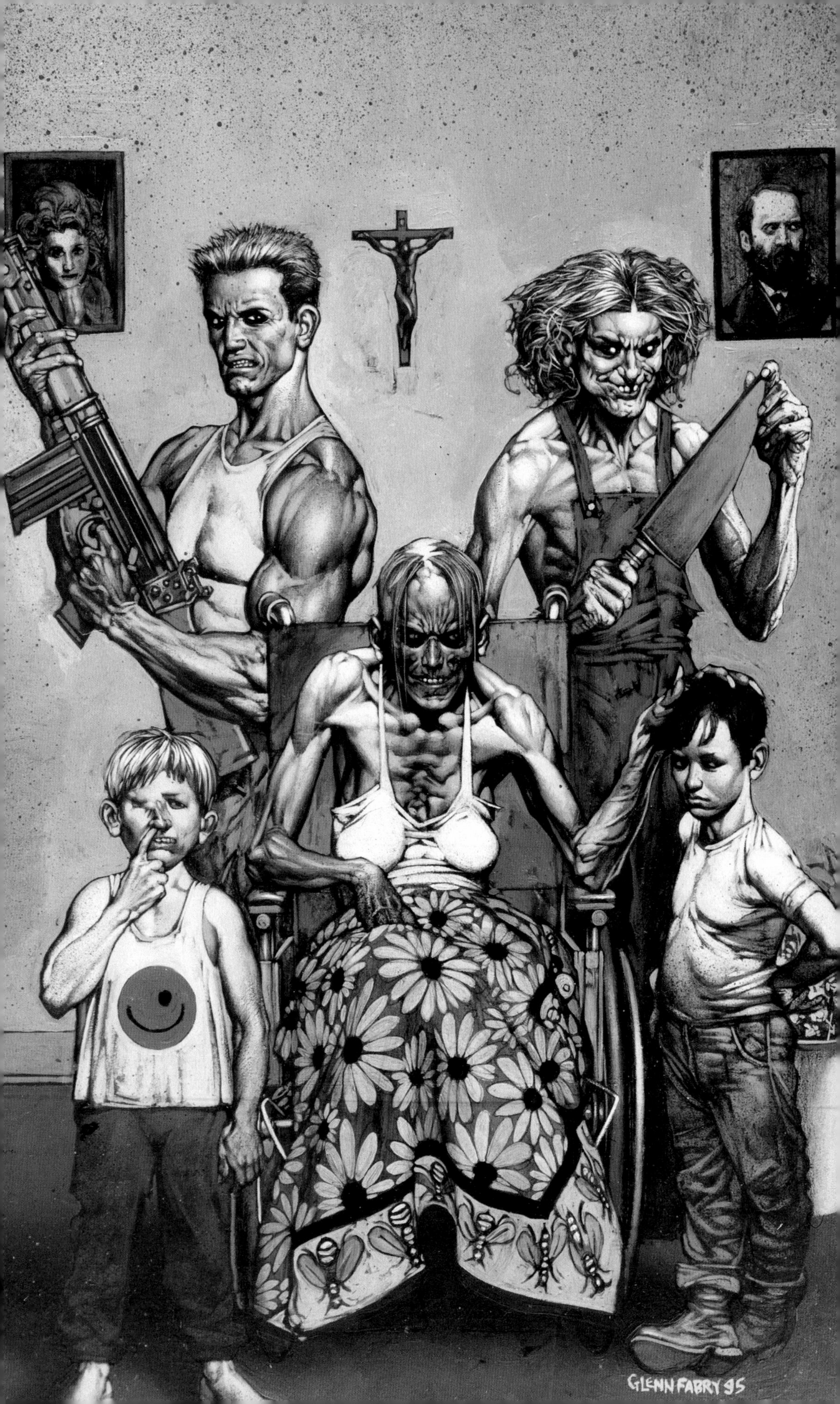
GLENN FABRY 95

"You gotta be one of the good guys, son.
'Cause there's way too many of the bad."

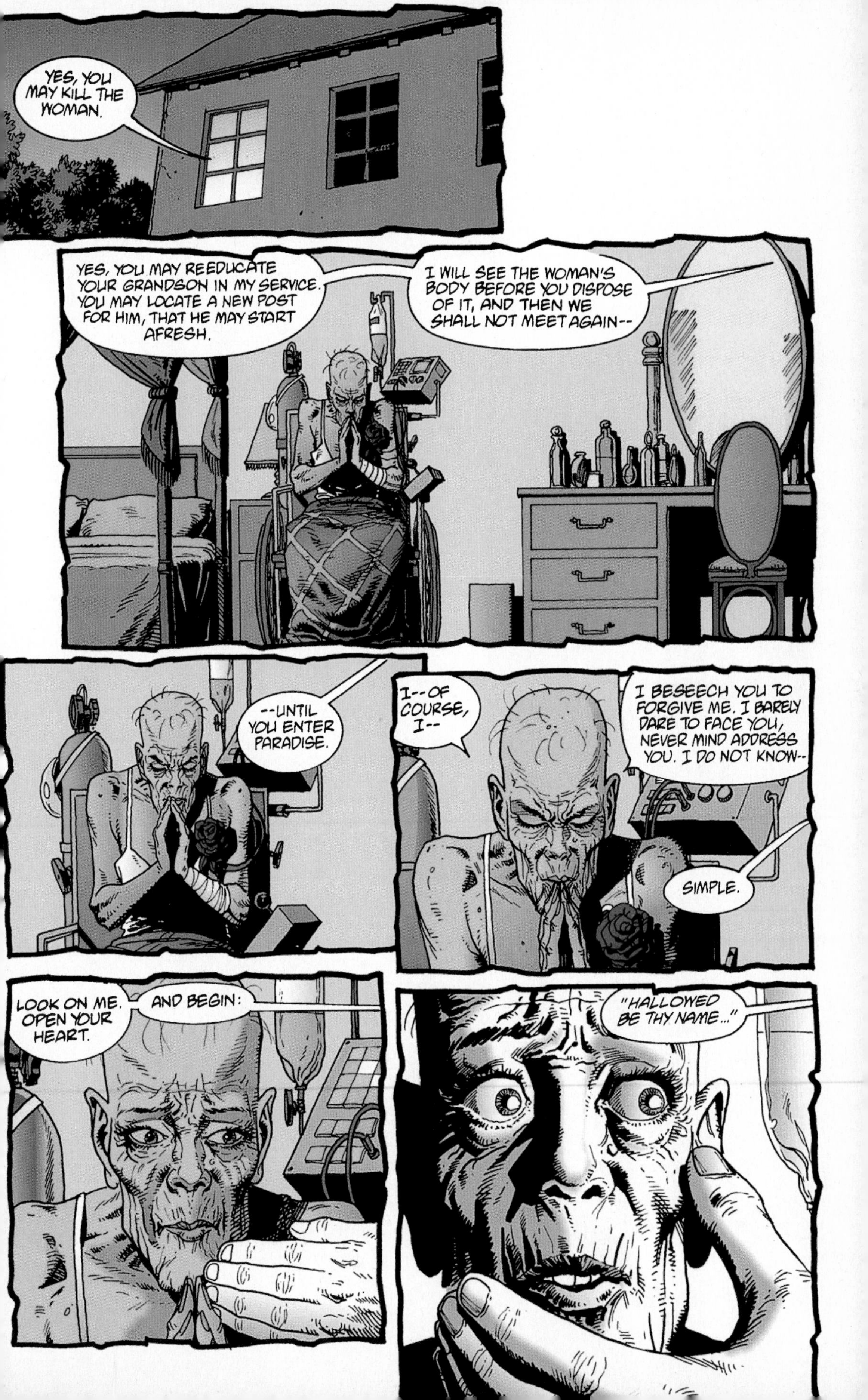
YES, YOU MAY KILL THE WOMAN.
YES, YOU MAY REEDUCATE YOUR GRANDSON IN MY SERVICE. YOU MAY LOCATE A NEW POST FOR HIM, THAT HE MAY START AFRESH.
I WILL SEE THE WOMAN'S BODY BEFORE YOU DISPOSE OF IT, AND THEN WE SHALL NOT MEET AGAIN--
--UNTIL YOU ENTER PARADISE.
I--OF COURSE, I--
I BESEECH YOU TO FORGIVE ME. I BARELY DARE TO FACE YOU, NEVER MIND ADDRESS YOU. I DO NOT KNOW--
SIMPLE.
LOOK ON ME. OPEN YOUR HEART.
AND BEGIN:
"HALLOWED BE THY NAME..."

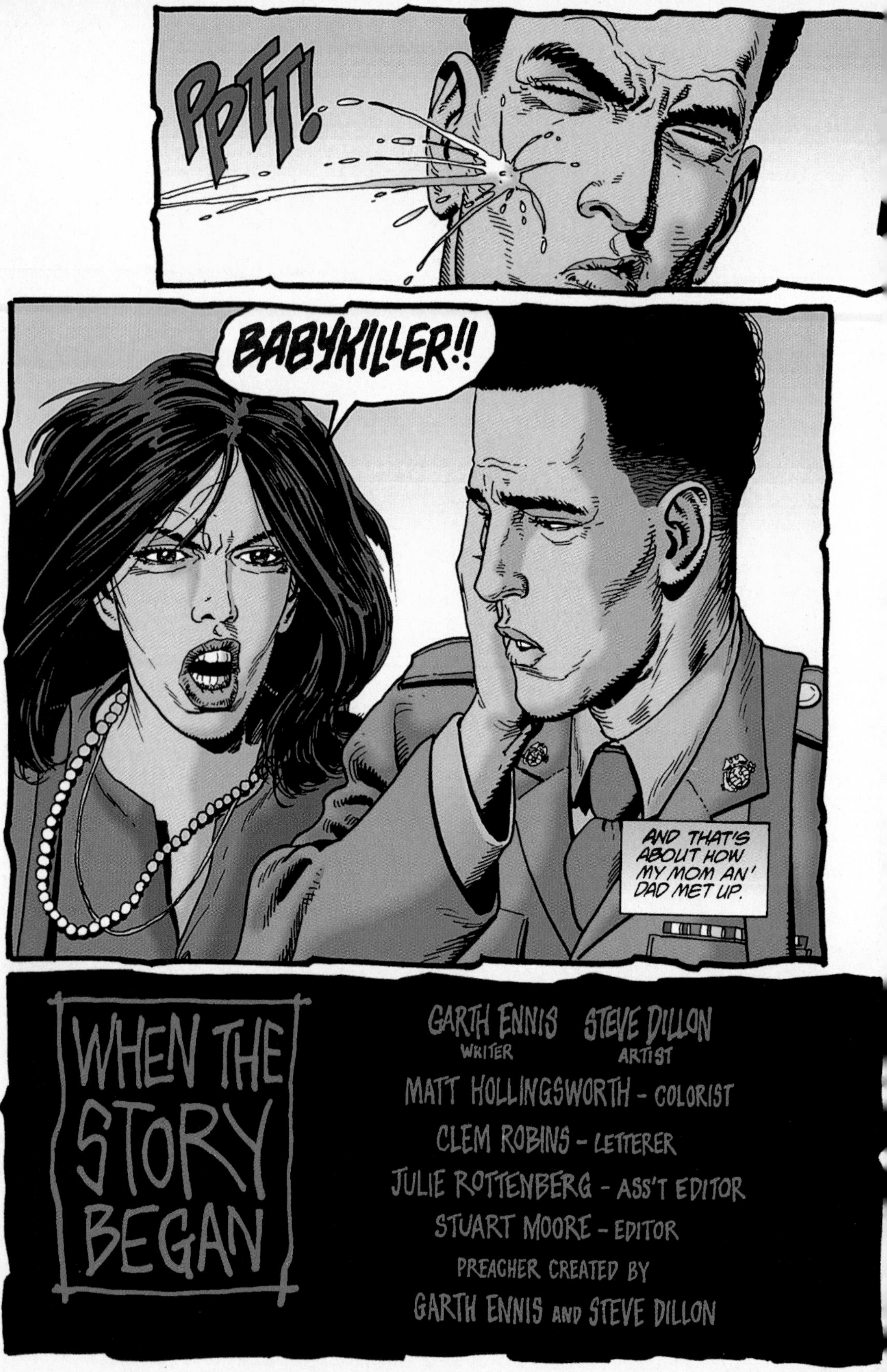
PPTT!
BABYKILLER!!
AND THAT'S ABOUT HOW MY MOM AN' DAD MET UP.
WHEN THE STORY BEGAN
GARTH ENNIS WRITER
STEVE DILLON ARTIST
MATT HOLLINGSWORTH - COLORIST
CLEM ROBINS - LETTERER
JULIE ROTTENBERG - ASS'T EDITOR
STUART MOORE - EDITOR
PREACHER CREATED BY
GARTH ENNIS AND STEVE DILLON

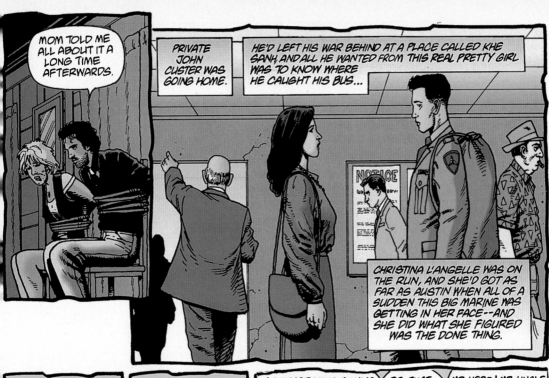

MOM TOLD ME ALL ABOUT IT A LONG TIME AFTERWARDS.

PRIVATE JOHN CUSTER WAS GOING HOME.

HE'D LEFT HIS WAR BEHIND AT A PLACE CALLED KHE SANH, AND ALL HE WANTED FROM THIS REAL PRETTY GIRL WAS TO KNOW WHERE HE CAUGHT HIS BUS...

CHRISTINA L'ANGELLE WAS ON THE RUN, AND SHE'D GOT AS FAR AS AUSTIN WHEN ALL OF A SUDDEN THIS BIG MARINE WAS GETTING IN HER FACE--AND SHE DID WHAT SHE FIGURED WAS THE DONE THING.

SO WHAT YOU GONNA DO, MAN? YOU GONNA HIT HER, *HUH?* YOU GONNA BEAT ON A WOMAN?

BE JUST ONE MORE, WOULDN'T IT?

MR. HERO! MR. UNCLE SAM'S FUCKING *MURDER MACHINE!*

FUCKING *ASSHOLE!*

NAZI BASTARD!

MURDERING PIECE OF SHIT!

FUCKING CRAWL BACK TO BOOT CAMP! LEARN HOW TO KILL SOME MORE!

CHRISTINA! BE COOL! ENOUGH!

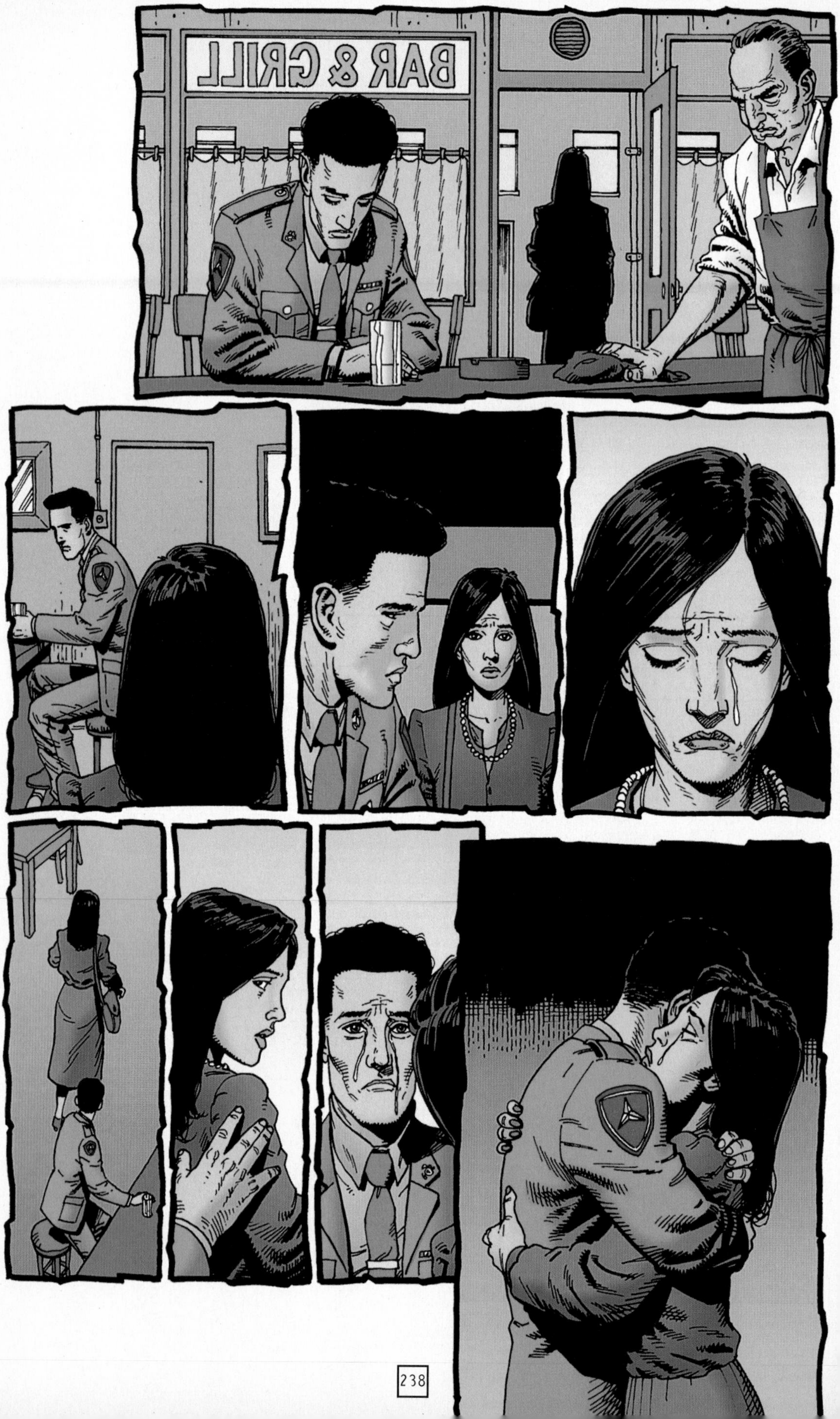
BAR & GRILL

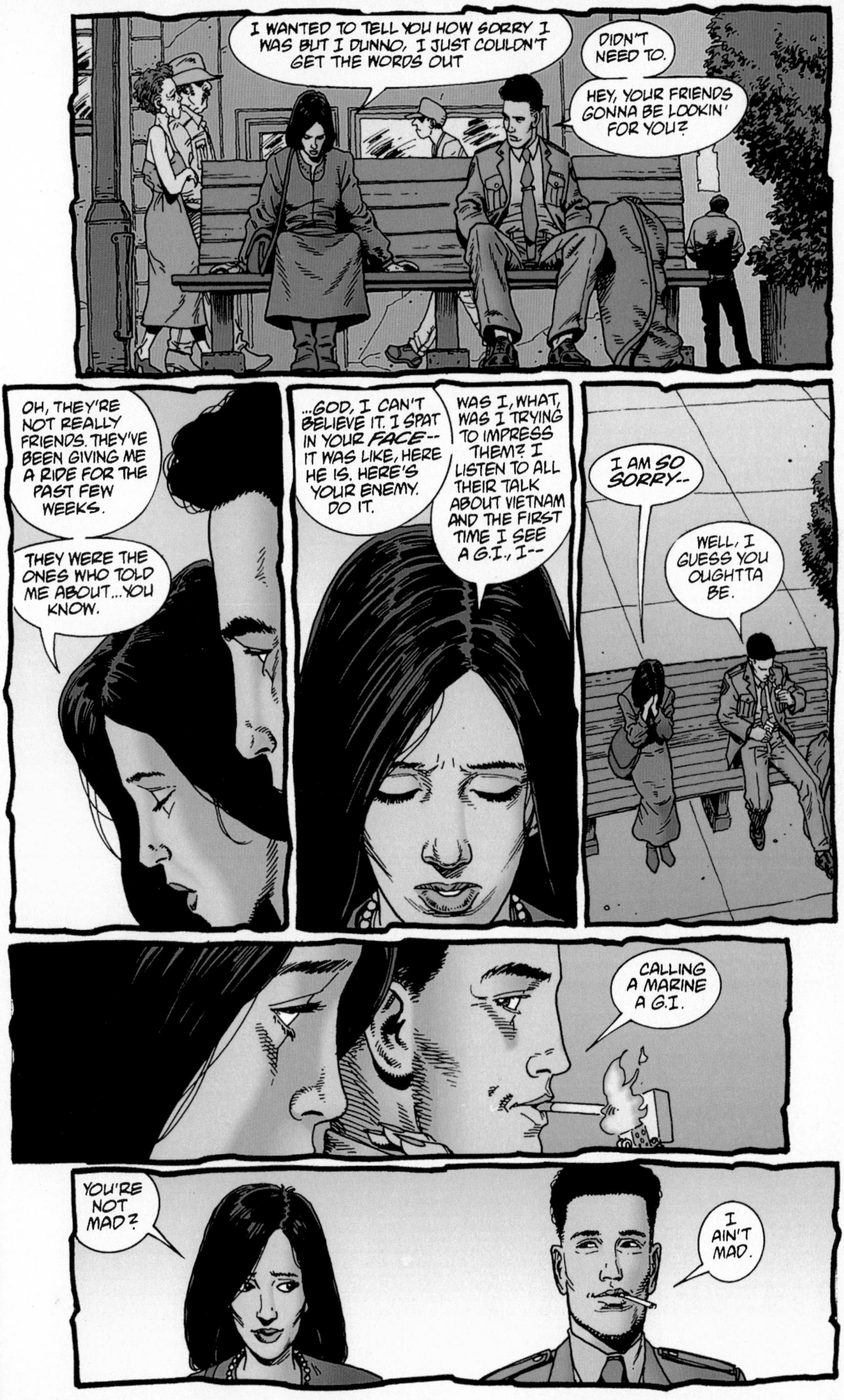
I WANTED TO TELL YOU HOW SORRY I WAS BUT I DUNNO, I JUST COULDN'T GET THE WORDS OUT
DIDN'T NEED TO.
HEY, YOUR FRIENDS GONNA BE LOOKIN' FOR YOU?
OH, THEY'RE NOT REALLY FRIENDS. THEY'VE BEEN GIVING ME A RIDE FOR THE PAST FEW WEEKS.
THEY WERE THE ONES WHO TOLD ME ABOUT...YOU KNOW.
...GOD, I CAN'T BELIEVE IT. I SPAT IN YOUR *FACE*-- IT WAS LIKE, HERE HE IS. HERE'S YOUR ENEMY. DO IT.
WAS I, WHAT, WAS I TRYING TO IMPRESS THEM? I LISTEN TO ALL THEIR TALK ABOUT VIETNAM AND THE FIRST TIME I SEE A G.I., I--
I AM *SO SORRY*--
WELL, I GUESS YOU OUGHTTA BE.
CALLING A MARINE A G.I.
YOU'RE NOT MAD?
I AIN'T MAD.

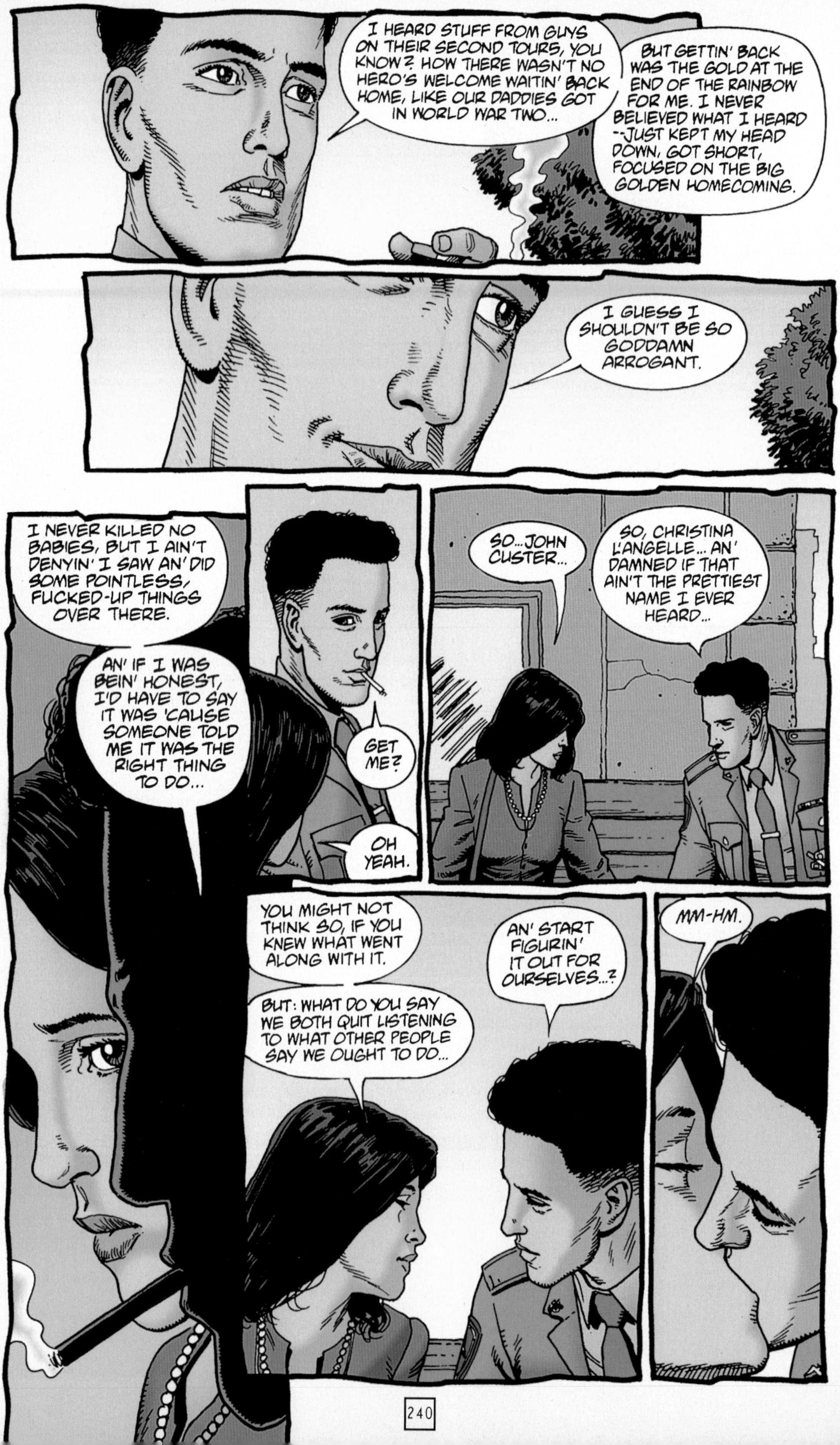
I HEARD STUFF FROM GUYS ON THEIR SECOND TOURS, YOU KNOW? HOW THERE WASN'T NO HERO'S WELCOME WAITIN' BACK HOME, LIKE OUR DADDIES GOT IN WORLD WAR TWO...
BUT GETTIN' BACK WAS THE GOLD AT THE END OF THE RAINBOW FOR ME. I NEVER BELIEVED WHAT I HEARD --JUST KEPT MY HEAD DOWN, GOT SHORT, FOCUSED ON THE BIG GOLDEN HOMECOMING.
I GUESS I SHOULDN'T BE SO GODDAMN ARROGANT.
I NEVER KILLED NO BABIES, BUT I AIN'T DENYIN' I SAW AN' DID SOME POINTLESS, FUCKED-UP THINGS OVER THERE.
AN' IF I WAS BEIN' HONEST, I'D HAVE TO SAY IT WAS 'CAUSE SOMEONE TOLD ME IT WAS THE RIGHT THING TO DO...
GET ME?
OH YEAH.
SO...JOHN CUSTER...
SO, CHRISTINA L'ANGELLE... AN' DAMNED IF THAT AIN'T THE PRETTIEST NAME I EVER HEARD...
YOU MIGHT NOT THINK SO, IF YOU KNEW WHAT WENT ALONG WITH IT.
BUT: WHAT DO YOU SAY WE BOTH QUIT LISTENING TO WHAT OTHER PEOPLE SAY WE OUGHT TO DO...
AN' START FIGURIN' IT OUT FOR OURSELVES...?
MM-HM.

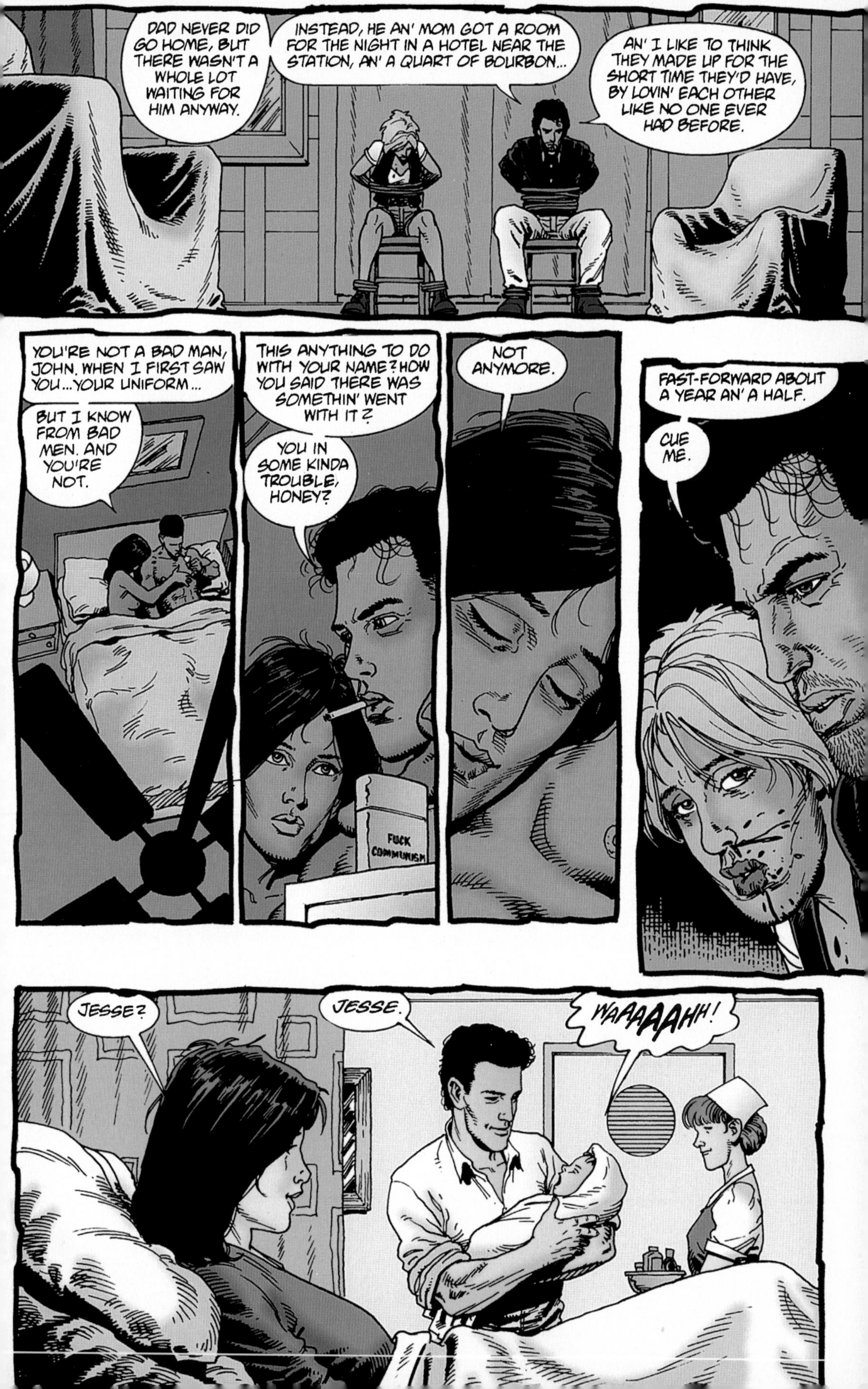

DAD NEVER DID GO HOME, BUT THERE WASN'T A WHOLE LOT WAITING FOR HIM ANYWAY.
INSTEAD, HE AN' MOM GOT A ROOM FOR THE NIGHT IN A HOTEL NEAR THE STATION, AN' A QUART OF BOURBON...
AN' I LIKE TO THINK THEY MADE UP FOR THE SHORT TIME THEY'D HAVE, BY LOVIN' EACH OTHER LIKE NO ONE EVER HAD BEFORE.
YOU'RE NOT A BAD MAN, JOHN. WHEN I FIRST SAW YOU...YOUR UNIFORM...
BUT I KNOW FROM BAD MEN. AND YOU'RE NOT.
THIS ANYTHING TO DO WITH YOUR NAME? HOW YOU SAID THERE WAS SOMETHIN' WENT WITH IT?
YOU IN SOME KINDA TROUBLE, HONEY?
FUCK COMMUNISM
NOT ANYMORE.
FAST-FORWARD ABOUT A YEAR AN' A HALF.
CUE ME.
JESSE?
JESSE.
WAAAAAHH!

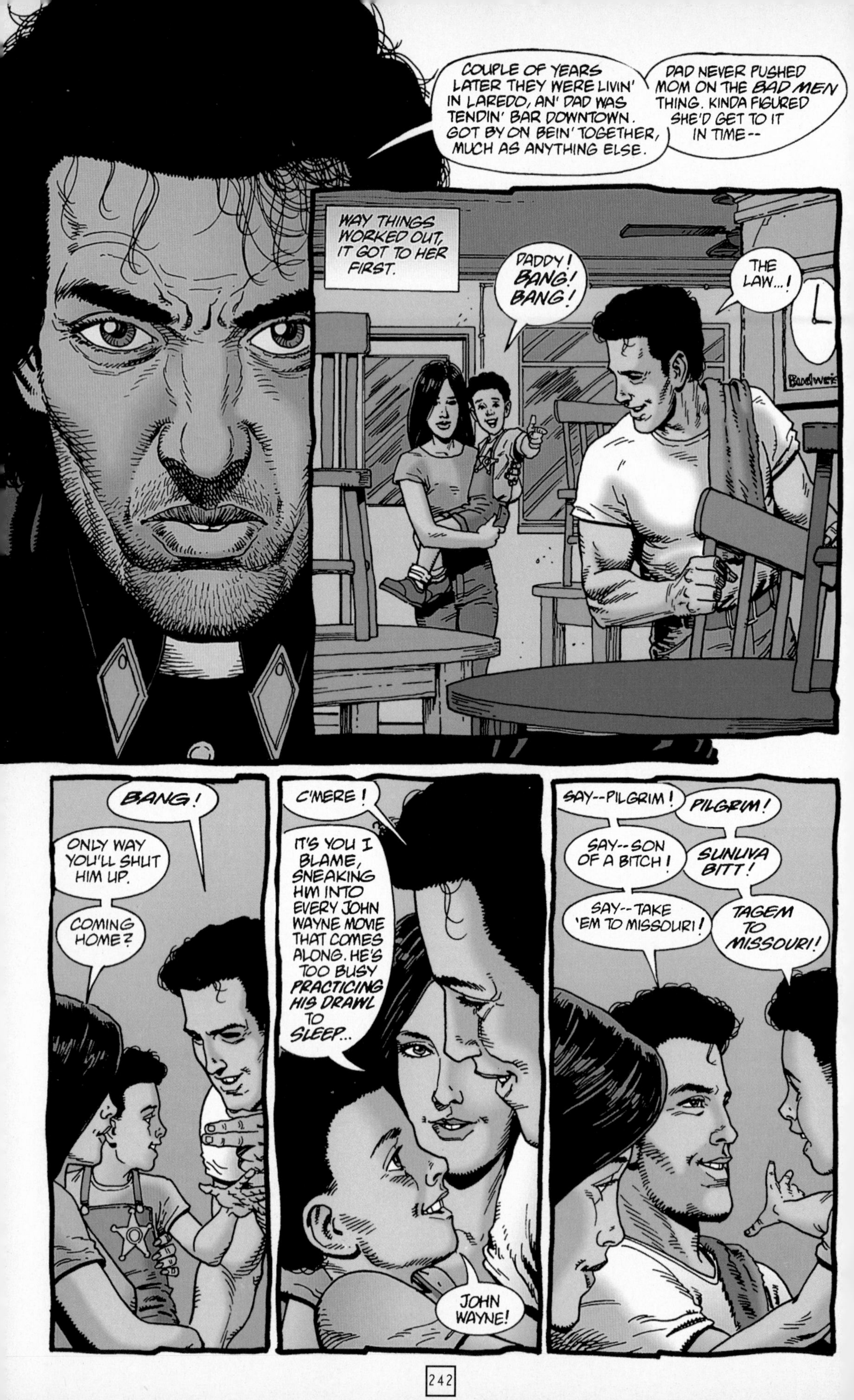
COUPLE OF YEARS LATER THEY WERE LIVIN' IN LAREDO, AN' DAD WAS TENDIN' BAR DOWNTOWN. GOT BY ON BEIN' TOGETHER, MUCH AS ANYTHING ELSE.
DAD NEVER PUSHED MOM ON THE BAD MEN THING. KINDA FIGURED SHE'D GET TO IT IN TIME--
WAY THINGS WORKED OUT, IT GOT TO HER FIRST.
DADDY! BANG! BANG!
THE LAW...!
BANG!
ONLY WAY YOU'LL SHUT HIM UP.
COMING HOME?
C'MERE!
IT'S YOU I BLAME, SNEAKING HIM INTO EVERY JOHN WAYNE MOVIE THAT COMES ALONG. HE'S TOO BUSY PRACTICING HIS DRAWL TO SLEEP...
JOHN WAYNE!
SAY--PILGRIM!
PILGRIM!
SAY--SON OF A BITCH!
SUNUVA BITT!
SAY--TAKE 'EM TO MISSOURI!
TAGEM TO MISSOURI!

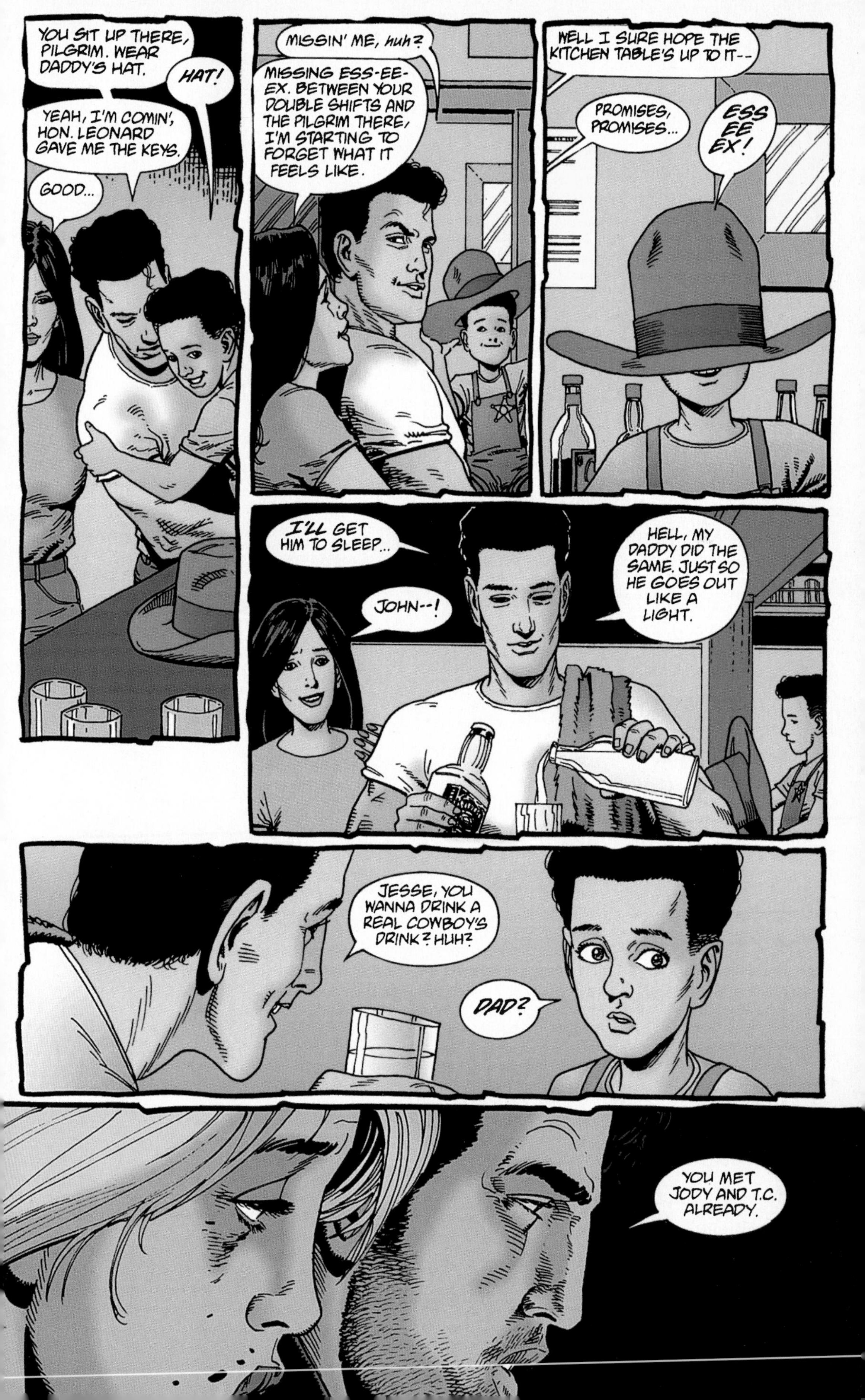
YOU SIT UP THERE, PILGRIM. WEAR DADDY'S HAT.
HAT!
YEAH, I'M COMIN', HON. LEONARD GAVE ME THE KEYS.
GOOD...
MISSIN' ME, huh?
MISSING ESS-EE-EX. BETWEEN YOUR DOUBLE SHIFTS AND THE PILGRIM THERE, I'M STARTING TO FORGET WHAT IT FEELS LIKE.
WELL I SURE HOPE THE KITCHEN TABLE'S UP TO IT--
PROMISES, PROMISES...
ESS EE EX!
I'LL GET HIM TO SLEEP...
JOHN--!
HELL, MY DADDY DID THE SAME. JUST SO HE GOES OUT LIKE A LIGHT.
JESSE, YOU WANNA DRINK A REAL COWBOY'S DRINK? HUH?
DAD?
YOU MET JODY AND T.C. ALREADY.

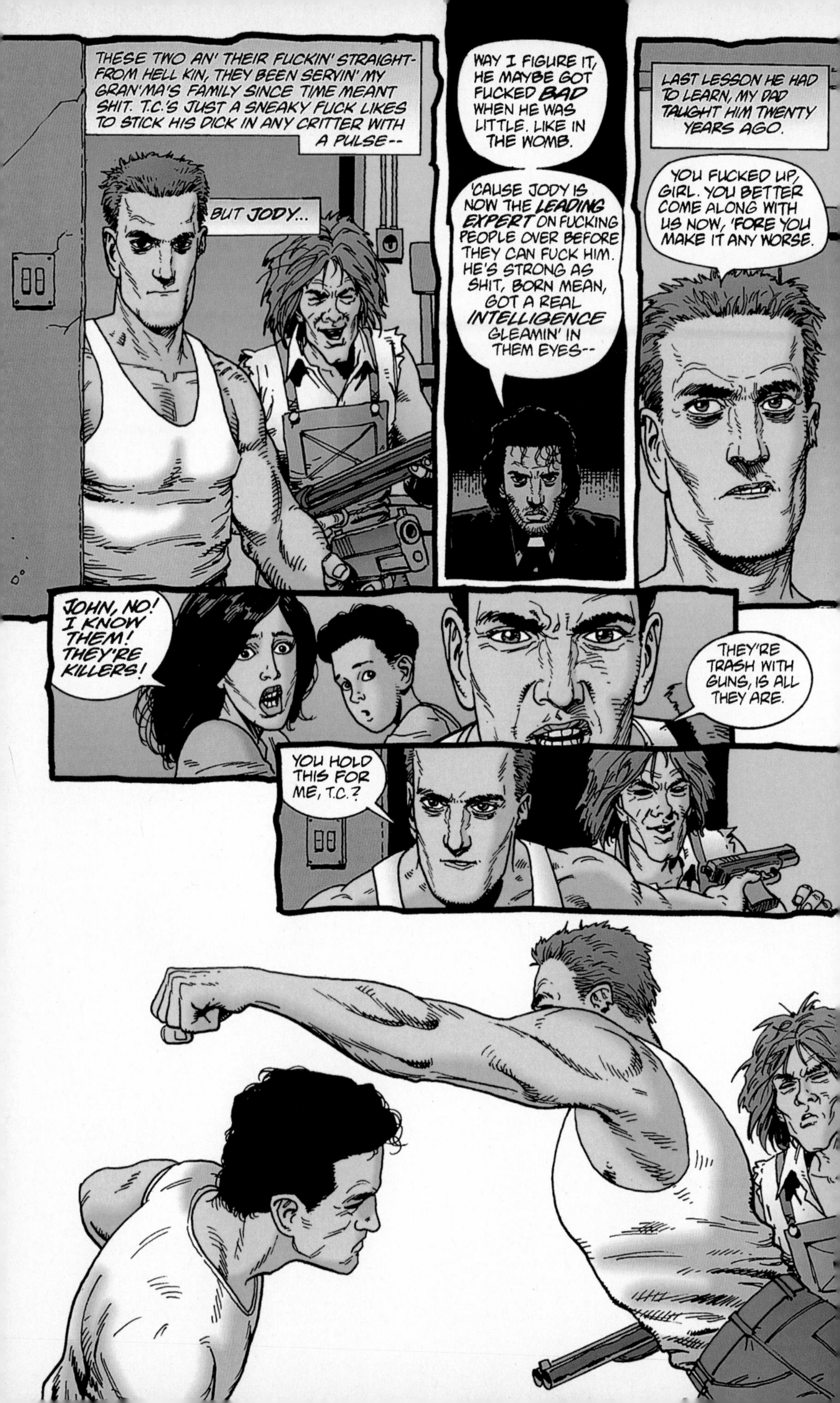
THESE TWO AN' THEIR FUCKIN' STRAIGHT-FROM HELL KIN, THEY BEEN SERVIN' MY GRAN'MA'S FAMILY SINCE TIME MEANT SHIT. T.C.'S JUST A SNEAKY FUCK LIKES TO STICK HIS DICK IN ANY CRITTER WITH A PULSE--
BUT JODY...
WAY I FIGURE IT, HE MAYBE GOT FUCKED BAD WHEN HE WAS LITTLE. LIKE IN THE WOMB.
'CAUSE JODY IS NOW THE LEADING EXPERT ON FUCKING PEOPLE OVER BEFORE THEY CAN FUCK HIM. HE'S STRONG AS SHIT, BORN MEAN, GOT A REAL INTELLIGENCE GLEAMIN' IN THEM EYES--
LAST LESSON HE HAD TO LEARN, MY DAD TAUGHT HIM TWENTY YEARS AGO.
YOU FUCKED UP, GIRL. YOU BETTER COME ALONG WITH US NOW, 'FORE YOU MAKE IT ANY WORSE.
JOHN, NO! I KNOW THEM! THEY'RE KILLERS!
THEY'RE TRASH WITH GUNS, IS ALL THEY ARE.
YOU HOLD THIS FOR ME, T.C.?

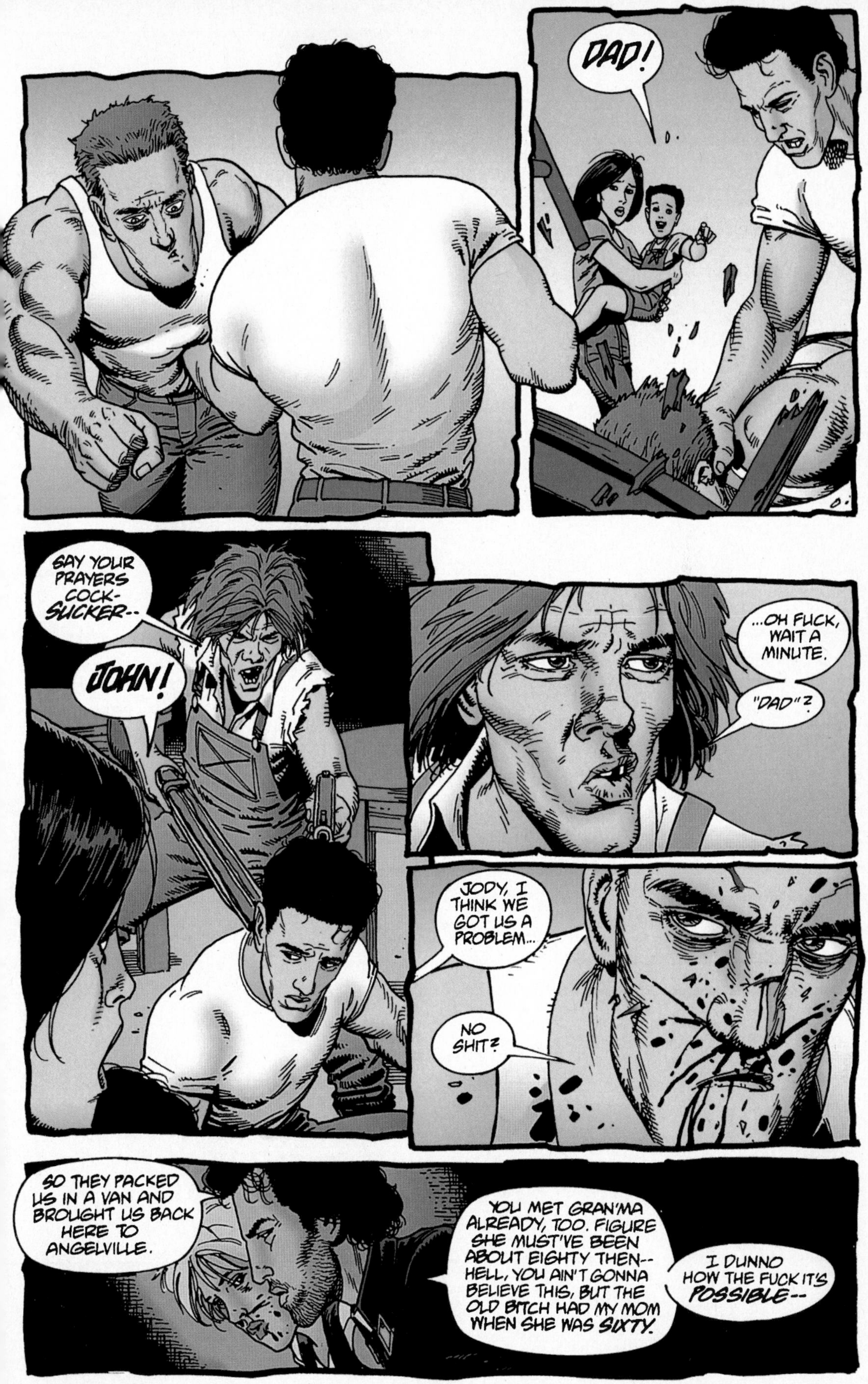
DAD!
SAY YOUR PRAYERS COCK-SUCKER--
JOHN!
...OH FUCK, WAIT A MINUTE.
"DAD"?
JODY, I THINK WE GOT US A PROBLEM...
NO SHIT?
SO THEY PACKED US IN A VAN AND BROUGHT US BACK HERE TO ANGELVILLE.
YOU MET GRAN'MA ALREADY, TOO. FIGURE SHE MUST'VE BEEN ABOUT EIGHTY THEN-- HELL, YOU AIN'T GONNA BELIEVE THIS, BUT THE OLD BITCH HAD MY MOM WHEN SHE WAS SIXTY.
I DUNNO HOW THE FUCK IT'S POSSIBLE--

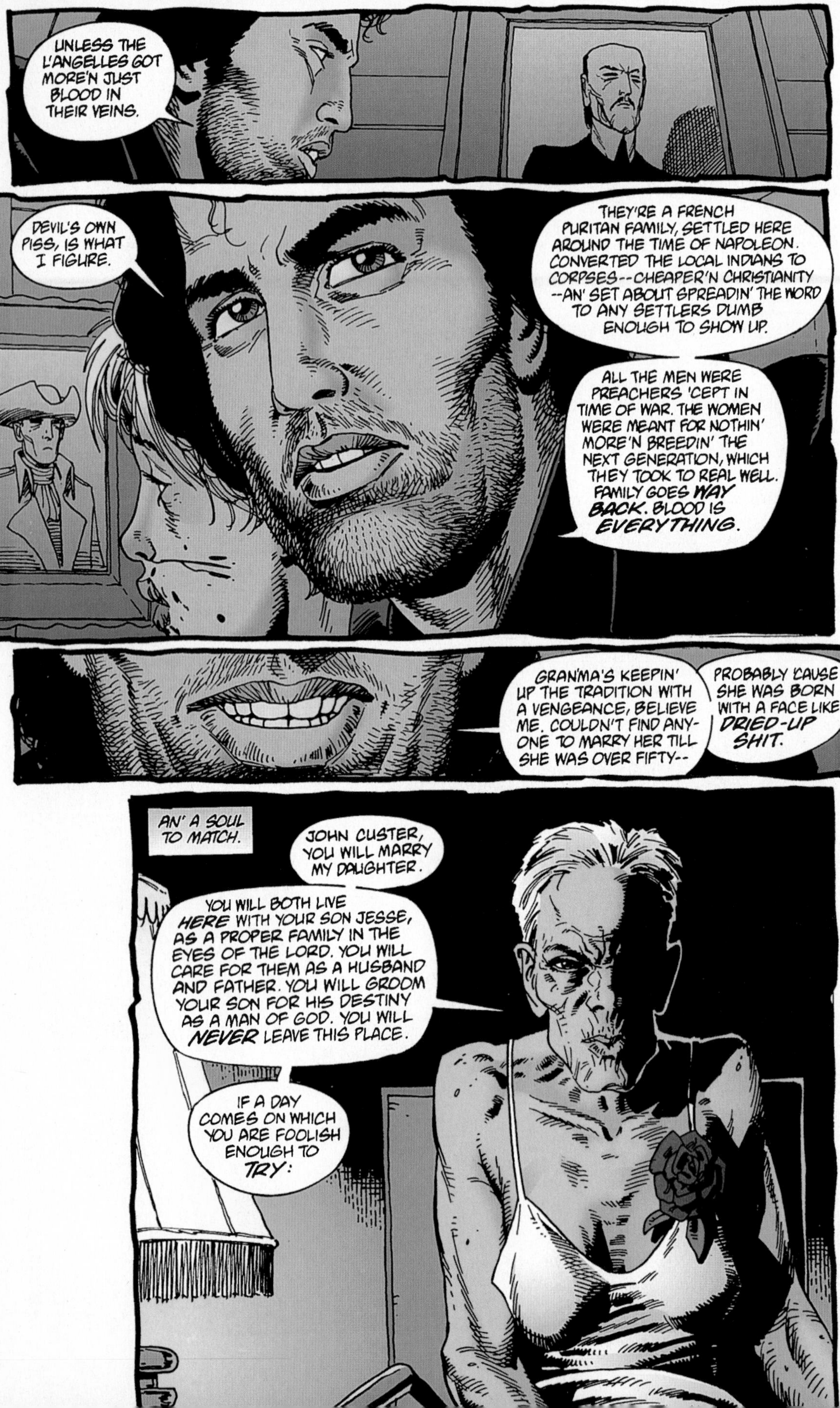
UNLESS THE L'ANGELLES GOT MORE'N JUST BLOOD IN THEIR VEINS.
DEVIL'S OWN PISS, IS WHAT I FIGURE.
THEY'RE A FRENCH PURITAN FAMILY, SETTLED HERE AROUND THE TIME OF NAPOLEON. CONVERTED THE LOCAL INDIANS TO CORPSES--CHEAPER'N CHRISTIANITY --AN' SET ABOUT SPREADIN' THE WORD TO ANY SETTLERS DUMB ENOUGH TO SHOW UP.
ALL THE MEN WERE PREACHERS 'CEPT IN TIME OF WAR. THE WOMEN WERE MEANT FOR NOTHIN' MORE'N BREEDIN' THE NEXT GENERATION, WHICH THEY TOOK TO REAL WELL. FAMILY GOES WAY BACK. BLOOD IS EVERYTHING.
GRAN'MA'S KEEPIN' UP THE TRADITION WITH A VENGEANCE, BELIEVE ME. COULDN'T FIND ANY-ONE TO MARRY HER TILL SHE WAS OVER FIFTY--
PROBABLY 'CAUSE SHE WAS BORN WITH A FACE LIKE DRIED-UP SHIT.
AN' A SOUL TO MATCH.
JOHN CUSTER, YOU WILL MARRY MY DAUGHTER.
YOU WILL BOTH LIVE HERE WITH YOUR SON JESSE, AS A PROPER FAMILY IN THE EYES OF THE LORD. YOU WILL CARE FOR THEM AS A HUSBAND AND FATHER. YOU WILL GROOM YOUR SON FOR HIS DESTINY AS A MAN OF GOD. YOU WILL NEVER LEAVE THIS PLACE.
IF A DAY COMES ON WHICH YOU ARE FOOLISH ENOUGH TO TRY:

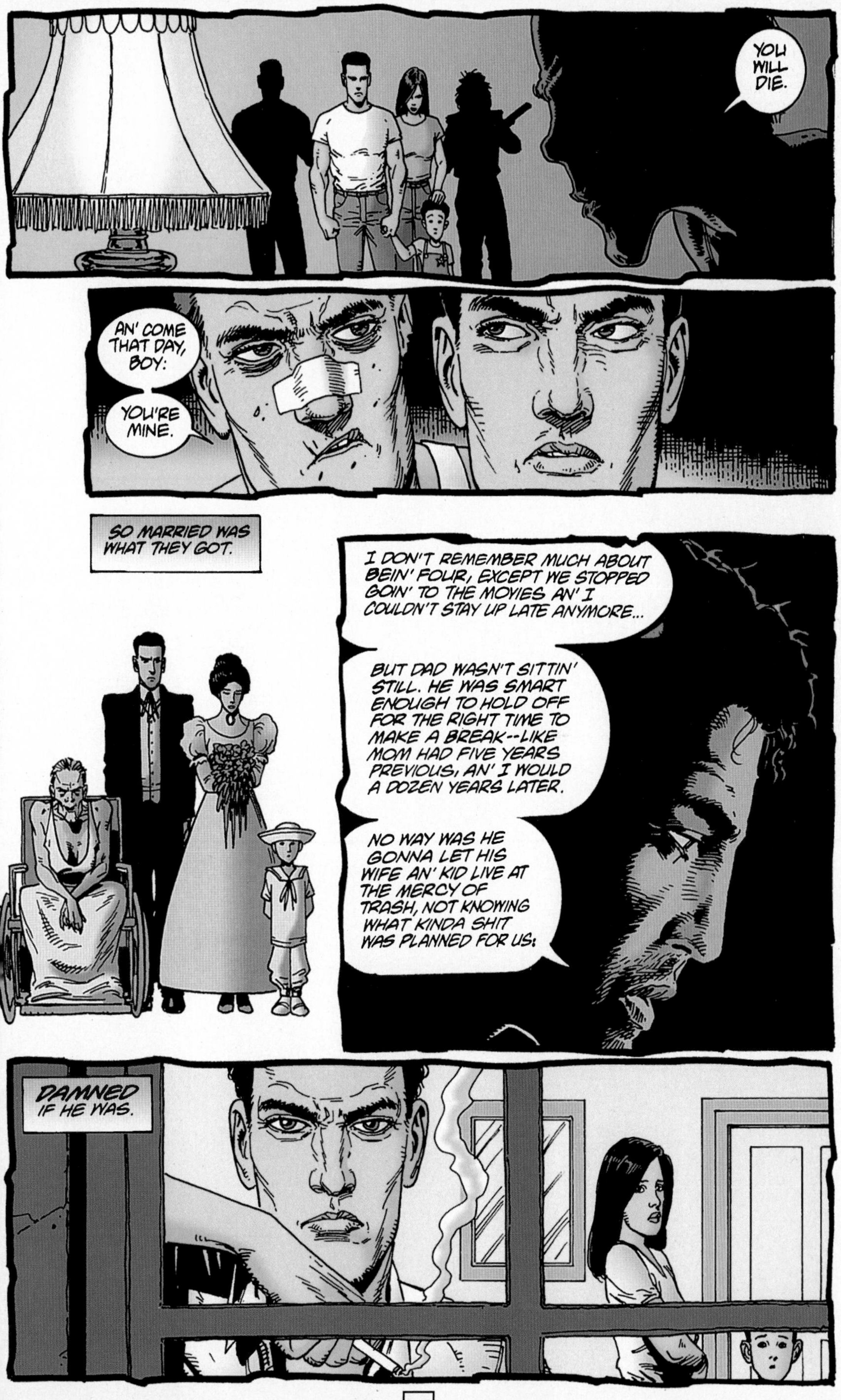
YOU WILL DIE.
AN' COME THAT DAY, BOY:
YOU'RE MINE.
SO MARRIED WAS WHAT THEY GOT.
I DON'T REMEMBER MUCH ABOUT BEIN' FOUR, EXCEPT WE STOPPED GOIN' TO THE MOVIES AN' I COULDN'T STAY UP LATE ANYMORE...
BUT DAD WASN'T SITTIN' STILL. HE WAS SMART ENOUGH TO HOLD OFF FOR THE RIGHT TIME TO MAKE A BREAK--LIKE MOM HAD FIVE YEARS PREVIOUS, AN' I WOULD A DOZEN YEARS LATER.
NO WAY WAS HE GONNA LET HIS WIFE AN' KID LIVE AT THE MERCY OF TRASH, NOT KNOWING WHAT KINDA SHIT WAS PLANNED FOR US:
DAMNED IF HE WAS.

SO ONE DAY, NOT LONG AFTER I TURNED FIVE, DAD CAME AN' TOLD ME WE WERE LEAVIN'.

I NEED YOU TO BE BRAVE FOR ME, SON.

AN' I NEED YOU TO KNOW SOME THINGS, IN CASE WE...WE DON'T GET A CHANCE TO TALK ABOUT 'EM LATER.

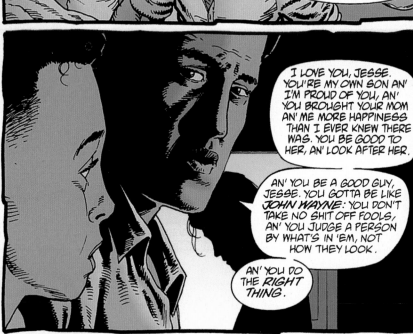

I LOVE YOU, JESSE. YOU'RE MY OWN SON AN' I'M PROUD OF YOU, AN' YOU BROUGHT YOUR MOM AN' ME MORE HAPPINESS THAN I EVER KNEW THERE WAS. YOU BE GOOD TO HER, AN' LOOK AFTER HER.

AN' YOU BE A GOOD GUY, JESSE. YOU GOTTA BE LIKE *JOHN WAYNE*: YOU DON'T TAKE NO SHIT OFF FOOLS, AN' YOU JUDGE A PERSON BY WHAT'S IN 'EM, NOT HOW THEY LOOK.

AN' YOU DO THE *RIGHT* THING.

YOU *GOTTA* BE ONE OF THE GOOD GUYS, SON:

'CAUSE THERE'S WAY TOO MANY OF THE BAD.

AN' THEY CAUGHT US BEFORE WE GOT TWO MILES, AN' THEY SHOT MY DADDY IN THE HEAD.

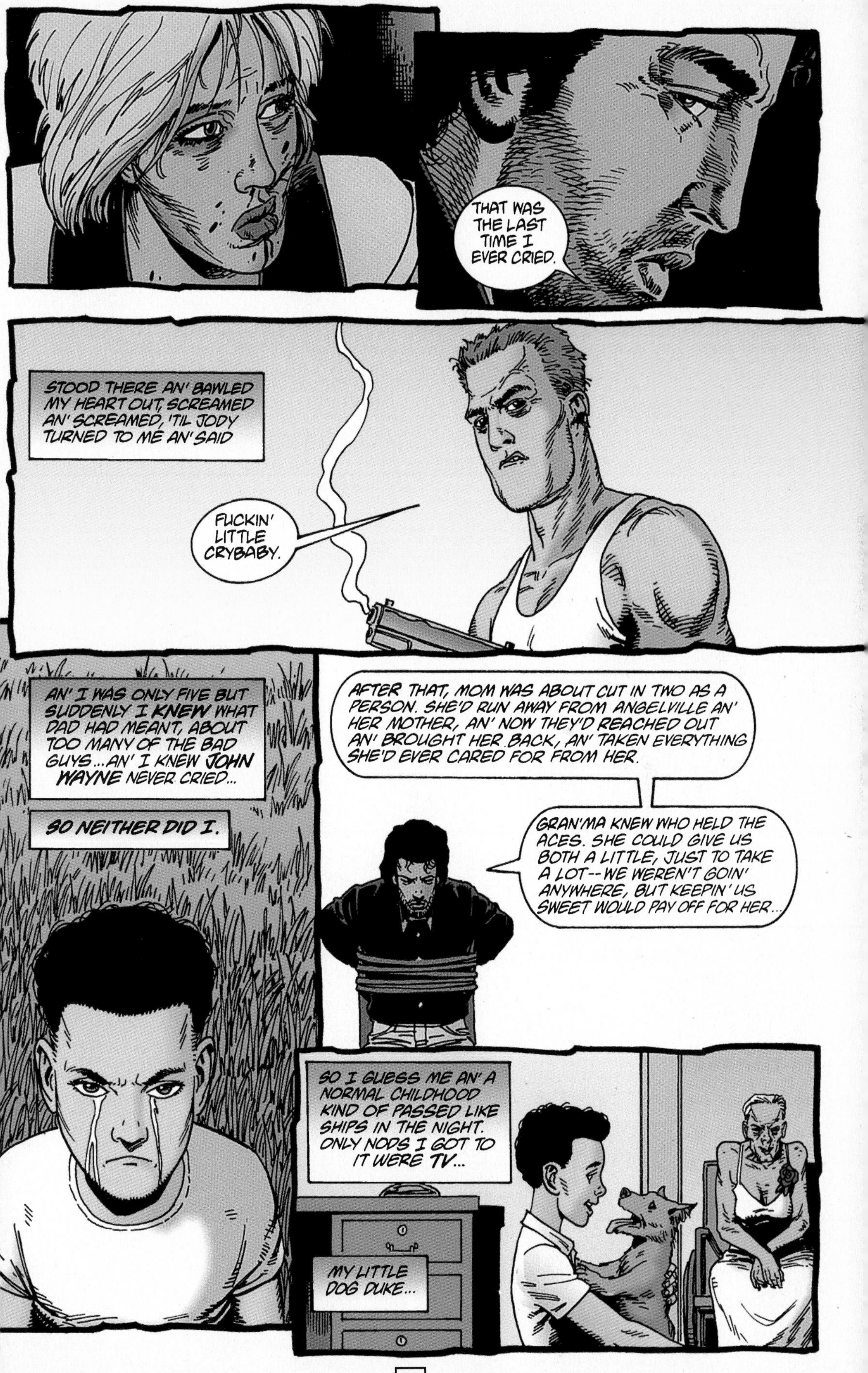
THAT WAS THE LAST TIME I EVER CRIED.
STOOD THERE AN' BAWLED MY HEART OUT, SCREAMED AN' SCREAMED, 'TIL JODY TURNED TO ME AN' SAID
FUCKIN' LITTLE CRYBABY.
AN' I WAS ONLY FIVE BUT SUDDENLY I KNEW WHAT DAD HAD MEANT, ABOUT TOO MANY OF THE BAD GUYS... AN' I KNEW JOHN WAYNE NEVER CRIED...
SO NEITHER DID I.
AFTER THAT, MOM WAS ABOUT CUT IN TWO AS A PERSON. SHE'D RUN AWAY FROM ANGELVILLE AN' HER MOTHER, AN' NOW THEY'D REACHED OUT AN' BROUGHT HER BACK, AN' TAKEN EVERYTHING SHE'D EVER CARED FOR FROM HER.
GRAN'MA KNEW WHO HELD THE ACES. SHE COULD GIVE US BOTH A LITTLE, JUST TO TAKE A LOT--WE WEREN'T GOIN' ANYWHERE, BUT KEEPIN' US SWEET WOULD PAY OFF FOR HER...
SO I GUESS ME AN' A NORMAL CHILDHOOD KIND OF PASSED LIKE SHIPS IN THE NIGHT. ONLY NODS I GOT TO IT WERE TV...
MY LITTLE DOG DUKE...

AND MY BEST FRIEND BILLY-BOB.

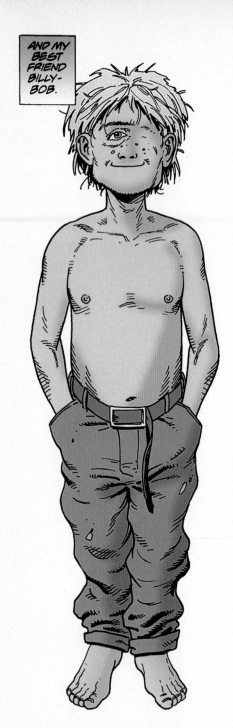

BILLY-BOB'S FOLKS LIVED WAY OUT IN THE BAYOU. I FIGURE HE LOOKED THE WAY HE DID 'CAUSE SOMEONE DUMPED CHEMICALS IN THE SWAMP, WAY IT HAPPENED IN THE CARTOONS.

TURNED OUT IT WASN'T THAT AT ALL...

YOU EVER WONDER WHO YOU'RE GONNA GROW UP TO MARRY, BILLY-BOB?

NOPE.

GONNA MARRY MY SISTER LORIE.

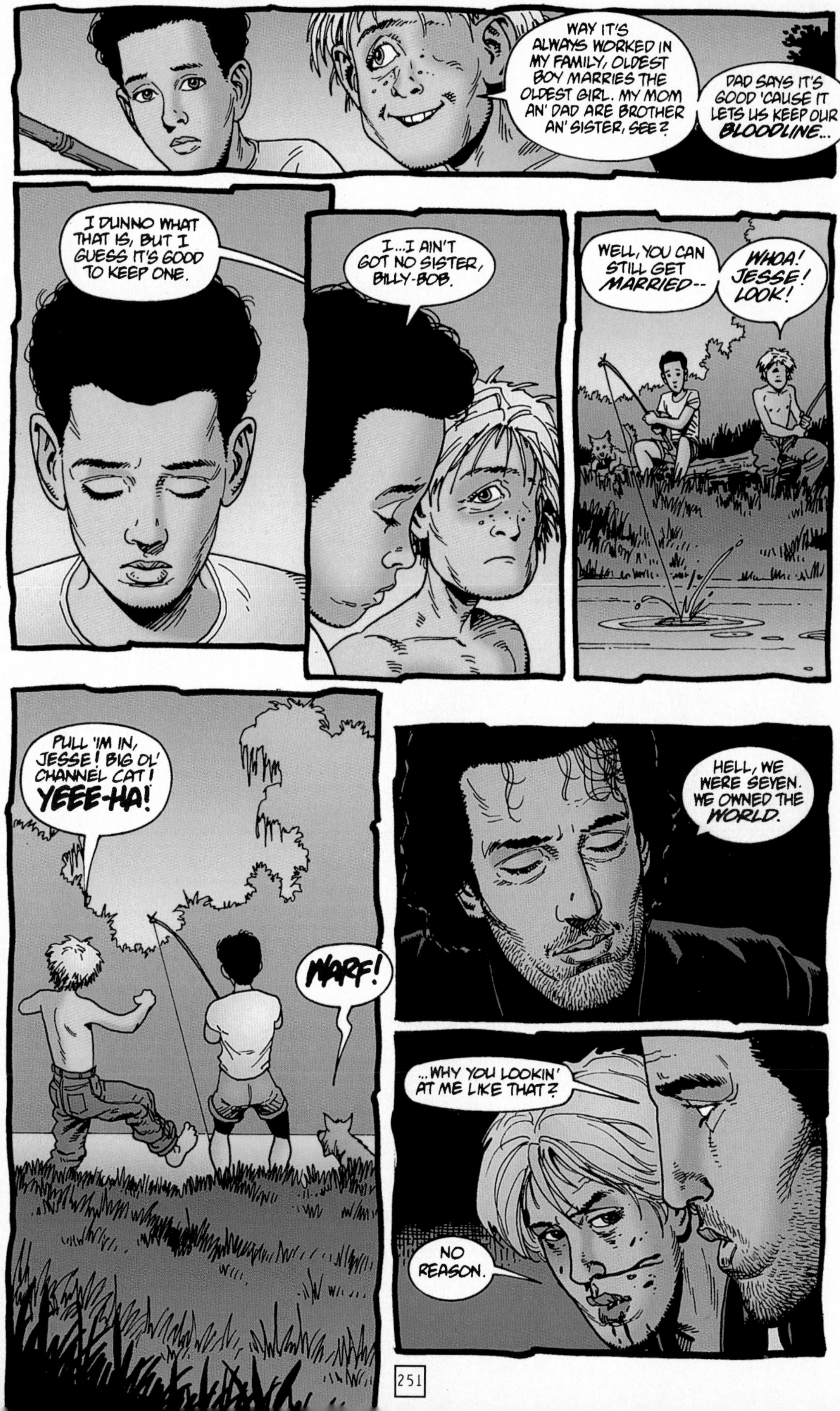
WAY IT'S ALWAYS WORKED IN MY FAMILY, OLDEST BOY MARRIES THE OLDEST GIRL. MY MOM AN' DAD ARE BROTHER AN' SISTER, SEE?
DAD SAYS IT'S GOOD 'CAUSE IT LETS US KEEP OUR BLOODLINE...
I DUNNO WHAT THAT IS, BUT I GUESS IT'S GOOD TO KEEP ONE.
I...I AIN'T GOT NO SISTER, BILLY-BOB.
WELL, YOU CAN STILL GET MARRIED--
WHOA! JESSE! LOOK!
PULL 'IM IN, JESSE! BIG OL' CHANNEL CAT! YEEE-HA!
WARF!
HELL, WE WERE SEVEN. WE OWNED THE WORLD.
...WHY YOU LOOKIN' AT ME LIKE THAT?
NO REASON.

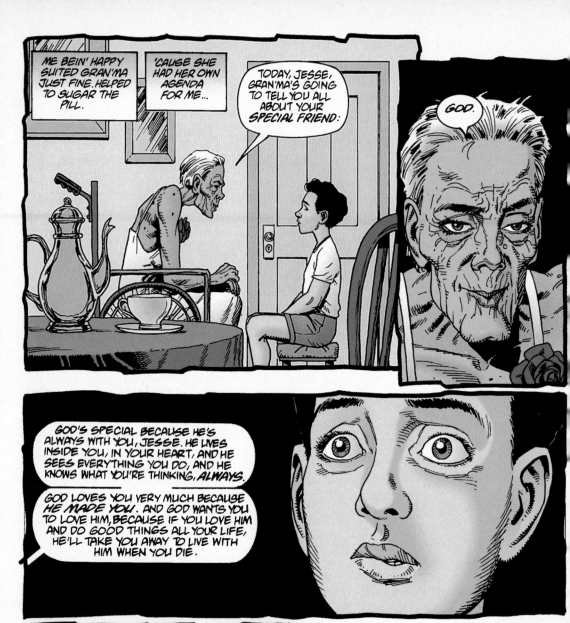

ME BEIN' HAPPY SUITED GRAN'MA JUST FINE. HELPED TO SUGAR THE PILL.

'CAUSE SHE HAD HER OWN AGENDA FOR ME...

TODAY, JESSE, GRAN'MA'S GOING TO TELL YOU ALL ABOUT YOUR SPECIAL FRIEND:

GOD.

GOD'S SPECIAL BECAUSE HE'S ALWAYS WITH YOU, JESSE. HE LIVES INSIDE YOU, IN YOUR HEART, AND HE SEES EVERYTHING YOU DO, AND HE KNOWS WHAT YOU'RE THINKING, *ALWAYS*.

GOD LOVES YOU VERY MUCH BECAUSE *HE MADE YOU*. AND GOD WANTS YOU TO LOVE HIM, BECAUSE IF YOU LOVE HIM AND DO GOOD THINGS ALL YOUR LIFE, HE'LL TAKE YOU AWAY TO LIVE WITH HIM WHEN YOU DIE.

NOW: ISN'T IT *NICE* TO HAVE A FRIEND LIKE GOD?

NO, GRAN'MA. IT'S KIND OF SCARY.

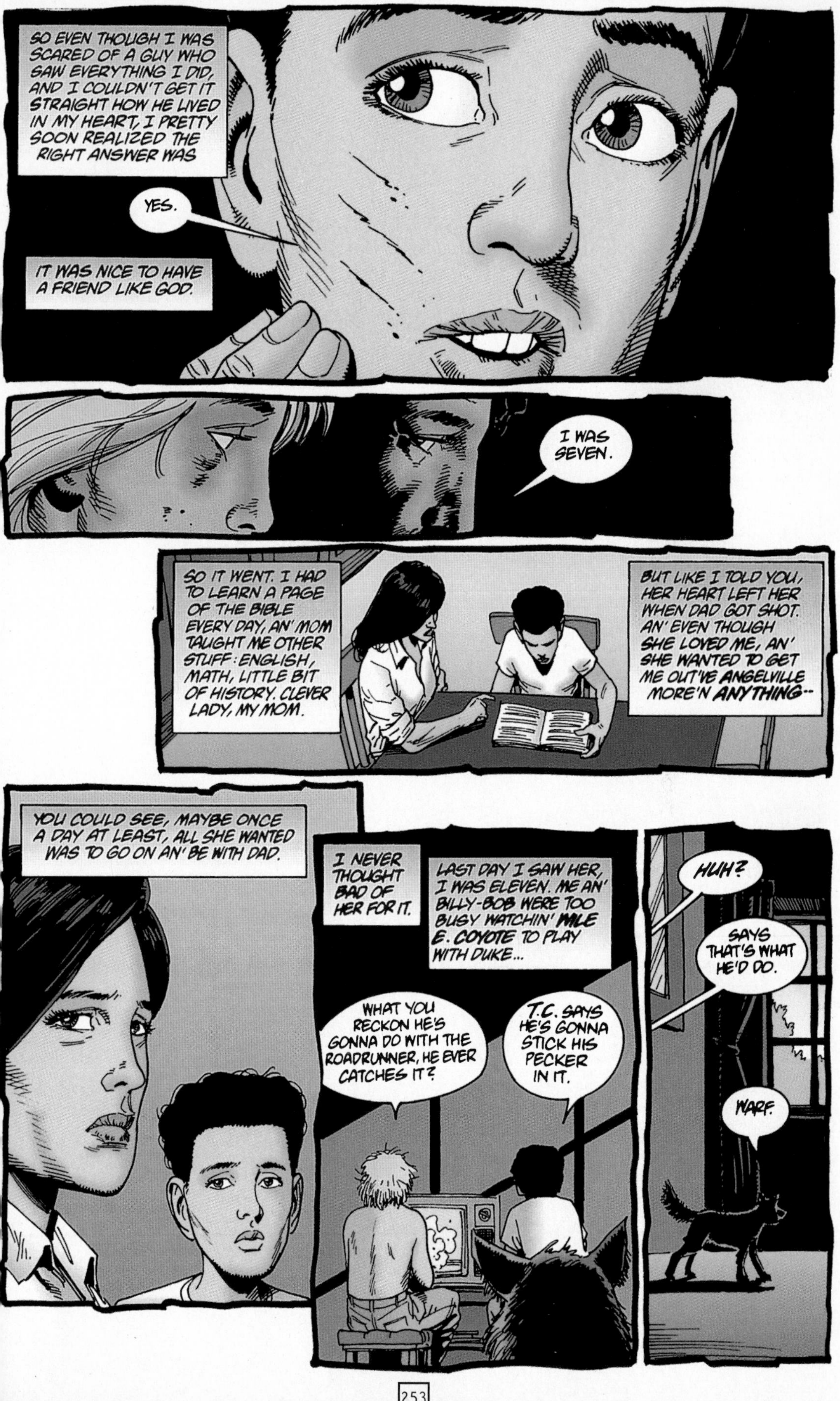
SO EVEN THOUGH I WAS SCARED OF A GUY WHO SAW EVERYTHING I DID, AND I COULDN'T GET IT STRAIGHT HOW HE LIVED IN MY HEART, I PRETTY SOON REALIZED THE RIGHT ANSWER WAS
YES.
IT WAS NICE TO HAVE A FRIEND LIKE GOD.
I WAS SEVEN.
SO IT WENT. I HAD TO LEARN A PAGE OF THE BIBLE EVERY DAY, AN' MOM TAUGHT ME OTHER STUFF: ENGLISH, MATH, LITTLE BIT OF HISTORY. CLEVER LADY, MY MOM.
BUT LIKE I TOLD YOU, HER HEART LEFT HER WHEN DAD GOT SHOT. AN' EVEN THOUGH SHE LOVED ME, AN' SHE WANTED TO GET ME OUT'VE ANGELVILLE MORE'N ANYTHING--
YOU COULD SEE, MAYBE ONCE A DAY AT LEAST, ALL SHE WANTED WAS TO GO ON AN' BE WITH DAD.
I NEVER THOUGHT BAD OF HER FOR IT.
LAST DAY I SAW HER, I WAS ELEVEN. ME AN' BILLY-BOB WERE TOO BUSY WATCHIN' WILE E. COYOTE TO PLAY WITH DUKE...
WHAT YOU RECKON HE'S GONNA DO WITH THE ROADRUNNER, HE EVER CATCHES IT?
T.C. SAYS HE'S GONNA STICK HIS PECKER IN IT.
HUH?
SAYS THAT'S WHAT HE'D DO.
WARF.

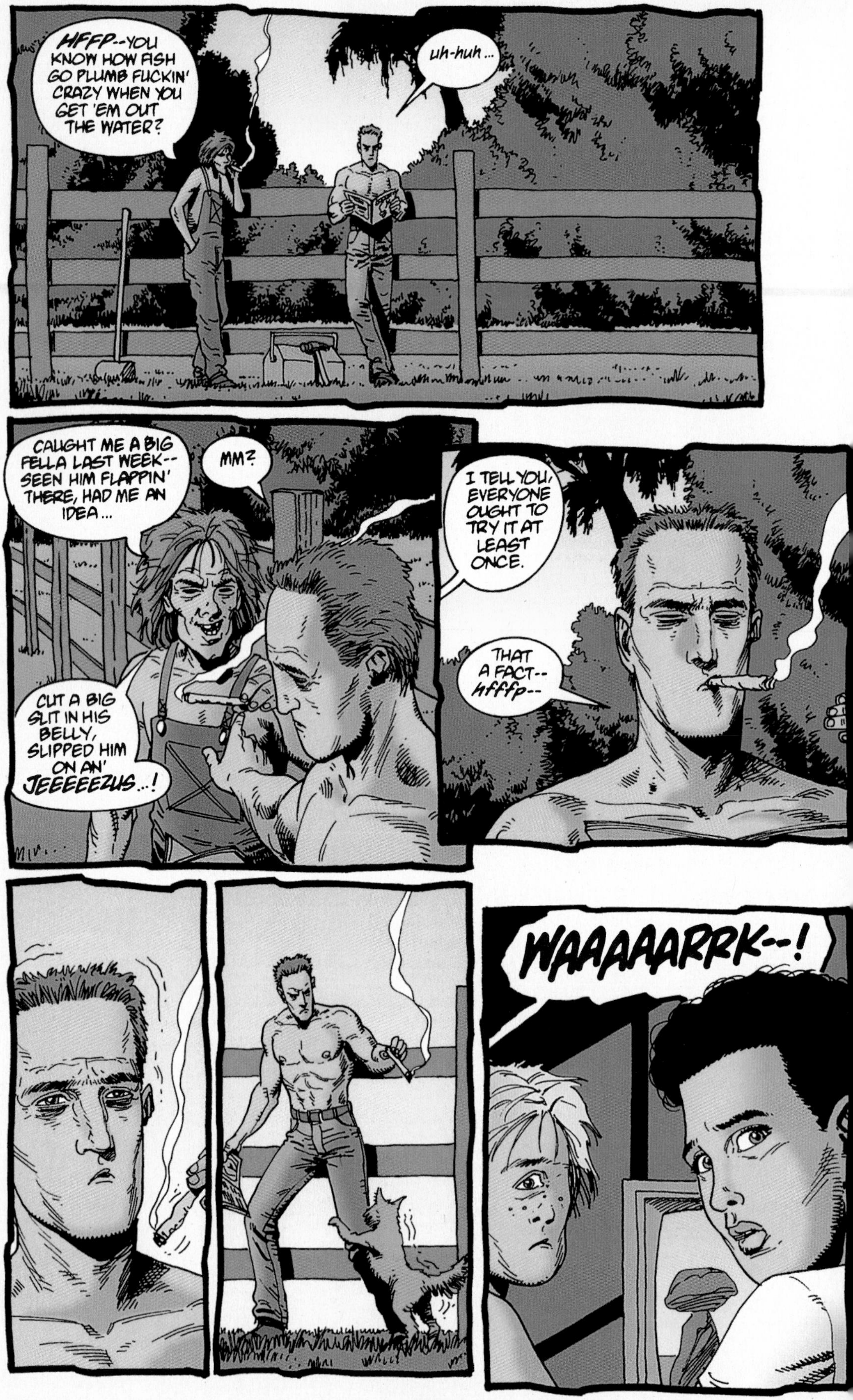
HFFP--YOU KNOW HOW FISH GO PLUMB FUCKIN' CRAZY WHEN YOU GET 'EM OUT THE WATER?
uh-huh...
CAUGHT ME A BIG FELLA LAST WEEK--SEEN HIM FLAPPIN' THERE, HAD ME AN IDEA...
MM?
CUT A BIG SLIT IN HIS BELLY, SLIPPED HIM ON AN' JEEEEEZUS...!
I TELL YOU, EVERYONE OUGHT TO TRY IT AT LEAST ONCE.
THAT A FACT--hfffp--
WAAAAARRK--!

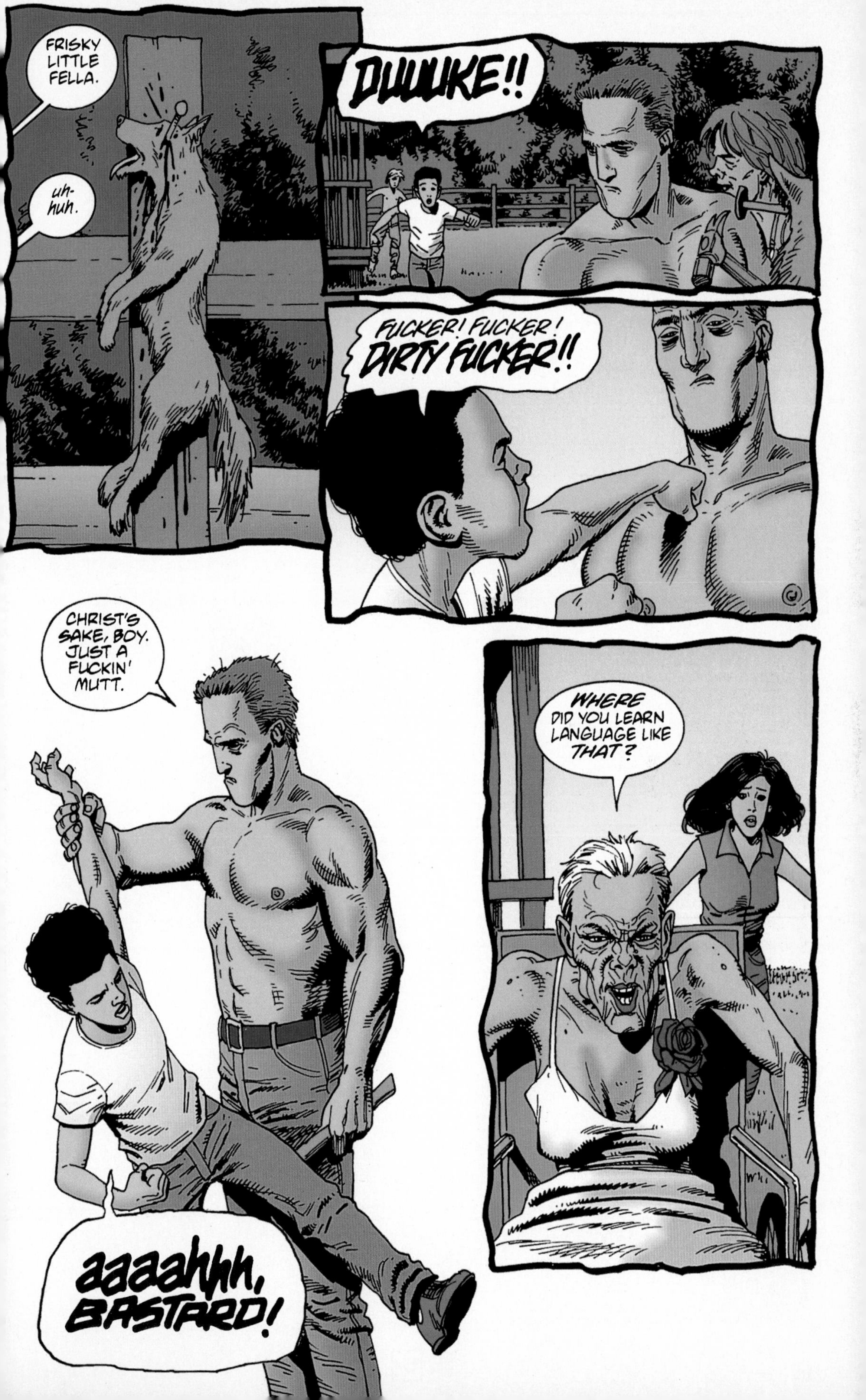
FRISKY LITTLE FELLA.
uh-huh.
DUUUKE!!
FUCKER! FUCKER! DIRTY FUCKER!!
CHRIST'S SAKE, BOY. JUST A FUCKIN' MUTT.
aaaahhh, BASTARD!
WHERE DID YOU LEARN LANGUAGE LIKE THAT?

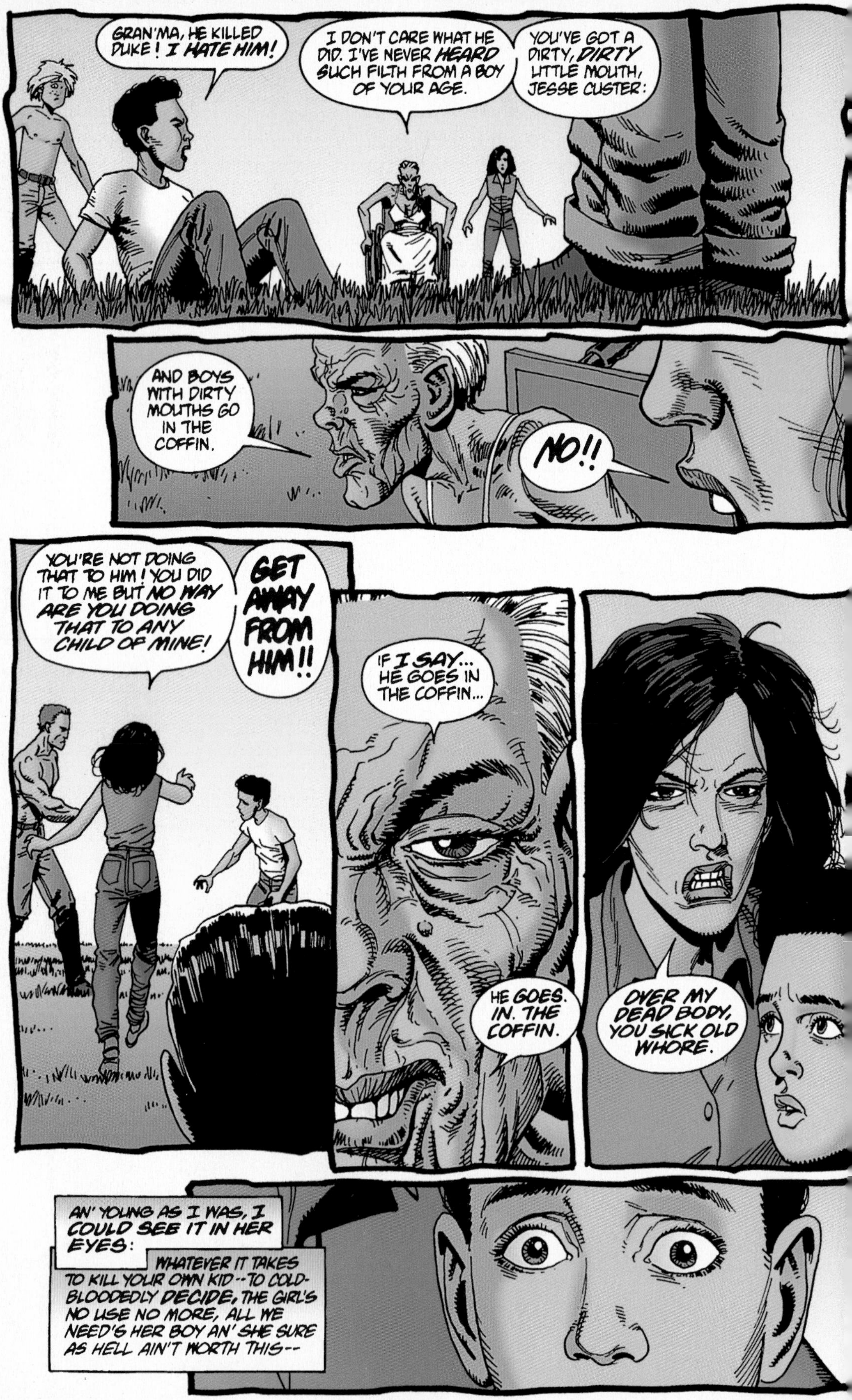

GRAN'MA, HE KILLED DUKE! I HATE HIM!
I DON'T CARE WHAT HE DID. I'VE NEVER HEARD SUCH FILTH FROM A BOY OF YOUR AGE.
YOU'VE GOT A DIRTY, DIRTY LITTLE MOUTH, JESSE CUSTER:
AND BOYS WITH DIRTY MOUTHS GO IN THE COFFIN.
NO!!
YOU'RE NOT DOING THAT TO HIM! YOU DID IT TO ME BUT NO WAY ARE YOU DOING THAT TO ANY CHILD OF MINE!
GET AWAY FROM HIM!!
IF I SAY... HE GOES IN THE COFFIN...
HE GOES. IN. THE COFFIN.
OVER MY DEAD BODY, YOU SICK OLD WHORE.
AN' YOUNG AS I WAS, I COULD SEE IT IN HER EYES:
WHATEVER IT TAKES TO KILL YOUR OWN KID--TO COLD-BLOODEDLY DECIDE, THE GIRL'S NO USE NO MORE, ALL WE NEED'S HER BOY AN' SHE SURE AS HELL AIN'T WORTH THIS--

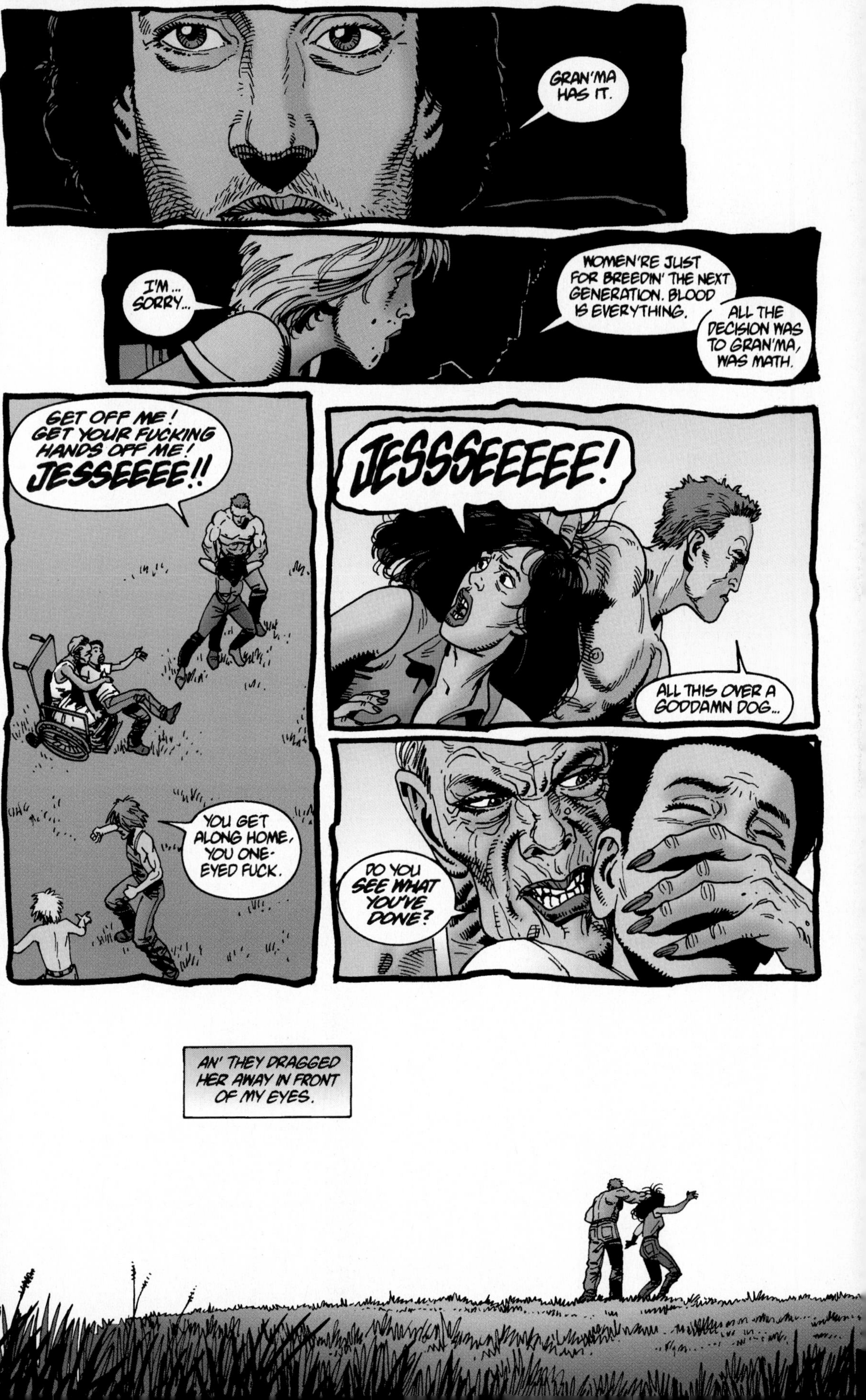
GRAN'MA HAS IT.
I'M... SORRY...
WOMEN'RE JUST FOR BREEDIN' THE NEXT GENERATION. BLOOD IS EVERYTHING.
ALL THE DECISION WAS TO GRAN'MA, WAS MATH.
GET OFF ME! GET YOUR FUCKING HANDS OFF ME! JESSEEEE!!
YOU GET ALONG HOME, YOU ONE-EYED FUCK.
JESSSEEEEEE!
ALL THIS OVER A GODDAMN DOG...
DO YOU SEE WHAT YOU'VE DONE?
AN' THEY DRAGGED HER AWAY IN FRONT OF MY EYES.

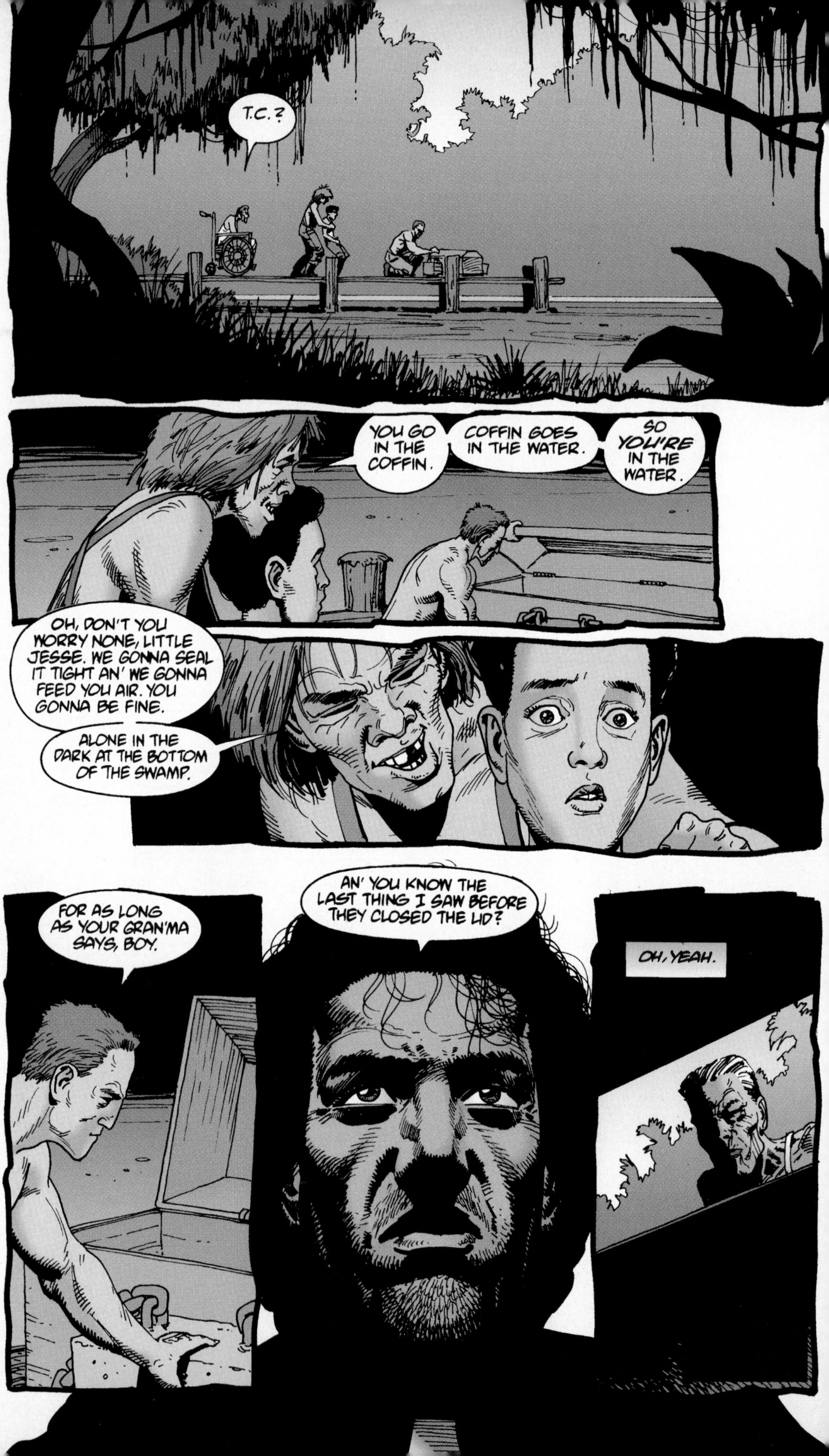
T.C.?
YOU GO IN THE COFFIN.
COFFIN GOES IN THE WATER.
SO YOU'RE IN THE WATER.
OH, DON'T YOU WORRY NONE, LITTLE JESSE. WE GONNA SEAL IT TIGHT AN' WE GONNA FEED YOU AIR. YOU GONNA BE FINE.
ALONE IN THE DARK AT THE BOTTOM OF THE SWAMP.
FOR AS LONG AS YOUR GRAN'MA SAYS, BOY.
AN' YOU KNOW THE LAST THING I SAW BEFORE THEY CLOSED THE LID?
OH, YEAH.

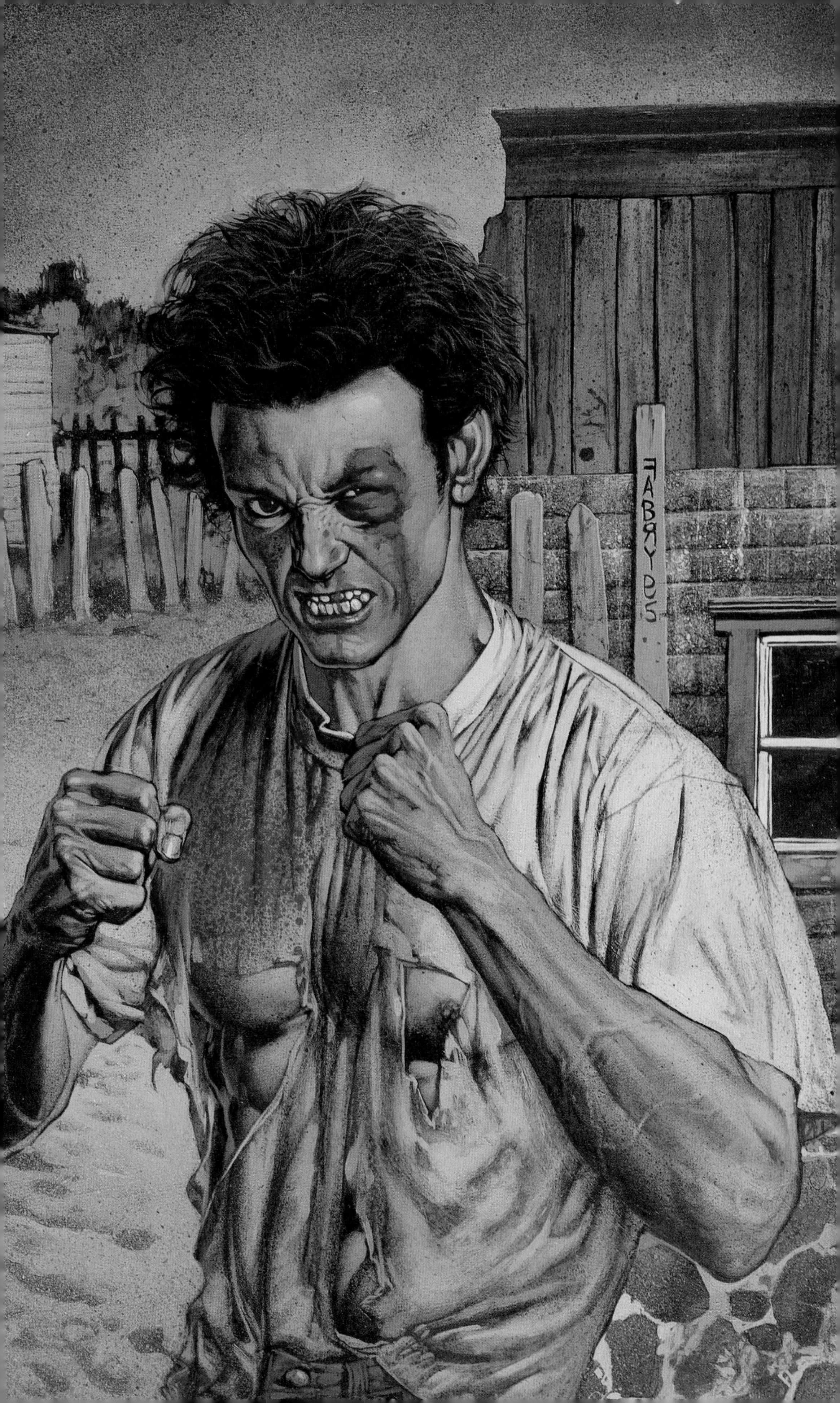
FABRY 05

"All you do is cause misery to folks. Always been that way. Snakes in the night, that's what you are."

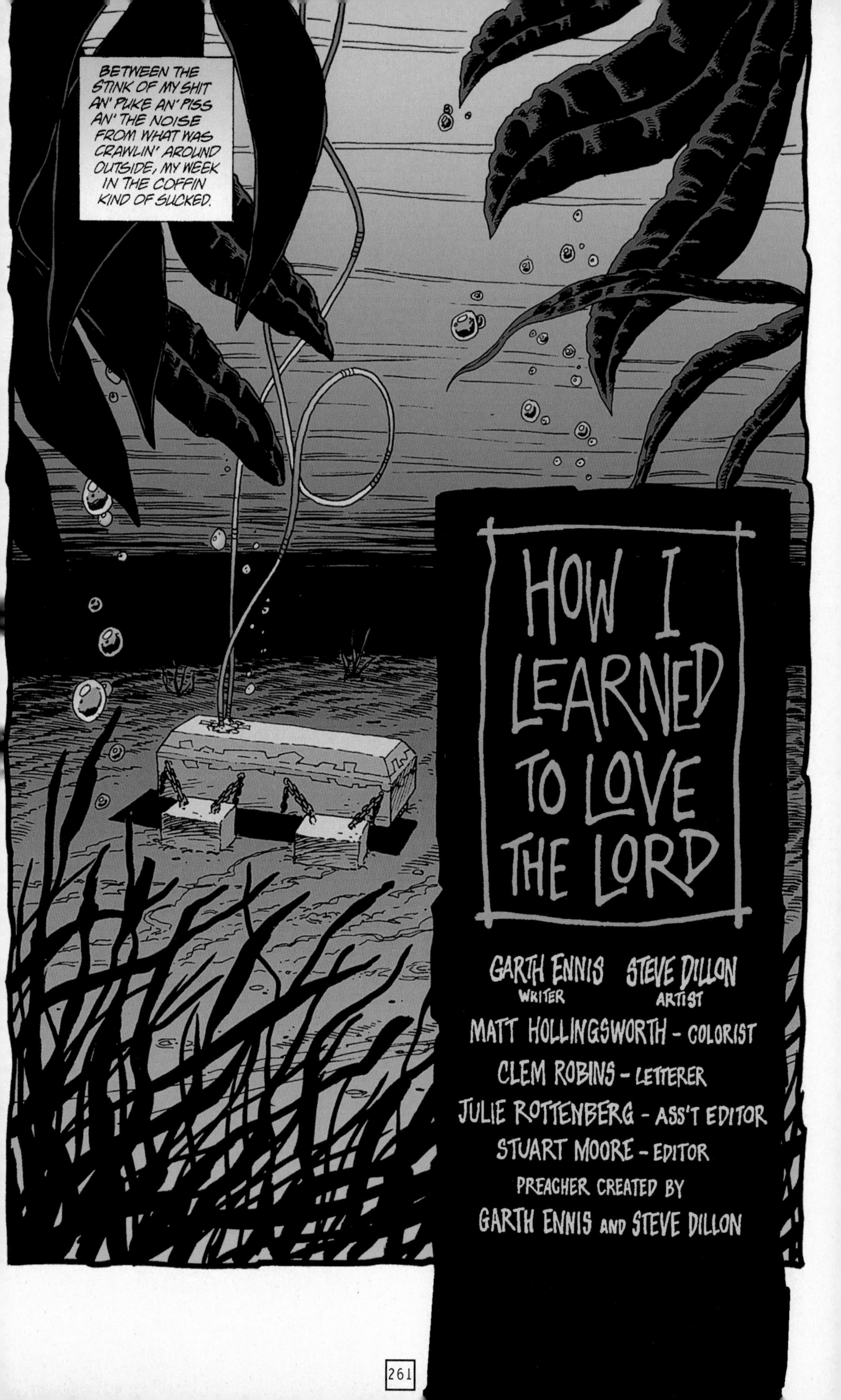
BETWEEN THE STINK OF MY SHIT AN' PUKE AN' PISS AN' THE NOISE FROM WHAT WAS CRAWLIN' AROUND OUTSIDE, MY WEEK IN THE COFFIN KIND OF SUCKED.
HOW I LEARNED TO LOVE THE LORD
GARTH ENNIS WRITER
STEVE DILLON ARTIST
MATT HOLLINGSWORTH - COLORIST
CLEM ROBINS - LETTERER
JULIE ROTTENBERG - ASS'T EDITOR
STUART MOORE - EDITOR
PREACHER CREATED BY
GARTH ENNIS AND STEVE DILLON

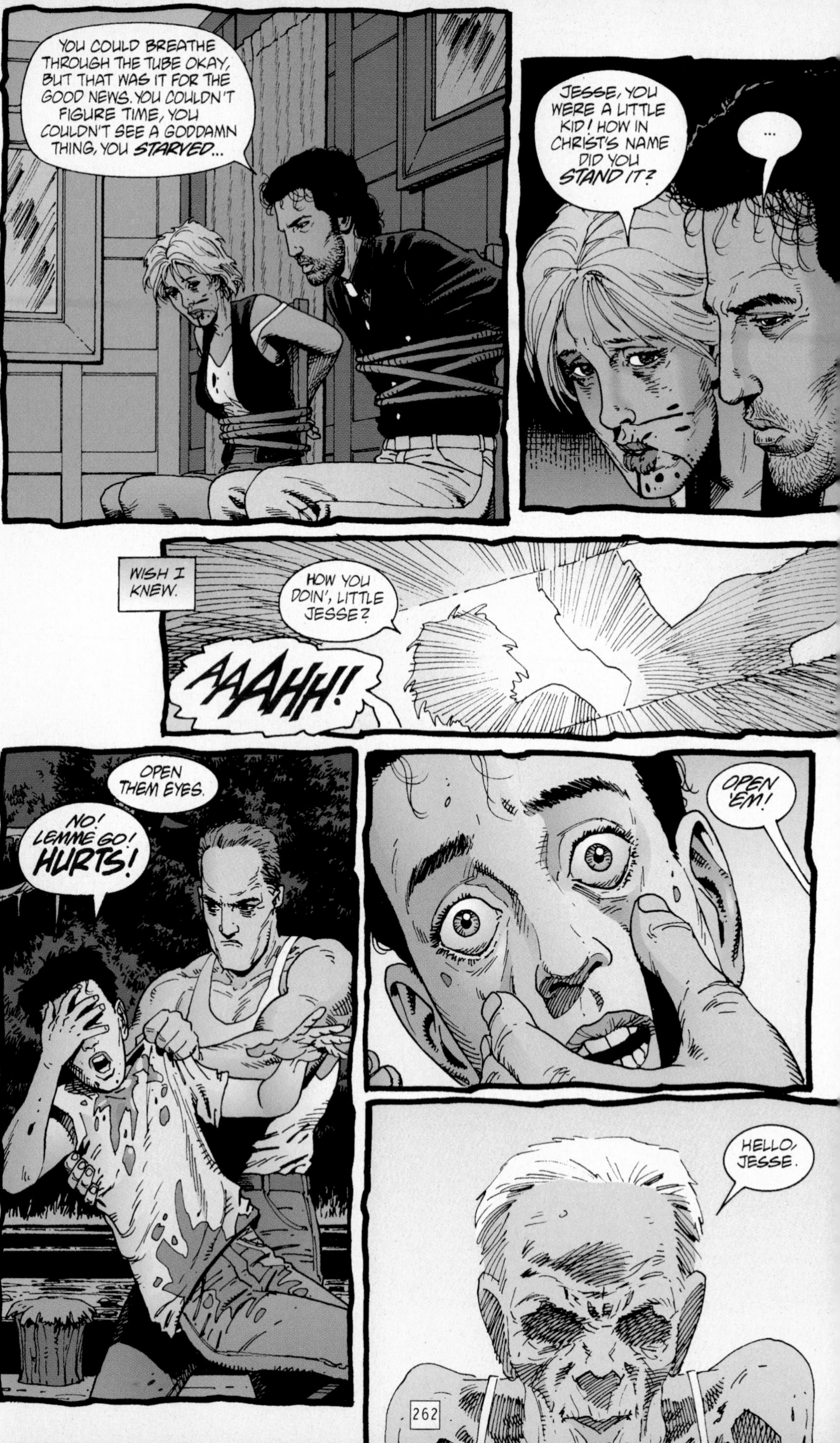

YOU COULD BREATHE THROUGH THE TUBE OKAY, BUT THAT WAS IT FOR THE GOOD NEWS. YOU COULDN'T FIGURE TIME, YOU COULDN'T SEE A GODDAMN THING, YOU STARVED...
JESSE, YOU WERE A LITTLE KID! HOW IN CHRIST'S NAME DID YOU STAND IT?
...
WISH I KNEW.
HOW YOU DOIN', LITTLE JESSE?
AAAHH!
OPEN THEM EYES.
NO! LEMME GO! HURTS!
OPEN 'EM!
HELLO, JESSE.

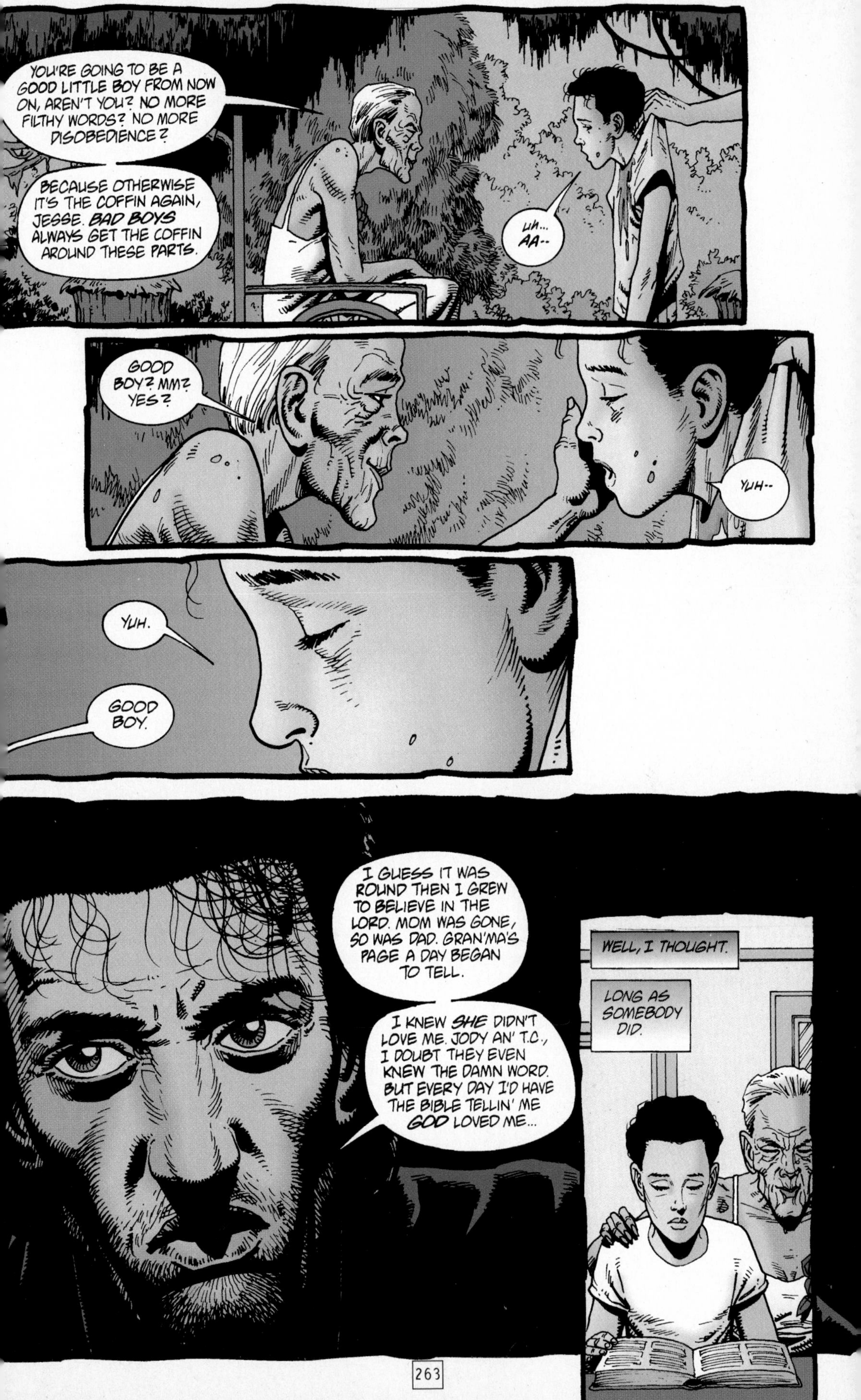
YOU'RE GOING TO BE A GOOD LITTLE BOY FROM NOW ON, AREN'T YOU? NO MORE FILTHY WORDS? NO MORE DISOBEDIENCE?
BECAUSE OTHERWISE IT'S THE COFFIN AGAIN, JESSE. BAD BOYS ALWAYS GET THE COFFIN AROUND THESE PARTS.
UH... AA--
GOOD BOY? MM? YES?
YUH--
YUH.
GOOD BOY.
I GUESS IT WAS ROUND THEN I GREW TO BELIEVE IN THE LORD. MOM WAS GONE, SO WAS DAD. GRAN'MA'S PAGE A DAY BEGAN TO TELL.
I KNEW SHE DIDN'T LOVE ME. JODY AN' T.C., I DOUBT THEY EVEN KNEW THE DAMN WORD. BUT EVERY DAY I'D HAVE THE BIBLE TELLIN' ME GOD LOVED ME...
WELL, I THOUGHT.
LONG AS SOMEBODY DID.

AN' THERE WAS STILL BILLY-BOB. I KNOW HE HAD THE EYE AN' ALL, BUT HE WAS STILL MY FRIEND AN' BELIEVE ME: WAY THINGS WERE, THAT MEANT A *LOT*.

HE WAS DUE TO MARRY HIS SISTER WHEN HE TURNED SIX-TEEN, AN' HE JUST COULDN'T WAIT...

SURE. I MEAN, I GUESS.

I GOTTA ASK GRAN'MA FOR TIME OFF MY STUDIES. GOTTA BE READY FOR PREACHER SCHOOL, END OF SUMMER. AN' JODY'S GOT ME WORKIN' REAL HARD AROUND THE PLACE...

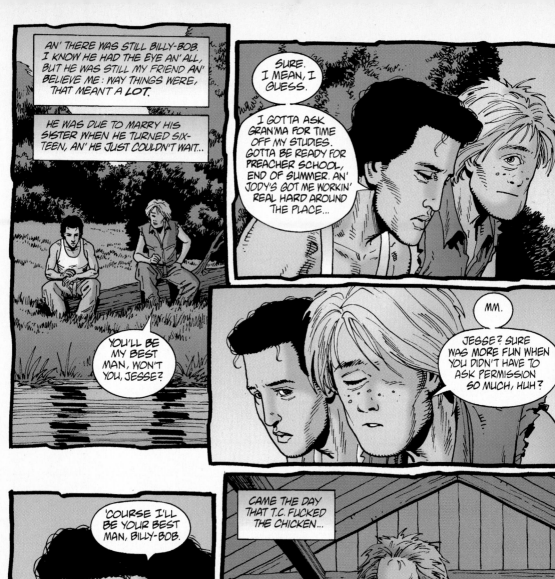

YOU'LL BE MY BEST MAN, WON'T YOU, JESSE?

MM.

JESSE? SURE WAS MORE FUN WHEN YOU DIDN'T HAVE TO ASK PERMISSION SO MUCH, HUH?

'COURSE I'LL BE YOUR BEST MAN, BILLY-BOB.

SO THERE WAS STILL A LITTLE' HOPE IN THE WORLD, SO LONG AS I HAD A FRIEND.

CAME THE DAY THAT T.C. FUCKED THE CHICKEN...

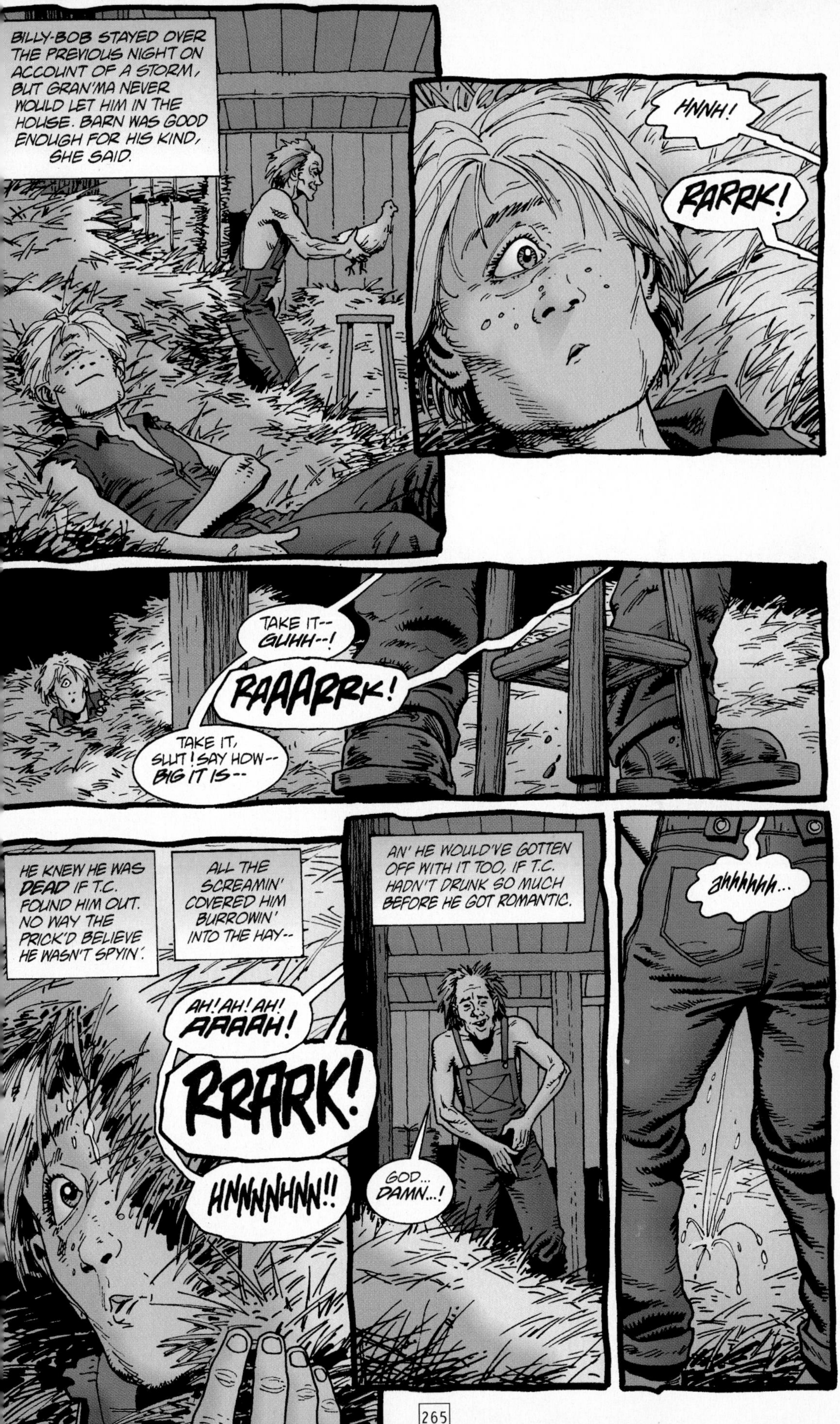
BILLY-BOB STAYED OVER THE PREVIOUS NIGHT ON ACCOUNT OF A STORM, BUT GRAN'MA NEVER WOULD LET HIM IN THE HOUSE. BARN WAS GOOD ENOUGH FOR HIS KIND, SHE SAID.
HNNH!
RARRK!
TAKE IT-- GUHH--!
RAAARRK!
TAKE IT, SLUT! SAY HOW-- BIG IT IS--
HE KNEW HE WAS DEAD IF T.C. FOUND HIM OUT. NO WAY THE PRICK'D BELIEVE HE WASN'T SPYIN'.
ALL THE SCREAMIN' COVERED HIM BURROWIN' INTO THE HAY--
AH! AH! AH! AAAAH!
RRARK!
HNNNHNN!!
AN' HE WOULD'VE GOTTEN OFF WITH IT TOO, IF T.C. HADN'T DRUNK SO MUCH BEFORE HE GOT ROMANTIC.
GOD... DAMN...!
ahhhhhh...

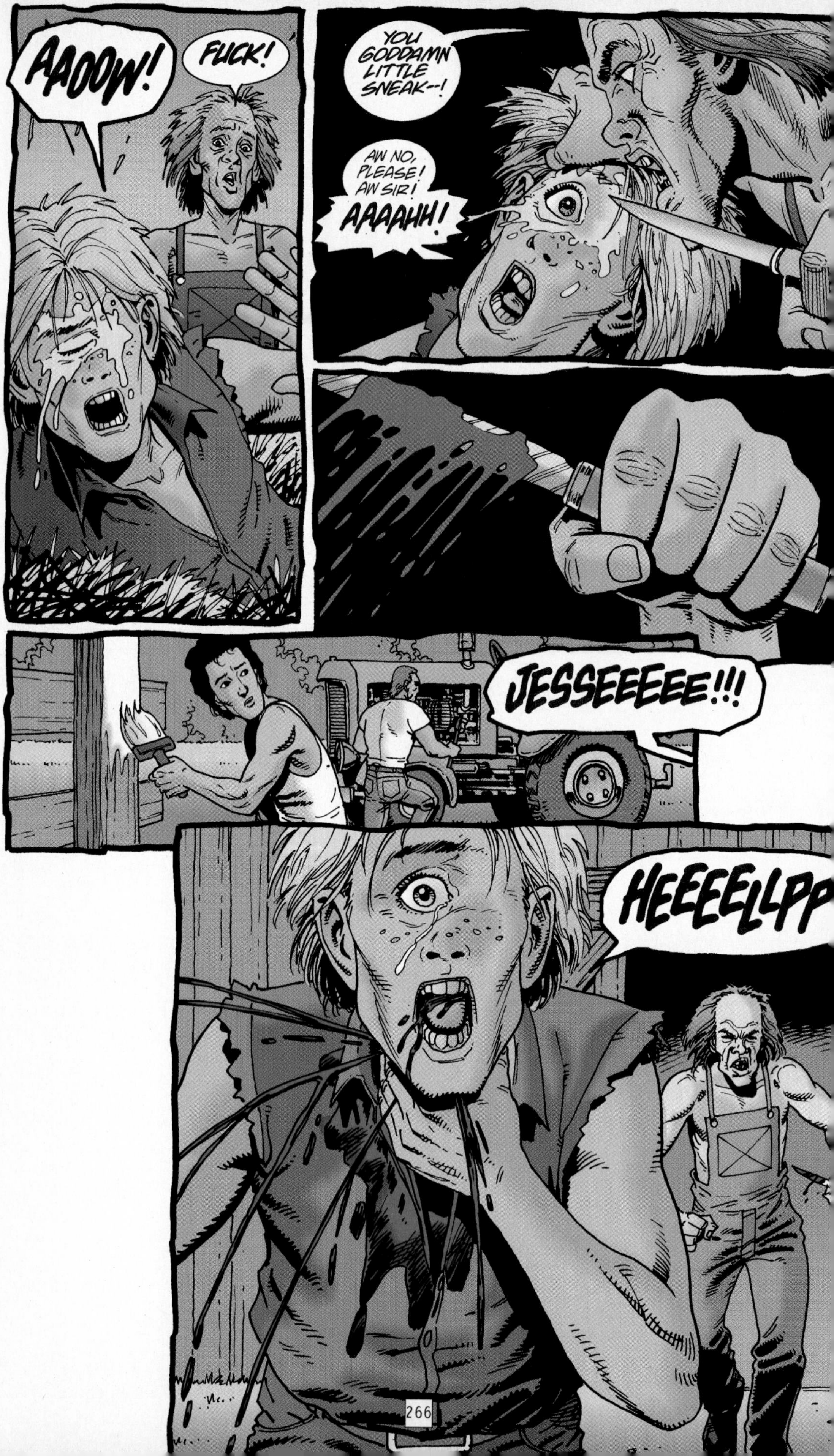
AAOOW!
FUCK!
YOU GODDAMN LITTLE SNEAK--!
AW NO, PLEASE! AW SIR! AAAAHH!
JESSEEEEEE!!!
HEEEELLPP

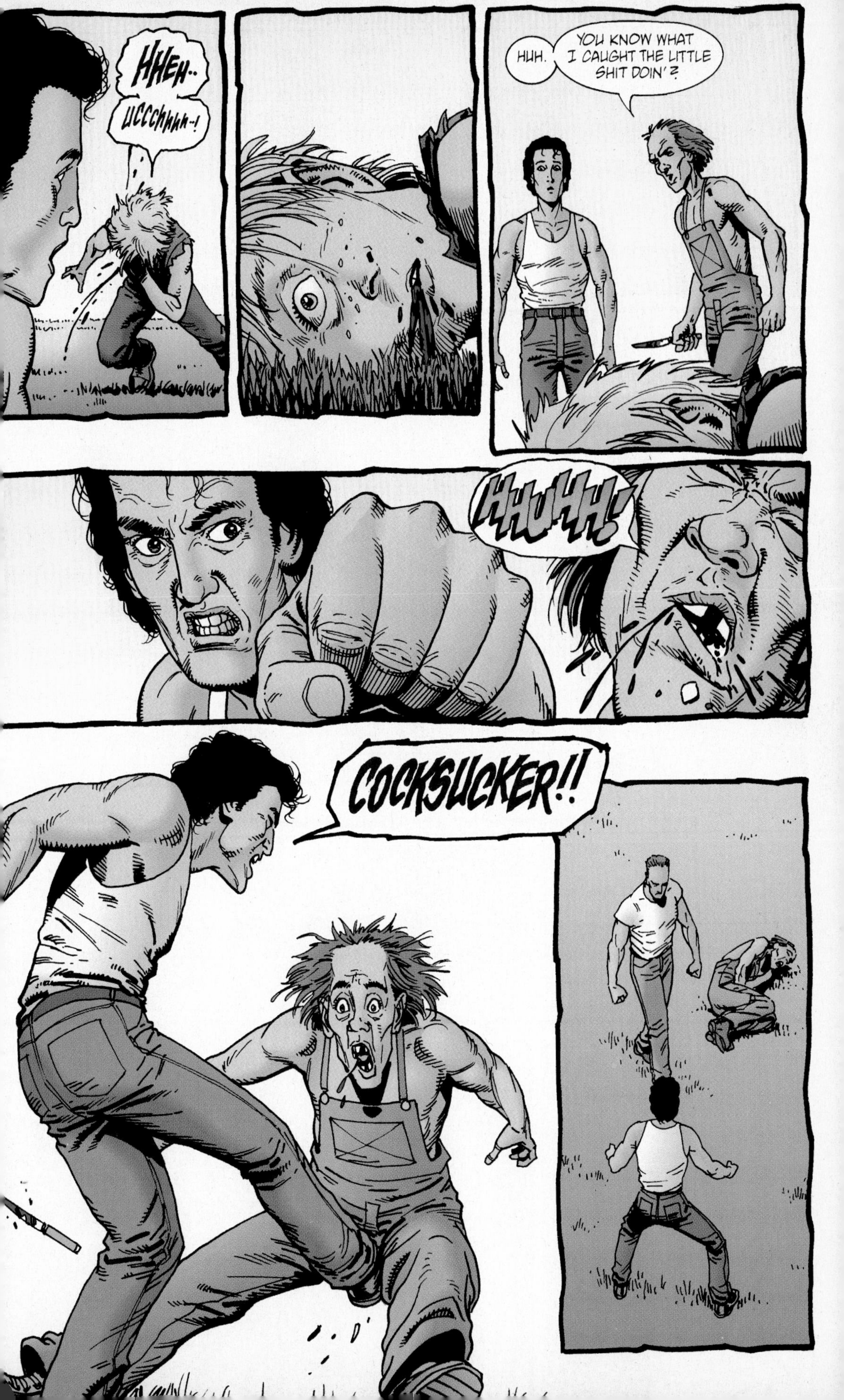
HHEH..
UCCChhh--!
HUH.
YOU KNOW WHAT I CAUGHT THE LITTLE SHIT DOIN'?
HHUHH!
COCKSUCKER!!

FUCK YOU, JODY.

YOU GET OUT OF MY WAY OR I'LL KICK YOUR REDNECK ASS WORSE THAN MY DADDY DID.

...YEAH.

FIGURE YOU'RE ABOUT OLD ENOUGH FOR THIS, BOY.

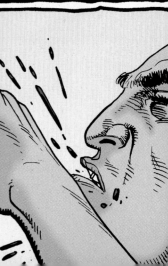

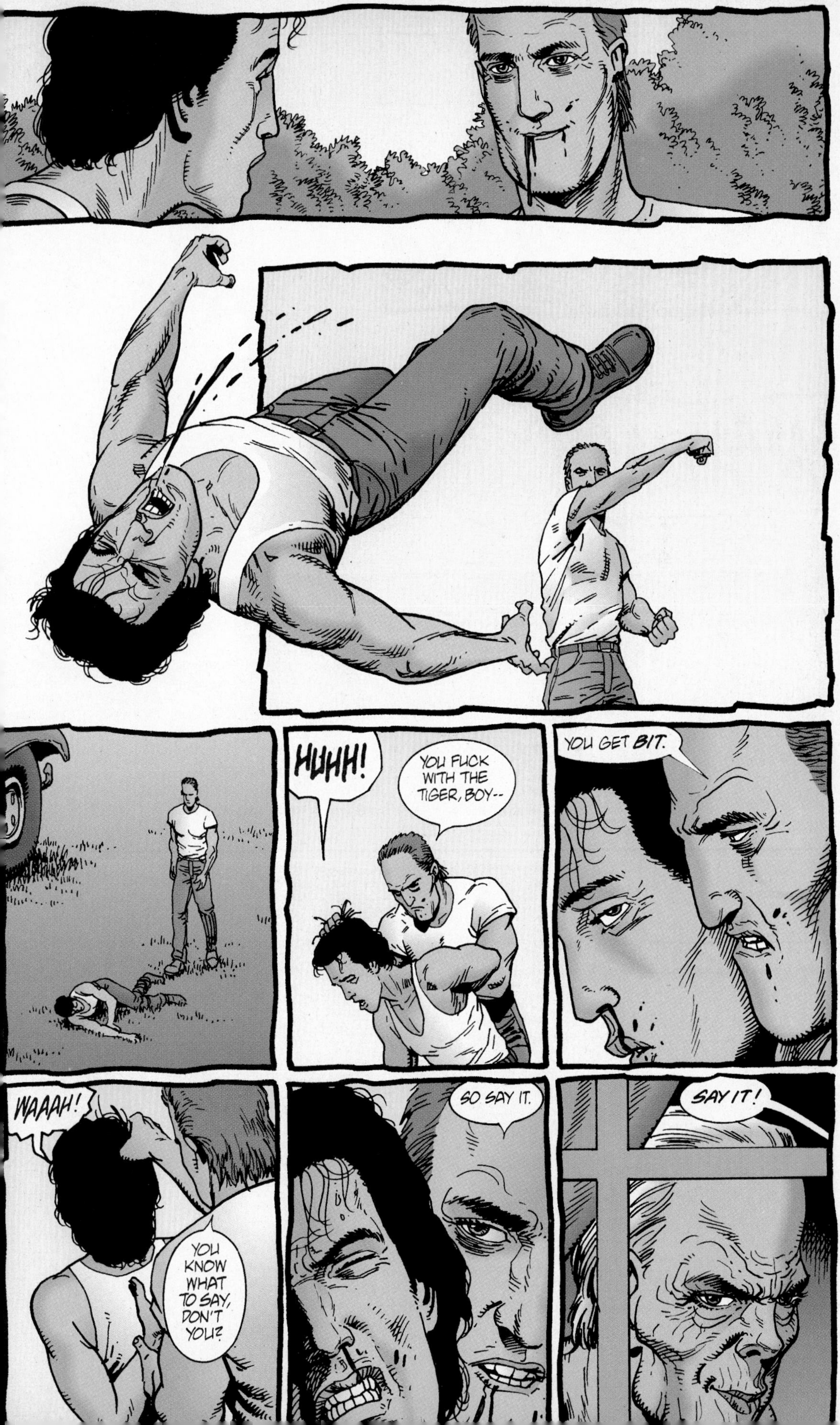
HUHH!
YOU FUCK WITH THE TIGER, BOY--
YOU GET BIT.
WAAAH!
YOU KNOW WHAT TO SAY, DON'T YOU?
SO SAY IT.
SAY IT!

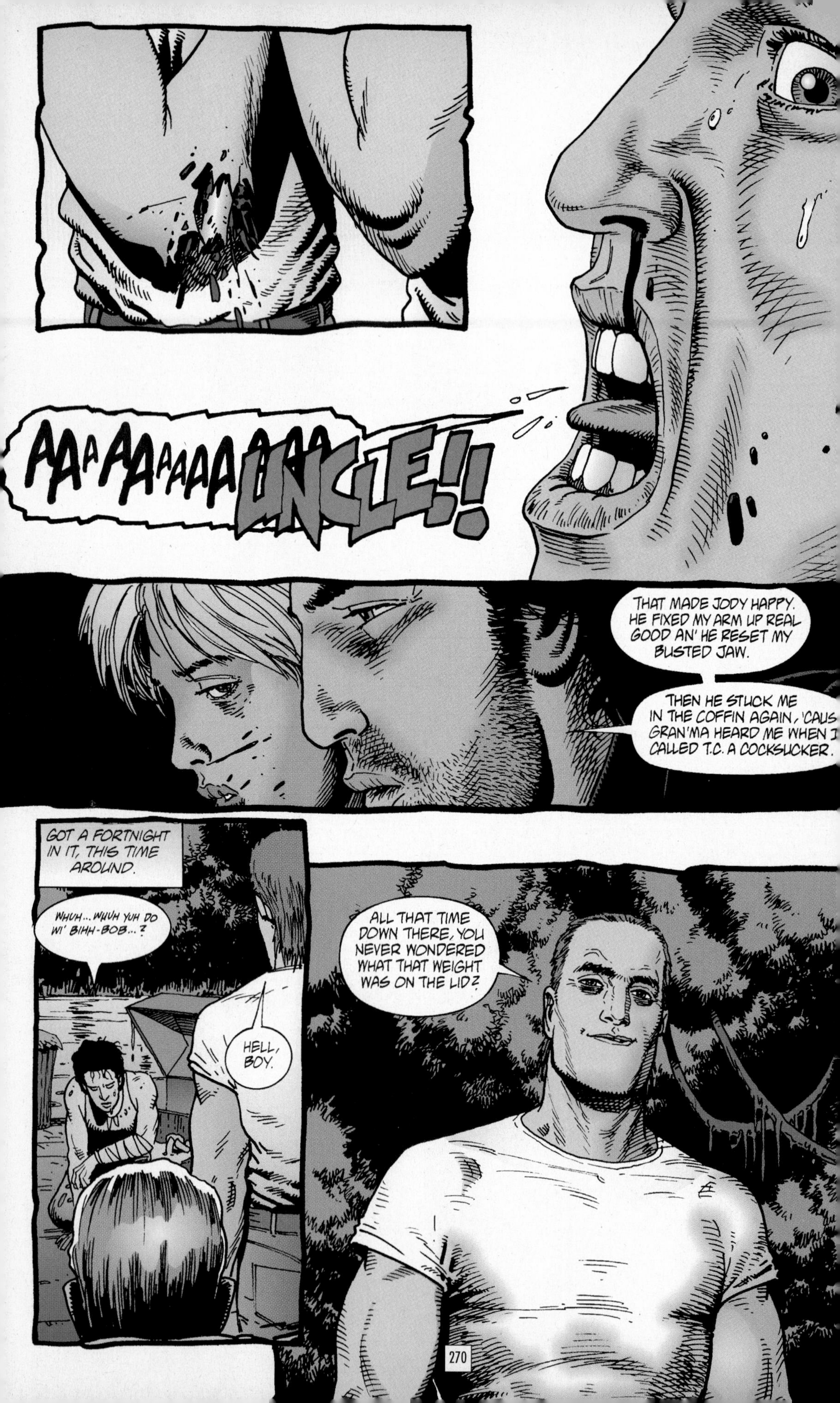
AAAAAAAAAAUNCLE!!
THAT MADE JODY HAPPY. HE FIXED MY ARM UP REAL GOOD AN' HE RESET MY BUSTED JAW.
THEN HE STUCK ME IN THE COFFIN AGAIN, 'CAUS GRAN'MA HEARD ME WHEN I CALLED T.C. A COCKSUCKER.
GOT A FORTNIGHT IN IT, THIS TIME AROUND.
WHUH... WHUH YUH DO WI' BIHH-BOB...?
HELL, BOY.
ALL THAT TIME DOWN THERE, YOU NEVER WONDERED WHAT THAT WEIGHT WAS ON THE LID?

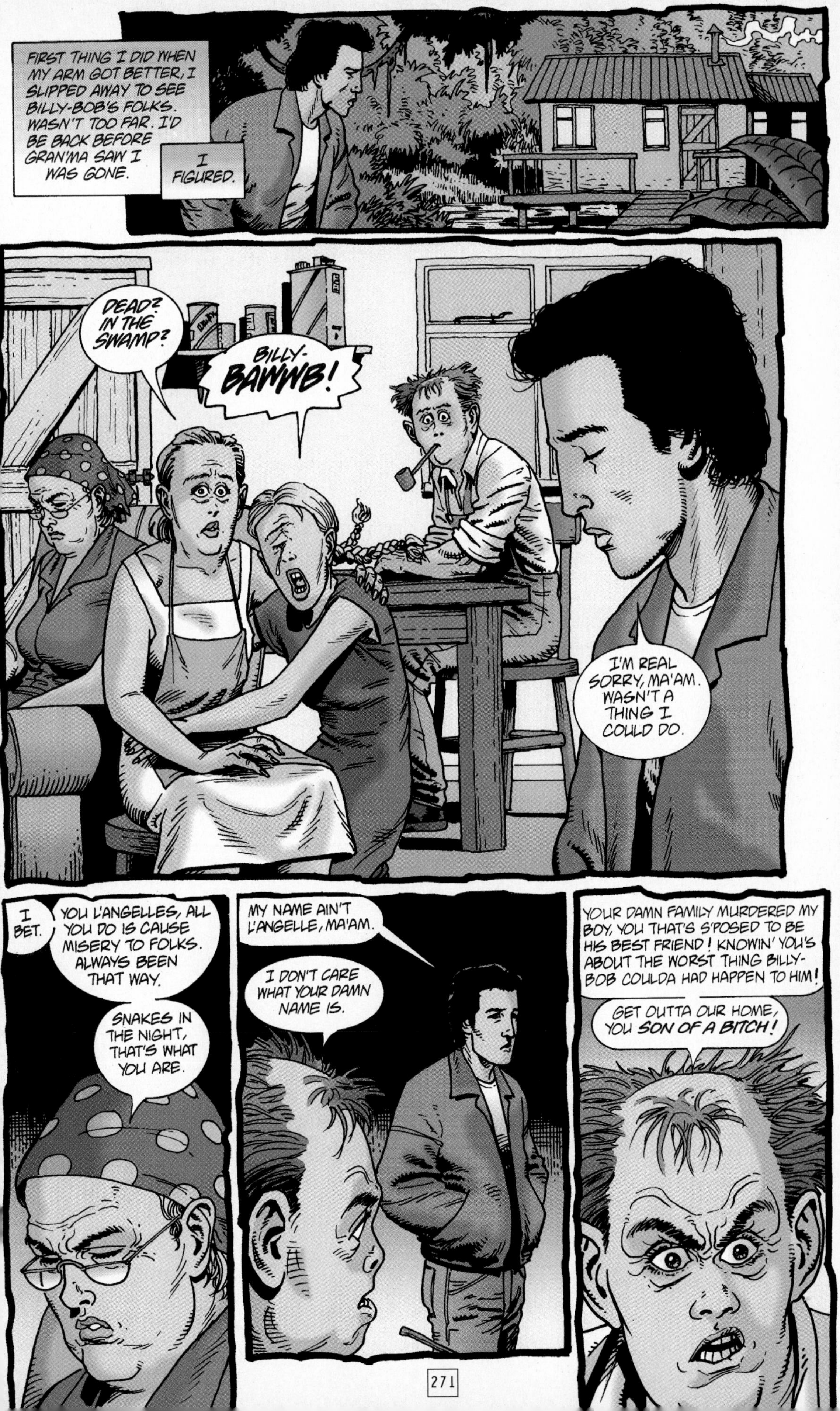
FIRST THING I DID WHEN MY ARM GOT BETTER, I SLIPPED AWAY TO SEE BILLY-BOB'S FOLKS. WASN'T TOO FAR. I'D BE BACK BEFORE GRAN'MA SAW I WAS GONE.
I FIGURED.
DEAD? IN THE SWAMP?
BILLY-BAWWB!
I'M REAL SORRY, MA'AM. WASN'T A THING I COULD DO.
I BET.
YOU L'ANGELLES, ALL YOU DO IS CAUSE MISERY TO FOLKS. ALWAYS BEEN THAT WAY.
SNAKES IN THE NIGHT, THAT'S WHAT YOU ARE.
MY NAME AIN'T L'ANGELLE, MA'AM.
I DON'T CARE WHAT YOUR DAMN NAME IS.
YOUR DAMN FAMILY MURDERED MY BOY, YOU THAT'S S'POSED TO BE HIS BEST FRIEND! KNOWIN' YOU'S ABOUT THE WORST THING BILLY-BOB COULDA HAD HAPPEN TO HIM!
GET OUTTA OUR HOME, YOU SON OF A BITCH!

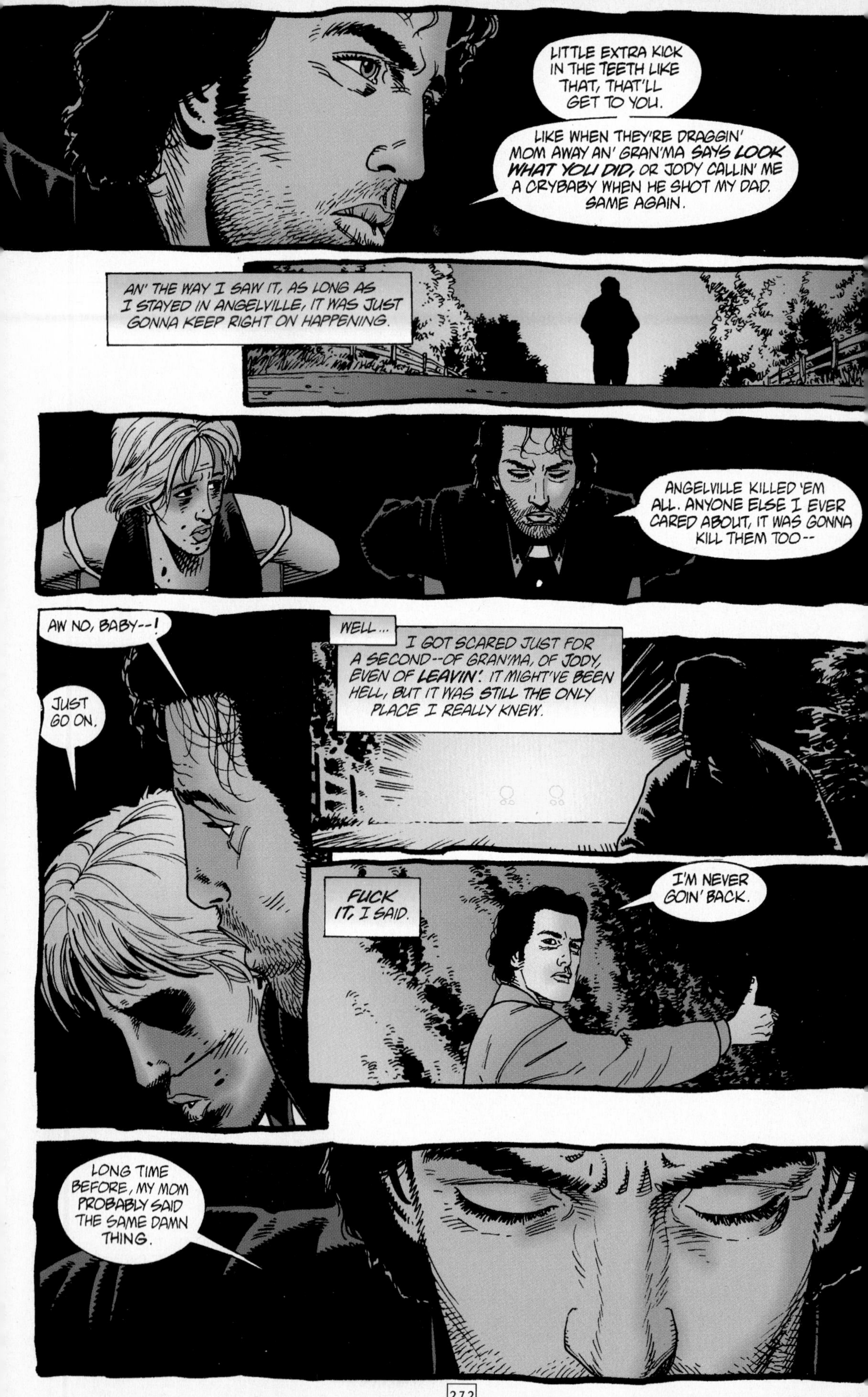
LITTLE EXTRA KICK IN THE TEETH LIKE THAT, THAT'LL GET TO YOU.
LIKE WHEN THEY'RE DRAGGIN' MOM AWAY AN' GRAN'MA **SAYS LOOK WHAT YOU DID,** OR JODY CALLIN' ME A CRYBABY WHEN HE SHOT MY DAD. SAME AGAIN.
AN' THE WAY I SAW IT, AS LONG AS I STAYED IN ANGELVILLE, IT WAS JUST GONNA KEEP RIGHT ON HAPPENING.
ANGELVILLE KILLED 'EM ALL. ANYONE ELSE I EVER CARED ABOUT, IT WAS GONNA KILL THEM TOO--
AW NO, BABY--!
JUST GO ON.
WELL...
I GOT SCARED JUST FOR A SECOND--OF GRAN'MA, OF JODY, EVEN OF **LEAVIN'.** IT MIGHT'VE BEEN HELL, BUT IT WAS **STILL** THE ONLY PLACE I REALLY KNEW.
FUCK IT, I SAID.
I'M NEVER GOIN' BACK.
LONG TIME BEFORE, MY MOM PROBABLY SAID THE SAME DAMN THING.

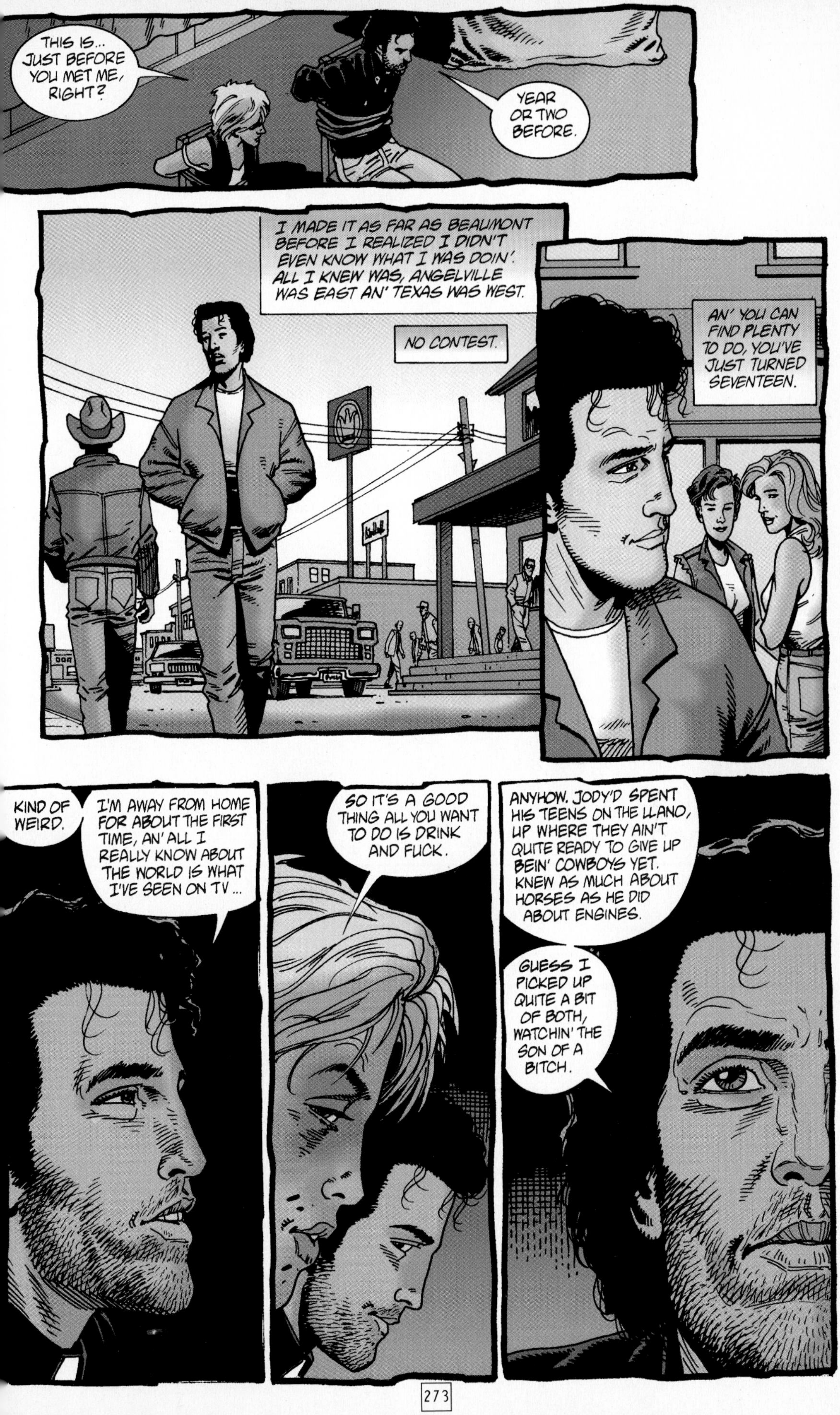
THIS IS... JUST BEFORE YOU MET ME, RIGHT?
YEAR OR TWO BEFORE.
I MADE IT AS FAR AS BEAUMONT BEFORE I REALIZED I DIDN'T EVEN KNOW WHAT I WAS DOIN'. ALL I KNEW WAS, ANGELVILLE WAS EAST AN' TEXAS WAS WEST.
NO CONTEST.
AN' YOU CAN FIND PLENTY TO DO, YOU'VE JUST TURNED SEVENTEEN.
KIND OF WEIRD.
I'M AWAY FROM HOME FOR ABOUT THE FIRST TIME, AN' ALL I REALLY KNOW ABOUT THE WORLD IS WHAT I'VE SEEN ON TV ...
SO IT'S A GOOD THING ALL YOU WANT TO DO IS DRINK AND FUCK.
ANYHOW. JODY'D SPENT HIS TEENS ON THE LLANO, UP WHERE THEY AIN'T QUITE READY TO GIVE UP BEIN' COWBOYS YET. KNEW AS MUCH ABOUT HORSES AS HE DID ABOUT ENGINES.
GUESS I PICKED UP QUITE A BIT OF BOTH, WATCHIN' THE SON OF A BITCH.

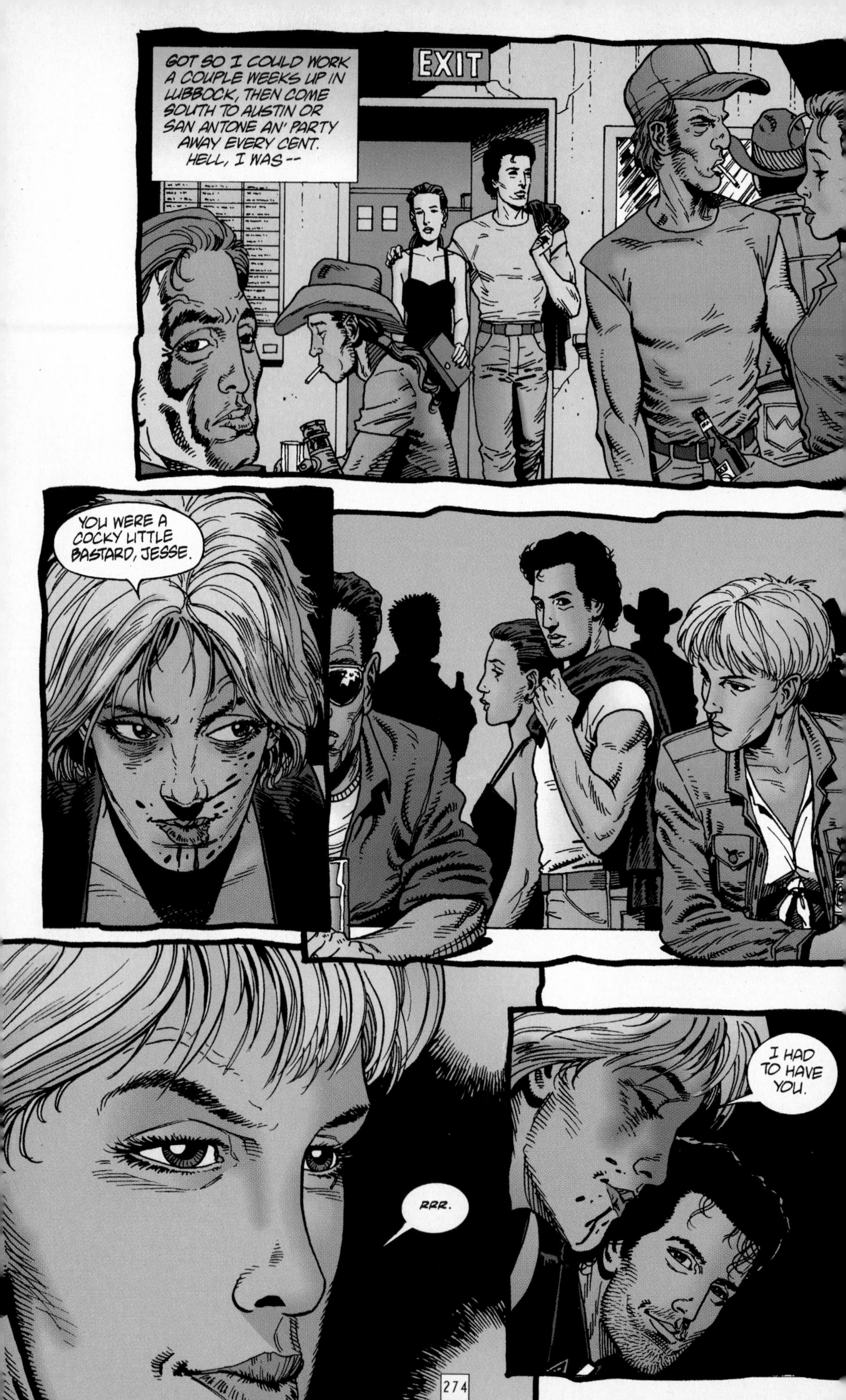
GOT SO I COULD WORK A COUPLE WEEKS UP IN LUBBOCK, THEN COME SOUTH TO AUSTIN OR SAN ANTONE AN' PARTY AWAY EVERY CENT. HELL, I WAS --
EXIT
YOU WERE A COCKY LITTLE BASTARD, JESSE.
RRR.
I HAD TO HAVE YOU.

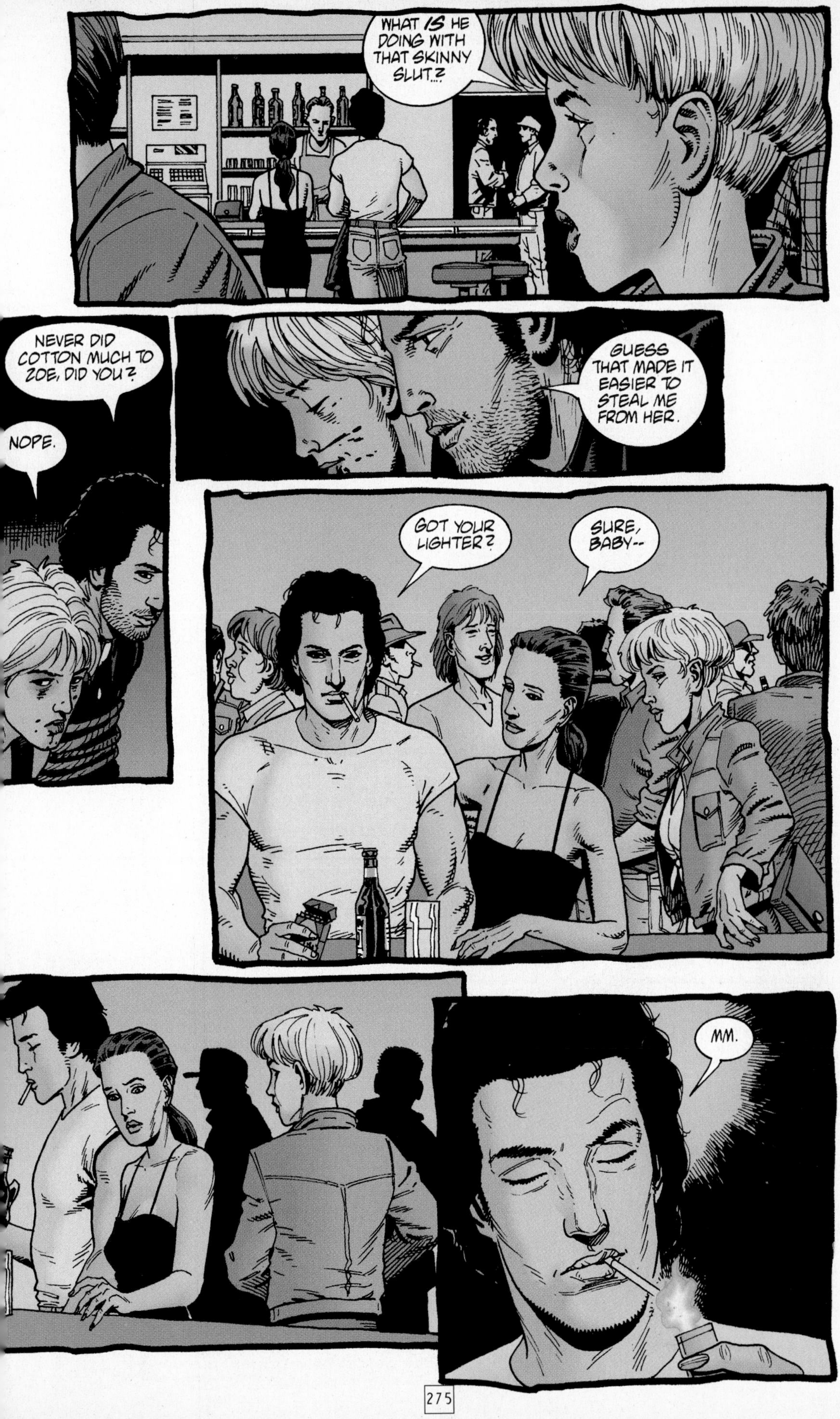
WHAT *IS* HE DOING WITH THAT SKINNY SLUT..?
NEVER DID COTTON MUCH TO ZOE, DID YOU?
NOPE.
GUESS THAT MADE IT EASIER TO STEAL ME FROM HER.
GOT YOUR LIGHTER?
SURE, BABY--
MM.

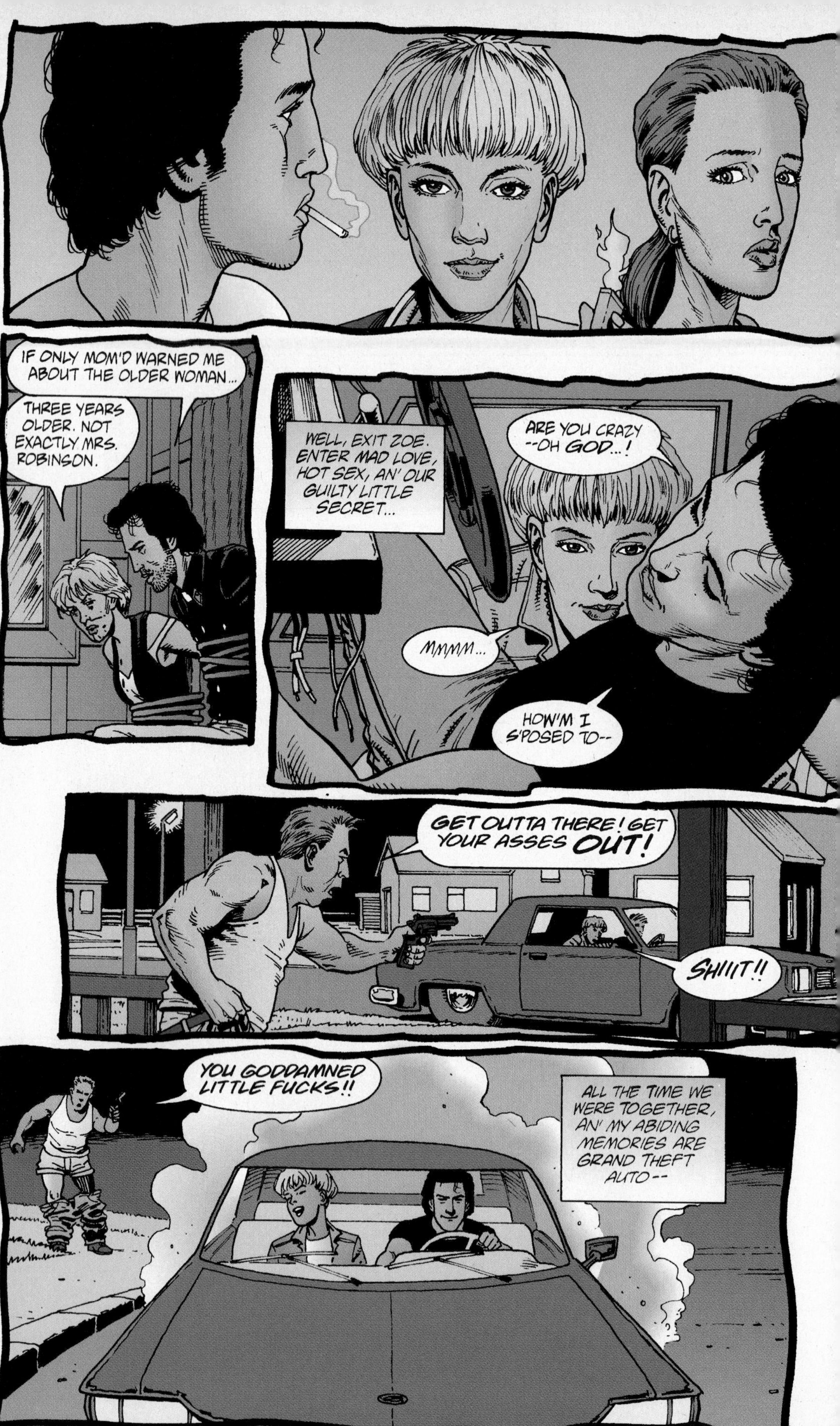
IF ONLY MOM'D WARNED ME ABOUT THE OLDER WOMAN...
THREE YEARS OLDER. NOT EXACTLY MRS. ROBINSON.
WELL, EXIT ZOE. ENTER MAD LOVE, HOT SEX, AN' OUR GUILTY LITTLE SECRET...
ARE YOU CRAZY --OH GOD...!
MMMM...
HOW'M I S'POSED TO--
GET OUTTA THERE! GET YOUR ASSES OUT!
SHIIIT!!
YOU GODDAMNED LITTLE FUCKS!!
ALL THE TIME WE WERE TOGETHER, AN' MY ABIDING MEMORIES ARE GRAND THEFT AUTO--

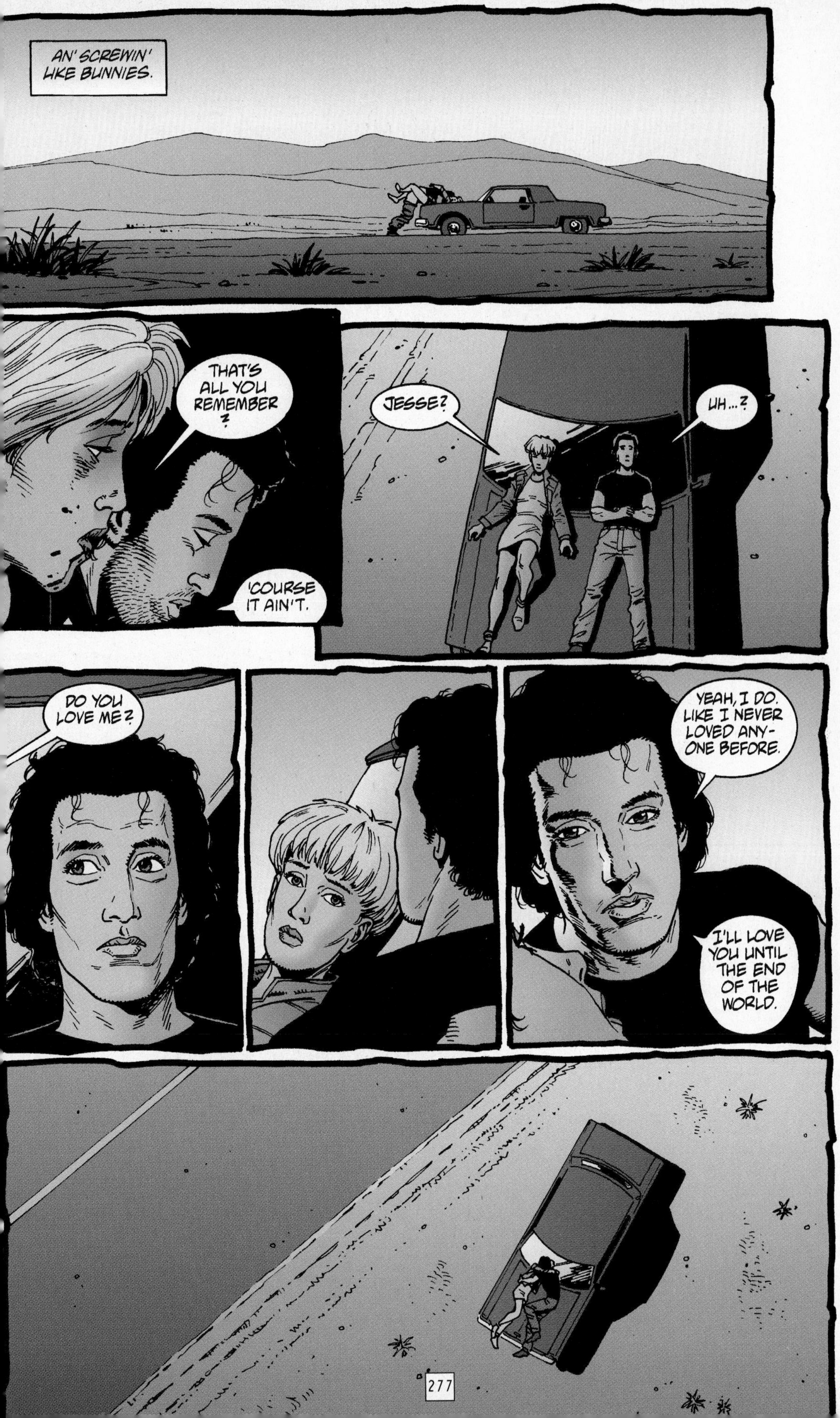
AN' SCREWIN' LIKE BUNNIES.
THAT'S ALL YOU REMEMBER?
'COURSE IT AIN'T.
JESSE?
UH...?
DO YOU LOVE ME?
YEAH, I DO. LIKE I NEVER LOVED ANY-ONE BEFORE.
I'LL LOVE YOU UNTIL THE END OF THE WORLD.

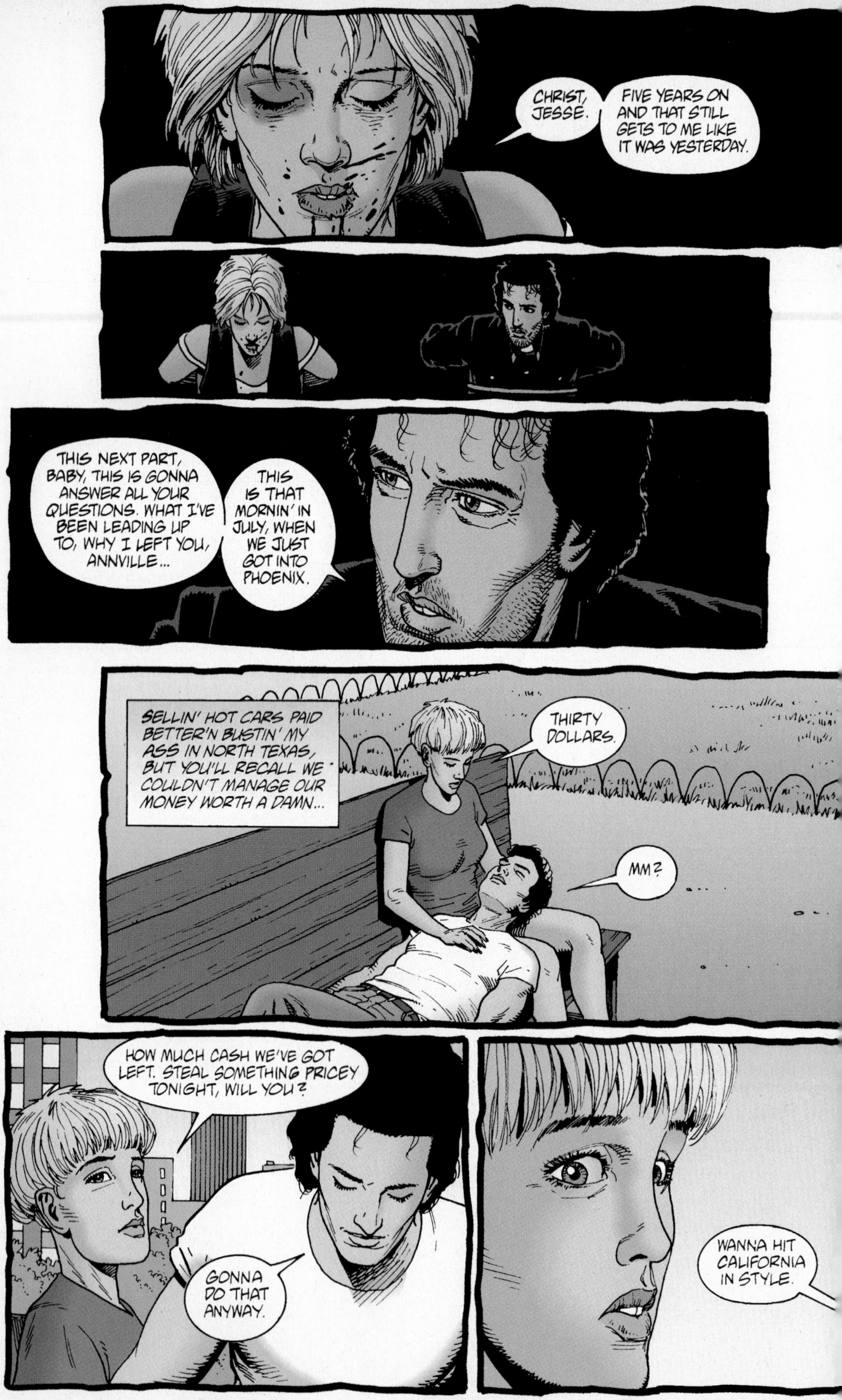
CHRIST, JESSE.
FIVE YEARS ON AND THAT STILL GETS TO ME LIKE IT WAS YESTERDAY.
THIS NEXT PART, BABY, THIS IS GONNA ANSWER ALL YOUR QUESTIONS. WHAT I'VE BEEN LEADING UP TO, WHY I LEFT YOU, ANNVILLE...
THIS IS THAT MORNIN' IN JULY, WHEN WE JUST GOT INTO PHOENIX.
SELLIN' HOT CARS PAID BETTER'N BUSTIN' MY ASS IN NORTH TEXAS, BUT YOU'LL RECALL WE COULDN'T MANAGE OUR MONEY WORTH A DAMN...
THIRTY DOLLARS.
MM?
HOW MUCH CASH WE'VE GOT LEFT. STEAL SOMETHING PRICEY TONIGHT, WILL YOU?
GONNA DO THAT ANYWAY.
WANNA HIT CALIFORNIA IN STYLE.

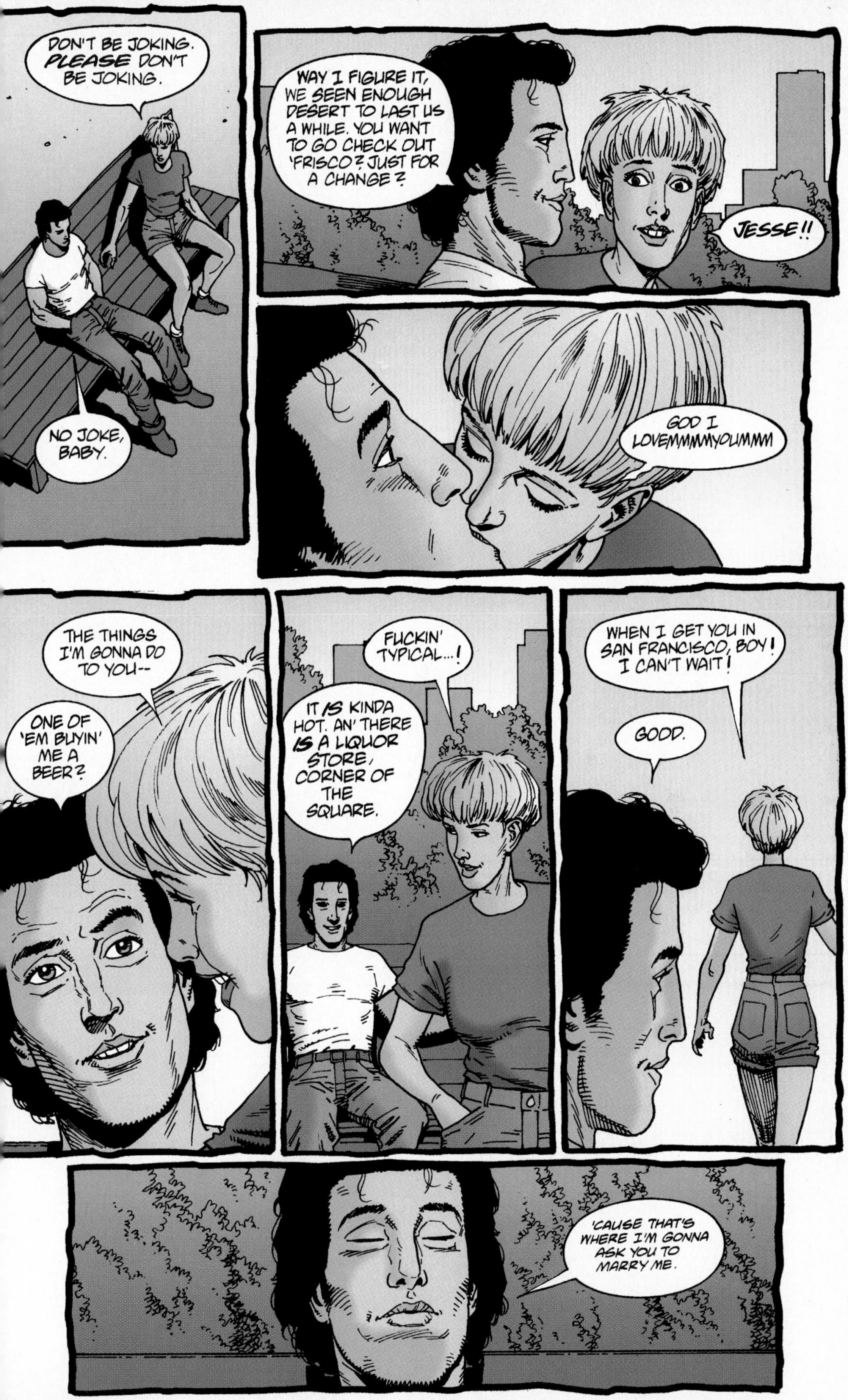
DON'T BE JOKING. PLEASE DON'T BE JOKING.
NO JOKE, BABY.
WAY I FIGURE IT, WE SEEN ENOUGH DESERT TO LAST US A WHILE. YOU WANT TO GO CHECK OUT 'FRISCO? JUST FOR A CHANGE?
JESSE!!
GOD I LOVEMMMMYOUMMM
THE THINGS I'M GONNA DO TO YOU--
ONE OF 'EM BUYIN' ME A BEER?
FUCKIN' TYPICAL...!
IT IS KINDA HOT. AN' THERE IS A LIQUOR STORE, CORNER OF THE SQUARE.
WHEN I GET YOU IN SAN FRANCISCO, BOY! I CAN'T WAIT!
GOOD.
'CAUSE THAT'S WHERE I'M GONNA ASK YOU TO MARRY ME.

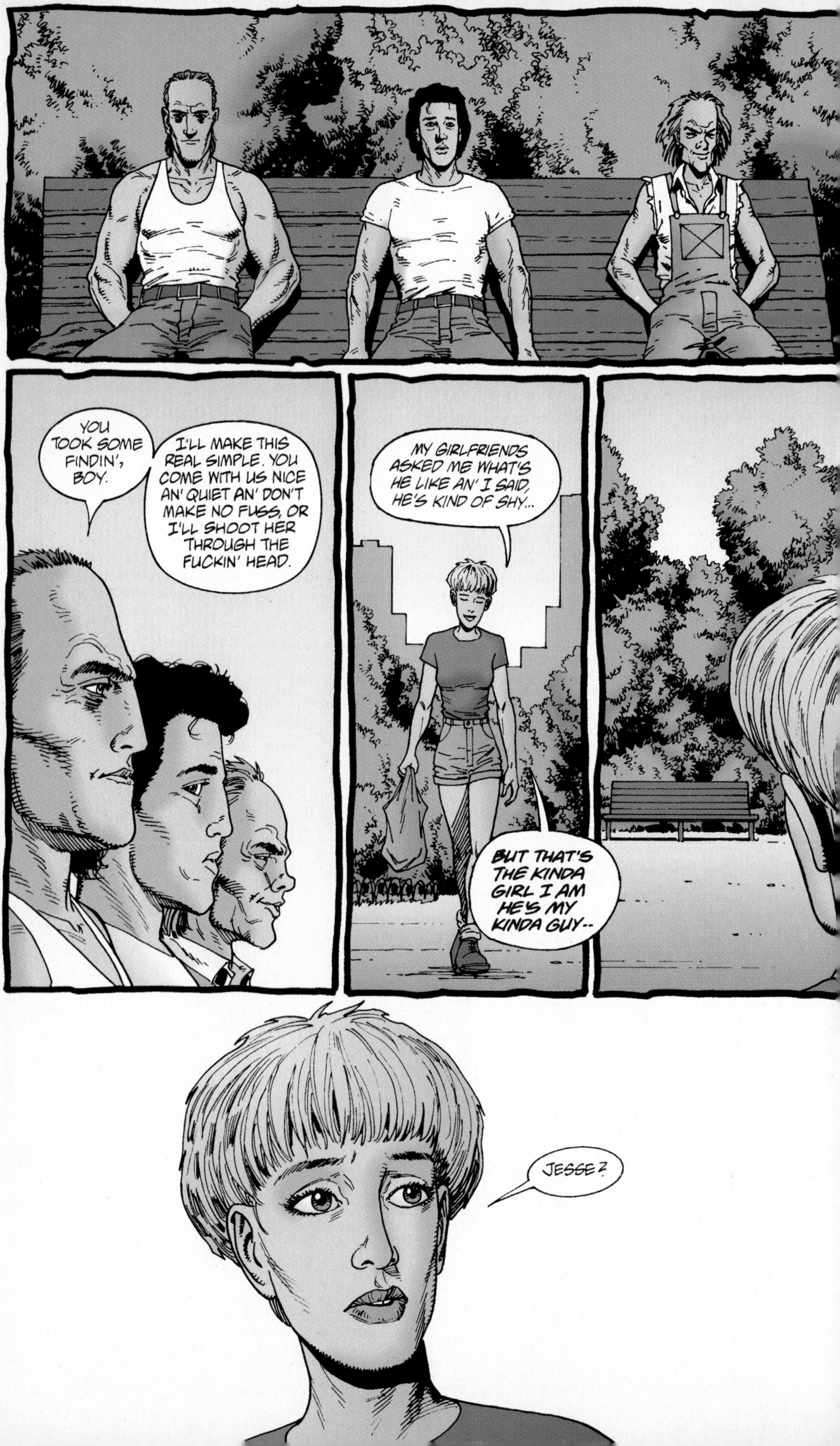
YOU TOOK SOME FINDIN', BOY.
I'LL MAKE THIS REAL SIMPLE. YOU COME WITH US NICE AN' QUIET AN' DON'T MAKE NO FUSS, OR I'LL SHOOT HER THROUGH THE FUCKIN' HEAD.
MY GIRLFRIENDS ASKED ME WHAT'S HE LIKE AN' I SAID, HE'S KIND OF SHY...
BUT THAT'S THE KINDA GIRL I AM HE'S MY KINDA GUY...
JESSE?

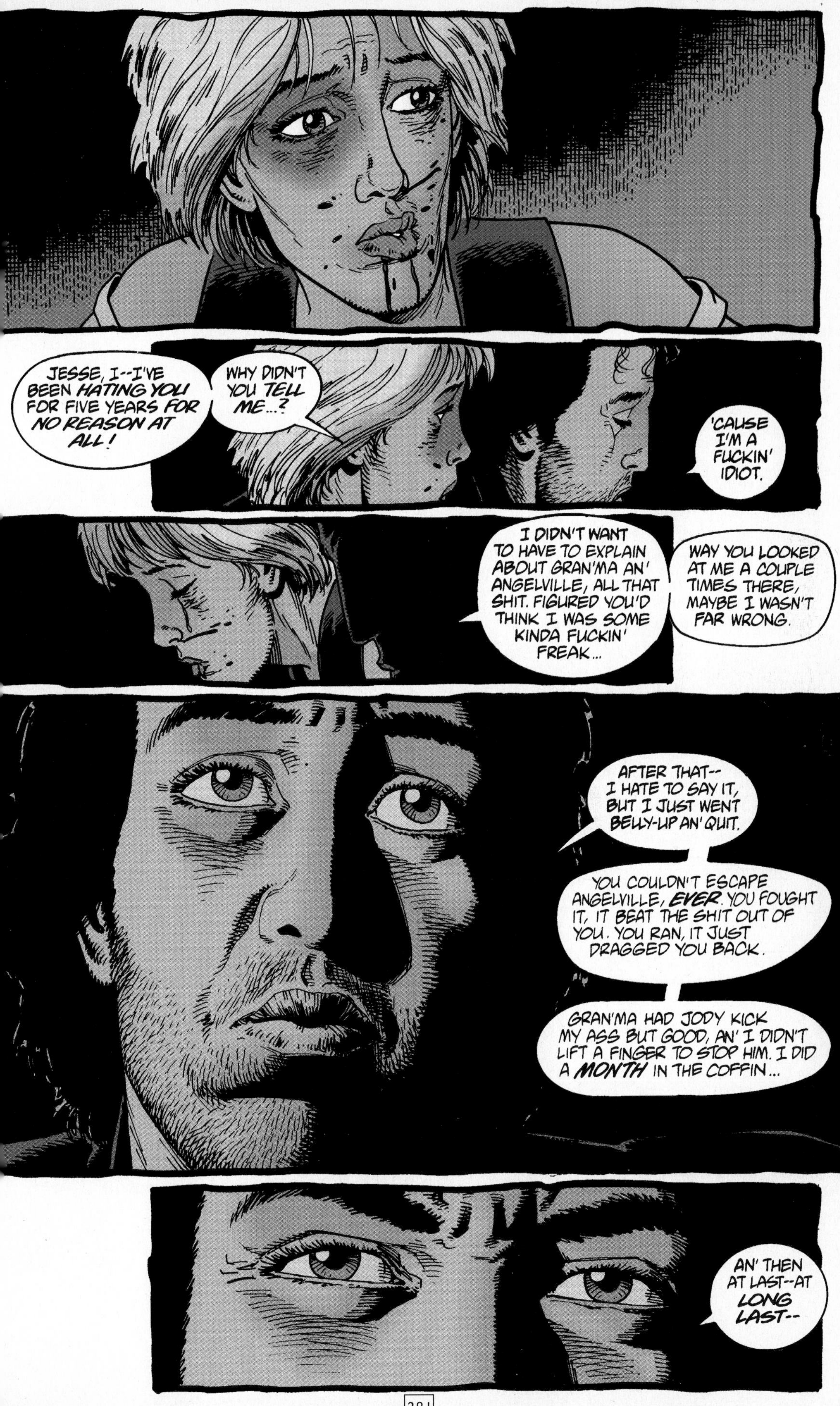

JESSE, I--I'VE BEEN HATING YOU FOR FIVE YEARS FOR NO REASON AT ALL!
WHY DIDN'T YOU TELL ME...?
'CAUSE I'M A FUCKIN' IDIOT.
I DIDN'T WANT TO HAVE TO EXPLAIN ABOUT GRAN'MA AN' ANGELVILLE, ALL THAT SHIT. FIGURED YOU'D THINK I WAS SOME KINDA FUCKIN' FREAK...
WAY YOU LOOKED AT ME A COUPLE TIMES THERE, MAYBE I WASN'T FAR WRONG.
AFTER THAT-- I HATE TO SAY IT, BUT I JUST WENT BELLY-UP AN' QUIT.
YOU COULDN'T ESCAPE ANGELVILLE, EVER. YOU FOUGHT IT, IT BEAT THE SHIT OUT OF YOU. YOU RAN, IT JUST DRAGGED YOU BACK.
GRAN'MA HAD JODY KICK MY ASS BUT GOOD, AN' I DIDN'T LIFT A FINGER TO STOP HIM. I DID A MONTH IN THE COFFIN...
AN' THEN AT LAST--AT LONG LAST--

I TRULY LEARNED TO LOVE THE LORD.

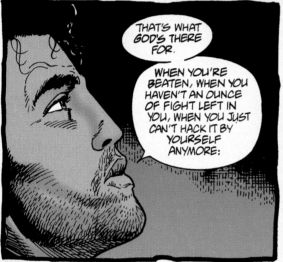

THAT'S WHAT GOD'S THERE FOR.

WHEN YOU'RE BEATEN, WHEN YOU HAVEN'T AN OUNCE OF FIGHT LEFT IN YOU, WHEN YOU JUST CAN'T HACK IT BY YOURSELF ANYMORE:

YOU TURN TO JESUS OR YOU STICK A FUCKIN' GUN IN YOUR MOUTH.

I WAS HAPPY. GRAN'MA WAS HAPPY. HELL, ALL OF US WERE FUCKIN' DELIRIOUS.

SHE PULLED A FEW STRINGS AN' GOT ME PUSHED THROUGH THE MINISTRY IN RECORD TIME. COUPLE OF YEARS AN' REVEREND JESSE CUSTER WAS DOING THE LORD'S WORK AMONG THE GOOD PEOPLE OF ANNVILLE...

AN' THEN, ONE NIGHT NOT SO LONG AGO:

FUCK 'EM.

COUPLE OF YEARS OF THAT, AN' HE WAS PUTTIN' AWAY A BOTTLE OF J.D. A NIGHT.

FUCK 'EM ALL.

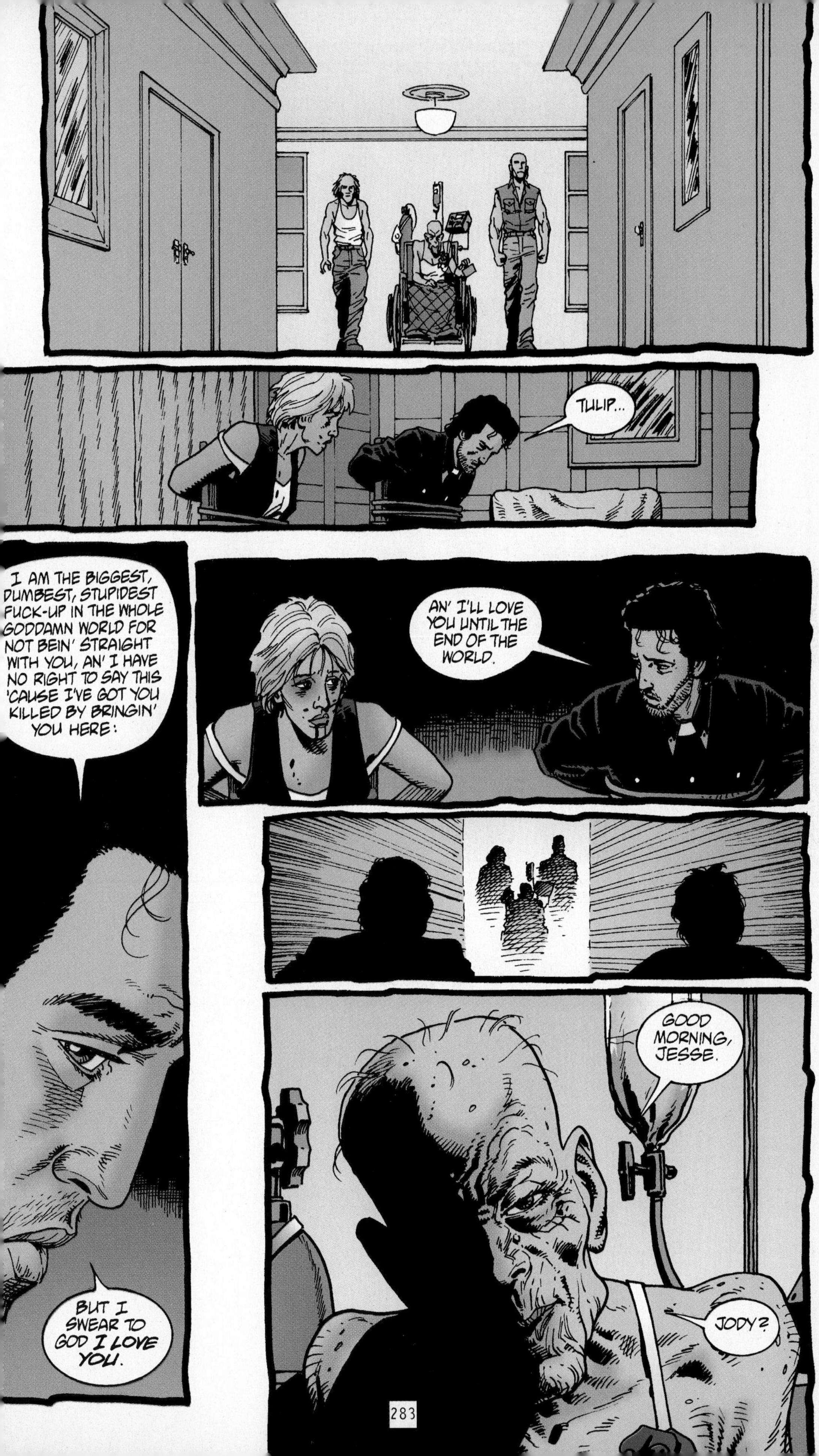
TULIP...
I AM THE BIGGEST, DUMBEST, STUPIDEST FUCK-UP IN THE WHOLE GODDAMN WORLD FOR NOT BEIN' STRAIGHT WITH YOU, AN' I HAVE NO RIGHT TO SAY THIS 'CAUSE I'VE GOT YOU KILLED BY BRINGIN' YOU HERE:
AN' I'LL LOVE YOU UNTIL THE END OF THE WORLD.
BUT I SWEAR TO GOD *I LOVE YOU.*
GOOD MORNING, JESSE.
JODY?

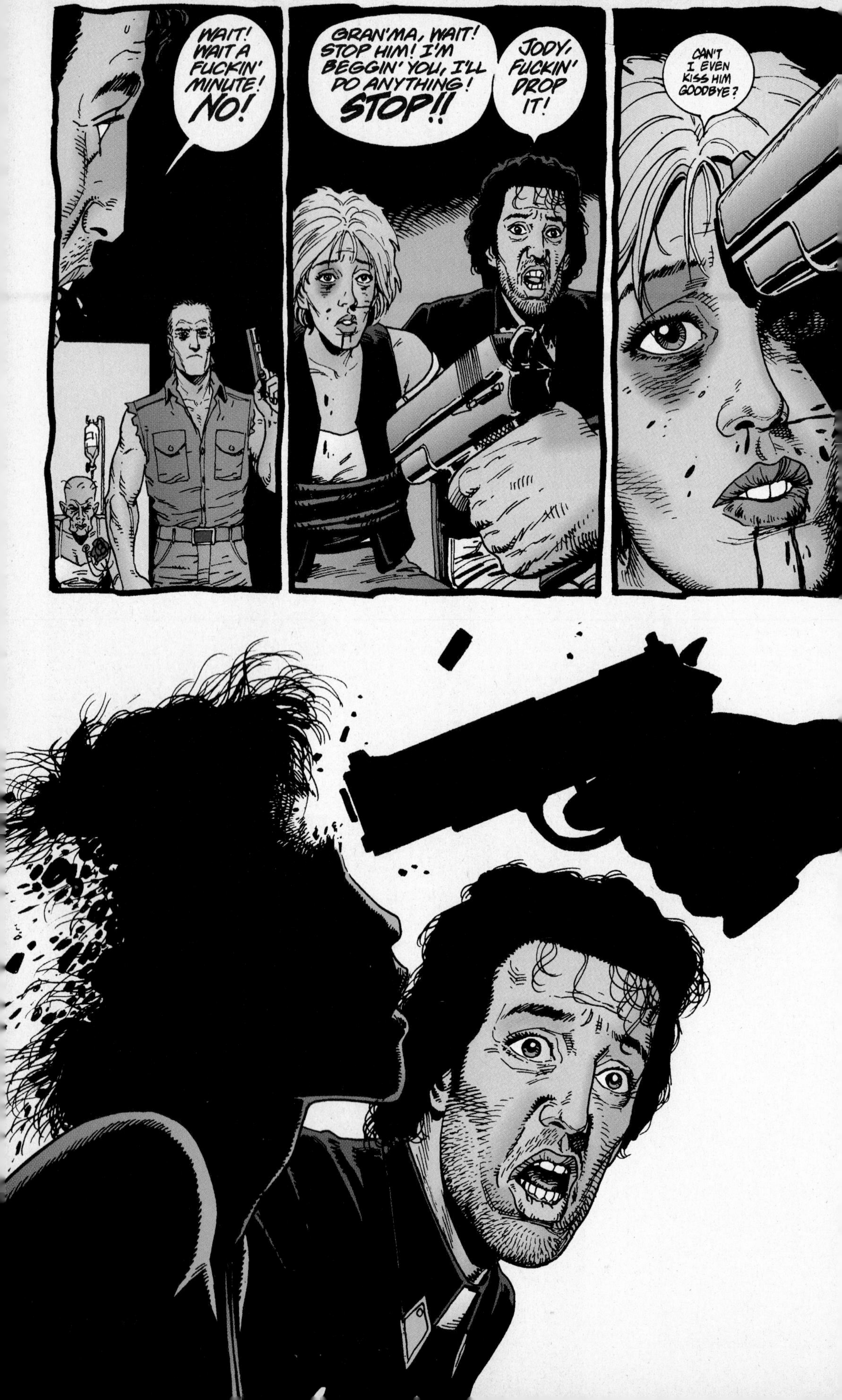
WAIT! WAIT A FUCKIN' MINUTE! NO!
GRAN'MA, WAIT! STOP HIM! I'M BEGGIN' YOU, I'LL DO ANYTHING! STOP!!
JODY, FUCKIN' DROP IT!
CAN'T I EVEN KISS HIM GOODBYE?

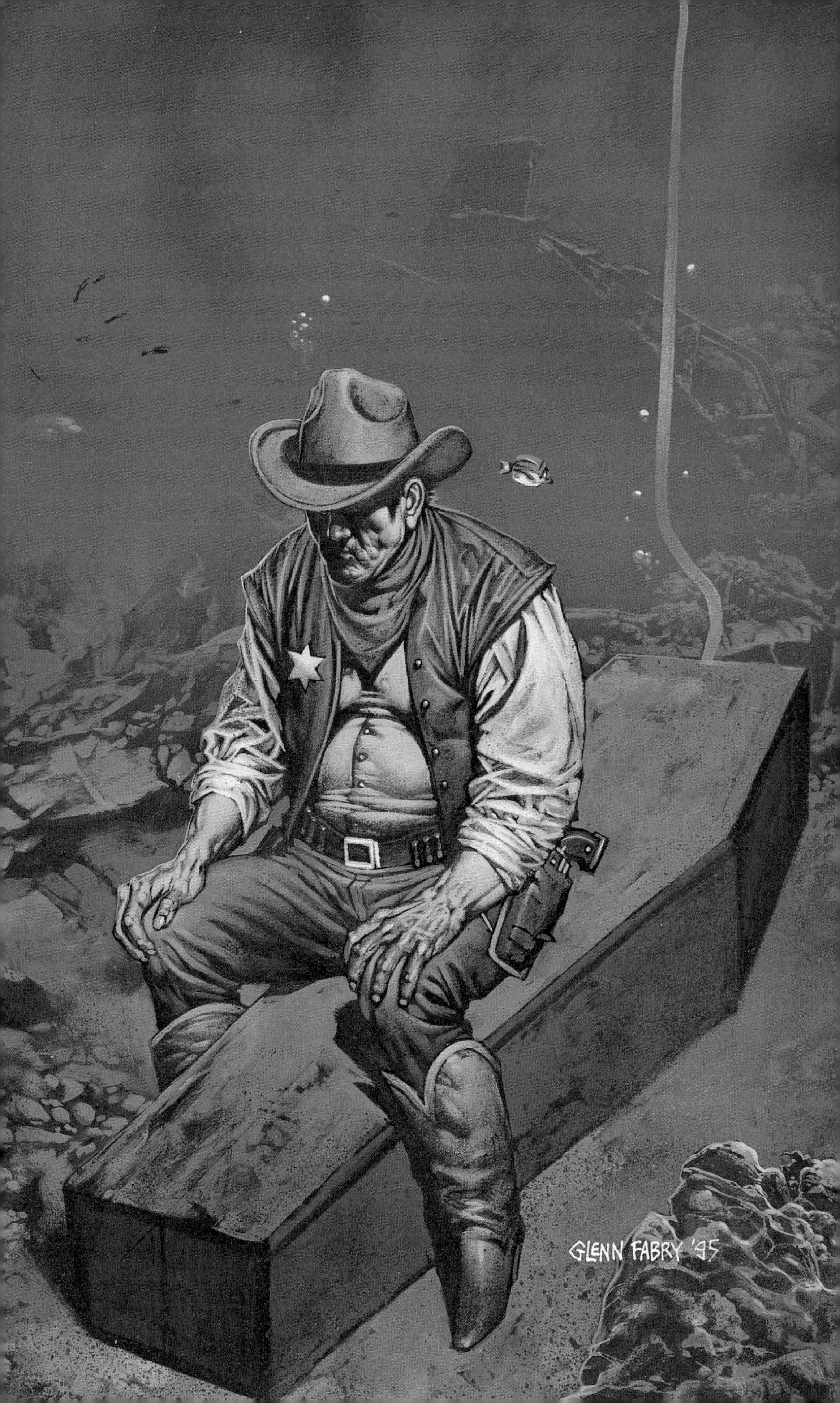
GLENN FABRY '95

"Christ, I think I'd grow old overnight if I lost you."

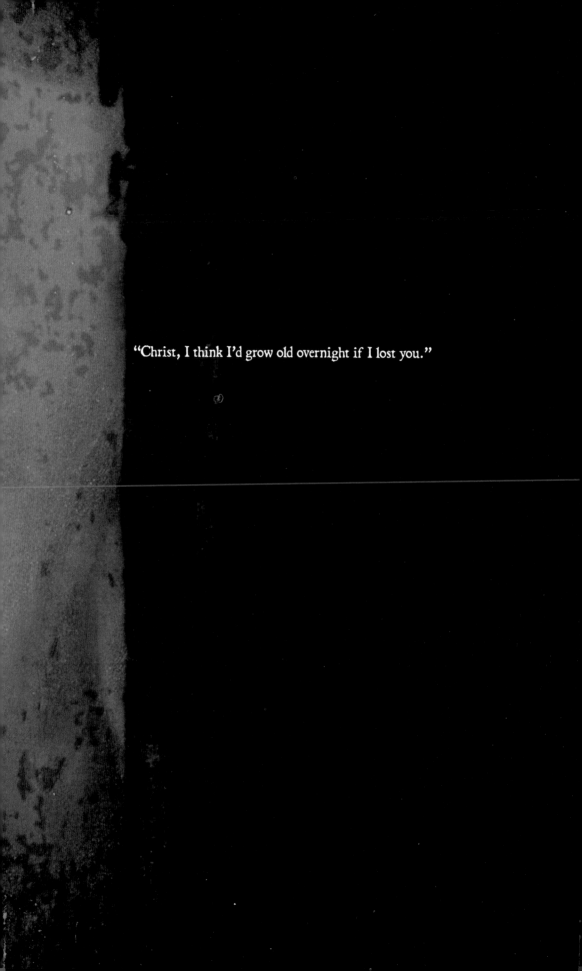

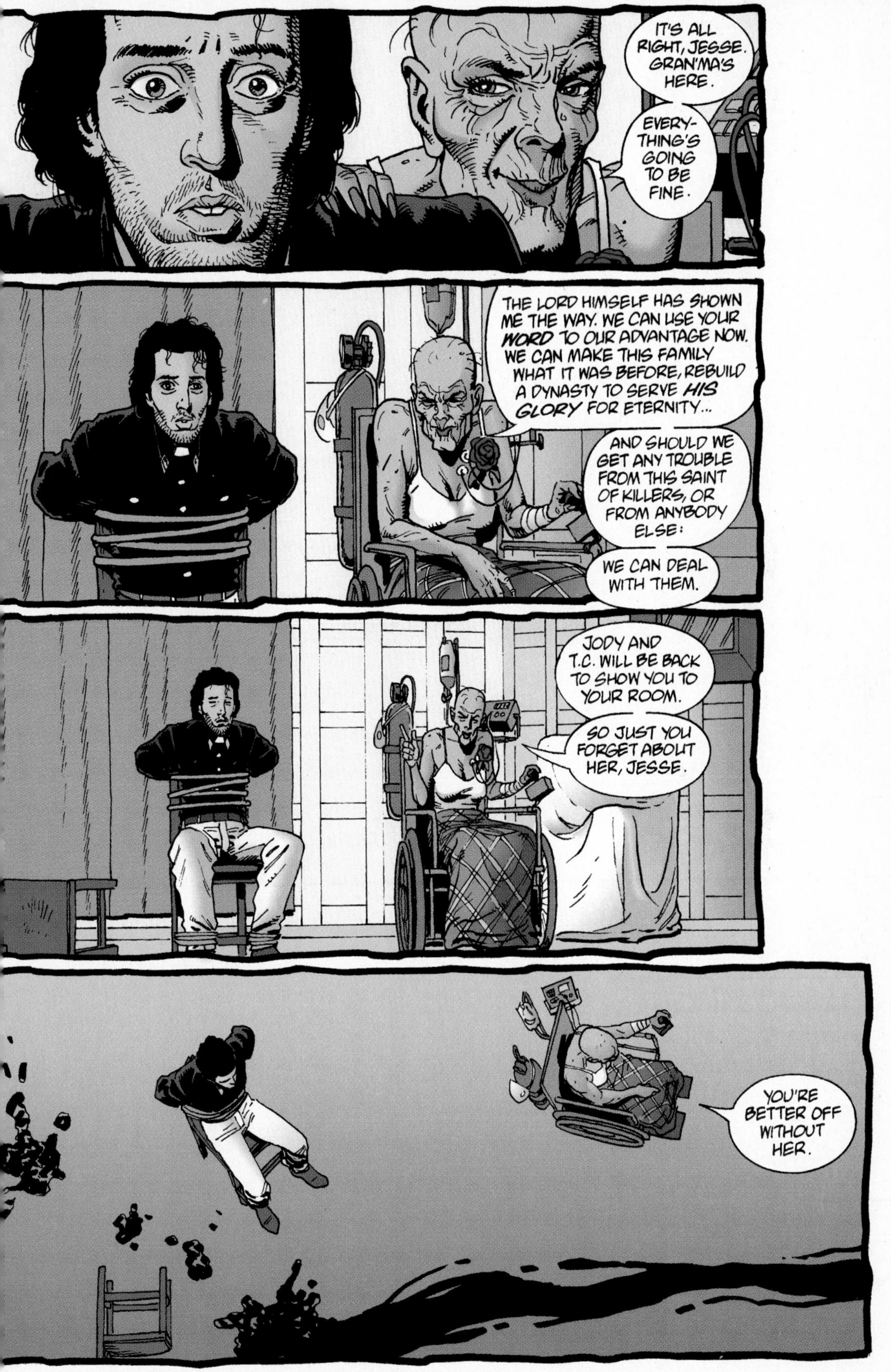
IT'S ALL RIGHT, JESSE. GRAN'MA'S HERE.
EVERY-THING'S GOING TO BE FINE.
THE LORD HIMSELF HAS SHOWN ME THE WAY. WE CAN USE YOUR WORD TO OUR ADVANTAGE NOW. WE CAN MAKE THIS FAMILY WHAT IT WAS BEFORE, REBUILD A DYNASTY TO SERVE HIS GLORY FOR ETERNITY...
AND SHOULD WE GET ANY TROUBLE FROM THIS SAINT OF KILLERS, OR FROM ANYBODY ELSE:
WE CAN DEAL WITH THEM.
JODY AND T.C. WILL BE BACK TO SHOW YOU TO YOUR ROOM.
SO JUST YOU FORGET ABOUT HER, JESSE.
YOU'RE BETTER OFF WITHOUT HER.

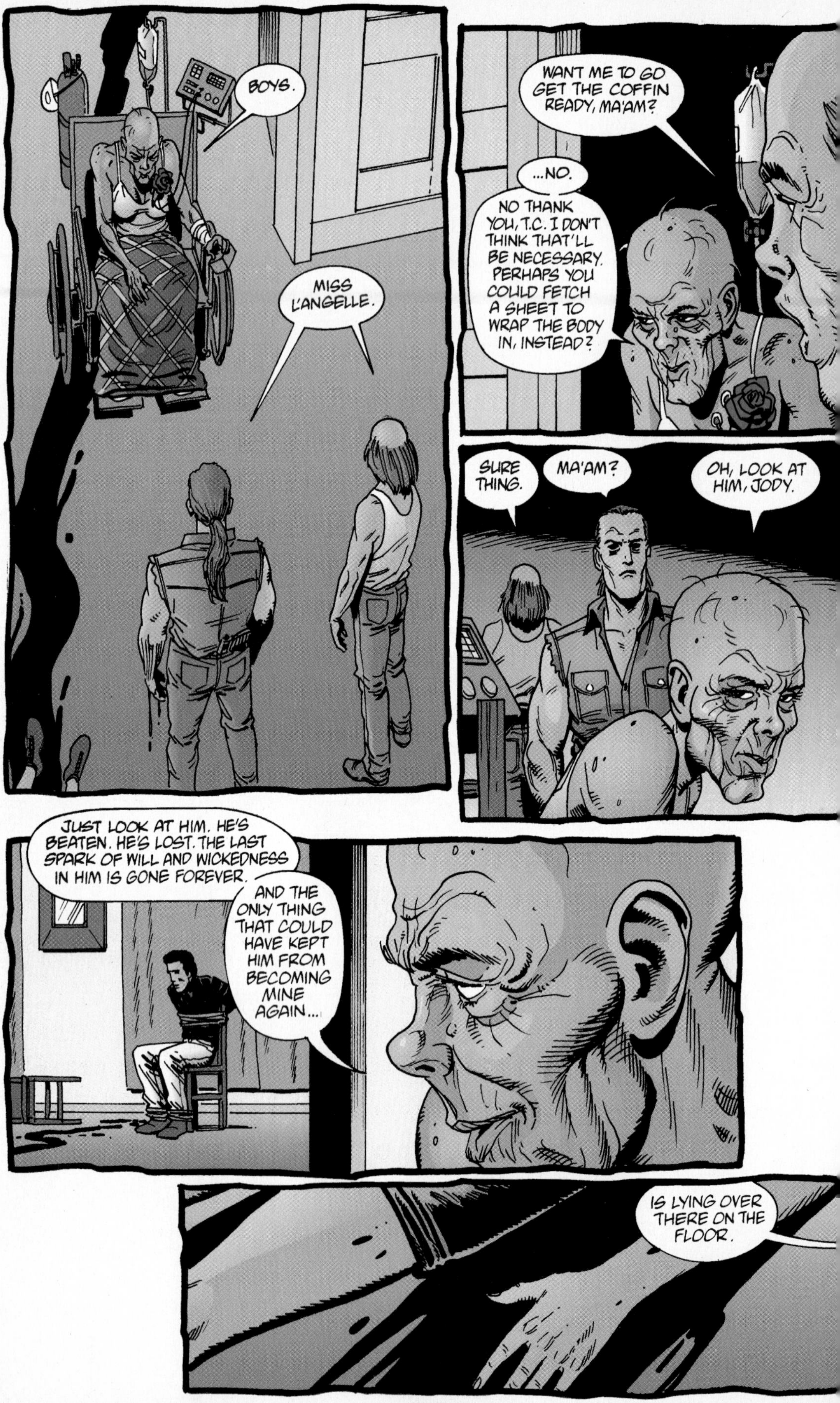

BOYS.
MISS L'ANGELLE.
WANT ME TO GO GET THE COFFIN READY, MA'AM?
...NO.
NO THANK YOU, T.C. I DON'T THINK THAT'LL BE NECESSARY. PERHAPS YOU COULD FETCH A SHEET TO WRAP THE BODY IN, INSTEAD?
SURE THING.
MA'AM?
OH, LOOK AT HIM, JODY.
JUST LOOK AT HIM. HE'S BEATEN. HE'S LOST. THE LAST SPARK OF WILL AND WICKEDNESS IN HIM IS GONE FOREVER.
AND THE ONLY THING THAT COULD HAVE KEPT HIM FROM BECOMING MINE AGAIN...
IS LYING OVER THERE ON THE FLOOR.

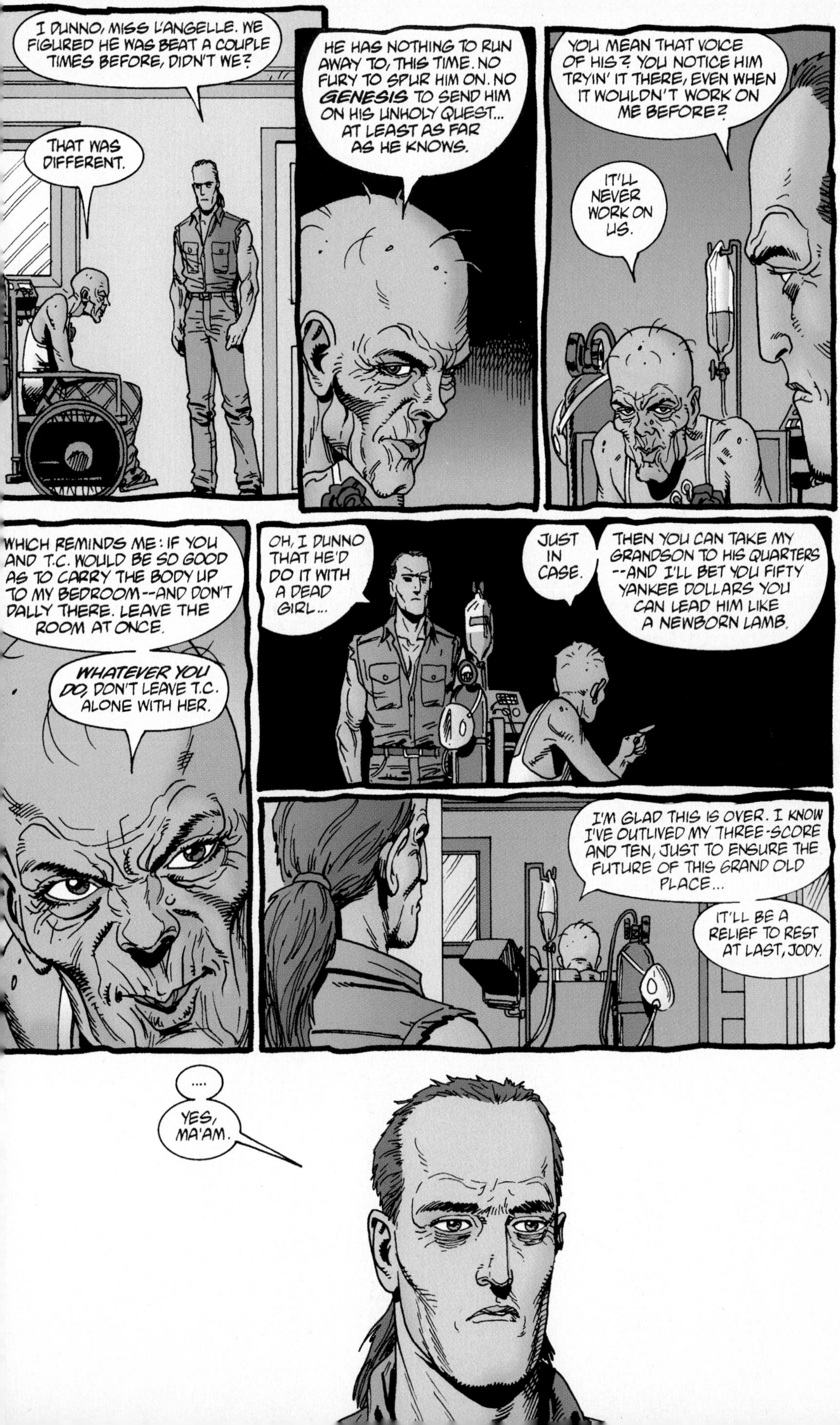
I DUNNO, MISS L'ANGELLE. WE FIGURED HE WAS BEAT A COUPLE TIMES BEFORE, DIDN'T WE?
THAT WAS DIFFERENT.
HE HAS NOTHING TO RUN AWAY TO, THIS TIME. NO FURY TO SPUR HIM ON. NO GENESIS TO SEND HIM ON HIS UNHOLY QUEST... AT LEAST AS FAR AS HE KNOWS.
YOU MEAN THAT VOICE OF HIS? YOU NOTICE HIM TRYIN' IT THERE, EVEN WHEN IT WOULDN'T WORK ON ME BEFORE?
IT'LL NEVER WORK ON US.
WHICH REMINDS ME: IF YOU AND T.C. WOULD BE SO GOOD AS TO CARRY THE BODY UP TO MY BEDROOM--AND DON'T DALLY THERE. LEAVE THE ROOM AT ONCE.
WHATEVER YOU DO, DON'T LEAVE T.C. ALONE WITH HER.
OH, I DUNNO THAT HE'D DO IT WITH A DEAD GIRL...
JUST IN CASE.
THEN YOU CAN TAKE MY GRANDSON TO HIS QUARTERS --AND I'LL BET YOU FIFTY YANKEE DOLLARS YOU CAN LEAD HIM LIKE A NEWBORN LAMB.
I'M GLAD THIS IS OVER. I KNOW I'VE OUTLIVED MY THREE-SCORE AND TEN, JUST TO ENSURE THE FUTURE OF THIS GRAND OLD PLACE...
IT'LL BE A RELIEF TO REST AT LAST, JODY.
....
YES, MA'AM.

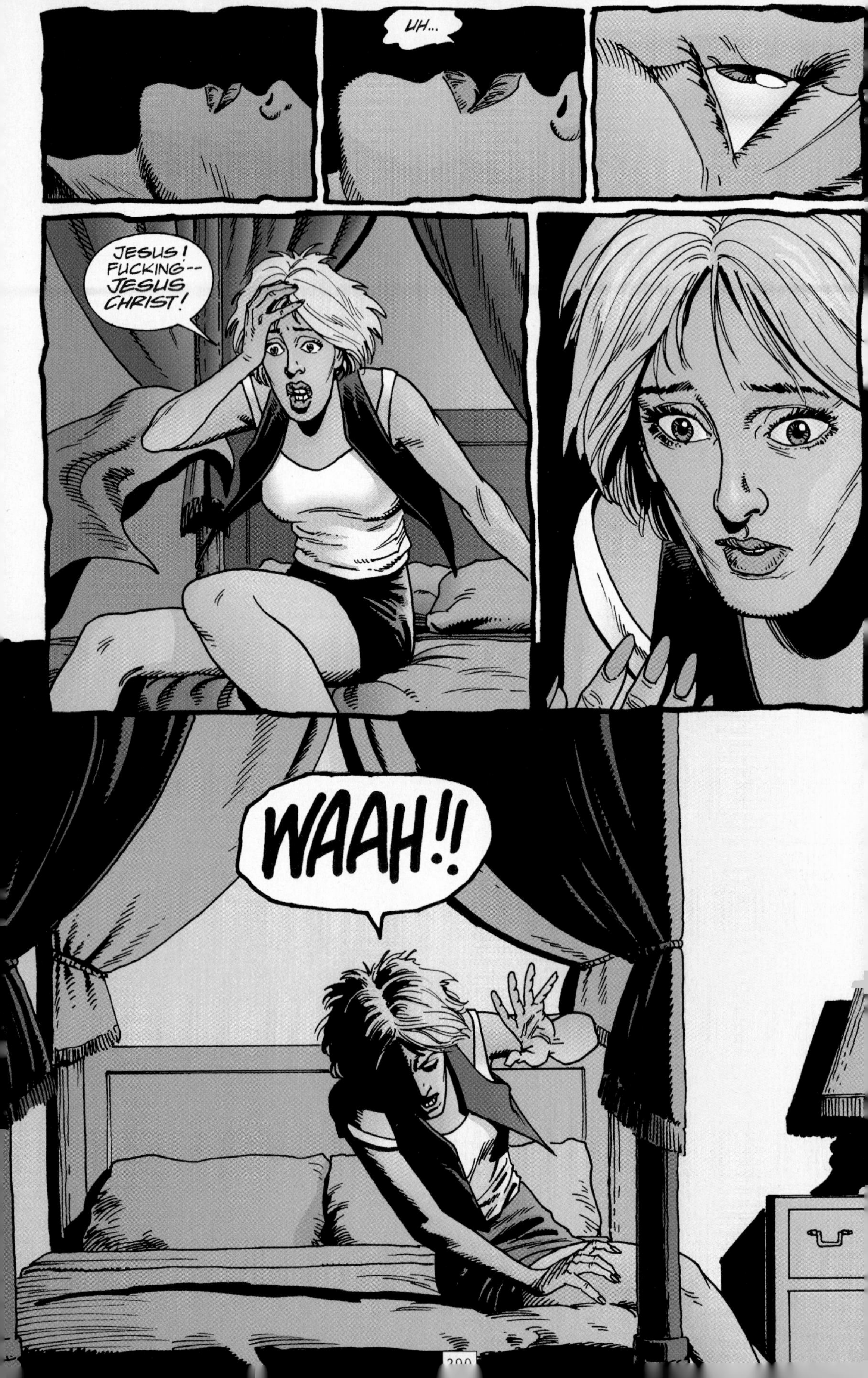
UH...
JESUS! FUCKING-- JESUS CHRIST!
WAAH!!

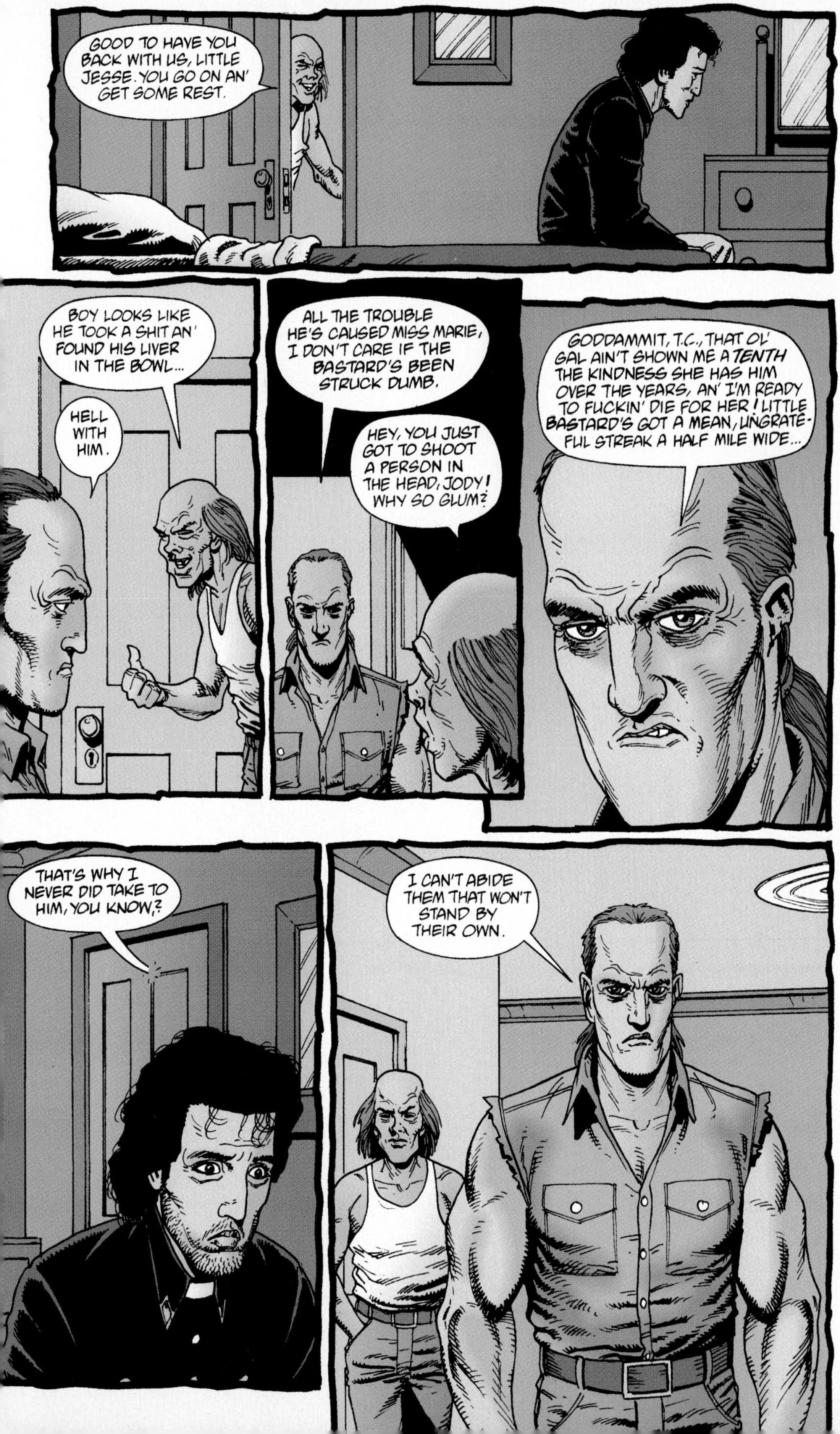

GOOD TO HAVE YOU BACK WITH US, LITTLE JESSE. YOU GO ON AN' GET SOME REST.
BOY LOOKS LIKE HE TOOK A SHIT AN' FOUND HIS LIVER IN THE BOWL...
HELL WITH HIM.
ALL THE TROUBLE HE'S CAUSED MISS MARIE, I DON'T CARE IF THE BASTARD'S BEEN STRUCK DUMB.
HEY, YOU JUST GOT TO SHOOT A PERSON IN THE HEAD, JODY! WHY SO GLUM?
GODDAMMIT, T.C., THAT OL' GAL AIN'T SHOWN ME A TENTH THE KINDNESS SHE HAS HIM OVER THE YEARS, AN' I'M READY TO FUCKIN' DIE FOR HER! LITTLE BASTARD'S GOT A MEAN, UNGRATEFUL STREAK A HALF MILE WIDE...
THAT'S WHY I NEVER DID TAKE TO HIM, YOU KNOW?
I CAN'T ABIDE THEM THAT WON'T STAND BY THEIR OWN.

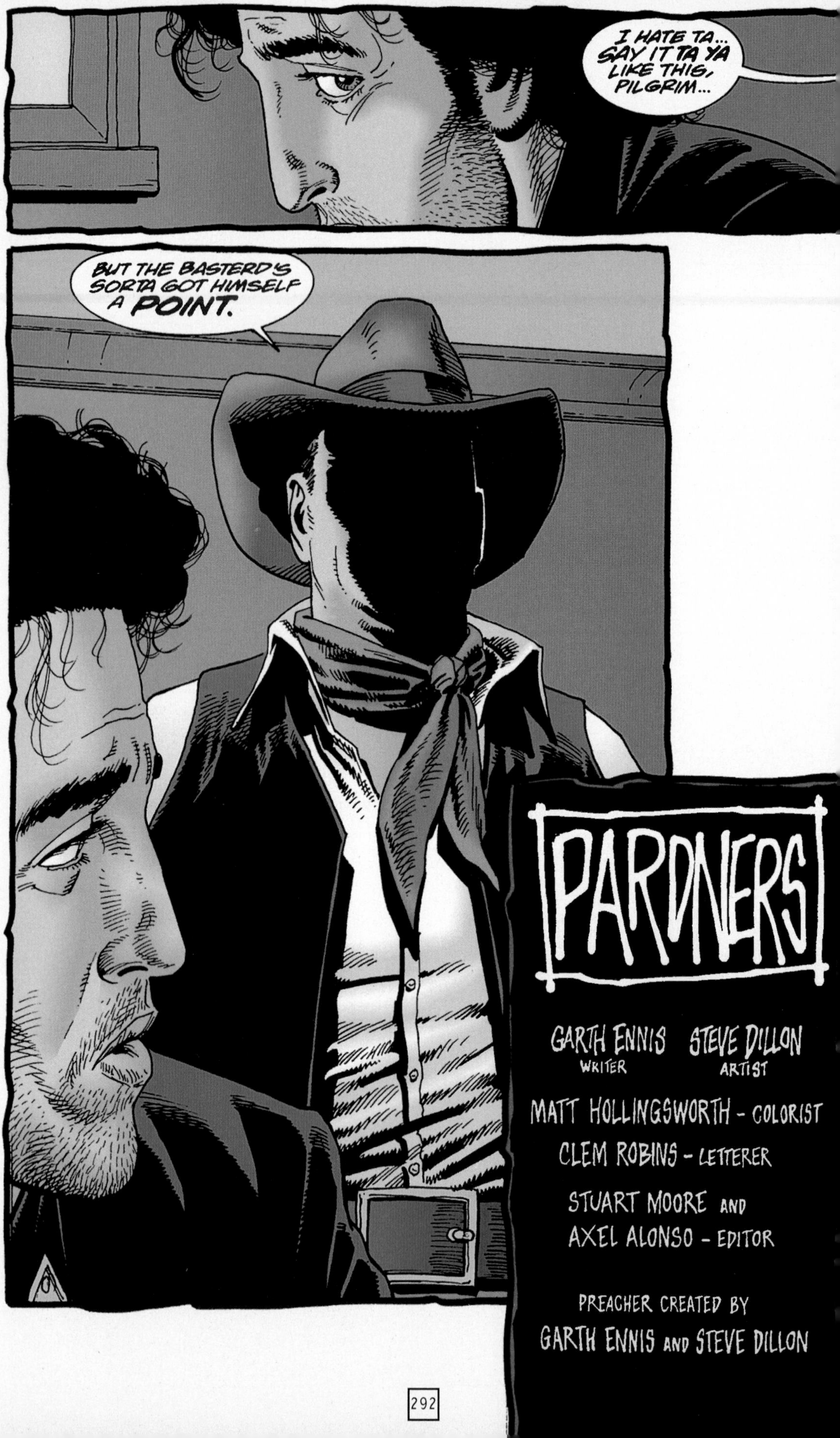
I HATE TA... SAY IT TA YA LIKE THIS, PILGRIM...
BUT THE BASTERD'S SORTA GOT HIMSELF A POINT.
PARDNERS
GARTH ENNIS WRITER
STEVE DILLON ARTIST
MATT HOLLINGSWORTH - COLORIST
CLEM ROBINS - LETTERER
STUART MOORE AND
AXEL ALONSO - EDITOR
PREACHER CREATED BY
GARTH ENNIS AND STEVE DILLON

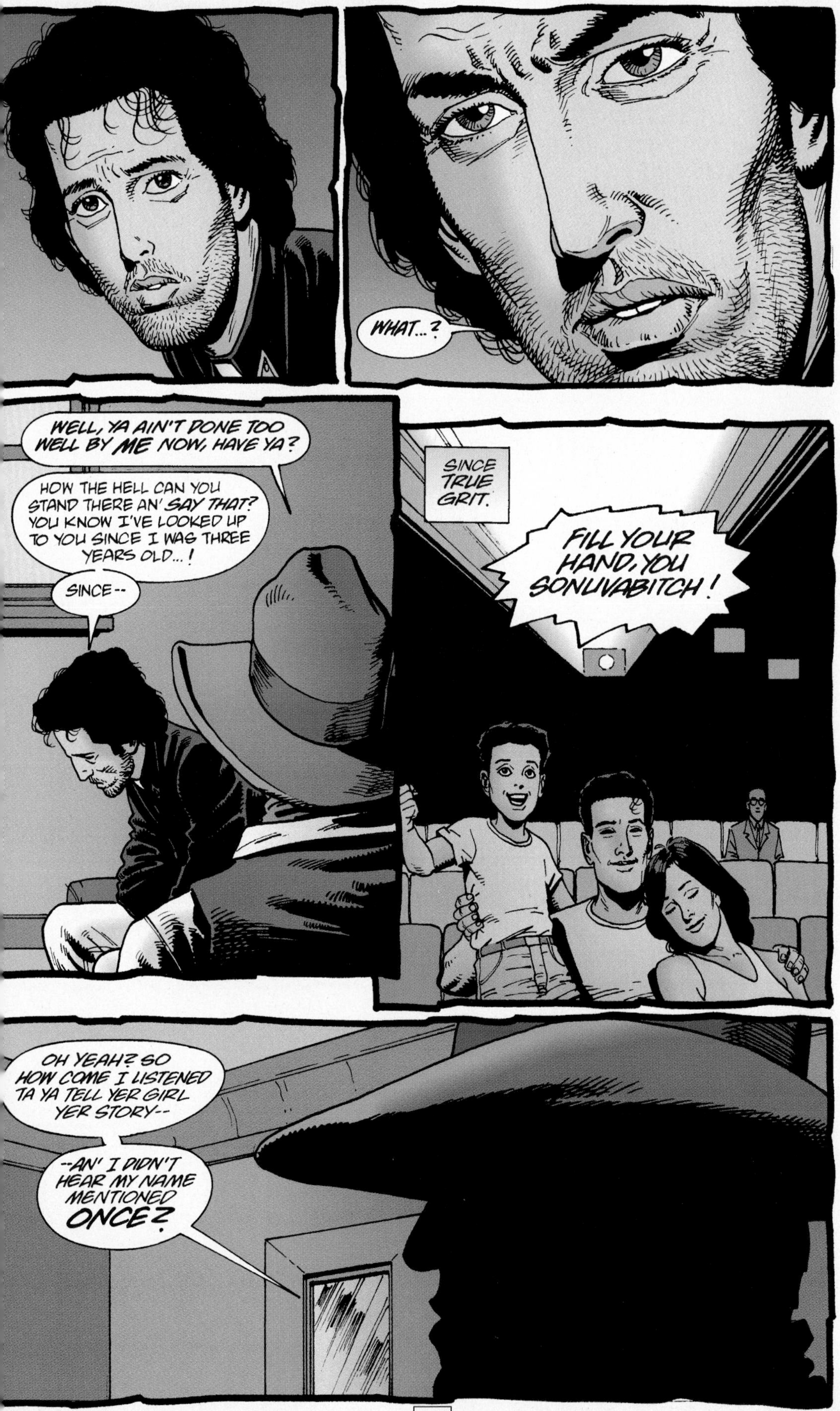
WHAT...?
WELL, YA AIN'T DONE TOO WELL BY ME NOW, HAVE YA?
HOW THE HELL CAN YOU STAND THERE AN' SAY THAT? YOU KNOW I'VE LOOKED UP TO YOU SINCE I WAS THREE YEARS OLD...!
SINCE--
SINCE TRUE GRIT.
FILL YOUR HAND, YOU SONUVABITCH!
OH YEAH? SO HOW COME I LISTENED TA YA TELL YER GIRL YER STORY--
--AN' I DIDN'T HEAR MY NAME MENTIONED ONCE?

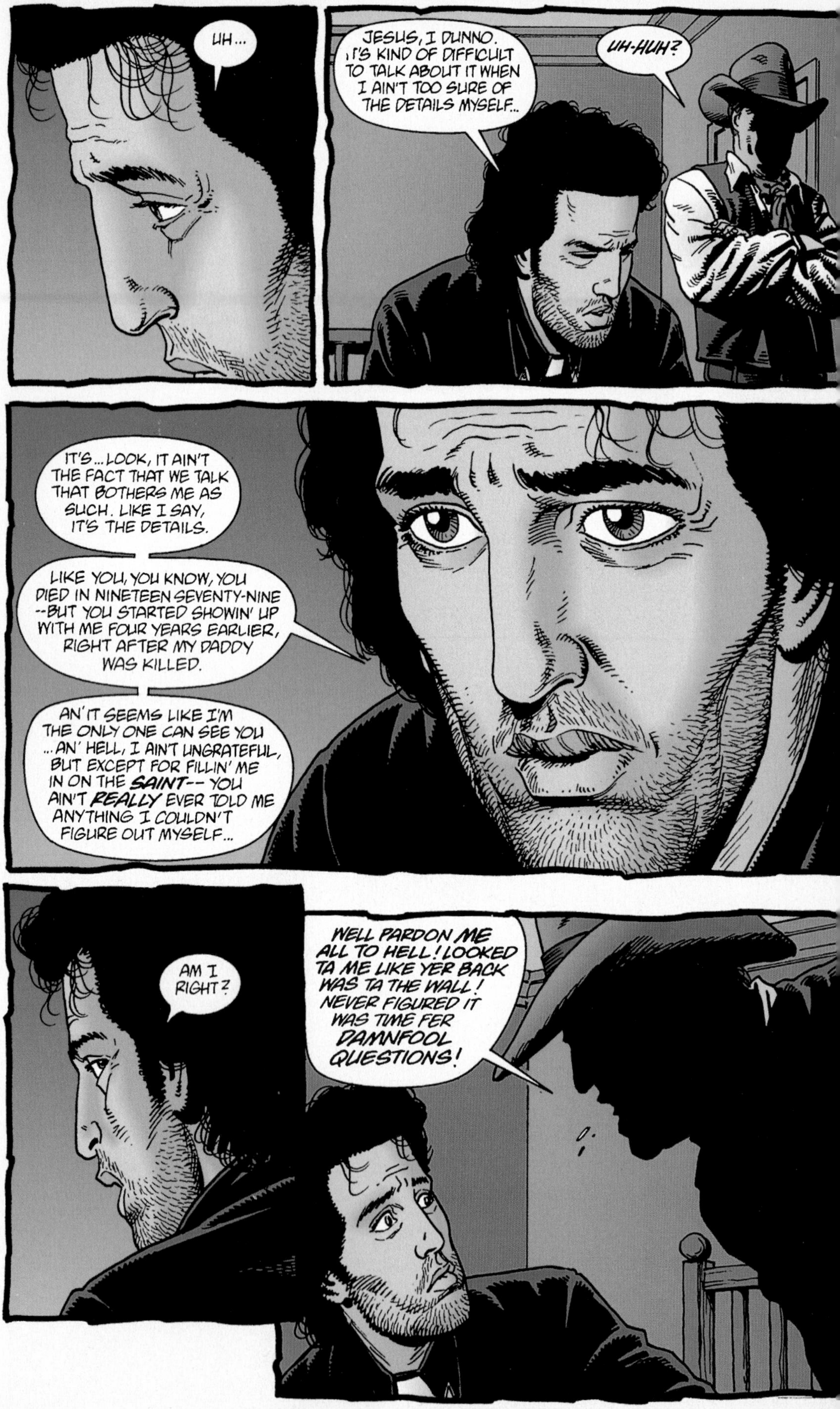
UH...
JESUS, I DUNNO. IT'S KIND OF DIFFICULT TO TALK ABOUT IT WHEN I AIN'T TOO SURE OF THE DETAILS MYSELF..
UH-HUH?
IT'S... LOOK, IT AIN'T THE FACT THAT WE TALK THAT BOTHERS ME AS SUCH. LIKE I SAY, IT'S THE DETAILS.
LIKE YOU, YOU KNOW, YOU DIED IN NINETEEN SEVENTY-NINE --BUT YOU STARTED SHOWIN' UP WITH ME FOUR YEARS EARLIER, RIGHT AFTER MY DADDY WAS KILLED.
AN' IT SEEMS LIKE I'M THE ONLY ONE CAN SEE YOU ...AN' HELL, I AIN'T UNGRATEFUL, BUT EXCEPT FOR FILLIN' ME IN ON THE SAINT-- YOU AIN'T REALLY EVER TOLD ME ANYTHING I COULDN'T FIGURE OUT MYSELF...
AM I RIGHT?
WELL PARDON ME ALL TO HELL! LOOKED TA ME LIKE YER BACK WAS TA THE WALL! NEVER FIGURED IT WAS TIME FER DAMNFOOL QUESTIONS!

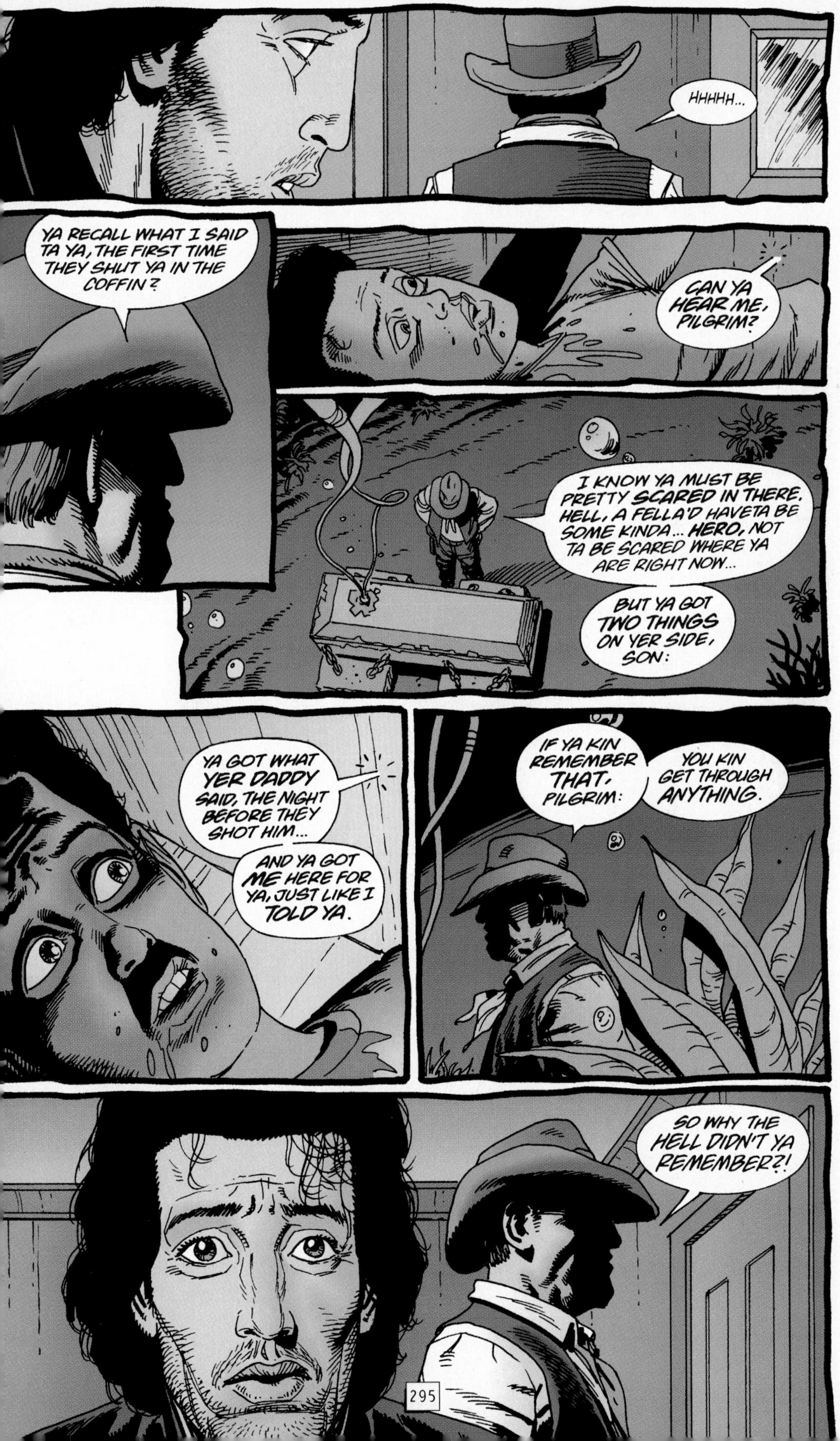
HHHHH...
YA RECALL WHAT I SAID TA YA, THE FIRST TIME THEY SHUT YA IN THE COFFIN?
CAN YA HEAR ME, PILGRIM?
I KNOW YA MUST BE PRETTY SCARED IN THERE. HELL, A FELLA'D HAVETA BE SOME KINDA... HERO, NOT TA BE SCARED WHERE YA ARE RIGHT NOW...
BUT YA GOT TWO THINGS ON YER SIDE, SON:
YA GOT WHAT YER DADDY SAID, THE NIGHT BEFORE THEY SHOT HIM...
AND YA GOT ME HERE FOR YA, JUST LIKE I TOLD YA.
IF YA KIN REMEMBER THAT, PILGRIM:
YOU KIN GET THROUGH ANYTHING.
SO WHY THE HELL DIDN'T YA REMEMBER?!

TALKING TO HIMSELF?

YES, MA'AM. I'M WALKIN' PAST HIS ROOM WHEN I HEAR HIM, SO I TAKE A PEEK THROUGH THE KEYHOLE. BOY'S SITTIN' ON HIS BED, MUMBLIN' AWAY LIKE A FOOL.

DAMN WORDS DON'T EVEN MAKE SENSE...

AH.

THINK MAYBE WE GOT HIM A LITTLE TOO BEAT, MISS L'ANGELLE?

POSSIBLY SO.

IT'D BE A SHAME. I HAD SUCH HOPES FOR JESSE...

BUT EVEN A MADMAN CAN STILL FATHER CHILDREN.

WE'LL SEE HOW HE IS AFTER A DAY'S REST. LOOK IN ON HIM AT SUNDOWN, T.C.

YES, MA'AM.

AN' TAKE THE TWELVE-GAUGE, 'CASE THE SON OF A BITCH IS FAKIN'.

JODY?

MA'AM?

WHEN YOU LEFT THE BODY OF THE WHORE IN MY BEDROOM ...DID YOU HAPPEN TO NOTICE ANY-ONE ELSE THERE?

NO MA'AM.

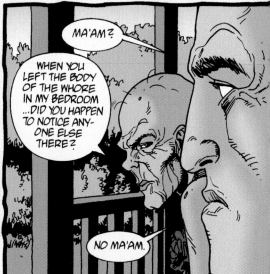

296

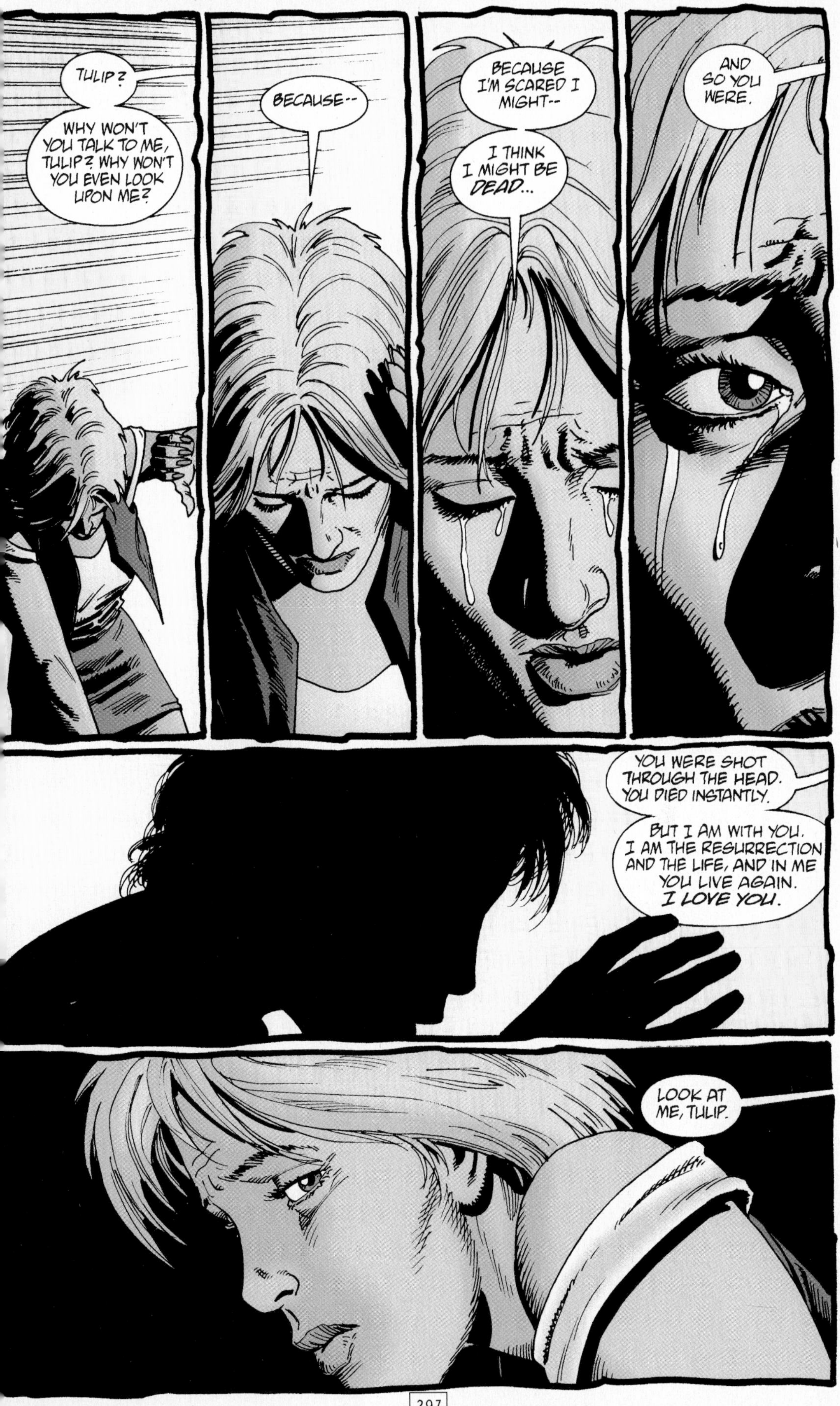
TULIP?
WHY WON'T YOU TALK TO ME, TULIP? WHY WON'T YOU EVEN LOOK UPON ME?
BECAUSE--
BECAUSE I'M SCARED I MIGHT--
I THINK I MIGHT BE DEAD...
AND SO YOU WERE.
YOU WERE SHOT THROUGH THE HEAD. YOU DIED INSTANTLY.
BUT I AM WITH YOU. I AM THE RESURRECTION AND THE LIFE, AND IN ME YOU LIVE AGAIN. I LOVE YOU.
LOOK AT ME, TULIP.

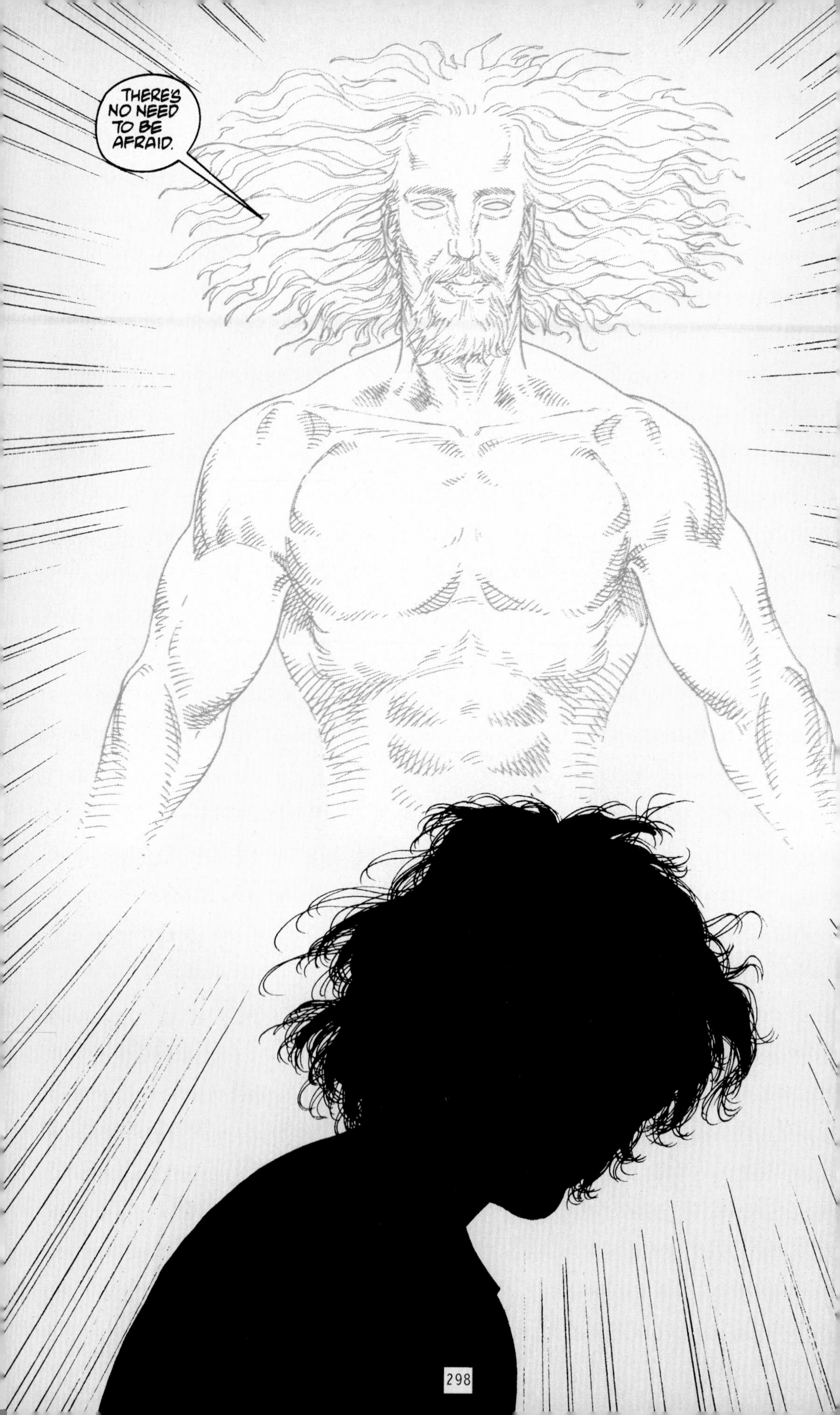
THERE'S NO NEED TO BE AFRAID.

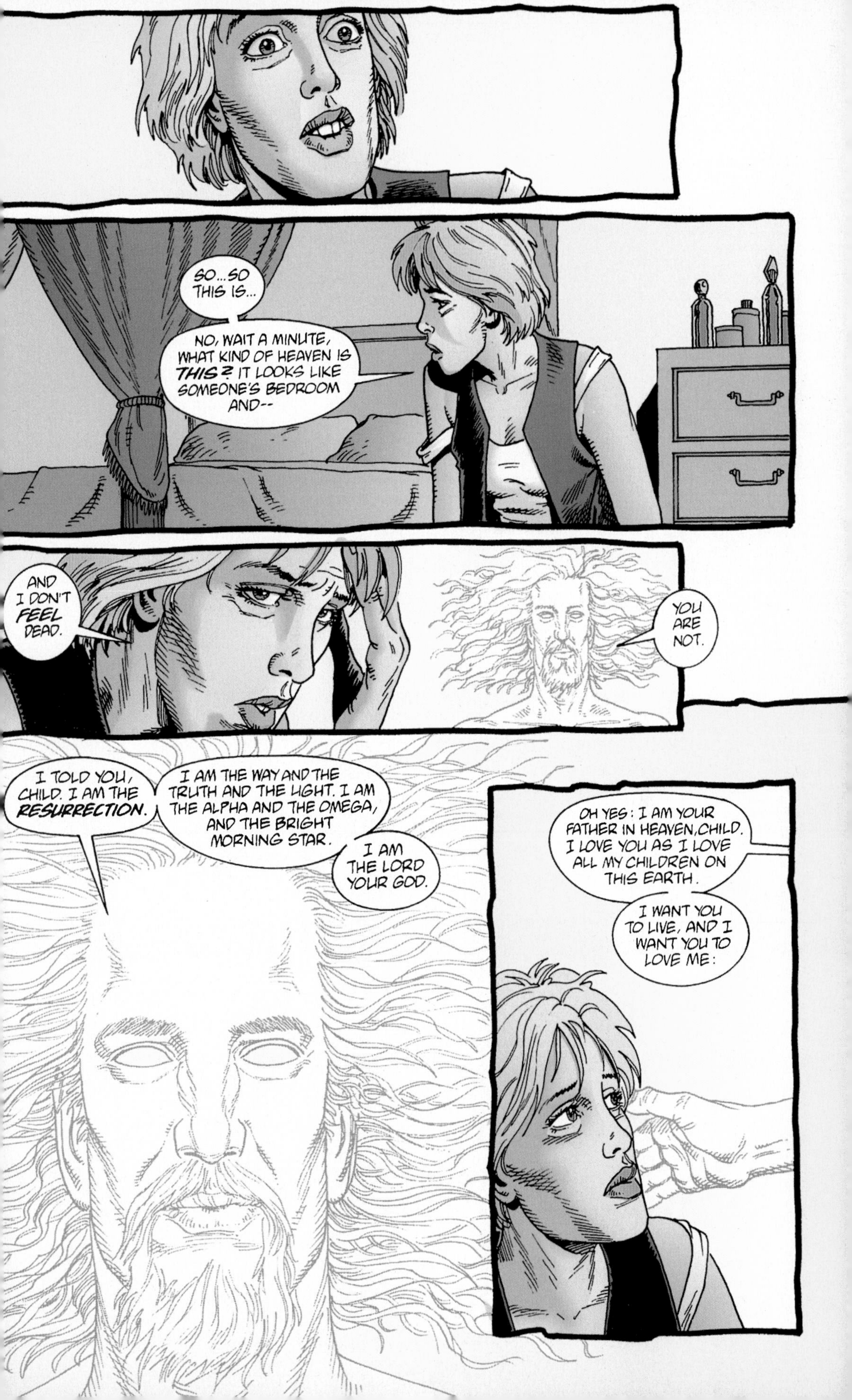
SO...SO THIS IS...
NO, WAIT A MINUTE, WHAT KIND OF HEAVEN IS THIS? IT LOOKS LIKE SOMEONE'S BEDROOM AND--
AND I DON'T FEEL DEAD.
YOU ARE NOT.
I TOLD YOU, CHILD. I AM THE RESURRECTION.
I AM THE WAY AND THE TRUTH AND THE LIGHT. I AM THE ALPHA AND THE OMEGA, AND THE BRIGHT MORNING STAR.
I AM THE LORD YOUR GOD.
OH YES: I AM YOUR FATHER IN HEAVEN, CHILD. I LOVE YOU AS I LOVE ALL MY CHILDREN ON THIS EARTH.
I WANT YOU TO LIVE, AND I WANT YOU TO LOVE ME:

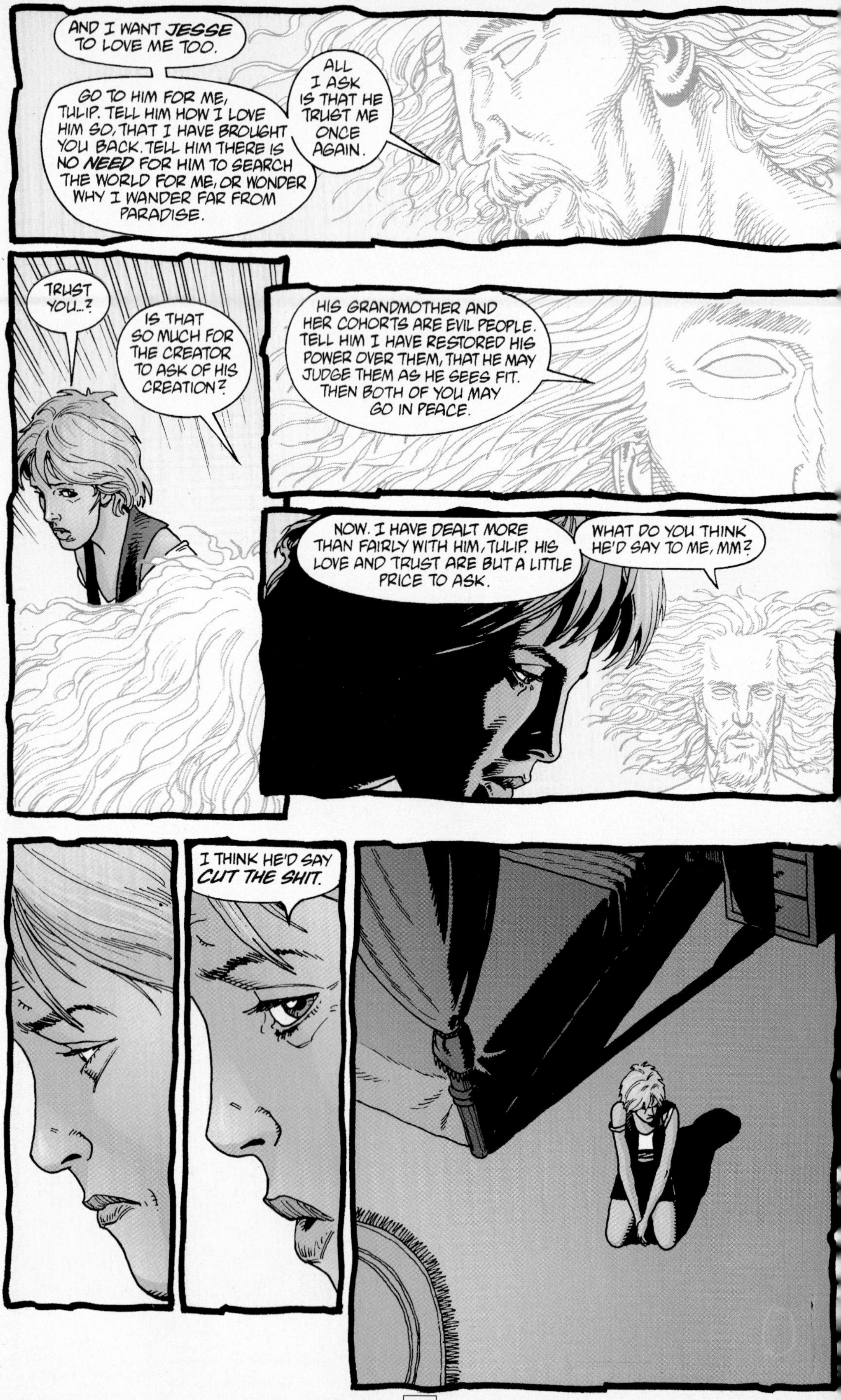

AND I WANT JESSE TO LOVE ME TOO.
GO TO HIM FOR ME, TULIP. TELL HIM HOW I LOVE HIM SO, THAT I HAVE BROUGHT YOU BACK. TELL HIM THERE IS NO NEED FOR HIM TO SEARCH THE WORLD FOR ME, OR WONDER WHY I WANDER FAR FROM PARADISE.
ALL I ASK IS THAT HE TRUST ME ONCE AGAIN.
TRUST YOU...?
IS THAT SO MUCH FOR THE CREATOR TO ASK OF HIS CREATION?
HIS GRANDMOTHER AND HER COHORTS ARE EVIL PEOPLE. TELL HIM I HAVE RESTORED HIS POWER OVER THEM, THAT HE MAY JUDGE THEM AS HE SEES FIT. THEN BOTH OF YOU MAY GO IN PEACE.
NOW. I HAVE DEALT MORE THAN FAIRLY WITH HIM, TULIP. HIS LOVE AND TRUST ARE BUT A LITTLE PRICE TO ASK.
WHAT DO YOU THINK HE'D SAY TO ME, MM?
I THINK HE'D SAY CUT THE SHIT.

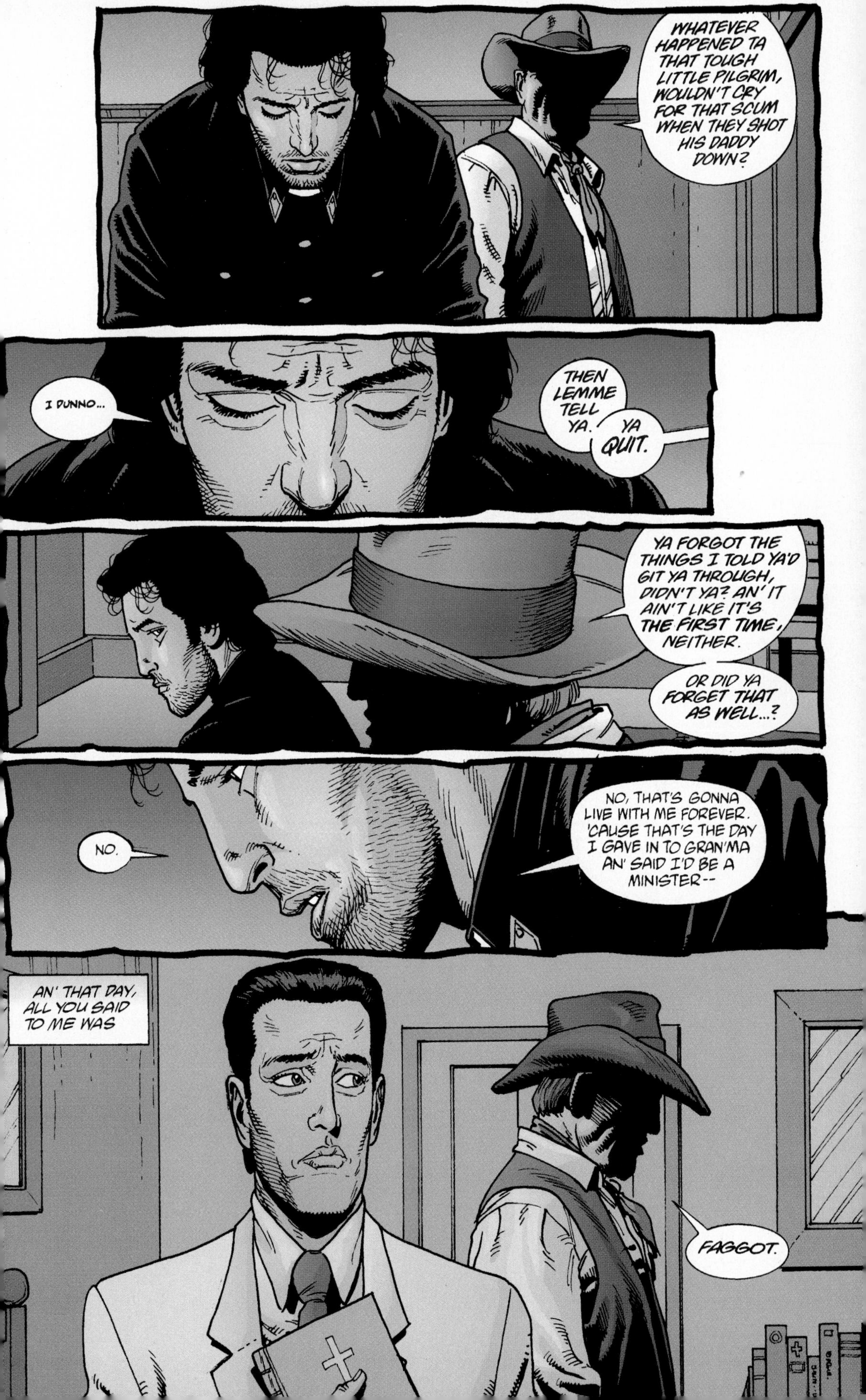
WHATEVER HAPPENED TA THAT TOUGH LITTLE PILGRIM, WOULDN'T CRY FOR THAT SCUM WHEN THEY SHOT HIS DADDY DOWN?
I DUNNO...
THEN LEMME TELL YA.
YA QUIT.
YA FORGOT THE THINGS I TOLD YA'D GIT YA THROUGH, DIDN'T YA? AN' IT AIN'T LIKE IT'S THE FIRST TIME, NEITHER.
OR DID YA FORGET THAT AS WELL...?
NO.
NO, THAT'S GONNA LIVE WITH ME FOREVER. 'CAUSE THAT'S THE DAY I GAVE IN TO GRAN'MA AN' SAID I'D BE A MINISTER--
AN' THAT DAY, ALL YOU SAID TO ME WAS
FAGGOT.

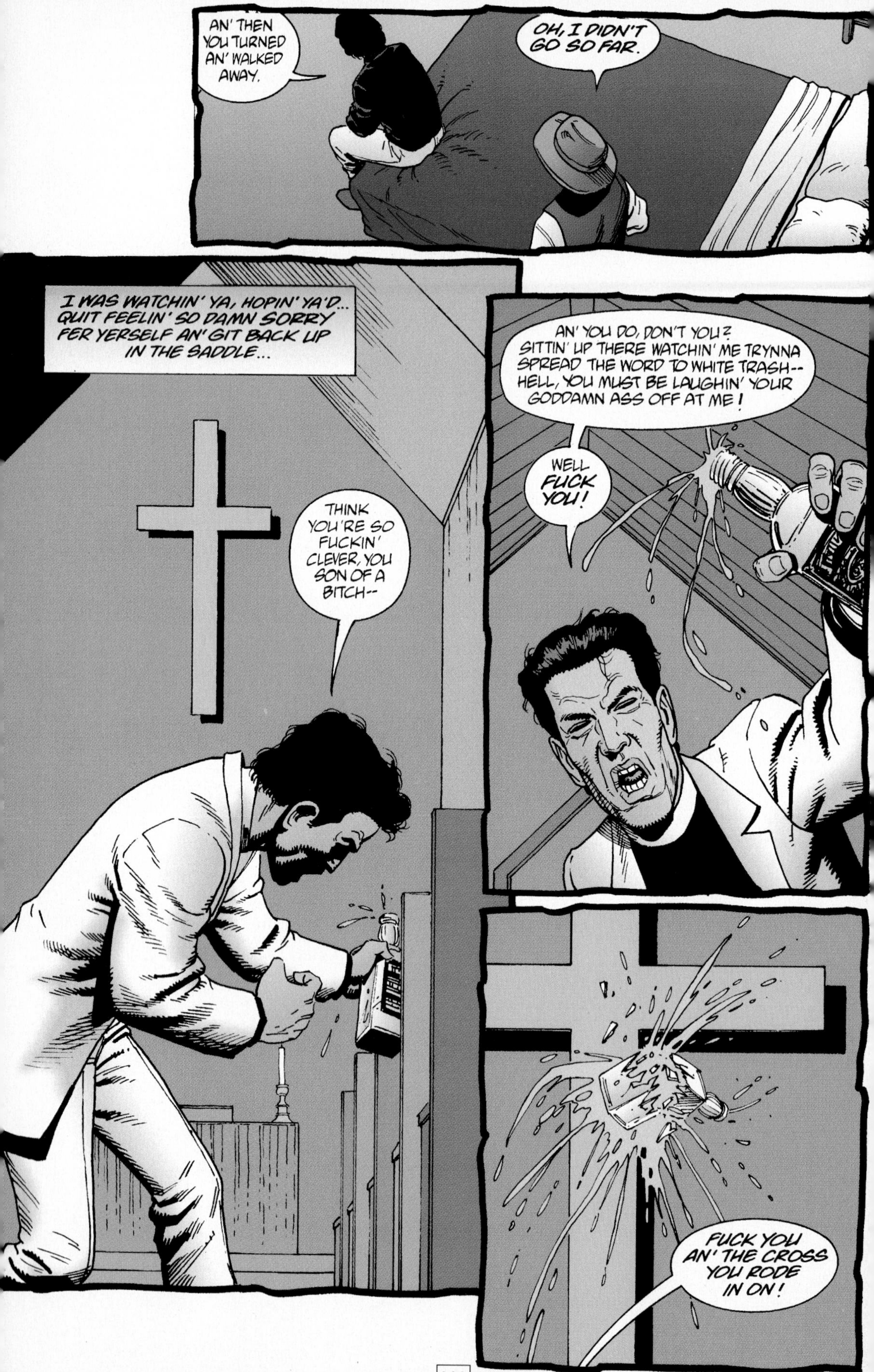
AN' THEN YOU TURNED AN' WALKED AWAY.
OH, I DIDN'T GO SO FAR.
I WAS WATCHIN' YA, HOPIN' YA'D... QUIT FEELIN' SO DAMN SORRY FER YERSELF AN' GIT BACK UP IN THE SADDLE...
THINK YOU'RE SO FUCKIN' CLEVER, YOU SON OF A BITCH--
AN' YOU DO, DON'T YOU? SITTIN' UP THERE WATCHIN' ME TRYNNA SPREAD THE WORD TO WHITE TRASH-- HELL, YOU MUST BE LAUGHIN' YOUR GODDAMN ASS OFF AT ME!
WELL FUCK YOU!
FUCK YOU AN' THE CROSS YOU RODE IN ON!

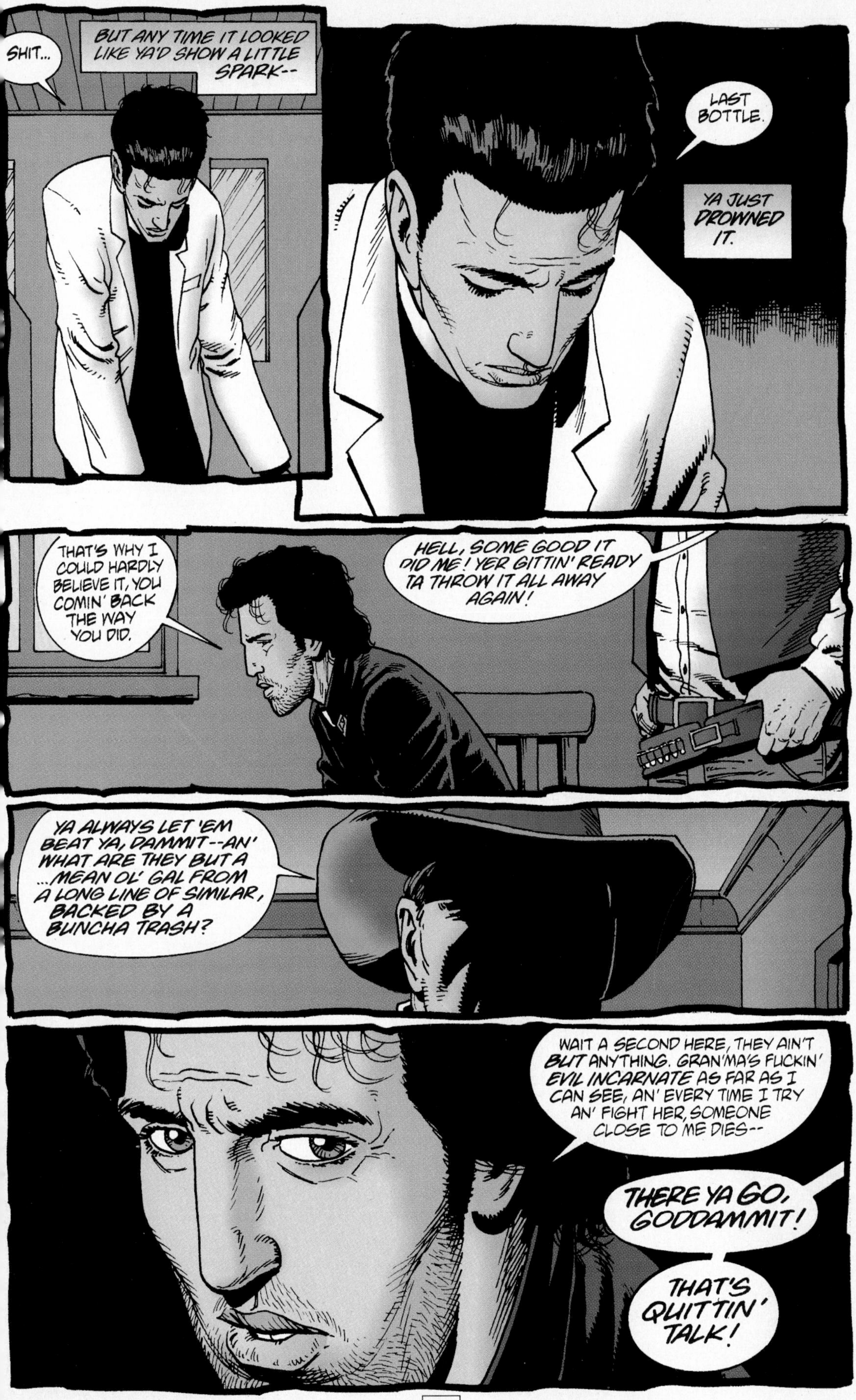
SHIT...
BUT ANY TIME IT LOOKED LIKE YA'D SHOW A LITTLE SPARK--
LAST BOTTLE.
YA JUST DROWNED IT.
THAT'S WHY I COULD HARDLY BELIEVE IT, YOU COMIN' BACK THE WAY YOU DID.
HELL, SOME GOOD IT DID ME! YER GITTIN' READY TA THROW IT ALL AWAY AGAIN!
YA ALWAYS LET 'EM BEAT YA, DAMMIT--AN' WHAT ARE THEY BUT A ...MEAN OL' GAL FROM A LONG LINE OF SIMILAR, BACKED BY A BUNCHA TRASH?
WAIT A SECOND HERE, THEY AIN'T BUT ANYTHING. GRAN'MA'S FUCKIN' EVIL INCARNATE AS FAR AS I CAN SEE, AN' EVERY TIME I TRY AN' FIGHT HER, SOMEONE CLOSE TO ME DIES--
THERE YA GO, GODDAMMIT!
THAT'S QUITTIN' TALK!

YER GRAN'MA'S GOT YA BROKE LIKE YA WERE A HEADSTRONG BRONCO. KNOWS WHEN TA ...GIVE YA ROPE AN' WHEN TA PULL YA IN--

AN' SHE KNOWS EXACTLY WHEN TA KICK YA WHEN YER DOWN.

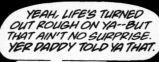

YEAH, LIFE'S TURNED OUT ROUGH ON YA--BUT THAT AIN'T NO SURPRISE. YER DADDY TOLD YA THAT.

SAID YA GOTTA BE ONE OF THE GOOD GUYS--

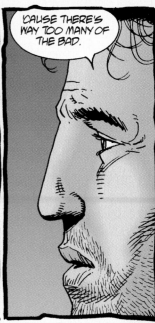

'CAUSE THERE'S WAY TOO MANY OF THE BAD.

YOU'RE RIGHT.

I LET 'EM BEAT ME. I QUIT ON MY DAD AN' I QUIT ON YOU.

I DON'T KNOW WHY YOU DIDN'T JUST DO THE SAME.

DERN IT, PILGRIM.

IT'S 'CAUSE WE'RE PARDNERS.

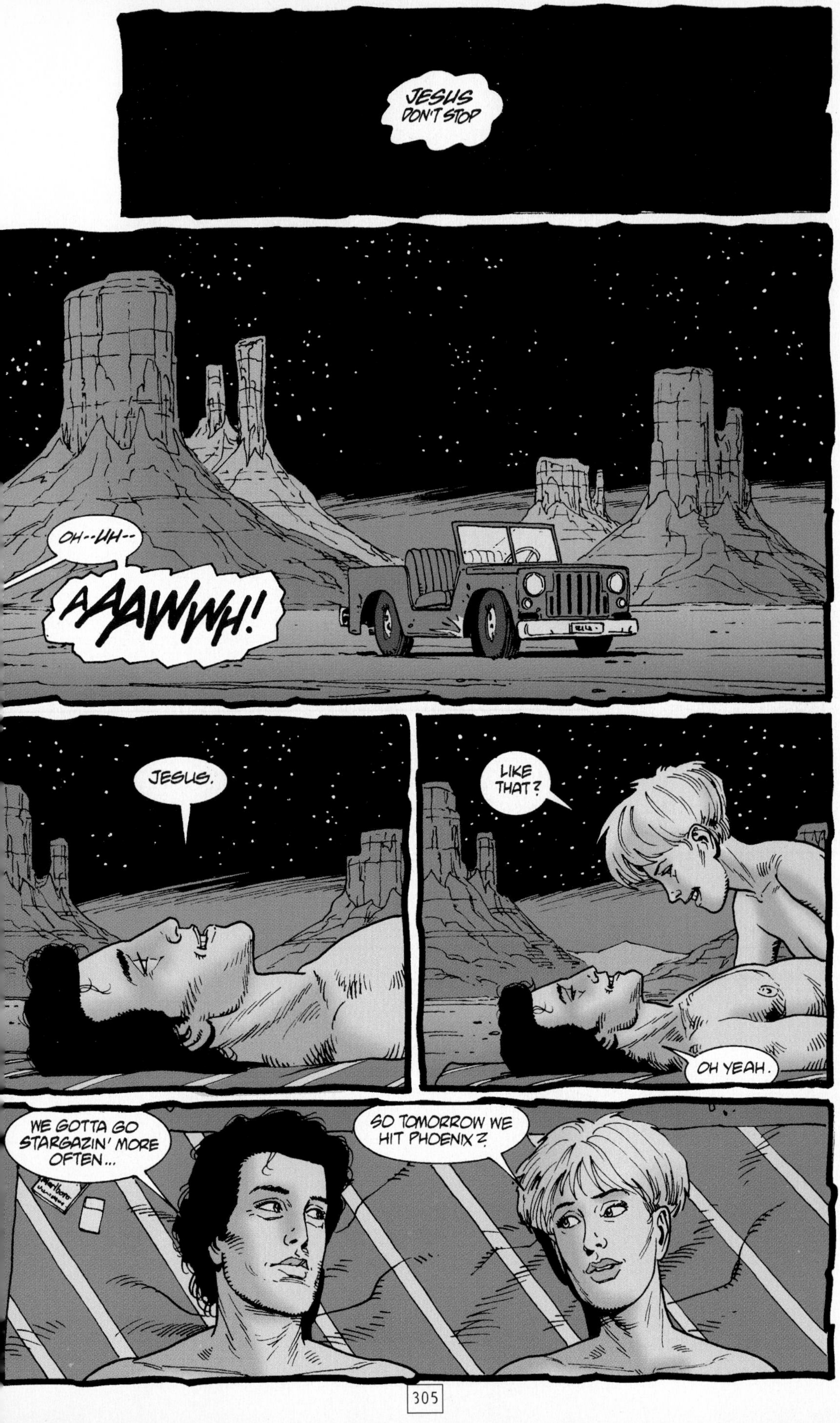
JESUS
DON'T STOP
OH--UH--
AAAWWH!
JESUS.
LIKE THAT?
OH YEAH.
WE GOTTA GO STARGAZIN' MORE OFTEN...
SO TOMORROW WE HIT PHOENIX?

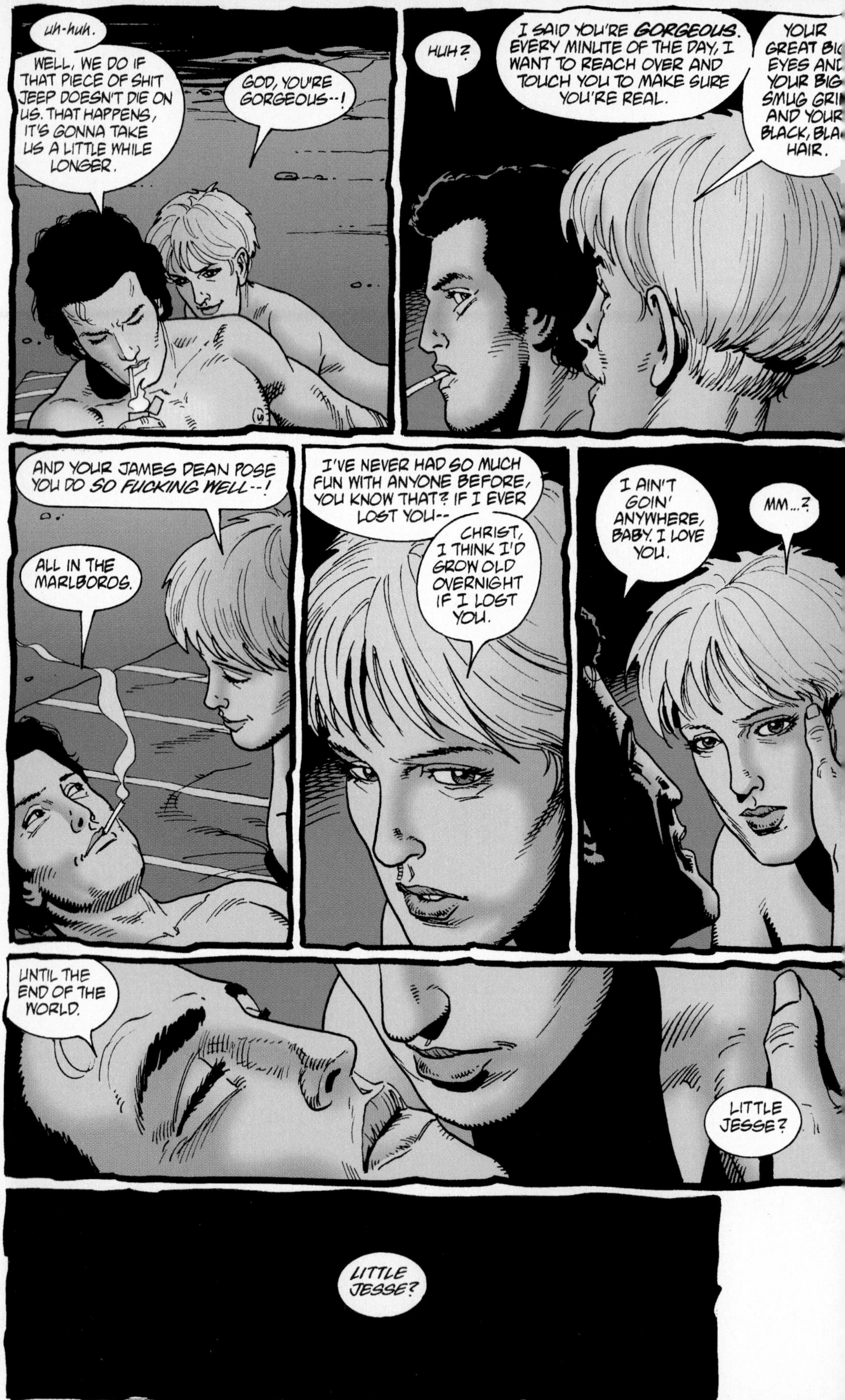
uh-huh.
WELL, WE DO IF THAT PIECE OF SHIT JEEP DOESN'T DIE ON US. THAT HAPPENS, IT'S GONNA TAKE US A LITTLE WHILE LONGER.
GOD, YOU'RE GORGEOUS--!
HUH?
I SAID YOU'RE GORGEOUS. EVERY MINUTE OF THE DAY, I WANT TO REACH OVER AND TOUCH YOU TO MAKE SURE YOU'RE REAL.
YOUR GREAT BIG EYES AND YOUR BIG SMUG GRIN AND YOUR BLACK, BLACK HAIR.
AND YOUR JAMES DEAN POSE YOU DO SO FUCKING WELL--!
ALL IN THE MARLBOROS.
I'VE NEVER HAD SO MUCH FUN WITH ANYONE BEFORE, YOU KNOW THAT? IF I EVER LOST YOU--
CHRIST, I THINK I'D GROW OLD OVERNIGHT IF I LOST YOU.
I AIN'T GOIN' ANYWHERE, BABY. I LOVE YOU.
MM...?
UNTIL THE END OF THE WORLD.
LITTLE JESSE?
LITTLE JESSE?

UNTIL--*UH?*

WHUZZAT?

AW *FUCK*...!

SAY, YOU KNOW WHAT? WE THOUGHT YOU'D GONE FUCKIN' *LOCO* ON US!

SURE IS A RELIEF--

POINT THAT FUCKIN' THING SOMEWHERE ELSE, WILL YOU?

ER...

DROP IT.

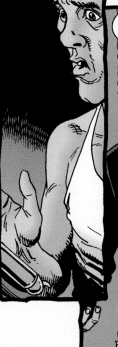

WELL, WELL, *WELL*....!

JUH-- *JODY*--

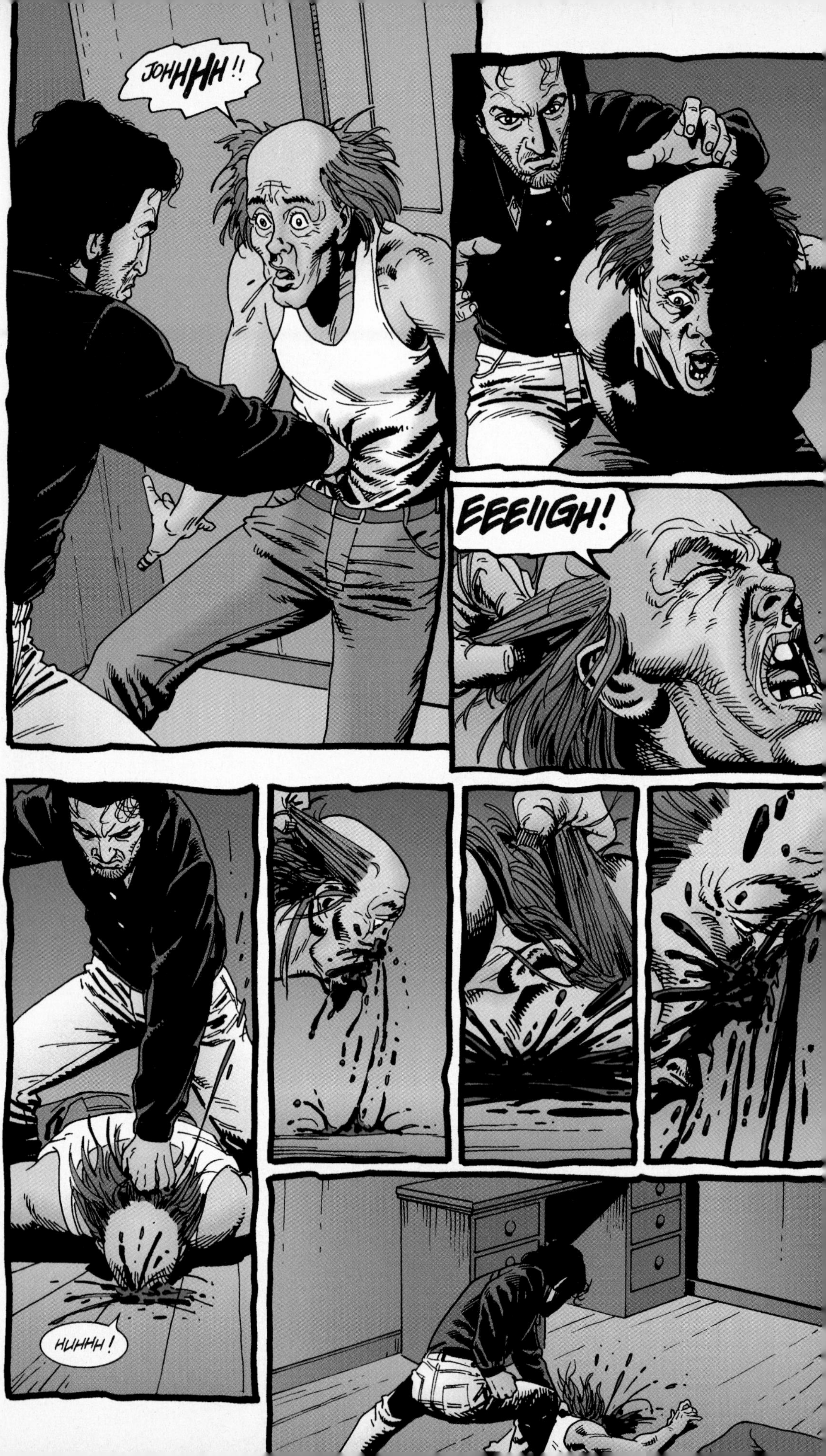
JOHHHH!!
EEEIIGH!
HUHHH!

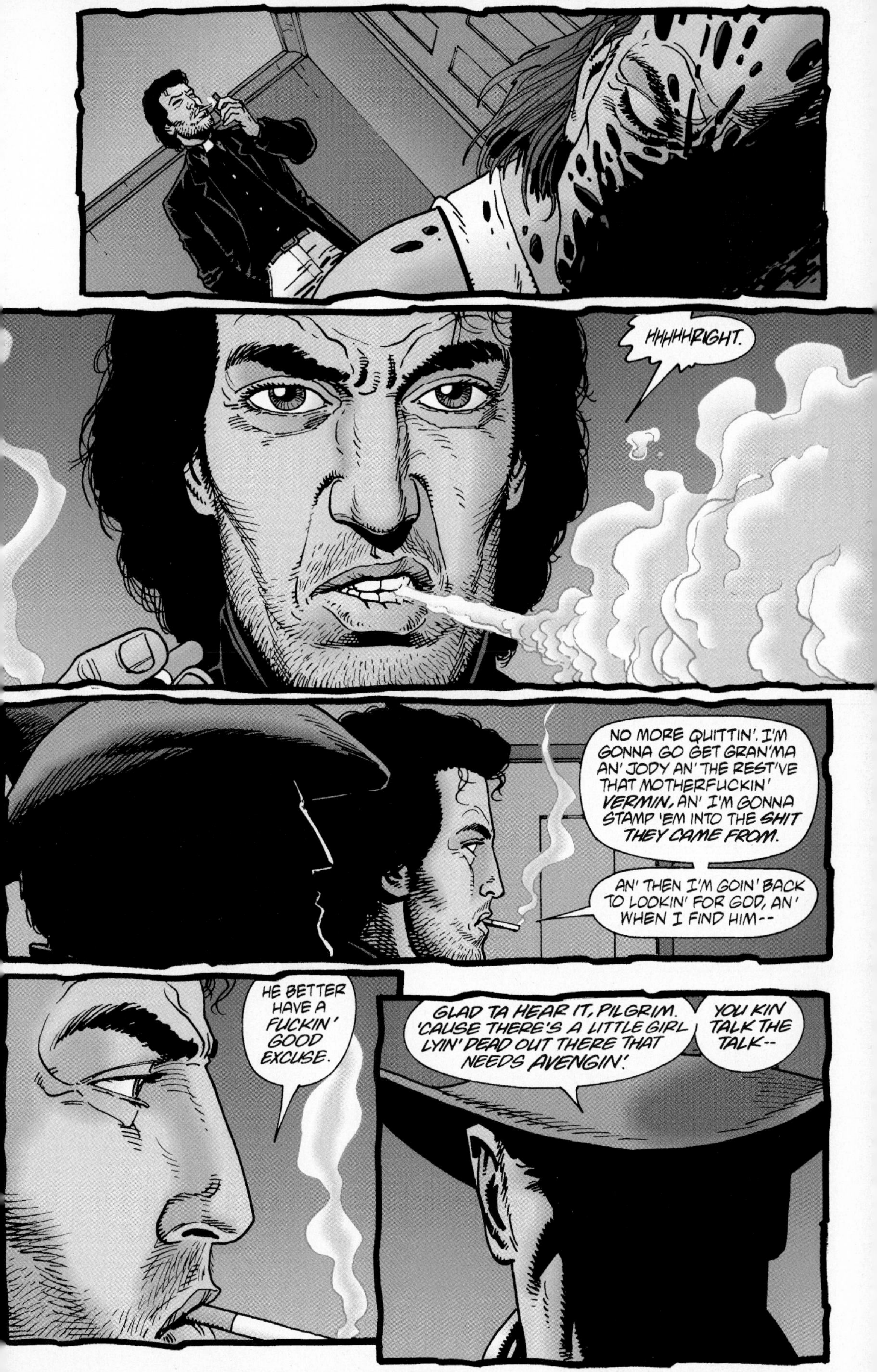
HHHHHRIGHT.
NO MORE QUITTIN'. I'M GONNA GO GET GRAN'MA AN' JODY AN' THE REST'VE THAT MOTHERFUCKIN' VERMIN, AN' I'M GONNA STAMP 'EM INTO THE SHIT THEY CAME FROM.
AN' THEN I'M GOIN' BACK TO LOOKIN' FOR GOD, AN' WHEN I FIND HIM--
HE BETTER HAVE A FUCKIN' GOOD EXCUSE.
GLAD TA HEAR IT, PILGRIM. 'CAUSE THERE'S A LITTLE GIRL LYIN' DEAD OUT THERE THAT NEEDS AVENGIN'.
YOU KIN TALK THE TALK--

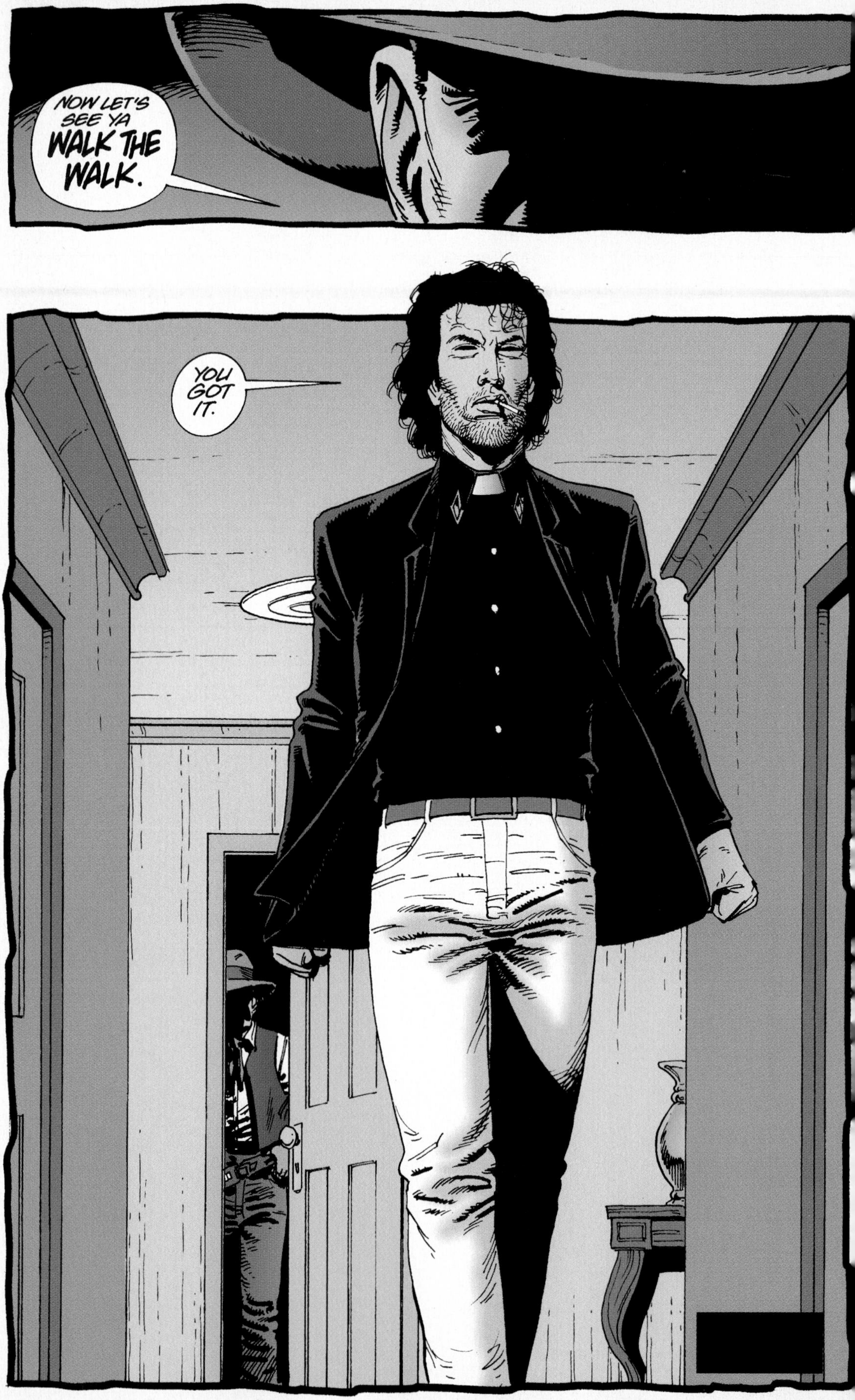
NOW LET'S SEE YA WALK THE WALK.
YOU GOT IT.

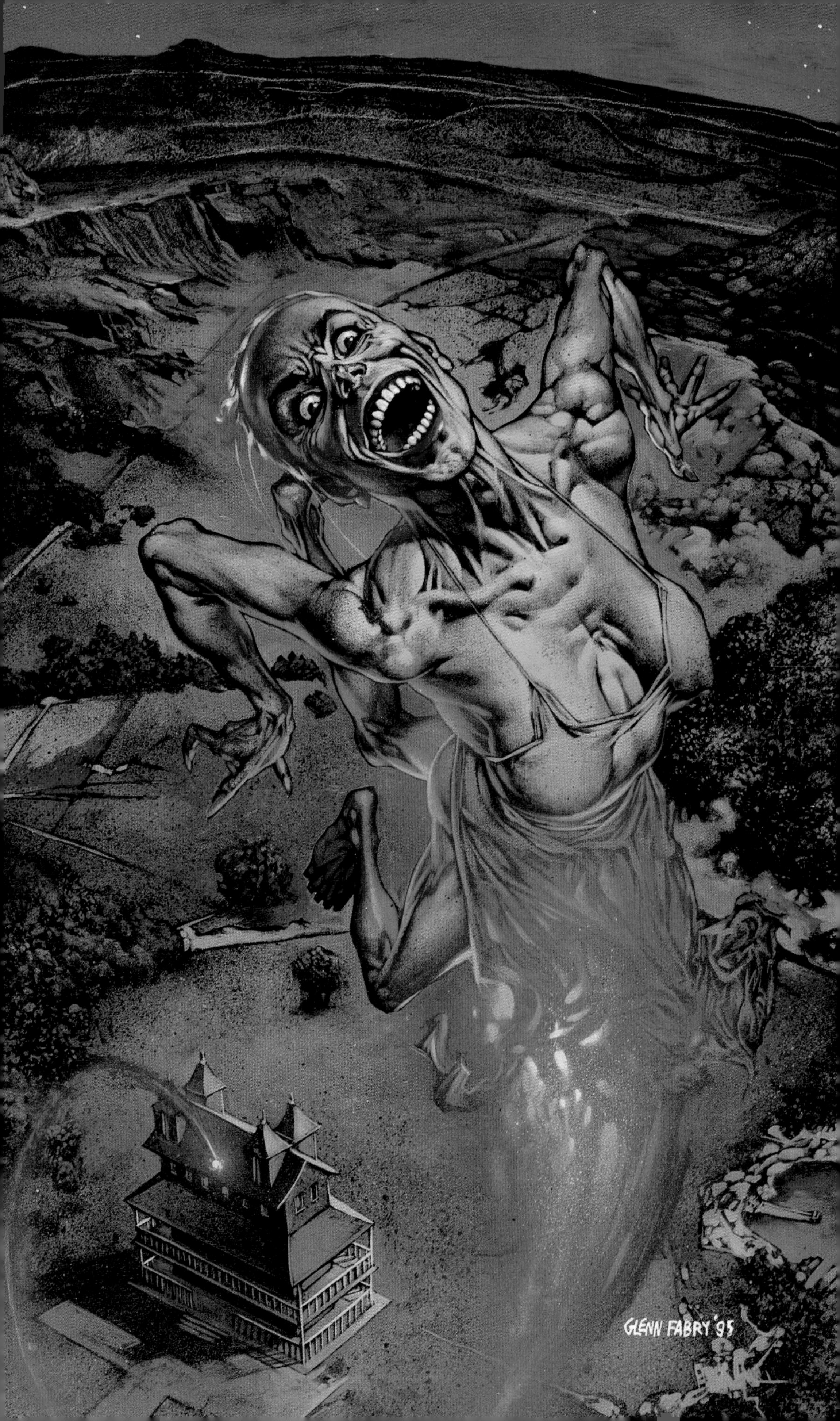
GLENN FABRY '95

"So who wants to get his ass kicked first?"

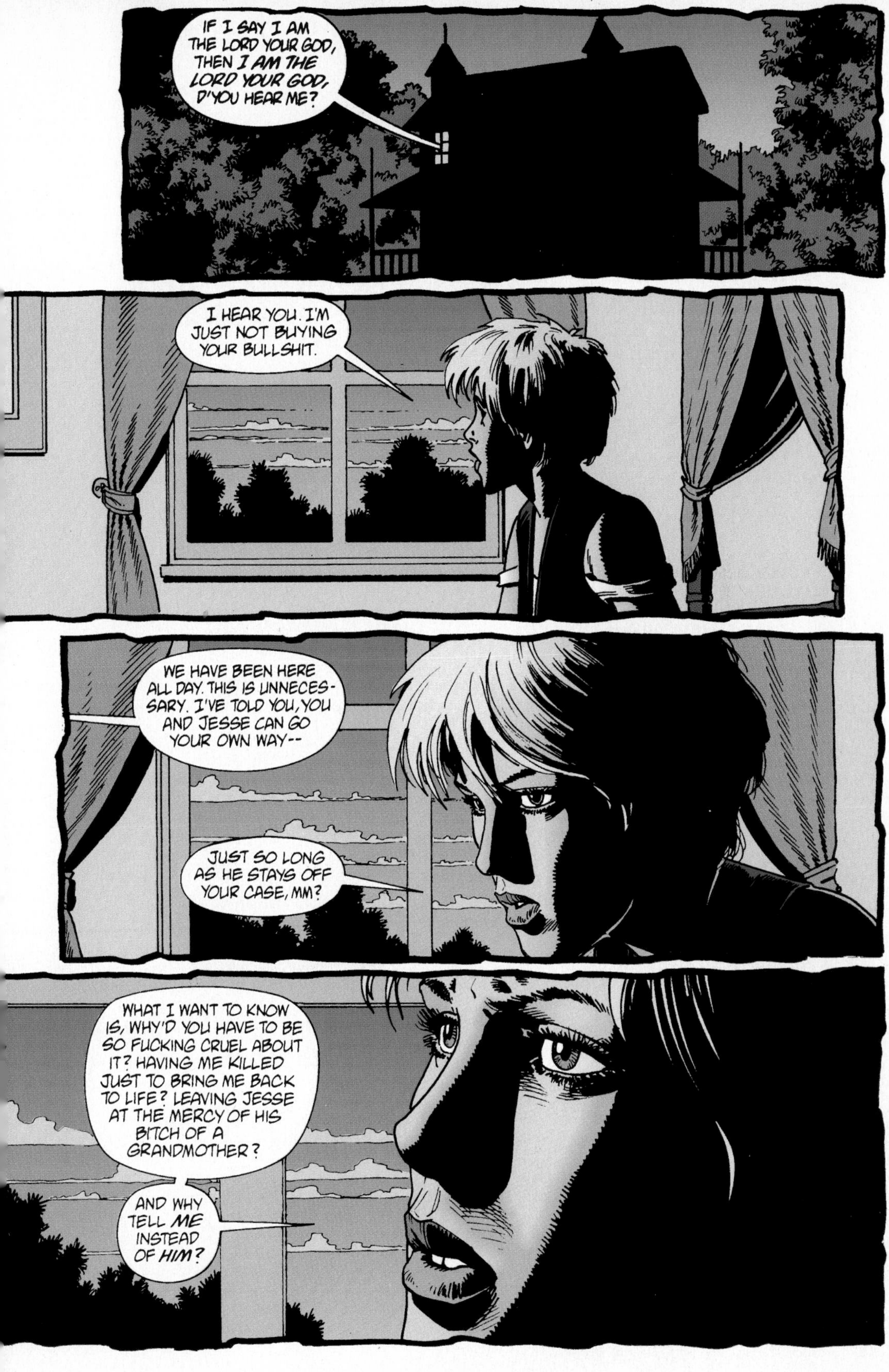
IF I SAY I AM THE LORD YOUR GOD, THEN *I AM THE LORD YOUR GOD,* D'YOU HEAR ME?
I HEAR YOU. I'M JUST NOT BUYING YOUR BULLSHIT.
WE HAVE BEEN HERE ALL DAY. THIS IS UNNECES-SARY. I'VE TOLD YOU, YOU AND JESSE CAN GO YOUR OWN WAY--
JUST SO LONG AS HE STAYS OFF YOUR CASE, MM?
WHAT I WANT TO KNOW IS, WHY'D YOU HAVE TO BE SO FUCKING CRUEL ABOUT IT? HAVING ME KILLED JUST TO BRING ME BACK TO LIFE? LEAVING JESSE AT THE MERCY OF HIS BITCH OF A GRANDMOTHER?
AND WHY TELL *ME* INSTEAD OF *HIM*?

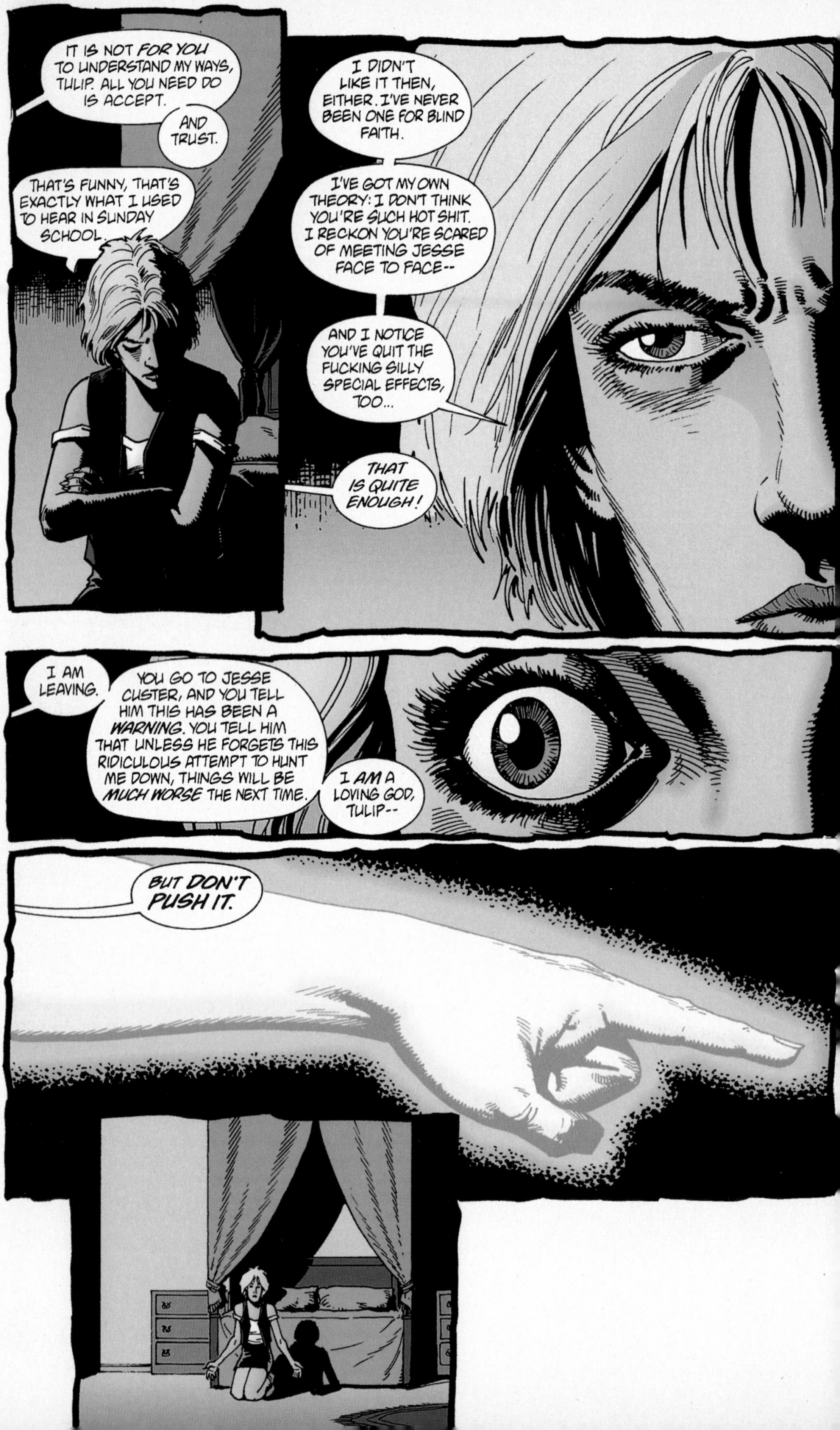

IT IS NOT *FOR YOU* TO UNDERSTAND MY WAYS, TULIP. ALL YOU NEED DO IS ACCEPT.
AND TRUST.
THAT'S FUNNY, THAT'S EXACTLY WHAT I USED TO HEAR IN SUNDAY SCHOOL.
I DIDN'T LIKE IT THEN, EITHER. I'VE NEVER BEEN ONE FOR BLIND FAITH.
I'VE GOT MY OWN THEORY: I DON'T THINK YOU'RE SUCH HOT SHIT. I RECKON YOU'RE SCARED OF MEETING JESSE FACE TO FACE--
AND I NOTICE YOU'VE QUIT THE FUCKING SILLY SPECIAL EFFECTS, TOO...
THAT IS QUITE ENOUGH!
I AM LEAVING.
YOU GO TO JESSE CUSTER, AND YOU TELL HIM THIS HAS BEEN A *WARNING*. YOU TELL HIM THAT UNLESS HE FORGETS THIS RIDICULOUS ATTEMPT TO HUNT ME DOWN, THINGS WILL BE *MUCH WORSE* THE NEXT TIME.
I *AM* A LOVING GOD, TULIP--
BUT *DON'T PUSH IT.*

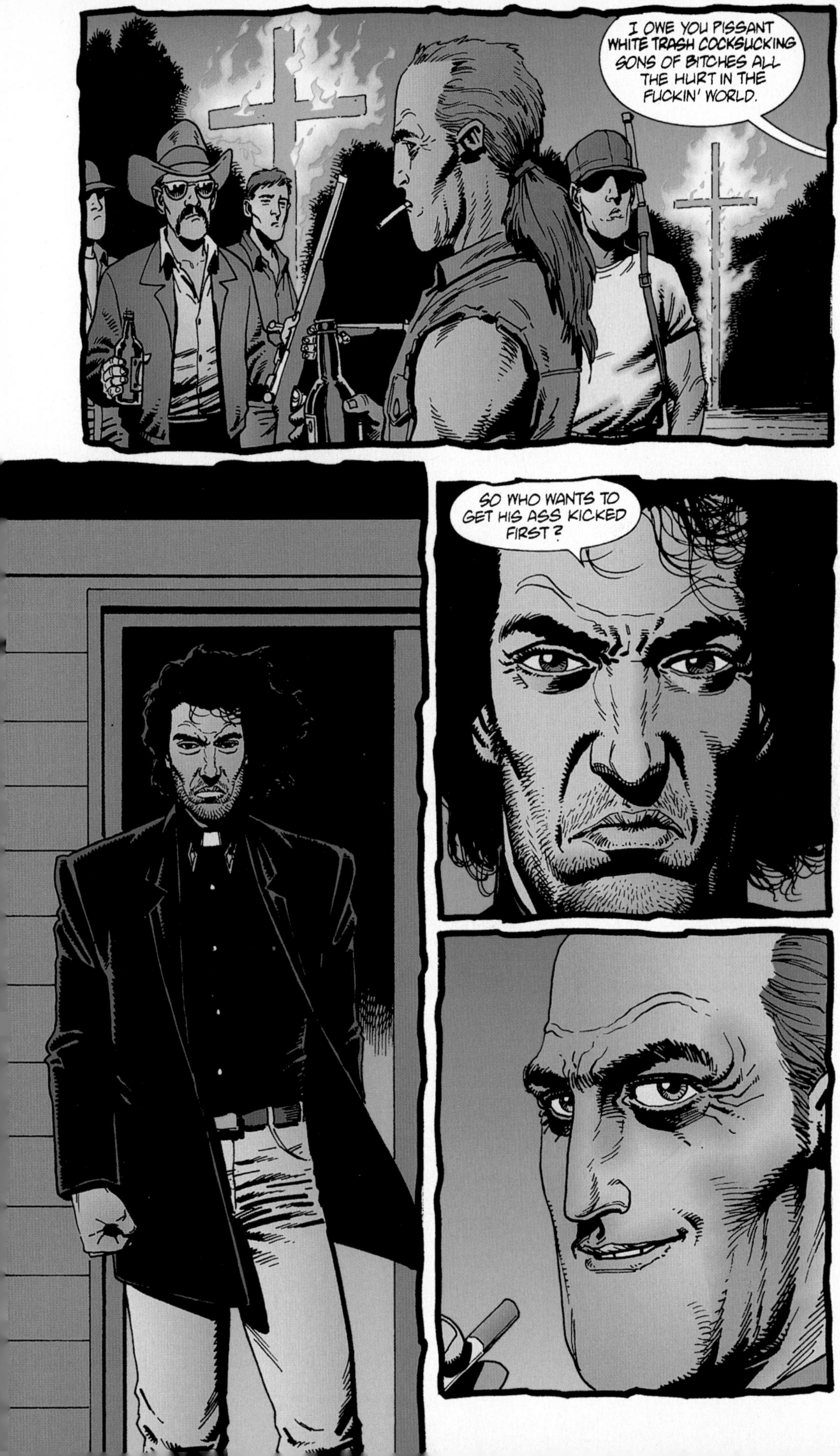
I OWE YOU PISSANT WHITE TRASH COCKSUCKING SONS OF BITCHES ALL THE HURT IN THE FUCKIN' WORLD.
SO WHO WANTS TO GET HIS ASS KICKED FIRST?

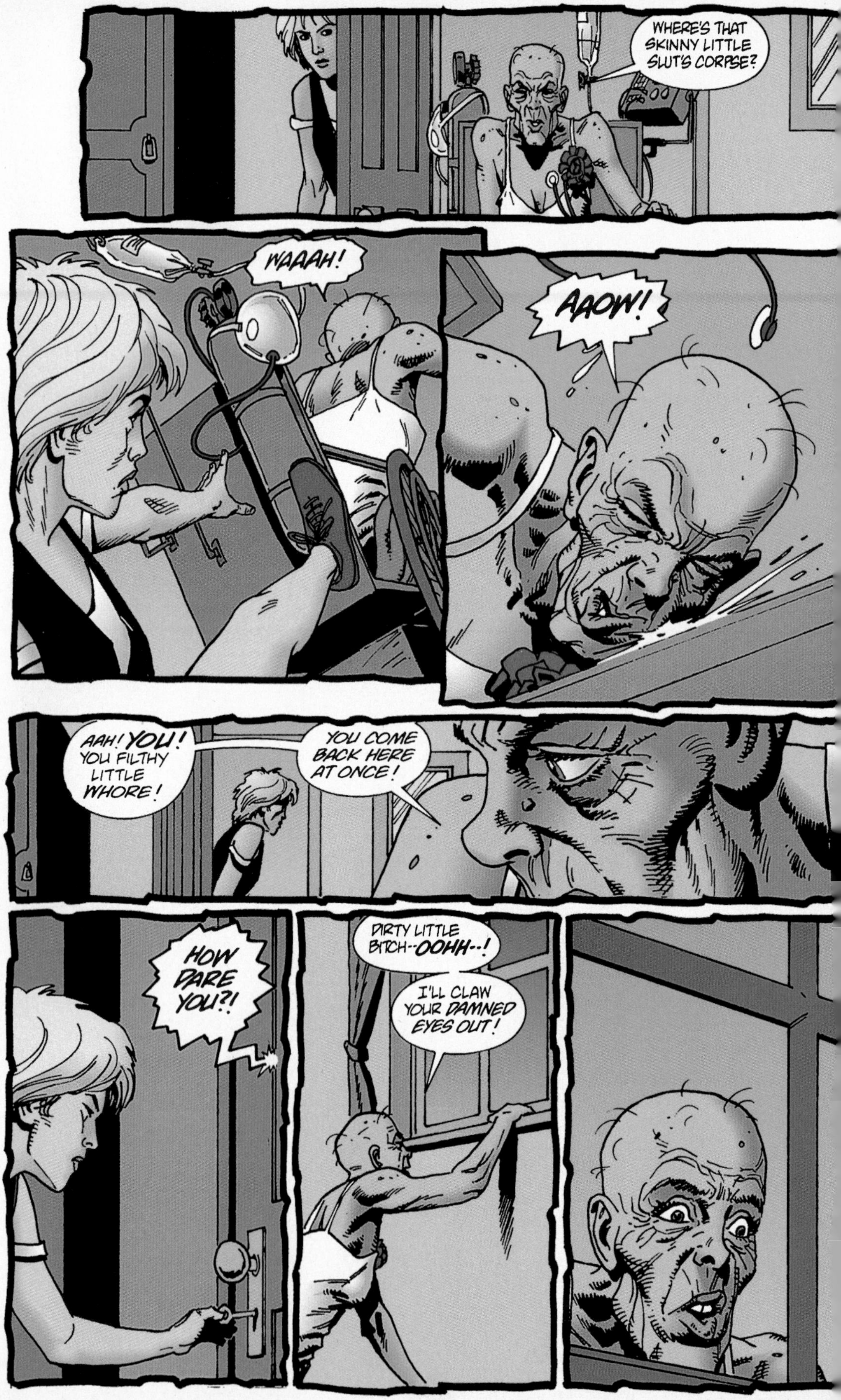
WHERE'S THAT SKINNY LITTLE SLUT'S CORPSE?
WAAAH!
AAOW!
AAH! YOU! YOU FILTHY LITTLE WHORE!
YOU COME BACK HERE AT ONCE!
HOW DARE YOU?!
DIRTY LITTLE BITCH--OOHH--!
I'LL CLAW YOUR DAMNED EYES OUT!

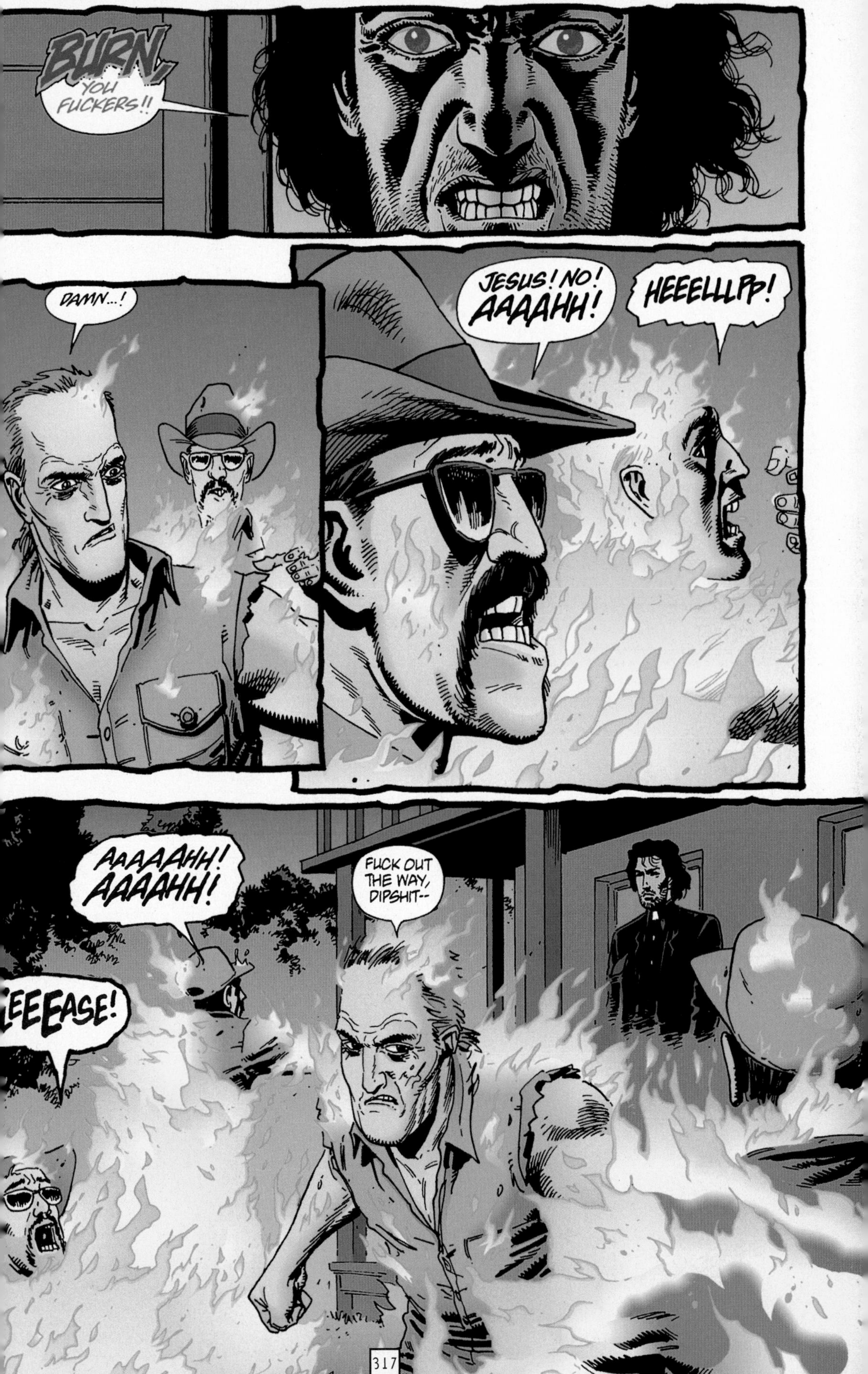
BURN, YOU FUCKERS!!
DAMN...!
JESUS! NO! AAAAHH!
HEEELLLPP!
AAAAAHH! AAAAHH!
FUCK OUT THE WAY, DIPSHIT--
LEEEASE!

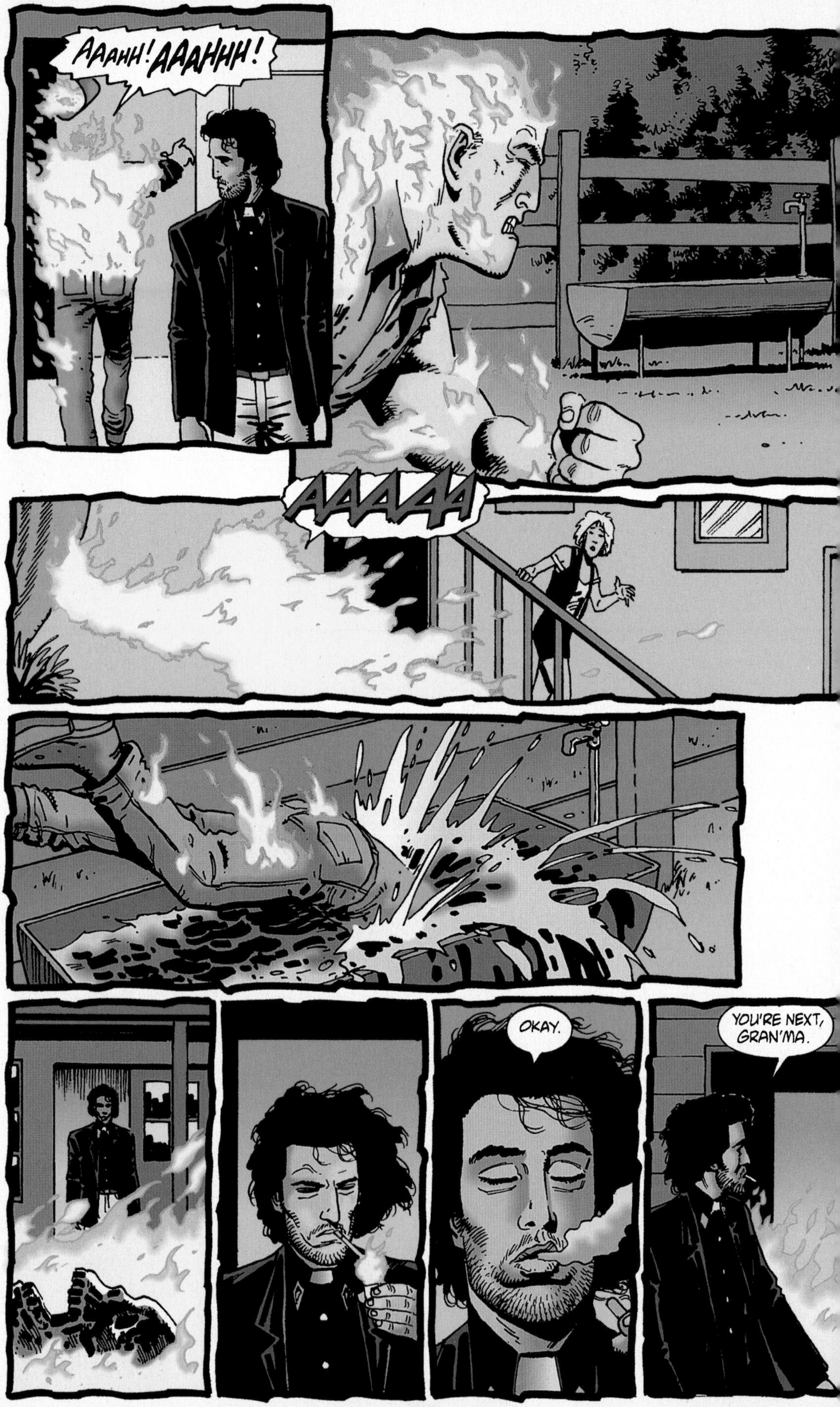
AAAHH! AAAHHH!
AAAAA
OKAY.
YOU'RE NEXT, GRAN'MA.

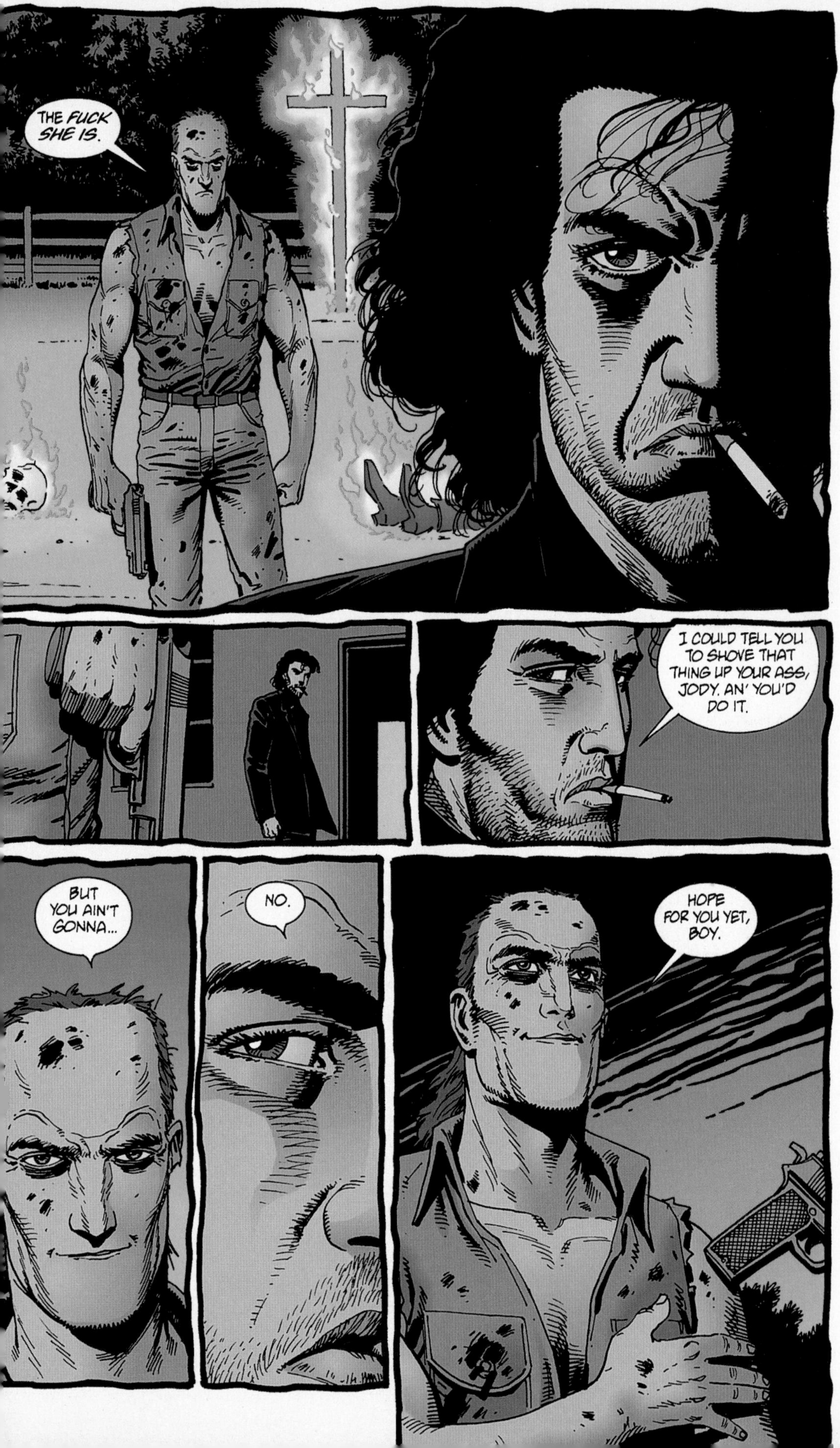
THE FUCK SHE IS.
I COULD TELL YOU TO SHOVE THAT THING UP YOUR ASS, JODY. AN' YOU'D DO IT.
BUT YOU AIN'T GONNA...
NO.
HOPE FOR YOU YET, BOY.

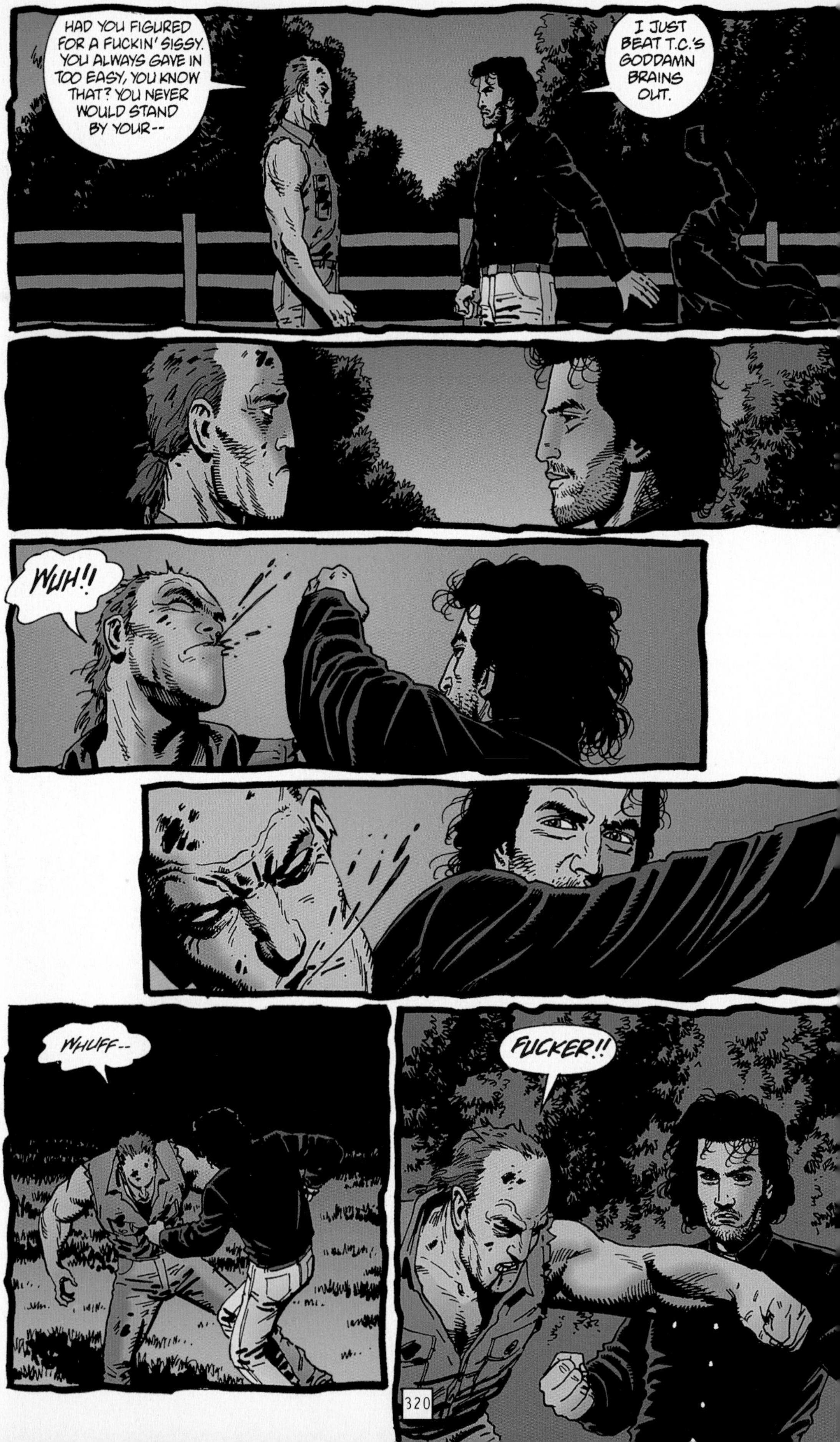
HAD YOU FIGURED FOR A FUCKIN' SISSY. YOU ALWAYS GAVE IN TOO EASY, YOU KNOW THAT? YOU NEVER WOULD STAND BY YOUR--
I JUST BEAT T.C.'S GODDAMN BRAINS OUT.
WUH!!
WHUFF--
FUCKER!!

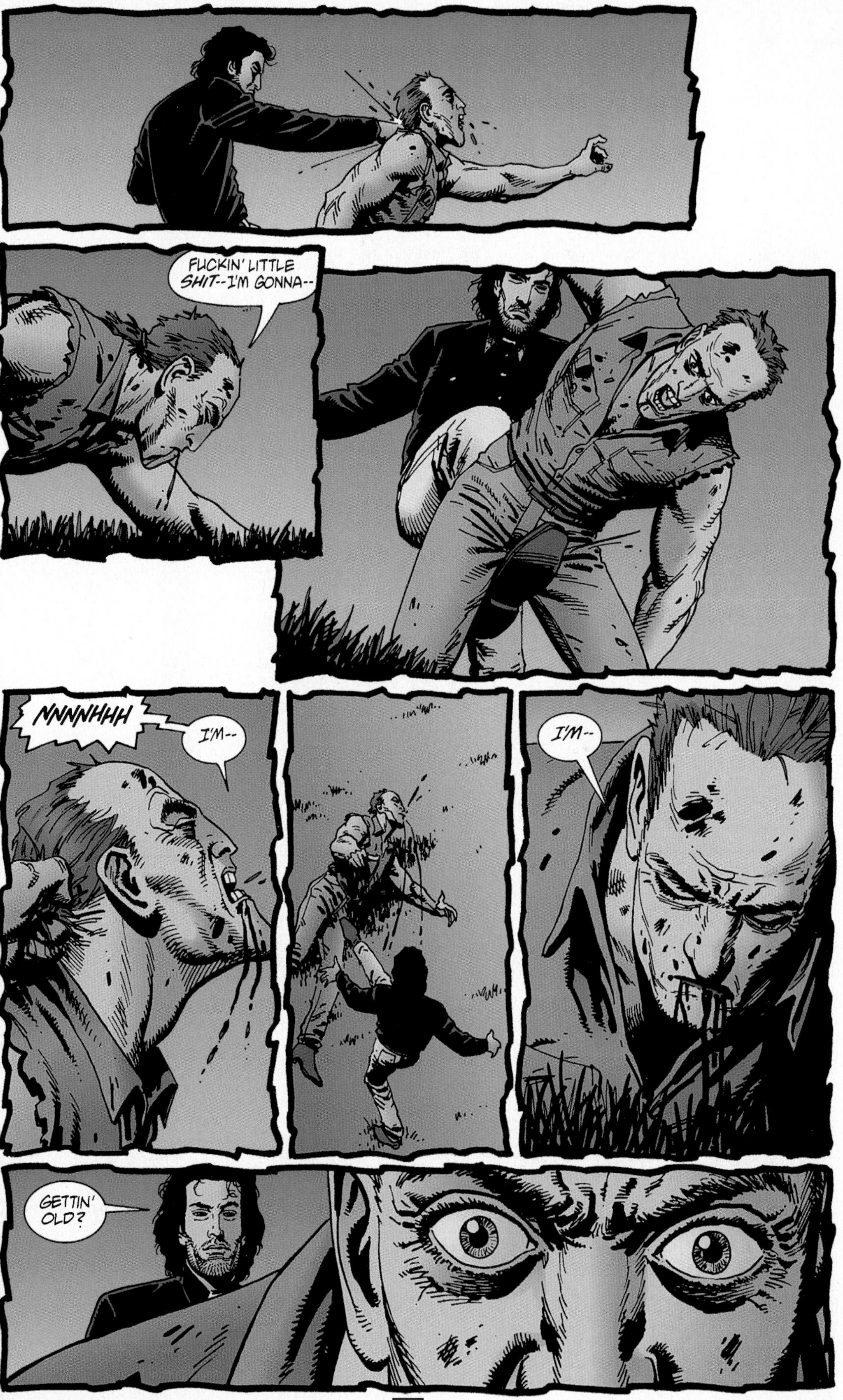
FUCKIN' LITTLE SHIT--I'M GONNA--
NNNNHHH
I'M--
I'M--
GETTIN' OLD?

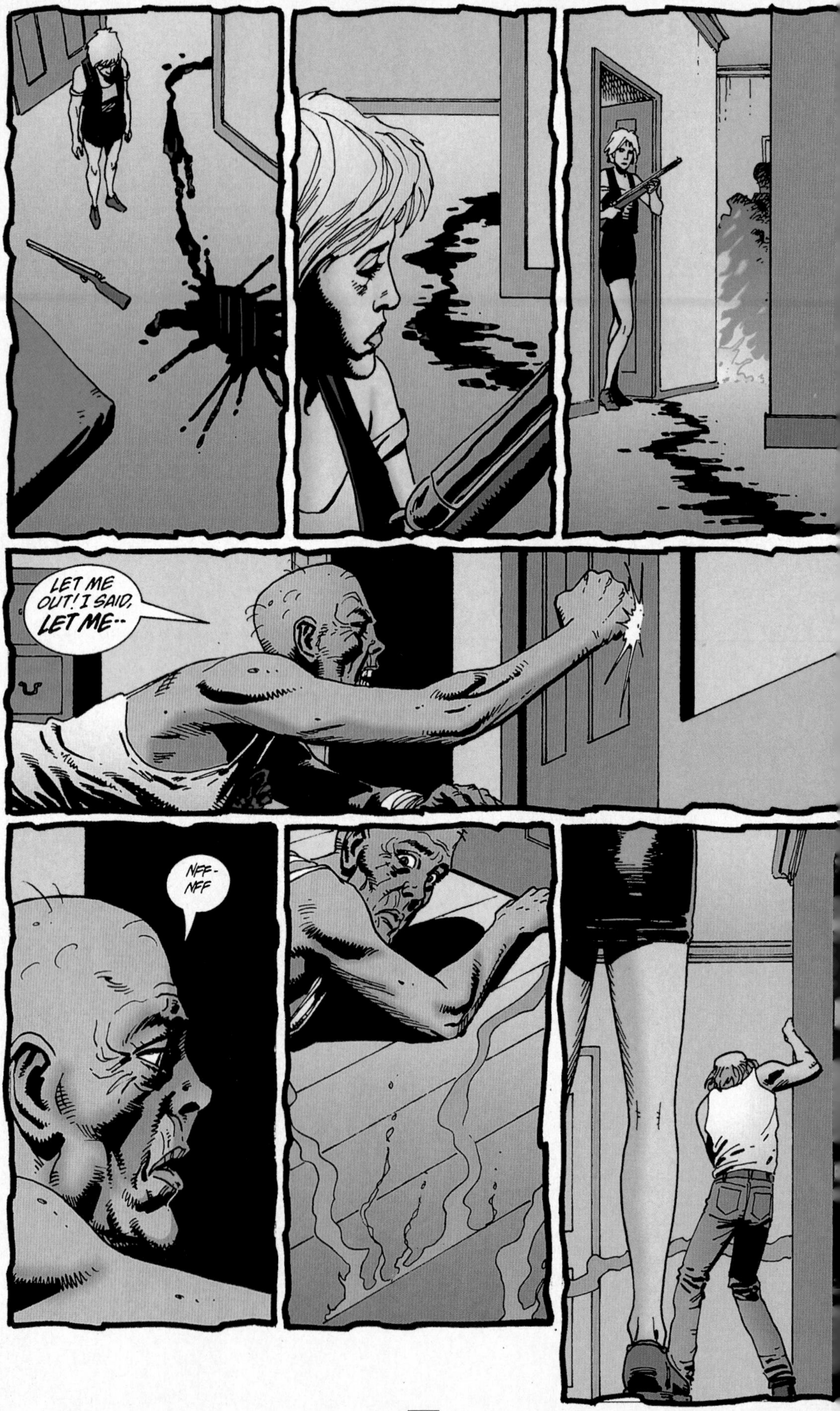
LET ME OUT! I SAID, LET ME--
NFF-NFF

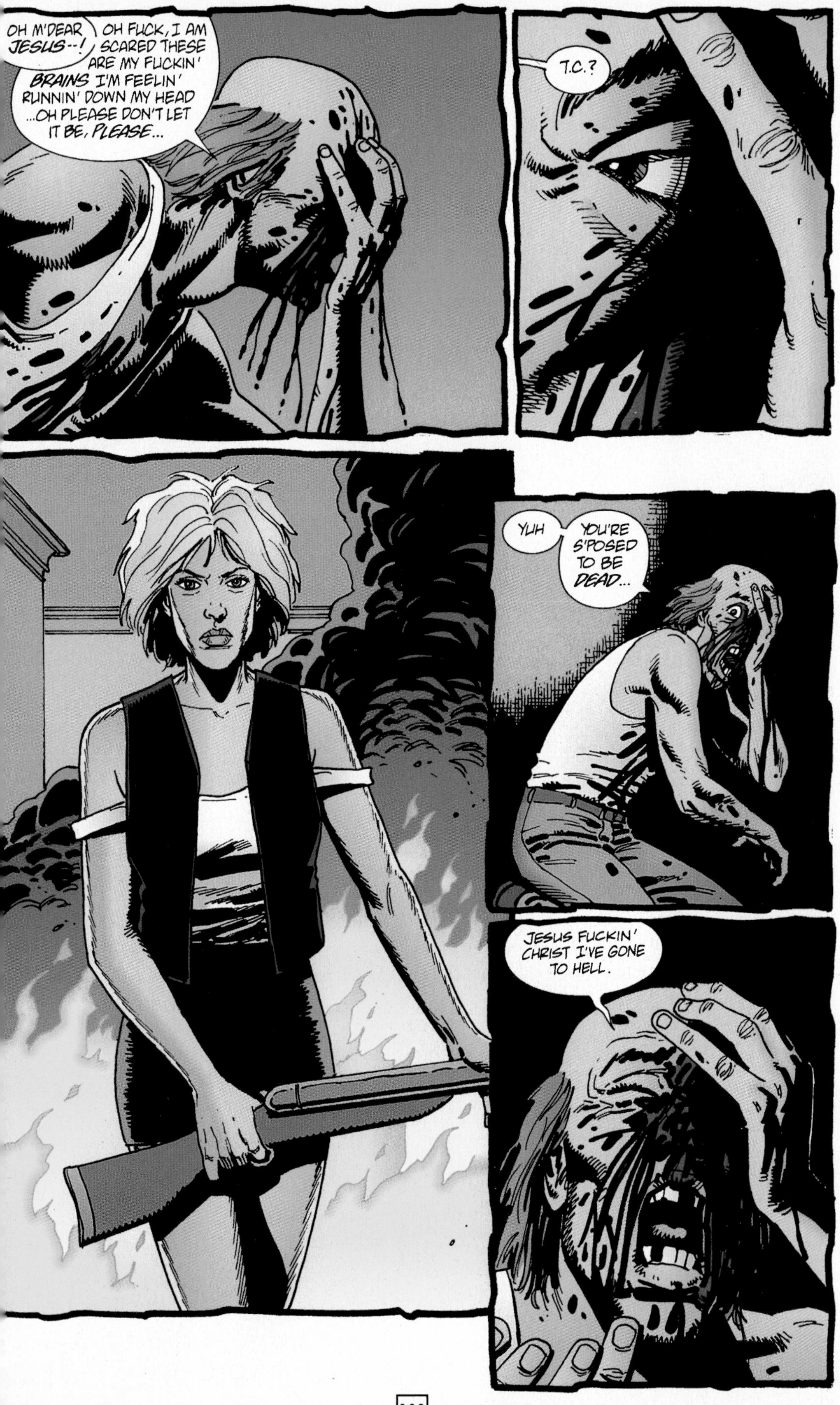
OH M'DEAR JESUS--!
OH FUCK, I AM SCARED THESE ARE MY FUCKIN' BRAINS I'M FEELIN' RUNNIN' DOWN MY HEAD ...OH PLEASE DON'T LET IT BE, PLEASE...
T.C.?
YUH
YOU'RE S'POSED TO BE DEAD...
JESUS FUCKIN' CHRIST I'VE GONE TO HELL.

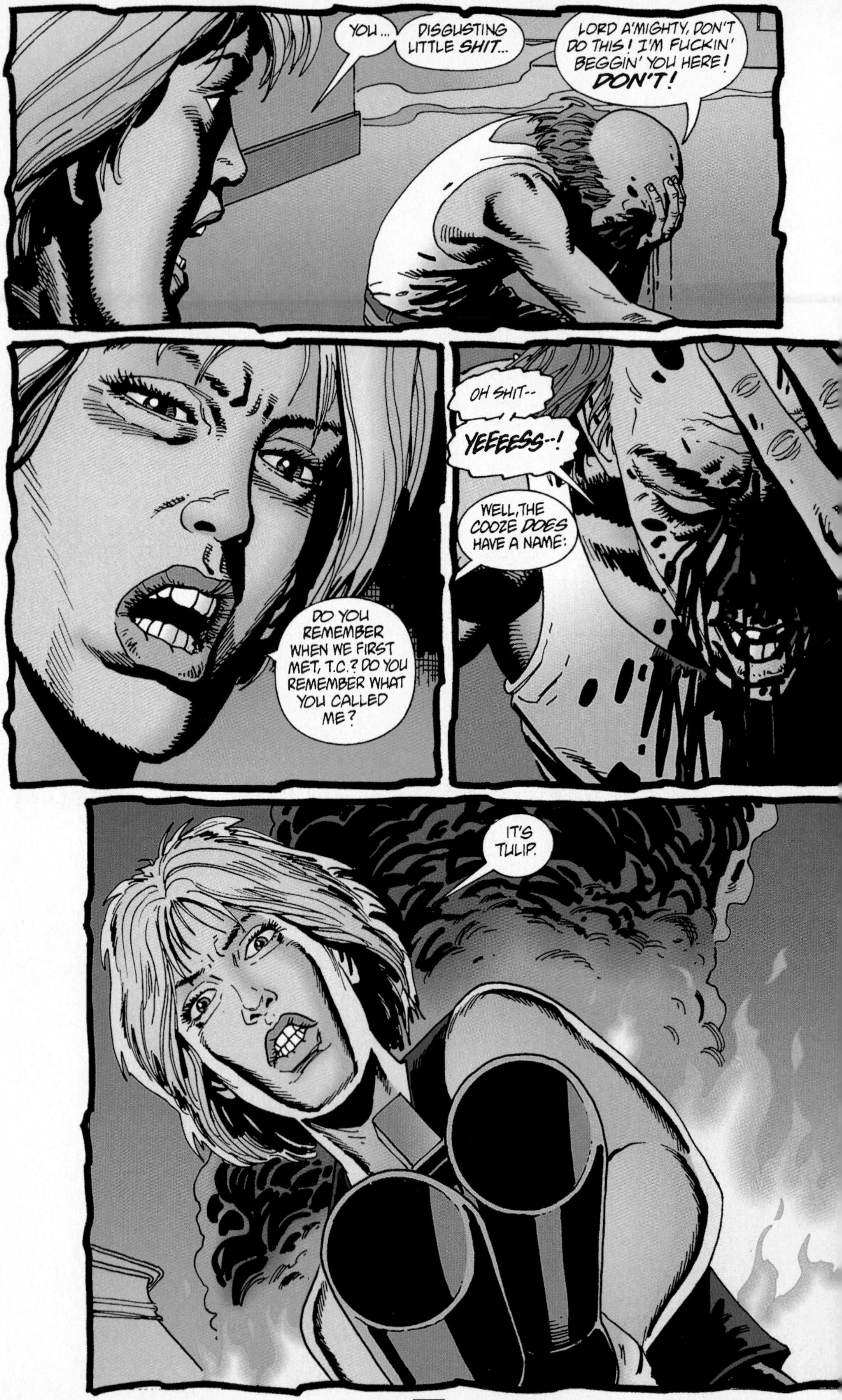
YOU...
DISGUSTING LITTLE SHIT...
LORD A'MIGHTY, DON'T DO THIS! I'M FUCKIN' BEGGIN' YOU HERE! DON'T!
DO YOU REMEMBER WHEN WE FIRST MET, T.C.? DO YOU REMEMBER WHAT YOU CALLED ME?
OH SHIT--
YEEEESS--!
WELL, THE COOZE DOES HAVE A NAME:
IT'S TULIP.

BADAMMM

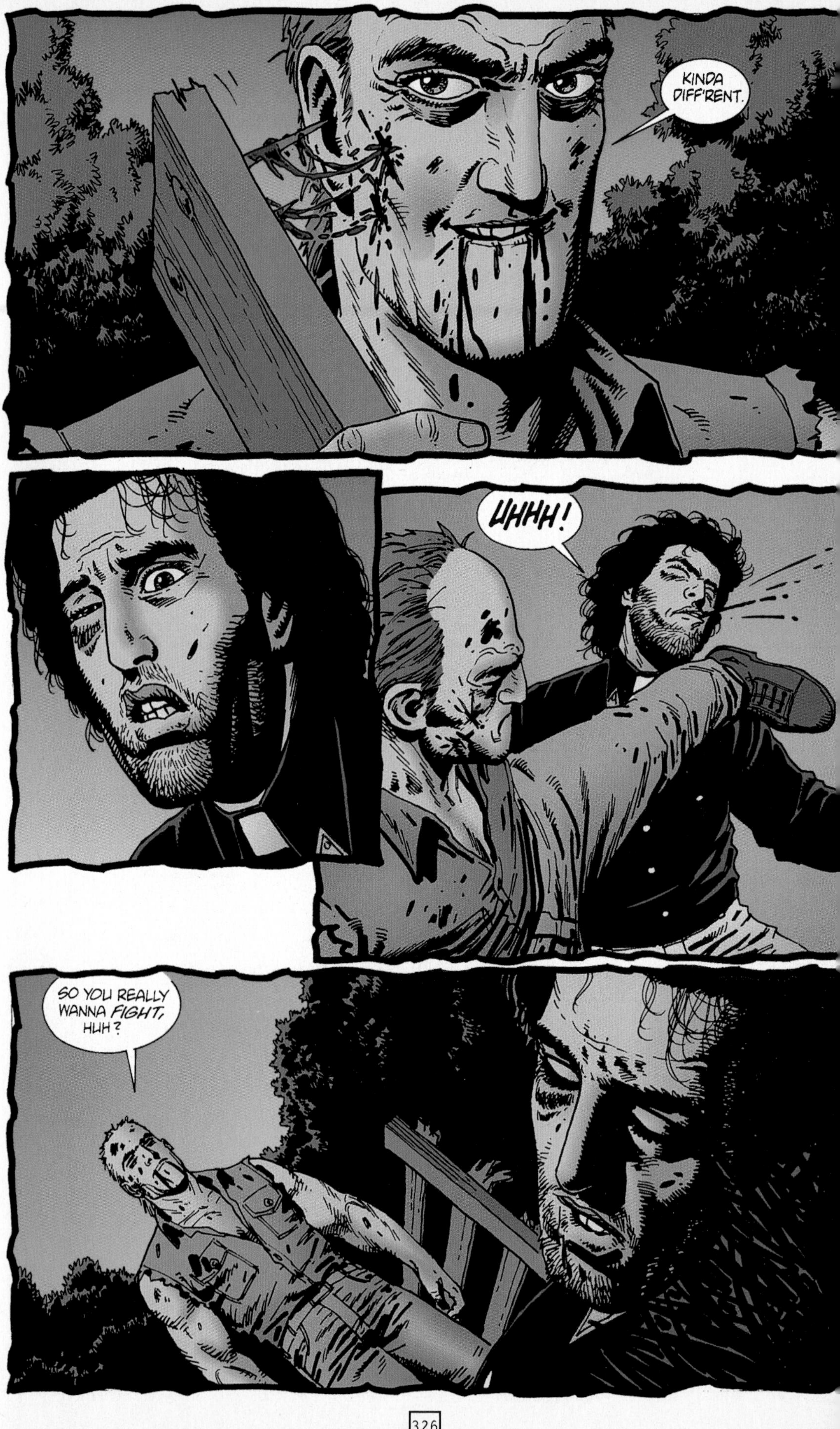
KINDA DIFF'RENT.
UHHH!
SO YOU REALLY WANNA *FIGHT*, HUH?

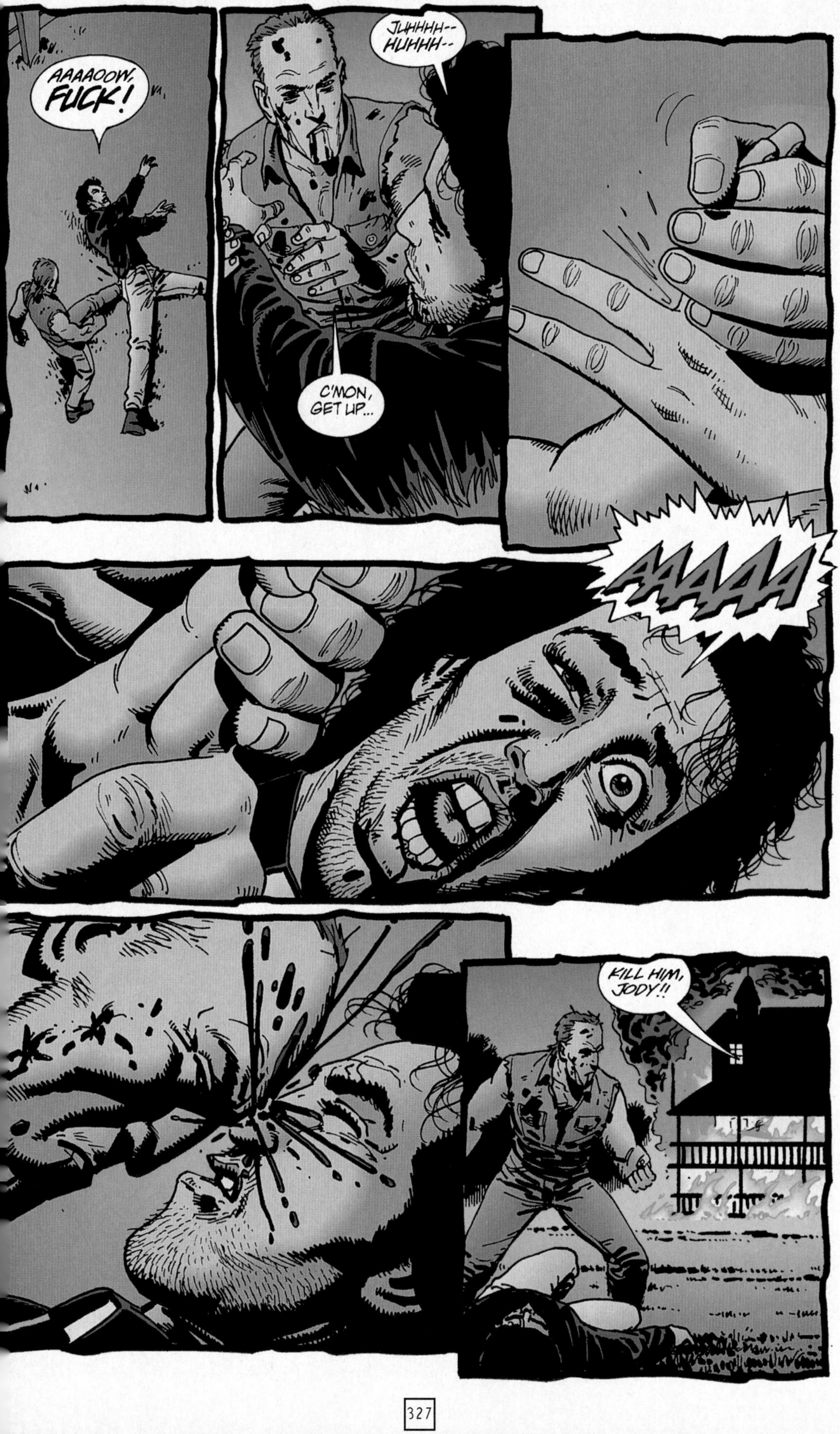
AAAAOOW, FUCK!
JUHHHH-- HUHHH--
C'MON, GET UP...
AAAAA
KILL HIM, JODY!!

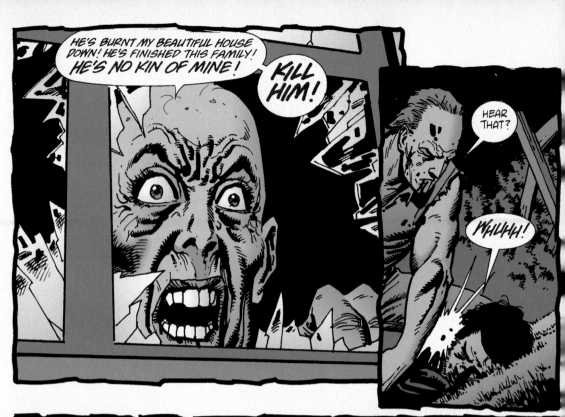

HE'S BURNT MY BEAUTIFUL HOUSE DOWN! HE'S FINISHED THIS FAMILY! **HE'S NO KIN OF MINE!**

KILL HIM!

HEAR THAT?

WHUHH!

BROUGHT IT ON YERSELF, BOY. YOU KNOW IT.

COULDN'T DO LIKE YOU WERE TOLD, COULD YOU? *HAD TO* GO YORE OWN WAY. YOU'D'VE LISTENED TO ME, WE COULDA MADE SOMETHIN' OUTTA YOU...

A FUCKIN'-- KILLER LIKE YOU?

YOU *PRICK...*

AW SHIT, I'M A KILLER!

SURE AM GLAD YOU BEEN PAYIN' ATTENTION!

S'POSE NOW YOU GONNA START WHININ' 'BOUT ME SHOOTIN' YORE ASSHOLE OF A FATHER, HUH?

FUCKER!

BEHAVE...!

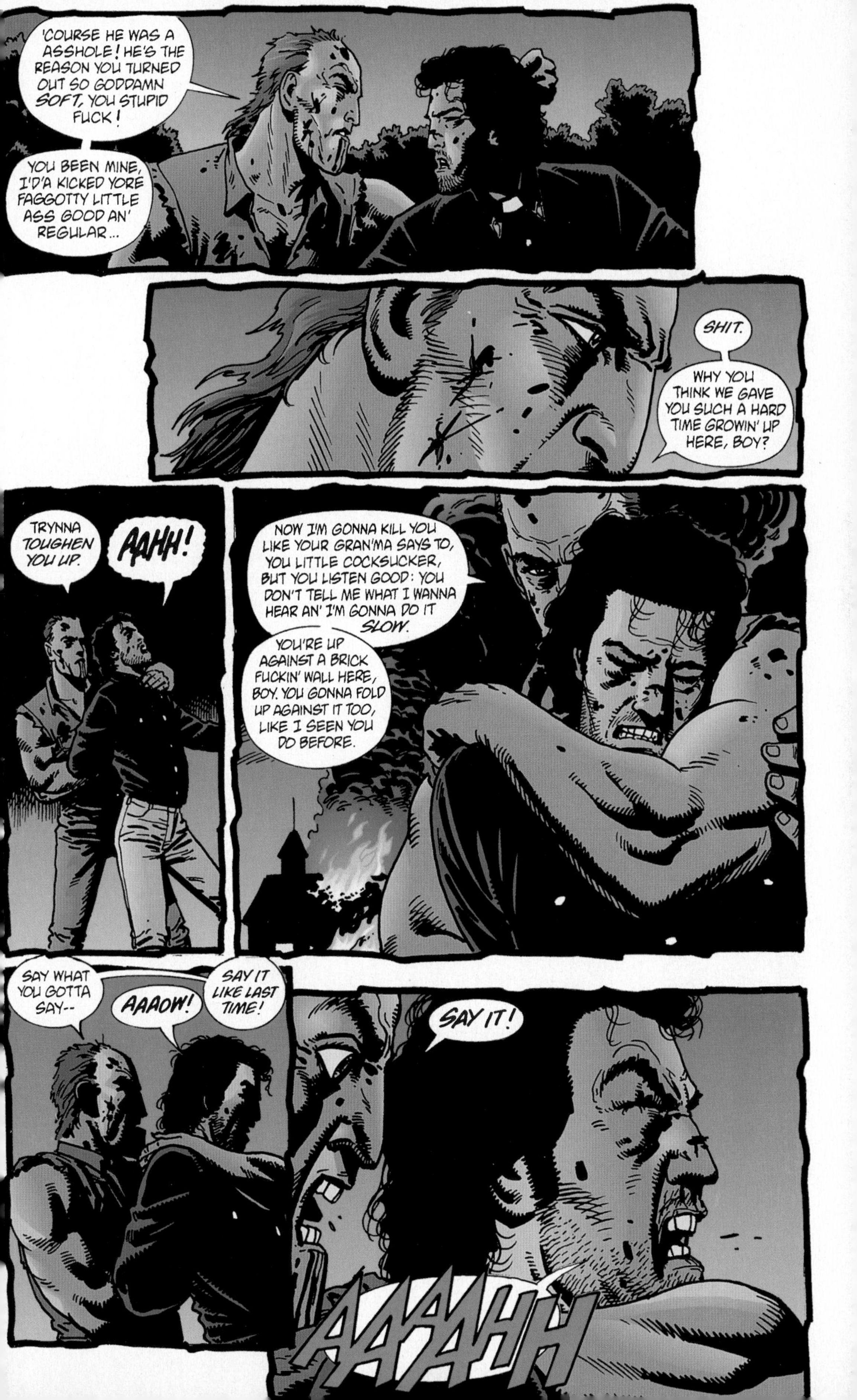
'COURSE HE WAS A ASSHOLE! HE'S THE REASON YOU TURNED OUT SO GODDAMN SOFT, YOU STUPID FUCK!
YOU BEEN MINE, I'D'A KICKED YORE FAGGOTTY LITTLE ASS GOOD AN' REGULAR...
SHIT.
WHY YOU THINK WE GAVE YOU SUCH A HARD TIME GROWIN' UP HERE, BOY?
TRYNNA TOUGHEN YOU UP.
AAHH!
NOW I'M GONNA KILL YOU LIKE YOUR GRAN'MA SAYS TO, YOU LITTLE COCKSUCKER, BUT YOU LISTEN GOOD: YOU DON'T TELL ME WHAT I WANNA HEAR AN' I'M GONNA DO IT SLOW.
YOU'RE UP AGAINST A BRICK FUCKIN' WALL HERE, BOY. YOU GONNA FOLD UP AGAINST IT TOO, LIKE I SEEN YOU DO BEFORE.
SAY WHAT YOU GOTTA SAY--
AAAOW!
SAY IT LIKE LAST TIME!
SAY IT!
AAAAHH

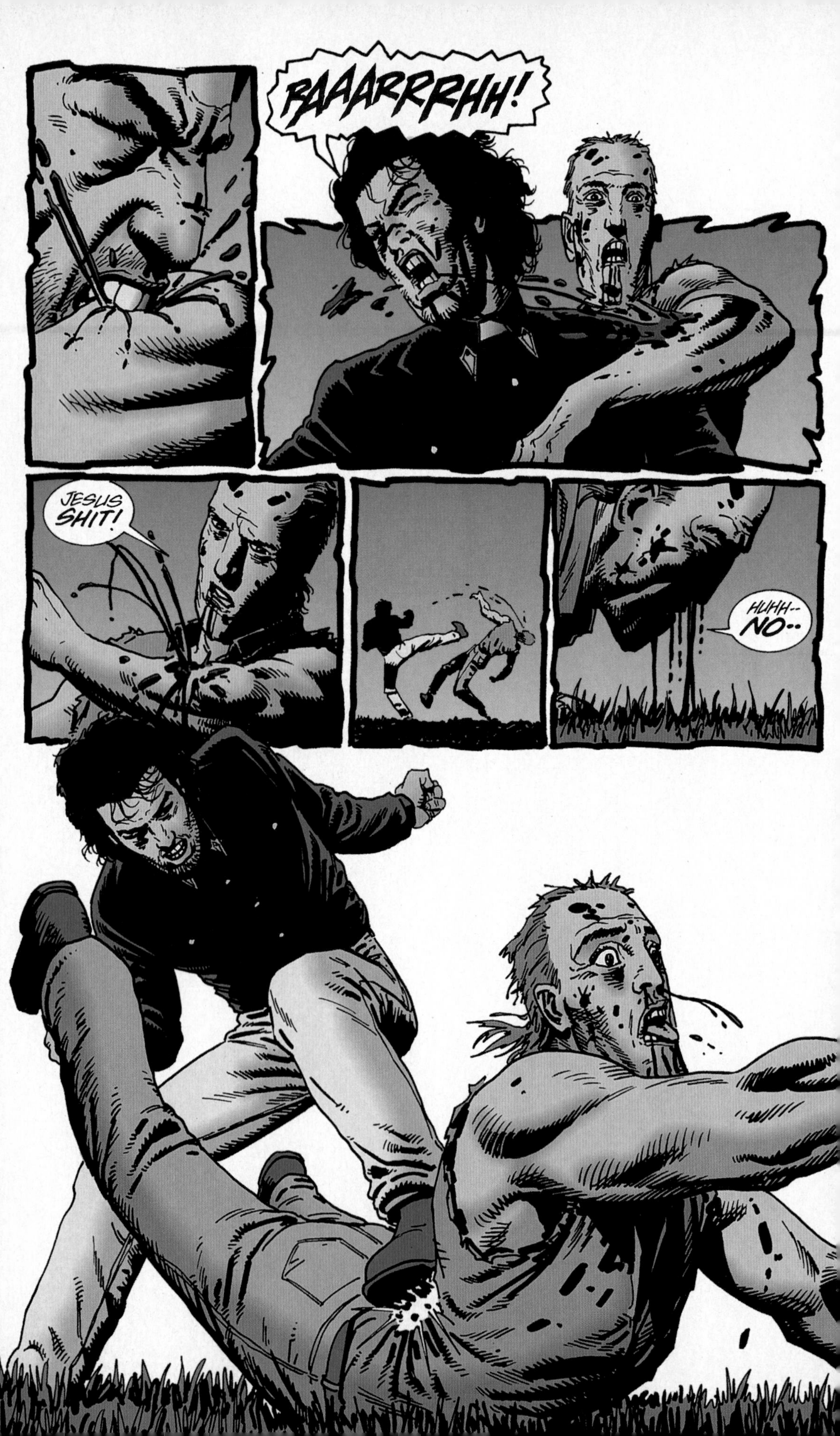
RAAARRRRHH!
JESUS SHIT!
HUHH-- NO--

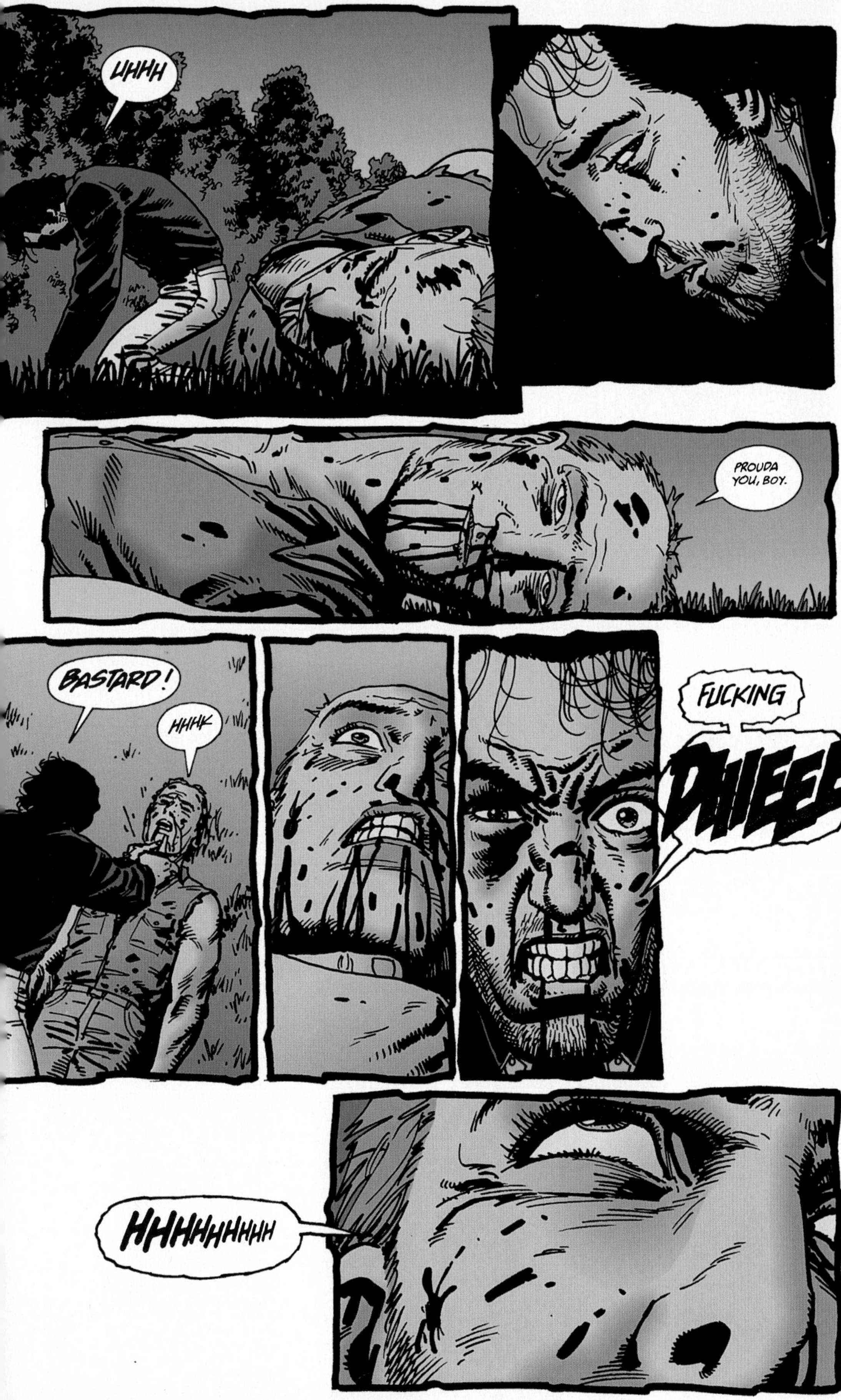
UHHH
PROUDA YOU, BOY.
BASTARD!
HHHK
FUCKING
DHEEE
HHHHHHHHH

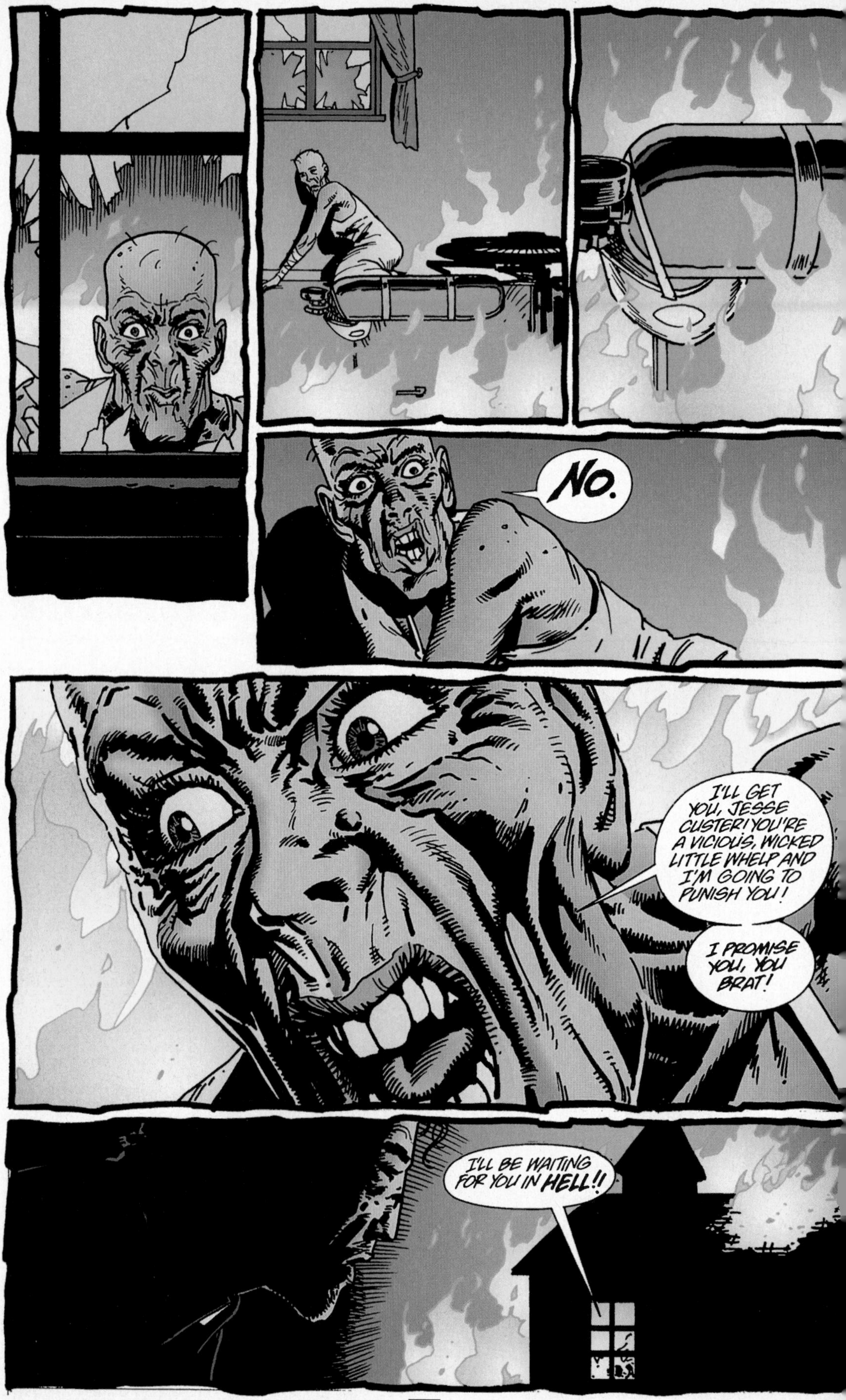
NO.
I'LL GET YOU, JESSE CUSTER! YOU'RE A VICIOUS, WICKED LITTLE WHELP AND I'M GOING TO PUNISH YOU!
I PROMISE YOU, YOU BRAT!
I'LL BE WAITING FOR YOU IN HELL!!

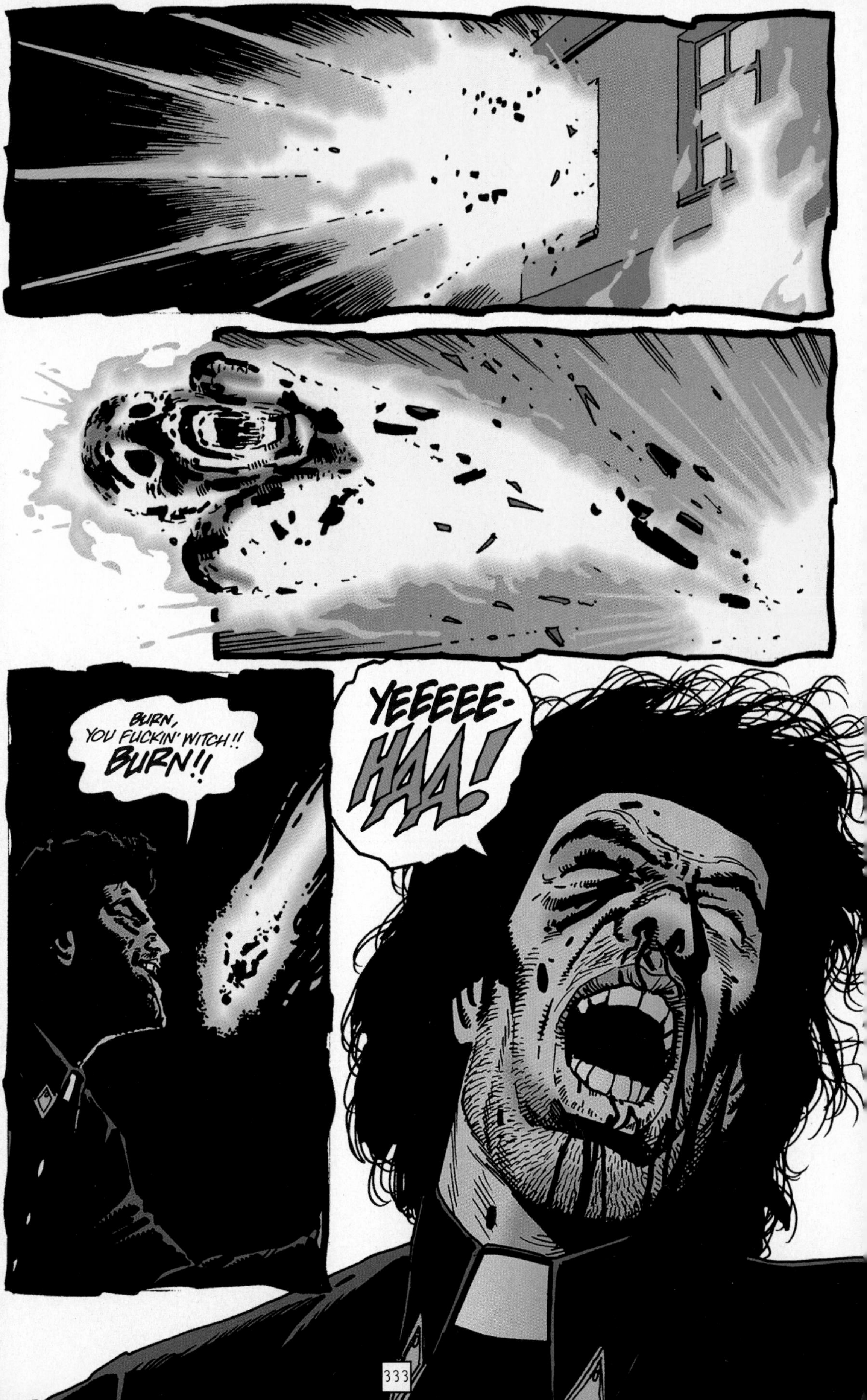
BURN, YOU FUCKIN' WITCH!! BURN!!
YEEEEE-HAA!

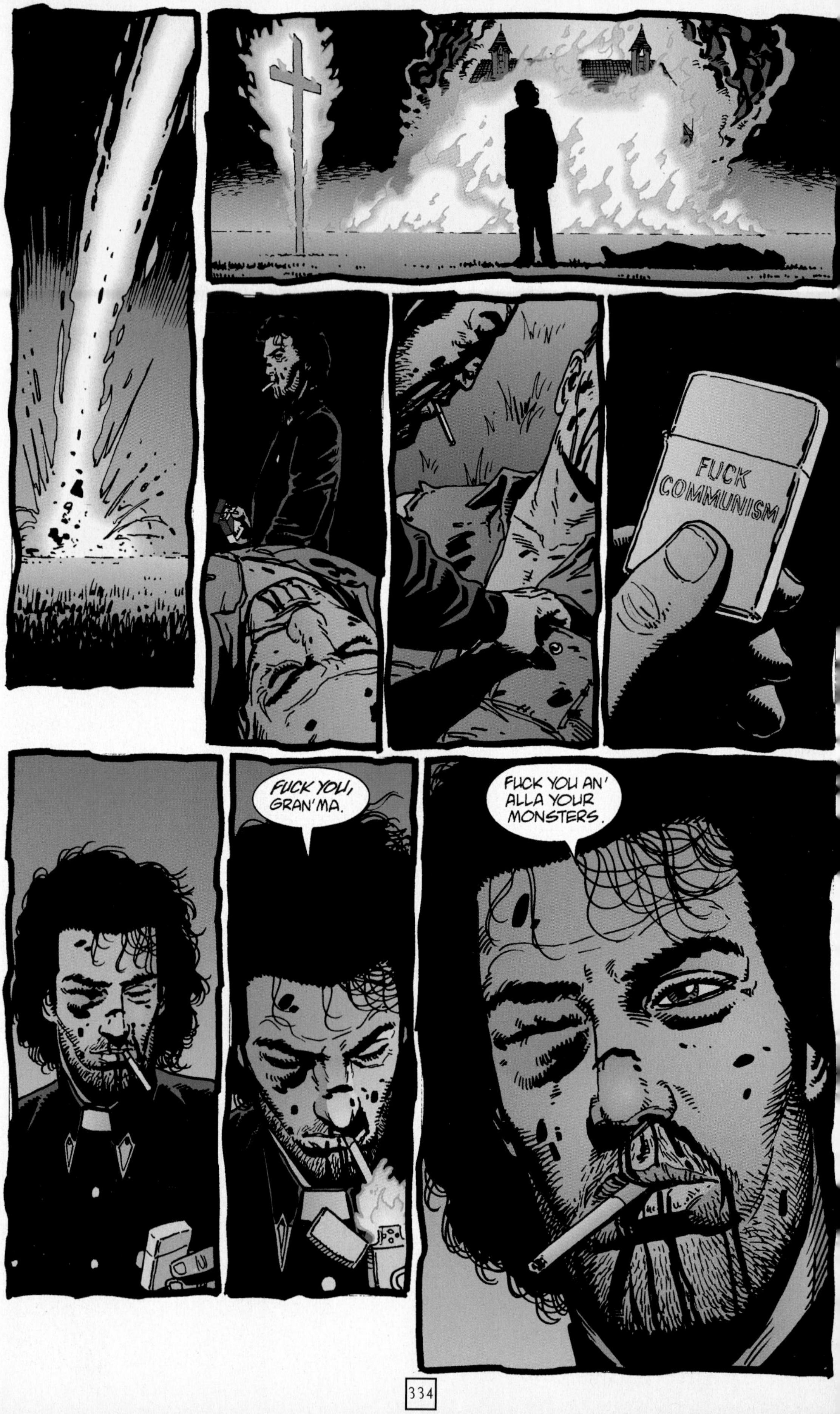
FUCK COMMUNISM
FUCK YOU, GRAN'MA.
FUCK YOU AN' ALLA YOUR MONSTERS.

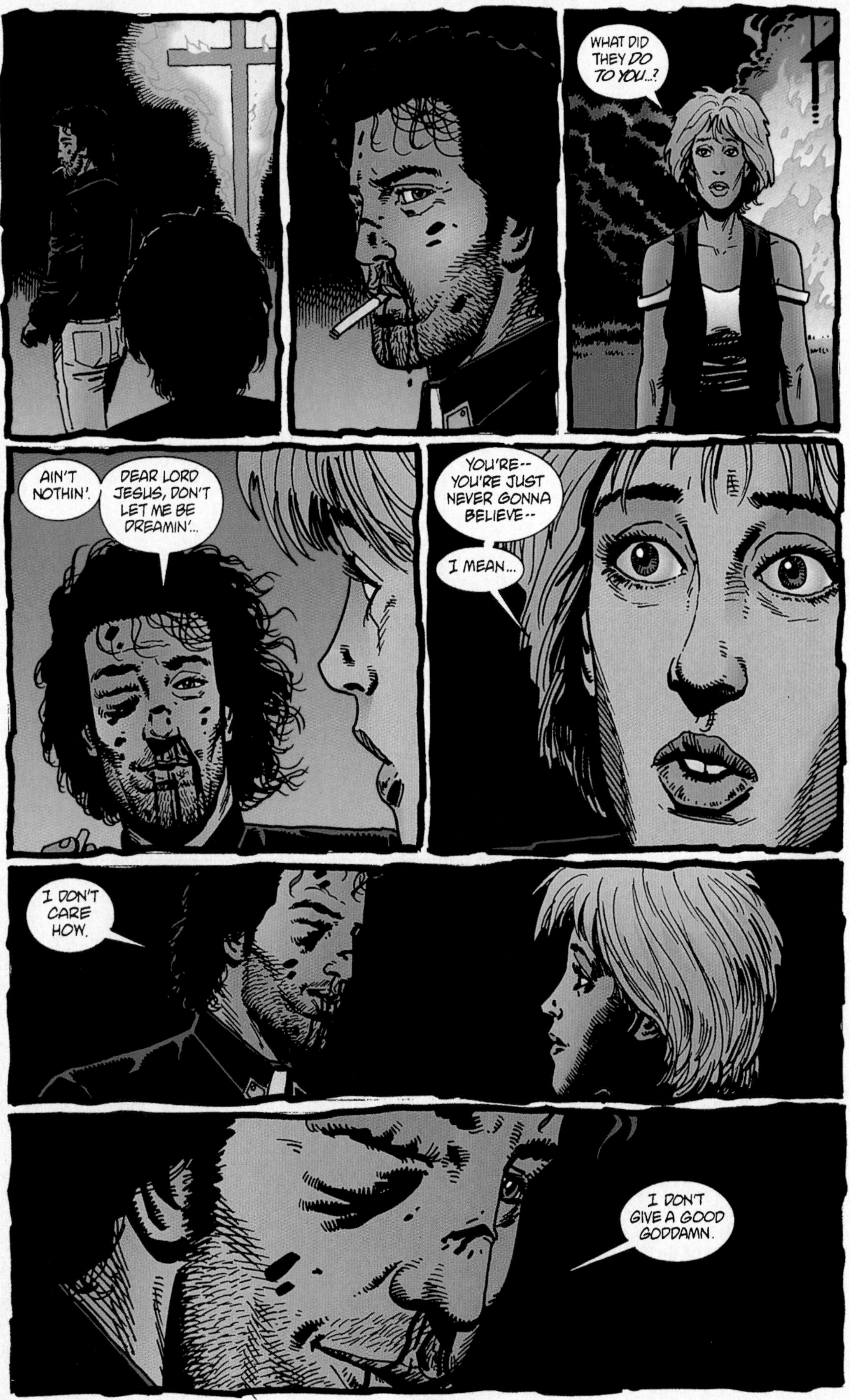
WHAT DID THEY *DO* TO YOU...?
AIN'T NOTHIN'.
DEAR LORD JESUS, DON'T LET ME BE DREAMIN'...
YOU'RE-- YOU'RE JUST NEVER GONNA BELIEVE--
I MEAN...
I DON'T CARE HOW.
I DON'T GIVE A GOOD GODDAMN.

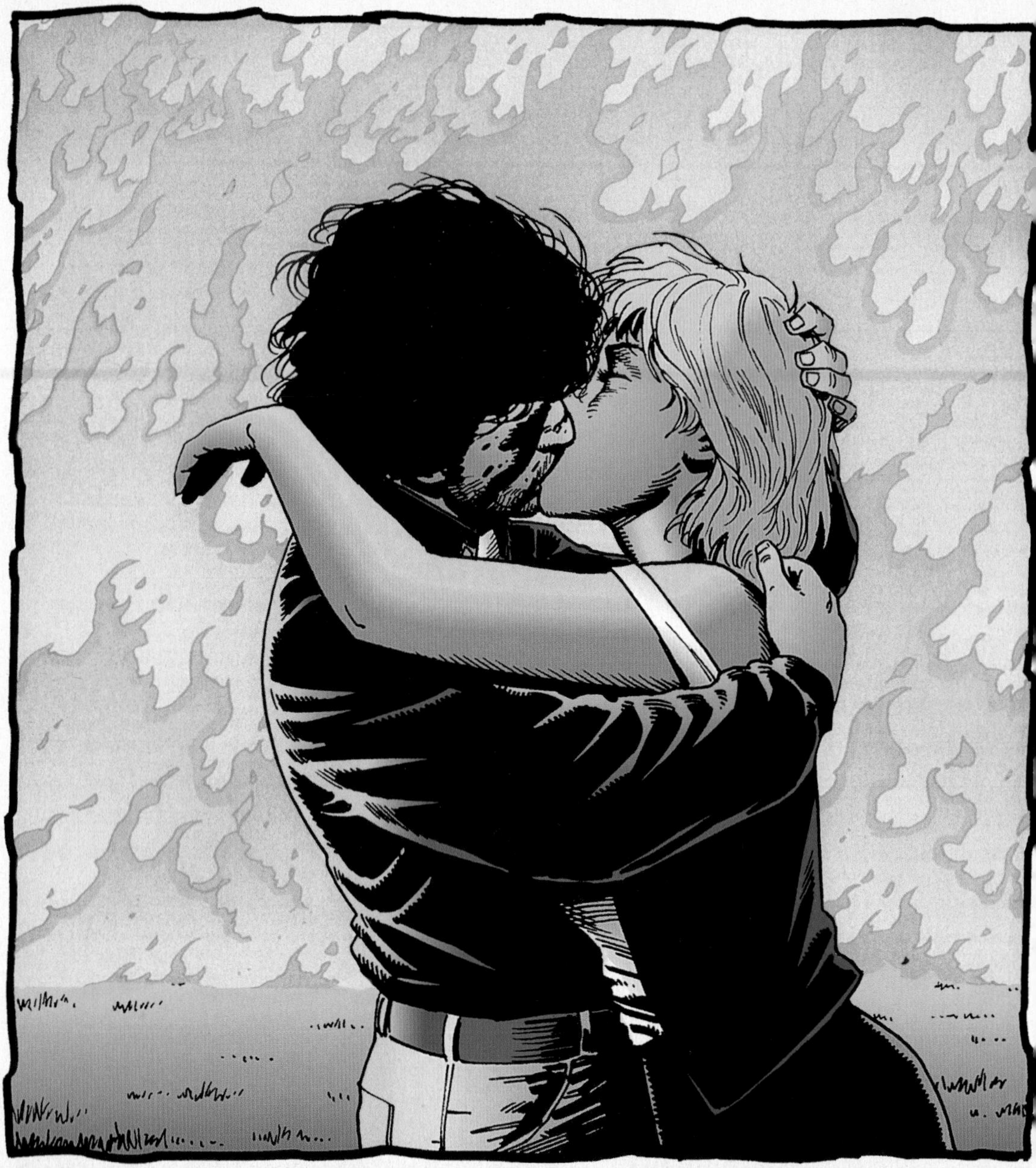

UNTIL THE END OF THE WORLD

GARTH ENNIS
WRITER

STEVE DILLON
ARTIST

MATT HOLLINGSWORTH - COLORIST

CLEM ROBINS - LETTERER

STUART MOORE
AND
AXEL ALONSO
- EDITORS

PREACHER CREATED BY
GARTH ENNIS AND STEVE DILLON

WANTED
A PREACHER Gallery

art by **Tim Bradstreet**
color by Matt Hollingsworth
338

art by **Glenn Fabry**
color by Matt Hollingsworth
339

art by **John McCrea**
color by Matt Hollingsworth
340

art by **Doug Mahnke**
color by Matt Hollingsworth
341

pencils by **Joe Quesada** · inks by **Jimmy Palmiotti**
color by Matt Hollingsworth
342

art by **Kieron Dwyer**
color by Matt Hollingsworth
343

pencils by **Jim Lee** · inks by **Scott Williams**
color by Tad Ehrlich
344

art by **Dave Gibbons**
color by Matt Hollingsworth
345

pencils by **Amanda Conner** · inks by **Jimmy Palmiotti**
color by Matt Hollingsworth
346

art by **Carlos Ezquerra**
color by Matt Hollingsworth
347

art by **John Higgins**
color by Matt Hollingsworth
348

art and color by **Dave Johnson**
349

art by **J.G. Jones**
color by Matt Hollingsworth
350

art by **Brian Bolland**
color by Matt Hollingsworth
351

art by **Bruce Timm**
color by Matt Hollingsworth
352

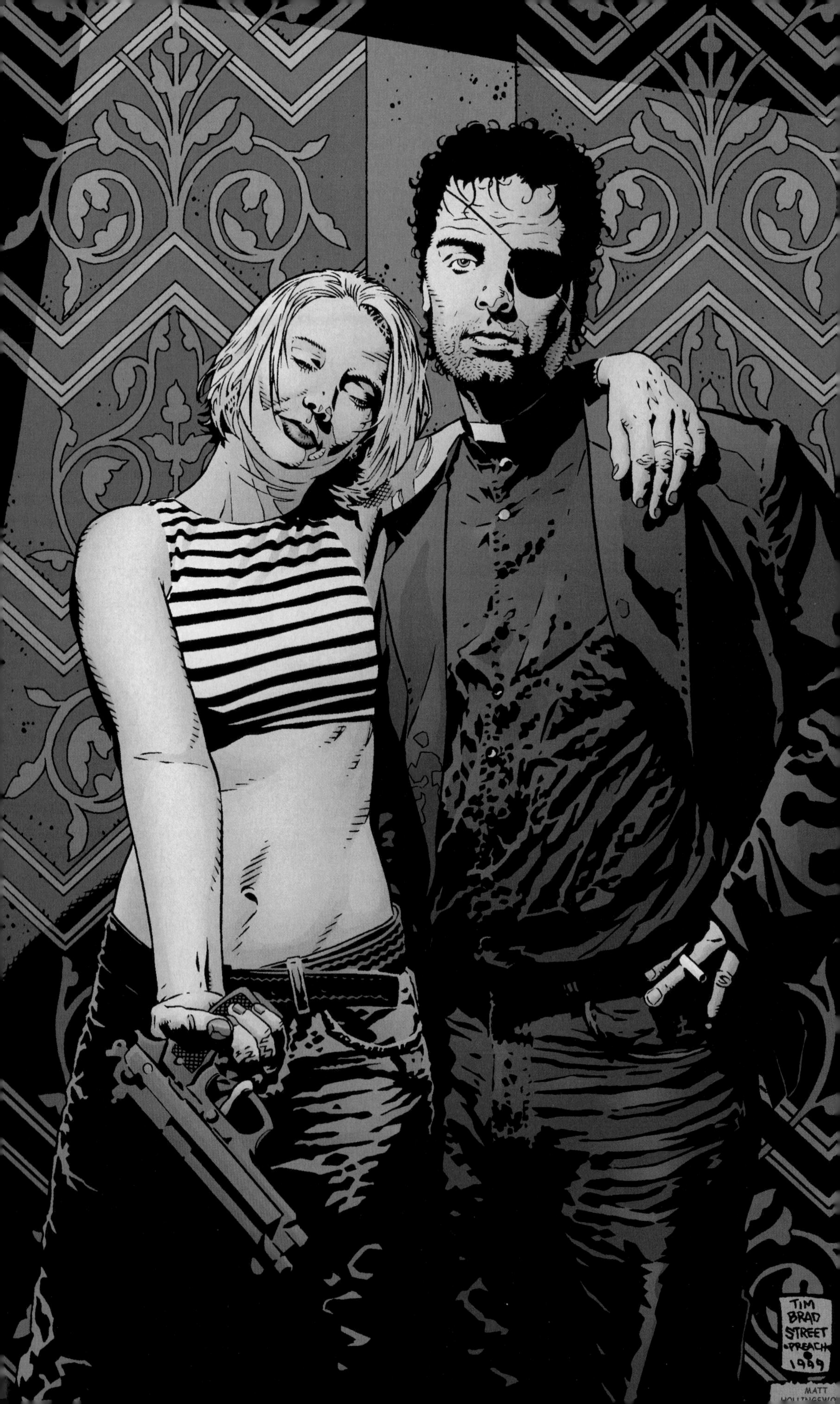
TIM BRAD STREET
•PREACH
1999
MATT

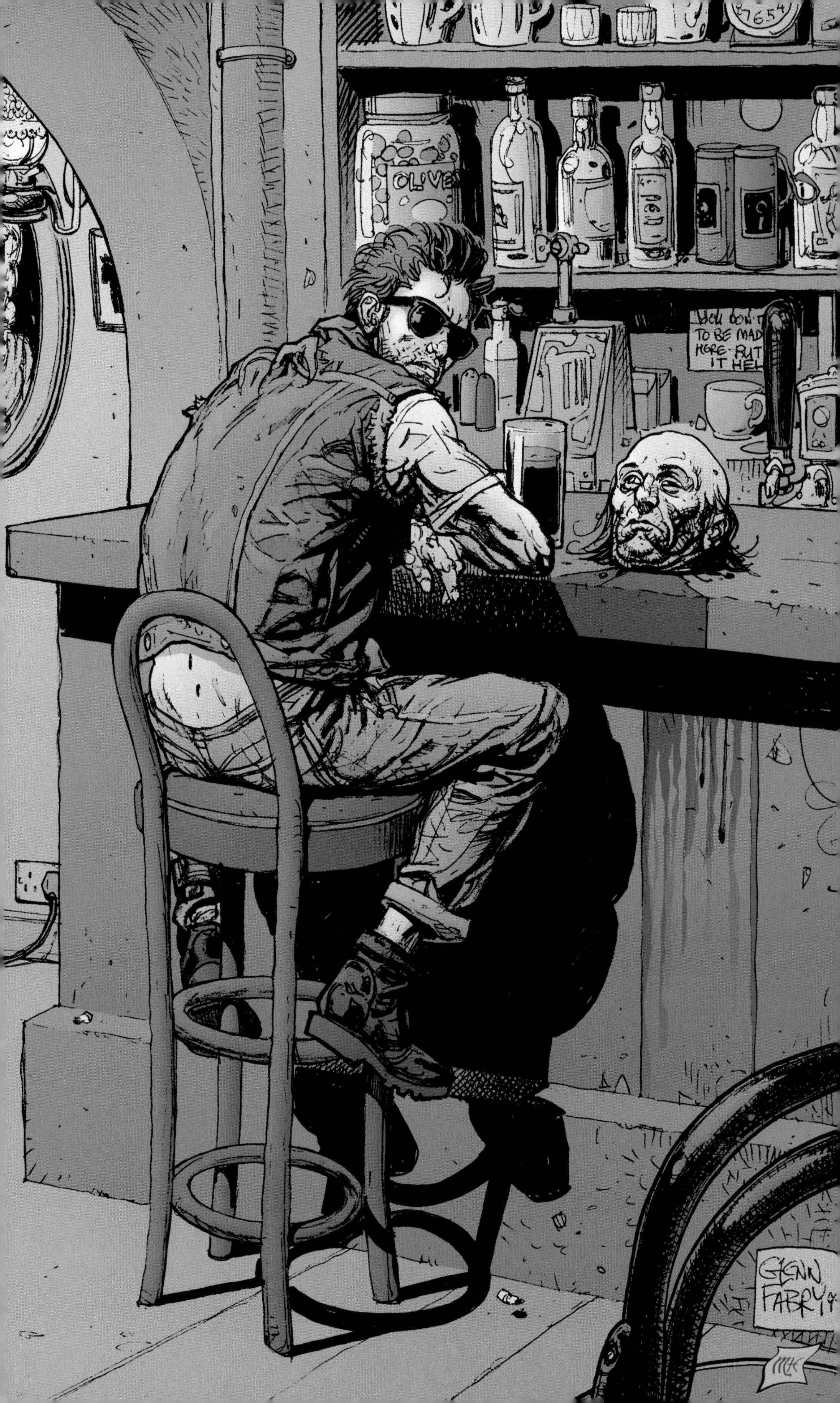
OLIVES
YOU DON'T
TO BE MAD
HERE--BUT
IT HEL
GLENN FABRY

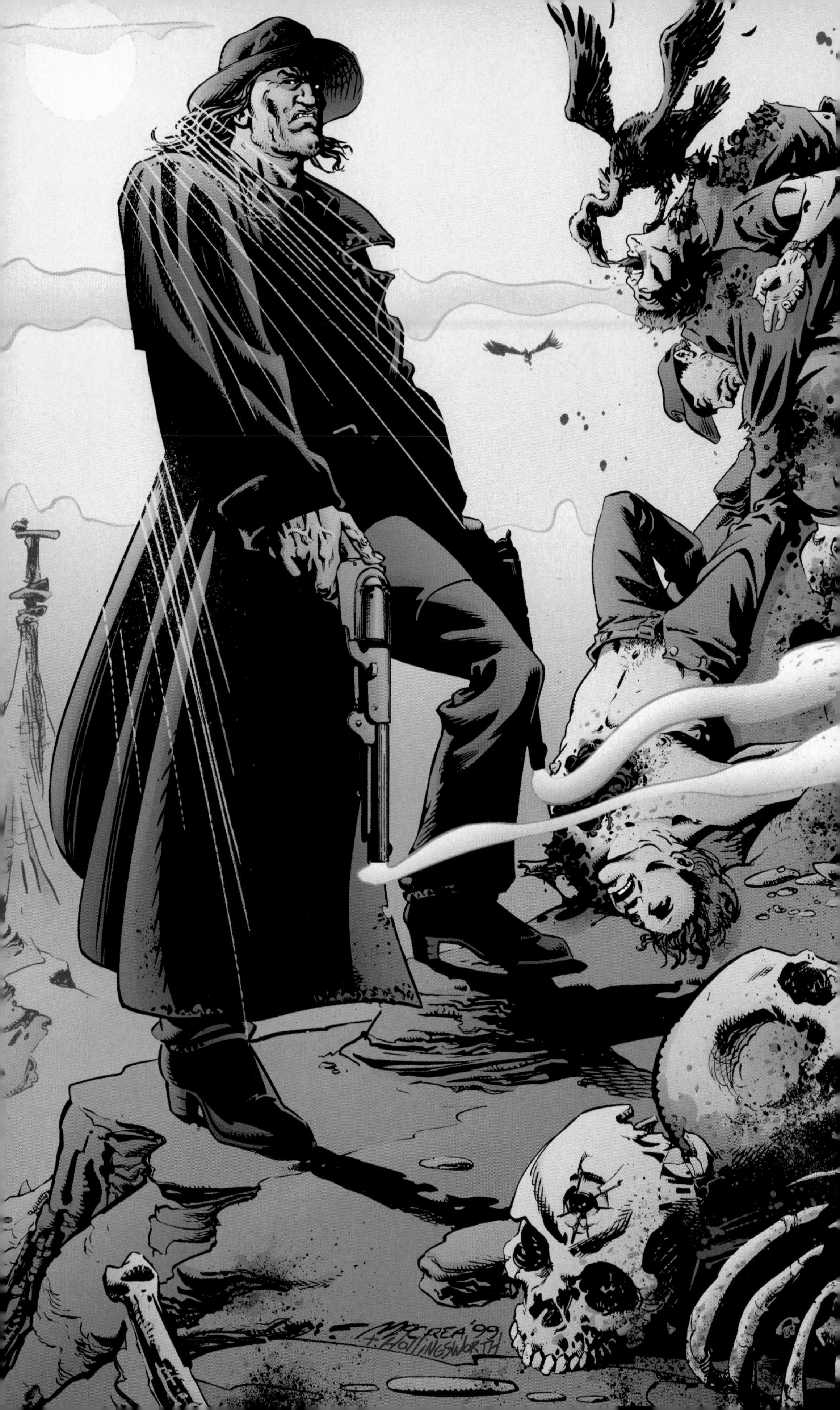
McCREA '99
+ HOLLINGSWORTH

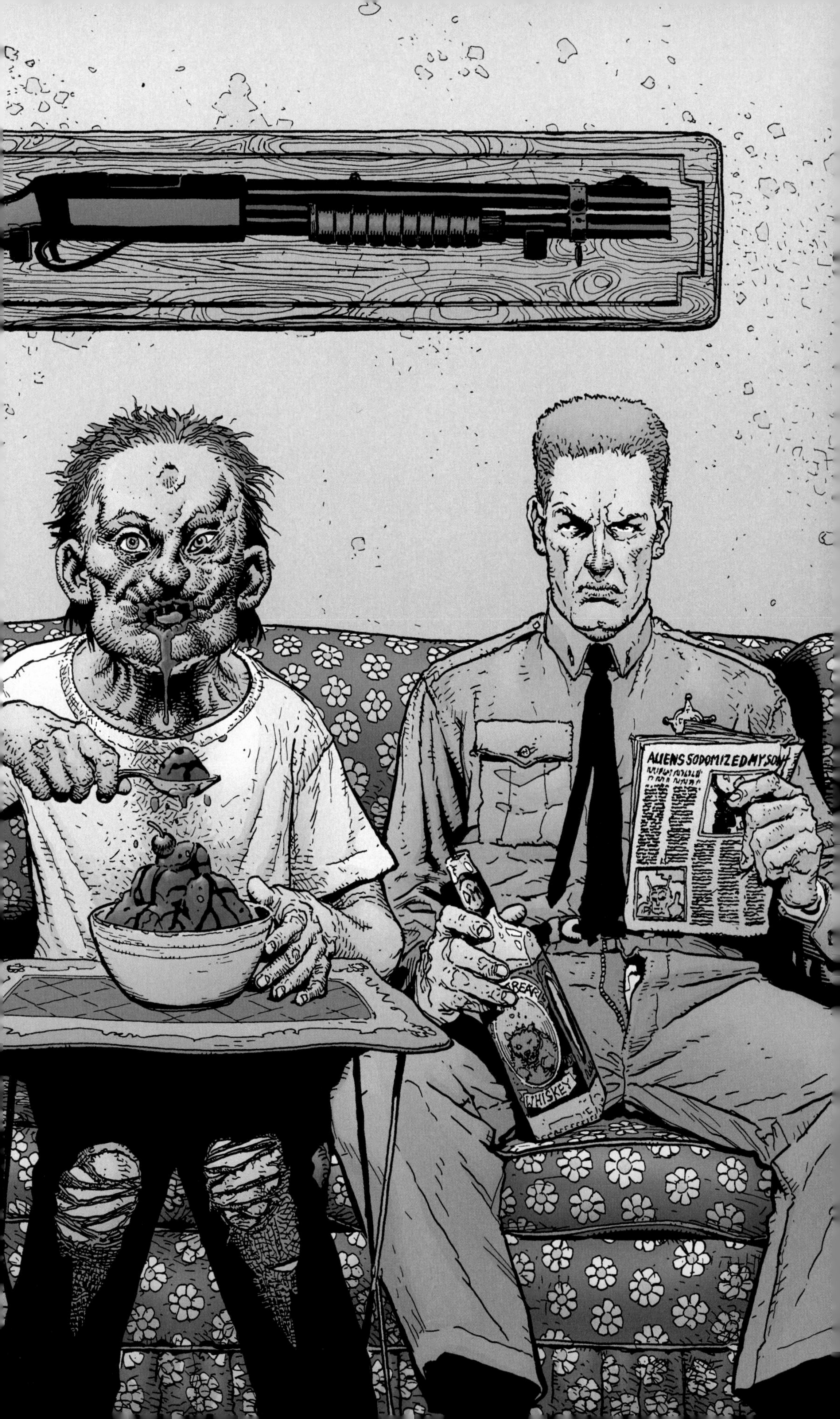
ALIENS SODOMIZED MY SON
WHISKEY

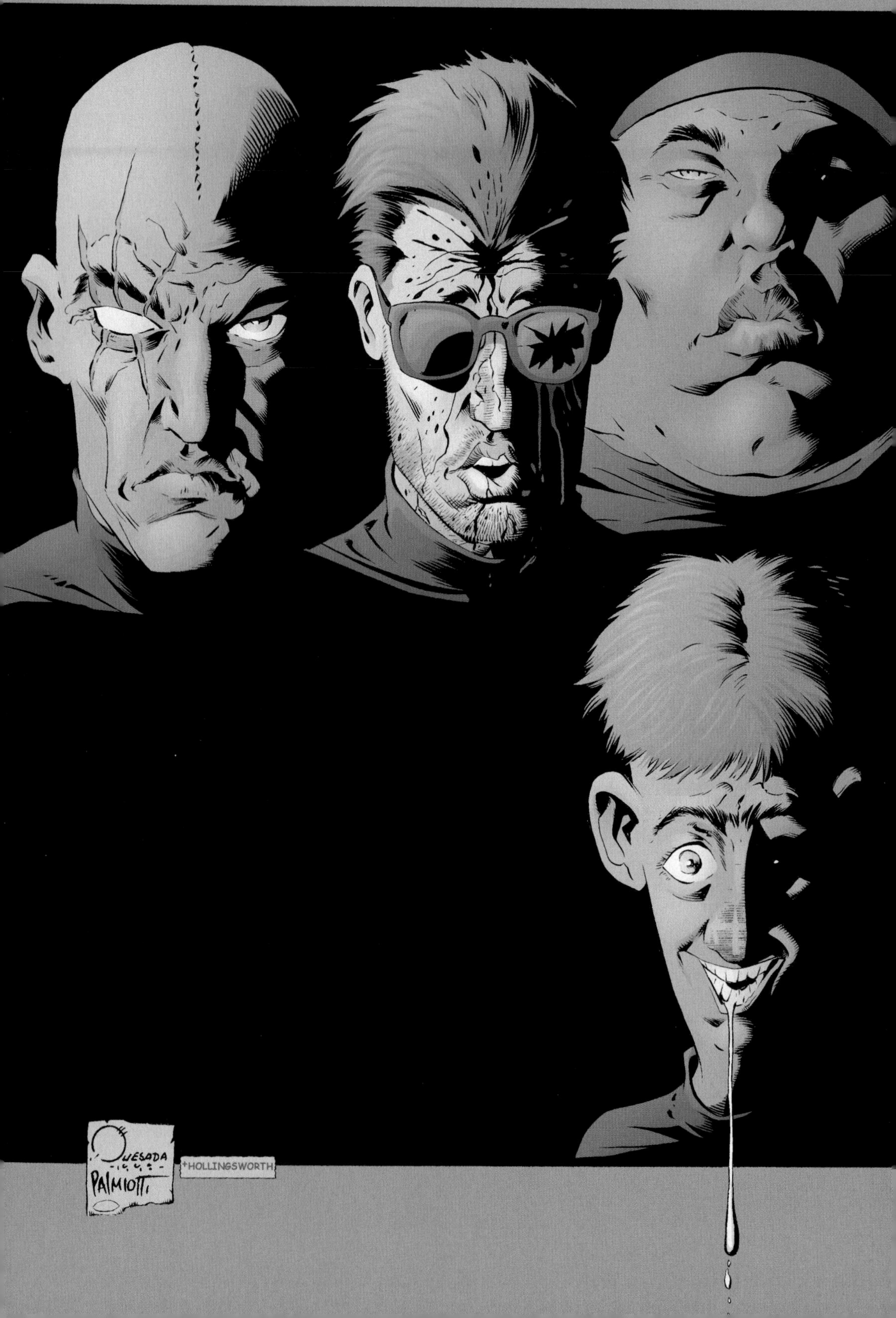
QUESADA
PALMIOTTI
+HOLLINGSWORTH

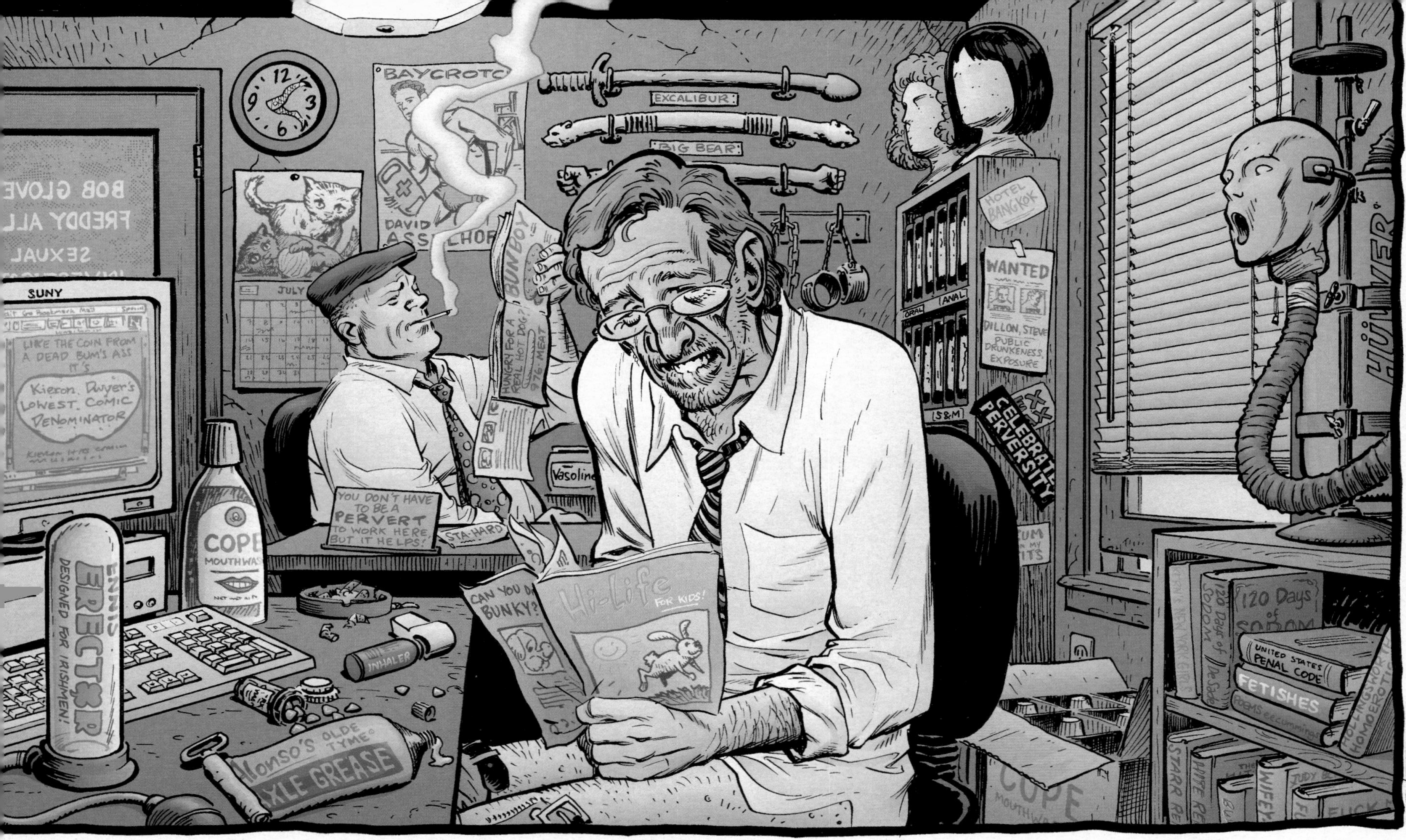
BAYCROTC
DAVID ASS LHOR
EXCALIBUR
BIG BEAR
HOTEL BANGKOK
WANTED
DILLON, STEVE
PUBLIC DRUNKENESS, EXPOSURE
ORAL
ANAL
S&M
CELEBRATE PERVERSITY
HÜVVER
JULY
BOB GLOVE
FREDDY ALL
SEXUAL
SUNY
LIKE THE COIN FROM A DEAD BUM'S ASS IT'S
Kieron Dwyer's LOWEST COMIC DENOMINATOR
HUNGRY FOR A REAL HOT DOG? 976-MEAT
BUNBOY
Vasoline
YOU DON'T HAVE TO BE A PERVERT TO WORK HERE, BUT IT HELPS!
STA-HARD
COPE MOUTHWASH
ENNIS ERECTOR DESIGNED FOR IRISHMEN!
INHALER
Alonso's OLDE TYME AXLE GREASE
CAN YOU DRAW BUNKY?
Hi-Life FOR KIDS!
120 Days of SODOM
120 Days of SODOM De Sade
NEW YORK GIRLS
UNITED STATES PENAL CODE
FETISHES
HOLLINGSWORTH HOMOEROTIC
WIFEY
STARR RE
HITE RE
COPE MOUTHWASH
99

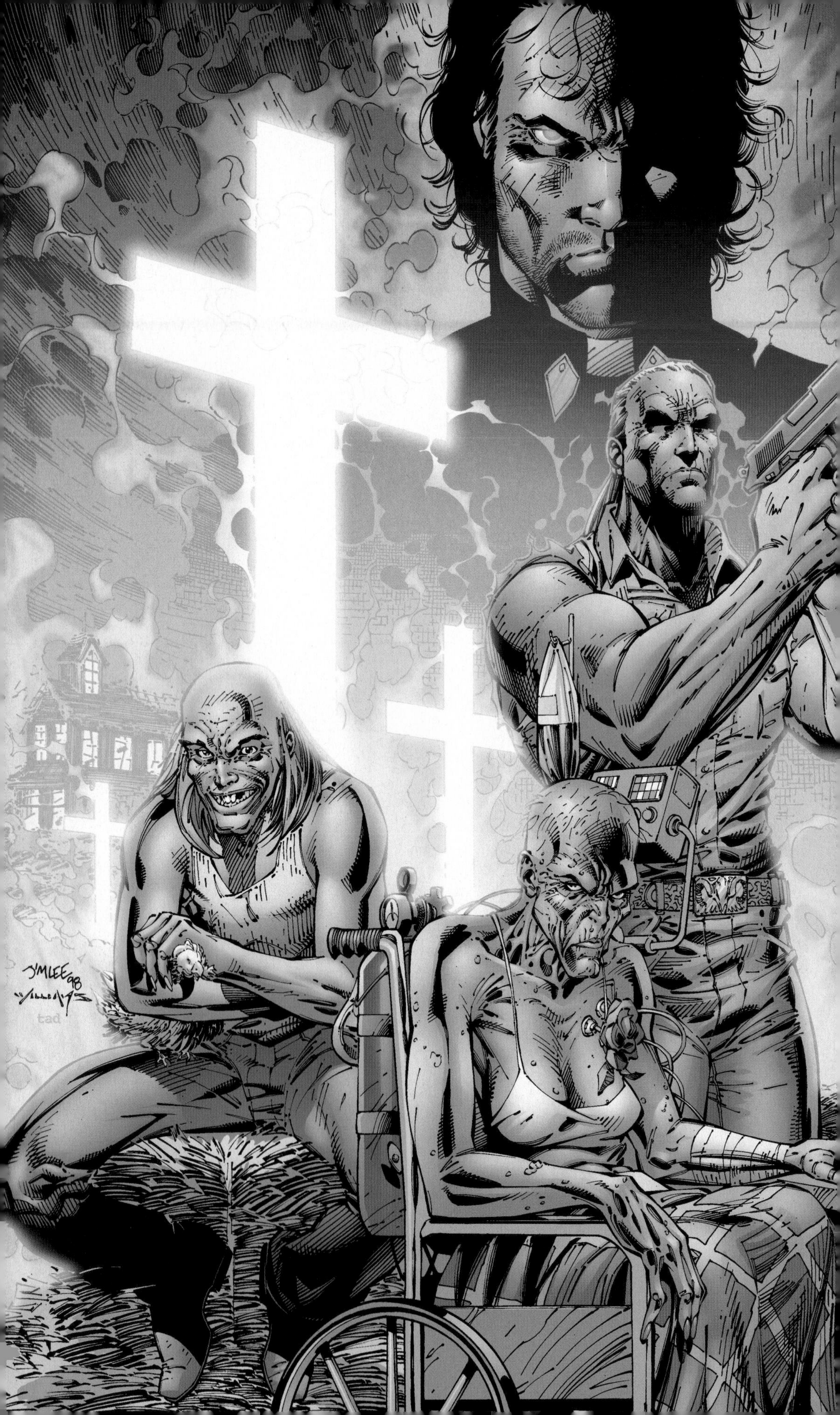
tad

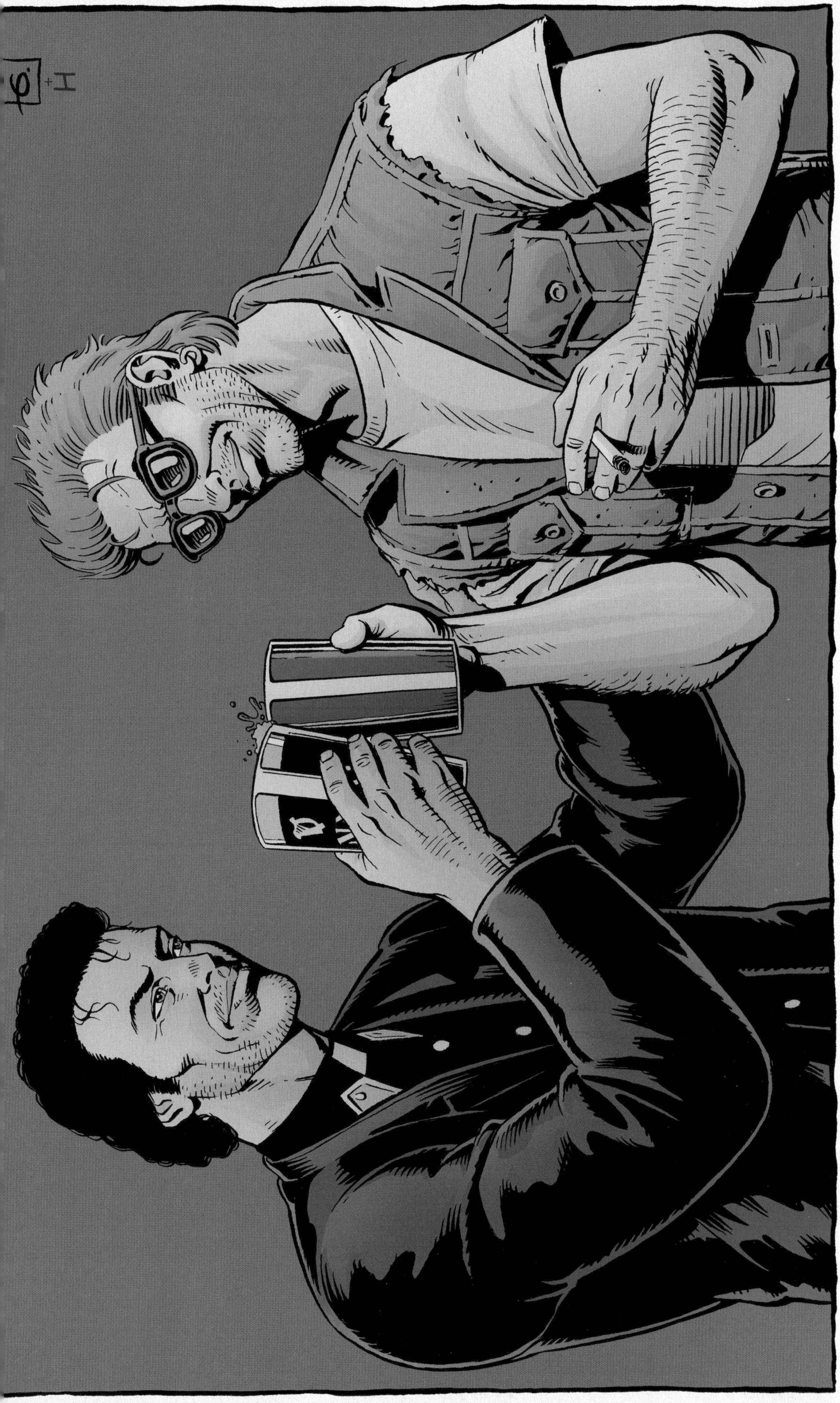

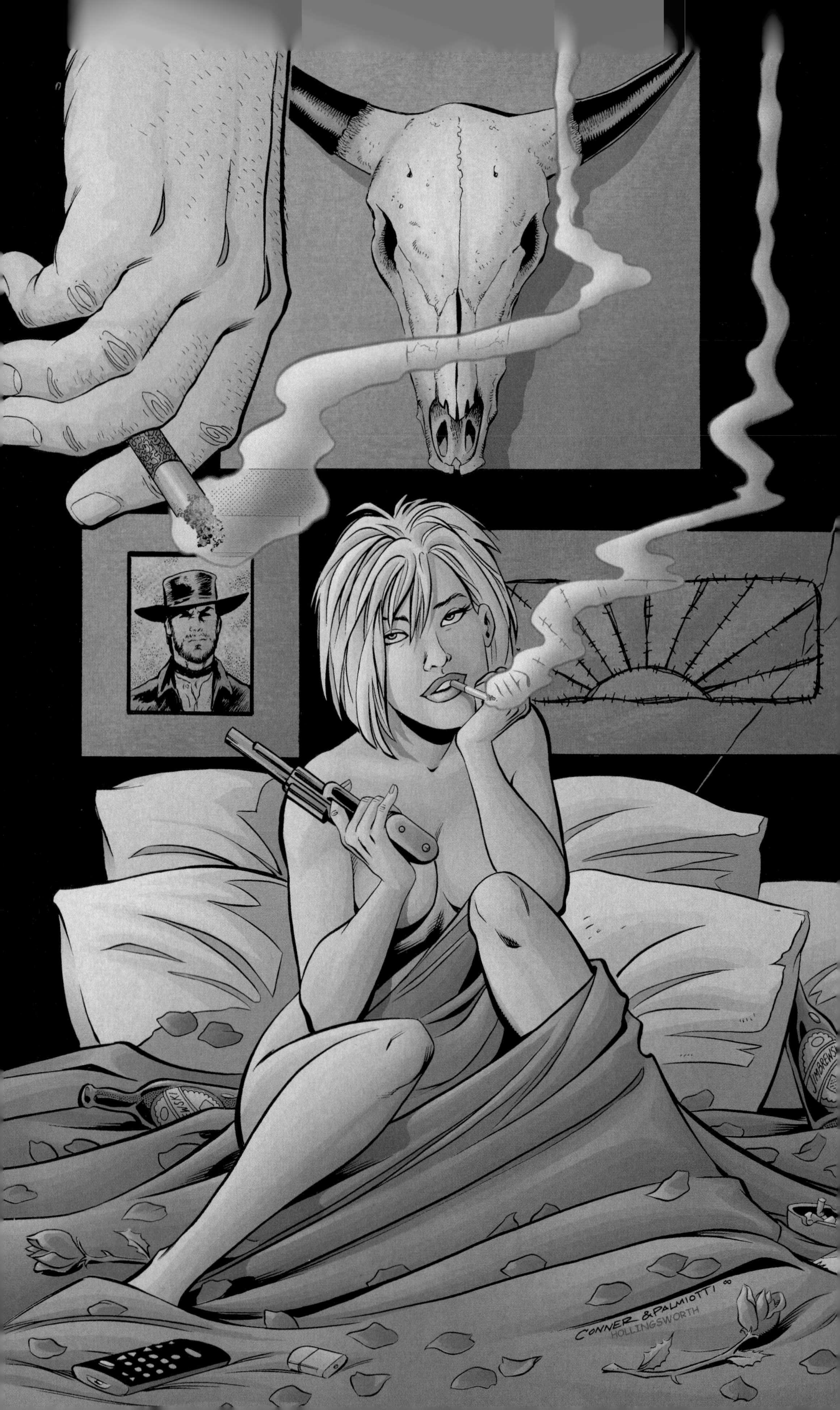
CONNER &PALMIOTTI
HOLLINGSWORTH

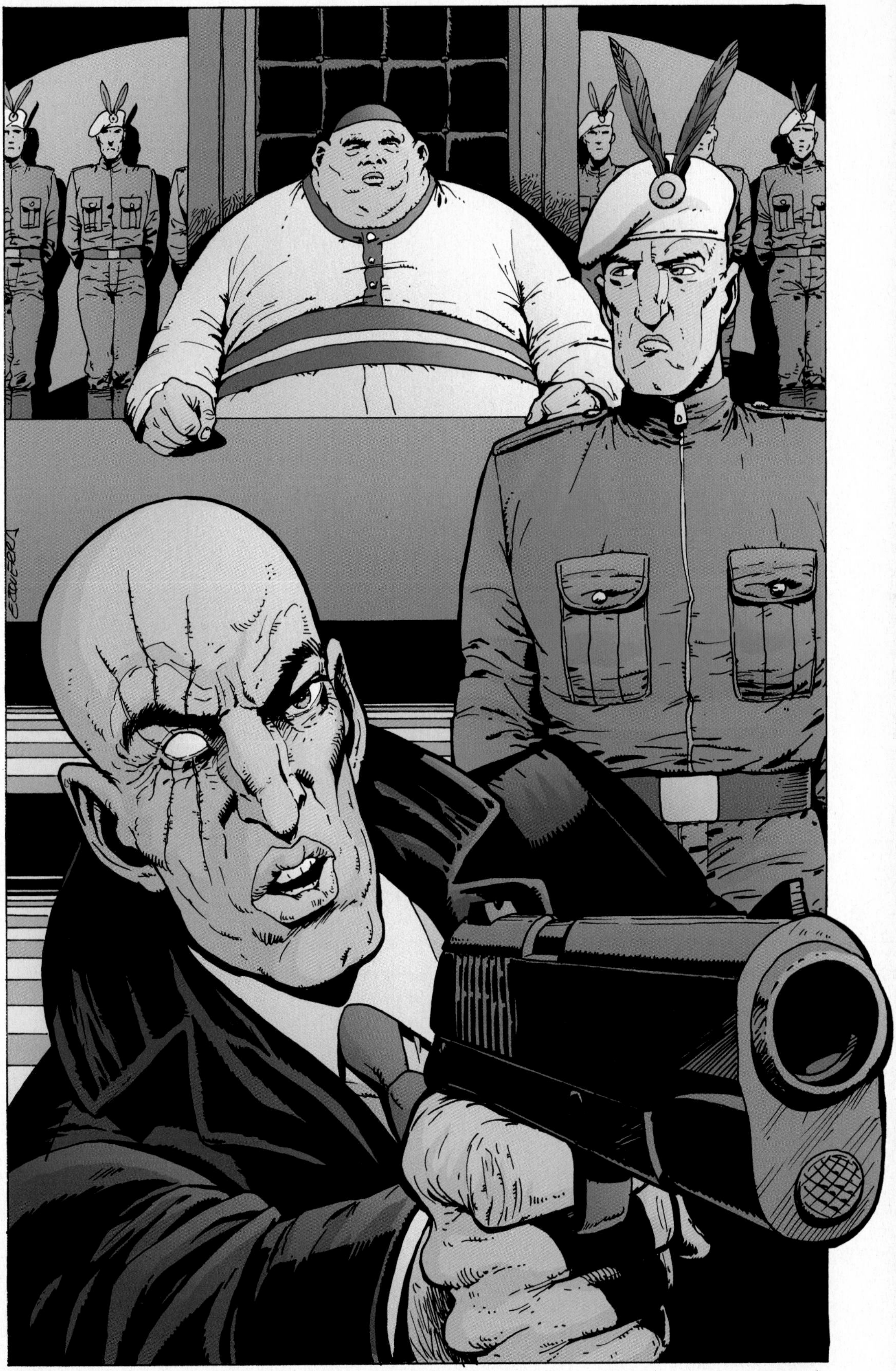

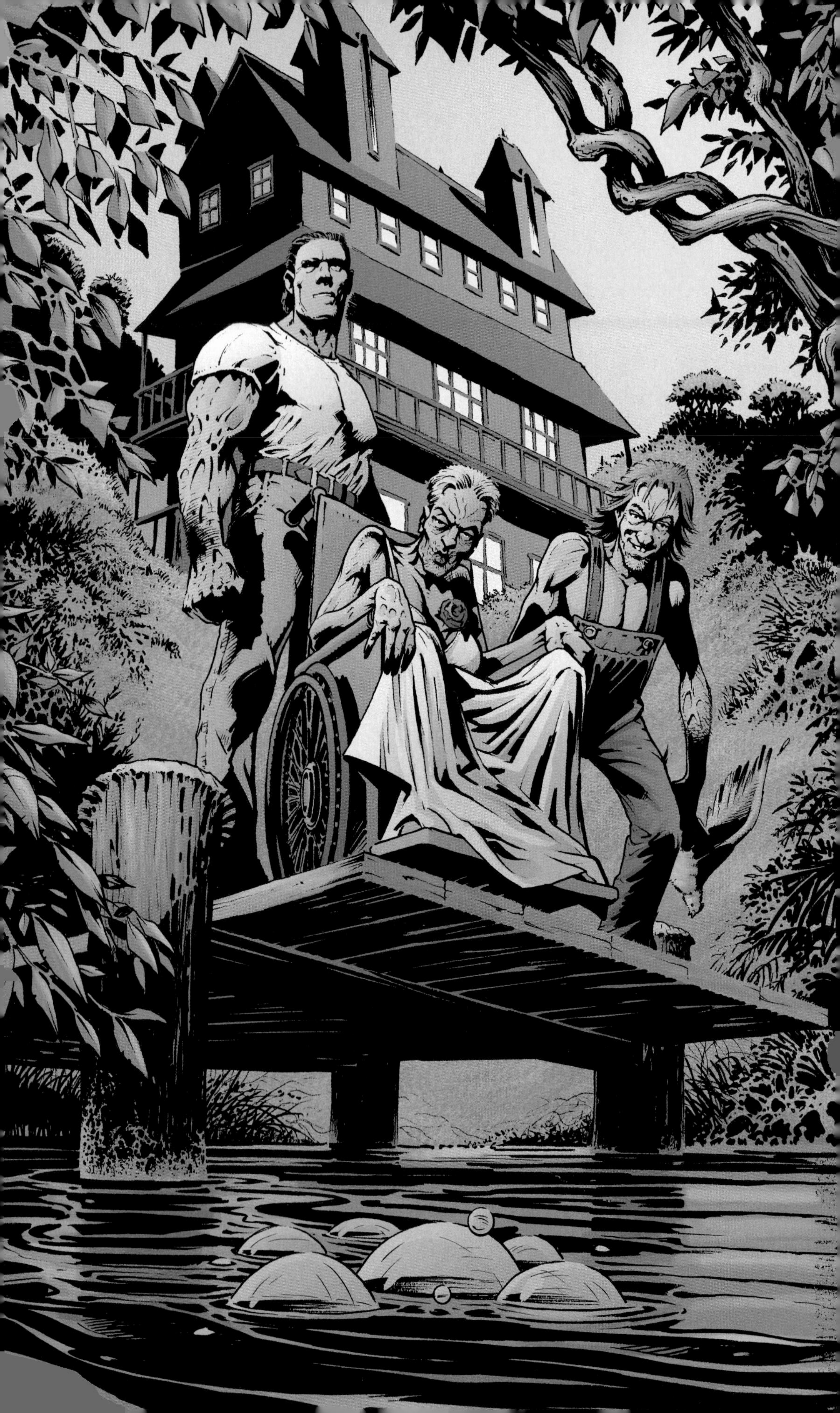

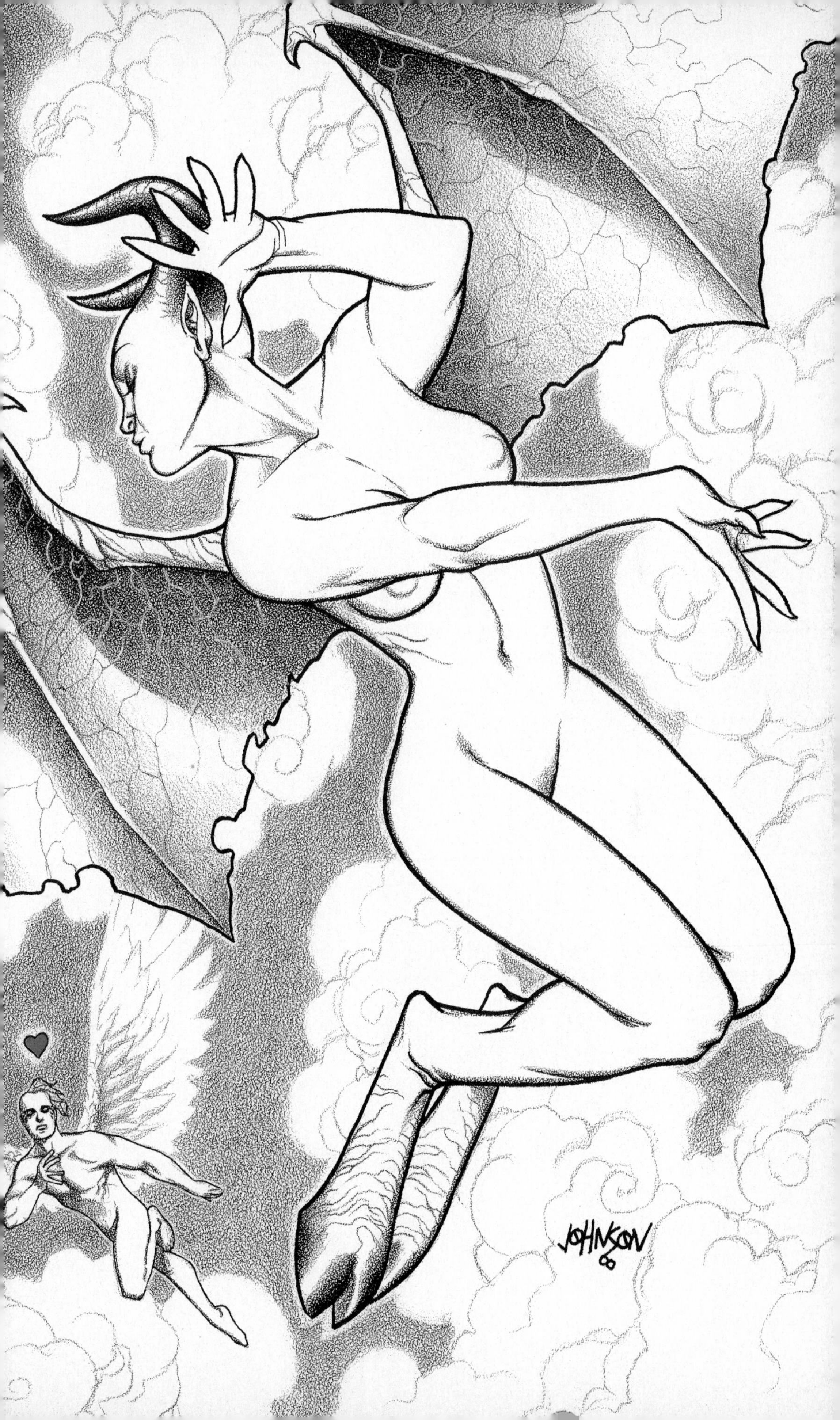
JOHNSON
06

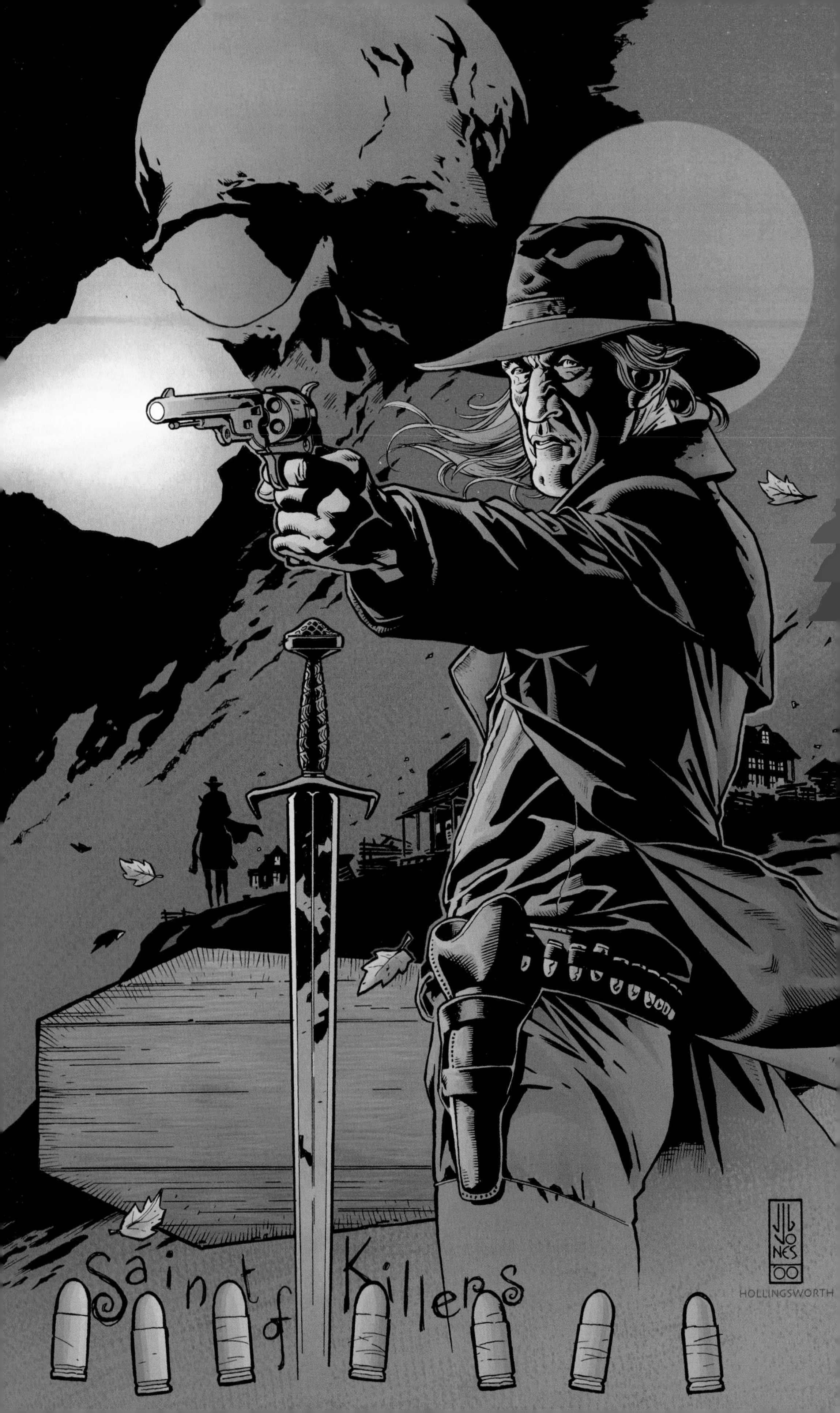
Saint of Killers
JG JONES 00
HOLLINGSWORTH

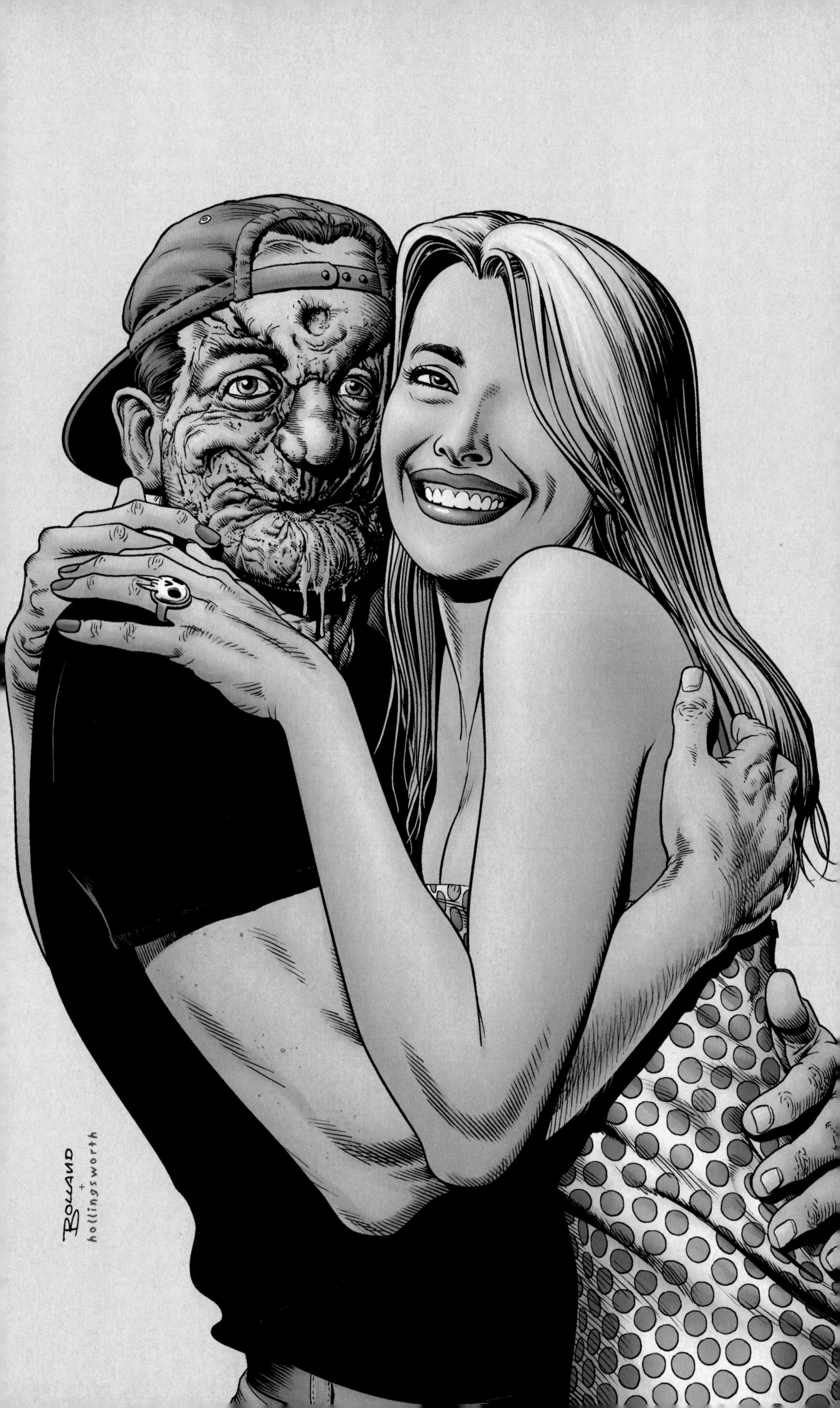
BOLLAND
+
hollingsworth

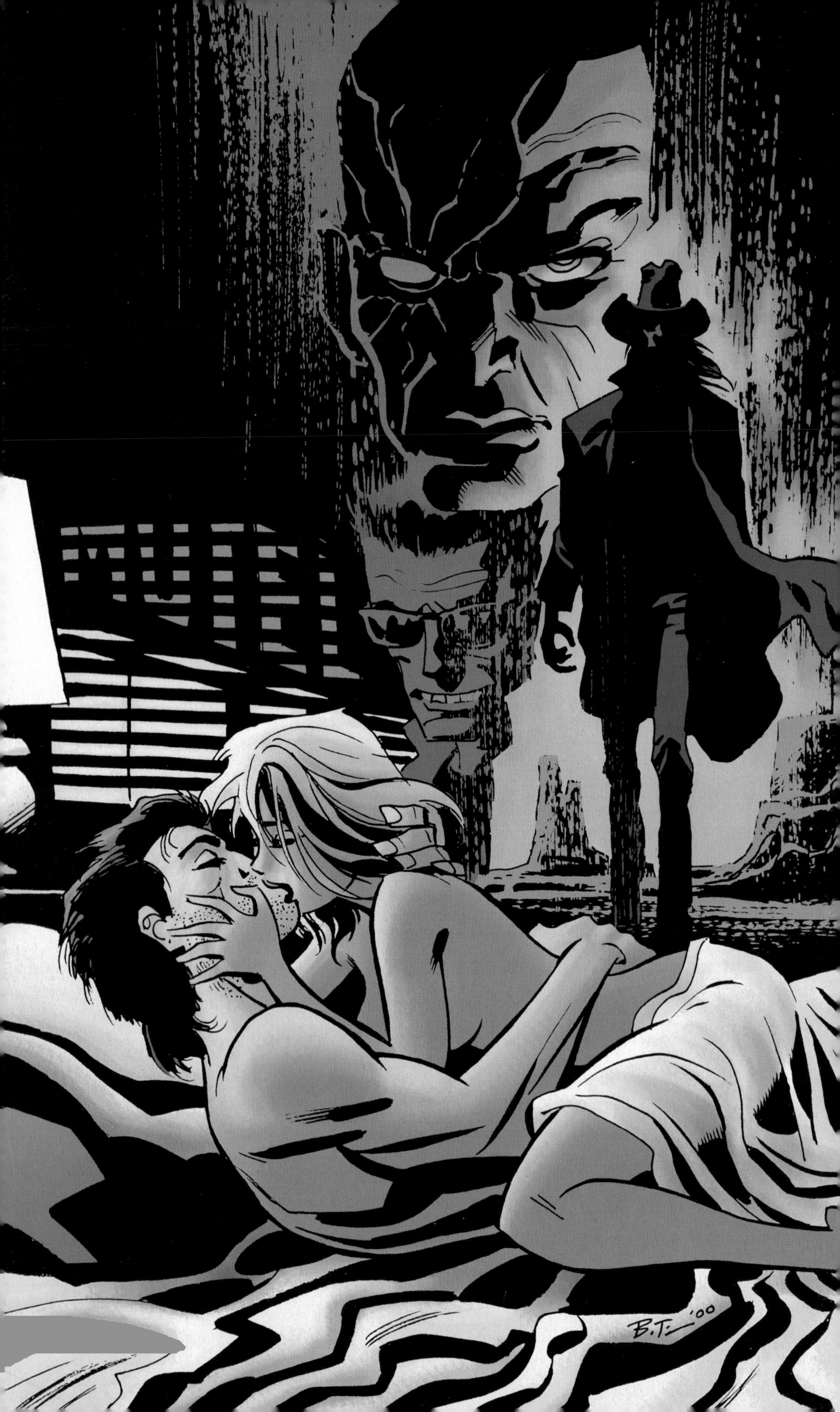

B.T. '00